Aristocracy of Armed Talent

"We in Singapore are fortunate that we do not subscribe to the aristocracy of pedigree, class or caste, but to the aristocracy of talent. Hence the high social mobility which is one of the outstanding characteristics of our Republic."[1]

> — His Excellency Chengara Veetil Devan Nair (1923–2006)
> President of the Republic of Singapore (1981–85)

---

[1] "The Scholars' Debt", *Straits Times*, 2 July 1982, p. 1.

Aristocracy of Armed Talent

The Military Elite in Singapore

Samuel Ling Wei Chan

NUS PRESS
SINGAPORE

Published by:

NUS Press
National University of Singapore
AS3-01-02, 3 Arts Link
Singapore 117569

Fax: (65) 6774-0652
E-mail: nusbooks@nus.edu.sg
Website: http://nuspress.nus.edu.sg

ISBN 978-981-3250-07-9 (paper)

National Library Board, Singapore Cataloguing in Publication Data

Name(s): Chan, Samuel Ling Wei.
Title: Aristocracy of armed talent: the military elite in Singapore / Samuel Ling Wei
    Chan.
Description: First edition. | Singapore: NUS Press, [2019] | Includes bibliographical
    references and index.
Identifier(s): OCN 1048269367 | ISBN 978-981-32-5007-9 (paperback)
Subject(s): LCSH: Singapore--Armed Forces. | Scholars--Singapore.
Classification: DDC 355.5095957--dc23

Typeset by: Ogma Solutions Pvt Ltd
Printed by: Ho Printing Singapore Pte Ltd

Key appointments in MINDEF

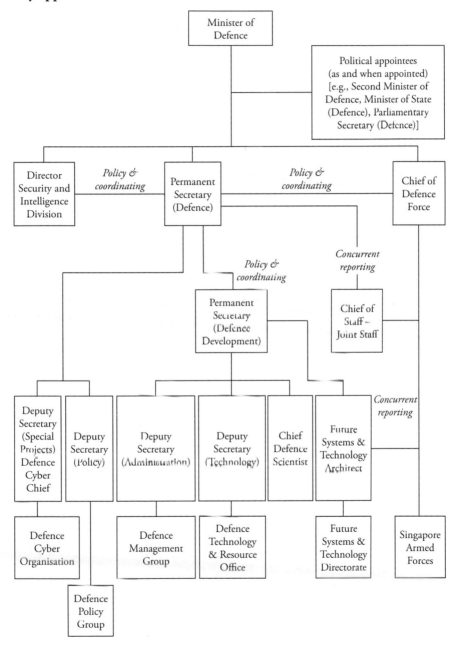

Key appointments in the SAF HQ

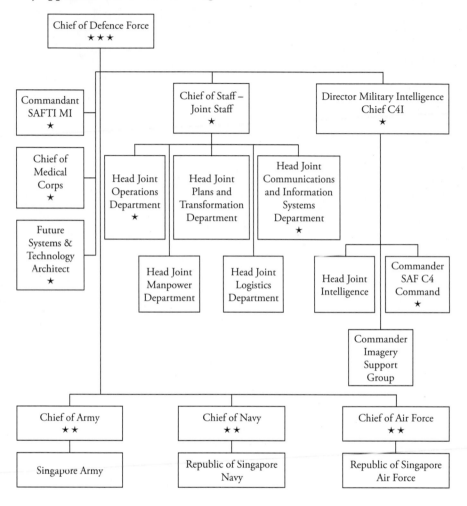

Contents

List of Tables

List of Graphs

List of Appendices

Singapore Armed Forces Act (Chapter 295) Regulation 2(1)

Singapore Armed Forces (Ranks of Servicemen) (Amendment) Regulations 2012 (Uniformed rank hierarchy in order of seniority)

1. General (GEN)/Admiral (ADM) [*authorised but not bestowed on any officer to date*]
2. Lieutenant-General (LG)/Vice Admiral (VADM)
3. Major-General (MG)/Rear-Admiral (Two-Star) (RADM2)
4. Brigadier-General (BG)/Rear-Admiral (One-Star) (RADM1)/Military Expert 8 (ME8)
5. Colonel (COL)/Military Expert 7 (ME7)
6. Senior Lieutenant Colonel (SLTC)
7. Lieutenant Colonel (LTC)/Military Expert 6 (ME6)
8. Major (MAJ)/ Military Expert 5 (ME5)
9. Captain (CPT)/Military Expert 4 (ME4)
10. Lieutenant (LTA)
11. Second Lieutenant (2LT)
12. Chief Warrant Officer (CWO)
13. Senior Warrant Officer (SWO)
14. Master Warrant Officer (MWO)
15. First Warrant Officer (1WO)/Military Expert 3 (ME3)
16. Second Warrant Officer (2WO)
17. Third Warrant Officer (3WO)
18. Master Sergeant (MSG)/Military Expert 2 (ME2)
19. Staff Sergeant (SSG)
20. First Sergeant (1SG)
21. Second Sergeant (2SG)/Military Expert 1 (ME1)
22. Third Sergeant (3SG)
23. Corporal (First Class) (CFC)
24. Corporal (CPL)

25. Lance-Corporal (LCP)
26. Private (First Class) (PFC)
27. Private (PTE)[2]
28. Recruit (REC)

---

[2] An officer cadet (OCT), a midshipman (MID), a specialist cadet (SCT), a military expert senior trainee/apprentice or a military expert trainee/apprentice is equivalent in rank to a private.

Abbreviations

1	Numerical designator for manpower branch or department (e.g., S1, G1, J1)
1 FLOT	First Flotilla
2	Numerical designator for intelligence branch or department (e.g., S2, G2, J2)
2IC	Second-in-Command
2LT	Second-Lieutenant
3	Numerical designator for operations branch or department (e.g., S3, G3, J3)
3 FLOT	Third Flotilla
3G	Third-Generation
4	Numerical designator for logistics branch or department (e.g., S4, G4, J4)
5	Numerical designator for plans branch or department (e.g., G5, J5)
5BX	Five Basic Exercises
6	Numerical designator for training branch or department (e.g., G6)
A*STAR	Agency for Science, Technology and Research
ABG	Armoured Battle Group (a mechanized battalion)
ABSD	Applied Behavioural Science Department
ACC	Air Combat Command
ACCORD	Advisory Council on Community Relations in Defence
ACGS	Assistant Chief of General Staff
ACP	Assistant Commissioner of Police
ADA	Air Defence Artillery
ADB	Air Defence Brigade (presently Air Defence Group [ADG])
ADF	(1) Army Developmental Force, or (2) Army Deployment Force
ADG	Air Defence Group (formerly Air Defence Brigade)

ADOC	Air Defence and Operations Command (formerly Air Defence Systems Division [ADSD] and before that Singapore Air Defence Artillery [SADA])
ADTF	Air Defence Task Force
AELG	Air Engineering and Logistics Group
AELO	Air Engineering and Logistics Organisation led by Head Air Engineering and Logistics (HAEL) (formerly Air Logistics Organisation and before that Air Logistics Department, both led by Head Air Logistics [HAL])
AELS	Air Engineering and Logistics Squadron (formerly Air Logistics Squadron [ALS])
AFC	Armed Forces Council
AFOG	Air Force Operations Group (presently Air Operations Control Group [AOCG])
AFR	Annual Feedback Report
AFSB	Air Force Systems Brigade (presently Air Surveillance and Control Group [ASCG])
Ag	Acting
ALS	Air Logistics Squadron (presently Air Engineering and Logistics Squadron [AELS])
AO	(1) Administrative Officer (a member of the Administrative Service [AS]), or (2) Additional Officer (naval appointment known today as Officer Under Training (OUT)]
AOAS	Army Officers Advanced School [formerly School of Advanced Training for Officers [SATO])
AOCG	Air Operations Control Group (formerly Air Force Operations Group [AFOG])
AOMC	Army Officers Management Centre
APGC	Air Power Generation Command
ARMCEG	Army Combat Engineer Group
AS	(1) Administrative Service (the bureaucratic elite with the Public Service Division [PSD]), or (2) Air Staff
ASCG	Air Surveillance and Control Group (formerly Air Force Systems Brigade [AFSB])
ATA	Academic Training Award
AWO	Air Warfare Officer

AWOL	Absent Without Official Leave
BG	Brigadier-General
BMT	Basic Military Training
Bn	Battalion
BTC	Battalion Tactics Course
C2D	Commitment to Defence
C3	Command, Control and Communications
C4	Command, Control, Communications and Computers
C4I	Command, Control, Communications, Computers and Intelligence
C4OG	Command, Control, Communications and Computers Operations Group
CAB	Changi Air Base
CAD	Combined Arms Division
CAF	Chief of Air Force
CARMO	Chief Army Medical Officer
CAS	Compulsory Active Service
CAT	(Operations) Category (for a pilot ranging from D [entry] to A [highest])
CDF	Chief of Defence Force (nomenclature for the defence chief since 1990)
CDG	Cyber Defence Group
CDO Bn	Commando Battalion
CE	Chief Executive
CEO	(1) Chief Engineer Officer, or (2) Chief Executive Officer
CEP	Current Estimated Potential
CGO	Chief Guards Officer
CGS	Chief of the General Staff (as the defence chief was known from 1978 to 1990)
CGSC	Command and General Staff College (Fort Leavenworth, Kansas)
CHOD	Alternative designation for the Chief of Defence Force (CDF)
CI	Chief Instructor (an appointment in a training school/centre/institute)
CIO	(1) Chief Infantry Officer, or (2) Chief Information Officer

CMC	Chief of Medical Corps
CMEO	Chief Maintenance and Engineering Officer
CMPB	Central Manpower Base
CMR	Civil-Military Relations
CNB	Changi Naval Base (subsequently renamed RSS Singapura – Changi Naval Base)
CNV	Chief of Navy
CO	Commanding Officer
COA	Chief of Army (formerly Deputy Chief of General Staff [Army])
COCC	Combat Officer Cadet Course
COL	Colonel
COMD	Commander
COMDT	Commandant
COS-AS	Chief of Staff – Air Staff
COS-GS	Chief of Staff – General Staff (formerly Chief of Staff of the General Staff)
COS-JS	Chief of Staff – Joint Staff
COS-NS	Chief of Staff – Naval Staff
COSCOM	Coastal Command (presently Maritime Security Task Force [MSTF])
CPT	Captain
CSA	Cyber Security Agency of Singapore
CSC	Command and Staff Course
CSH	Combat Support Hospital
CSSCOM	Combat Service Support Command
CTC	Company Tactics Course
CTF-151	Combined Task Force 151
CTO	Chief Transport Officer
DBS	Development Bank of Singapore
DCGS	Deputy Chief of General Staff
DCO	Defence Cyber Organisation
DEFCO	Defence Council
DGS	Director General Staff (as the defence chief was known from 1965 to 1978)

DIR	Director
DISO	Defence Industry and Systems Office
DIV	Division
DIV ARTY	Division Artillery (an artillery brigade)
DIV COMD	Division Commander
DJID	Director Joint Intelligence Directorate
DJO	Director Joint Operations (formerly Head Joint Operations [HJO])
DJOPD	Director Joint Operations and Planning Directorate
DMG	Defence Management Group
DMI	Director Military Intelligence
DMO	Defence Materials Organisation
DMRI	Defence Medical Research Institute
DMS	Defence Merit Scholarship
DPG	Defence Policy Group
DPM	Deputy Prime Minister
DPO	Defence Policy Office
DS	Deputy Secretary
DSO	Defence Science Organisation
DSTA	Defence Science and Technology Agency
DTRO	Defence Technology and Resource Office
DXO	Defence Executive Officer
ECA	Extra-Curricular Activity (plural form is ECAs)
EDB	Economic Development Board
FMC	Federation Military College (Malaysia)
FSTD	Future Systems and Technology Directorate headed by the Future Systems and Technology Architect (FSTA) (formerly Future Systems Directorate [FSD] headed by the Future Systems Architect [FSA])
FTS	Flying Training School
GBAD	Ground Based Air Defence (formerly Air Defence Artillery [ADA])
GDP	Gross Domestic Product
GDS	Guards

GKSCSC	Goh Keng Swee Command and Staff College (formerly Singapore Command and Staff College [SCSC])
GLC	government-linked company
GM	General Manager
GMKE	General Military Knowledge Exams
GS	General Staff
GSMB	General Support Maintenance Base
HDB	Housing and Development Board
HJL	Head Joint Logistics
HJO	Head Joint Operations (presently Director Joint Operations)
HNL	Head Naval Logistics
HNO	Head Naval Operations
HNP	Head Naval Personnel
HNPL	Head Naval Plans
HNW	Hotel New World
HQ	Headquarters
HRC	High Readiness Core
HUDC	Housing and Urban Development Company
I/O	Institution/Occupation
ICT	In-Camp Training
IDF	Israeli Defense Forces
IDTF	Island Defence Task Force
IMT	Initial Military Training
IPPT	Individual Physical Proficiency Test
ISEAS	Institute of Southeast Asian Studies
ISG	Imagery Support Group
JCISD	Joint Communications and Information Systems Department (J6) led by Head Joint Communications and Information Systems (HJCIS) (formerly Joint Communications and Electronics Department [JCED])
JFC	Junior Flying Club (presently the Singapore Youth Flying Club [SYFC])
JID	(1) Joint Intelligence Directorate, or (2) Joint Intelligence Department (J2) led by Head Joint Intelligence (HJI) (subordinate within the Military Intelligence Organisation)

JLD	Joint Logistics Department (J4) led by Head Joint Logistics (HJL)
JMPD	Joint Manpower Department (J1) led by Head Joint Manpower (HJMP)
JOD	Joint Operations Department (J3) led by Director Joint Operations (DJO)
JOPD	Joint Operations and Planning Directorate led by Director Joint Operations and Planning Directorate (DJOPD) (The title of DJOPD seems to be defunct)
JPTD	Joint Plans and Transformation Department (J5/J7) led by Head Joint Plans and Transformation (HJPT) (formerly Joint Plans Department [JPD] headed by Head Joint Plans [HJP])
JS	Joint Staff
JTC	Jurong Town Corporation
KL	Kuala Lumpur
LG	Lieutenant-General
LKY	Lee Kuan Yew
LMS	Local Medicine Scholarship
LMV	Littoral Mission Vessel (type of naval vessel)
LSA	Local Study Award
LST	Landing Ship Tank (type of naval vessel)
LTA	(1) Lieutenant, or (2) Land Transport Authority
LTC	Lieutenant Colonel
MA UN	Military Adviser at the Permanent Mission of Singapore to the United Nations
MAF	Malaysian Armed Forces
MAJ	Major
MCV	Missile Corvettes (type of naval vessel)
MDES	Military Domain Expert Scheme
MFA	Ministry of Foreign Affairs
MG	Major-General
MGB	Missile Gun Boat (type of naval vessel)
MIB	Malaysian Infantry Brigade
MID	(1) Midshipman, or (2) Ministry of Interior and Defence
MINDEF	Ministry of Defence

MIO	Military Intelligence Organization led by Director Military Intelligence (DMI) (formerly Joint Intelligence Directorate [JID] led by Director Joint Intelligence Directorate [DJID])
MND	Ministry of National Development
MO	Medical Officer
MOCC	Medical Officer Cadet Course
MOE	Ministry of Education
MOH	Ministry of Health
MP	(1) Member of Parliament, or (2) Military Police (Provost)
MSD	Military Security Department
MSTD	Midshipman Sea Training Deployment
MSTF	Maritime Security Task Force (formerly Coastal Command [COSCOM])
MTA	Military Training Award
MTS	Minimum Term of Service
NALCOM	Naval Logistics Command led by Commander NALCOM
NCC	National Cadet Corps
NDP	National Day Parade
NDU	Naval Diving Unit
NLD	Naval Logistics Department led by Head Naval Logistics (HNL)
NLO	Naval Logistics Organisation
NOD	Naval Operations Department led by Head Naval Operations (HNO)
NPD	Naval Personnel Department led by Head Naval Personnel (HNP)
NPLD	Naval Plans Department led by Head Naval Plans (HNPL)
NS	(1) National Service, or (2) Naval Staff
NSAD	National Service Affairs Department
NSF	National Service Full-time (full-time active-duty conscript; plural form is NSFs)
NSman	Operationally Ready National Serviceman (formerly and colloquially referred to as reservist; plural form is NSmen)
NTU	Nanyang Technological University
NUH	National University Hospital

NUS	National University of Singapore
OC	Officer Commanding
OCC	Officer Cadet Course
OCS	Officer Cadet School
OCT	Officer Cadet Trainee
OMS	Overseas Merit Scholarship
OP	Observation Post
OPC	Officers Personnel Centre
OR	Operations Research
ORBAT	Order of Battle
ORD	Operationally Ready Date (i.e., completion of active military service, formerly known as Run-Out Date [ROD])
OSA	Official Secrets Act
OTA	Overseas Training Award
OUT	Officer Under Training (junior naval officer appointment formerly known as Additional Officer [AO])
PA	(1) Promotion Authority, or (2) People's Association
PAP	People's Action Party
PC	(1) Participation Command, (2) Platoon Commander, (3) Promotion Council, or (4) Peace Carvin (RSAF training arrangement in the United States)
PDF	People's Defence Force
PLA	People's Liberation Army
PLAB	Paya Lebar Air Base
PM	Prime Minister
PMO	Prime Minister's Office
PMR	Performance Management Report
PPL	Private Pilot Licence
PR	Permanent Residents
PRB	Promotion Recommendation Board
PS	Permanent Secretary
PS (D)	Permanent Secretary (Defence)
PS (DD)	Permanent Secretary (Defence Development)
PSA	Port of Singapore Authority

PSC	Public Service Commission (which "oversees the recruitment, promotion and terms of service of civil servants")
PSD	Public Service Division (the "central people agency of the Singapore Public Service")
PSLE	Primary School Leaving Examination
PSO	Principal Staff Officer
PUB	Public Utilities Board
QFI	Qualified Flying Instructor
RAAF	Royal Australian Air Force
RADM1	Rear-Admiral (One-Star) (formerly Commodore [CDRE])
RADM2	Rear-Admiral (Two-Star)
RAF	Royal Air Force
REME	Royal Electrical and Mechanical Engineers (corps of the British Army)
RET	Retired
RI	Raffles Institution
RMN	Royal Malaysian Navy
ROC	Republic of China (also referred to as Taiwan)
ROCAF	Republic of China Air Force
ROD	Run-Out Date (i.e., completion of active military service, presently known as Operationally Ready Date [ORD])
RSAF	Republic of Singapore Air Force (formerly Singapore Air Defence Command [SADC])
RSM	Regimental Sergeant Major
RSN	Republic of Singapore Navy
RSS	Republic of Singapore Ship
S/O	Son of
SA	Singapore Artillery
SAB	Singapore Armoured Brigade
SAF	Singapore Armed Forces
SAFE	SAF Enterprise
SAFES	Singapore Armed Forces Engineering Scholarship
SAFMC	Singapore Armed Forces Medical Corps
SAFOS	Singapore Armed Forces Overseas Scholarship

SAFOS-PS	Singapore Armed Forces Overseas Scholarship-President's Scholarship
SAFRA	Singapore Armed Forces Reservist Association
SAFTI	Singapore Armed Forces Training Institute
SAFTI MI	SAFTI Military Institute
SAR	(1) Singapore Armoured Regiment, or (2) Search and Rescue
SAS	(1) SAF Academic Scholarship (formed from the amalgamation of the Academic Training Award [ATA] and Military Training Award [MTA]), or (2) Singapore Advanced Schools
SATO	School of Advanced Training for Officers (presently Army Officers Advanced School [AOAS])
SBAB	Sembawang Air Base
SC	Special Constabulary
SCDF	Singapore Civil Defence Force
SCE	Singapore Combat Engineers
SCR	Staff Confidential Report
SCSC	Singapore Command and Staff College (presently Goh Keng Swee Command and Staff College [GKSCSC])
SIA	Singapore Airlines
SIB	Singapore Infantry Brigade
SID	Security and Intelligence Division (agency for external intelligence)
SIG	Signals
SIR	Singapore Infantry Regiment
SIT	Singapore Improvement Trust
SLOC	Sea Lines of Communication
SLTC	Senior Lieutenant Colonel
SMC	Standard Military Course
SMS	SAF Merit Scholarship (formerly Overseas Training Award [Academic])
SOH	Sword of Honour
SOF	Special Operations Force
SP	Special Projects
SPF	Singapore Police Force

SPFOS	Singapore Police Force Overseas Scholarship
SQN	Squadron (a unit designator applicable in the RSAF and RSN)
SSSO	Senior Specialist Staff Officer
SVC	Singapore Volunteer Corps
TAB	Tengah Air Base
TASC	Tactical Air Support Command (1991–2007, forerunner of present UC)
TASG	Tactical Air Support Group (subordinate unit of Participation Command)
TNB	Tuas Naval Base
TPT Bn	Transport Battalion
TRADOC	Army Training and Doctrine Command
TSWC	Tri-Service Warfighter Course (formerly Tri-Service Course and before that the Joint Junior Staff Course [JJSC])
UAV	Unmanned Aerial Vehicle
UC	Unmanned Aerial Vehicle Command
UK	United Kingdom
UN	United Nations
UNIKOM	United Nations Iraq-Kuwait Observation Mission
UNMISET	United Nations Mission of Support in East Timor
UNPKO	United Nations Peacekeeping Operations
VADM	Vice Admiral
VC	Vigilante Corps
VOL	Volunteer
WO1	Warrant Officer Class 1 (no longer in use)
WO2	Warrant Officer Class 2 (no longer in use)
WOSPEC	Warrant Officer and Specialists
WSO	Weapon Systems Officer

Preface

I first heard the word "scholar" used as a pronoun when I enlisted for National Service in the Singapore Armed Forces (SAF) on 15 February 1996, Total Defence Day. A fellow recruit described a particular officer as a "scholar", to which I remarked "Aren't we all" only to receive a rather perplexed look in return. This was a rather naive assumption on my part after eight years abroad that we were all bound for tertiary studies after 30 months of conscription. Unbeknownst to me, my fellow recruit was referring to a recipient of a top-tier SAF scholarship. This "scholar" phenomenon was to take a back seat all throughout basic military training (BMT), where the sergeant was king, the physical training instructor feared, and the lieutenant revered. The company Officer Commanding was a regular lieutenant who was hardly seen with the exception of live fire practice at the rifle range. The school's Commanding Officer (CO) in the rank of major (MAJ) was almost mythical, sighted only from a distance and distinguished by the red beret worn by members of the elite commando fraternity.

It was a few months later, in June 1996, that I first saw pictures of the military elite—the generals and admirals at the apex of the SAF's uniformed hierarchy. Framed portraits of the most senior among them hung proudly in the main auditorium at Officer Cadet School in SAFTI Military Institute. Their uniforms were resplendently adorned with badges and ribbons, yet the most distinguishing features were the fine embroidery of the stars on their epaulettes and their youthful-looking faces. The portraits changed a month later. Bey Soo Khiang (Chief of Defence Force) received his third star as Lieutenant-General. Goh Yong Siang (Chief of Air Force) and Han Eng Juan (Chief of Army) received their second stars as Major-Generals. The new Chief of Navy Richard Lim, then a one-star, had succeeded the two-star Rear-Admiral Kwek Siew Jin. The word "scholar" was mentioned again. Some but not all of them were.

The military elites were as mythical to officer cadet trainees (OCTs) as the COs of the BMT school were to recruits. It was only when Commandant SAFTI MI, Brigadier General (BG) Stephen Wong, chided the school of cadets for the lack of martial bearing and discipline that we OCTs crossed paths with a general officer. Our day-to-day concerns centred around training at the platoon level within the framework of a rifle company under the erudite supervision of Captain Tan Kee Heng and later MAJ Chan Wing Kai. The latter was fresh from his tour as a battalion S3 (operations officer) and in 2010 made BG. As OCTs we would meet generals only on another two occasions before receiving our commissions as officers. The first was on an overseas training exercise observed by BG Wong, an infantry officer, who imparted the finer points of terrain appreciation. The second was at the Army Certificate Presentation Ceremony in March 1997, where we were presented with officer appointment scrolls and ceremonial swords by BG Lam Joon Khoi, Director Joint Operations and Planning Directorate, and concurrently Chief of Staff - General Staff. The alphabet soup proved more a tongue twister than an appreciation of the heavy responsibilities that accompanied the appointments. The word "scholar" was once again mentioned somewhere.

It was only during my post-commissioning tours of duty in 1997–98 and 2001–02 that a larger picture began to form. I made a habit of perusing through issues of *Pioneer* magazine and *Pointer* journal from cover to cover. Initially this was due in part to their availability within the camp confines. It was also the implied responsibility of service personnel regardless of whether they were regulars, conscripts or reservists to keep abreast of developments in the SAF. These reasons soon gave way to a genuine interest in the armed forces as an organization and in particular the leaders, their biographies (or lack of), and manpower issues in general. The command rolls of honour of various units proved a great source of interest, especially when certain names repeated themselves across different issues of service newsletters. The last general I came across while serving full-time National Service was BG Andrew Tan, Commander 6th Singapore Division, when he visited the subordinate 2nd Singapore Infantry Brigade commanded by Lieutenant Colonel Loh Wai Keong. Both men paid very close attention to the storied 1st Battalion, Singapore Infantry Regiment, as the CO MAJ Philip Lim led the "leopards" in an evaluation exercise. Loh and Lim made BG in 2003 and 2007 respectively. Yes, the word "scholar" surfaced once again.

As the word "scholar" became intrinsically linked to the military elites, many queries surfaced since I first began cursory observations through open-source literature in 1997. The first, having read statistics as an undergraduate, was whether being a scholar was a necessary or sufficient condition for ascension to the top. But cognizance of the different tiers of scholarships invariably led to the second query, which in many ways should have been the first, of "Who is a 'scholar'?" This in turn opened the floodgates for many more questions: How many individuals are there, both in terms of these "scholars" and military elites? What are the common variables, if at all? Is there causality or mere correlation between any pair of variables? How can an individual be identified in their late teens and groomed for a position they would hold only in their late 30s and early 40s? Does this not contradict the oft-mentioned practice of meritocracy that is championed as Singapore's great social equalizer? Or does meritocracy mean different things at different times to different groups? Alas, these were but rhetorical questions.

Those questions alone, while interesting, did not prove to be the catalyst for this book. This book is the alignment of unique circumstances because it was never my intention to write on any aspect of Singapore's military establishment. The initial dissuasion came when I was a graduate student of strategic studies and any such undertaking was painted as unwise at best. The sagacity of such advice came to fruition in 2010 when a chapter I was invited to write on the evolution of SAF peace support operations as part of a monograph initiative was censored. This was initially over 40 words but eventually covered any references to Singapore. It was clear that if any defence-related topic ever crossed my path again I would, in the words of the eminent British military historian Sir Michael Howard, need "considerable moral courage to state conclusions highly unwelcome to the (Defence) Ministry".[1] Within such an environment it is perhaps unsurprising that the former *Straits Times* defence correspondent David Boey once observed:

> The SAF can also do more to ensure that institutional knowledge is safeguarded. The professional reading list used by SAFTI Military Institute has only one book on the SAF and that—*Defending the Lion City*—is written by a foreigner, Dr Tim Huxley. Books published by the SAF have so far been of coffee-table genre. Most were written to commemorate various anniversaries.[2]

Under such circumstances it is unsurprising that little is known of the military elite in Singapore. It is no exaggeration to say that it is easier for Singaporeans to learn about American and European military leaders, or even those in Israel and South Korea where conscription is significant in length of service and for national survival. Singapore's retired top brass are also not in the habit of publishing (auto)biographies because of the information they were once privy to, the possible repercussions arising from any such candid publication, and the intention to avoid any hint of self-aggrandizement. Yet, these untold stories of Singapore's military leaders are an important part of Singapore's history. They have, after all, led at the highest levels of an organization that impacts the lives of almost every single Singaporean male and by extension every Singaporean family. Their lived experiences and accompanying empirical evidence also serve to address myths and correct inaccuracies circulating in print, cyberspace and

---

[1] Michael Howard, *Captain Professor: A Life in War and Peace* (London: Continuum UK, 2006), p. 140.

[2] David Boey, "Old Soldiers Still Have Something to Teach", *Straits Times*, 28 Sept. 2004, p. 12.

thought. A few members of the top brass have also departed. Any words not captured are lost.

This book, like many others, is an account and an interpretation of people and events. It stands at the confluence of history, politics, sociology and statistics to address several pertinent queries. First, what motivated the military elites to join the SAF as regular officers? So far only career personnel have served in the ranks of one-star and above, whereas reservists have made colonel in the course of their NS duties. Second, why were the military elites committed to stay on as regulars? Certain junctures in SAF history have indicated that two-thirds of officers leave active duty after completing their initial terms of engagement or first contracts. The voices from conversations with 28 retired generals and admirals offer verisimilitude in their respective explanations of choices. The third enquiry is concerned with the manpower processes (software) and force structure (hardware) that govern rank mobility within the SAF Officer Corps. The processes address individual officer performances and potential, which in turn determine postings and promotions. The force structure determines the distribution of appointments and echelons. The fourth area covers the statistics and unique cases revealed by empirical data on the SAF Overseas Scholarship and the military elite. The fifth query contained in the penultimate chapter covers social aspects in Singapore that have an impact on the present SAF and with possible repercussions for the future.

This book is not about extraordinary individuals. It is a collection of story fragments from ordinary individuals who found meaning and purpose in the profession of arms. It speaks of those whose values and deep-seated care for their soldiers, sailors and airmen gave them perseverance to weather the troughs and show humility at the crests of their careers. It is the story of those who made the most of opportunities they had, who were noticed by the system and/or their superiors, and whose selflessness made extraordinary achievements possible with the teams they led. Yet, this portrait is also a partial painting of Singapore's military elites because a segment of 28 can, at very best, only hope to resemble the whole. The voices contained within portions of the following pages are of those willing to preserve aspects of their lived experiences within academic amber for those with an interest in their thoughts, feelings and historical contexts. I am extremely thankful for those who helped me along this journey and made this book possible. My hope is that I justified the time and effort that they invested in me.

Samuel Ling Wei Chan
Singapore, September 2018

CHAPTER 1

Generally Speaking

"If we do not remember our heroes, we will produce no heroes. If we do not record their sacrifices, their sacrifices would have been in vain ... the greatest strength we have as a people is our common memories of the past and our common hopes for the future ... For without those memories, the next generation will not have the fighting spirit to carry on."[1]

— BG (NS) George Yeo Yong Boon
Minister for Information and the Arts (1991–99)

1.1   Introduction

It is generally regarded as a privilege and an honour to serve as a commissioned officer in the Singapore Armed Forces (SAF). The President has commissioned tens of thousands in the Republic's first 50 years of independence, but only 170 individuals have had the opportunity to serve as flag officers between 1965 and 2018 (Appendix A).[2] To wear one "star" or more on epaulettes and be addressed as General or Admiral is an acknowledgement of having reached the pinnacle of the profession of arms, and an embodiment of the finest uniformed leadership within the SAF and the Ministry of Defence (MINDEF). These ranks bear testament to technical, tactical and operational competencies, and further reflect a unique blend of irreproachable character, military professionalism, critical responsibility, strategic foresight, diplomatic acumen and political trustworthiness. The advice of such officers is crucial to the civilian bureaucracy and elected leadership on all matters pertaining to military defence, which forms one of the five pillars

---

[1] Speech by BG (NS) George Yeo, Minister for Information and the Arts, at the launch of the SCCI publication "The Price of Peace", 21 June 1997. Inscription at the Bukit Chandu Memorial for the Malay Regiment, Singapore.

[2] The term "flag officer" is used in the SAF to reference "senior commanders holding the rank of one-star general (or its equivalent) and above". See "Navy Day: 'Charting the Future'", *Pioneer* (June 1994): 16. The term was most recently used to encompass "General or Admiral" in a speech by defence minister Dr Ng Eng Hen at the Committee of Supply Debate on 3 March 2017.

in Singapore's concept of Total Defence.[3] Most important, these members of the military elite bear the duty of ensuring that the country's technologically advanced war machine stands ready to deter aggression in times of peace and, as the last resort, to manage the calibrated application of violence in war.

This book is inspired in many ways by the 1971 Morris Janowitz classic *The Professional Soldier: A Social and Political Portrait*. The late American military sociologist examined aspects of generals in the US Army, from the one-star Brigadier-General (BG) through to the four-star General (GEN). His completed portrait is an amalgamation of the variations he uncovered among the officers, including but not restricted to their family backgrounds, the rural-urban divide, reasons for joining the armed forces, commissioning sources, military occupation speciality, and career progression. Janowitz provides an insightful and entertaining account of those who prepared, led and reached the apex of the US Army. The pages that follow offer to do the same for Singapore by capturing socio-historical aspects of its military development and painting a collective portrait of its military elites through the "lived" realities of 28 interviewees, an exhaustive survey of open-source information on MINDEF-SAF, and concomitant empirical data. A detailed examination of military elites in Singapore has never been undertaken, and this book was made possible only through the first-hand accounts of those who graciously shared their personal journeys in armed service to their country.

This portrait is formed from a collective rather than an individual and takes form through an extended narrative that begins in the second chapter, with the contextualization of national defence and the profession of arms. Singapore became a British colony in 1819, but the local population only assumed complete responsibility for defence after independence on 9 August 1965. Singapore's military history was until that epochal moment merely a section in the annals of British colonial, Japanese imperial, Commonwealth, and Malaysian military history. An indigenous military culture was non-existent except for those who braved service in various volunteer outfits. Furthermore, the very idea of a military career did not sit well with the Chinese ethnic group, which accounted for three-quarters of the population. Attracting adequate numbers of quality Regulars (regular personnel) for an ethnically balanced SAF also proved difficult in the aftermath of independence. Conscription—known today as National Service or NS—was introduced under a cloud of uncertainty in a piecewise manner commencing in 1967. The notion of the "scholar" military officer was established in 1971 via the top-tier SAF (UK) Scholarship—later renamed the

---

[3] Total Defence consists of military defence, civil defence, economic defence, social defence and psychological defence.

SAF Overseas Scholarship (SAFOS) and most recently the vague-sounding SAF Scholarship—to appeal to the Confucian ethics of the Chinese majority. That same year lower-tiered local university study awards were offered to officers with potential to contribute as Regulars. The variety and tiers of military scholarships and awards on offer have since expanded significantly, most notably with the inclusion of the SAF Merit Scholarship (SMS) in 1983, a scheme almost identical to the SAFOS and second only in prestige.

The invisible bifurcation of Regulars within the SAF Officer Corps into scholars and non-scholars has at times been confusing, contentious and controversial. Scholar-officers are the individuals offered prestigious undergraduate scholarships and emplaced on a specially managed and accelerated career path. Only the recipients of the 332 SAFOS and to an extent the 462 SMS awarded as of 2018 are considered scholar-officers.[4] The remaining officers have been cast colloquially as "farmers", which initially encompassed non-graduates but in contemporary terms is used loosely for all non-scholar-officers. Some recipients of the lower-tiered scholarships and study awards have humorously deprecated themselves as graduating from *sekolah attap* (Malay for "village school"), which traditionally lacked resources. This delineation has spawned countless rumours and myths that litter conversations, Internet chatrooms and even academic literature. The Australian academic Michael Barr, in his observation of SAFOS recipients, maintains: "it should not be surprising that since its inception, winners have come to dominate the SAF hierarchy completely. It is more surprising that they have also come to make up about 10 per cent of the civilian Administrative Service, thanks to the practices of routinely seconding serving SAF officers into the Administrative Service."[5]

Barr continues that on the strength of the "scholar-officers" "it might be more accurate to think of the officer corps as armed bureaucrats, rather than soldiers".[6] However, a blind preference for promoting officers based on the scholarship awarded would be a certain recipe for disquiet among Regulars and the consequential erosion of the SAF's warfighting capabilities. The empirical

---

[4] One publication has presented errors and incomplete figures. There were 277 SAFOS awarded between 1971 and 2010, not 283. There were nine non-Chinese SAFOS recipients between 1971 and 2017: Wesley Gerard D'Aranjo (1972), Gaurav Keerthi (1998), Jacques Wei-Ren Erasmus (1999), Letchumanan Narayanan (2001), Robert Khoon Liat Colflesh (2005), John Nehemiah Samuel (2005), Mikail Kalimuddin (2005), Geeva S/O Gopal Krishnan (2011) and Satesh Kumar S/O Sukumar (2017). Michael D. Barr, *The Ruling Elite of Singapore: Networks of Power and Influence* (London and New York: I.B. Tauris, 2014), pp. 44, 67, 69, 76–7, 79.

[5] Barr, *Ruling Elite of Singapore*, p. 44.

[6] Ibid., p. 81.

evidence shows that the majority of one-star officers are not SAFOS recipients. It is a common fallacy to equate scholars with elites and vice versa, because one hears frequently of successes but less so of failures. One must remember that the SAFOS is an investment in *potential* for service at the highest echelons but those promoted to general and admiral are the ones who realized their potential in *reality*.

After situating national defence and the military elites in historical context, the focus of the book shifts to the lived experiences of 28 retired generals and admirals in chapters 3 and 4, and portions of 5. The underlying tripartite query is concerned with the eclectic reasons why they joined the military, why they remained on active duty, and how they came to be members of Singapore's Aristocracy of Armed Talent.[7] It would be comforting if the reasons given for joining and remaining—essentially two broad dimensions of career satisfaction— in regular military service were purely altruistic, but that would also be self-deceiving. The interviewees on the contrary provide detailed accounts of their individual contexts, which allows readers to step into their shoes at a particular point in time and understand their respective intentions. Chapter 5 also delves into personnel movement and the formal processes that regulate power within the SAF Officer Corps.[8] These processes comprise performance appraisals and potential estimations, which in tandem determine the postings and promotions essential for hierarchical mobility. Chapter 6 follows on with an examination of the organizational structure across the tri-service SAF and MINDEF that supports the concomitant appointments and rank hierarchy. Although military ascension is predicated on processes and structure, one must be mindful of the stochastic variable sometimes referred to as luck because it is usually the best person available who is appointed and promoted.

Chapter 7 provides a quantitative account of various aspects regarding the SAFOS recipients and members of the military elite in five sections. The first is concerned with the schools and institutions at which the SAFOS recipients completed their secondary education. Next, the SAFOS retention and attrition rates as well as flag officer ascension rates are examined, and the cases of high attrition in signals and armour vocations are presented. This is followed by a comparison of SAFOS and non-SAFOS flag officers with specifics on the age of wearing their first star, the years of active flag officership, and the estimated

---

[7] The phrase "Aristocracy of Talent" has been used to depict a societal "aristocracy" based on merit instead of birth. Lewis K. Killian, "Generals, the Talented Tenth, and Affirmative Action", *Society* (Sept./Oct. 1999): 33; Stephen J. McNamee and Robert K. Miller Jr., *The Meritocracy Myth* (Lanham: Rowman & Littlefield, 2004), p. 101.

[8] Terence Lee, *Defect or Defend: Military Responses to Popular Protests in Authoritarian Asia* (Singapore: ISEAS Publishing and Johns Hopkins University Press, 2015), p. 35.

age of leaving active service. The post-career destinations of flag officers are then examined, but estimates of the officers' loyalty to the armed forces and powers to influence public policy are ultimately inconclusive. The sole SAFOS recipient to be stripped of the scholarship also presents a unique insight into career costs and benefits. The fourth section presents outliers in the Aristocracy of Armed Talent to include those with unique career advancements, the bestowment and rescission of "local" ranks, colonels bypassed for promotion despite holding established flag appointments, and on the flip side a one-star sitting in an appointment usually held by a colonel (COL). The chapter rounds out with the transition from one-star officer into the elite nucleus as a two-star service chief. The Chief of Defence Force (CDF) is then selected from among the three to lead as the SAF's most senior uniformed officer.

The penultimate chapter of this book considers the changing society and manpower challenges as Singapore moves on from the Golden Jubilee milestone in nationhood. The city-state is an undeniable economic miracle, but in many ways some of the steps taken along the way to success are today potential hurdles to maintaining a disciplined and credible defence force. The changing social character of Singapore has created obstacles in the form of materialism, discontentment with meritocracy, and self-centredness. Economic success and globalization have thrown up the twin challenges of locals emigrating abroad and the influx of migrants. Finally, the human capital required for defence is perceived as declining in quality and decreasing in quantity. One solution is to increase female participation in defence, but the long-term implications of such an initiative remain to be seen.

1.2   The Elite and the Military Elite

Before commencing the narrative journey, it is imperative to address the terms "elite" and "military elite" and their application in the Singaporean context. The issue with "elite" as a noun or an adjective is the inimical connotations associated with the noun "elitism". This association has altered the meaning of "elite" and made it a dirty word in Singapore and even abroad.[9] A definition of the word usually contains two parts. The first refers to a segment of society or an organization considered superior to the rest.[10] This superiority is normally a

---

[9] Tan Weizhen, "Get to Know Koh First: PM", *TODAY*, 29 Jan. 2013, pp. 1–2; "Should 'Elite' Cease to Be a Dirty Word?" *The Guardian*, 18 Mar. 2008. Another word in the crosshairs seems to be "meritocracy", which is increasingly seen as benefiting only a selected few. Siau Ming En, "Avoid Making Meritocracy a Dirty Word, Says Heng", TODAY, 29 Jan. 2014.

[10] Judy Pearsall, ed., *The Concise Oxford Dictionary*, 10th ed. (Oxford: Oxford University Press, 1999), p. 463.

quality or ability that makes the segment the best within the reference group.[11] The second part consists of perceived benefits such that "an elite group has a high status because it contains the best of its kind".[12] The result of combining ability and status is that the elite are usually "a small group of people who have a lot of power or advantages".[13]

The dictionary offers various definitions of "elitism" according to the angle of emphasis. It can mean "the belief that a small group of people who have a lot of advantages should keep the most power and influence".[14] It can also refer to "the belief that a society or system should be run by an elite" or "the superior attitude or behaviour associated with an elite".[15] The latter reference points to the crux of the issue where the superiority complex and sense of entitlement arising from elitism intertwines itself with the word "elite". An elite entity does not necessarily display elitism but is today frequently guilty by association.[16] The Singaporean academic Kenneth Paul Tan expands on the notion:

> Elitism sets in when the elite class develops an exaggerated "in-group" sense of superiority, a dismissive attitude toward the abilities of those who are excluded from this in-group, a heroic sense of responsibility for the well-being of what the in-group "laments" as the "foolish" and "dangerous" masses, and a repertoire of self-congratulatory public gestures to maintain what is sometimes merely a delusion of superiority.[17]

In practical terms elitism raises its ugly head when "the best, the cream of society, [look] after themselves and their kind, ensuring their own progress and successes, if necessary at the expense of the rest of society".[18] In Singapore elitism is frequently seen as the condition of a segment of "upper-middle or upper-class public servants with impeccable academic grades but out of touch with the very people they are supposed to serve".[19]

---

[11] *MacMillan English Dictionary for Advanced Learners*, International Student Edition (Oxford: Macmillan Education, 2002), p. 450.

[12] Ibid.

[13] Ibid.

[14] Ibid.

[15] Pearsall, *Concise Oxford Dictionary*, p. 463.

[16] "Should 'Elite' Cease to Be a Dirty Word?"

[17] Kenneth Paul Tan, "Meritocracy and Elitism in a Global City: Ideological Shifts in Singapore", *International Political Science Review* 29, 1 (Jan. 2008): 10.

[18] Speech by Minister of Defence Dr Yeo Ning Hong at the MINDEF Workplan Seminar, 26 Mar. 1994, MINDEF, Gombak Drive. Reported in "An SAF That Strives for Excellence", *Straits Times*, 1 July 1994, p. 4.

[19] Han Fook Kwang, Zuraidah Ibrahim, Chua Mui Hoong, Lydia Lim, Ignatius Low, Rachel Lin and Robin Chan, *Lee Kuan Yew: Hard Truths to Keep Singapore Going* (Singapore: Straits Times Press, 2011), p. 102.

It is stressed that elites and elitism are not necessarily synonymous, but this begs the question of who forms society's elites. Classical theorists such as Gaetano Mosca, Vilfredo Pareto and Robert Michels focused on the rule of political elites (the "organised minority") over the masses (the "disorganised majority") and examined themes of superiority, force, manipulation, wealth, class, familial ties, achievements, revolutions and political parties.[20] These themes influenced subsequent research work, including the classification of social functions (e.g., political, organizational, intellectual, artistic, moral, religious, business, education, cultural, military and legal); cooperation and integration among the elites; the familial backgrounds, selection and recruitment education of elites; and the notion of meritocracy.[21]

Wide-ranging definitions of the word "elite" have proliferated in tandem with the expansion in research emphasis. Consideration is given to those with the most influence based on power, wealth, respect and knowledge.[22] Others view elites as the minority who exert disproportionate influence and make "major decisions" in political and social affairs.[23] In functional terms elites include "political leaders; administrators of the state; those in charge of the economy; leaders of the people; and military chiefs".[24] Leaders in the media, academia and labour unions are also included as elites.[25] Such an indiscriminate use of the term has resulted in conceptual overstretch, as John Scott observes:

> At the height of its popularity almost any powerful, advantaged, qualified, privileged, or superior group or category might be described as an elite. The term became one of the most general —and, therefore, one of the

---

[20] Michael Hartmann, *The Sociology of Elites* (Abingdon and New York: Routledge, 2004), pp. 8–21.

[21] John Scott, *Power* (Cambridge: Polity Press, 2001), p. 39; Pierre Bourdieu, *The State Nobility: Elite Schools in the Field of Power* (Stanford: Stanford University Press, 1996); Robert L. Cutts, *An Empire of Schools: Japan's Universities and the Molding of a National Power Elite* (Armonk: M.E. Sharpe, 1997); Hartmann, *Sociology of Elites*, pp. 22–40, 61–88; Mitchell L. Stevens, *Creating a Class: College Admissions and the Education of Elites* (Cambridge: Harvard University Press, 2009).

[22] Harold D. Lasswell, Daniel Lerner and C. Easton Rothwell, "The Elite Concept", in *Political Elites in a Democracy*, ed. Peter Bachrach (New York: Atherton Press, 1971), p. 14; Harold D. Lasswell, *On Political Sociology*, ed. and intro. Dwaine Marvick (Chicago: University of Chicago Press, 1977), p. 115.

[23] Geraint Parry, *Political Elites* (Colchester: European Consortium for Political Research, 2005), pp. 13, 28.

[24] Nada K. Kakabadse, Andrew Kakabadse and Alexander Kouzmin, "From Local Elites to a Globally Convergent Class: A Historical Analytical Perspective", in *Global Elites: The Opaque Nature of Transnational Policy Determination*, ed. Andrew Kakabadse and Nada Kakabadse (Basingstoke: Palgrave Macmillan, 2012), p. 2.

[25] Hartmann, *Sociology of Elites*, p. 3.

most meaningless—terms used in descriptive studies. It was applied to
such diverse groups as politicians, bishops, intelligent people, aristocrats,
lawyers, and successful criminals.[26]

Barr similarly notes that in Singapore the term "elites" extended from political
leadership to the civil service and legal profession and today "encompasses
virtually the entire upper echelon of society, though the apex of the elite was
always restricted to the decision-makers, primarily the managers of resources
and people".[27] Scott proposes the term be applied only to those who hold
and exercise a degree of "power", the authority to issue orders, to direct, and
to expect compliance from others.[28] Concepts consistent with this proposal
include Suzanne Keller's "strategic elites" whose "decisions and actions have
many consequences for many members of society".[29] An even narrower and
more succinct concept is C. Wright Mills' "power elites", namely, the "economic,
political, and military" triumvirate who are the "real centers of power" affecting
the whole of society.[30]

The military elite as a group are counted among society's elite, independent
of broad or narrow definitions—perhaps by all except classical theorists, who
focused exclusively on the ruling class or political elites. In some cases the military
and political elites are one and the same, as in post-coup juntas or preparation
for democratic transitions.[31] In most cases military elites are subservient to
the political echelons, and this holds true across the varying forms of political
systems (democratic, authoritarian, sovereign, etc.).[32] In terms of vested power,

---

[26] John Scott, "Modes of Power and the Re-conceptualization of Elites", in *Remembering Elites*, ed. Mike Savage and Karel Williams (Malden: Blackwell Publishing, 2008), p. 27; Scott, *Power*, pp. 31–2.

[27] Michael D. Barr, *Lee Kuan Yew: The Beliefs behind the Man* (Richmond: Curzon Press, 2000), p. 98.

[28] Scott, *Power*, p. 31; Scott, "Modes of Power", p. 28.

[29] Hartmann, *Sociology of Elites*, p. 31.

[30] Ibid., p. 41; Scott, *Power*, p. 38; Scott, "Modes of Power", p. 35; Kakabadse et al., "From Local Elites to a Globally Convergent Class", p. 6.

[31] See, for example, Eva Etzioni-Halevy, "Civil-Military Relations and Democracy: The Case of the Military-Political Elites' Connection in Israel", *Armed Forces & Society* 22, 3 (Spring 1996): 401–17; Nil S. Satana, "Transformation of the Turkish Military and the Path to Democracy", *Armed Forces & Society* 34, 3 (Spring 2008): 357–88; Mark Beeson, "Civil-Military Relations in Indonesia and the Philippines: Will the Thai Coup Prove Contagious?" *Armed Forces & Society* 34, 3 (Spring 2008): 474–90; and Jonathan M. Powell and Clayton L. Thyne, "Global Instances of Coups from 1950 to 2010: A New Dataset", *Journal of Peace Research* 48, 2 (Mar. 2011): 249–59.

[32] Hartmann, *Sociology of Elites*, pp. 32–3.

military elites are expected to exercise authority over the armed forces in a manner consistent within the state's constitutional framework and expectations of the profession.[33] In times of conflict, the most conspicuous application of this power—and a metric by which military elites are often judged—lies in the actions taken and advice given to achieve conditions for victory.[34] In times of peace, military elites exercise power through the authority of their respective appointments in preparing the armed forces to fight and win the nation's wars.

Identifying members of the military elite is a subjective process, even though military elites are recognized among the various groups of social elites. Military analysts sometimes refer to "elite" units, which further confuses matters:

> … the whole question of what constitutes a military elite is not as clear as many people may believe. Due to a lack of understanding, the term is often misused by the press and public, and also by military personnel. Many different groups, including submariners, search and rescue technicians, paratroopers, fighter pilots, specific combat arms units, and even military police have been labelled as elites, just to name a few.[35]

In this book the term "military elite" is used to refer to specific senior military officers and not to units. Janowitz defines the military elite—whom he also calls an "elite cadre"—as officers at the apex of the rank hierarchy "responsible for the management of the armed forces".[36] Within this esteemed group lies the strategic core—"the elite nucleus"— that provides the armed forces with direction.[37] The concept is broad, and the composition of military elites unsurprisingly differs across countries and researchers. Janowitz considers one-to four-star general officers as the United States' military elite.[38] Scott uses the same group of officers in his study of power in the United States.[39] Eva Etzioni-Halevy qualifies "colonels and above" as military elites in the Israeli Defense Forces (IDF).[40] Oren Barak and Eyal Tsur, on the other hand, limit their

---

[33] Peter Bachrach, "Introduction", in *Political Elites in a Democracy*, ed. Peter Bachrach (New York: Atherton Press, 1971), pp. 2–3.

[34] Ibid.

[35] Bernd Horn, "The Dark Side to Elites: Elitism as a Catalyst for Disobedience", *Canadian Army Journal* 8, 4 (Winter 2005): 67; Bernd Horn, "Love 'Em or Hate 'Em: Learning to Live with Elites", *Canadian Military Journal* 8, 4 (Winter 2007–08): 34.

[36] Morris Janowitz, *The Professional Soldier: A Social and Political Portrait* (New York: Free Press, 1971), pp. 11, 58.

[37] Ibid.

[38] Ibid., p. 147.

[39] Scott, *Power*, p. 37.

[40] Etzioni-Halevy, "Civil-Military Relations and Democracy": 403.

definition to IDF officers in the ranks of the two-star Major-General (MG) and three-star Lieutenant-General (LG).[41] Others use specific appointments as the delimiter. Li Cheng and Scott Harold group officers from Colonel to General in the Central Committee and Central Military Commission as China's military elite.[42] Nicholas Jans et al. do not classify their officers of interest as military elites but restrict their study of Australian Defence Force officers to those of two- to four-star seniority who served in the capacity of a "military strategist rather than that of senior operational commander".[43] There is no single prescribed way of distinguishing military elites; this remains a matter of definition and context.[44]

1.3   The Military Elite in Singapore

The fear of being tagged as an "elite" within Singapore's context arises from semantic associations with "elitism" at best, or perceptions of a deeper and more sinister malaise at worst. Yet it was Dr Goh Keng Swee—the chief architect of Singapore's economic, defence and education policies and Singapore's first defence minister—who specifically applied the term "military elite" to the SAF.[45] In 1972 he revealed the "deliberate creation of military elites in the Republic ... the most skilled, most competent and most successful ... the ultimate guardians of the independence of sovereign states".[46] Goh was cognizant of elitism and cautioned Singapore's elites, including its senior military officers: "The prejudice against elites is a natural one because the majority of people in any social group have to remain outside the select circle. However, in a democratic society, elites while providing leadership do not enjoy special privileges other than bigger incomes and better working conditions which their superior performance entitles them to."[47]

---

[41] Oren Barak and Eyal Tsur, "The Military Careers and Second Careers of Israel's Military Elite", *Middle East Journal* 66, 3 (Summer 2012): 473.

[42] Li Cheng and Scott W. Harold, "China's New Military Elite", *China Security* 3, 4 (Autumn 2007): 62.

[43] Nicholas Jans with Stephen Mugford, Jamie Cullens and Judy Frazer-Jans, *The Chiefs: A Study of Strategic Leadership* (Canberra: Centre for Defence Leadership and Ethics, Australian Defence College, 2013), p. 7.

[44] Scott, *Power*, p. 38.

[45] Melanie Chew and Bernard Tan Tiong Gie, *Creating the Technology Edge: DSO National Laboratories, Singapore 1972–2002* (Singapore: DSO National Laboratories, 2002), p. 26.

[46] Speech by Dr Goh Keng Swee, Minister of Defence, at the Promotion Ceremony at MINDEF HQ on 2 May 1972. Reproduced in "Creating a Military Elite", *Pioneer* (June 1972): 13–4.

[47] Ibid., p. 13.

The military elites in Singapore are defined in this book as uniformed SAF officers authorized to wear one or more stars. These ranks reflect the Military's judgement of the individual's abilities to lead at the highest and most important echelons of the defence establishment. The elite nucleus within the group includes the CDF, who is responsible for the entire SAF, and the three service chiefs: Chief of Army (COA), Chief of Navy (CNV) and Chief of Air Force (CAF), at the helm of the Singapore Army, Republic of Singapore Navy (RSN) and Republic of Singapore Air Force (RSAF) respectively. Statutory laws do not prescribe or cap the number of flag officers, but MINDEF actively controls promotions to this level to avoid brass-creep.[48]

The identification of Singapore's military elites has been a perennial challenge. In *Defending the Lion City* Tim Huxley referred to a BG by the name of "Tan Seck Khim".[49] Huxley, assuming a spelling error most likely gleaned from open sources, was referring to then-Assistant Commissioner of Police (ACP) Tan Teck Khim, who served as the first Director General Staff (DGS) in the former Ministry of Interior and Defence (MID) from 1966 to 1968.[50] Ross Worthington, in *Governance in Singapore*, confused the ranks of various individuals, making BGs of two non-general officers while demoting a third.[51] The late Singapore President S.R. Nathan in his memoirs with Timothy Auger mentioned an "M. S. Gill from Tangkak in Johore, who later became a brigadier-general in the Singapore Armed Forces".[52] The stated individual is believed to have been the late Mancharan Singh Gill, who held the then-second

---

[48] Interviews No. 25 and No. 15.

[49] Tim Huxley, *Defending the Lion City* (St Leonards: Allen & Unwin, 2000), p. 74.

[50] The MID was established in 1965 and on 11 August 1970 was divided into the Ministry of Defence (MINDEF) and the Ministry of Home Affairs (MHA). The legacy of MID is preserved in the number plates on MINDEF vehicles, which begin with the prefix "MID". See "An Assistant Commissioner of Police at Age of 38", *Straits Times*, 5 Sept. 1963, p. 18; "Police Chief to Get Envoy's Post", *Straits Times*, 7 July 1971, p. 8; Lee Kuan Yew, *From Third World to First: The Singapore Story: 1965–2000* (Singapore: Times Media and Straits Times Press, 2000), p. 36; and Ramachandran Menon, ed., *One of a Kind: Remembering SAFTI's First Batch* (Singapore: SAFTI Military Institute, 2007), p. 31.

[51] Worthington cited BGs Foo Kok Swee, Ho Meng Kit and Lim Chuan Poh. Foo was a lieutenant colonel (LTC) who retired in the mid-1970s. Ho was a COL who left the SAF in the early 1990s. Former CDF Lim made BG in 1997, MG in 1999 and LG in 2001. See Ross Worthington, *Governance in Singapore* (London and New York: RoutledgeCurzon, 2003), pp. 209, 215–7, 222.

[52] S.R. Nathan with Timothy Auger, *An Unexpected Journey: Path to the Presidency* (Singapore: Editions Didier Millet, 2011), p. 153.

highest uniformed appointment as Deputy Chief of General Staff (DCGS) in 1982 before retiring as a COL in 1986.[53]

Such confusions are unavoidable because information on Singapore's military elite is neither readily available nor accessible. This is unlike Israel—to which Singapore is often compared—where "[o]ccasionally derided for their failings, but more often worshipped for their achievements, Israel's generals become household names and popular heroes in a way that is unimaginable in most liberal democracies".[54] This is especially so in times of conflict when Israeli society is uncompromising in judgement of IDF leaders. Singapore's military elites are not as well known. At times queries have even surfaced as to why so many flag officers are required.[55] Furthermore, only a few have seen any direct action, which renders any questions of "combat motivation" moot.[56] Commitment can be viewed only in terms of staying on or leaving active service, and not as "commitment to the point of death" during operations.[57] In fact, it was once reported that war-gaming exercises are "the closest to a major military deployment as they (SAF officers) will ever get".[58]

Independent of war, peace or that which lies between, Janowitz opined that "the career experiences of generals and admirals are matters of public record, and this information is an essential part of the civilian control of the military profession".[59] This obviously does not apply to Singapore, even as it prides itself on being an information hub. Official biographies of its military

---

[53] Gill made COL in 1972. "No. 1 Soldier Col. Vij Promoted to Brigadier", *Straits Times*, 3 May 1972, p. 1; "Deputy SAF Chief Retires", *Straits Times*, 20 Oct. 1986, p. 9. Another possible "M.S. Gill" is LTC (RET) Mejar Singh Gill, who is usually referred to as "Mejar" and not by the initials "M.S."

[54] "The IDF's New Chief of Staff: Israel's Feuding Generals", *The Economist*, 15 Feb. 2011.

[55] Li Xueying, "Save Money by Having Fewer Generals? No Way", *Straits Times*, 11 Mar. 2007, p. 8; "Every Soldier Counts: PM", TODAY, 12 Mar. 2007, p. 3.

[56] Officers with "direct action" experience include BG (RET) Thomas Campbell in World War II, BG (RET) Patrick Sim and LG (RET) Winston Choo during *Konfrontasi* (1963–66), and BG (RET) Lam Shiu Tong as part of Operation Thunderbolt to free hostages on SQ117 (26 Mar. 1991).

[57] Bernard Morris Bass, *Transformational Leadership: Industrial, Military and Educational Impact* (Mahwah: Lawrence Erlbaum Associates, 1998), p. 20.

[58] Chua Hian Hou, "SAF Warriors Train on Virtual Front", *CT* (*Straits Times*), 9 Aug. 2000, p. 12.

[59] Janowitz, *Professional Soldier*, p. 125. The most famous war heroes are MG Lim Bo Seng (1909–44) of Force 136 and LTA Adnan Bin Saidi (1915–42) of the 1st Battalion, Malay Regiment, who made the ultimate sacrifice in World War II. See Kevin Blackburn, "Colonial Forces as Postcolonial Memories: The Commemoration and Memory of the Malay Regiment in Modern Malaysia and Singapore", in *Colonial Armies in Southeast Asia*, ed. Karl Hack and Tobias Retting (Abingdon and New York: Routledge, 2006), pp. 320–3.

leaders are rare, and the few in existence are often abridged either by design or by sloppiness.[60] Public access to the thoughts of military leaders is in even shorter supply. It should not be surprising if Singaporeans cannot recognize their military elites, despite official reports of overwhelming support for national defence. This situation is due largely to the luxuries afforded by a long peace and sustained prosperity, which have removed matters of national defence from society at large and fostered benign civil-military relations (CMR). Nevertheless, constructing a database of Singapore's military elites is possible albeit time consuming. Tedious sifting through open-source information and subsequent data triangulation resulted in a list of 170 SAF officers—169 males and 159 ethnically Chinese—who wore at least one star between 1965 and 2018. This list of 94 army generals (55.29 per cent of the total), 31 admirals (18.24 per cent) and 45 air force generals (26.47 per cent) excludes those with honorific titles and foreign officers on loan or hired on contract to the early SAF (Appendix B).[61]

1.4 Literature

The vast majority of literature on Singapore's military defence focuses on technological acquisition, CMR, ethnicity, leadership development, and studies of active-duty conscripts conducted by Regular officers. Under the acquisition umbrella, pundits have traditionally examined Singapore's defence spending, arms procurement, indigenous military-industrial complex, and improvement in war-fighting capabilities. Since the 1970s numerous publications have ranked the SAF, and especially the RSAF, as the best-equipped and best-organized defence force in Southeast Asia.[62] Tim Huxley's *Defending the Lion City: The Armed Forces of Singapore* remains the most holistic, albeit dated, reference on

---

[60] Despite an Internet presence since the late 1990s, it was only on 22 October 2012 that a revamped MINDEF website contained the biographies of the CDF and service chiefs. The biographies of other flag officers are also sketchy and piecewise information is released only on an ad hoc basis. See Rachael Lim, "MINDEF's Revamped Website User-Friendly on Multiple Platforms", *Cyberpioneer*, 29 Oct. 2012.

[61] Air Commodores Geoffrey Millington and John Langer were on loan from the Royal Air Force to help develop the Singapore air force. Lim Bo Seng's bravery and sacrifice in World War II earned him a posthumous promotion to MG from the Chinese Nationalist Kuomintang.

[62] Willard A. Hanna, "The New Singapore Armed Forces", *Fieldstaff Reports* 21, 1 (1973): 6; John Keegan, *World Armies* (London: Macmillan, 1983), p. 520; Huxley, *Defending the Lion City*, pp. 172–95; Felix K. Chang, "In Defense of Singapore", *Orbis* 47, 1 (Winter 2003): 107–23.

the SAF from infancy to the dawn of its Third-Generation (3G) manifestation.[63] The monograph *Defence* by Ho Shu Huang and Samuel Chan Ling Wei provides further but brief coverage of the topic.[64] Authorized commemorative books play complementary roles and provide the most updated open-source information available.

The second widely covered topic is CMR in Singapore. Many foreign authors seem fixated on Singapore's deliberate practice of channelling military scholar-officers and retired senior officers into the civil service and politics.[65] Their conclusions invariably question the professionalism of the SAF Officer Corps but also recognize the symbiotic relationship between the military and the government. One writer queries whether Singapore is headed towards a military-administrative state where civil servants and military personnel (both active duty and retired) in senior government positions hold the authority to set policy albeit without the public accountability faced by politicians.[66] Another depicts the election of retired military elites into the Cabinet as a "silent semi-putsch by the Brigadier-Generals".[67] History shows that to the contrary no putsch of any sort has taken place. Military men have never dominated the Cabinet by numbers, and their ranks have been trimmed by electoral defeat (2011), resignation from politics (2015), or reassignment from the Cabinet (2017). Nevertheless, these publications and others indicate that civilian control

---

[63] The 1G SAF existed from independence until the early 1980s and grew in terms of manpower and equipment. The key focus was on doctrine development, achieving operational capability of individual units, and elementary combined arms operations. The SAF HQ was run by the General Staff. The 2G SAF consolidated combined arms capabilities and ventured into the realm of joint operations. The Joint Staff ran the SAF HQ and coordinated the capabilities of the tri-service outfit. From the early years of the 21st century the hallmarks of the 3G SAF have been service sensor-shooter integration matched with unprecedented information superiority and weapon lethality.

[64] Ho Shu Huang and Samuel Chan Ling Wei, *Defence* (Singapore: Straits Times Press and Institute of Policy Studies, 2015).

[65] Tai Ming Chung, "Soldiers and Scholars: Bright Officers Form New National Elite", *Far Eastern Economic Review* 154, 49 (5 Dec. 1991): 15–8; Tim Huxley, "The Political Role of the Singapore Armed Forces' Officer Corps: Towards a Military-Administrative State", Strategic and Defence Studies Centre Working Paper, No. 279 (Dec. 1993); Richard A. Deck, "Singapore: Comprehensive Security—Total Defence", in *Strategic Cultures in the Asia-Pacific Region*, ed. Ken Booth and Russell Trood (New York: St. Martin's Press, 1999), pp. 247–69; Huxley, *Defending the Lion City*, pp. 232–40; Sean P. Walsh, "The Roar of the Lion City: Ethnicity, Gender, and Culture in the Singapore Armed Forces", *Armed Forces & Society* 33, 2 (Jan. 2007): 265–85; Barr, *Ruling Elite of Singapore*, pp. 80–6.

[66] Huxley, "Political Role of the Singapore Armed Forces' Officer Corps", pp. 3, 19.

[67] Deck, "Singapore: Comprehensive Security", p. 254.

of the military apparatus is an undeniable characteristic of CMR in Singapore although the "Civil-Military Problematique" remains a perennial concern for other countries.[68]

Singaporean authors do not seem fussed over civilian control of the SAF.[69] Chan Heng Chee reckoned "dissatisfied young officers do not stage coups. They merely resign to join the lucrative private sector with their highly marketable skills."[70] Tan Tai Yong coined the term "civil-military fusion" to describe an SAF that is integrated into the civilian structure and plays "an essentially complementary role in the social and economic functions of the state. The upshot is a military establishment that does not possess its own independent political or ideological ambitions but instead identifies fully with the values, interests, and national goals set by the civilian government."[71]

Alan Chong and Samuel Chan venture beyond this perceived civil-military harmony and examine the tension between ideals and reality.[72] They argue that CMR in Singapore is predicated on temperate social militarization through state institutions—namely, MINDEF and the more visible SAF—and discuss "crises" within calibrated (as opposed to rampant and unchecked) nationalism. CMR is essentially kept at the correct temperature to maintain strong self-defence capabilities despite the high opportunity costs in terms of land, labour and capital.

When it comes to CMR in Singapore, the bottom line is that the state gave birth to the military and not vice versa. In fact, it was an almost insurmountable

---

[68] Peter D. Feaver, "The Civil-Military Problematique: Huntington, Janowitz, and the Question of Civilian Control", *Armed Forces & Society* 23, 2 (Winter 1996): 149–78; Peter D. Feaver and Richard H. Kohn, "The Gap: Soldiers, Civilians and Their Mutual Misunderstanding", *National Interest* (Fall 2000): 29–37; Muthiah Alagappa, "Asian Civil-Military Relations: Key Developments, Explanations, and Trajectories", in *Coercion and Governance: The Declining Political Role of the Military in Asia*, ed. Muthiah Alagappa (Stanford: Stanford University Press, 2001), p. 436; Worthington, *Governance in Singapore*, p. 247.

[69] Chan Heng Chee, "Singapore", in *Military-Civilian Relations in South-East Asia*, ed. Zakaria Haji Ahmad and Harold Crouch (Singapore: Oxford University Press, 1985), p. 136; Tan Tai Yong, "Singapore: Civil-Military Fusion", in *Coercion and Governance: The Declining Political Role of the Military in Asia*, ed. Muthiah Alagappa (Stanford: Stanford University Press, 2001), pp. 276–93; Tan Tai Yong, "The Armed Forces and Politics in Singapore: The Persistence of Civil-Military Fusion", in *The Political Resurgence of the Military in Southeast Asia: Conflict and Leadership*, ed. Marcus Mietzner (Abingdon and New York: Routledge, 2011), pp. 148–66; Alan Chong and Samuel Chan Ling Wei, "Militarizing Civilians in Singapore: Preparing for 'Crisis' within a Calibrated Nationalism", *Pacific Review* 30, 3 (2017): 365–84.

[70] Chan, "Singapore", p. 147.

[71] Tan, "Singapore: Civil-Military Fusion", p. 278.

[72] Chong and Chan, "Militarizing Civilians in Singapore": 365–84.

challenge to establish and a perennial struggle to maintain the conscript-based SAF. The military has never had any reason to step into politics given the years of unhindered peace (notwithstanding the ethno-religious struggles of the early years), although Lee Kuan Yew did speculate once or twice, as Senior Minister, that an opposition victory at the polls might require the army to step in. The domestic political climate has proven to be relatively benign due to the longevity and cohesiveness of the ruling party. It would take a very unlikely event, such as a violent grassroots uprising, or extremely incompetent governance, or a decapitation strike on the combined civil service and political leadership, for the military to step into politics. Any politically ambitious officer is at liberty to run for office after leaving active duty. History indicates that a handful will receive an invitation from the ruling regime. So far none have chosen to pick up the gauntlet on an opposition ticket.

The third topic that receives a fair amount of attention is the underrepresentation of Malay Muslims in the upper echelons and sensitive areas of the military establishment. This is a reflection of deliberate policies in the past, but mention of these policies has become *sine qua non* in studies on Singapore's practice of meritocracy, the minority Malay Muslim community, and at times Singapore-Malaysia relations.[73] The Australian academics Michael Barr and Lily Zubaidah Rahim have proven the most persistent and scathing critics of Singapore in this regard. Rahim cites the two-decade-long practice of "exclusion and discrimination" against Malays as a "contradiction" of meritocracy and multiculturalism.[74] Barr depicts the underrepresentation of minorities (especially Malays) among recipients of major government scholarships as a "charade of meritocracy".[75] Yet the contextual circumstances for the marginalization of Malay Muslims in the SAF's early days and their socio-economic and educational disadvantages are little discussed in these one-sided and increasingly

---

[73] Elizabeth Nair, "Nation-Building through Conscript Service in Singapore", in *The Military in the Service of Society and Democracy*, ed. Daniella Ashkenazy (Westport: Greenwood Press, 1994), p. 103; Alon Peled, *A Question of Loyalty: Military Manpower Policy in Multiethnic States* (Ithaca and London: Cornell University Press, 1998); Deck, "Singapore: Comprehensive Security", p. 263; Barr, *Lee Kuan Yew*, p. 203; Carl A. Trocki, *Singapore: Wealth, Power and the Culture of Control* (Abingdon and New York: Routledge, 2006), p. 142; Michael D. Barr, "The Charade of Meritocracy", *Far Eastern Economic Review* 169, 8 (Oct. 2006): 18–22; Sean P. Walsh, "The Roar of the Lion City: Ethnicity, Gender, and Culture in the Singapore Armed Forces", *Armed Forces & Society* 33, 2 (Jan. 2007): 265–85; Lily Zubaidah Rahim, "Governing Muslims in Singapore's Secular Authoritarian State", *Australian Journal of International Affairs* 66, 2 (Apr. 2012): 181.

[74] Rahim, "Governing Muslims in Singapore's Secular Authoritarian State": 181.

[75] Barr, "Charade of Meritocracy": 18–22.

anachronistic and parochial studies.[76] The gradual advancement of Malays into the upper echelons of the officer corps has remained conspicuously unremarked upon by this group of scholars.

The fourth area of research covers leadership development and sociological aspects of active-duty conscripts. The majority of these studies were conducted by personnel at MINDEF's Applied Behavioural Science Department (ABSD) and the SAF Centre for Leadership Development (CLD) at SAFTI Military Institute (SAFTI MI). The studies varied in size and focus to cover topics such as how NS fostered racial integration; motivation for leadership positions; the evolution of perceptions, beliefs and values over the course of Basic Military Training (BMT); team composition and the effects of processes and performances of infantry sections; job satisfaction among Regulars serving in active battalions; and how initial training experiences and the way conscripts coped affected their perceptions of, and commitment to, NS in terms of time and energy.[77] Despite such efforts, the in-depth examination of SAF history and the sociological aspects of its top brass have remained conspicuously absent.[78] Derek Da Cunha paints a macro-sociological portrait of the SAF and includes several paragraphs on the unique scholar-officer phenomenon used to groom senior military leaders.[79] Tim Huxley includes a chapter in *Defending the Lion City* that broadly addresses SAF manpower policies. Publications commemorating Dr Goh Keng Swee also

---

[76] Adrian Lim, "Malays Make Strides in SAF", *MyPaper*, 30 May 2014; "Malay-Muslim Community against Tokenism: Maliki", *Straits Times*, 31 May 2014, p. B16.

[77] Nair, "Nation-Building through Conscript Service in Singapore", pp. 101–10; Kim-Yin Chan, "Toward a Theory of Individual Differences and Leadership: Understanding the Motivation to Lead", PhD dissertation, University of Illinois at Urbana-Champaign, 1999; Star Soh, "Organizational Socialization of Newcomers: A Longitudinal Study of Organizational Enculturation Processes and Outcomes", PhD dissertation, Ohio State University, 2000; Beng Chong Lim, "Do the Leader and Member Make the Team? The Role of Personality and Cognitive Ability", PhD dissertation, University of Maryland, 2003; Don Willis, "The Structure & Antecedents of Organisational Commitment in the Singapore Army", presentation at the 45th International Military Testing Association Conference, Pensacola, 3–6 Nov. 2003; Chiang Hock Woon, "Young Singaporeans' Perspectives of Compulsory Military Conscription: How They Manage the National Service Experience in Relation to Their Education, Development and Careers", PhD dissertation, University of Leicester, 2011.

[78] Irvin Lim Fang Jau, "Viewpoints: Pointers from the Past, Foresight into the Future", *Pointer* 30, 3 (2004); Tan Peng Ann, "Viewpoints: Learning from the Past: An Old Soldier's Advice", *Pointer* 30, 3 (2004).

[79] Derek Da Cunha, "Sociological Aspects of the Singapore Armed Forces", *Armed Forces & Society* 25, 3 (Spring 1999): 459–75.

mention certain manpower policies he implemented.[80] The autobiography of the late John Francis Langer (1925–2016), a retired RAF Air Commodore and fighter pilot on loan service to Singapore from January 1973 to April 1975, provides insightful reading into the state and variety of challenges faced in leading the republic's infant air force.[81]

The paucity of insights into the military elite is illustrated by the fact that very few sociological sketches are available. Leong Choon Cheong includes BG (RET) Lee Hsien Yang, then an Officer Cadet Trainee (OCT) at the SAF Training Institute (SAFTI), in *Youth in the Army*, which presents biographical sketches of 11 conscripts.[82] Leslie Terh's *Sons and Officers* records the lived experiences of Singaporean trainees, including LG (RET) Winston Choo Wee Leong, at the Federation Military College (FMC) in Malaya between 1957 and 1965.[83] BG (RET) Tan Yong Soon's *Living the Singapore Dream* is a short autobiography that includes partial biographical sketches of his peers.[84] It remains the only book of its kind by an SAF general officer. A 2011 monograph by the SAF CLD titled *Called to Lead* represents the then-largest account by the SAF's senior leadership—six army generals and five admirals—to champion introspection about the profession among active-duty officers.[85] The interviews with the top brass yielded a scant collection of six explanations for signing on and four for staying on. There is no mention of officer ascension, but this is not a shortcoming as the monograph was never intended to paint a portrait of the military elite in Singapore.

---

[80] Ooi Kee Beng, *In Lieu of Ideology: The Intellectual Biography of Goh Keng Swee* (Singapore: Institute of Southeast Asian Studies, 2010); Dhoraisingam S. Samuel, *Working for Dr. Goh Keng Swee: Collection of Anecdotes* (Singapore: Dhoraisingam S. Samuel, Nov. 2011); Barry Desker and Kwa Chong Guan, eds, *Goh Keng Swee: A Public Career Remembered* (Singapore: World Scientific Publishing, 2012).

[81] J.F. Langer, *From the Spitfire Cockpit to the Cabinet Office: The Memoirs of Air Commodore J F "Johnny" Langer CBE AFC DL* (Barnsley: Pen & Sword Aviation, 2016), pp. 205–30.

[82] Leong Choon Cheong, *Youth in the Army* (Singapore: Federal Publications, 1978).

[83] Leslie Terh, *Sons and Officers: Life at Prestigious Military College* (Singapore: Sea Sky Books Enterprise, 2000).

[84] Tan Yong Soon, *Living the Singapore Dream* (Singapore: SNP International Publishing, 2007).

[85] Ng Zhi-Wen, Adrian Chan, Sukhmohinder Singh and Lim Teck Yin, *Called to Lead: A Reader for Aspiring SAF Leaders* (Singapore: Pointer: Journal of the Singapore Armed Forces, 2011). The interviewees were LG Lim Chuan Poh, LG Ng Yat Chung, RADM2 Kwek Siew Jin, RADM2 Ronnie Tay, BG Hugh Lim, BG Ong Boon Hwee, BG Ravinder Singh, BG Winston Toh, RADM1 Sim Gim Guan, RADM1 Tan Kai Hoe and RADM1 Tay Kian Seng.

1.5 Data

Publications on the military elite in Singapore are conspicuously absent, but this is not the case for other countries. There are numerous biographies and autobiographies of military leaders, usually retired from active service, in the English-speaking world. Some are focused on the unique political and military milieu of a particular period, conflict or government. Others are centred on criticisms of military leaders in times of conflict. The literature also covers prestigious military colleges and academies that serve as cradles for various officer corps. In terms of military sociology, there are three core authors who stand out among the literary kaleidoscope and provide sensitizing concepts or "signposts" to approach the cases studied and uncover empirical evidence.[86] The works of these doyens are not utilized as definitive concepts to test hypotheses, nor do they present a rigid framework for approaching the inquiries undertaken.[87]

The political scientist Samuel Huntington in his early classic *The Soldier and the State* framed the motivational basis expected of the professional American military officer in the mid-20th century:

> Does the officer have a professional motivation? Clearly he does not act primarily from economic incentives. In western society the vocation of officership is not well rewarded monetarily. Nor is his behavior within his profession governed by economic rewards and punishments. The officer is not a mercenary who transfers his services wherever they are best rewarded, nor is he the temporary citizen soldier inspired by intense momentary patriotism but with no steadying and permanent desire to perfect himself in the management of violence. The motivations of the officer are a technical love for his craft and the sense of social obligation to utilize his craft for the benefit of society. The combination of these drivers constitutes professional motivation. Society, on the other hand, can only assure this motivation if it offers its officers continuing and sufficient pay both while on active duty and when retired.[88]

These Huntingtonian ideals demand professionalism though a lifelong devotion to the profession of arms and the triumph of altruism (improving the welfare of others) grounded in societal obligation and benefit over egoism (improving personal welfare) based on economic and monetary considerations.

---

[86] Martin Bulmer, "Concepts in the Analysis of Qualitative Data", in *Sociological Research Methods: An Introduction*, 2nd ed., ed. Martin Bulmer (Piscataway: Transaction Publishers, 1984), pp. 242–3.

[87] Ibid., p. 243.

[88] Samuel P. Huntington, *The Soldier and the State: The Theory and Politics of Civil-Military Relations* (Cambridge: Belknap Press of Harvard University Press, 1964), p. 15.

Janowitz theorized that officer motivation for service varied according to models of political-military elites. His 1957 study attributes power and the preservation of social status as motivating factors within the aristocratic model.[89] The democratic model assumes officers are motivated by "professional ethics alone". Officers in the totalitarian model have no alternatives to military service. Finally, those in the garrison-state model are motivated by "national survival and glory". Janowitz continues with a thorough examination of American military elites within the democratic model in *The Professional Soldier*. He argues that individuals with the potential to serve as commissioned officers face "extensive tension" in their decision to realize this potential. Certain social circles (usually in urbanized areas) consider the military "a berth of mediocrity" attracting only those keen to "avoid the competitive realities of civil society", whereas "the best minds are attracted to more positive endeavours".[90] Yet others hold a countervailing view that military officers fulfil "some special mission", namely, the mastery of military craft necessary to fight and win the nation's wars.[91]

During his interviews with 277 army generals, Janowitz uncovered four main and not necessarily mutually exclusive patterns of motivation to join the army. These included "tradition, or more precisely family and social inheritance; sheer desire for education and social advancement, with or without a career commitment to the military; experience in a military setting; and 'boyhood' ambition".[92] Those who cited motivation from a "calling" were, however, "outnumbered by a greater concentration of individuals for whom the military is just another job".[93] With specific reference to commitment, Janowitz highlighted the numbers of "junior officers who resign after completing their required services" as a clear challenge to retention but did not provide specific reasons for those who chose to remain on active service.[94]

Janowitz also investigated the ascension of the United States' military elites. Their careers followed prescribed—or cookie-cutter—routes "performed with high competence", but three- and four-star generals in the elite nucleus required

> innovating perspectives, discretionary responsibility, and political skills ...
> unconventional and adaptive careers ... developed within the framework
> of existing institutions, since officers who express too openly their desire

---

[89] Morris Janowitz, "Military Elites and the Study of War", *Conflict Resolution* 1, 1 (Mar. 1957): 10–1.

[90] Janowitz, *Professional Soldier*, pp. 104–5, 107.

[91] Ibid., p. 104.

[92] Ibid., p. 108.

[93] Ibid., p. 117.

[94] Ibid., p. 122.

to innovate or to criticize are not likely to survive. All types of elites must be skilled in managing interpersonal relations, in making strategic decisions, and in political negotiations, rather than in the performance of technical tasks.[95]

While these are expectations, the reality is often more complicated. Other hidden and presumably less meritocratic factors that influenced an officer's ascension included being in "the appropriate academy class" and the good fortune to be "at the right spot when new opportunities suddenly develop".[96] Aspiring officers also needed to create informal communication channels with influential officers and establish a reputation to attract superiors who could position them in subordinate command and staff billets.[97] Competency and visibility proved essential as officers were constantly observed and assessed, and "it is impossible to separate the formal procedures from the elaborate informal screening that goes on simultaneously".[98] Furthermore, success came not only to those who demonstrated technical competence but also to those with the initiative to drive their careers by seeking appointments required for success. This meant "command duty, and to be involved in operations when assigned to staff duty".[99] While command was necessary, it was insufficient on its own as military elites also "displayed an early and persistent propensity for staff work".[100]

Janowitz's empirical evidence stands in contrast to Huntington's ideal professional soldier. Charles Moskos captures the departure from the Huntingtonian ideals in his Institution/Occupation (I/O) thesis, where the motivation and commitment for military service lie between opposite poles. The institutional pole is rooted in values and norms where individuals act presumably for a greater good, follow a "calling", and view their profession as "being different or apart from the broader society".[101] The occupational pole is

---

[95] Ibid., pp. 11–2.

[96] Ibid., p. 126. The significance of attendance at specific academies in officer ascension has been noted at various times and in different countries. See, for example, David R. Segal, "Selective Promotion in Officer Cohorts", *Sociological Quarterly* 8, 2 (Mar. 1967): 199–205; and Insoo Kim and Tyler Crabb, "Collective Identity and Promotion Prospects in the South Korean Army", *Armed Forces & Society* 40, 2 (Apr. 2014): 295–309.

[97] Janowitz, *Professional Soldier*, p. 145.

[98] Ibid., p. 145–6.

[99] Ibid., p. 147.

[100] Ibid., p. 166.

[101] Charles C. Moskos, "Institutional and Occupational Trends in Armed Forces", in *The Military: More Than Just a Job?* ed. Charles C. Moskos and Frank R. Wood (New York: Pergamon Press, 1988), p. 16.

predicated on rational calculations and prioritized self-interests over the military as an employer.[102] This is not mere semantics; Moskos and Frank Wood note that "occupationalism" threatens to replace

> ... the intrinsic motivation of an institution with the extrinsic motivation of an occupation ... the difference between intrinsic motivation, as in action due to personal values, and extrinsic motivation, as in behavior brought about by pay. The interaction of intrinsic and extrinsic rewards can be quite complex; not only may these rewards be nonadditive, but also inducing members to perform tasks with strong extrinsic rewards may create behavior that will not be performed in the future except for even greater extrinsic rewards. Extrinsic rewards, moreover, can weaken intrinsic motivation.[103]

With regard to officer ascension, Moskos reasons that "[a]n institutional military tends to evaluate its personnel in 'whole person' categories and rely heavily on qualitative and subjective evaluations. An occupational military tends toward judgments relating to specific performance standards and prefers numerical or quantitative evaluations."[104] He concludes that there is no dominant pole and a clear bifurcation between the poles is absent. Characteristics of both are present in the military community, with implications for personnel attitudes, behaviour, socialization, preservation of professional values, and CMR.[105] The I/O mix was evident in various empirical studies conducted on militaries in the United States, Europe, Israel and Taiwan.[106] Singapore is not spared this perennial struggle (despite contextual differences) as the following chapters will attest.

The ideas and observations from Huntington, Janowitz and Moskos, in conjunction with psychology, sociology and management science were utilized

---

[102] Ibid., p. 17.

[103] Charles C. Moskos and Frank R. Wood, "Introduction", in *The Military: More Than Just a Job?* ed. Charles C. Moskos and Frank R. Wood (New York: Pergamon Press, 1988), p. 5.

[104] Charles C. Moskos, "Institutional/Occupational Trends in Armed Forces: An Update", *Armed Forces & Society* 12, 3 (Spring 1986): 381.

[105] Moskos, "Institutional Occupational Trends", pp. 6, 15.

[106] See, for example, David R. Segal and Mady Wechsler Segal, "Change in Military Organization", *Annual Review of Sociology* 9 (1983): 152, 154; David R. Segal, "Measuring the Institutional/Occupational Change Thesis", *Armed Forces & Society* 12, 3 (Spring 1986): 358; Giuseppe Caforio and Marina Nuciari, "The Officer Profession: Ideal-Type", *Current Sociology* 42, 3 (Winter 1994): 36, 41–2; Bernard Morris Bass, *Transformational Leadership: Industrial, Military and Educational Impact* (Mahwah: Lawrence Erlbaum Associates, 1998), p. 2; Reuven Gal, "The Motivation for Serving in the IDF: In the Mirror of Time", *Strategic Assessment* 2, 3 (Dec. 1999); Eliot A. Cohen, "Twilight of the Citizen-Soldier", *Parameters* (Summer 2001): 23–4; and Kuo-Wei Lin, Chia-Mu Kuan and Chi-Hao Lu, "Analysis of Intention to Continue Services among Recruited Voluntary Soldiers", *Journal of Social Sciences* 8, 4 (2012): 479–80.

as sensitizing concepts in this study. The primary sources of information were obtained from a maximum variation sample across the services and vocations (Table 1.1). A list of 125 flag officers from 1965 to 2012 was drawn up for possible interviews between July 2012 and February 2013. The list was trimmed on the assumption that retired officers and those not in politics had the greatest liberty to speak candidly without needing to take an official stance.[107] Some will invariably scoff at this suggestion, but realities determine such action. As retired civil servant Bilahari Kausikan, a former Permanent Secretary (PS) at the Ministry of Foreign Affairs, explained at the monthly Singapore Platform for East-West Dialogue:

> Here, I have to acknowledge that there is something of a quandary. I can educate you in this closed group, and because I am a pensioner after all, I can say anything I want. I have a title that is meaningless. Don't ask me what Ambassador-at-Large means because I have no idea. In the colloquial sense of the term, "at large" means not-yet-called. But I am a pensioner, I have no authority, I have no official position. So I can say what I just said to you. It's very hard for a government to say these things because you don't want to go and roil the official track unnecessarily. If it is necessary, of course, we have to hold firm to this fundamental bedrock of what makes Singapore, even if it causes tensions in the first track, and that's what we did over the last year-and-a-half and 2004. A few months ago, Mr Chan Chun Sing was asked a question about foreign influence in politics in parliament. He had to give a very circumspect answer. So circumspect that, unless you already knew, you won't know what he was talking about. I can't blame him, you know? But in small groups like this, I can try to educate you.[108]

For this reason, the 30 officers on active service and the five holding political office were excluded from consideration. The list was further shortened with the exclusion of two deceased officers and an estimated ten who were not resident in Singapore.[109] Forty-six of the remaining 78 were approached, resulting in 28 (62.2 per cent) one-off semi-structured and opened-ended interviews. Of the

---

[107] The author made email requests for information through two official channels, but neither replied.

[108] Talk by Bilahari Kausikan, Ambassador-at-Large at the Ministry of Foreign Affairs, titled "Why Small Countries Should Not Behave Like a Small Country", Singapore Platform for East-West Dialogue, 11 Oct. 2017, https://blogs.ntu.edu.sg/paralimes/2018/03/26/bilahari-smallcountries, accessed 4 Apr. 2018.

[109] The deceased officers were BG (RET) Thomas James Duncan Campbell and BG (NS) (Dr) Wong Yue Sie (d. 28 May 2010). The names of the officers residing overseas are withheld to maintain their privacy.

other 18 invitees, four responded with good wishes but declined to participate, 12 did not respond, and two responded favourably but were not interviewed.[110]

Table 1.1. Service and rank distribution of interviewees

Rank	Army	Navy	Air Force	Total
BG/Rear-Admiral (One-Star) (RADM1)	15	3	6	24
MG/ Rear-Admiral (Two-Star) (RADM2)	1	1	–	2
LG	1	–	1	2
Total	17	4	7	28

There are three noteworthy points regarding the interviews and interviewees. First, the interviewees' voices in chapters 3 to 5 provide the reader with vicarious experiences through narrative and description. Transcripts of interview data are presented as verbatim facsimiles and include observations of expression and non-verbal communication of feelings. The difficulty is that

> [v]erbal interactions follow a logic that is different from that for written prose, and therefore tend to look remarkably disjointed, inarticulate, and even incoherent when committed to the printed page. Inherent differences between the spoken tongue and the written word mean that transcripts of verbal conversations do not measure up well to the standards we hold for well-crafted prose (or even formal speeches), with the result that participants often come across as incoherent and inarticulate … The disjuncture between what coheres in natural talk and what demonstrates communicative competence in written prose comes as a shock to many respondents when they are asked or are offered the opportunity to review the transcripts of their interviews.[111]

This was the case with participants who requested a copy of notes taken during their interviews and subsequently revised the text into well-crafted prose. For the other interviews, the recommendation followed was to tidy the text by editing—for instance, through the use of square brackets to add words not used by the original speaker—for readability without altering the message and meaning.[112]

---

[110] An interview with BG (RET) (Dr) Lim Meng Kin was arranged for 30 November 2012. The same morning he was hospitalized for pneumonia, and he passed away on 31 January 2013 from a cancer-related illness aged 62. An interview with the second officer did not take place as his schedule did not permit an interview before the author left Singapore.

[111] James A. Holstein and Jaber F. Gubrium, "Inside Interviewing: Transcription Quality", *SAGE Research Methods* (Thousand Oaks: Sage Publications, 2003), p. 11.

[112] Ibid.

The second point is the possibility for interviewees to avoid unbridled self-aggrandizement and project—not necessarily false—modesty to give legitimacy to "both their own positions of power and the system of social relations within the military itself".[113] James Dowd coined the term "rhetoric of modesty" after interviews with 62 active-duty US Army generals, where he observed:

> When officers talk about successful military careers, they face a dilemma. They must uphold the integrity of the promotion system and their faith in its wisdom while, at the same time, acknowledging the critical importance of the timely intervention of sponsors ... However, the Army cannot acknowledge this intervention, let alone recommend it, because of its close resemblance to careerism and favouritism.[114]

Dowd further noted the officers' explanations for successful careers were centred on care for subordinates, the help of sponsors (mentor-protégé relationship), and "good" ambition to seek "hard jobs".[115] This is not entirely unexpected given an environment that emphasizes service above self through the explicit values system and promotion board observations.[116] The voices from the 28 interviews are kept anonymous, and any "rhetoric of modesty" is successfully minimized should their candour allow readers to find verisimilitude in the pages that follow.

Finally, only information of contextual and specific relevance to the motivation, commitment and ascension of uniformed officers was noted. This excludes details such as the character of flag officers —personality traits, behaviour patterns and leadership styles—and their impact on organizational outcomes. Relationships between rivals have at times festered and reached comical levels thanks to egos and vicarious bravado made possible by Singapore's very own "long peace" (absence of inter-state armed conflict). The details of such internecine clashes are peripheral and at most serve only to blemish the collective portrait of the military elite. "Professionalism" in terms of tactical prowess as junior officers, abilities to manoeuvre forces as senior officers, or strategize as flag officers was similarly avoided. The technological aspects—from platforms to networks and systems and the wider military-industrial complex—are mentioned in passing

---

[113] James J. Dowd, "Hard Jobs and Good Ambition: U.S. Army Generals and the Rhetoric of Modesty", *Symbolic Interaction* 23, 2 (2000): 184.

[114] Ibid., p. 191.

[115] Ibid., p. 188.

[116] A promotion board is an authorized panel of uniformed officer and/or civilian bureaucrats convened to address issues related to the promotion of individuals junior in rank and appointment vis-à-vis panel members. Civilian public officers fall under the respective personnel boards of various ministries listed under the Public Service (Personnel Boards) Order, Constitution of The Republic of Singapore (Article 110D(1) AND (2)).

out of contextual necessity. Similarly, the SAF's ability to achieve a swift and decisive victory in the event of armed conflict remains speculative at best.

Civilian employees who serve as Defence Executive Officers (DXO) and operatives from Singapore's external intelligence agency—the Security and Intelligence Division (SID)—make valuable contributions to defence but are excluded from discussion in this book. Even though DXOs were recognized as "regular servicemen" in 1994, they provide non-combat services (e.g., corporate communications, policy, human resources, information technology, logistics and medical services) within a defence setting.[117] They do not command, do not bear arms, and are not asked to stand in harm's way. Their roles, while important, cannot be compared to those of uniformed personnel. The shroud of secrecy that covers SID and the dearth of open-source material are straightforward reasons for their exclusion in this discussion.

The primary source interviews are augmented with open sources such as official MINDEF, SAF and other government publications (e.g., websites, newsletters, annual reports and books), sanctioned commemorative anniversary books published by SAF units, and interview transcripts from the Oral History Centre at the National Archives of Singapore. Newspapers, academic books and journals provide additional historical information to confirm or raise queries where necessary. Readers not familiar with Singapore must be cognizant that a Freedom of Information Act (or equivalent) does not exist. Anyone who requests information on defence and other security-related matters is likely to be stonewalled or ignored. As a former Harvard doctoral candidate noted in his thesis-turned-book on a comparative study of ethnic minorities:

> Before travelling to Singapore, I called a journalist who had worked there many years to ask for his advice on how to facilitate my research. The journalist, who knew nothing about the topic of my work, attempted to allay my fears. "The reports in the West on the so-called Singaporean secrecy are grossly exaggerated," he told me. "You can research anything you wish to research in Singapore with the exception of two topics: the military and ethnic relations."[118]

Gaining access to information and willing witnesses to history are perennial challenges.[119] This applies to the military, where the information flow was further restricted in early 2016. Personnel movement has been securitized and removed from army, RSN and RSAF newsletters. The Singapore Government Directory

---

[117] "Non-Uniformed Staff Regular Servicemen Too", *Straits Times*, 1 Nov. 1994, p. 20.

[118] Peled, *A Question of Loyalty*, p. xiv.

[119] Loh Kah Seng and Liew Kai Shiun, eds, *The Makers & Keepers of Singapore History* (Singapore: Ethos Books and Singapore Heritage Society, 2010).

interactive portal is outdated at times, and official websites are left neglected in favour of other forms of social media. Nevertheless, there is a portrait to paint despite the challenges of incomplete information. The restrictive infoscape makes this book even more timely and relevant in many ways.

CHAPTER 2

The Profession of Arms and Society

"The guns we provide the SAF are as effective as the soldiers who fire them. The soldiers are as effective as the officers who lead them. The officers are as effective as the society which nurtures them."[1]

— Dr Goh Keng Swee (1918–2010)
Minister for Defence (1965–67, 1970–79)

2.1   Introduction

National security has been a cornerstone of Singapore's economic success and a mandatory obsession among its political leaders. Defence sits on a pedestal festooned with an unquestionable raison d'être, given funding priority with the expectation of prudence, and high degrees of domestic and international visibility.[2] The SAF today is a far cry from the "two battalions and three ships" on hand when Singapore went from being a British colony (1819–1963) to a state within Malaysia (1963–65) and finally an independent republic.[3] Indeed, defence spending and organization have forged the city-state into a quasi-"Nation in Arms" over the last five decades.[4] The obstacles to

---

[1] *SAFTI Leadership Journal* (Singapore: Centre for Leadership Development, SAFTI Military Institute, 2003), p. 81.

[2] 2015 Global Militarization Index ranking of military expenditure in relation to Gross Domestic Product and national budget: 1. Israel, 2. Singapore, 3. Armenia, 4. Jordan, 5. Republic of Korea, 6. Russia, 7. Cyprus, 8. Azerbaijan, 9. Kuwait, 10. Greece. Jan Grebe and Max M. Mutschler, eds, *Global Militarization Index 2015* (Bonn: Bonn International Center for Conversion, 2015), p. 5.

[3] "Yusof Charts Way ahead and Warns of Twin Dangers", *Straits Times*, 9 Dec. 1965, p. 14.

[4] One definition of Nation in Arms is the "codependency between the military and society. This codependency includes, but is not limited to, almost full national conscription of men and women of service age, harnessing the nation's economy to the country's war efforts, and even conscription of personal property (such as personal possessions, vehicles, and land) at times of war." See Gabriel Ben-Dor, Ami Pedahzur, Daphna Canetti-Nisim, Eran Zaidise, Arie Perliger and Shai Bermanis, "I versus We: Collective and Individual Factors of Reserve Service Motivation during War and Peace", *Armed Forces & Society* 34, 4 (July 2008): 587.

creating a credible defence force seemed insurmountable at times, but the early generations prevailed against the odds. The impressive and sometimes pompous arsenal put on display every SAF Day (1 July) and National Day (9 August) and at various Open House events testifies to the investments in defence independent of the prevailing economic climate. The symbiotic practice of consistency and prudence over one of "feast or famine" in defence spending is perhaps the simpler portion of the equation. Defence must be viewed beyond the impressive hardware and consider the various manpower challenges, as Dr Goh frequently cautioned. This chapter captures the growing pains of Singapore's defence establishment and features certain military figures who led the SAF in its formative years, the majority of whom joined the military before conscription was introduced in 1967.

2.2 Defence: The Sacrosanct Pillar

The nature of defence in independent Singapore was shaped by the tumultuous events between the fall of Singapore on 15 February 1942 and its separation from Malaysia on 9 August 1965.[5] The myth of British colonial supremacy was shattered by Japanese imperialism as the Eastern power occupied Syonan-to for a long three and a half years. Some 20,000 to 30,000 men in Syonan-to were massacred, while the surviving population faced hunger on a scale unimaginable for Singaporeans today. Communist subversion and insurgency along the Malayan peninsula followed soon after, in 1948, and led to a struggle that officially concluded only in 1989. Indonesia was also at odds with the newly independent Malaysia, which resulted in a low-intensity *Konfrontasi* (Indonesian Confrontation) from 1963 to 1966. Few Singaporeans remember that eight of their own soldiers perished and another five were wounded in Operation Oak Tree when a 25-man detachment was ambushed by Indonesian infiltrators in Bukit Lebam, Kota Tinggi, Johore, at dusk on 28 February 1965. These key events firmly entrenched Singapore's vulnerabilities into the collective psyche of the nation's early leaders amidst the myriad of post-independence domestic political and socio-economic challenges.[6] Furthermore, Singapore did not exist in a "strategic vacuum" despite relative poverty and underdevelopment, as

---

[5] Alex Josey, *Lee Kuan Yew: The Struggle for Singapore* (Sydney: Angus & Robertson, 1976), pp. 225–6; Bilveer Singh, "The Communist Threat in Perspective", *Straits Times*, 5 Jan. 2015.

[6] Lee Boon Hiok, "Leadership and Security in Singapore: The Prevailing Paradigm", in *Leadership Perceptions and National Security: The Southeast Asian Experience*, ed. Mohammed Ayoob and Chai-Anan Samudavanija (Singapore: Institute of Southeast Asian Studies, 1989), pp. 161–9; Chin Kin Wah, "Singapore: Threat Perception and Defence Spending in a City-State", in *Defence Spending in Southeast Asia*, ed. Chin Kin Wah (Singapore: Institute of Southeast Asian Studies, 1987), p. 196.

geography placed it "at the gateway to the Indian Ocean and the South China Sea, the ante-room to the Pacific".[7]

History provided the experience and future considerations laid the foundations for Singapore's seemingly unflinching devotion to defence. First, defence was of utmost importance if Singapore wanted to remain independent. This was long an afterthought for the local population during the colonial years when Singapore—the "Gibraltar of the East"—served as an important trading port, naval base and satellite earth station for the British empire. Such concerns remained peripheral during the short-lived merger with Malaysia, but the security umbrella folded rather suddenly as irreconcilable political differences led to separation.[8] The subsequent phased withdrawal of British military forces "east of the Suez" reflected London's strategic realignment after World War II, which had drained a quarter of its national wealth.[9] Nevertheless, Singapore assumed Downing Street would honour any political assurances.[10] The visiting British defence minister declared "no naval pull-out from Singapore in the foreseeable future" in October 1966, but by 15 January 1968 the UK announced a complete withdrawal of forces by December 1971.[11] The Singapore government was shocked and disappointed as plans for self-defence fell into disarray. State revenue from British bases was also sizable. In 1970, the 36,685-strong garrison occupied 72 installations covering 6,507 hectares and

---

[7] George G. Thomson, "Britain's Plan to Leave Asia", *Round Table: Commonwealth Journal of International Affairs* 58, 230 (1968): 123–4.

[8] Issues included special rights for Malays, equality, citizenship for non-Malays, governance (Malay political domination and monarchical system), choice of national language(s), and ideology (both domestic and external). Lee, *From Third World to First*, pp. 257–91; Lau Teik Soon, "Malaysia-Singapore Relations: Crisis of Adjustment, 1965–68", *Journal of Southeast Asian History* 10, 1 (Mar. 1969): 157, 159; Chan Heng Chee, "Singapore's Foreign Policy, 1965–1968", *Journal of Southeast Asian History* 10, 1 (Mar. 1969): 179; Menon, *One of a Kind*, pp. 21–5.

[9] Greg Behrman, *The Most Noble Adventure: The Marshall Plan and the Reconstruction of Post-War Europe* (London: Aurum Press, 2008), pp. 15–6.

[10] Derek McDougall, "The Wilson Government and the British Defence Commitment in Malaysia-Singapore", *Journal of Southeast Asian Studies* 4, 2 (Sept. 1973): 229–40; Leonard Rayner, "A Review of British Defence and Foreign Policies and Their Effects on Singapore and the Rest of the Region", *Southeast Asian Affairs* (1976): 348–53.

[11] Lim Suan Kooi, "Full Steam Ahead for the Future", *Straits Times*, 9 Aug. 1972, p. 2; Lui Pao Chuen, ed., *Engineering Land Systems 50* (Singapore: Ministry of Defence, 2016), p. 6.

accounted for around one-fifth of Singapore's gross domestic product (GDP).[12] An irate Dr Goh—whom Singapore's first Prime Minister (PM) Lee Kuan Yew (LKY) depicted as his "alter ego"—called the episode "a disgraceful breach of an undertaking given to us".[13]

In contrast to the British forces leaving Singapore prematurely in 1971, Malaysian infantry units lingered in Singapore after independence in 1965. Singapore also had great difficulty recovering equipment that was merged into the Malaysian Armed Forces while Singapore was part of the federation (1963–65).[14] The 1st Battalion, Royal Malay Regiment, of the Malaysian Armed Forces (MAF) occupied Camp Temasek (which existed from 1963 to 1977) at Ulu Pandan, while the 2nd Battalion, Singapore Infantry Regiment (2 SIR), was deployed to Sabah from August 1965 to February 1966 during *Konfrontasi*. The officers and men of 2 SIR found themselves without accommodation after returning from their tour of duty and ended up living under canvas at Farrer Park. A fleet of the unit's vehicles "found their way" to Batu Gajah in Malaysia as the battalion pitched tents. Kuala Lumpur (KL) was adamant that Malaysian forces would not vacate Camp Temasek until suitable alternative accommodation was available. Temporary barracks were constructed at Bukit Sembawang to house

---

[12] The British Far East Command stood down on 31 October 1971, and remaining units were withdrawn between September 1975 and March 1976. "Lee: We Have Five to 10 Years to Build Sinews …", *Straits Times*, 20 July 1967, p. 1; "Britain's Pullout Decision Will Stay", *Straits Times*, 17 Jan. 1970, p. 5; R. Chandran, "Lee's Tribute to British Peace-keeping Role in S-E Asia", *Straits Times*, 17 Oct. 1971, p. 1; Leslie Fong, "Britain's Bombshell", *Straits Times*, 24 Nov. 1974, p. 10; Chin Kin Wah, "Singapore: Threat Perception and Defence Spending in a City-State", in *Defence Spending in Southeast Asia*, ed. Chin Kin Wah (Singapore: Institute of Southeast Asian Studies, 1987), p. 195; Malcolm H. Murfett, John H. Miksic, Brian P. Farrell and Chiang Ming Shun, *Between Two Oceans: A Military History of Singapore from First Settlement to Final British Withdrawal* (Oxford: Oxford University Press, 1999), pp. ix, 280, 322–3; Lui, *Engineering Land Systems 50*, p. 123.

[13] Lee Kuan Yew, *The Singapore Story: Memoirs of Lee Kuan Yew* (Singapore: Times and Simon & Schuster, 1998), p. 510; Lee, *From Third World to First*, pp. 49, 61; Thomson, "Britain's Plan to Leave Asia": 124. At the tribute foyer of the Goh Keng Swee Command and Staff College, SAFTI Military Institute, Lee Kuan Yew was quoted on 4 June 2010 as having said: "Keng Swee was my alter ego, never daunted, never intimidated. We reinforced each other's resolve. It was a partnership that lasted from the London Forum days in 1949 until he resigned in 1984."

[14] See Mei-Lin Chew, "Crack Unit to Move House", *Straits Times*, 3 Feb. 1975, p. 6; "Malaysian CDF at Woodlands Base", *Pioneer* (Feb. 1992): 23; Peled, *A Question of Loyalty*, p. 103; Lee, *From Third World to First*, pp. 32–3; and Menon, *One of a Kind*, pp. 29–30.

MAF troops who eventually withdrew in 1971.[15] The problem was compounded by the fact the land belonged to Singapore but the British government handed the new camp over to the Malaysians.

The situation was no better for 1 SIR, whose drivers from the 4th Malaysian Infantry Brigade (4 MIB) were unable to act without orders from KL. Armoured cars from Singapore had been absorbed into the MAF's 1st Independent Reconnaissance Regiment, and attempts to "unscramble" them proved unsuccessful. Even the Singapore naval vessel *Panglima* was temporarily unaccounted for. The unscrambling of citizens from both states within each other's respective armies proved slightly easier. Some 300 Singaporeans were in the MAF, with the 4 MIB alone accounting for 60.[16] An agreement was reached in mid-1966 to repatriate citizens, and at the end of the year some 700 officers and men were transferred from the SAF to the MAF.[17] Dr Goh diplomatically described the episodes as "symptomatic of a deeper malaise in the relations between the two governments on defence matters".[18] Military relations would improve in due time, leading to a consultative grouping of Australia, Malaysia, New Zealand, Singapore and the UK under the auspices of the Five Power Defence Arrangements.[19]

The preceding events make clear that Singaporeans were responsible for defending themselves if they were to chart their own destiny.[20] It was prescient for *The Straits Times* on 9 August 1964 to cover Switzerland's devotion of a third of its annual budget to defence, exactly a year before Singapore's exit from Malaysia.[21] The inaugural post-independence budget borne completely

---

[15] The Royal Malaysian Navy Training School (KD Sri Pekandok) continued operations at Khatib Camp until relocation to Lumut in Perak state of West Malaysia. Khatib Camp was transferred to the Singapore government on 2 February 1982. The Royal Malaysian Navy also housed its Recruits Training Centre (PULAREK Berek TLDM Woodlands), formerly known as KD Malaya, at Woodlands Barracks. The Malaysian Navy, however, continued using bases under agreements made during the formation of the Federation and subsequently after separation.

[16] "Call for a New Malaysian Attitude to Singapore", *Straits Times*, 24 Feb. 1966, p. 4.

[17] Sia Cheong Yew, "Sack: 427 Now Up", *Straits Times*, 2 Apr. 1967, p. 2.

[18] "Call for a New Malaysian Attitude to Singapore", p. 4.

[19] Carlyle A. Thayer, "The Five Power Defence Arrangements at Forty (1971–2011)", in *Southeast Asian Affairs 2012*, ed. Daljit Singh and Pushpa Thambipillai (Singapore: Institute of Southeast Asian Studies, 2012), pp. 61–72.

[20] Military control was transferred from the British to the Singapore government on 29 October 1971, with the latter fully responsible upon the standing down of the Far East Command on 31 October 1971. See Murfett et al., *Between Two Oceans*, p. 280.

[21] "A Third of Nation's Budget for Armed Forces to Protect Its Neutrality", *Straits Times*, 9 Aug. 1964, p. 25.

by Singaporean taxpayers apportioned $40 million to the police, while the military received $30 million for national defence.[22] Convincing the general population of this pressing need was not as simple as publishing an article in the press or passing budgets in parliament, as consecutive defence ministers found. During the second and third readings of the Singapore Army Bill in late 1965, Dr Goh underlined:

> "British military protection today has made quite a number of our citizens complacent about the need to carry out our own defence preparations. These people assume that this protection will be permanent. I regard it as the height of folly to plan our future on this assumption and, indeed, the only rational basis on which we, as an independent country, can plan our future is on the opposite assumption, that is, the removal of the British military presence at some time in the future. Nobody, neither we nor the British, can say when this will be. It may be five, 10, 15 years; maybe more, maybe less. Whatever the time may be, it would be useless then to think about building up out defence forces. The time to do so is now."[23]

This sentiment was echoed by Dr Goh's successor as defence minister (1967–70), Lim Kim San, who explained in 1969:

> "… one reason why some people in Singapore were insensitive to problems of defence was that for 150 years the British had been the power responsible for security, largely with soldiers brought from outside Singapore. So generations of Singaporeans had been conditioned to believe that defence was not their personal concern. They had been taught to take it for granted."[24]

Those in power were far-sighted and viewed a strong defence as necessary to safeguard against revanchism, irredentism and suzerainty. This would also guarantee Singapore's sovereignty across the political, economic and territorial spectrum and provide the freedom to manoeuvre independent of external interference or opposition.[25] A steady stream of conspicuous domestic and

---

[22] "Pause for Thought", *Straits Times*, 3 Jan. 1966, p. 8.

[23] "Dr. Goh: If It Isn't for the British Bases in Singapore …", *Straits Times*, 24 Dec. 1965, p. 22.

[24] "At the Floodgates of History … We Stand Prepared", *National Pioneer* (Aug. 1969): 5–6.

[25] Incidents include the 17 October 1968 execution of two Indonesia infiltrators responsible for bombing MacDonald House, killing three and wounding 30 during *Konfrontasi* (March 1965); the 7 May 1988 expulsion of E. Mason "Hank" Hendrickson (First Secretary [political] at the US Embassy in Singapore) for meddling in domestic politics; the 5 May 1994 caning of Michael Fay for vandalism; and the 17 March 1995 hanging of Flor Contemplacion (Filipina domestic helper) for the double murder of Delia Maga and Nicholas Huang.

foreign events over the last 50-plus years would underpin and perpetuate the need for Singapore to possess a strong defence force.[26]

The immediate question facing the government in the days after separation was how a credible defence capability could urgently be cobbled together. Singapore lacked any martial heritage—perhaps with the exception of the Malay and Sikh minorities—and retained various traditions inherited from the British but also looked abroad to adopt best practices.[27] The search for a suitable model to build the army proved fruitless in India, Egypt, Sweden and Switzerland.[28] It was the Israelis who gave a direct helping hand from 1965 to 1974 and left an indelible IDF imprint on Singapore's NS system.[29] In hindsight, this was a blessing in disguise in the sense of Israel's similarities with Singapore. Both are geographically small and relatively young states formed post-World War II in regions where history, race and religion are sensitive and often divisive fault lines. Back then Israel also contended with malevolent neighbours bent on its extirpation, while Singapore feared its neighbours' intentions that ranged from suzerainty to brinksmanship and outright revanchist tendencies.[30] Israel's performances against an eclectic mix of regional military forces during the Six-Day War (1967), War of Attrition (1969–70) and Yom Kippur War (1973) also

---

[26] Incidents included the Laju Ferry hijacking by two members of the Japanese Red Army and another two from the Popular Front for the Liberation of Palestine (1974); and the hijacking of Singapore Airlines Flight SQ117 en route from Kuala Lumpur to Singapore by four members of the Pakistani People's Party (1991). Visible periods of tension in bilateral relationships included the official visit by Israeli President Chaim Herzog, which led to protest riots in Malaysia (1986), and the bilateral military exercise *Malindo Darsasa 3AB* between Malaysia and Indonesia, which culminated in an airborne exercise 18km from the Singapore-Malaysia border (1991).

[27] Patrick M. Mayerchak, "The Role of the Military in Singapore", in *The Armed Forces in Contemporary Asian Societies*, ed. Edward A. Olsen and Stephen Jurika Jr. (Boulder and London: Westview Press, 1986), pp. 170–2; Huxley, "Political Role of the Singapore Armed Forces' Officer Corps", pp. 1–2; *Our Army: Customs and Traditions* (Singapore: Ministry of Defence, 2006).

[28] Then PM Lee Kuan Yew personally wrote to Indian PM Lal Bahadur Shastri to help build up five army battalions and Egyptian President Gamal Abdel Nasser to help with Singapore's coastal defence, but only the Israelis acquiesced. Lee, *From Third World to First*, pp. 30–1; Mickey Chiang, *SAF and 30 Years of National Service* (Singapore: MINDEF Public Affairs, 1997), pp. 57–9.

[29] See Lam Peng Er and Kevin Yew Lee Tan, *Lee's Lieutenants: Singapore's Old Guard* (St Leonards: Allen & Unwin, 1999), p. 58; Ooi, *In Lieu of Ideology*, pp. 135–6; and Tng Ying Hui, *Not Born in Singapore: Fifty Personalities Who Shaped the Nation* (Singapore: Epigram Books for Institute of Policy Studies, Lee Kuan Yew School of Public Policy, 2015), pp. 178–83.

[30] Lee, *From Third World to First*, pp. 26–41.

inspired confidence in its system. Perhaps most important, Israel provided an example of a state that not only survived but flourished economically on the strength of the IDF. As Jean-Louis Margolin observed:

> Among the attractions of Israel, it appeared to have succeeded in integrating immigrants from many countries; its unions were strong, but responsible and co-operative; its powerful armed forces (a true citizens' army, quick to mobilise, and strictly subordinated to the civilian authorities) provided efficient protection in a hostile environment, which included much more populous adversaries. Israel constituted an oasis of competence and development in the middle of backwardness and poverty.[31]

The journalist Thomas Plate recalled that LKY "admires no one more than the Israelis for their hard-scrabble, high-IQ survivalism".[32] Claims of Singapore being an "Israel in Southeast Asia" raised fears among neighbours, but the city-state proactively assuaged concerns with care in its conspicuous dealings with Tel Aviv/Jerusalem.[33]

Defence has been a sacrosanct priority in Singapore because its leaders, while not warmongers, subscribe to a Hobbesian worldview where "covenants, without the sword, are but words, and of no strength to secure a man at all".[34] Two themes in particular are consistently highlighted. First, reminders for vigilance are perpetuated based on Singapore's inherent vulnerabilities, a siege mentality and use of the rhetoric of "war" to include events such as the 2003 SARS epidemic.[35] LKY cautioned that "[b]oth our northern and southern neighbours are much larger than us. Both have Muslim majorities and are differently organized. Both have not completely accepted their ethnic Chinese citizens. This accentuates the religious and cultural divide, and a subconscious sense of being a

---

[31] Jean-Louis Margolin, "Foreign Models in Singapore's Development and the Idea of a Singaporean Model", in *Singapore Changes Guard: Social, Political and Economic Directions in the 1990s*, ed. Garry Rodan (Melbourne: Longman Cheshire, 1993), p. 89.

[32] Thomas Plate, *Conversations with Lee Kuan Yew: Citizen Singapore: How to Build a Nation* (Singapore: Marshall Cavendish, 2010), p. 110.

[33] Chan Heng Chee, "Singapore's Foreign Policy, 1965–1968", *Journal of Southeast Asian History* 10, 1 (Mar. 1969): 185, 187; Nair, "Nation-Building through Conscript Service in Singapore", p. 106; Lee, "Leadership and Security in Singapore", p. 169. Some characteristics of the relationship include Singapore's reluctance to establish an embassy in Israel and posting of a residential ambassador; and that SAF officers attending IDF courses are not publicized and wear civilian clothing on official trips.

[34] Thomas Hobbes, *Leviathan or The Matter, Forme and Power of a Common-Wealth Ecclesiasticall and Civill* (1651), Chapter 17: Of the Causes, Generation, and Definition of a Commonwealth.

[35] Yasmin Ibrahim, "SARS and the Rhetoric of War in Singapore", *Crossroads: An Interdisciplinary Journal of Southeast Asian Studies* 18, 2 (2007): 90–119.

nut in a nutcracker."[36] Such views undoubtedly demand that the SAF maintain its edge as an "effective war machine" to ensure Singapore's survival in "a Malay[/Muslim] sea".[37]

The second theme is that Singapore has been able to consistently attract foreign investors in part due to its strong emphasis on national defence. No one would put money into a state—be it the underdeveloped Singapore of yesteryear or the contemporary prosperous manifestation—without guarantee of stability. A strong SAF is seen as a foundational pillar to provide such a guarantee. A lack of natural resources has proven a non-issue in achieving a high standard of living. Yet it would not be farfetched to say that "[i]f people believed that Singapore was weak and defenceless even wealthy Singaporeans would move part of their capital abroad".[38] The national narrative has consistently attributed Singapore's high standard of living to its sovereignty and a secure climate that would otherwise retard economic growth, resulting in "a poorer people and instability".[39] In 1983 LKY cautioned the state that

> "Beirut was a banking centre, a prosperous oasis in the Middle East. Look at it. Cambodia was an oasis in Indochina. Now a third of the Cambodians are dead and its cities are in ruins. After 30 years of war, the Vietnamese are still suffering, risking their lives in small boats to get out. So we are resolved we will not be boat people. We will have the best airforce, the most advanced equipment in the area."[40]

In 1984 Dr Goh reiterated: "We must never forget that our existence as an independent sovereign state cannot be made to depend on the sufferance of others. The most dependable guarantee of our independence is a strong SAF. A strong SAF, in turn, depends on the political will to make the effort and pay the price."[41]

Singapore has matched words with deeds through prudent investments in its defence capabilities over the years. Australia, Israel, New Zealand, Taiwan,

---

[36] Plate, *Conversations with Lee Kuan Yew*, pp. 109–10.

[37] Alagappa, "Asian Civil-Military Relations", pp. 444–5.

[38] Josey, *Lee Kuan Yew*, p. 221.

[39] Li Xueying and Teo Wan Gek, "From Improbable to Reality", *Straits Times*, 16 Aug. 2010. These sentiments are expressed also in various government publications, such as Martin Choo, ed., *The Singapore Armed Forces* (Singapore: Public Affairs Department, Ministry of Defence, 1981), pp. 6–7; "SAF Day Message 1983", *Pioneer* (July 1983): 2; and *Defending Singapore in the 21st Century* (Singapore: Ministry of Defence, 2000), pp. 5–6.

[40] "The Only Way to Survive", *Straits Times*, 7 Apr. 1983, p. 14.

[41] Speech by Dr Goh Keng Swee at the Establishment Dinner, Singapore, 25 Sept. 1984. Reproduced in "Defence and the Establishment", *Pioneer: Journal of the Singapore Armed Forces* 11, 2 (Jan.–Mar. 1985): 11.

the United Kingdom and the United States provided much needed military assistance in the early days. Its unflinching dedication to harness and maintain its technological edge has turned the SAF into what most pundits would consider the most advanced defence force in Southeast Asia. The price has been steep, with a quarter of the annual budget consistently devoted to defence independent of economic conditions. The need for a strong defence is continually and explicitly emphasized because, as incumbent PM Lee Hsien Loong explained: "Without the SAF, the good life and the opportunities that young people enjoy would disappear like Cinderella's coach at midnight."[42] So long as the ruling People's Action Party (PAP) remains in power, the trend of "more guns to secure more butter" looks likely to remain a key priority and defence set to receive choice portions of the yearly budget.

2.2.1 National Service: Conscription by Any Other Name

The most pressing concern in Singapore's quest for a credible defence force was the manpower required for running a war machine to deter in peace and secure victory in war. Money could purchase impressive military hardware but not necessarily the men and women needed to use the equipment. Conscription was certainly not a given at independence, and the MID initially sought a brigade-sized force of part-time reservists with a small cadre of Regulars at the core.[43] Debates on the future defence structure continued within the political elite, and while views differed, the underlying urgency was clear in light of the accelerated British withdrawal. Dr Goh envisioned a professional all-volunteer army of 12 battalions: seven infantry, two wheeled reconnaissance, one engineer, one artillery and one commando.[44] LKY, on the other hand, favoured conscription on the following grounds:

> "If you are only a soldier, you do not contribute to the productivity of the place. So we train. Every man who is chosen becomes a soldier or sailor for two years. Then he goes back to earn a living in a factory or office and, for the next 10 to 15 years, he is part of a reservoir of people who understand discipline, who know the mechanics of self-defence and who, in an emergency, help to defend their own country. It will take many years—perhaps five, seven or 10 years—before we can get the whole machine into gear."[45]

---

[42] Nazry Bahrawi, "Battle for Bright Minds", *TODAY*, 7 Aug. 2008, p. 8.

[43] Some 3,000 volunteered between October and December 1965. See also "Volunteers Drive in Singapore", *Straits Times*, 7 Nov. 1965, p. 8; and "S'pore to Have Volunteer Fighting Force", *Straits Times*, 31 Dec. 1965, p. 4.

[44] Lui, *Engineering Land Systems 50*, p. 1.

[45] "Singapore Call-Up: Military Training for the Girls, Too", *Straits Times*, 26 Feb. 1967, p. 1.

Lee also considered universal conscription to include both males and females, but Goh objected to NS for the latter.[46] Alex Josey, Lee's one-time press secretary, further reasoned that "Lee also believed that an army based upon national service is an army that will never be able to stage a successful coup d'état. His task was to create a citizens' army which involved everyone in a family sense, while at the same time elevating the status of the soldier."[47]

The lean economic years of early independence shelved Dr Goh's proposal because "[t]he two existing battalions were already costing us $20 million a year, a princely sum of money. 12 battalions would have bankrupted the treasury."[48] Conscription was the solution, the cheapest way to maintain the expensive business of defence without draining state coffers.[49] Goh also viewed NS as an invaluable tool for nation-building because "participation in defence and membership in the armed forces" could efficiently and effectively inculcate "loyalty and national consciousness" in a young nation.[50] He was well aware that Singaporeans were not yet "a nation, we are a community, a society, a group of people living in the island of Singapore".[51] Citizens needed to believe in the construct that was Singapore and that NS was the ideal "school of the nation".[52] This was especially significant post-independence when "Singaporeans had very little in common except financial aspirations and a sorrowful history of racial riots ... citizens lacked a common loyalty, patriotism, history, or tradition".[53] The basic premise is that communal living during NS—most conspicuous

---

[46] Ibid.; Lee, *From Third World to First*, p. 35; Ooi, *In Lieu of Ideology*, p. 135.

[47] Josey, *Lee Kuan Yew*, pp. 219–20. See also Lam and Yew, *Lee's Lieutenants*, p. 59.

[48] Speech by Prime Minister Goh Chok Tong at the "35 Years of National Service Commemoration Dinner", 7 Sept. 2002, http://www.mindef.gov.sg/imindef/news_and_events/nr/2002/sep/07sep02_nr/07sep02_speech.html (no longer available).

[49] Kirpa Ram Vij quoted in Tan Guan Heng, *100 Inspiring Rafflesians 1823–2003* (Singapore: World Scientific Publishing, 2008), p. 88. See also Ng Pak Shun, "'Why Not a Volunteer Army?' Reexamining the Impact of Military Conscription on Economic Growth for Singapore", *Singapore Economic Review* 50, 1 (2005): 47–67.

[50] Ooi, *In Lieu of Ideology*, p. 134; Ng Kai Ling, "SAF Needs the Best Leaders: DPM Teo", *Straits Times*, 18 Aug. 2010; Jon S.T. Quah, "Singapore: Towards a National Identity", *Southeast Asian Affairs* (1977): 209; "The SAF Then", *Straits Times*, 27 Mar. 1988, p. 2.

[51] Speech by Dr Goh Keng Swee at a seminar on "Democracy and Communism" sponsored by the Ministry of Education for pre-university students, Singapore Conference Hall, 24–29 Apr. 1971. Reproduced in Goh Keng Swee, *The Economics of Modernization* (Singapore: Federal Publications, 1995), p. 146.

[52] Anna Leander, "Drafting Community: Understanding the Fate of Conscription", *Armed Forces & Society* 30, 4 (Summer 2004): 577.

[53] Peled, *A Question of Loyalty*, p. 94.

during BMT—forces conscripts from all walks of life to interact independent "of economic, ethnic, religious, cultural and language differences" and forges unity by eliminating prejudices and stereotypes.[54] It was possible that over time society—at least the male half—would be disciplined and obsequious, and the workforce more efficient and professional.[55]

Conscription eventually provided Singapore with a total mobilized defence force some seven times larger than peacetime numbers and a figure far greater than a purely professional defence force. This addressed the imbalances vis-à-vis Singapore's neighbours, as Dr Goh rationalized:

> "It is foolish to allow ourselves to be hypnotised by the disparity in the population ratios between Singapore and her neighbours. What counts is the fighting strength of the armed forces, not the size of populations. After five years of conscription, we can field an army of 150,000 by mobilising those on the reserve service. By using older persons and women for non-combatant duties, we should eventually be able to field an army with a combat strength of 250,000 consisting of men between the ages of 18 and 35. The war-making potential of a small, vigorous, well-educated and highly motivated population should never be underestimated."[56]

While NS saved the treasury, the costs were not eliminated as the burden was simply redistributed broadly among citizens. Conscription is, after all, "the legal and regulated form of forced labour for the state" in the uniformed services.[57] NS initially ameliorated unemployment, but opportunity costs soon became apparent.[58] Common gripes were an individual's youth, lost employment potential, disruption in education, and career nuisance if called up for reservist training.[59] The MID acknowledged in 1967 that "an enlarged standing army

---

[54] Chan Heng Chee, *Singapore: The Politics of Survival 1965–1967* (Singapore: Oxford University Press, 1971), p. 57; Elizabeth Nair, "Conscription and Nation-Building in Singapore: A Psychological Analysis", *Journal of Human Values* 1, 1 (1995): 96, 98; Lam and Yew, *Lee's Lieutenants*, p. 59.

[55] "An Efficient SAF Makes for Better Work Force", *Straits Times*, 13 Nov. 1986, p. 20.

[56] "Building an Army from Scratch", *Straits Times*, 9 Sept. 2000, pp. 62–3.

[57] Casey B. Mulligan and Andrei Shleifer, "Conscription as Regulation", *American Law and Economics Review* 7, 1 (2005): 88. NS in Singapore commenced with the SAF in 1967 and was extended to the SPF in 1975, and fire brigade (now SCDF) in 1981. See *Supporting Our NSmen: An Employers' Guide* (Singapore: MINDEF Public Affairs, n.d.), pp. 7, 10.

[58] Chan, *Singapore: The Politics of Survival 1965–1967*, p. 57; Amnon Barzilai, "A Deep Dark, Secret Love Affair", *Haaretz*, 16 July 2004.

[59] Nair, "Nation-Building through Conscript Service in Singapore", p. 106; Mulligan and Shleifer, "Conscription as Regulation": 85–111.

would be better from the point of view of combat efficiency".[60] Others voiced concerns over the professionalism of a defence force that "has to look after a large number of conscripts" and was besieged with training and deployment constraints.[61] Yet the longevity of conscription is testament to its balancing role between economic viability and defence credibility.

The greatest hurdle to implementing conscription was for society to buy into the idea of citizen-soldiers. Political leaders faced a gamut of challenges thanks to socio-historical antecedents. The British colonial administration's attempt at part-time conscription in 1954 was strongly resisted even though there were a few keen individuals. Chinese Middle School students vented their anger and ran amok at policy designed to "defend the same British order that had discriminated against them and in which they saw no future".[62] Only 400 men enlisted before the NS Ordinance Act was abrogated in 1955. The failure of this episode cautioned LKY and his colleagues to the sensitivities of military service. Dr Goh reasoned: "We wanted the people to regard our soldiers as their protectors—a reversal from the days when army and police uniforms aroused fear and resentment as symbols of colonial coercion. People must admire military valour."[63] Students, parents and businesses had to be convinced of the country's vulnerabilities and the need to defend themselves and their collective interests. Politicians worked the ground to assure concerned citizenry, hosted NS dinners for enlistees, and graced send-off ceremonies at enlistment centres.[64] The Chinese Chamber of Commerce even minted special gold medallions for the first 5,000 recruits. The political leadership was quick to address fears as conflict gripped Indo-China. At one send-off ceremony in November 1967, Parliamentary Secretary to the Ministry of Culture Fong Sip Chee emphasized: "The only things we will send to Vietnam are eggs, meat, pork, plywood and

---

[60] "National Service in Singapore", *Straits Times*, 28 Feb. 1967, p. 10.

[61] Lee Hsien Loong quoted in Chan Kim Yin, "Professionalism in a National Service Army: An Uneasy Combination?" *Pointer* 15, 2 (Apr.–June 1989): 30; Goh Kee Nguan, "The Singapore Army Moving Decisively beyond the Conventional", *USAWC Strategy Research Project* (Carlisle Barracks: US Army War College, 2004), p. 14.

[62] Twenty of the 500 students who protested in front of Government House (Istana Negara) on 18 May were injured and 45 arrested in the ensuing clash with riot police. Six policemen were also injured. Another 1,000 students locked themselves in Chung Chen High School but were evicted on 19 May by police. Another lock-in three days later involved 2,500 student protesters but was eventually settled peacefully. See Nor-Afidah Abd Rahman, "National Service Riots of 1954", *InfopediaTalk* (National Library Board Singapore), 28 July 2006, http://infopedia.nl.sg/articles/SIP_1202_2006-07-28.html (accessed 28 May 2014).

[63] "Building an Army from Scratch", *Straits Times*, 9 Sept. 2000, p. 3.

[64] R. Chandran, "Call-Up Youths Report for Training", *Straits Times*, 27 Dec. 1967, p. 11.

other goods. We will not send you ... You cannot go anywhere. This is our land and this is where we fight for our survival."[65]

State administrators pre-empted the unpopular decision and prepared the population psychologically for the impending NS announcement by setting examples for others to follow. Early leaders joined the part-time militia and even marched in uniform at the first National Day Parade (NDP) on 9 August 1966.[66] LKY recalled that his cabinet and parliamentary colleagues "put up a brave show and were cheered enthusiastically by those behind the saluting dais and by the crowds lining the streets as they recognised their suntanned ministers and MPs in uniform, eager in their stride if lacking in martial bearing."[67]

On 29 November 1966 all civil servants were decreed eligible for Compulsory Active Service (CAS), which commenced on 1 January 1967.[68] NS communiqués followed swiftly on 21 February 1967. Nine thousand eligible males born between 1 January and 30 June 1949 received official reminders by 17 March requiring them to register for NS at any of the four centres between 28 March and 18 April.[69] Uncertainty shrouded the inaugural enlistment exercise, but Dr Goh repeatedly stressed the importance of national defence and cogently warned that reliance on others meant "that Singapore must revert to a colony or satellite of whoever wishes to afford it protection". The indefatigable defence minister continued: "If you are in a completely vulnerable position anyone disposed to do so can hold you to ransom and life for you will become very tiresome. I consider it wrong to believe that there is nothing we can or should do about defending ourselves, even though we cannot achieve complete invulnerability by our unaided efforts."[70]

---

[65] "Singapore Soldiers Get 'No Service in Vietnam' Pledge", *Straits Times*, 3 Nov. 1967, p. 11.

[66] Jek Yeun Thong (Minister for Labour), Othman Wok (Minister for Culture and Social Affairs), Ong Pang Boon (Minister for Education), Wee Toon Boon (Minister of State for Defence), Fong Sip Chee (Parliamentary Secretary to the Ministry of Culture); MPs such as R.A. Gonzales, S.V. Lingam, Rahmat Kenap, Toh Weng Cheong and Ho Cheng Choon; and unionist Mahmud Bin Awang all stepped forward to serve in the People's Defence Force. Dr Goh was himself the honorary colonel of the 20th Regiment, PDF (Artillery). See "Ministers in Uniform", *Straits Times*, 25 Aug. 1966, p. 11; "Ministers on Parade ...", *Straits Times*, 30 Nov. 1966, p. 4; and "The Heroes Catch the Eye at a Passing Out Parade", *Straits Times*, 12 Oct. 1969, p. 6.

[67] Lee, *From Third World to First*, p. 34.

[68] "First 'New Look' Civil Servants on Parade", *Straits Times*, 18 June 1967, p. 7; Lim Beng Tee, "Rewards for the 'Military' Civil Servant", *Straits Times*, 21 June 1967, p. 9.

[69] "All Set for Call-Up of First Batch", *Straits Times*, 14 Mar. 1967, p. 20.

[70] Ibid.

The 9,000 young men called up were channelled into four different service streams. Only 900 enlisted for a full-time two-year tour in the SAF, with the first batch of 200 reporting for duty on 14 August 1967.[71] They were considered the "top 10 per cent" of national servicemen—even labelled "an elite"—with the majority (838 men) channelled into 3 and 4 SIR.[72] These infantrymen received the same salary and allowances as regular counterparts of the same rank and were further assured of post-NS employment "either in Government service, statutory boards or large firms".[73] The remaining 90 per cent of the pioneering national servicemen rendered part-time service in the People's Defence Force (PDF), Special Constabulary (SC) and Vigilante Corps (VC) according to their respective schedules (Table 2.1).[74]

The CAS initiative was extended in 1968 to increase the SAF's full-time intake and targeted those with the greatest opportunity costs. This meant all civil servants (1967), followed by university graduates (1968) and subsequently those with 12 (A-level) and 10 (O-level) years of schooling.[75] Precedent was set immediately so that members of high society would not receive any special treatment. Lee Hsien Loong enlisted into 2 SIR after his secondary schooling and was subsequently awarded the President's Scholarship in 1970. Edwin Charles Hinghwee Sheares, the second son and youngest of then-President

---

[71] The 3rd and 4th Battalions, Singapore Infantry Regiment (3 and 4 SIR), each received 419 conscripts. On 16 August 1969 they became the first operationally ready "reservists". The remaining National Servicemen were spread among 1 and 2 SIR, and SAFTI. See "200 Recruits for New Battalions", *Straits Times*, 4 Aug. 1967, p. 4; "Top 10 Per Cent", *Straits Times*, 31 Aug. 1967, p. 8; Mickey Chiang, *Fighting Fit: The Singapore Armed Forces* (Singapore: Times Editions, 1990), p. 40; and "Not Just in Reserve", *Army News* 113 (Oct.–Nov. 2004): 6.

[72] "Singapore Call-Up: Military Training for the Girls, Too", p. 1; "Top 10 Per Cent", *Straits Times*, 31 Aug. 1967, p. 8.

[73] "Call-Up: 4,000 Youths Have Registered", *Straits Times*, 6 Apr. 1967, p. 4.

[74] Ong Eng Chuan, "National Service in Singapore: Early Years", *InfopediaTalk* (National Library Board Singapore), 1 Feb. 2005, http://infopedia.nl.sg/articles/SIP_692_2005-02-01. html, accessed 28 May 2014.

[75] Those enlisted under the CAS received their last drawn salary (if applicable) instead of the (lower) NS allowance. A-level and HSC students were enlisted almost year-round in January, April and July of 1970 due to the basic infrastructure in place at the point in time. A cycle was soon established with A-level students enlisting in December and polytechnic graduates in June. All other education levels were dependent on their date of birth, or when they completed their studies. From 1981 onwards, A-level enlistments took place in December and March; and from 1987 onwards, polytechnic intakes took place in June and September. See Chandran, "Call-Up Youths Report for Training", p. 11; "Academic Training Scheme (Higher Learning Scheme) for NSF Officers", *National Pioneer* (Mar. 1971): 3; "New NS Enlistment Policy for 'A' Level Students", *Pioneer* (Sept. 1981): 8; "Two NS Intakes for Poly Grads", *Pioneer* (Mar. 1987): 33.

Benjamin Sheares' three children, enlisted with 2 SIR on 18 July 1972 at the age of 23 after reading law and economics in England.[76] Chelva Rajah, son of High Commissioner in London Arumugam Ponnu Rajah, also received his enlistment papers.[77]

Table 2.1. Service schemes for the pioneering intake of national servicemen in 1967[78]

Scheme	Full-time	Part-time	Reserve	Allowances
SAF	2 years	–	10 years	Same as SAF Regulars $118.50 (REC) to $321.50 (WO2)
PDF	–	12 years First 6 months: Two 3-hour training periods per week and In-Camp Training (ICT) once per month. Subsequently: One 3-hour training period per week and one week of ICT per year.	–	$2.50 (REC) to $4 (officers) per parade
SC	–	12 years First 6 months: Two 4-hour training periods per week (at one of 5 training centres) and up to a fortnight of ICT. Subsequently: Up to 4 days of duty per week and one week of ICT annually.	–	$2 to $3 each parade
VC	–		–	Nil[79]

---

[76] "Mrs. Sheares Sends Off Son Edwin", *New Nation*, 18 July 1972, p. 1; "Sheares' Son Called Up for N-Service", *Straits Times*, 18 July 1972, p. 7; Christina Cheang, "President's Son off for N-Service", *Straits Times*, 19 July 1972, p. 9.

[77] Yeo Toon Joo, "Students in U.K. Get a N-Service Reminder", *Straits Times*, 10 Aug. 1970, p. 30.

[78] "Call-Up: 4,000 Youths", p. 4; "Top 10 Per Cent", p. 8.

[79] "Call-Up: 4,000 Youths", p. 4. Members of the VC were not eligible for allowances because "Their training is done close to homes, and much of the activity consists of playing games and learning useful things such as first-aid, law and self-defence."

The patchwork of initiatives designed to meet desperate manpower needs lasted until 21 May 1970, when the NS Enlistment Act (1970) covered all males in the 18–40 age group. On 1 January 1971 the Enlistment (Amendment) Act (1970) rendered all male citizens and permanent residents (PRs) born on or after 1 January 1949 eligible for NS, with a few exceptions such as full-time clergymen and those with certain classes of physical or mental disabilities.[80] Service lengths varied between two and three years at different junctures, and close to a million men have since rendered NS.[81] Current estimates place the active strength of the tri-service SAF at 50,000–60,000, comprising 15,000 to 20,000 Regulars and 35,000–40,000 active-duty conscripts (officially termed National Servicemen Full-time or NSFs). One source places an "active" figure of 82,000 with 10,000 career personnel, 40,000 NSFs, and reservists (officially termed Operationally Ready National Servicemen or NSmen) who render service equal to 32,000 NSFs.[82] The estimated mobilized strength lies somewhere between 300,000 and 385,000 personnel under arms.[83] Such numbers would certainly prove impossible without conscription.

2.2.2 Soldiering: Not an Honoured Profession

Singaporeans slowly and reluctantly accepted NS as a disruptive necessity where men were put through the paces of military—and later also law enforcement and civil defence—training for the national good.[84] Yet, unsurprisingly, draft evasion manifested itself in various forms despite the initial fanfare and even assurances of post-service employment.[85] Ephemeral loopholes allowed parents to send their sons overseas for education, while others tried illicit drug

---

[80] Edwin Lee, *Singapore: The Unexpected Nation* (Singapore: Institute of Southeast Asian Studies, 2008), pp. 282–5; "Dilemma of the Conscientious Objector", *Straits Times*, 7 June 1968, p. 14.

[81] Seow Bei Yi, "National Service: 50 Years, One Million Memories", *Straits Times*, 13 Mar. 2017.

[82] Ng Pak Shun, "'Why Not a Volunteer Army?' Reexamining the Impact of Military Conscription on Economic Growth for Singapore", *Singapore Economic Review* 50, 1 (2005): 48, 54.

[83] Current estimates place 300,000 NSmen in the SAF, 21,000 in the Singapore Police Force (SPF), and 23,000 in the Singapore Civil Defence Force (SCDF). *Supporting Our NSmen: An Employers' Guide* (Singapore: MINDEF Public Affairs, n.d.), pp. 3, 8, 10; Huxley, *Defending the Lion City*, p. 93; *Defending Singapore in the 21st Century* (Singapore: Ministry of Defence, 2000), p. 27.

[84] "Call-Up: 'Elite' Youths for a Full-time Army", *Straits Times*, 17 Mar. 1967, p. 8.

[85] "First Six Charged with Call-Up Dodging", *Straits Times*, 5 May 1967, p. 18; "Assurance of Jobs for National Servicemen", *Straits Times*, 30 June 1969, p. 6; William Campbell, "Towards Higher Levels in Singapore's Forces", *Straits Times*, 12 Oct. 1970, p. 12.

consumption or exemptions on medical grounds.[86] Conscientious objection and maladjustment did not pass muster as valid reasons for exemption.[87] Stiff penalties were imposed for those who flouted the rules, but the SAF had its work cut out as former CDF (1974–92) LG (RET) Winston Choo recalled: "We were so busy just trying to raise units, convincing parents that National Service was okay, taking in soldiers who were mostly ill-equipped, ill-motivated and ill-educated, to train them for the SAF."[88] It was little wonder that morale and motivation were low in the early SAF.[89] Discipline was also in short supply and resulted in amendments to the SAF Act in 1975 and 1978. The SAF Detention Barracks were established, a framework for court martials and summary trials of servicemen by rank was formalized, and punishments were listed for the ever-growing litany of offences.[90]

The unfortunate circumstances were compounded by issues over basics such as infrastructure and logistics. One general with first-hand experiences lamented: "In those days some of the equipment items issued were inferior. The *chankol* (entrenching tool) broke easily so we had to use our steel helmets to dig. Logistics was not so good. Firelighters did not work in the wet. Quality Control [was] not that great. Inferior buys irritates people. Why should it be like that?"[91]

Methods of instruction ranged from "mediocre to appalling"; there was no common medium of communication, which resulted in the segregation of personnel into platoons based on mother tongue.[92] It was difficult to mask

---

[86] Yeo, "Students in U.K. get a N-Service Reminder", p. 30; "N-Service: What Else Is Needed From", *Straits Times*, 12 Oct. 1970, p. 21; "N-Service: No 'Privileged Families,' Says Dr. Goh", *Straits Times*, 13 Mar. 1973, p. 6.

[87] "Dr. Goh Wants Fairness for All in Army", *Straits Times*, 11 Sept. 1978, p. 9.

[88] Chew and Tan, *Creating the Technology Edge*, p. 26. Penalties in the early days included a $2,000 fine, six month jail term, or both. See "A Roundup of Call-Up Dodgers", *Straits Times*, 19 Apr. 1967, p. 5.

[89] "The Typical Soldier: By Dr. Goh", *Straits Times*, 18 Sept. 1975, p. 8; Stu Glauberman, "10-Year-Late PR Job for SAF", *Straits Times*, 6 Mar. 1985, p. 9.

[90] "When SAF Men May Be Caned", *Straits Times*, 28 Mar. 1975, p. 1; "Murder Charge Soldiers Can Be Court-martialled", *Straits Times*, 30 July 1975, p. 9; "Protected Info: Court Can Try These Cases", *Straits Times*, 24 Mar. 1978, p. 8.

[91] Interview No. 24.

[92] "Whitlam Praises S'pore Defence Build-up", *Straits Times*, 31 Jan. 1968, p. 16; R. Chandran, "Govt to Improve Army Training", *Straits Times*, 21 Sept. 1973, p. 1; "Language Badge", *Pioneer* (May 1975): 10; "Best Taking Root Rapidly in the SAF", *Straits Times*, 29 Mar. 1983, p. 13. The lack of a common language of communication necessitated the introduction of a "language badge", which had two parts: "[t]he background colour of the badge indicates the main language spoken while the strips or bars at the side identified additional languages spoken." The main colours covered the most widely spoken languages: English (green), Mandarin (orange), Malay (blue), Hokkien (red) and Tamil (yellow).

the fact that conscripts were forced into soldiering, even though they tried. Dr Goh shared in May 1978 that "[i]n the course of my work, I often visit military camps. One of the lasting impressions I get on these occasions is the image of the National Serviceman on sentry duty—a bespectacled youth of slender proportions, ill at ease in an unaccustomed environment but trying to conceal it. An improbable soldier."[93]

While legislation kept men in uniform for a limited period, they were never obliged to take up a military career. The stigma of military service was amplified by the negative experiences of British colonialism, Japanese imperialism and "the Chinese tradition that good sons do not become soldiers, plus the fact that most of the Singapore Indian community were from non-warrior castes".[94] Others associated the military with negative influences in the form of smoking, drinking, drug abuse and other forms of social mischief.[95] The Malay community, which displayed a greater predilection for military service, was restricted in numbers until the mid-1980s to maintain the SAF's ethnic balance and due to security concerns related to the racial and religious composition of neighbouring Malaysia and Indonesia.[96] BG (RET) Kirpa Ram Vij, who led the SAF as DGS (1970–74), further described the conundrum:

> "The main function of the military is to protect the people of the country; yet in times of peace they will not be able to demonstrate the importance of their responsibility ... It is only in time of war that the soldiers become heroes in the eyes of the people. Only then will they receive the respect and admiration of the public ... In our society the status of the military is still not highly respected. Army personnel at present do not receive the admiration and respect of other professionals like doctors and engineers ... From the psychological point of view, the reluctance of university graduates to join the army as regulars may be due to fear. The military is a new profession in the country; furthermore it is a profession that has little direct connection with what is learnt in school."[97]

---

[93] Leong Choon Cheong, *Youth in the Army* (Singapore: Federal Publications, 1978), p. iii.

[94] Josey, *Lee Kuan Yew*, p. 219.

[95] Philip Lee, "For Youths Without Too Much Schooling—The Army's Offer Is Best ...", *Straits Times*, 7 May 1978, p. 12.

[96] See, for example, Stanley S. Bedlington, "Ethnicity and the Armed Forces in Singapore", in *Ethnicity and the Military in Asia*, ed. DeWitt C. Ellinwood and Cynthia H. Enloe (New Brunswick: Transaction Books, 1981), p. 257; "This Is a Singapore Problem. We Will Solve It Ourselves ...", *Straits Times*, 18 Mar. 1987, p. 10; Gillian Koh and Ooi Giok Ling, "Singapore: A Home, A Nation?" *Southeast Asian Affairs* (2002): 260; Azmi Hassan, "Best Personnel for Defence, Regardless of Race", *Straits Times*, 25 Sept. 2003, p. 20; Han et al., *Lee Kuan Yew*, pp. 221–2.

[97] Pang Cheng Lian, "Soldiers Must Be Bi-lingual", *New Nation*, 8 Sept. 1971, p. 6.

In 1972 Dr Goh noted that "a great deal remains to be done before the military profession can occupy the honoured position that it does in modern states" simply because "[a]s a community of traders with no military traditions there was little conception of the role of the military in Singapore".[98] He chided those who belittled servicemen: "Some businessmen are apt to regard soldiers as little better than hired *jagas* (security guards). They know little about the motivations of the military profession. They know nothing about how a defence force operates."[99] Some of those the army sought to recruit in the late 1970s also held the view that "[l]ife in the army is too tough, officers bully their men too much, there is little freedom and precious little free time".[100] IDF adviser Lieutenant Colonel (LTC) Moshe Shefi's observation of the SAF was congruent with the preceding sentiments: "We discovered that there was psychological resistance to conscription in Singapore ... Of 10 professions, that of soldier was ranked last. In first place was the artist, followed by the philosopher, the teacher and the merchant, and the thief was in ninth place. Soldiering was considered a contemptible profession."[101] It was hardly surprising that conscripts tended "to shy away from a military career because it was just not worth it unless you were desperate".[102]

Dr Goh gave his personal attention to raising the profile and prestige of the military career given the unfavourable circumstances. An exclusive "Luncheon Club" was initiated for civilian defence bureaucrats and senior officers in the rank of Major (MAJ) and above.[103] Mercedes-Benz sedans—still a rarity in the 1970s—ferried brigade and division commanders on official duties, as status symbols of senior officership. Cadence was introduced in the units to raise morale, the Music and Drama Company entertained soldiers, and the SAF Reservist Association (SAFRA) handled various initiatives to recognize the contributions of national servicemen.[104] SAF Enterprise (SAFE) supermarkets were established and catered to the household needs of defence personnel.

---

[98] "Raising Status of Armed Forces: By Dr. Goh", *Straits Times*, 2 July 1971, p. 1.

[99] Ibid.

[100] Lee, "For Youths Without Too Much Schooling—The Army's Offer Is Best ...", p. 12.

[101] Barzilai, "A Deep Dark, Secret Love Affair".

[102] "Great Little Army", *Straits Times*, 3 July 1987, p. 22.

[103] Dhoraisingam, *Working for Dr. Goh Keng Swee*, p. 36.

[104] Dr Goh Keng Swee inaugurated the SAF Reservist Association, or SAFRA, on 2 July 1972. In 1994 SAFRA was renamed SAFRA National Service Association. See "One Roof for Reservists", *Straits Times*, 3 July 1972, p. 9; Dhoraisingam, *Working for Dr. Goh Keng Swee*, pp. 49–52; and Hoong Bee Lok, ed., *Without Reserve: Commemorating 30 Years of SAFRA* (Singapore: SAFRA National Service Association, 2002), pp. 278, 283.

The SAF's official magazine, *Pioneer*—initially launched as *National Pioneer* in 1969—contained numerous photographs and underlined the serious business of defence.[105] Government statutory boards were roped in to foster relationships between the military and non-security sectors with the aim of inculcating a sense of community among uniformed personnel.[106] The now-defunct MINDEF Book Club was created in 1976 and proved vastly popular with officers.[107]

If serving as an officer in the SAF was a calling, it would certainly be one with benefits. Officer salaries were relatively attractive in the 1960s and early 1970s and were enhanced with vocational, medical, clothing, food and housing allowances. The *Straits Times* observed:

> These liberal terms are seldom available elsewhere. On retirement from active service, their skills and training will serve them in good stead for continued employment in other sectors if they so desire. Although not generally known, total incomes of officers and other ranks in the Singapore Army compare favourably, and, in fact, are often better than for similar qualifications in commerce, industry or the civil service.[108]

This view was seconded by Willard Hanna, whose fieldwork in Southeast Asia prompted his conclusion that:

> The personnel of the SAF itself enjoy excellent conditions of service rivalled in the region only by those in nearby Malaysia or rich little Brunei. Quarters, rations, uniforms, and equipment are absolutely first class, as are medical services and sports, entertainment, and educational facilities ... The Army Captain, drawing S$720–995, ranks with the junior executive; he is much, much better compensated than are his counterparts in Indonesia, Thailand, or the Philippines.[109]

While Dr Goh increased the attractiveness of the SAF career, he never compromised on standards of military professionalism and character or entertained frivolous indulgences to confuse form for content. It was little wonder that "[t]he over-sized parade, the medal-laden officer corps and

---

[105] Dhoraisingam, *Working for Dr. Goh Keng Swee*, pp. 42–6.

[106] The six statutory boards involved were the Housing and Development Board (HDB), Port of Singapore Authority (PSA), Public Utilities Board (PUB), Jurong Town Corporation (JTC), Tourist Promotion Board, and Singapore Telephone Board. See "Statutory Bodies Adopt SAF Units under Mindef Scheme", *Straits Times*, 4 May 1971, p. 5.

[107] "Where History Isn't Bunk", *Pioneer* (Feb. 1977): 8–9; "MINDEF Book Club Sales Take Off", *Pioneer* (Aug. 1977): 23.

[108] "Professional Training for Army Officers", *Straits Times*, 4 Feb. 1968, p. 9.

[109] Hanna, "New Singapore Armed Forces": 7.

other gaudy trappings of illusory pomp are also not its style".[110] One source observed, "Goh expressed a deep dislike for blind imitations, be it of Western permissive behaviour, trendy economic theories or pompous military uniforms and reviews."[111] Officers deemed incompetent and detrimental to the SAF were swiftly demoted or replaced.[112]

Despite such initiatives, it was apparent that the military still suffered from an image crisis in the early 1980s. It reached a point where active personnel seemed ashamed of the uniform, as shown by rhetorical questions in a 1979 issue of *Pioneer*: "Are you the kind of soldier who hates to be seen in uniform once he leaves camp? Do you jump into civilian clothes the first chance you get? Would you be caught dead walking with your girlfriend or boyfriend if you were in uniform?"[113]

Defence Minister (1982–91) Goh Chok Tong concluded, "the preference values of society at present do not put soldiering high on the priority of professions".[114] Another defence minister (1991–94), Dr Yeo Ning Hong, recalled that "many service personnel changed to *civvies* (civilian clothing) before they left [MINDEF] because of the public's negative attitude of those in uniform".[115] Despite 15-plus years of NS, with personnel drawn from different social strata, it was evident "that we have not yet built up a close and natural relationship between the SAF and the people. There is still inadequate appreciation of the importance of SAF officers. Our society as a whole does not accord SAF officers the esteem they deserve."[116] Then-COL Lee Hsien Loong (SAFOS 1971) cited the lack of respect for the profession of arms in addition to the SAF's inexperience (non-battle tested) as distinct disadvantages of Singapore's military establishment.[117]

---

[110] "Great Little Army", p. 22.

[111] Ooi, *In Lieu of Ideology*, p. 133.

[112] Dhoraisingam, *Working for Dr. Goh Keng Swee*, p. 45.

[113] "Uniform Pride: Taking It beyond the Camp Gates", *Pioneer* (May 1979): 7

[114] "Let Us Find Hearts and Minds of SAF: Chok Tong", *Straits Times*, 4 July 1982, p. 10.

[115] Speech by Minister of Defence Dr Yeo Ning Hong at the MINDEF Workplan Seminar, MINDEF, Gombak Drive, 26 Mar. 1994. Reported in "An SAF That Strives for Excellence", *Straits Times*, 1 July 1994, p. 4.

[116] "'Use Your Rank in Civilian Life'", *Straits Times*, 30 June 1982, p. 8.

[117] "The Straits Times Says More Than a Fighting Chance", *Straits Times*, 3 May 1984, p. 16.

2.3   Commitment to Defence: A Perennial Challenge

Certain challenges have persisted even though the SAF is now an established institution of almost 50 years. Conscription has consistently provided the critical mass for an impressive bean-counting entry in the International Institute for Strategic Studies' annual defence almanac *The Military Balance*. What matters most, however, is the pulse of the SAF and the support it expects from the society it pledges to defend—in short, society's Commitment to Defence (C2D). In 1968 Lim Kim San reminded the SAF that "[o]ur military leaders should never be aloof or isolated from the people of Singapore. There must always be an interaction between them, an interaction that is necessary to maintain the vitality of the armed forces and their combat strength. The days of arrogant commanders are over."[118]

The British military historian Sir Michael Howard, on his 1986 visit to Singapore, also emphasized society's crucial role in defence: "A purely military defence is of no use unless there is a sense of social solidarity and social support behind it—unless the armed forces feel they have the support of the entire population, and the entire population does feel involved in the activities of the armed forces."[119]

More recently, MG (RET) Chan Chun Sing (SAFOS 1988) emphasized, as the outgoing COA (2010–11):

> "The strength of our Army lies not just in the people that are currently serving. It also lies in the strength of the support from all walks of society—those that have come before us and those that will come after us. We must never forget that we are part of society. We must continue to connect with society to uphold the belief in the importance of our defence, the ethos to serve and spirit to defend what we have."[120]

Official sources have often painted positive and rosy pictures of C2D. MINDEF surveys have conveyed favourable public opinions of the SAF and support for NS.[121] LKY declared in his 2000 memoirs, "Annual in-camp training is taken seriously by everyone, including employers."[122] The official *Army News* proclaimed in 2009, "Even though we are predominantly a conscript force,

---

[118] "The Army Chiefs We Need: By Kim San", *Straits Times*, 2 Oct. 1968, p. 9.

[119] Paul Jacob, "'Educate the Public on Role of Armed Forces'", *Straits Times*, 28 Apr. 1986, p. 14.

[120] Jonathan Chan, "MG Chan Hands Over Command of Our Army to BG Ravinder", *Army News* 186 (Mar. 2011): 2.

[121] Owyong Eu Gene, "What Do Singaporeans Think about National Service?" *Pioneer* (July 1977): 16–7; "It's Worth the Time and Money", *Straits Times*, 24 Aug. 1982, p. 1; "People Think Well of SAF Prowess, Survey Shows", *Straits Times*, 6 Mar. 1985, p. 40.

[122] Lee, *From Third World to First*, p. 44.

our National Servicemen are well-trained and possess the will to fight."[123] In 2013 incumbent Defence Minister Dr Ng Eng Hen said, "Commitment is high but we want to continue to talk to different groups—employers, parents and NSmen themselves—to see how we can increase this commitment."[124] Another politician expressed similar sentiments after a dialogue session that supposedly confirmed "that commitment to NS is strong. All stakeholders acknowledge the importance of NS."[125] The great unknown is whether this expressed support is grounded in genuine personal ownership and action or is merely a Pavlovian response steeped in political correctness. Furthermore, could respondents and stakeholders say otherwise?

Other sources, in contrast, convey guarded pessimism over unbridled optimism. Even though the SAF had become a technologically advanced outfit by 1983, a foreign periodical recognized that "[m]obilising the population for participation in national defence—never an easy task in a society which has traditionally accorded a low priority to a military career—has become more difficult. Morale in the services, at least among conscripts, is not what the senior leadership would like it to be."[126]

In 1986 Elizabeth Nair, then the head of MINDEF's Personnel Research Department, wrote in the SAF journal *Pointer*:

> War seems to be far from the minds of the public in Singapore ... Surveys carried out in Singapore, with various sectors of the general public, has reflected a general lack of appreciation of the primary objectives of national service and reserve service. Lip-service is paid to the necessity for national service in Singapore. However, mothers still hope that their sons will be clerks rather than riflemen so that they can return home every night rather than stay in camp. Teachers and principals still voice their fears that their brighter students may be diverted from pursuing their studies at university, and national service is seen as an interruption in their academic pursuit. Employers are not happy when their reservist employees are required to be away from their work places for reservist in-camp training. Not all mothers, educators and employers are of such a mind, but a good number are.[127]

---

[123] Tan Wee Meng, "A World Class Army: Building Capacity, Creating Value", *Army News* 163 (Feb.–Mar. 2009): 7.

[124] Ong Hong Tat, "Committee to Strengthen NS Hold First Meeting", *Cyberpioneer*, 8 May 2013.

[125] Rachael Lim, "Views on Strengthening NS Sought from Community Groups", *Cyberpioneer*, 20 May 2013.

[126] Patrick Smith and Philip Bowring, "The Citizen Soldier: Singapore Stresses Security as an Arm of Nation-Building", *Far Eastern Economic Review* 119, 2 (13 Jan. 1983): 26.

[127] Elizabeth Nair, "The Singapore Soldier", *Pointer* 12, 2 (Jan.–Mar. 1986): 85–6.

By 1994 things had not changed. Then-COA BG Lim Neo Chian explained: "If we can get our NSmen to be better motivated and to better understand their roles in national defence, then there is no doubt that this will lead to a more capable SAF."[128] A decade later Star Soh, then a uniformed military psychologist with the ABSD, reasoned:

> With a trend towards smaller families and western pop culture, more youths today do not have a sibling, are doted on by their parents (who can provide because of fewer children and strong economic growth of Singapore) and are brought up with western child-rearing styles. As a result, more youths conscripted today are self-focus[ed] and questioning, have enjoyed good life and lots of freedom at home, and are obese. Their values, habits and fitness are generally in contrast to the culture and expectations of the military. Youths are aware of the contrast and this in turn affects their commitment to national service.[129]

Other foreign observers have also weighed in on the issues of NS and C2D. One visiting physician at a local hospital lamented that "[t]he health-seeking behaviour and conduct of the NS men were sometimes interesting or disappointing".[130] Malaysian academics writing on the outcome of potential armed conflict between the neighbours argued that "Malaysia is deemed to survive when a war breaks compare [*sic*] to Singapore for the spirits of Singapore citizen patriotism is weak … it is still lacking in terms of nationalism or patriotic spirit."[131] Even the United States' Cable News Network (CNN) chimed in with a report that "[t]he Singapore government has been criticized for responding to worried parents by making military service safer and softer for recruits—in one case a conscript was famously snapped making his maid carry his military pack".[132] One company took this further and began offering personal equipment storage and concierge

---

[128] Mathew Pereira, "SAF Units Pitted against Each Other in Realistic Battle Games", *Straits Times*, 5 June 1994.

[129] Star Soh, "Applications of Psychology in HR and Training in a Conscript Army", presentation at the 46th International Military Testing Association Conference, Brussels, 26–28 Oct. 2004. Parentheses in original.

[130] Khalilah Bullock, "Reflection on Tan Tock Seng Hospital Clinical Fellowship Experience", *Singapore Medical Association News* (Mar. 2010): 16.

[131] Mohamad Faisol Keling, Md. Shukri Shuib and Mohd Na'eim Ajis, "The Impact of Singapore's Military Development on Malaysia's Security", *Journal of Politics and Law* 2, 2 (June 2009): 71–2.

[132] Peter Shadbolt, "Taiwan Protests Throw Spotlight on Asia's Military Service", CNN, 13 Aug. 2013.

services to reservists reporting for ICT.[133] Perhaps the most corrosive element to weaken C2D is the number of fatalities among service personnel. The actual deaths are often overshadowed by scant information, a perception of secrecy shrouding investigations, and the subsequent speculative obfuscation between fact and fiction.

It is comforting to think of those who wear the uniform—whether Regular, conscript or reserve—as being monolithic in motivation and commitment to defence and service; yet this is also self-deception. There are certainly patriots who give their all—but the question is whether they can make up for dead weight and maintain the substance and not merely the style of a formidable defence force. What would be the hypothetical signs of a defence establishment that has hit rock bottom in peacetime? For starters, the Regular cadre is plagued by careerism, which in turn requires more ranks, more medals and more prestige appointments. The solution to recruitment and retention is always more money, more scholarships and more benefits. Others get by on minimum effort, content with the handsome spoils of a career in uniform. Profession and occupation become conflated and confused. Conscription becomes so unpopular that departments dealing with NS administration and public communications are greatly expanded with the sole mission to provide palliative care to a seemingly parochial and anachronistic institution. Surveys still show strong support for defence, but the premise of this lip service is that someone else takes the risks and makes the sacrifices. On a larger scale, the nation-in-arms soon forgets the reason for a defence establishment because the possibility of armed conflict is far from the public's conscience. With societal indifference and a prolonged peace, the very thought of armed conflict and the concept of war become completely alien to the establishment raised for that very purpose. Training safety then takes precedence over operational standards, which invariably atrophy. The downward spiral is arrested only with the integrity to acknowledge the problem and the will to correct the malaise. To pretend that all is copacetic is tantamount to treason. Thankfully, Singapore is nowhere near this precipice.

Opinions on society's commitment to NS and defence will continue to be divided for the time being, without any clear conclusion. The reality probably lies between the optimistic and pessimistic ends of the spectrum. The challenges in the days ahead lie with the changing character of society in terms of the values and achievements emphasized, and the solutions adopted to address pressing issues. These discussions are revisited at length in chapter 8. It is sufficient for the moment to note that NS is neither as welcomed as officialdom

---

[133] Justin Ong, "NSmen 'Should Consider Carefully' Proposed Concierge Service, Says Singapore Army", Channel NewsAsia, 19 May 2017.

would paint it nor as detestable as certain circles would have us believe. NS remains an essential insurance policy of state, but the premiums paid in terms of time, effort, risks and opportunity costs in a globalized world are increasingly seen as too costly.[134] Efforts to recognize and maintain service commitment are ever growing.[135] Singapore's socio-economic advancement does not help the NS cause, as the British military sociologist Christopher Dandeker reasons:

> It is a well-established finding in military sociology that the long-term shift away from conscription and mass armed force model dating from the 1789–1945 era is caused by a combination of societal and international factors. From a societal point of view, the growth of affluence, individualism, and differing conceptions of citizenship have all undermined the idea that the primary basis of citizenship is military service.[136]

The "good" news is that Dandeker also attributes membership of an alliance, distance from threat to national sovereignty, and frequent participation in peacekeeping operations as external factors of this shift.[137] Those factors have remained opaque within the Singaporean context. Even so, the government has continually sought to pre-empt and arrest problems in maintaining a conscript-based defence force and society's C2D.

The most effective and appropriate channel has been to educate the nation— literally termed "National Education"—by shaping "the attitudes and values towards a loyal and committed citizenry" with the message that Singapore can be defended and to instil a "sense of affiliation and belonging to the country".[138]

---

[134] Seah Chee Meow, "National Security", in *Management of Success: The Moulding of Modern Singapore*, ed. Kernial Singh Sandhu and Paul Wheatley (Singapore: Institute of Southeast Asian Studies, 1990), pp. 959–60.

[135] These include the establishment of the Advisory Council on Community Relations in Defence (ACCORD) in January 1984; Committee to Recognise the Contribution of Operationally Ready National Servicemen to Total Defence in 1990; National Service Affairs Department (NSAD) in 2001; and Committee to Strengthen National Service in March 2013.

[136] Christopher Dandeker, "Building Flexible Forces for the 21st Century: Key Challenges for the Contemporary Armed Services", in *Handbook of the Sociology of the Military*, ed. Giuseppe Caforio (New York: Kluwer Academic/Plenum Publishers, 2003), p. 410.

[137] Ibid., p. 411.

[138] Quah, "Singapore: Towards a National Identity": p. 212; Lee, "Leadership and Security in Singapore", pp. 170–1; Terence Lee, "The Politics of Civil Society in Singapore", *Asian Studies Review* 26, 1 (Mar. 2002): 100; Charissa Tan, Beng Chong Lim and Star Soh, "Understanding Attitudes towards National Defence and Military Service in Singapore", presentation at the 45th International Military Testing Association Conference, Pensacola, 3–6 Nov. 2003; Jasmine B-Y. Sim and Murray Print, "Citizenship Education in Singapore: Controlling or Empowering Teacher Understanding and Practice?" *Oxford Review of Education* 35, 6 (Dec. 2009): 705–23.

It is no surprise "[t]he Singapore government has not faltered in its conscious and consistent program of political socialization, beginning particularly with the schools".[139] Schools were approached to mentally prepare students for NS, and since 1979 familiarization visits to military installations have formed part of the education curriculum.[140] In 1981 parents first visited their sons during BMT, which further served to ameliorate concerns and reiterate the importance of NS. That same year MINDEF reached out to employers and stressed their important role within the defence ecosystem.[141]

The message would be more easily emphasized if Singapore had an identifiable enemy like other states with conscript-based militaries since the conclusion of World War II. The price of peace has afforded no such concessions, and for Singapore to name potential enemies is to make actual enemies.[142] The historical cards of British colonialism and Japanese imperialism have never been played to stir nationalism. Their confluence is revisited annually on Total Defence Day (15 February) but otherwise resides mainly in the pages of history books, monuments, commemorative plaques, and contested and possibly fading memories.[143] The Singapore government, after all, "accepted Japan's atonement which took the form of a grant of $25m and the loan of another $25 million on liberal terms" post-independence.[144] Decolonization has never gained traction beyond the scheduled handover of land, infrastructure and institutions. The flip side to not having any identifiable enemies, either historical or contemporary, is that "train[ing] hard and seriously was difficult in peacetime especially when there is no immediate threat to your security".[145]

Two other key avenues have helped in the quest to strengthen C2D. The annual National Day Parade (NDP) "with its emphasis on spectacle and discipline has been institutionalized as a national symbol" and has entailed

---

[139] Chan, *Singapore: The Politics of Survival 1965–1967*, p. 57; H.E. Wilson, "Education as an Instrument of Policy in Southeast Asia: The Singapore Example", *Journal of Southeast Asian Studies* 8, 1 (Mar. 1977): 75–84.

[140] Edmund Teo, "Military Training Plan for Schools", *Straits Times*, 18 Oct. 1980, p. 1.

[141] Lee, *Singapore: The Unexpected Nation*, pp. 289–90.

[142] Thomson, "Britain's Plan to Leave Asia": 123; Paul Jacob, "'Educate the Public on Role of Armed Forces'", *Straits Times*, 28 Apr. 1986, p. 14.

[143] Kevin Blackburn and Karl Hack, *War Memory and the Making of Modern Malaysia and Singapore* (Singapore: NUS Press, 2012).

[144] Ibid., p. 9; Josey, *Lee Kuan Yew*, p. 16.

[145] Ronnie Wai, "More Stress on Personnel Development", *Straits Times*, 27 May 1982, p. 1.

greater fanfare and monetary costs with each passing year.[146] The show of military strength and organizational efficiency is a subtle hint to foreign dignitaries that Singapore is prepared to defend itself. A message of solidarity and the "can-do" spirit that enabled Singapore to defy the odds of survival and success is also woven into the accompanying mass performances. Then there is the National Cadet Corps (NCC), which was formed in 1969 with a traceable lineage to the first army cadet corps established in 1902.[147] The organization served to inculcate values, as former Parliamentary Secretary (Education) Mohammed Ghazali Ismail rationalized in 1971: "The National Cadet Corps provides the means to shape Singapore youths to be resourceful, resilient, and responsible citizens … the corps prevented local youths from being led astray by the unhealthy, outside influences caused by Singapore's rapid urbanisation and strategic position."[148] NCC has also provided a solid foundation for NS through military regimentation and outdoor activities, and it has at times offered wider opportunities than those available to conscripts.[149]

Participation in NCC does not necessarily lead to a military career, but it provides a pivotal introduction to the military, as various flag officers have attested. A medical officer (MO) who would one day become the Chief of Medical Corps (CMC) recalled: "I was in NCC land for six years including being a cadet lieutenant in JC (Junior College) one and two (the penultimate and final years of secondary school). This was a shaping experience in terms of familiarity with the SAF and an appreciation for both discipline and regimentation."[150]

---

[146] Chan, *Singapore: The Politics of Survival 1965–1967*, p. 57. The annual cost of the NDP between 2010 and 2014 was around $20 million, while $40 million was set aside for the Golden Jubilee celebrations in 2015. Jermyn Chow, "NDP 2015 to Recreate Nation's First Parade; Free Funpacks for 1.25m Households", *Straits Times*, 5 Mar. 2015.

[147] The NCC has roots in the army cadet corps formed in 1902, which was subsequently formed into land, sea, air, girls and police units in 1969. The bifurcation of the MID in 1970 resulted in the NCC's affiliation with MINDEF, and the National Police Cadet Corps with the Ministry of Home Affairs. The NCC Council formed in 1973 with representatives from the Ministries of Education and Defence. HQ NCC provides governance and oversight through centralized leadership, administration and training activities. See Tan Wang Joo, "Developing Leaders from Cadets", *Straits Times*, 7 July 1974, p. 12; and Ivan Fernandez, "Kids Who Are Tough and Disciplined to Boot", *Straits Times*, 20 Oct. 1980, p. 6.

[148] "Ghazali on the Role of the NCC in Turning Out Model Citizens", *Straits Times*, 27 Sept. 1971, p. 8.

[149] The SAF allocates more billets on the Basic Airborne Course at HQ Commando and the Basic Diver Course at the Naval Diving Unit for NCC cadets than NSFs not in commando or diver vocations. NSmen are rarely eligible for airborne training.

[150] Interview No. 18.

Former COA (2011–14) MG (RET) then-BG Ravinder Singh S/O Harchand Singh reasoned:

> "I joined the SAF because I wanted to be a soldier and a leader. I guess in some ways it's related to what I did when I was in school. I was in NCC (Sea) when I was in secondary school and I knew from that experience that I enjoyed leading and getting things done. When I was offered the SAF scholarship, it was very much in line with what I wanted to do … So for me it was a natural choice."[151]

BG (RET) Lim Yeow Beng, former Head Air Logistics (HAL), similarly explained: "I realized that my NCC days have influenced the later chapters of my life in more than one way. Firstly, it inculcated in me a set of values and traits that have helped me throughout my life, even till to-date. Secondly, it provided me with opportunities to greater leadership roles. Thirdly, it influenced my decision of a career choice."[152]

A fourth officer who also joined the air force highlighted how NCC catered to his interests and prepared him for enlistment: "Prior to NS I was looking to be a pilot or something in the air force like engineer or controller, something that deals with the air in some way. NCC and outdoor activities prepared me for NS and mentally knowing it was part of the process to defend Singapore."[153]

The means of conveying the National Education message to foster strong commitment among citizens to Singapore has evolved over the years, and the message is now transmitted through various programmes. The Temasek Seminar (renamed Temasek Dialogue in 2010) was initiated in 1991 to inculcate the importance of national security among student leaders from junior colleges and polytechnics. The focus on the responsibilities of being a citizen began in 1996. Since February 1999, a senior SAF officer usually in the rank of COL has headed NEXUS—formerly called the Central National Education Office—with the responsibility for synergizing NE initiatives across various government ministries and agencies. In 2007 the MINDEF Scholarship Centre and respective service recruitment centres established the MINDEF Internship to offer pre-NS students insights into military life in a thinly veiled attempt to recruit. Finally, the SAF-Schools Partnership Programme paired active army battalions and schools, which "not only helped the students and teachers to

---

[151] Ng et al., *Called to Lead*, p. 22.

[152] "National Cadet Corps (NCC) Affirmation Ceremony", *Air Force News* 82 (July 2002): 20.

[153] Interview No. 14.

better understand the Army's role in defending Singapore, it also allowed the servicemen involved to appreciate their contribution in national defence".[154]

Many challenges remain despite the efforts and resources devoted to NE activities. Some observers have warned that complacency is the greatest threat to Singapore.[155] Others lament Singaporeans' knowledge of their own history.[156] Yet another decries that "[i]n Singapore, many of us are prone to a certain navel-gazing, obsessing over domestic concerns".[157] Most recently, Lee Hsien Loong acknowledged the need to "help younger generations of Singaporeans who have grown up in a more stable and affluent environment to understand ... strategic realities, and prepare them for their part in defending Singapore, our home".[158] The importance of C2D has taken on greater significance with the unprecedented surge of immigrants in recent years. This is especially the case with naturalized citizens and PRs; no effort is spared in emphasizing to them the rationale and importance of NS. Visits to military units are arranged for parents and potential enlistees to assuage concerns.[159] There are some who question the strategic wisdom and impact on operational security of conscripting PRs, who are essentially citizens of another country. Nevertheless, NS serves as a peacetime test of their commitment to Singapore and partially satisfies the criteria for citizenship should they decide to stay.[160] Indeed, official publications and local media frequently laud dual citizens and foreign nationals with PR status who

---

[154] Tan Wee Meng, "Ready, Relevant and Decisive", *Army News* 187 (Apr. 2011): 7; Ling Wei Chao, "Many Faces One Identity", *Army News* 197 (Feb. 2012): 5–8.

[155] "Complacency Greatest Threat to S'pore's Defence: Dr Yeo", *Straits Times*, 1 July 1994, p. 30.

[156] Chua Lee Hoong, "Never Too Late for S'poreans to Learn about Country's Past", *Straits Times*, 10 Aug. 1996, p. 26; Kwa Chong Guan, "A New Generation Rewrites History, Doubts Singapore's Vulnerability", *Straits Times*, 30 Jan. 2015.

[157] Chua Mui Hoong, "We're Living in the Most Dangerous Region in the World", *Straits Times*, 28 Sept. 2014.

[158] Goh Chin Lian and Jermyn Chow, "National Service a Part of Singapore Identity: PM Lee", *Straits Times*, 23 Oct. 2012.

[159] Terence Lim, "First-Generation PRs Assured after BMTC Visit", *Pioneer* (Aug. 2006): 14; "PRs Get National Service Insights at BMTC", *Army News* 138 (Jan.–Feb. 2007): 3.

[160] Official figures showed that there were 13,000 NS-eligible male PRs between 2006 and 2011. Of them, 8,800 (67.7 per cent) enlisted for NS while the other 4,200 (32.2 per cent) renounced their PR status; 6,100 (69.3 per cent who enlisted for NS or 46.9 per cent of all NS-eligible PRs) of those who enlisted became Singaporean citizens, while the remaining 2,700 held on to their foreign passports. See "Written Reply by Minister for Defence Dr Ng Eng Hen to Parliamentary Question on Permanent Residents in National Service", MINDEF, 22 Nov. 2011, http://www.mindef.gov.sg/imindef/press_room/official_releases/ps/2012/15oct12_ps.html, accessed 7 Nov. 2016.

have enlisted for service in the SAF.[161] Yet their enlistment in tandem with the establishment of the SAF Volunteer Corps for non-NS liable individuals (certain PRs and female citizens) has only blunted but not silenced the critics of liberal migration policies and their claims of "NS for locals and jobs for foreigners".

The SAF has also addressed the intra-organizational aspects of C2D on the individual level and conscientiously sought to provide all personnel with "meaningful and positive experiences".[162] Former CDF (2007–10) LG (RET) Desmond Kuek Bak Chye (SAFOS 1982) stressed this necessity:

> "The Positive Army Experience is part of our mission. We need the commitment of our people to take our defence seriously ... Without commitment we will not have mission effectiveness, competency or readiness ... [soldiers must] feel good, proud, passionate and committed. This comes about when our soldiers perform roles that are personally rewarding, and when they feel satisfied and appreciated for their contributions."[163]

It was recognized as far back as 1985 that "[a]n enlightened reservist or national serviceman who speaks well of his experience was the SAF's best ambassador".[164] Such experiences are presently encapsulated in routing BMT graduation marches past famous landmarks and holding parades within view of Singapore's central business district.[165] This further serves to remind society at large that the SAF is ready to defend Singapore. Another initiative is the proliferation of uniform insignia, which the SAF of yesteryear actively minimized so as to reflect a "citizen's army".[166] A simple heraldic tradition is no longer in vogue, and the

---

[161] Kelvin Kow, Chia Han Sheng, Samuel Cheam and Marcus Ho, "Our Army, Our People, Our Edge", *Army News* 172 (Jan. 2010), p. 6; "Our People, Our Edge", *Army News*, Special Supplement #2 (Oct. 2010), p. 4; "The Tiger Family", *Army News*, Special Supplement #11 (Sept. 2011), p. 4; Saifulbahri Ismail, "NS Enlistment Expected to Dip to 19,500 in 2025", Channel NewsAsia, 30 June 2012; Hariz Baharudin, "Uprooted Idyllic Life in UK to Serve National Service in Singapore", *New Paper*, 31 Jan. 2016.

[162] Star Soh, "Applications of Psychology in HR and Training in a Conscript Army", presentation at the 46th International Military Testing Association Conference, Brussels, 26–28 Oct. 2004.

[163] Poon Shou Yi, "Our Army Experience", *Army News* 113 (Oct.–Nov. 2004): 4–5.

[164] Glauberman, "10-Year-Late PR Job for SAF", p. 9.

[165] Samuel Cheam, "Recruits Graduate at Floating Platform", *Army News* 181 (Oct. 2010): 4.

[166] Military regalia such as lanyards, ceremonial belts, brass insignias, and oversized epaulettes were removed. Today a different aspect has been revived with the proliferation of formation sleeve patches, vocation collar insignia, multiple confidence badges, new vocation brevets, and even a new coloured beret for those in the infantry vocation.

anachronism is seen as a hindrance in the quest to foster positive experiences and strengthen C2D.

The effort to create an overwhelming positive environment is perhaps best illustrated at the Army Museum of Singapore (ARMS), where the thoughts of former CDF (1992–95) LG (RET) Ng Jui Ping on a terrorist hijacking are angled to project optimism over candour. In a 2010 paper presented at an international conference by then-MAJ Psalm Lew, former ARMS Chief Researcher (2005–07), Ng's recollection of Operation Thunderbolt in March 1991 to retake hijacked flight SQ117 allegedly read: "… between the time that I gave the order to start the process of assaulting and the actual lifting up of the ladders … and the beginning of the assault, I had a few minutes. In that few minutes, I was composing a letter I would write if the assault in any way would end in disaster."[167]

The raw candour and guarded possibility of mission failure certainly had no place in a publicly accessible museum. Only unbridled optimism would pass muster for consumption by locals and foreigners alike. The account that sits astride the portrait of the SAF's second COA at the "Reflections of Our Chiefs of Army" gallery proudly proclaims:

> … I never had doubts that once the doors were opened, our SOF troopers were that well trained that they would nail the terrorists. I was looking at the SOF approaching the aircraft. The ladders to storm the aircraft went up. They scaled the ladders and I suddenly realized that my heart was beating so fast. That was when I thought it would burst because the tension was, for me, the opening of the doors. After the incident, I spoke to PM Lee (then 2nd Minster for Defence). The gist of it was, how glad we were that years ago when we were General Staff officers, the SAF had worked on the development, training and operational efficiency of the SOF … the special attention we placed upon the group, the special training, so on and so forth, it was all worthwhile.[168]

The contrast is plain to see.

2.4   The Pioneers

The challenges of creating a credible defence within Singapore's historical context are clear, and three pertinent points must be reiterated. First, Singapore did not have an established military tradition or martial spirit even though it

---

[167] Quoted in presentation by Psalm B.C. Lew, "Preparing Values Based Commanders for the 3rd Generation Singapore Armed Forces", 52nd International Military Testing Association Conference, Lucerne, 29 Sept. 2010, pp. 15–6.

[168] Quote obtained from the "Reflections of Our Chiefs of Army" gallery during the author's visit to the ARMS in 2012.

was a British colony. Second, Singapore benefited from the presence of foreign military forces—British and later Commonwealth, namely Australian and New Zealand—for defence and deterrence until the mid-1970s even though self-rule (11 April 1957) and independence were achieved earlier.[169] Third, circumstances dictated the political will and decision to implement NS with the primary reason to overcome manpower and treasury constraints in building a credible defence capability. The SAF could purchase equipment and enlist soldiers to fill the rank and file, but the issue of finding officers before the maturation of the SAF Officer Corps proved challenging.

A combined Ministry of Interior and Defence (MID) from 1965 to 1970 proved optimal as the ministry tackled manpower and budgetary constraints. Local police and army units addressed domestic issues, while the British military umbrella remained open. Civilian bureaucrats held the most senior MID positions because of personnel constraints and by design "to ensure that the SAF remained subordinate to the political leadership by keeping important functions such as manpower and finance under civilian officers in the defence ministry".[170] Indeed, the first Director General Staff (DGS), Tan Teck Khim, was a newly minted Assistant Commissioner of Police (ACP) seconded to MID in 1965. The 39-year-old rose through the police ranks as a Constable (1945), Inspector (1946), Deputy Superintendent (1956), Superintendent (1961) and ACP (1965). His experience as a police officer was essential, as Singapore faced internal security problems such as communal violence and Communist subversion. His role as the Commandant of the Police Academy (then called the Police Training School) from 1958 to 1960 also came in handy as one of the SAF's first priorities was the establishment of training schools. Tan became the inaugural DGS (1966–68) while at MID and subsequently served as the acting Permanent Secretary (PS) at the Ministry of Health. He then returned to the Singapore Police Force (SPF), where he became the Commissioner in 1971.[171]

Officers from foreign militaries on service loan or on contract to the SAF also held command, staff and instructional billets until Singaporeans could assume responsibility. Some of the higher-ranking officers included Air Commodores Geoffrey Millington and John Langer; Group Captains William Kelly, David Rhodes and Basil Fox from the Royal Air Force (RAF); Group Captain Murray

---

[169] Australian infantry battalions rotated through Singapore during the Vietnam War. A New Zealand infantry battalion was stationed in Singapore until 1989. From the early 1990s the gradual shift towards hosting American naval and air assets at Sembawang and Paya Lebar respectively took place.

[170] Lee, *From Third World to First*, p. 36.

[171] "Security", *Business Times*, 2 Oct. 1978, p. 21.

Turnbull from the Royal Australian Air Force (RAAF); and Liu Ching Chuan, a retired Republic of China Air Force (ROCAF) officer who was bestowed the rank of COL. Singaporeans took on more senior roles as the MID tapped officers from three areas: citizen-soldiers from the pool of volunteers, the smaller pool of professional officers from the Old Guard of the SIR, and bureaucrats from the Administrative Service (AS) placed on temporary secondment to the SAF. Members of SAFTI's First Batch would in due course relieve the early pioneers and pave the way for the maturation of a self-generating SAF Officer Corps underpinned by the NS system.

2.4.1 A Volunteer and World War II Veteran

The second DGS from the military was Brigadier (known today as BG) Thomas James Duncan Campbell. The former literature teacher was born in Singapore in 1922 and served two terms (1961–66, 1971–73) as the principal of St Stephen's School.[172] Information is rather scant on this pioneering general of the SAF, but there is adequate evidence of his physical hardiness, penchant for the outdoors, and motivation to serve in uniform albeit on a part-time basis. Campbell joined the 1st Battalion, Straits Settlement Volunteer Force, as a private in 1940 after graduating from St Joseph's School and was issued service number 20274. The infantryman was taken prisoner during World War II and on 28 April 1943 sent to Siam (Thailand), where he survived forced labour on the infamous "Death Railway". He was interned at Singapore's infamous Changi Prison on 21 December 1943.[173]

Campbell's post-war actions and decisions spoke volumes of his commitment to military service. Soldiering was not his profession, and his health suffered as a prisoner-of-war—yet he did not hang up the uniform.[174] Campbell instead earned an officer's commission in 1950 while teaching at St Patrick's Secondary School and made LTC in January 1962 as Commanding Officer (CO) of the 1st Battalion, Singapore Volunteer Corps (SVC).[175] In 1965 he was promoted to Brigadier and given command of the Singapore Infantry Brigade (SIB). Campbell could have taken his leave for the West when Singapore gained independence.

---

[172] St Stephen's School opened 1957 and is one of the six Christian Brothers' School of the De La Salle Order in Singapore.

[173] Jonathan Moffatt and Paul Riches, *In Orient Primus: A History of the Volunteer Forces in Malaya and Singapore* (Trowbridge: Cromwell Press Group, 2010), p. 74.

[174] "Ex-Army Chief, BG Campbell, Dies in Australia", *Straits Times*, 22 Oct. 1989, p. 17.

[175] "S'pore's Former SAF Chief Dies in Australia", *New Paper*, 21 Oct. 1989, p. 6; "Col Vij Is New General Staff Director", *Straits Times*, 10 Sept. 1970, p. 2; "Former SAF Director of General Staff Passes Away", *Pioneer* (Nov. 1989): 43.

He chose instead to stay and served faithfully as Commander (COMD) 1 SIB (1968–69) before becoming the top soldier as Acting DGS (1968–69) and then DGS from December 1969 to September 1970. He was then appointed Director (DIR) of the Singapore Command and Staff College (SCSC)—renamed the Goh Keng Swee Command and Staff College (GKSCSC) on 1 February 2011—where he stayed until March 1971, when he hung up the olive greens for good.[176] Campbell returned to St Stephen's School and in 1973 emigrated to Perth, Australia, where he remained until his death from heart complications in 1989.[177]

2.4.2 The Old Guard of the Singapore Infantry Regiment

The SIR occupies a special place in the annals of SAF history. The first two SIR battalions formed Singapore's corps of professional infantrymen and were raised pre-independence in 1957 and 1962. The first recruitment drive for the 1st Battalion, SIR (1 SIR) on 4 March 1957 witnessed long queues of eager young men at the recruitment centre. Of the 1,420 applications received, only 237 were accepted.[178] Like the rest of the then-Singapore Military Forces (SMF)—formed in 1952 and the predecessor of the SAF—the SIR's officer billets required time to be filled by locals. The first Singaporean officer in 1 SIR was COL (RET) then-Lieutenant (LTA) Ronald Wee, who joined the Australian Imperial Forces in 1942 and subsequently the battalion on 6 November 1957.[179] The other junior officers were recruited locally and received pre-commissioning training at either Officer Cadet School (OCS) Portsea in Victoria, Australia, or the Federation Military College (FMC) at Port Dickson, Malaysia.[180]

---

[176] SCSC was resident at Fort Canning (February 1970 to August 1976), Marina Hill (August 1976 to April 1981) and Seletar Camp (April 1981 to June 1995) and is currently at SAFTI MI (since June 1995). *SAFTI 50: Developing Leaders since 1966* (Singapore: SAFTI Military Institute, 2016), pp. 95, 97.

[177] "S'pore's Former SAF Chief Dies in Australia", p. 6; "Ex-Army Chief, BG Campbell, Dies in Australia", p. 17.

[178] Ashley Seek, "Infantry 60th Anniversary", *Army News* 243 (2017): 12.

[179] R. Chandran, "Valiant Wees", *Straits Times*, 17 Oct. 1971, p. 3; "Perm-Sec Told Me to Take on Extra Work", *Straits Times*, 16 Apr. 1981, p. 10.

[180] Forty Singaporeans completed pre-commissioning training at OCS Portsea between 1957 and 1985. Thirty-five attended the FMC (29 for the full-course and 16 on the short-service commissioning course) between 1957 and 1965. See Neville Lindsay, *Loyalty and Service: The Officer Cadet School Portsea* (Kenmore: Historia Productions, 1995); and Leslie Terh, *Sons and Officers: Life at Prestigious Military College* (Singapore: Sea Sky Books Enterprise, 2000).

The career officers who filled billets in the professionally manned SIR came to be known as the Old Guard.[181] LG (RET) Winston Choo and the late BG (RET) Patrick Sim Hak Kng (1936–2017), both veterans of *Konfrontasi*, emerged from their ranks and became generals in the 1970s. Sim was a trainee at the Teachers' Training College when he came across the recruitment advertisement by coincidence in the local papers seeking candidates for OCS Portsea.[182] The opportunity for pre-commissioning training overseas instantly piqued the interest of the all-rounder who excelled in sports and was an active member of the Boy Scouts. The excitement was amplified by Sim's earlier visit Down Under for the international Scouts Jamboree in 1952 and his receipt of the Queen Scout Award the following year. Ninety-eight responded to the advertisement, 20 were shortlisted, 13 were interviewed, and three including a reserve candidate were selected. Sim and COL (RET) Peter Lim Poh Weng eventually made the trip, and the inaugural Singaporeans at Portsea completed their training in July 1958.[183] Sim holds the distinction of serving two command tours each at the battalion (10th Battalion PDF, 5 SIR), brigade (2 SIB, 3 SIB) and division (6 DIV, 3 DIV) echelons. He retired in 1981 after 24 years in uniform, including the last three as DCGS, the SAF's number two soldier.

For LG (RET) Winston Choo—arguably Singapore's most well-known and highly decorated officer—a career in uniform with either the police or the military was always on the cards. The avid sportsman's childhood was grounded in many outdoor-oriented activities, and he also benefited from a long association with the Boys' Brigade. Choo's inclination and affinity for the military led him to sign up with the SVC as a rifleman during his final year of high school. He later chanced upon and responded to an advertisement for the FMC prior to his A-level examinations in 1959. Choo and three other successful applicants

---

[181] 1 and 2 SIR were raised as all-regular battalions on 12 March 1957 and 16 July 1962 respectively and became conscript battalions in 1968. The other infantry battalions raised for NS intakes were: 3 SIR (1 April 1967), 4 SIR (1 April 1967), 5 SIR (1 November 1968), 6 SIR (2 April 1969), 7 SIR (1 August 1970) and 8 SIR (1 April 1974). On 1 December 1969 the SAF Regular Battalion was established, and it became the SAF Commando Unit a year later on 1 December 1970. On 16 July 1971 the unit was renamed the 1st Commando Battalion, and due to the recruitment shortfall of Regulars it received its first NS company on 15 January 1973.

[182] See "Public Appointments—Singapore Infantry Regiment", *Straits Times*, 30 Mar. 1957 and 1 Apr. 1957, p. 10.

[183] "Australia Will Help Train New Army", *Straits Times*, 28 June 1956, p. 7; "Public Appointments—Singapore Infantry Regiment", p. 10; "13 Interviewed for Two Awards", *Straits Times*, 16 May 1957, p. 7; "3 Cadets to Train 'Down Under'", *Singapore Free Press*, 24 May 1957, p. 5.

formed the fourth batch of Singaporeans at FMC and completed their training in 1961.[184] The lure of a military career and Choo's misplaced proclivity towards the outdoors over academic pursuits were evident as he later admitted: "My first thought on becoming a soldier was that I did not have to study anymore. As it turned out, while in military service, I never stopped studying. I received my training in Malaysia, England and in various parts of the United States."[185]

General Choo became the first SAF officer to attend the US Army's Command and General Staff College (CGSC) at Fort Leavenworth (1972), and he later studied Military History and International Relations at Duke University (1981–82). His storied career included CO 1 SAF Signals Battalion (1967–68), Head of Operations, Organisation and Training (1969), Chief of Communications and Electronics Department (1969, 1970–71), CO 4 SIR (1971), CO 1 SIR (1972), COMD 2 SIB (1972–73), and Head of Training and later Head of Organisation and Plans Departments (1973–74). He was appointed defence chief at the age of 33 over peers and seniors from the 1st Command and Staff Course (CSC) such as Lim Poh Weng, Donald Jambu, Mancharan Singh Gill, George Mitchell, Seah Peng Yong, Charles Chew and April Wee.[186] General Choo would go on to lead the SAF as DGS between 1974 and 1978, Chief of the General Staff (CGS) from 1978 to 1981 and 1982 to 1988, and CDF from 1988 to 1992. His unrivalled longevity as the SAF's number one soldier is testament to his abilities as a military professional, the trust he earned within the political echelons, and the dearth of worthy successors.

2.4.3 Secondment from the Administrative Service

The third talent pool tapped was the Administrative Service (AS) and its complement of Administrative Officers (AOs). These bureaucratic elites are recruited based on stringent Public Service Commission (PSC) criteria, and their careers are closely managed by the Public Service Division (PSD). AOs are tried and tested through a crucible of postings in government, with only the "best" appointed PS of a ministry. A handful of AOs were personally tapped by Dr Goh for secondment to the SAF, with Kirpa Ram Vij and Tan Chin Tiong both making BG.

---

[184] The inaugural batch of three candidates—Peter Tang Hong Whye, George Mitchell and Ahmad Hassan—left for FMC on 31 December 1957 and completed their training in 1958.

[185] Winston Choo, "A Soldier in Diplomacy", in *The Little Red Dot: Reflections by Singapore's Diplomats*, ed. Tommy Koh and Chang Li Lin (Singapore: World Scientific Publishing, 2008), p. 171.

[186] *SAFTI 50*, p. 98.

The story of BG (RET) Kirpa Ram Vij—or "Kip", as the IDF advisers referred to him—is one of an immigrant who made the most of opportunities and sunk roots in his newfound homeland.[187] A barely teenage Vij and his family fled from an area in modern-day Pakistan during the tumultuous 1947 partition of India and arrived in Singapore later that year.[188] He was educated at Rangoon Road Primary School, Victoria Afternoon School and the premier Raffles Institution (RI). The student prefect proved to be a capable sportsman, favouring hockey and rugby, and was the quartermaster in the cadet corps. Despite his abilities, he was preoccupied with how the family could make ends meet within the context of Singapore's "era of poverty": "My father was a petty trader. I was the eldest of eight children and had no great ambition. It was merely a question of survival. I intended to be a teacher to support the family. It was Mr Philip Liau who advised me to enrol in the university that changed the course of my life."[189] Vij took the advice and earned an honours degree in geography at the former University of Singapore in 1959. In 1960 he made the grade as an AO and was appointed Collector of Land Revenue at the Land Office before another promotion in 1963 to Assistant Secretary for Methods and Organisation at the finance ministry.[190]

Vij participated in the uniformed services as a part-time volunteer despite his hectic schedule as an AO and President of the University of Malaya Geographical Society.[191] He was commissioned as an officer in the Singapore Volunteer Artillery Regiment in 1960 and earned the Sword of Honour (SOH) as the top graduate.[192] Singapore's independence and the embryonic SAF presented a unique opportunity for full-time service, but Vij also recognized the uncertainties:

> "They were actively looking for [individuals] who knew something about military affairs to take up positions in the Defence Ministry. After three years in the Finance Ministry, I was happy to make the change but was unsure whether I should be going there in uniform. I have only a few years

---

[187] Ramachandran Menon, ed., *One of a Kind: Remembering SAFTI's First Batch*, 2nd ed. (Singapore: SAFTI Military Institute, 2015), p. 64.

[188] Patrick Jonas, "In Command of His Life", *AsiaOne*, 7 Jan. 2011.

[189] Tan Guan Heng, *100 Inspiring Rafflesians 1823–2003* (Singapore: World Scientific Publishing, 2008), p. 87.

[190] Arthur Richards, "Seven Civil Servants Take 'Induction Course' at Political Study Centre", *Singapore Free Press*, 30 June 1960, p. 4; "No. 1 Soldier Col. Vij Promoted to Brigadier", p. 1; "Kirpa Ram Appointed Envoy to Egypt", *Straits Times*, 16 May 1975, p. 1.

[191] "Study Group to Visit Christmas Island", *Singapore Free Press*, 13 Jan. 1960, p. 7.

[192] "Seven Civil Servants Take 'Induction Course'", p. 4; *SAFTI Silver Jubilee 1966–1991* (Singapore: Ministry of Defence, 1991), p. 42.

of uniform experience and was a captain in the volunteers. So I did not think I was senior enough for any high-level position in the ministry."[193]

Dr Goh had other ideas and directed the artillery officer with a clear albeit difficult task: "We are starting a new training school for soldiers, officers, and we want you to head the project."[194] Vij was swiftly seconded to the MID in 1965 with the rank of LTC and commenced a two-month mission in Israel with ACP Tan Teck Khim to study the IDF systems and training institutions.[195] Upon their return Vij became the inaugural DIR SAFTI with help from a team of IDF advisers.[196] Service in this capacity from February 1966 to May 1968 was enough for him to sit on the Army Board—which in 1972 was renamed the Armed Forces Council (AFC)—chaired by the defence minister.[197] His reward, however, was simply the opportunity to serve: "We had a kind of a vision, we wanted to build a nation ... and that fired us on! ... The proudest moment of my entire career as a soldier was when the first batch passed out. I almost cried that Sunday afternoon—we were all so filled with emotion."[198]

In 1967 General Vij received military (to COL) and civil service (to Principal Assistant Secretary) promotions as a seconded AO.[199] In June 1968 he was appointed the first DGS from the military, but he relinquished the post in December to BG Campbell. The Israeli academic Alon Peled noted:

> Lim Kim San, the minister of defence, in a most unusual move, asked Kirpa Ram Vij to give up his position temporarily as the director of general staff (the most senior staff position at the time) and take personal charge of constructing the new brigade's buildup. Vij completed this task in nine months and, after attending a short staff course, returned to his newly named post of chief of staff.[200]

---

[193] Desker and Kwa, *Goh Keng Swee*, p. 94.

[194] Ibid.

[195] "Another Step up the Scales for 10 Top Men", *Straits Times*, 1 Aug. 1970, p. 6; Pang, "Soldiers Must Be Bi-lingual", p. 6.

[196] The acronym SAFTI has over the decades morphed into a pronoun with its current manifestation as SAFTI Military Institute. "Last 3 Israeli Advisers Leaving in May", *Straits Times*, 14 Apr. 1974, p. 1; "Pasir Laba Camp is Now Safti Once Again", *Straits Times*, 3 July 1986, p. 14; *SAFTI Silver Jubilee 1966–1991*, p. 42; Menon, *One of a Kind*, p. 39; *SAFTI 50*, p. 9.

[197] "Army Board Members", *Straits Times*, 2 May 1966, p. 4; "New Army Board Members Named", *Straits Times*, 20 Nov. 1967, p. 4.

[198] *SAFTI Silver Jubilee 1966–1991*, p. 42.

[199] "Up the Ladder for Six S'pore Govt. Officers", *Straits Times*, 6 Aug. 1967, p. 12; "Col Vij is New General Staff Director", *Straits Times*, 10 Sept. 1970, p. 2.

[200] Peled, *A Question of Loyalty*, p. 114.

Vij's conspicuous efforts and results at SAFTI made him known among the political echelons. He was tapped as DIR SCSC from March 1969 to September 1970 and became the inaugural COMD 3 SIB from September 1969 to January 1970.[201] Vij even attended the CSC as a student while leading the very same Staff College due to the SAF's rapid expansion.[202] In September 1970 he was reappointed DGS and made BG in 1972. BG (RET) Kirpa Ram Vij retired from the SAF in 1974 at age 39 and returned to the civil service.[203]

Another AO tapped for secondment was BG (RET) Tan Chin Tiong, whose career trajectory provided a blueprint for the ascension pathway mirrored later by deserving SAFOS officers. Tan completed a history degree with first class honours at the University of Singapore before joining the AS. He served in the finance ministry from March to September 1967 before the CAS made him eligible for NS by virtue of being a civil servant. Even if he had joined the private sector he would have been conscripted the next year by virtue of his tertiary qualifications. Tan enlisted in 1967 and penned a prize-winning essay in the 1968 SAFTI Director's Essay Competition while still a recruit.[204] His post-commissioning tours included platoon commander (PC) in 6 SIR and staff officer in military intelligence. He attended the School of Advanced Training for Officers (SATO) in preparation for company command and rounded off NS with a promotion to Captain (CPT) in 1970.

General Tan returned to the AS with postings at the law and defence ministries but, together with other AOs, received an offer of secondment from Dr Goh to serve in uniform.[205] Goh recognized that graduates in the SAF Officer Corps were essential to attract other bright individuals for regular service but was under no illusions that a graduate equalled a good officer. Tan was under no obligation and received no promises but rejoined the SAF in 1972 motivated with the opportunity to help build the nascent SAF. Later the same year he attended the British Army's Command and Staff College at Camberley, and his career took off thereafter with rapid promotions to LTC (1973), COL (1976)

[201] Jackie Sam, "S'pore Gets a New Infantry Brigade", *Straits Times*, 27 June 1969, p. 1.

[202] Pang, "Soldiers Must Be Bi-lingual", p. 6; *SAFTI 50*, p. 95.

[203] "Col. Choo Gets Top Job", *Straits Times*, 31 May 1974, p. 10; "NOL's Management Team", *Straits Times*, 30 Dec. 1983, p. 3.

[204] *The Scimitar: Magazine of the Singapore Armed Forces Training Institute* (Mar. 1968), pp. 80–7.

[205] Oral History Centre, National Archives of Singapore, interview with COL (RET) Ramachandran Menon for "The Civil Service—A Retrospection" project, Accession No: 003250, Reel 8 of 17 (2007), p. 178.

and BG (1979).[206] His path of advancement included CO 4 SIR (1973–74), CO OCS (1974), Head of Training (1976) and Plans (1977), and finally DCGS (1980–82) including 14 months as the acting CGS (1981–82).[207] BG (RET) Tan Chin Tiong retired from the SAF in August 1982, aged 38, and returned to the civil service.[208]

2.4.4 The Vanguard: SAFTI's First Batch

While the MID could fill officer shortages by tapping volunteers, the SIR Old Guard and seconded AOs, these were merely short-term stopgap measures. The volunteers had zeal but were at times found wanting in experience, knowledge and skill. The SIR Old Guard, while professional and operationally experienced, were small in number and overwhelmingly non-graduates. The AOs were undoubtedly intelligent, but few had what it took to hold senior military appointments. The opportunity cost of AOs in the SAF was counted by their absence in other government ministries. Furthermore, one general observed that drawing "amateurs" from the ranks of civil servants and the SVC created tensions with professionals from the SIR: "In the early days we were short on professionals so sometimes we had volunteers who came in as Lieutenant Colonels. There was unhappiness with those who were clueless (about the military profession) but still had rank. But the important thing is to do your job as a professional. Don't make a big deal over who gets promoted and why. Just work in peace."[209]

This was especially pronounced when SVC "part-timers" were seen to leapfrog their Regular counterparts to more senior appointments. Dr Goh saw this as a necessary, temporary and practical solution to buy time. He needed most of the Old Guard on the ground working as the professional cadre to develop the next generation of officers. But this arrangement also posed its own problems, between combat officers "who were always dirty from being in the field while the service officers were in the office environment and clean".[210]

The work of BG (RET) Vij and his associates in establishing SAFTI provided a firm foundation for the indigenous pre-commissioning training and education

---

[206] "Five New Colonels in SAF", *Straits Times*, 1 Dec. 1973, p. 17; Ronnie Wai, "Man Who Became No. 2 in 10 Years", *Straits Times*, 7 Sept. 1981, p. 16.

[207] Esther Lew, ed., *The Spirit of the Cobra: 6 Division Silver Jubilee* (Singapore: Headquarters 6 Division, 2001), p. 60; "Changes in the General Staff", *Pioneer* (Sept. 1983): 2.

[208] "Farewell to BG Tan", *Pioneer* (Oct. 1982): 4.

[209] Interview No. 01.

[210] Interview No. 03.

of SAF and in particular army officers.[211] The 1966 recruitment drive for Regular officer cadets attracted more than 2,500 applications, one-fifth of whom held Senior Cambridge School Certificates.[212] Eventually only 117 of the famed all-Regular First Combat Officer Cadet Course (COCC) at SAFTI—commonly called the First Batch—were commissioned as officers on 16 July 1967 and formed the vanguard in preparation for the first conscripts in August 1967.[213] The Second COCC commissioned 107 officers on 17 March 1968, and SAFTI received its first NS officer cadets in time for the Third COCC.[214] This freed FMC graduates to replace SVC officers in the higher echelons, and eventually conscripts allowed the First Batch to relieve the FMC graduates. In time the SAFTI pipeline delivered a steady and self-renewing stream of commissioned officers. Subsequent batches who enlisted between 1967 and 1970 either actively sought a military career or were liable under the CAS initiative. From 1970 onward, all male SAF personnel enlisted under NS obligations and independent of any intentions for a military career.

So what would motivate a young man in 1966 to join an organization in its infancy without a track record or history and tasked to defend a society that frowned on the military profession? For starters, there is anecdotal evidence that a number were teachers who seized the opportunity for adventure, uniformed service and better career prospects.[215] Eleven members of the SPF and five from the People's Association (PA) also jumped into the fray. A number attributed their predilection for "army life and the better promotion prospects offered by the army" as reasons for signing up.[216] Next, the absence of childhood ambitions

---

[211] Midshipmen were sent to academies overseas, notably Britannia Royal Naval College in Dartmouth, UK, and the Royal Canadian Navy at Canadian Forces Base Chilliwack and the Fleet School at Esquimalt. The SAF midshipman school was established at Jervois Block, Terror Barracks, Sembawang, in 1974 with help from the Royal New Zealand Navy. Pilot training was conducted by the British RAF, and air force officers attended the Royal Air Force College at Cranwell. The Flying Training School was established at RAF Tengah only in 1969. See "A Report from Canada", *Pioneer* (Feb. 1972): 17; and "Our Men Training at Cranwell", *Pioneer* (Mar. 1972): 21.

[212] "500 Apply to Join up as Cadet Officers", *Straits Times*, 5 Apr. 1966, p. 8.

[213] "Officers for New Battalions on Parade", *Straits Times*, 17 July 1967, p. 7; "Goh at Commissioning Parade", *Straits Times*, 18 July 1967, p. 6; "President Presents Swords in Historic Ceremony", *Straits Times*, 19 July 1967, p. 6.

[214] Ajit Singh Nagpal, ed., *The Pioneers of SAFTI: Singapore Golden Jubilee* (Singapore: Innoprint & Gifts, 2015), pp. 23–30, 42.

[215] Some of the more well known included LG (RET) Ng Jui Ping, BG (RET) Patrick Choy, BG (RET) Colin Theseira and COL (RET) Ramachandran Menon.

[216] "200 Recruits for New Battalions", *Straits Times*, 4 Aug. 1967, p. 4.

and the scant availability of information and options regarding military service were enduring themes up until the 1980s. It was a leap of faith for members of the First Batch, and five from their ranks—LG (RET) Ng Jui Ping, BG (RET) Gary Yeo Ping Yong, BG (RET) Patrick Choy Choong Tow, BG (RET) Colin George Theseira and BG (RET) Chin Chow Yoon—eventually became generals. Three shared their stories; and while similarities persist, the contextual nuances are also clear and present.

The first general grew up in the rough neighbourhood of Chinatown, where his father, a resistance fighter who fought the Japanese in China during World War II, worked as clerk for an import-export company and did double duty as a bookkeeper at night. The financial burden to provide for six children also obliged his mother to seek part-time employment as a hairdresser. He recollected:

> "Growing up, I had no aspirations at that time. I was a very ordinary student. I won't tell people I had a dream and all that. The aim was to pass exams and see which opportunities presented themselves after that. I mean, I didn't have the luxury. My parents were not well-to-do. I just wanted to do well, pass and whatever it is it will be. I took one step at a time. Work? Study? I don't think my father could afford (tertiary education). I was not really a good student. I was more active outdoors than studious. I passed exams but did not excel, but I still think I needed to go upward (in terms of education) ... I completed my A's (A level) and concurrently [trained] to be a teacher. Back then it was not difficult to be a teacher. You just attend Teachers' College. It was steady, a respectable, steady job. But I felt teaching was not very exciting. I am an outdoor person, and what could I possibly be as a teacher? With my qualifications and the (teaching) environment, the army sounded interesting. The job was different, where assessment and selection is based on leadership. This was the key to upward mobility instead of education. So you think to yourself: 'I have a chance to be somebody.' Between the two (teaching or soldiering), I decided to give soldiering a try. I thought my inclination was that way. Maybe I have what it takes to excel, so I decided to try— and the SAF provided this opening. Of course, looking at the perks and recruitment brochure with 'Clarence Tan in the red sports car' <laughs> and the salary premium over civil servants—all this enticed me to try. I didn't know anything (about the SAF) so try."[217]

The second general similarly came from what he described as a poor background: his father was a clerk and mother a housewife who returned to employment to support the family of four girls and one boy. The family lived in the Magna Road *kampong* (Malay for "village"). He recalled:

---

[217] Interview No. 27.

"As a kid I wanted to be a bus conductor so that I could collect money from everybody. <laughs> I was a rascal. I would go under the *wayang* (Javanese for 'shadow puppetry') stage to gamble, and every three weeks I would also have a 'new' bicycle. <laughs> As a student I failed my O-levels so I had to take them as a private candidate. What happened was this: I was a student at St Joseph's, and in those days there was this teacher who used to smack students on the back of the head. I am not sure why he did this at all. <frowns and shakes his head> So one day I thought to myself: 'If he ever smacked me one more time I would punch him.' And I did, so I got expelled. I went to take my O-levels at night school and then became a teacher. It was my girlfriend at that time who helped me through by patiently tutoring me. Eventually I became an English teacher but found it boring. One day a neighbour down the street by the name of Colonel April Wee mentioned about prospects in the army, and I thought why not give it a shot."[218]

The third general was the eldest of eight children with a father who worked in the clerical line of the family business and a housewife mother. The "poor" lower-middle-class family lived in Kampong Bukit Timah in Jurong Kechil and later a terrace house in Fu Yong Estate. The sense of comparison was not lost on him:

"Being the eldest and having a big [extended] family, you see cousins doing well; [so] in a sense it came down to me that I must use the academic route as a way forward. I never expected to be in the (particular service) or the SAF. I was on bursary at (an educational institute), and at the end of the course we were directed toward the SAF. They needed people to go into service, and I guess as a bursary holder I felt obliged and went in on that basis. I was small and scrawny, so I supposed going in it was a different culture. I didn't quite like the culture during the initial training. The whole organizational culture was to make men of boys. The instructors were old soldiers trained by FMC. The approach was to belittle as a form of motivation. For some it did not go quite well. Quite a number left initial training. I did consider leaving, but I was under bond so it was a little hard to leave. The pay was also not so attractive compared to my contemporaries (in the private sector). I told myself if I must be in service then I better make the best out of it. I was out to show that it was something to improve myself; if I can make the grade as an officer. That was the way of advancing. Work hard, perform well and achieve your status as a commissioned officer. I had no preconceived ideas that this is the organization for me and that I would one day make general. It was very much more to prove I was able to make it (to get commissioned)."[219]

Nothing quite prepared these generals for the shock of training at SAFTI even though they were motivated to give the unknown and newly established SAF

---

[218] Interview No. 26.

[219] Interview No. 24.

a shot. Indeed, SAFTI's inaugural SOH recipient from the First Batch, COL (RET) Kwan Yue Yeong, recollected two decades later:

> "I never expected soldiering to be so tough. Our officers and NCO's (non-commissioned officers) were either British or Malayan army-trained ... Two o'clock in the morning and you had this preparation for boots inspection! Even in the brightest moonlight, you would not be able to see your boots ... Every day, it was 5BX (five basic exercises) at 5:45 am ... Now things are very different; we don't think such practices are necessary for the training of good soldiers."[220]

The rationales behind certain actions were questioned and intestinal fortitude demanded from the officer cadets to overcome the physical and mental challenges. Such actions would be classified as "ill-treatment" today and form the basis of myths and legends about the SAF's past. For one who was there, it was anything but mythical:

> "There were silly things like polishing boots until you could see your face in the reflection. If you did not meet standards the instructor would throw the pair outside and forced you to leopard crawl and retrieve them. By then your effort was ruined, and your starched uniform was too. It was a waste of time. I also remember that being late to fall-in resulted in punishment in the form of running around the parade square. We ran until the officer told the RSM (Regimental Sergeant Major) to stop. Culturally the approach sought to turn boys into men, but I would do it differently ... People at SAFTI had a job to do, but the approach was quite distasteful to some. You [had] to show you can stomach it and show you can do what they wanted you to do."[221]

These practices can be viewed in two ways. On one hand, they reflected the training philosophy of breaking and then moulding and building an individual into a soldier. It was a part of military socialization. On the other, and more congruent with contemporary expectations, this was nothing more than brazen ill treatment which in the West is termed "bastardization" or "hazing". Such practices invariably decreased in intensity but persisted, as another general who enlisted in the 1970s attested:

> "In the past, ill treatment of soldiers by commanders up the chain of command was rampant. When you go through the army in the '70s and '80s officers made decisions and were not held responsible for the injuries to the soldiers. They also make you do duck walk, star jumps, leopard

---

[220] Michael Lim, "Col Kwan Recalls Pioneering Days", *Straits Times*, 6 Aug. 1986, p. 2.

[221] Interview No. 24.

crawl across the parade square until your elbows and knees were scarred with abrasion. It was just ill treatment."[222]

For other officers, the physical hardships were tolerable but it was the mental aspect that proved challenging. Even the hardiness of the *kampong* lifestyle sometimes proved inadequate:

> "I wanted to quit in the first week of training during the First Batch. We were asked to do stupid things. Go up the hill to find a leaf and when you return they told you it is the wrong leaf and asked you to go again. I thought it was just stupid. When I went home I saw my dad almost in tears. I asked him what happened and he said he was praying for me. He later told me: 'You are my only son; how can you give up? At least have the balls and the guts.' So I said, 'OK I will try' and just hung in there."[223]

LG (RET) Ng Jui Ping expressed similar views in *SAFTI 50*, the official publication to commemorate SAFTI's Golden Jubilee:

> "Everything had to be done to perfection, to the satisfaction of instructors. Everyone had to do his part of the drill correctly and you get to repeat it until you got it right and then the group has to repeat it until we got it right … And of course in this kind of training, it's never easy to get it right the first time. You always take a number of times and so for not getting it right, you always get punished and again that means more running up and down of the hills and so on. But it toughened us, it shaped our characters … it taught us to face adversity and to overcome."[224]

For another First Batch graduate the problem was not the physical exertion or questionable intentions behind certain practices, but more the taxing nature of leadership assessments:

> "I was a rascal but also a shy person. In a small group I am good but big group it was hard for me. I just joined and be part of it. Army does change you [and] draw[s] out your latent leadership. Army forces you into certain situations and draws it out. It matured me because I was able to exploit my innate capabilities. When I joined I was ordinary but I tried to make the most of it. The trainers with Israeli advisers gave us hell but I was quite determined. The physical part I can endure. Waking up early and getting shouted at; I can also take. <grins> My challenge was when you are being assessed. There was a tension and you are exposed to situations you are not used to. You start to doubt your own capabilities but still try your best. You had Israelis who went to war so you learned. <nods>"[225]

---

[222] Interview No. 28.

[223] Interview No. 26.

[224] *SAFTI 50*, p. 18.

[225] Interview No. 27.

On the whole, SAFTI's First Batch produced 117 quality Regular officers who left an indelible mark on the formation and growth of the SAF through the harnessing of conscript manpower. This vanguard also exploited the technological edge in cooperation with partners from the defence industry, and spearheaded pioneering projects to streamline and modernize the military infrastructure.

2.5   Summary

This chapter juxtaposed defence against Singapore's historical context and highlighted the reasons for conscription as the most expedient means to address geopolitical conditions within socio-economic constraints. NS was deemed the most affordable solution to the expensive business of defence by apportioning the burden among citizens. The initiative has become indispensable to sustaining the SAF Officer Corps despite the hurdles in securing society's C2D. The SAF's early leaders who stepped forward to serve in uniform had an array of reasons and contexts despite the taboo associated with military service. These generals were drawn from the ranks of the volunteers and the Old Guard of the SIR, or were Administrative Officers seconded to the SAF on Dr Goh's initiative. Their motivations included a mix of duty, adventure which suited their outdoor-oriented upbringing, and a sense of guiding the defence force through its infancy. The establishment of SAFTI in 1966 attracted young men to sign up with promises of adventure and potentially better career prospects. Joining the army was a leap of faith for most in the famed all-Regular First Batch. They did not know what to expect and relied on fortitude and determination to earn their commissions as officers in 1967. The foundation of the SAF Officer Corps was established. This was the basis on which to develop future military elites.

CHAPTER 3

Motivations for Military Service

"How well do we know our people? Do we know what makes them say, stay and strive? Do we give them a reason to join, a reason to give?"[1]

— COL Tan Cheow Han, Bernard (1967–2006)
Assistant Chief of General Staff (Personnel) (2004–06)

3.1 Introduction

There were those who decided to throw in their lot with the SAF despite the stigma associated with the profession and issues surrounding rapid expansion, personnel policy and morale. It was a leap of faith for many. This chapter is concerned with the select few who rose to the very top and why they were motivated to sign on. There is a kaleidoscope of motivations to join the military, ranging from Huntingtonian ideals and the urban-rural divide to the altruistic and egotistic reasons noted by Janowitz and encapsulated in Moskos' I/O thesis, the role of parents, and meeting a hierarchy of needs. The importance of cultural-historical contexts must be stressed, and motivation must be understood through personal circumstances that shape decision making. Empirical data revealed several thematic categories divided into primary and secondary motivations. The first part of this chapter deals with the challenges in recruiting officers for regular service in the SAF. The second looks at categories of primary motivation that were necessary and sufficient for an individual to sign on. The third contains categories of secondary motivation that were necessary but insufficient reasons depending on individual circumstances.

3.2 The Challenges of Recruitment

Singapore implemented conscription as a means to raise the required manpower within budgetary constraints. NS would in due course provide a pipeline of

---

[1] Bernard Tan, "Putting People First in Our Army", *Pointer* 30, 3 (2004): 18.

conscripts from which the patchwork of personnel would be replaced and a steady stream from which to recruit Regulars. Yet the challenges of recruitment would remain. The hurdles were manifested in a general lack of ambition and dearth of information regarding a military career. The stigma associated with the profession of arms certainly did not help. These issues were partially addressed through advertising campaigns, generous scholarships and an array of attractive service benefits, but these "solutions" in turn created new problems. The quest has always been for getting people with the right motivations and values—but who is to decide what is right?

3.2.1 National Service

The announcement of NS took the nation by surprise. Even though policies were implemented in a stepwise manner, the situation was fluid and shrouded in uncertainties, which caught some off guard. A general who enlisted under the CAS scheme recounted:

> "My batch did not *siam* (Hokkien for "avoid") [service]. When we went in, we were told that Basic Military Training was for four months and then we would return to civilian life. But during BMT a law was passed for NS of two years. During our officer cadet course, during the section leader phase, this was changed again to three years for officers. The British withdrawal was used as a justification. <grins> As we were not yet commissioned many tried not to do well so they didn't have to serve three years. I enlisted in September (year X) and was commissioned in November (year X+1), a 14-month OCS course. I remember in those days during OCS training that the failure to evacuate a casualty was grounds for failing the mission because the Israeli advisers wanted to inculcate the value of 'leaving no man behind'."[2]

While this general was surprised with enlistment and the extensions in service obligations, another was caught up in the maelstrom of policy changes and ended up serving NS twice. It would certainly test anyone's view of fairness, as he recollected:

> "In 1967 I was in the constabulary on a part-time basis and then went to work after my A-levels ... Those were turbulent days. You grumbled like hell. Three nights a week you reported for duty with the Special Constabulary while those younger and the girls did not have to. But we took it in our stride. After BMT I was selected for leadership training. During the course we satirised NS and got hauled up the next day and were called 'subversive elements' ... At the announcement (of NS) I had no choice. I could not go to university because I could not afford it.

---

[2] Interview No. 03.

You could not get a job as they (potential employers) asked if you have completed NS. I reached the final interview for an accountant executive position at an advertisement company. The starting salary was $270 a month, which was then considered big. I was one of the few with a full A-level certificate and able to go to university. They asked why I did not go and I explained that I did not have money for university studies. I wanted to go to university. I was half-decided that after NS I would go, but things changed and I stayed on (in the SAF)."[3]

For the "younger" ones, policies and infrastructure capacity constraints also threw up uncertainties. The immediate future for those who completed their A-levels in the late 1960s was decided by ballot. Some proceeded directly to university before NS, with the remainder scheduled to complete NS before their tertiary studies. This arrangement proved disruptive to both students and the SAF, as another general experienced:

"In secondary school some classmates, some had to do NS on a part-time basis in the Special Constabulary. There were some rather old students. I was not in the Constabulary, but we knew we had to do NS. There was a balloting system for those who could do university before NS. Half of my JC class went to [university], while the rest enlisted for NS. It was April [year X] when we started [our studies]. I was enlisted during my studies in May of [year X+1], during the long semester break between [X+1] and [X+2]. In our second year, the rest who were enlisted earlier [were disrupted for studies] after one year plus in the army … We knew at the onset we would serve NS after graduation. We were informed of this in university but did not realize BMT would happen between studies in year one and two."[4]

Uncertainties hovered also over those who were born overseas and held foreign identification papers. A segment of them were initially informed of their exemption from NS but later received notifications to register and enlist.[5]

The Enlistment (Amendment) Act (1970) ended any uncertainties and clearly stipulated the terms of NS.[6] From then onward NS became the conduit through which the military elites would first render service in the SAF. An overwhelming majority of those interviewed expressed similar sentiments prior to their enlistment. First, they possessed a quiet confidence that they could cope with the training regime as most of them were physically fit by virtue of their

---

[3] Interview No. 13.

[4] Interview No. 20.

[5] Interview No. 15.

[6] Commissioned officers and those with A-level and above education were liable to render two-and-a-half years of service while all others served two years. The length of NS was standardized at two years regardless of rank and education level with effect from December 2004.

active participation in sports, outdoor activities, and uniformed groups like the Boys' Brigade, Scouts and NCC. Second, they viewed NS as a rite of passage even though there was little information regarding military life and simply sought to make the most of their time in service. One officer remarked: "I accepted NS as a matter of fact. It was compulsory. There was no way out of it. I did not have any negative feelings. It was something that has to be done; two-and-a-half years. <nods>"[7]

Another recalled:

> "I did not pay much attention to NS in primary school. In secondary school I was in NCC Land, and that provided some exposure to things military. I enjoyed firing the M16 as part of the rifle team. Like many boys my age then, and maybe even now, there was a fascination with all things military. Apart from uncles who did NS and showed me their uniform, I did not have many older friends so I did not know much. I saw it as something that needs to be done. So go with the flow. <smiles>"[8]

A third officer had this to say:

> "I would say people think of going to the army when they think of NS ... At the point in time of enlistment there was not much communication of 'duty, honour, country'. The imagery captured of the '70s and '80s were of truckloads of NSFs being ferried to camp. Dempsey Road for those going to OCS and SISPEC (School of Infantry Specialists for non-commissioned officers training) or the community centres near the camps for those who went directly to the battalions. MPs (members of parliament) would grace the send-offs, but later it was centralized at CMPB (Central Manpower Base). My personal view about NS? It was a rite of passage and part of the growing up process. There was no thought of whether you were Singaporean or PR. There was also not much information (about NS), and people didn't think too deeply about it. In the good old days life was a lot simpler. <laughs>"[9]

NS and military life were particularly welcomed by those who faced great hardships during their formative years. One general who grew up in a single-parent household with half a dozen siblings recollected:

> "I would say NS was fairly well accepted. Overall it was viewed as "must have". There were some protective parents. I remembered visiting my brother during his BMT confinement. Some parents were crying. At another time one parent actually followed behind us in a car during route march. <laughs> But in those days (late 1960s, early 1970s) kids were

---

[7] Interview No. 17.

[8] Interview No. 21.

[9] Interview No. 18.

rugged, more rough-and-tumble. I actually got my first bed in the army camp. Before enlistment I used to sleep on the floor. There were also better food and amenities. <smiles>"[10]

Another who grew up on a farm in a family of six explained: "During schooldays I helped my parents with their work, and the rural lifestyle built up my physical strength. When I enlisted in the army life actually got better in that I had more time to myself. The rural upbringing also gave me a sharp sense of the terrain. Because of the *kampong* community, I was also comfortable walking and talking to anybody."[11]

The interview participants unanimously underlined that NS was, and continues to be, essential for national defence and took an optimistic approach towards the endeavour. This consistency cuts across the spectrum of vocations, from the majority who never considered a military career to the handful who intended to sign on prior to or during the initial stages of NS. A few officers additionally cited regional conflicts that heightened their sense of purpose, especially those who enlisted as the Vietnam War raged on. It seemed far off until US withdrawal gave way to Communist consolidation and the subsequent refugee crisis captured local headlines. One officer who kept abreast of current affairs offered an insight into the physical distance but psychological proximity of conflict:

> "During primary and secondary school it was the height of the Vietnam War. There was also intense fighting in Cambodia, and when Pol Pot came to power atrocities were committed in Cambodia. You also read about the Domino Theory in newspapers. As a student in NCC and one with interest in the military it was good to be in uniform. I was looking forward to NS and to serve with purpose."[12]

The first Gulf War in 1991 similarly seeded curiosity in the mind of another officer when Singapore deployed a 30-strong medical contingent to Saudi Arabia in support of international efforts to restore Kuwaiti independence.[13]

Among the many who did not initially consider a military career, very few expressed any NS-specific aims beyond hopes of making it into Officer Candidate School. For one officer the prospects of OCS trumped service in the famous commando formation with their famous red berets: "I was selected for Commando, but I opted for direct entry into OCS where I was with (a particular

---

[10] Interview No. 10.

[11] Interview No. 05.

[12] Interview No. 14.

[13] Interview No. 23.

cadet course). I indicated earlier an interest for OCS and Commando, but since OCS was direct entry it seemed a more attractive posting. <smiles>"[14]

Even if one made it to OCS the array of post-commissioning possibilities were unknown and bounded one's aspiration(s):

> "I was not in any uniform group at school before NS, but I was active in sports and took part in outdoor activities. I thoroughly enjoyed BMT. As a recruit my aim was to get into OCS. That was one of the drivers in BMT. At that point in time there was not a very differentiated need in OCS because it was a single-minded track to train infantry platoon commanders. In OCS the goal was to be an OCS instructor after you are commissioned. You're influenced by what you know and we did not have many ideas beyond our immediate scope. We never met a PC from the unit before. In OCS then, a cadet had no exposure to other arms let alone the air force or navy. There was very little knowledge beyond OCS."[15]

It took on-the-job experience and exposure to the wider SAF for officers to identify possible career challenges and opportunities at hand. Former CNV (1985–91) RADM1 (RET) James Leo Chin Lian noted: "People of my vintage started off in the SAF by doing National Service. During my NS with the Navy I saw the many challenges ahead, like the work that was being done, and so decided to stay on."[16]

While NS proved beneficial in recruiting certain members of the military elite, negative experiences—both personal and vicarious—hindered recruitment efforts. For some it came from misconceptions of "not wanting a desk job" and the romantic ideal of "defending the country". For others, NS was simply discouraging. Furthermore, former PS (Defence) (1981–94) Lim Siong Guan cited the limited and peripheral experiences gained during NS:

> "Very often a man only knows the SAF through the eyes of a national service officer or other rank. What then happens is that in his national service he is in his unit as a platoon commander, for example, and that is all he knows about the SAF. It would be very unfortunate if that was also the basis on which he decides whether the SAF offers him a lifetime career. What he is exposed to in the field is not all that the SAF is about. And when we talk about the higher levels the work expands much more than what he can see at ground level."[17]

---

[14] Interview No. 11.

[15] Interview No. 23.

[16] "Interview with COL James Leo Commander RSN", *Navy News* (Oct. 1985): 3.

[17] Ronnie Wai and Paul Jacob, "Pay Boost for SAF Officers", *Straits Times*, 1 Apr. 1982, p. 1.

Incumbent COA BG then-LTC Goh Si Hou (SAFOS 1997) similarly affirmed: "When we first enlist into the Army at 19, our perspective of the SAF can be limited by our personal experience at the basic training stage."[18] Negative experiences before, during and after NS do not help recruitment efforts either. SLTC then-OCT Narayanan Letchumanan (SAFOS 2001) explained: "I was quite sceptical about the scholarship, and in particular about working in the forces … There are a lot of impressions that people get when they deal with the SAF during their time in National Service, and not all of them are flattering."[19] CPT (NS) Toh Weisong (SAFOS 2001) similarly argued that mandatory NS "has produced attitudes toward military service that that [sic] make it difficult to recruit regulars … this grudging acceptance of NS is accompanied by a perception of it as two years of drudgery, which dilutes the regard for regular military service."[20]

What can one say about NS and the making of Singapore's military elites? First, it is undeniable that NS has provided the defence establishment with access to the total talent pool of male Singaporeans and PRs. It offers the SAF an edge in the war for talent as these men render two to three years of service independent of whether they decide on a military career or simply serve out their terms as conscripts. Second, the military elites harboured a positive outlook of NS but the overwhelming majority did not initially consider a career in the SAF. They certainly possessed the latent talent, as their careers and pinnacle ranks attest. But why did they not consider a career in the forces? The answers are found in their ambitions (or lack of) up until the point of enlistment and the channels through which they learned about career possibilities in the SAF.

3.2.2 Ambitions and Advertisements

It might be common nowadays for Singaporean children to speak of ambitions, but this was hardly the case for the interview participants, all of whom were born between the Japanese occupation (1942) and national independence (1965). Ambition, if it could be considered as such, was simply to obtain the highest education level possible as a means to upward social mobility. Limited financial resources commonly obliged one or more siblings to forgo tertiary education. Once an individual reached an education plateau, it was his duty to help ease

---

[18] Alex Lim, "Leading with Distinction", *Straits Times*, 5 Mar. 2010.

[19] Noel Hidalgo Tan, "Unique Chance", *With Honour: A MINDEF/SAF and DSTA Scholarship Special (Straits Times)*, 10 Mar. 2002, p. R4.

[20] Toh Weisong, "High Flyers: Implications of Short Officer Careers in the SAF", *Pointer* 38, 3 (2012): 11–2.

the family's financial burden and repay parental hardships. This practice was encapsulated in the childhood of former COA (1992–05) MG (RET) Lim Neo Chian (SAFOS 1972):

> "My father was the manager of a rattan shop in Boat Quay. We lived in a two-room SIT flat in St Michael's road, and I was the second of 7 children. My father had the added responsibility of looking after us when my mother died of breast cancer when I was 10 years old. He impressed upon us the importance of studying hard as this was the path to a better life. He gave us prize money whenever we did well in school, and I really appreciated the hard life he must have led. I attended Towner Road Primary School. One day, as we were travelling in a bus when it passed Bras Basah Road, my father pointed RI out to me and said he hoped that I would study there."[21]

RADM1 (RET) Tan Kai Hoe (SAFOS 1985) similarly recalled when he received the scholarship: "My mother had to toil from dawn to dusk for the family and I had always told myself that I must push myself to succeed in order to add meaning to her tireless efforts."[22]

The completion of pre-tertiary education is in much the same way almost a given for any Singaporean child today but was by no means the case for generations past.[23] Even those with the intelligence were uncertain of how far they could go. At times it was about clearing the next set of exams and the "luck" of the birth order within the family:

> "For us at that time, standard seven was the leaving school [certificate], which was the equivalent of [secondary] three, or today. We had little ambition. My father sent me to an English school (English medium of instruction) for a better future. I went to [a De LaSalle school] for moral training. The schools then were also limited. There were very few English schools. My ambition was to get to standard seven, then onward to O-levels, from O's to pre-university, and from there to university. At each stage it was on the condition that my parents could support me, [bearing

---

[21] Tan, *100 Inspiring Rafflesians 1823–2003*, p. 131. The Singapore Improvement Trust (SIT) was an initiative by the colonial government to address housing needs of the indigenous population. "Singapore Improvement: Report of Trust for the Year 1924", *Straits Times*, 11 Aug. 1925, p. 11.

[22] "Educational Opportunities and a Challenging Career", *Pioneer* (Oct. 1986): 2.

[23] Sherlyn Quek, "Training Every Soldier to Be a Leader", *Cyberpioneer*, 27 July 2011. The share of National Servicemen with 12 years of pre-tertiary schooling (A-level) or specialized education (diploma) rose steadily from 30 per cent (1980s) to 75 per cent (2011) and was projected to reach 85 per cent (2015). The most recent percentages are not available.

in mind they] had two boys and five girls. I went to university, but the opportunity cost was that my (younger) brother did not."[24]

Another officer relied on bursaries and scholarships without which it would have been impossible for him to realize his educational aspirations:

"Ambition? In those days you 'take things as they come'. When you are in primary six, you aim to take secondary four. Those who pass were usually listed in the newspapers. Then you go to work and earn a few hundred dollars. After secondary four you considered the options. To be honest in school I was usually in the top three. In fact I was in primary one for only a few months, then my mother got me transferred to primary two. In terms of the calendar year I was one year ahead of my cohort. When I was at [school] you take life a step at a time. Ask yourself after A's what is possible. If you don't do so well, perhaps join the Maritime Command. <smiles> Perhaps take the opportunity of training at an overseas academy. You read about the heroes who went to Dartmouth. So that was one career option. The other was admission to the University of Singapore, where I could earn a degree. In those days you also needed a certificate of suitability to get into university because they wanted to weed out those with Communist inclinations. Option three was to get a scholarship. In those days naval architecture and nautical studies were in demand. It was also something out of the ordinary. In the end, since I received a scholarship I took it. I also did not need my uncle to support me. Anyway for pre-university I got by on an ASEAN scholarship. In secondary school days I also received the Tan Jiak Kim scholarship for less well-off families."[25]

The experiences of others were rather consistent. One officer who described his family as "lower socio-economic" but "not struggling" and the usual "man on the street" explained: "I had no real ambition. I did not have an ambitious mind, and I just hoped to earn a decent living. I did desire for university education. All the primary and secondary schools I went to while growing up are already gone. <smiles> They were neighbourhood schools. I did well for my [O-levels] but did not take part in any uniform groups."[26]

Another officer, the grandson of a fruit and vegetable farmer and son of an automobile spray-painter, highlighted the years of studying hard but without many signposts in life:

"Growing up I did not have any real ambitions. There were limited options and also a lack of information or exposure to possibilities. I am the only graduate in my family, and there wasn't really anyone to look to

---

[24] Interview No. 03.

[25] Interview No. 15.

[26] Interview No. 17.

for advice or guidance. So I looked to peers and friends. All my cousins went to one school, so I followed. For secondary school I followed others in applying to RI, but I could not get in so I followed my neighbour to Thompson secondary. <laughs> I was prepared to attend [polytechnic] if I did not do well, but I was one of the top students and was admitted to [a prestigious secondary school] where I took science and maths. I also considered being an air steward because I wanted to see the world."[27]

Three categories emerged from interviewees who expressed any sort of ambition. To be a pilot was most common, but as seen later in this chapter this was more a dream, a childhood fantasy, and for many proved a mere secondary motivation for joining the SAF. The second category was to do something "scientific", meaning science or engineering. Personal interests and ability coupled with the fact they performed well in school spawned this ambition. It was standard practice to place top students in the science stream (as opposed to arts) to read subjects in the natural and physical sciences. Some may have toyed with professions such as law or architecture, but this gave way to what they did best at school. The government's early initiative to train more engineers as part of national industrialization efforts in the 1960s and 1970s reinforced such thinking. One officer elaborated:

> "When you are 17 and 18 you listened to the government. The only source of information was through reading newspapers, and the government wanted to train more engineers, so I wanted to be an engineer. The key focus as a student was to do well and then get an engineering degree. Even though I took one step at a time I hoped to get a scholarship for overseas study. But the immediate aim in school was to do well for A-level and then to do well in university."[28]

Another officer's penchant for things scientific came from his interests and abilities as well as the role model provided by his father:

> "My father is a doctor, still practising even though he is 79 already. One reason. In terms of ambition I was always interested in science and by extension science and technology. I was a science nerd in school, and medicine has a scientific angle to it. Engineering also has a scientific angle. Since my father was a doctor and a father figure I tried medicine, but I did not get admitted. So engineering. The one common theme throughout my life is science. You could say it was my motivation in life."[29]

---

[27] Interview No. 11.

[28] Interview No. 10.

[29] Interview No. 21.

Medical Officers (MOs) expressed an ambition specific to their pursuit of medicine. Early life experiences were instrumental in driving one MO:

> "Ever since I was in primary school, around primary four and five, I decided I wanted to do medicine. I had a younger brother who was sick with asthma and admitted frequently to hospital. When we visited the hospital we would see the poor guy standing in the doorway. I would also see other children there. So you could say I had a one-track mind all the way. In my time the top students wanted to do engineering. I applied for Colombo Plan (a now-defunct scholarship tenable at various universities in the Commonwealth), and during the interview they told me to give up med[icine] and do psychology instead. Of course I rejected it! <laughs> Some classmates of mine decided to follow the trend and do engineering."[30]

A second MO wanted to be a pilot, but when his eyesight became less than perfect he simply sought

> "… to be a good person. It was only in junior college that I seriously looked at medicine. You know, at JC you need to evaluate career options by looking at your strengths and possibilities. All my older siblings furthered their education. My oldest sister earned her ACCA (professional accountancy qualification) but did not go to uni[versity] and so did not burden the family in any way. My second sister was awarded a PSC merit scholarship to study medicine. My brother was awarded a SAF Training Scholarship … My two other sisters were funded by my parents to NUS (National University of Singapore) … Yes, 'papa mama' (parental-funded) scholarship. <smiles> I am the youngest and was funded by the rest of the family. <laughs> $100 per month from each sibling. <laughs> I was thinking of a non-bonded scholarship. PSC was restrictive and only gave out a few. The bond for medicine was for five years including NS but not houseman. Fees were manageable at $1,000 for medicine and dentistry, while the others were $700, which was affordable back then."[31]

For a third MO, the son of a professional architect, it was a not-so-simple process of deduction:

> "Like most kids I did not know what I wanted to be. In secondary school I had the inclination to be a doctor. The thought of being a Regular officer came only after medical school and after I re-enlisted for NS during MOCC (Medical Officer Cadet Course). Why did I decide I wanted to be a doctor in secondary school? Good question. I would not say there was

---

[30] Interview No. 20. The Colombo Plan Scholarships gave bright students the opportunity to earn an undergraduate degree in participating Commonwealth countries, mainly the UK, Australia, Canada and New Zealand. See Nancy Byramji, "The Colombo Plan Scholars", *Straits Times*, 4 July 1976, p. 17.

[31] Interview No. 18.

some seminal event that made me want to be a doctor. I thought it was something I could do. Maybe I was inclined to the biological sciences and could do well. I was also less inclined to be an engineer or in finance. So partly it was a process of elimination. I also wanted to do something that deals with people. There was a tussle between medicine and humanities such as law, architecture. In JC I took triple science, which made medicine a tangible goal. I was also not financially motivated, and money was definitely not a factor … My dad did say 'don't do architecture'. <laughs> I think it is one of those things when fathers tell their sons not to join them in the same industry. <laughs> I did adequately well in secondary school and pre-U[niversity] to apply for medicine but not well enough to be eligible for a PSC scholarship. In those days medicine was perhaps a little less competitive than today."[32]

Regardless of ambitions while growing up, one consistent and common theme was the lack of information regarding SAF career possibilities. The defence establishment's need for consistent investments in advertising campaigns and the competitive employment environment becomes clear when juxtaposed against other sectors of employment. The early leaders of the SAF relied on newspaper advertisements, recruitment brochures, radio and the word of mouth. These avenues of communication were soon widened by virtue of NS with circulars in routine orders and periodic recruitment talks. Additionally, the pre- and post-NS audiences (including females) were exposed to career possibilities through security-related seminars at schools, recruitment talks at universities, and the former Junior Flying Club (JFC) which is known today as the Singapore Youth Flying Club.

Advertisements were especially important in the early days when the SAF was synonymous with the army while the air and naval services were still in the embryonic stages of development. One of those earmarked for a possible career in the RSAF reminisced:

"After commissioning there was a circular in SAFTI regarding the initiative to set up the air force. A handful of us, 20 to 30, went for aptitude tests. [A number] were eventually selected for air force training and sent to MID. There was no air force yet, and the infrastructure was rudimentary, so we were temporarily posted to MID as staff officers. I spent my time writing letters to senior officers and staff papers, but not training. <laughs> My claim to fame was that I got the SAF to buy the Unimog. <laughs> Ronald Wee was the department head, and he struck me as a kind, nice, gentle and encouraging individual. I could also draw, so he tasked me to design formation patches, and I ended up with

---

[32] Interview No. 23.

insignias like cobra, marlin, etc. It was a labour of love. It was not an official job, but I had an interest in these kinds of things."[33]

The navy was also an unknown entity in search of a few good men. As one officer recalled, "I went to BMT, and three months after, I was selected for section leaders' course. One day I saw an advertisement on the company-line notice board about navy scholarships. It was for studies in university and asking interested recruits to reply. Successful candidates would transfer to the navy."[34] It did not help that the nascent navy then had fewer ships than most had fingers on two hands and paled in comparison to the merchant fleet. Another officer recalled his time flipping through the broadsheet in search of opportunities: "There were quite a few advertisements for careers at sea with companies such as NOL (Neptune Orient Lines). Some advertisements also with the Maritime Command. <smiles>"[35]

With all but eight of the military elites having entered the SAF via the CAS and NS, it is evident that conscription has become the chief conduit for military service. But how do ambitions and advertisements add to the contextual role of NS and the motivation to sign on? First, the majority of the interview participants did not have much by way of ambitions with the exception of studying hard and securing the highest education level possible. The minority with ambitions were interested in flying, an occupation related to the sciences, and medicine. These ambitions provided a direction but for most were neither concrete nor certain. Second, information pertaining to military careers proved scant, or was simply inefficient in reaching the target audience. Any pre-NS avenues of communication were subsequently reinforced with recruitment talks and circulars in routine orders. Today, such efforts are extended to various social media platforms and followed up with unsolicited mailers, career brochures, scholarship tea sessions, and visits to different units across the SAF despite the packed training schedule. Recruitment efforts can bear fruit even after an individual has completed NS when a dormant interest is present and perhaps when economic circumstances prove less fortuitous.

3.2.3 Scholar-Officers: Appealing to Confucian Values

A critical problem for the SAF was that a military career seemed to fail in its quest for rightful status as an "honoured" profession. This invariably hindered the

---

[33] Interview No. 24. See also "Singapore Forces Get New Badges", *Straits Times*, 4 July 1967, p. 9.

[34] Interview No. 17.

[35] Interview No. 15.

recruitment of the "right" candidates for officership, namely, "highly educated men with disciplined minds and a higher level of general knowledge, articulation and mental training … necessary to improve the army's calibre".[36] In the shadow of an impending British withdrawal, Lee Kuan Yew highlighted the urgency and challenge of recruiting quality individuals: "… we got to break down this prejudice, the pre-conception, you know, that the armed forces comprise of people who can't make the grade in the professions or in the traditional occupations like lawyer, doctor, engineer and the armed forces, particularly in a developing country, comprise one of the most important sectors of life."[37]

The undesirable nature of a career in uniform was most apparent when "superior candidates" opted instead for public service, government-linked companies (GLCs) and the private sector.[38] This problem was compounded by the ephemeral albeit unpopular policy in 1969 where a commission attracted three years of NS due to large numbers of unfilled officer billets while other ranks served only two.[39] As a result and "[n]ot unnaturally, some of the smartest opted for the anonymity of followership rather than the spotlight of leadership, taking their first steps toward becoming captains of industry a year ahead of their colleagues".[40] This problem persisted in the early 1980s, when a segment of those who had the "academic ability, physical fitness, alertness and ability to cope under stress" deliberately avoided any path towards an officer's commission.[41] Regular NCOs also voiced displeasure over serving with, and taking orders from, reluctant national servicemen who were pushed for officer training.[42]

---

[36] "SAF University Scholarship Details", *Straits Times*, 19 May 1971, p. 9.

[37] "When Scholars Become Officers", *Straits Times*, 15 Oct. 1971, p. 18.

[38] Among the more attractive public sector employers were the Administrative Service, Economic Development Board (EDB), JTC, Development Bank of Singapore (DBS), Telecommunication Authority of Singapore, and PUB. "Ensuring Quality of Leadership in the Armed Forces", *Straits Times*, 7 Sept. 1981, p. 16; *Manpower Policies Affecting the SAF Officer*, The Pointer Special Issue (Singapore: Ministry of Defence, Mar. 1982), p. 16.

[39] MINDEF stood firm on the decision (based on the recommendations of IDF advisers) despite strong reactions from graduates and the Chinese Chamber of Commerce on behalf of employers. See "Why Graduate Refuses to Be an Officer", *Straits Times*, 15 Aug. 1970, p. 9; "Goh: We Must Preserve Our Reputation", *Straits Times*, 11 July 1975, p. 15; Edwin Lee, *Singapore: The Unexpected Nation* (Singapore: Institute of Southeast Asian Studies, 2008), p. 282; Nagpal, *Pioneers of SAFTI*, p. 59.

[40] Ramachandran Menon, *To Command: The SAFTI Military Institute* (Singapore: HQ SAFTI Military Institute and Landmark Books, 1995), pp. 112, 115.

[41] "Officer Rank 'Should Not Be Avoided'", *Straits Times*, 26 Oct. 1982, p. 10.

[42] William Campbell, "Towards Higher Levels in Singapore's Forces", *Straits Times*, 12 Oct. 1970, p. 12.

The "scholar" tag grounded in Confucian values, which resonated with Singapore's Chinese-ethnic majority, was utilized in an attempt to attract the country's "top brains".[43] The scheme was reminiscent of imperial China's selection of scholars and the recruitment of military officers and civil servants in medieval Korea.[44] Lee Onn Pong, then MINDEF's Director of Employment and an architect of the scheme, elaborated:

> "During one meeting in 1970, Dr. Goh discussed with me the problem of very few NSmen, particularly university graduates, wanting to become officers. After 1970 it was decided to call up A-level passes for NS. I suggested that SAF should attract the best A-level holders to become officers, by giving them scholarships for their higher studies. They would be bonded to serve in the SAF. My recommendation was to give SAF scholarship more money, though President's scholarship would still be higher in status. The scholars would sign up as regulars before they went off to university; they would get their rank pay and the scholarship, plus any other scholarship that they won, such as the President's or PSC scholarship. Dr. Goh asked about the likely pitfalls; I said there would eventually be a logjam of SAF scholar officers in the upper echelons of the SAF, which, if not managed well, could cause a big problem, possibly even a coup! So after serving their bond in SAF some of the senior officers should be assigned to the Administrative Service. Dr. Goh liked the idea and, after discussing it with senior MINDEF directors, took it up with the Prime Minister and Cabinet for approval."[45]

The Prime Minister embraced the idea wholeheartedly and in a written reply to Goh reiterated: "If annually we can get four to five for the Army, two to three for the Air Force and Navy each, we shall really have first class staff officers by 1980, creative and imaginative."[46] Cabinet approval came swiftly enough for the

---

[43] George Yeo quoted in Warren Fernandez, *Without Fear or Favour: 50 Years of Singapore's Public Service Commission* (Singapore: Times Media for the Public Service Commission, 2001), p. 78.

[44] "Ancient Chinese Examination System Made Relevant", *Straits Times*, 16 Mar. 1996, p. 24; Benjamin A. Elman, *A Cultural History of Civil Examinations in Late Imperial China* (Berkeley and Los Angeles: University of California Press, 2000); Eugene Y. Park, *Between Dreams and Reality: The Military Examination in Late Chosŏn Korea, 1600–1894*, Harvard East Asian Monograph No. 281 (Cambridge: Harvard University Press, 2007).

[45] Desker and Kwa, *Goh Keng Swee*, p. 108. The President's Scholarship remains the most prestigious scholarship awarded by the Public Service Commission. That said, at least one student has declined the scholarship. See "Temasek JC Maths Whiz Turns Down President's Scholarship", *Straits Times*, 11 Aug. 1991, p. 3.

[46] Speech by Minister for Defence Dr Ng Eng Hen at the MINDE/SAF Scholarship Awards Ceremony on 29 July 2015, https://www.mindef.gov.sg/imindef/press_room/official_releases/sp/2015/29jul15_speech.html, accessed 7 Nov. 2016.

inaugural batch of five officers, including Lee Hsien Loong, to receive the SAF Overseas Scholarship (SAFOS) in 1971. This clearly highlighted the importance placed on defence.[47] A candid Lee explained after the scholarship ceremony:

> "The decision was made by my eldest son. He is already 19 1/2 years old and he should determine his own life. I encouraged him to join the army because I believe in it, in the future, it will benefit him and also the country ... I think in a developing country, the army and the police are the two most important sectors of the nation. Therefore, if my son wishes to join the army, I don't have to interfere with his decision or stop him doing that ... Anyway he has to do national service for 2 1/2 years. And with another six years and three months which means a total of eight years and nine months, I think he can become a more sophisticated army officer."[48]

If the scholarship was good enough for the PM's son, it was surely good enough for anyone and led to this early observation by Willard Hanna: "There are already certain signs that the stress upon elitism may eventually lend to the military career a certain éclat. The much publicized decision of Lee Hsien Loong, eldest son of the Prime Minister, to make the Army his career is the most dramatic recent evidence."[49] The establishment of the SAFOS enhanced the image of a military career and attracted a portion of the nation's brightest students each year.[50] The law enforcement apparatus was also keen to net its share of talent. Three SAFOS officers were transferred to the SPF in September 1977 and fast-tracked to senior positions, as it was argued "Criminal 'masterminds' need to be countered by superior forces".[51] The SPF Overseas Scholarship (SPFOS) was first awarded in 1979 and by 2018 counted more than 80 recipients.

The terms and conditions of the SAFOS proved extremely attractive at a time when scholarships were a rare commodity and most of society belonged to the lower socio-economic strata. For the overwhelming majority of recipients it was a windfall that catered to all the financial needs of an undergraduate and

---

[47] In 1982 the SAF (UK) Scholarships were extended to universities in the United States, Canada, Australia and New Zealand and renamed the SAFOS. Ronnie Wai, "SAF Scholars Given Wider Choice than Just Oxbridge", *Straits Times*, 30 Apr. 1982, p. 14.

[48] "When Scholars Become Officers", *Straits Times*, 15 Oct. 1971, p. 18.

[49] Hanna, "New Singapore Armed Forces": 5.

[50] Martin Choo, ed., *The Singapore Armed Forces* (Singapore: Public Affairs Department, Ministry of Defence, 1980), p. 144.

[51] "Superior Police Force", *Straits Times*, 16 June 1973, p. 14.

more.[52] In return, recipients were bonded to the SAF for eight years—which was subsequently revised to six in line with other government scholarships; and in earlier times, there was even a caveat on marriage to Singaporean citizens only.[53] This scholarship system is a unique sociological aspect of Singapore, as Derek Da Cunha observed:

> Elsewhere around the world, "scholars" are people who are university academics where a measure of respect is accorded to them and their views. In Singapore, however, the general attitude elevates the "government scholar" onto a pedestal far beyond the reach of the ordinary man. This observation highlights the technocratic nature of the Singaporean state, in which the technical competence of an individual is highly prized.[54]

The profile of SAF officership rose over time but was invariably overshadowed by the conspicuous careers of successful scholar-officers. Since its inception the SAFOS has served as an investment in leadership potential and the avenue for transporting its recipients to the apex of the SAF. Various authors have noted the rapid promotion of scholar-officers, with the fastest among them making COL by their early 30s.[55] The earliest such examples were Lee Hsien Loong, Boey Tak Hap and Sin Boon Wah, who received the SAFOS in 1971 and made LTC in 1981, COL a year later, and subsequently BG.[56] Precedence and repetition created an atmosphere and assumption whereby

> The scholars automatically became the *crème de la crème* of the SAF and could reasonably expect to attain the rank of Colonel within ten years after they returned from their degree studies … Around the beginning of the 1980s, the issue gained notoriety due to the categorization of career officers in the SAF into "scholars" and "farmers", but the outcome of

---

[52] The scholarship included air travel, tuition fees, college fees (if applicable), an annual stipend, a regular salary which differed from the rest of the officer corps (until 1982), and other allowances. "16 Get SAF Study Grants", *Straits Times*, 22 Sept. 1972, p. 21; *Manpower Policies Affecting the SAF Officer*, p. 2.

[53] "'Marriage to S'pore Citizens Only' for SAF Award Holders", *Straits Times*, 31 Dec. 1970, p. 3.

[54] Da Cunha, "Sociological Aspects of the Singapore Armed Forces": 466–7.

[55] See, for example, Da Cunha, "Sociological Aspects of the Singapore Armed Forces": 467; Ng Pak Shun, "From 'Poisonous Shrimp' to 'Porcupine': An Analysis of Singapore's Defence Posture Change in the Early 1980s", Strategic and Defence Studies Centre Working Paper, Australian National University, No. 397 (2005), p. 26; and Sean P. Walsh, "The Roar of the Lion City: Ethnicity, Gender, and Culture in the Singapore Armed Forces", *Armed Forces & Society* 33, 2 (Jan. 2007): 270.

[56] "Salute the Young Top Brass!" *Straits Times*, 30 Aug. 1980, p. 1; "Pips & Crests", *Pioneer* (Aug. 1981): 8; "Promotion: Ranks and Responsibilities", *Pioneer* (Aug. 1982): 6; Menon, *One of a Kind*, pp. 337–8.

the debate about who would inherit the highest strata of the SAF was a foregone conclusion.[57]

This conclusion, however, was not necessarily as "foregone" as it would seem given the empirical evidence presented in chapter 6.

While the SAFOS attracted "bright" individuals, it was necessary to maximize the perceived talents of this group not just for the SAF but also for Singapore at large.[58] The Dual-Career Scheme allowed SAFOS recipients to join the AS, and those who made the cut as AOs became civil servants seconded to the military. At the conclusion of their SAF careers they could continue to serve in other areas of public service.[59] By the late 1980s this career scheme facilitated the rise of former SAFOS officers into the upper echelons of unelected government. Recruitment advertisements proudly declared that the SAFOS "is not just a passport to one pyramid—the SAF—but the first stepping stone to that pyramid and beyond. The world is the scholar-officer's oyster."[60] This scholarship took on trophy-like status for the top schools, and at one point a senior civilian defence official even declared: "We will not require an application … those who are eligible for consideration will be invited."[61] By the first decade of the 21st century the SAFOS sale pitch promised "a pedigree education, a challenging career and maximum satisfaction".[62] The ultimate endorsement, as if one was required, came from Lee Kuan Yew, who shared that if he were to relive his life

> … he would opt for a Singapore Armed Forces (SAF) or Overseas Merit Scholarship (OMS) to study at a top American university, followed by a career in the SAF or civil service and a stint in one of the statutory boards

[57] Menon, *One of a Kind*, pp. 337–8.

[58] Leslie Fong and Ronnie Wai, "Top Officers Given Exposure", *Straits Times*, 17 Sept. 1982, p. 1; "The SAF Personnel Management Philosophy", *Pioneer* (Feb. 1984): 4; "SAF Will Free Staff to All Civilian Posts if Required: Lt-Gen Choo", *Straits Times*, 12 Aug. 1990, p. 3; "National Day Honours", *Pioneer* (Sept. 1990): 22.

[59] Speech by PM Lee Kuan Yew at the SAF Day Dinner, 1 September 1981. Reproduced in "Ensuring Quality of Leadership in the Armed Forces", *Straits Times*, 7 Sept. 1981, p. 16; Paul Jensen, "Getting the Best Brains into SAF", *Straits Times*, 7 Sept. 1981, p. 1; "For Potential SAF Scholars—No Application Required", *Pioneer* (June 1992): 27.

[60] "A Complete Employer", *Straits Times*, 19 Mar. 1989, p. 19.

[61] "For Potential SAF Scholars", p. 26.

[62] Edmund Tee, "The Leading Edge", *With Honour: A MINDEF/SAF and DSTA Scholarship Special* (*Straits Times*), 10 Mar. 2002, p. R2. From the mid-1990s SAFOS recipients were allowed to pursue a master's degree as long as it was completed within four years inclusive of the undergraduate degree. See "Revised SAF Scholarships and Awards", *Army News* 15 (Apr. 1996): 3.

or government-linked companies. Then, he would enter politics and serve as a minister for two or three terms.[63]

He reiterated that "what you want in life is a passport you can flash".[64] The SAFOS is quite simply that passport. The difficulty for the defence establishment is always, as discussed in more detail in later chapters, to keep the individual scholar engaged and committed to service within an ever-changing society.

3.2.4 Pandora's Box

The pressing need to raise the general education level of the SAF Officer Corps persisted even though the SAFOS attracted a premium slice of secondary school leavers annually. The key to increasing the number of graduates within officer ranks was a two-pronged effort to offer more opportunities for university education coupled with higher salaries and benefits. The Local Study Award (LSA) tenable at local universities and the Overseas Training Award (OTA) for pre-commissioning training at foreign military academies commenced in tandem with the SAFOS in 1971.[65] It is no surprise, however, that opportunities for tertiary education have proliferated steadily over the years and a multi-tiered system established based on prestige and associated visibility within the organization (Table 3.1). The current order of prestige for combat officers is the SAF Scholarship followed by SMS, SAS, and MTA/MSA/LSA. The PSC administers the SAFOS together with other high-level government-sponsored scholarships for the three civil service career streams—Uniformed Service (SAFOS and SPFOS), Public Administration and Professional Service (e.g., foreign, legal and specialist)—to ensure consistency in rewarding the most deserving applicants. The term "deserving" simply meant academic excellence in days past and today further encompasses extra-curricular activities (ECAs) and character. It would seem that Singapore citizenship is mandatory only upon receipt of the scholarship.[66] All other scholarships and awards have similar albeit less stringent criteria and fall under the purview of the respective ministries.

---

[63] Chua Mui Hoong, "Schooled for Leadership", *Straits Times*, 13 Aug. 1994, p. 30.

[64] Quoted from an SAF Recruitment Advertisement, *Straits Times*, 5 Mar. 1996, p. 7.

[65] The first two OTA recipients received their training at the Royal Military College, Sandhurst. The OTA has since included academies in Australia, Canada, Germany, Japan, the Philippines, India and the United States. "SAF University Scholarship Details", *Straits Times*, 19 May 1971, p. 9.

[66] Tracy Sua, "Born in China, Now an SAF Scholar", *Straits Times*, 27 Aug. 2006, p. 12; Sara Grosse, "Four Outstanding Persons Get President's Scholarships", Channel NewsAsia, 12 Aug. 2011.

Table 3.1. Evolution of the SAF scholarship hierarchy and nomenclature for combat officers[67]

1970s–1980s	1980s–1990s	1990s–2010s	Present
SAF (UK) Scholarship	SAF Overseas Scholarship (SAFOS)	SAFOS	SAF Scholarship
	OTA (Academic)[68]	SAF Merit Scholarship (SMS)[69]	SMS SMS (MDES)
Overseas Training Award (OTA)	OTA (Graduating)[70]	MTA (Graduating)	SAF Academic Scholarship (SAS) (Military) SAS (MDES)
	OTA (Non-graduating)[71]	MTA (Non-graduating)	MTA (Non-graduating)

---

[67] Other scholarships include the SAF Medicine Scholarship, SAF Dentistry Scholarship, Defence Merit Scholarship (DMS), and SAF Engineering Scholarship (SAFES). The first two are for SAF medical officers, the DMS is designed for grooming civilian defence bureaucrats, and the fourth for uniformed engineers from the Military Expert Corps.

[68] OTA (Academic)—initially given the confusing name "SAF Overseas (Non-Oxbridge) Scholarships"—was tenable at renowned universities abroad. See *Manpower Policies Affecting the SAF Officer*, p. 17.

[69] The SMS is tenable at both foreign civilian universities and military academies and open to both A-level and diploma holders. See "Scholarship for Outstanding Officers", *Pioneer* (Nov. 1990): 15; "Cream of the Crop", *Pioneer* (Oct. 1992): 18; and "Revised SAF Scholarships and Awards", *Army News* 15 (Apr. 1996): 3.

[70] OTA (Graduating) was tenable at military academies where undergraduate tertiary education was provided, such as the US Military Academy, US Naval Academy, US Air Force Academy, the Philippines Military Academy, Japanese Naval Academy, and Royal Military College, Duntroon. See *Manpower Policies Affecting the SAF Officer*, p. 17.

[71] The OTA (Non-graduating) was for training at military academies where tertiary education was not included, such as RMC Sandhurst and subsequently the RMC Duntroon after the establishment of the Australian Defence Force Academy. See *Manpower Policies Affecting the SAF Officer*, p. 17.

1970s–1980s	1980s–1990s	1990s–2010s	Present
Nil	Academic Training Award (ATA)[72]	ATA (Overseas) ATA (Local)	SAS (Overseas)[73] SAS (Local)
Local Scholarship	Local Study Award (LSA)[74]	LSA	SAF LSA SAF MDES Study Award (Degree)

While the scholarships invariably attracted a fair share of intelligent individuals to the military, they created two problems. The first, and the Achilles heel of the scholarship system, was evident early on. As Martin Choo, one of the pioneering writers on the SAF, pointed out: "It is ultimately a question of commitment and dedication to the SAF. The last thing the SAF needs is clock-watching officers who are not interested in their work, but bent on spending much of their time counting the days when their contract with the SAF expires so that they can leave the military for greener pastures elsewhere."[75]

The second problem came from perceptions that an officer's career prospects were based not on abilities but on the scholarship received. Indeed, in 2011 an SAF recruiter questioned what those considering regular service would

> … think if presented with the above scholarships and information concerning their terms and eligibility? Beyond any politically correct message, which we in the SAF tend to dismiss quickly in any case, can we truly expect him to give a sterling military performance, trusting that the award which he will obtain subsequently will not affect his career progression? If one isolates and points out the rare individual who painstakingly clawed his way up without the 'doors of opportunities' opened up by a more prestigious scholarship … [one can cite] the prevalence of luck and low probability and thus concluding that this example is not reflective of the norm.[76]

---

[72] The Academic Training Award (ATA) was tenable at approved local and foreign universities.

[73] Chia Han Sheng, "At the Pinnacle of West Point", *Army News* 167 (June–July 2009): 8.

[74] The SAF Local Study Award (LSA) was introduced in 1987 to attract combat officers. It was initially offered only to OCTs within three to six months of NS but in 1989 offered to reserve officers and also NCOs who performed well. See "A Chance to Advance: The SAF Local Study Award for Aspiring Combat Officers", *Pioneer* (Mar. 1988): 26; "SAF Launches New Study Scheme to Woo Promising A-Level Holders", *Straits Times*, 6 Mar. 1988, p. 1; "Local Study Award Now Open to Undergrad Reservist NCOs", *Pioneer* (Apr. 1989): 13; and "Leader of Leaders: MINDEF/SAF Scholarships", *Scholars' Choice III (Straits Times)*, Mar. 2010, p. 5.

[75] Martin Choo, ed., *The Singapore Armed Forces* (Singapore: Public Affairs Department, Ministry of Defence, 1980), p. 145.

[76] Stanley Lim Wee Tong, "Discourse on Army Recruitment: In the Context of Generation Y", *Pointer* 36, 3–4 (2011): 67.

Aside from those scholarship issues, challenges remained and recruitment hit rock bottom in 1981. The recruitment of combat officers fell from "199 in 1978, 145 in 1979, 74 in 1980, to a mere 32 in 1981" despite overt political support and proactive publicity from advertisement campaigns.[77] Of the 450 officers recruited in this period, only ten were graduates.[78] The decision to raise the minimum education level for officers from O- to A-levels in 1981 played a part, but so did uncompetitive salaries that were pegged at O-level expectations.[79] This led increasing numbers of active service officers to "request early release or [decline] to extend their contracts, in most cases due to better terms offered them in the private sector".[80]

The simple and practical solution was to raise salaries and benefits. This worked out well on paper in the mid-1970s, when pay increases led to more than 1,000 applications—three-fifths from NSFs and 40 per cent from NSmen—to fill shortages within the ranks of Regular NCOs.[81] The year 1982 proved a watershed for the SAF's officer recruitment efforts as MINDEF conducted its second salary restructuring exercise after 1969 and its first comprehensive revision of salaries and benefits.[82] Officer salaries increased "by an average of 26 per cent" as compensation for the "tough physical demands, irregular working hours and regimentation of military life".[83] Those in the ranks of LTA and CPT with tertiary qualifications received the greatest increases.[84] Deserving scholar-officers were slated for promotions more quickly than civil service scholars from the same cohort serving in other areas of government.[85]

---

[77] "Brighter Pay Days for SAF Officers", *Pioneer* (May 1982): 2–3.

[78] "Salaries for Regular SAF Officers: 1982 Revision", *The Pointer: SAF Officers' Quarterly, Special Issue* (1982): 1.

[79] Leslie Fong, "Salute the Young Top Brass!" *Straits Times*, 30 Aug. 1980, p. 1; Wai and Jacob, "Pay Boost for SAF Officers", p. 1.

[80] Wai and Jacob, "Pay Boost for SAF Officers", p. 1.

[81] "The Typical Soldier", p. 8.

[82] In June 1969 the SAF revised the salary scheme by eliminating various allowances (e.g., marriage, ration, rent, utilities) and based the monthly pay for all service personnel on "rank" and where applicable a "vocation" component (to reflect education, expertise). See William Campbell, "Pay Conversion: Problems of Adjustment", *Straits Times*, 13 Oct. 1970, p. 10.

[83] Wai and Jacob, "Pay Boost for SAF Officers", p. 1; "Towards a Dynamic, Thinking Man's Army", *Straits Times*, 27 May 1982, p. 10.

[84] The revisions differentiated between graduates and non-graduates, and also degree classes within graduates (e.g., honours classes and basic) at junior officer ranks. Convergence took place in senior (MAJ and above) ranks so that there was no differentiation between graduates at the rank of MAJ, and at LTC a cessation differentiation between graduates and non-graduates. See Wai and Jacob, "Pay Boost for SAF Officers", p. 1.

[85] Speech by PM Lee Kuan Yew at the SAF Day Dinner, 1 Sept. 1981.

As a guide, civil service salaries were pegged to the private sector, and in 1984 SAF officer salaries attracted a 20 per cent premium above the civil service and 10 per cent above the SPF.[86] Such perks were extended to graduates and civil servants who had performed well in NS and rejoined the SAF as Regulars.[87] More grades were also created within each rank to enable more frequent salary increments.[88] Other tangible benefits included priority in purchasing government housing, medical and dental care for officers and their immediate family members, recreational facilities, welfare amenities, and heraldic decorations.[89] Salary increments have since taken place periodically, with the last comprehensive revision in 1998, when all Regular officers were placed on the Savings and Employment Retirement (SAVER) Plan designed to aid post-SAF career transitions. This was especially important for combat officers whose skills and experiences were "less directly marketable" and hence "the expected greater difficulties in career transition".[90]

---

[86] In line with the civil service, military officers also received bonuses predicated on individual performances and the national economy. Paul Jensen, "Getting the Best Brains into SAF", *Straits Times*, 7 Sept. 1981, p. 1; "High Priority on Expertise", *Straits Times*, 17 Mar. 1984, p. 18; "Pay Rise for Servicemen", *Pioneer* (Jan. 1994): 24; "New Service Schemes for SAF Officers", *Pioneer* (Jan. 1994): 25.

[87] The Combat Graduate Officers Scheme was formulated to entice NSmen holding at least a second-class upper honours degree to join the SAF at the rank of captain for an initial three-year contract with a salary pegged at 20 per cent higher than the civil service. NSmen in the civil service and government-affiliated units were offered a 20 per cent pay increase if they accepted a three-year voluntary secondment to the SAF with job guarantees and no loss in salary increments should they opt to return to the civil service. Those who stayed on as a Regular also had salaries backdated where applicable. See Ahmad Osman, "Join-As-Captain Plan to Attract Top Talent into SAF", *Straits Times*, 10 Jan. 1982, p. 1; and "Secondment Scheme for Graduate Reservists", *Straits Times*, 25 Apr. 1982, p. 9.

[88] "Colonels Get $9,000 a Month in New Grade", *Singapore Monitor*, 1 Mar. 1985, p. 2; "New SAF Salary Grade for Regular Colonels", *Straits Times*, 2 Mar. 1985, p. 15.

[89] "Are You Suited for Command?" *Straits Times*, 5 Dec. 1983, p. 21. Other perks included an increasing plethora of education opportunities and heraldic expansion. Prior to 2007, an officer with 25 years of service would receive two medals: the Good Conduct Medal after five years and the Long Service and Good Conduct Medal after 12 years, with a clasp after 22 years. A third, the Long Service Medal, was bestowed after 30 years. The 2007 heraldic revisions now schedule four medals within a 25-year career: the Good Conduct Medal after five years, the Long Service and Good Conduct (10 Years) Medal after ten years with a clasp after 15 years, the Long Service and Good Conduct (20 Years) Medal after 20 years, and the Long Service Medal (Military) after 25 years. A clasp is added to the Long Service and Good Conduct (20 Years) Medal after 30 years. See "We Wear 'Em Ribbons with Pride!" *Navy News* 4 (2006): 11; and Gail Wan, "SAF Medals: Recognising Dedication, Reflecting the Time", *Pioneer* (Jan. 2007): 7–9.

[90] "Savings & Employee Retirement Plan (SAVER)", MINDEF, 12 Jan. 1998, www.mindef.gov.sg/imindef/press_room/official_releases/nr/1998/jan/12jan98_nr.htm, accessed 7 Nov. 2016.

Generous salaries succeeded in stabilizing recruitment numbers but created their own problems. In 1982, then-Defence Minister Goh Chok Tong cautioned: "Singaporeans are pragmatic people. They respond to tangible incentives. But we do not want to over-emphasise the material rewards. They are important but not the most important. To over-emphasise the monetary aspects is to stand the risk of attracting the wrong types of candidates."[91] The public would certainly be none the wiser if the "wrong types" were recruited, as detailed metrics of officer recruitment and attrition are non-existent in the open domain. Nevertheless, getting the "right people" remains a perennial concern, as one former service chief attested: "The issue of grooming leadership is not so simple. There is the need to balance motivation and incentives. You get what you pay for, but you cannot make salary so high that people only do it for the money. The career is front-loaded because if you cannot get people in you have no chance of getting people to stay."[92]

Others have voiced similar concerns. In 1991, BG (RET) then-MAJ Tay Lim Heng (SAFOS 1982) asked:

> … how to maintain military professionalism, with its implicit notions of self-sacrifice, in an affluent society in times of peace, where the pursuit of self-interest has become pervasive and all important … most clearly manifested in the increasing need to resort to monetary incentives to recruit and retain regular service, just so to compensate for 'additional hardship' of military service. Monetary remunerations feature strongly in our recruitment advertisements.[93]

Tan Tai Yong concurred that "[m]ore and more the SAF must resort to monetary incentives and generous scholarships to recruit and retain regular servicemen as compensation for the hardship that is associated with military service".[94]

The SAF continued to struggle with challenges in retaining officers, with temporary respites during infrequent economic downturns despite generous scholarship opportunities and handsome remuneration.[95] The government acknowledged in the late 1990s: "To have a strong SAF, MINDEF needs to

---

[91] "Let Us Find Hearts and Minds of SAF", p. 10; Ronnie Wai, "Mass-Media Drive", *Straits Times*, 7 Jan. 1983, p. 18.

[92] Interview No. 15.

[93] Tay Lim Heng, "The Regular Military Career: From Profession to Occupation?" *Pointer* 17, 2 (Apr.–June 1991): 96–7. For a more recent and congruent view on the importance of benefits to officer recruitment, see Yip Kin Cheng, "The Professional Soldier: Organisational and Occupational Commitment of Regular Officers in the Singapore Army", honours thesis, National University of Singapore, 2002, p. 34.

[94] Tan, "Singapore: Civil-Military Fusion", p. 289.

[95] Tay Lim Heng, "The Regular Military Career: From Profession to Occupation?" *Pointer* 17, 2 (Apr.–June 1991): 97.

recruit and retain sufficient numbers of good officers from each cohort. Past trends have shown that despite efforts to enhance the attractiveness of the SAF career MINDEF is still falling short of its required recruitment and retention targets. If this trend continues, the future operational capability of the SAF will be affected."[96]

There are two key areas that have thrown up obstacles to recruitment in the past and continue to do so. The first is the difficult mixture of limited knowledge of what the military career entails coupled with negative NS experiences, society's lack of respect for the profession of arms, and the lure of long-term earning potential beyond the military career. For starters, the tyranny of peace has had a somewhat paradoxical effect on defence. Defence is portrayed as essential to Singapore but, in a way congruent with insurance policies, is seen by society as a luxury when its benefits are not immediately required. The premiums paid in economic terms of land, labour and capital always seem too steep in peace. This combination has created a milieu where members of other professions and civil servants "ordinarily enjoy esteem from the larger society, [but] regulars in the SAF apparently do not enjoy such esteem".[97]

Second, every Regular officer must accept that service in the SAF is not a lifelong commitment and in all likelihood a "second career" is necessary. The shifting mandatory ages of retirement have not helped as the pendulum has swung between "50 for MAJ and below, and 55 for LTC and above" to "retirement at 40 for MAJ and below and 45 for LTC and above".[98] In 1997 MINDEF acknowledged the difficulty of mid-life career transition: "Owing to the policy to keep the SAF young, younger officers do not see any incentive to stay until the age of 40 to 45 when transition to a second career will be more difficult. About two-thirds of every cohort leave after the first contract to start a new career."[99]

The following year the New Partnership Scheme, which rolled out the SAVER plan, was implemented with a 23- or 25-year route of advancement.

---

[96] "Factsheet: Dr Tony Tan's Announcement at the SAF Day Dinner for Senior Officers", MINDEF, 4 July 1997, www.mindef.gov.sg/imindef/press_room/official_releases/nr/1997/jul/04jul97_nr/04jul97_fs.html, accessed 7 Nov. 2016.

[97] Aaron Chia Eng Seng, "Are We Military Professionals or Professionals in the Military?" *Pointer* 23, 2 (Apr.–June 1997): 56.

[98] William Campbell, "Towards Higher Levels in Singapore's Forces", *Straits Times*, 12 Oct. 1970, p. 12; "When a Colonel Can Call It a Day", *Straits Times*, 29 Jan. 1978, p. 5; *Manpower Policies Affecting the SAF Officer*, p. 24; "Pay Rise for Servicemen", *Pioneer* (Jan. 1994): 24; "New Service Schemes for SAF Officers", *Pioneer* (Jan. 1994): 25; "New Office Formed to Develop Second Careers for Retiring Personnel", *Pioneer* (Mar. 1995): 16–7.

[99] "Factsheet: Dr Tony Tan's Announcement".

Monetary incentives were also more enticing, "because the skills and experience gained by combat officers are less directly marketable and the extra amounts are to help these officers because of the expected greater difficulties in career transition".[100] For an 18-year-old this meant retirement at 41 or 43 (for pilots and ranks of COL and above).[101] The benefit to MINDEF with the introduction of SAVER has certainly been the consolidation of service schemes into one and the complete financial separation (in contrast to the pension) once an officer retires from active service.[102]

In 2010 the Enhanced Officer Scheme revised and standardized the retirement age for officers at 50.[103] This does not necessarily equate to the

---

[100] MINDEF, as the employer, contributes 15 per cent of the officer's gross salary to CPF on a monthly basis. Under the SAVER plan MINDEF foots an additional 5 per cent into an officer's CPF Top-Up Account, thereby increasing its total contribution rate from 15 per cent to 20 per cent to ensure parity with the private sector. The second is the Savings Account, in which MINDEF places 8 per cent of an officer's annual gross salary for the first six years of service and gradually decreases before ceasing in the tenth year. Funds in this account may be withdrawn in stages from the seventh year onwards (assuming the officer remains in service). The third is the Retirement Account, where 5 per cent of an officer's gross salary is deposited from the seventh year of service onwards and gradually increases until a ceiling is reached with a lump-sum payment made only upon retirement. Officers are also emplaced on a Flexible Benefits Program with 500 to 900 credits ($500–$900) depending on length of service for use on approved expenses. David Miller, "New SAF Rewards Package", *Straits Times*, 13 Jan. 1998, p. 3, "New Retirement Savings Plan for SAF Uniformed Officers", *Straits Times*, 21 Mar. 1998, p. 40.

[101] "SAF Pay 'Not Competitive Enough'", *Straits Times*, 5 July 1997, p. 39; Miller, "New SAF Rewards Package", p. 3; "Career Management in 'The New Partnership'", *Army News* (Sept. 1998), p. 5; Ansley Ng, "New Ranks, Pay Benchmark in SAF Career Scheme Overhaul", *TODAY*, 8 Oct. 2009, p. 6. Before 1998 officers were placed on one of the following service schemes: (1) Contract (MINDEF and officer each contribute 15 per cent of the officer's gross monthly salary to CPF with gratuity based on 9 per cent of last-drawn basic rank pay and length of service); (2) Full-CPF (MINDEF and officer each contribute 20 per cent of the officer's gross monthly salary into CPF and the officer receives a special gratuity calculated on last-drawn salary); and (3) Pension (MINDEF and officer pay equal amounts into CPF based on a pensionable and non-pensionable component. On retirement pension calculated is based on pensionable component of last-drawn salary).

[102] SAVER has been "enhanced" through various monetary initiatives since inception in 1998. For example, the Variable Market Bonus (based on Singapore's GDP growth above 4 per cent and officer's performance; pegged at a maximum of twice last-drawn salary), the Full Savings Vesting bonus once an officer completed the first ten years of service (pegged at five times the officer's last-drawn monthly salary), and an increase in the tiered allocation of annual FLEX credits at 600 (first to sixth year of service), 800 (seventh to 11th year), and 1,000 (12th year onwards). See Terence Lim, "New Manpower Initiatives to Attract and Retain Talent", *Cyberpioneer*, 13 Sept. 2007.

[103] At the time of writing the retirement age ceilings were: 50 for Specialists, 55 for Warrant Officers, 50 for Officers, 60 for Military Experts, and 62 for civilian employees.

spreading out of a career, as the pace of advancement remains unchanged.[104] It instead allows those who choose to remain on active duty to serve additional tours that would previously have been impossible. Whether enticements via SAVER's monetary-based incentives and revising the retirement age to 50 have improved the retention rates of officers is unknown. Raising the retirement age does not necessarily improve the long-term prospects of second career transition. A typical career officer retiring as LTC or Senior Lieutenant Colonel (SLTC) might have more money in the pocket, but for the majority the need to retool and relearn later in life for another industry, as compared to their early- to mid-40s, is no mean challenge.

The difficulties associated with midlife career transition are exacerbated by the military profession offering limited skills beyond the oft-quoted "leadership and management". Regular service personnel already griped about not possessing the technical or commercial skills required for the civilian world as far back as 1970.[105] Even scholar-officers, who in the past had their career transition "managed in a more structured and systematic" manner, face the need to possess current and relevant skills and knowledge in the highly competitive job market.[106] In 2006 *The Straits Times* painted a broad and unflattering picture:

> Things are getting tougher for military or civil service high-fliers nearing or past their shelf life. Previously, most were absorbed by government-linked companies or statutory boards when it was time to leave. But these days, GLCs ... prefer to hire those who can hit the ground running from Day One. These would be people with experience in global banking, financial services, mergers and acquisitions, leisure entertainment and customer relations. Unfortunately, those leaving the military and civil service lack that global perspective and struggle to keep up ... Finding them a job in the private sector is also a problem. Singapore's contract manufacturing industry is shrinking and the growth of home-grown companies with pockets deep enough to hire such high-calibre candidates is just not able to keep pace with the conveyor belt of government scholars today.[107]

Hitting the ground running means industry-specific experiences, and these are undoubtedly accumulated the earlier an officer departs active service. While

---

[104] Toh Weisong, "High Flyers: Implications of Short Officer Careers in the SAF", *Pointer: Journal of the Singapore Armed Forces* 38, 3 (2012): 14.

[105] William Campbell, "Towards Higher Levels in Singapore's Forces", *Straits Times*, 12 Oct. 1970, p. 12.

[106] Goh Chin Lian, "Army Man Taking Over as Defence Force Chief", *Straits Times*, 7 Feb. 2003, p. 4.

[107] Ho Ai Li and Susan Long, "Don't Knock Us, Our Rice Bowls Are Not Iron", *Straits Times*, 16 Dec. 2006.

not all officers face challenges in transitioning to a second career, the potential negative publicity should there be a community of unemployed ex-Regulars obliged MINDEF to act. The Career Transition Resource Centre was established in 2009 to aid around three-fifths of the annual "100 to 200" retirees across all ranks to ease into second careers as "supervisors, managers or directors in defence manufacturers, banks and security firms, while others set up their own businesses".[108] That said, the individual always bears sole responsibility for his or her transition from active military service to any industry in the civilian world.

3.3 Primary Motivations

The interview participants were motivated to join the SAF due to a combination of primary and secondary factors despite the broad recruitment challenges faced by the armed forces. Primary factors are necessary and sufficient for an individual to join the SAF. Secondary motivations, on the other hand, are necessary but insufficient on their own merits. Five categories of primary motivations surfaced from the constant comparison of data. First, the scholarships proved the greatest lure for those who qualified. Second, non-scholarship recipients viewed the SAF as the best career opportunity at that point in time. Third, the military offered an atypical medical career for MOs. The fourth motivation came from opportunities to work on cutting-edge technology and gain technical competence, which attracted engineers and those in platform-centric vocations. Finally, there were the few who harboured interests in the military and entertained a possible career from an early age.

3.3.1 Scholarships

The opportunity for tertiary education (especially overseas) enticed many a scholar-officer into the SAF. Although the majority of NS-eligible males are channelled into the SAF, nothing obliges them to stay beyond statutory limits. Military scholarships commenced as a way for the SAF to attract and hopefully retain its fair share of the country's limited pool of "top brains". If the SAF did not secure their services, another employer certainly would through an ever-increasing plethora of scholarships, with more tenable overseas and some for local studies even bond-free. It was envisaged that these top brains would in turn attract others and in due time create a "talent pipeline" for the SAF. This would also eradicate the stigma that the finest in society avoided uniformed service. These top brains were undoubtedly book-smart and possessed top grades, which were once the top discriminating factors in the search for scholar-officers. The

---

[108] Jermyn Chow, "8 in 10 Land New Jobs within 6 Months", *Straits Times*, 27 Dec. 2011.

process evolved into a holistic approach that considered character and ECAs that indicated leadership potential (e.g., school student council, prefect, etc.) and military-relevant attributes (e.g., sports, uniform groups).

At a very basic level, one can understand that motivation came from the opportunity to earn a university degree on a government ticket. This was especially so for the lower socio-economic class, which in the days before Singapore's economic success encompassed virtually every scholar-officer. As one SAFOS recipient said: "It benefits the students by getting an overseas education they otherwise wouldn't be able to afford and on the part of the government, its way to attract the best and the brightest; it benefits both sides."[109] This simple explanation has strong historical echoes. MG (RET) Lim Neo Chian candidly stated his motivation was the opportunity for tertiary education overseas while his $1,500 monthly salary (a large amount in those days) contributed to the financial needs of his father and six siblings.[110]

For BG (NS) then-MAJ Gary Ang Aik Hwang (SAFOS 1986), the scholarship met twin aspirations:

> "My parents would not have been able to send me overseas; the SAF sent me to Oxford, one of the best universities in the world … I also had aspirations of serving the nation. The scholarship gave me the opportunity to see the big picture of life in Singapore and why defence is the backbone of the country. Not many people have the chance to understand the importance of military defence."[111]

Even the reflections of former Commissioner of Police (2010–15) Ng Joo Hee (SPFOS 1985) would not be out of place:

> "It was not my youthful ambition to be a police officer. But a place in Oxford changed all of that because my family was poor and I had no money to go. The police came along and paid for my Oxford education. In exchange, I had to do eight years on my return. I liked it, turned out to be a decent police officer and stayed on. That was 29 and a half years ago, and with the last five as Commissioner."[112]

---

[109] Jennifer Sabin, "Countries Fund Future Leaders' Yale Study", *Yale Daily News*, 26 Mar. 2004, www.yaledailynews.com/news/2004/mar/26/countries-fund-future-leaders-yale-study, accessed 28 May 2014.

[110] "From Chief to Chairman", *Straits Times*, 24 Feb. 2001, p. 24; Tan, *100 Inspiring Rafflesians 1823–2003*, p. 132.

[111] "Winning an Edge in Life", *Pioneer* (Nov. 1996): 25.

[112] Susan Sim, "Ng Joo Hee, Commissioner of Police, Singapore", in *Trends in Policing: Interviews with Police Leaders across the Globe*, Vol. 5, ed. Bruce F. Baker and Dilip K. Das (Boca Raton: CRC Press, 2017), p. 215.

These sentiments were echoed by MG (RET) Chan Chun Sing, whose mother, Kwong Kait Fong, struggled single-handedly as a cleaner and machine operator to raise him and his sister.[113] "When your back is against the wall and you don't have many options, your mind is more focused right?" asked the Cabinet minister; "[a]lso, if you see your mother working very hard to bring up the family, and if your heart is not made of stone, you'd want to do something".[114] He harboured a childhood ambition to be a librarian but credited the dual SAFOS and President's Scholarship (SAFOS-PS) with allowing the top student from Raffles to realize his "ridiculous dream" of a world-class education in economics.[115] Then-CPT Chan reasoned upon his return from Cambridge University that he "accepted the SAF Scholarship because it offered the best 'package deal'—not just the chance to pursue [his] subject of choice in a respected university, but also a very well-planned route of advancement in the SAF".[116]

The scholarship is a primary motivation because its presence or absence often, but not always, determines whether an individual opts for regular service. This explains why the multi-tiered scholarship system has endured and flourished since 1971. Only a few would say that the scholarship was not a primary motivation. For example, BG (RET) then-OCT Wesley D'Aranjo (SAFOS 1972), who also received the Colombo Plan Scholarship, maintained: "I've always wanted to make a career in the army. It's an interesting life. I guess the scholarship is more of an incentive to me."[117] Yet for the other flag officers, a scholarship contained significance beyond mere educational opportunities. Two characteristics are particularly notable. First, scholarship applications took precedence over inclinations for a military career. The opportunities and benefits were too good to pass up, and there was "nothing to lose". The scholarship application net was cast far and wide and decisions based on what was reeled in. Second, the prestige associated with a scholarship was a differentiating factor for those with multiple offers. A pecking order established itself after the initial batches of scholarships were awarded. The nascent manifestation of this order started with government declarations, eligibility, associated benefits and word of mouth. In time, the success of earlier recipients cemented the prestige of a particular scholarship.

---

[113] "Chun Sing: 'Ridiculous Dream' Comes True", *Straits Times*, 20 Aug. 1988, p. 18.

[114] Wong Sher Maine, "The Boy Who Scored with Ds", *Voices: Magazine for the Central Singapore District* 61 (Nov.–Dec. 2011): 8.

[115] Ibid., p. 8; "Chun Sing: 'Ridiculous Dream' Comes True", *Straits Times*, 20 Aug. 1988, p. 18.

[116] "No Blues at All about Scholarship and Career Choices", *Straits Times*, 20 Feb. 1995, p. 4.

[117] "From a Mangrove Swamp to a Military Byword", *Pioneer* (July 1972): 19.

Nothing to Lose

There was nothing to lose and very much to gain given the primacy of education in sorting out potential members of Singapore's civil and military elite from the remainder of the public service. In colonial times, "those who had performed best in school exams were admitted to Singapore's elite school, Raffles, and then went to England for further training, with the expectation that they would return and serve the government".[118] In early post-independent Singapore the relatively small crème de la crème of pre-university students were enticed into government service through the President's Scholarship and the Colombo Plan Scholarship, tenable at universities across the Commonwealth. Military scholarships arrived somewhat belatedly in 1971. Most families then could ill afford tertiary education for their children. Local tertiary education was limited to the University of Singapore and Nanyang University, while foreign institutions were a pipe dream for most.[119]

Over time, the concentration of the brightest in only a handful of top schools have led to concerns over potential breeding grounds for "elitism and complacency".[120] Eligible students are actively encouraged to accept scholarships to maintain or improve the standing of their respective schools. Publicity events are held annually for organizations to court students with scholarships and challenge those with potential to consider possible futures. Male students shortlisted for PSC-administered scholarships based on school assessments and ECAs are then enlisted for NS in December or early January.[121] This schedule allows the SAF to assess and confirm potential military scholars based on performances in BMT (December to March) and the junior term in OCS (March to August). Dreams take a step closer to reality (or become nightmares) when examination results are released in the first quarter of the year. By July the annual list of selected PSC scholarship holders is released, and the overwhelming

---

[118] Ezra F. Vogel, *The Four Little Dragons: The Spread of Industrialization in East Asia* (Cambridge: Harvard University Press, 1991), pp. 78–9.

[119] The University of Malaya in Singapore (1949–61) became the University of Singapore (1962–79). The latter and Nanyang University (Nantah) subsequently merged to form the present-day National University of Singapore (NUS) in 1980. In 1981 part of NUS formed Nanyang Technological Institute, which in 1991 became the present-day Nanyang Technological University (NTU). See Low Kar Tiang and Peter K. G. Dunlop, eds, *Who's Who in Singapore* (Singapore: Who's Who Publishing, 2000), pp. xix–xx.

[120] Woo Sian Boon, "Spread Young Talent among Schools", *TODAY*, 30 Aug. 2012, p. 4.

[121] These scholarships presently include: the President's Scholarship, the SAFOS, the SPFOS, the Overseas Merit Scholarship, the Local-Overseas Merit Scholarship, the Local Merit Scholarship (Medicine) and the Singapore Government Scholarship (Open).

majority commence their undergraduate studies between August and October the same year. The United Kingdom and United States are the two prime destinations of choice.

This schedule is double-edged for the defence establishment. The advantage of conscription allows close scrutiny of all potential candidates and their mandatory attendance at various recruitment-oriented events. In practical terms, an OCS "scholars platoon" of individuals earmarked for the SAFOS, PSC merit and Colombo Plan Scholarships was conceived back in 1972 "to induce 'top brains' already serving under National Service to stay on as regulars".[122] These scholars were put through their paces and tested for leadership potential. It proved far from easy, as one scholar from the initial platoon reflected: "Some of the other platoons thought we were privileged. But in fact, the pressure was intense: if we didn't perform the program would have been canned."[123] The platoon has since evolved into a company-sized wing of OCS at SAFTI MI and continues to fulfil the function of assessing and confirming scholarship recipients.[124]

The disadvantage is that the SAF usually only has one chance to net potential scholars, a difficulty exacerbated by increasing competition from other scholarships. For example, for an admiral whose parents ran a laundromat, his average performances during internal school assessments meant missing out on top-tier scholarships, which would have dashed any thoughts of regular service:

> "I was a unique case. When I applied for the scholarship most of my contemporaries had secured scholarships already. I did not do well for my school-level exams in my last year but my A's were superb, surprising everybody including myself. But by then all the scholarship applications were already closed. So I applied for it (military scholarship). I think the recruiters were happy to get a crop like me. If I had done well (for the school-level exams), I would have taken another scholarship and the navy career would not have happened."[125]

---

[122] "From a Mangrove Swamp to a Military Byword": 18.

[123] Li Xue Ying, "Star Platoon", *Straits Times*, 22 Aug. 2004, p. 12. In the first Scholars Platoon of 43 cadets, 42 eventually passed the cadet course.

[124] Officer Cadet Trainees (OCTs) in OCS were once organized by "companies" and headed by a "senior" CPT or MAJ. Between 2000 and 2009 they were redesignated "wings" under the supervision of a "senior" MAJ or LTC. The change in nomenclature did not affect subdivisions which remained as "platoons" (led by a LTA/CPT platoon commander) and "sections" (led by 2LT/LTA section instructor). Potential scholars were once attached to Charlie, Foxtrot and Delta companies at different points in SAF history. Delta wing is presently the designated scholar wing with an annual intake of OCTs in March and almost exclusively manned by platoon commanders who are themselves recipients of SAF scholarships or graduates of foreign military academies.

[125] Interview No. 17.

This instance proved fortuitous for both him and the navy, but the SAF certainly cannot rely on such instances to woo talent.

For most of the military elites who were also top students, their path was simple. One reasoned: "Results allowed you to apply so [I applied] for SAFOS. It was prestigious and there was nothing to lose."[126] The attraction of government-sponsored studies was there for another even if it was not a top-tier scholarship: "Of course. It made sense to do a degree, so I went to university. No ifs or buts."[127] The outcome at best would be a scholarship congruent with career aspirations (if any) at the point of leaving school. At worst, one decided on employment or local studies if the prospects for self-funded overseas education were ruled out. For the top students this was a rare contemplation. Consider this officer who once harboured ambitions of a medical career:

> "I was given brochures for SAFOS in school. Being one of the top students the principal gave us information on the PSC selection. My father encouraged me to take up the scholarship. If the government is willing to pay me to study why not? <smiles> I did not consider a career in the SAF, but the scholarship came along so why not? I had no particular ambition. I went through a couple of interviews. It was provisional based on results and interviews. Of course performance in OCS. They (PSC) wanted me to do management studies, but I thought: 'What the hell is management studies?' I also received information on PSC scholarships immediately after the medical thing fell through. We were invited to apply for local scholarships. They said: 'We give you a scholarship, just tell us what you want to do.' <smiles>"[128]

Former CNV (2007–11) Rear-Admiral (two-star) (RADM2) Chew Men Leong (SAFOS 1987) also considered medicine, but the issue of affordability intervened:

> "I joined the RSN while I was still in Officer Cadet School. Honestly at that point, I had no intention to join the SAF at all because I was more interested in pursuing medicine. I came from a pure science class, and my friends and I wanted to be doctors. Medicine is a good career with good prospects and you get to help people. However, I also realised that I could not afford medical school because bursaries and scholarships are very limited. Having said that, the navy was actually recruiting and they offered me a scholarship plus an adventure of a lifetime. They told me I could go to the UK and train with the Royal Navy as a Midshipman (MID). It was difficult weighing between being a doctor and joining the SAF, but in the end I took a leap of faith. I joined the navy in 1986, took a year to complete my MIDS course and in time was interviewed and

---

[126] Interview No. 12.

[127] Interview No. 22.

[128] Interview No. 21.

offered the SAF Overseas Scholarship. It was truly an opportunity of a lifetime and after that leap, I have not looked back since."[129]

Similarly, for another officer an SAF scholarship clinched his services that would otherwise have been directed elsewhere:

> "I started off life with changing ambitions: lawyer, psychologist, cartoonist and architect. I got good grades and secured a Colombo Plan Scholarship for physical sciences. The SAF also offered and gave me the choice to study anything. Growing up I was fascinated with all the great scientists like Oppenheimer, so I decided to take the SAF offer. My obligation was to be a good soldier, but any of my secondary school classmates will tell you they never expected me to be in the SAF. <laughs> I didn't want to join the army. I am the last person you would think who would join the army. It was easy to get straight A's in school. The defining moment for me was the scholarship to [a military academy]. I did not know what it meant to be in a military college … It seemed odd to all my friends, and no one really thought I would join. I was ill disciplined even though I was in the Boy Scouts."[130]

Even if one applied for a scholarship, there were no obligations attached at any point prior to contract signing. In certain cases this worked out well for both the individual and the SAF:

> "I applied for the SAF OTA scheme in the hope of attending the military academies in either Germany or Japan. I was asked to attend the interview, but it so happened that the day before the interview I received the admission to NUS medical school. So I informed PSC that I wanted to be a doctor and then join SAF later. The other option was to study to be a vet (veterinary surgeon) in Australia. I was aware that SAF was not offering medicine [scholarships] (at that point in time). My interest and passion was to do medicine, then the military, and then the public service."[131]

<u>The Pecking Order</u>

A decision eventually has to be made even though an individual has nothing to lose by applying for a scholarship. A pecking order is frequently utilized to

---

[129] Casey Rafael Tan, "At the Pinnacle of the RSN", *Navy News* 1 (2011): 33. Some other SAFOS recipients who harboured thoughts of a medical career included Yoon Kam Choon (SAFOS 1985), Frederick Chew (SAFOS 1994) and Kevin Siew (SAFOS 2002). See "Medicine's Loss was the Navy's Gain", *Scholars' Choice: A Special Feature on Scholarships (Straits Times)*, 17 Mar. 1994, p. 4; "The SAF Overseas Scholarships", *Pioneer* (Oct. 1994): 14; and "Leaders in the Making", *Army News* 89 (Aug.–Sept. 2002): 3.

[130] Interview No. 28.

[131] Interview No. 18.

discriminate and rank offers predicated on the awarding organization and the "exclusiveness"—in terms of quality and quantity—of recipients, which is in turn reflected in the terms and benefits.[132] This practice established itself early on. Lee Hsien Loong explained his decision in 1971 to opt for a military career over the civil service: "Well, I decided to apply but it was my decision. I came to the conclusion that between eight years serving in the government, in a government department on the President's Scholarship and eight years in the army under SAF Scholarship, I would be better off with the SAF Scholarship."[133]

A 1978 micro-sociological study of youth in the SAF by former MINDEF Chief Psychologist MAJ (RET) Leong Choon Cheong recounted that then-OCT Lee Hsien Yang "believe[d] in pursuing his interests, either at the practical or the research level and these, at the moment, are Physics and Engineering".[134] Several years later, however, then-MAJ Lee Hsien Yang (SAFOS 1976) revealed that his decision to join the army was an "obvious choice" as "[i]t seemed to be what a lot of people were doing and the SAF Scholarship was one of the most prestigious awards to apply for".[135] LG (RET) then-COL Lim Chuan Poh (SAFOS 1980) also considered the quality of past recipients:

> "The army had a good reputation when I joined. Many of the best people in my school, Raffles Institution, had gone before me. But it was in OCS that I really appreciate the infantry vocation … The SAF scholarship is definitely a premium scholarship. One important question is 'why the SAF?' It depends on how a person wants to contribute to society. If you want to contribute to the nation, the SAF scholarship or PSC scholarship is the best way to do so."[136]

The interview participants who joined the SAF via the NS and/or scholarship route did so between 1971 and 1981. The scholarship hierarchy during this time frame was limited to various offerings from the PSC, the SAF (such as SAFOS and OTA), and the Colombo Plan. A pecking order existed even though the list was short. One officer experienced the loss of the family home during the Bukit Ho Swee fire in 1961. He hailed from a poor and large family with eight siblings and explained his decision:

---

[132] At the apex is the President's Scholarship, which does not take applications and is awarded by the PSC based on their assessment of the annual A-level cohort. At one time the SAFOS also did not require an application, but this policy is not current. "For Potential SAF Scholars: No Application Required", *Pioneer* (June 1992): 26.

[133] "When Scholars Become Officers", *Straits Times*, 15 Oct. 1971, p. 18.

[134] Leong Choon Cheong, *Youth in the Army* (Singapore: Federal Publications, 1978), p. 187.

[135] "Major Lee Leads 46th Battalion", *Straits Times*, 27 Apr. 1985, p. 17.

[136] "Ready for Any Mission", *Straits Times (Scholarship Special)*, 7 Mar. 1997, p. 15.

"I just wanted to fly. I wanted to fly and be a test pilot because it allows me to push the envelope and exploring flying close to the edge. I cannot attribute this to any one 'trigger' point. Perhaps it was subconsciously linked to my elder brother's ambition to be a pilot, but we did not talk much about it. Growing up this was my aim, so I made sure of my physical condition was right, especially my eyesight. Besides that it was just to study hard and enjoy life. <laughs> ... My eldest brother joined the air force after his A-levels, but he was not selected for pilot training so he joined SIA (Singapore International Airlines) instead. I did not talk much about military life with my brother. Actually I did not have much knowledge about the SAF at all. I was applying for scholarships after my A's, and my brother was in the process of joining SIA. He had a $50 monthly trainee allowance. There was no way I could study on a 'papa' (parental-funded) scholarship. I applied for a range of scholarships, including the Colombo Plan. I selected Naval Architecture at Newcastle because I did my research and realized not many applied for the course so [there was a] higher chance (of receiving the scholarship). <laughs> I just applied for the scholarships and then decide later (once offers were made). There were a lot of uncertainties. I selected the SAF scholarship because it provided a salary and an allowance. I was prepared to test it due to my outdoor nature. They asked for my choices, and I put down air force, commando and then navy. It allowed me to fulfil my desire (to fly) and also help support my family. I later found out the British government was paying for my studies at [a British university]. <laughs> I think they gave quite a few, and so some were allocated to the SAF. <laughs>"[137]

Another officer, who was the seventh of ten children with only one breadwinner in the family, gave a similar account of maximizing scholastic opportunities:

"After OCS I went to [a battalion] as a PC. It was a good few months. Sometime in November [that year] MINDEF asked if I was keen on the Overseas Training Award. OPC (Officers Personnel Centre which used to managed the careers of all Regular SAF officers) at CMPB was in charge of the admin[istration]. Ya, why not? If it allows me to earn a degree within a military environment, why not? The options available included Duntroon (Australia), Japan, West Point (US) and Sandhurst (UK) ... Although I did not get SAFOS I also secured a Colombo Plan Scholarship for Manchester University in the UK or UNSW (University of New South Wales in Australia) for engineering. I could have disrupted from full-time NS to study at either, but since [the opportunity to attend a world-renowned military academy] came [along] I took the OTA ... I was open to either Colombo or OTA and not too concerned of a uniform or civilian career. Both provided a scholarship, monthly allowance, and importantly allowed me to study engineering. <pause> Plus both had a bonded period attached. <smiles>"[138]

---

[137] Interview No. 25.

[138] Interview No. 14.

A third officer also used a pecking order, but his intention was not just to secure an education but one that would immerse him in a completely different culture beyond the confines of Southeast Asia:

> "I did not decide to sign on because of the military. My aim was more to head overseas for exposure. If I did not secure the OTA I would not have joined the army. The other scholarships available then included the Colombo Plan, SAF and PSC. It was during a scholarship talk that the OTA was introduced with opportunities for Sandhurst, Philippines, Japan, Australia and India. I was interested in Sandhurst, Australia and Japan, as it was an opportunity to be schooled (further) overseas."[139]

The final example is an officer who encapsulated the ambition of doing well in school and also subjected the scholarship hunt to a pecking order:

> "I did not really have any specific ambitions in school. The aim was to do well and secure a scholarship. The top scholarships were the SAFOS and the OMS. The Colombo Plan was seen as a second-tier scholarship. I was open to a military scholarship. In school I was in NCC and also active in sports as a cross-country runner. If I did not secure the SAFOS I would have considered the OMS or the OTA. My parents were OK with me taking up the scholarship and a career in the military. If I did not get a scholarship then I would not be a Regular, but I would still put in my best effort during NS. The SAFOS was an extremely important part of my decision to sign on. The lure was the opportunity for overseas studies. It was also the promise of a new experience and independence."[140]

The above insights highlight the importance of scholarships in enticing and securing the services of bright individuals who would eventually become military elites. There were, however, individuals who took up scholarships with the intention of checking the contractual-binding boxes before leaving active service. They were frequently depicted as "not interested" and "lazy" by superiors despite the great resources expended by the state. Incumbent Speaker of the Parliament and former Cabinet minister BG (RET) Tan Chuan-Jin (SAFOS 1989) has consistently addressed this point. Even as a young lieutenant he emphasized that in taking up a scholarship, "The most important thing is that the person must be interested in carving a career in the SAF. If he signs-on, he must be prepared for the challenges ahead."[141] The benefits and limits of the scholarship scheme are further explored in subsequent chapters, but for now its importance in addressing the motivation for a military career is adequate.

---

[139] Interview No. 11.

[140] Interview No. 02.

[141] "SAF Scholars", *Pioneer* (Apr. 1991): 18.

3.3.2 *The Military Solution*

Although an increasing number of military elites took the NS-scholarship route, others were not beneficiaries of such opportunities. These individuals were instead motivated by their unique circumstances and sought to make the best of a given situation where the "solution" was to join the SAF. Non-graduates, graduates on SAF study awards (lower-tier "scholarships") tenable at local universities, and non-SAF scholarship recipients populated this category. What mattered most were the employment prospects, the people they led, and the military life. One officer lost his father during his O-level year, which left him and 12 siblings to meet the subsistence levels required by the household. Government policies had just given birth to conscription, and after performing well during NS he weighed his options:

> "I wanted to go to university. I was half-divided after NS I would go, but things changed and I stayed on. Why did I join the SAF? <pause> First, the pay was relatively good compared to outside. An OCT was $360 a month. A 2LT $460. Second, I liked the outdoors. It suited me. I grew up in a mixed *kampong*-city environment and took on a lot of leadership roles in school. I was the athletics 'A' division champion. In secondary school I was the captain of the football (soccer) team, Queen's Scout, Head Prefect, athletics. I used to be the second best high jumper, but today I cannot clear two feet. <laughs> I was relatively active then ... [a department head in MINDEF later] offered me the opportunity to go to university, but I decided it was wasting time."[142]

For RADM2 (RET) Kwek Siew Jin, who lost his father in secondary three, the choices were narrowed by the push from serving as a conscript in the army and the pull of a regular career in the navy when his flying aspirations failed to take off:

> "I had to look for a job after my HSC (Higher School Certificate, an A-level equivalent). National Service was beckoning. I thought that instead of spending three years in the army as a foot soldier, I could do better by signing up as a regular in the SAF for six years. I had always dreaded joining the army and having to crawl in the wet mud and dirt in a mosquito-infested jungle."[143]

The former CNV (1992–96) elaborated:

> When I was in school, I had always wanted to be an Electrical Engineer. However, I was not able to secure a scholarship to continue my studies after my A-levels. My family was poor and could not afford to support

---

[142] Interview No. 13.

[143] Tan, *100 Inspiring Rafflesians 1823–2003*, p. 96.

me through university, so I was faced with the prospect of serving two and a half years of full-time National Service. Two choices were available to me then: do full-time NS and then go to University if possible, or join the SAF as a regular. I decided to take the latter as the better option available to me at that time. Although I applied initially to be a pilot, and had passed all the medicals and tests, the Air Force decided that I was too vertically-challenged to meet their needs, and turned me down. Not wanting to be an Army officer, I joined the Navy.[144]

A third officer, the middle of three children with a housewife mother and father who worked as a clerk, spurned the option of returning to the civil service. Superiors noticed his exceptional NS performance and encouraged him to stay in uniform, an eventual decision aided by a lack of attractive alternatives:

> "Growing up I did not have any high ambition. After my A-levels I had a clerical job at MOH (Ministry of Health). I was NS liable but enlisted under the civil servant category so I was on civil service pay. This meant I received $180 a month instead of $60. Through NS I had no intention to sign on, but I did so on the last day before I ROD (completion of full-time NS). The Head MPO (manpower officer) asked me about signing on. It was straight away pensionable service then. I was the SOH ... I had job offers from the outside, but there was nothing interesting. I had a job offer at National Semiconductor as supervisor. What I wanted was to be an SIA steward, but I did not get the job. The MOH position was also kept for me until ROD. Life would have been different and I would not have realized my potential without the SAF. I would definitely be less confident. Signing on was simply the best thing I could do at that point in time."[145]

This need for a job and the role of superiors resonated with BG (RET) Ong Boon Hwee, who played an instrumental role in the 1997 non-combatant evacuation of Singaporean citizens from Cambodia:

> "I was enlisted in end 1974, Boxing Day 1974, and completed my National Service full time. Almost at the end of the two and a half years National Service, I signed on. That was about 1976. So, why did I sign on ... If I may put it in crisp form, number [one]: the need. I needed a job, to

---

[144] Speech by RADM2 (RET) Kwek Siew Jin, President of the National Council of Social Service, at the Singapore Institute of Management University Convocation Ceremony, 7 Oct. 2011, www.ncss.gov.sg/About_NCSS/download_file.asp?speechid=121 (no longer available).

[145] Interview No. 09. The date an individual completed full-time NS was known as ROD or "Run Out Date". This had the negative connotation that conscripts could not wait to "run out" of the army. The nomenclature changed in 1994 to the more positive-sounding ORD or "Operationally Ready Date". Similarly, the term "Reservist" was replaced with "Operationally Ready National Serviceman" to convey the positive idea that conscripts were not second-tier "reserves" but held an "operationally ready" frontline role.

support my family then. Number two: the inclination, meaning that I felt through serving my national service, having been commissioned, having led as a platoon commander, having been through overseas exercises, battalion exercises and so on, and having seen the way that I was able to perform in the military field related work, and having seen the effects of men and also superiors telling me that I should sign on; … I think I had the inclination for the military. So, there was this interest in the work, the yearning for adventure, which was reason number two. And number three: a sense of purpose, and indeed a tinge of 'duty, honour, country'. So, reasons for joining the Army: need, inclination, a sense of purpose."[146]

Another general, the only child of a bus inspector and housewife, grew up in a Ponggol *kampong* and considered the military as a means to further his studies overseas:

"During NS I was not interested in making the military a career. It was something we all had to do, and so you gave it your best shot. During the last six months of service I was selected to attend SATO as an NSF, so this was an indicator that I was doing quite OK. I considered signing on but only on a short-term contract. Finally, I signed a three-year contract one day before ORD (as ROD has been known since 1994), and this was driven by two circumstances. First, I qualified for entry into an arts degree, but all the while I was in science. At that time arts was viewed as for those who 'cannot make it'. I toyed with the idea of saving some money and then heading overseas for my studies. Second, I asked for an eight-to-five job, and my request was granted when I was posted to [a staff appointment]. I took a City and Guilds certificate for computer programming. Back then it was COBOL programming. It was the way people were heading, so I took this course via evening classes. The three-year contract was also a way for me to save money to get an overseas education."[147]

Finally, a sixth officer performed so well as a PC that he was judged one of the best officers in the battalion and also attended the School of Advanced Training for Officers (SATO) course as an NSF. It was circumstances in the immediate aftermath of leaving the army that provided the catalyst to return:

"I was actually offered a local study award, but I did not take it up because it did not cross my mind to be a Regular. I wanted to go through NS … (but) [w]hat should I do after completing NS? Should I go back to the farm and help my family? An insurance (sales) manager recruited me during my leave period before ROD. I found [insurance sales] very mercenary. It was like asking one person for a bowl of rice. I saw the satisfaction in the SAF of leading men, of achieving results. Then one day my CO … called

---

[146] Ng et al., *Called to Lead*, p. 24.

[147] Interview No. 06.

me and asked: 'Do you want to come back?' He immediately spoke to OPC and arranged for an interview … OPC (subsequently) offered me a contract including backdated pay for nine months, which was the middle of my PC tour."[148]

The satisfaction of leading men was most apparent for those in the army, especially within the combat arms of the infantry, commando, guards and armour. A green 2LT serving as a PC is responsible for around 30 soldiers, a larger number than counterparts in the navy and air force—perhaps with the exception of air defence artillery and field defence units. Satisfaction in leading men comes not only from meeting mission success but also from looking after the men. One general took this as a personal mission:

"I harboured the ambition to be a RSAF pilot, but it waned and eventually gave way to something of greater importance. I dropped the idea because I gained the satisfaction of influencing people in front of me and making it better for them. It was about making the difference for NSFs in the platoon who did not want to be there. This is the reason I decided to sign on and stay on. To make things better for them. I decided to sign on one month before we were to be commissioned. I was offered the Local Study Award and signed the contract in [year X], but it would take five months before there was confirmation that I was a Regular due to background checks by MSD (Military Security Department). And this has to be the way."[149]

Even non-SAF scholarship recipients were not spared the need to make the best of their respective situations.[150] For one, the option could have been to complete NS and serve out his bond elsewhere in a civilian occupation. This proved rather unpalatable:

"In those days returning scholars had to serve three years NS. When I returned home (to Singapore) after my studies I harboured the desire to serve in the navy. If I was going to spend three years in NS I might as well be in the navy as an NSF, after which I could work in the port industry or for shipping companies. I wrote in (to the authorities), but they never

---

[148] Interview No. 05.

[149] Interview No. 07.

[150] The practice of Colombo Plan scholars opting to transfer their bonds to the SAF commenced early in the 1970s. One of the first was Lye Heong Sai, who completed a Bachelor of Applied Science (First Class Honours) in Electrical Engineering from the University of British Columbia in Canada. He joined the navy as a Weapons and Electrical Officer serving in the Systems Integration and Management team after attending the weapons and electrical engineers application course at the Royal Naval Engineering College at Manadom, Plymouth in the UK. See "Two Officers for Technical Courses Overseas", *Pioneer* (Mar. 1973): 23; and "Maritime Command's Able Seaman", *Pioneer* (Apr. 1974): 3–4.

replied. I was posted to OCS, and during the SMC (Standard Military Course) I asked myself: 'What am I doing here? Why muck around the army for three years?' I would rather be in the navy, but I had to be a Regular and the navy intake was in December. In those days a lot of people came in (to the navy) as engineers, so I asked if I could come in as an engineer or logistician but I was told 'no'—I had to be in combat. So I signed up as a Regular on pensionable service. It did not bother me. If it did not work out I could always resign."[151]

There was no breaking of the scholarship bond as the PSC was flexible enough to accommodate this officer's desire to serve in uniform, demonstrated by his signing on in the SAF. For another officer, his decision to return to the SAF despite having completed NS and an outstanding non-SAF scholarship bond was made within the context of a trough in the economic cycle. He benefited from personal experiences, information, and the PSC's willing accommodation:

> "I had doubts where PSC would put me in. One of my friends told me about the air force. He was happy being there. It brought me back to my NS days. The RSAF also gave recruitment talks in university. They were trying to ramp up engineers in the air force, the air engineering officer vocation. So I applied in university or thereabouts and in May (of year X) signed on. The PSC bond was transferred to RSAF."[152]

The SAF provided the "solution" for these individuals, but each had unique reasons for signing on. For some it met the need for employment. For others it was about making a difference in the lives of those they led.

3.3.3 Not a Standard Medical Career

The MOs who earned their star as the Chief of Medical Corps (CMC) were exposed to career opportunities in the SAF after (re)enlistment upon completion of their medical degrees and houseman training. It could be during the Cadet Course or subsequently during their first tour. The Local Medicine Scholarship (LMS) is a relatively recent initiative, indicated by the fact that none of the first six CMCs who made one-star between 1994 and 2013 were recipients. The majority were also not recipients of bonded government scholarships for their medical studies. Scholarships certainly did not entice them to sign on, nor was it a matter of meeting bond obligations. These doctors were instead motivated by the opportunity to utilize their medical skills in different settings—beyond "four walls and a patient"—even though more lucrative paths lay elsewhere.[153]

---

[151] Interview No. 15.

[152] Interview No. 21.

[153] Interview No. 20.

For career MOs in the SAF, this translated at times to high-risk environments. As former CMC (2009–11) BG (RET) (Dr) Benjamin Seet Hun Yew summarized: "I joined the SAF to go on missions, to do something different with my life and to be more than just a clinic or hospital doctor … I have seen my share of war-torn countries, and have planned medical responses to numerous contingencies and disasters … I have a deep personal satisfaction of having achieved what I set out to do when I first joined the army."[154]

The theme of "doing something different" with their medical skills resonated with other CMCs. The late BG (RET) (Dr) Lim Meng Kin (1950–2013) joined the SAF in 1975, motivated by the unique opportunity to serve Singapore in a medical capacity. This conviction allowed the pioneer in aviation medicine to lay the professional foundations for the SAF Medical Corps (SAFMC) during his tenure as CMC (1986–95).[155] When the Hotel New World (HNW) collapsed in 1986 he embodied "leadership by example" and crawled through tunnels to save trapped survivors despite his status as a senior officer.[156] Lim, along with another future CMC (1995–2001), BG (RET) (Dr) Lionel Lee Kim Hock, and a third MO, were subsequently decorated for their tireless efforts.[157] The disaster also proved decisive for the late BG (RET) (Dr) Wong Yue Sie (1960–2010) to contribute his medical skills in uniform. The PSC Local Merit (Medicine) scholar was on track to complete NS and serve in a government ministry but instead transferred his bond to the SAF. A eulogy carried by the Singapore Medical Association captured seminal elements of Wong's motivation to do so:

> As an NSF medical officer, he spent days at the site of [HNW] collapse, helping to coordinate the medical resources mobilised. It was during crises like this, and in his daily NSF work as a medical staff officer when he realised that there was plenty of work to be done, and that good people needed to step forward. Not being one to sit back and complain, he

---

[154] Joy Wong, "New Chief for the SAF Medical Corps", *Cyberpioneer*, 20 July 2011.

[155] Gan Wee Hoe, Robin Low Chin Howe and Jarnail Singh, "Aviation Medicine: Global Historical Perspectives and the Development of Aviation Medicine Alongside the Growth of Singapore's Aviation Landscape", *Singapore Medical Journal* 52, 5 (May 2011): 324–9.

[156] Lai Yew Kong, "Nation Salutes Rescue Heroes", *Straits Times*, 26 Apr. 1986, p. 1; Lee Siew Hua, "Families Share Joy of Their Brave Men", *Straits Times*, 27 Apr. 1986, p. 9; "SAF Needs More Medical Volunteers", *Straits Times*, 29 Mar. 1987, p. 12; "A Doctor's Anguish", *Straits Times*, 5 Sept. 1987, p. 1; Melissa Lin, "Hotel Collapse Hero Loses Fight with Cancer", *Straits Times*, 8 Feb. 2013, p. B2.

[157] Beng Tan, "Two Who Had to Cut up a Corpse", *Straits Times*, 26 Apr. 1986, p. 13.

decided it was his duty to stand up and be counted upon, and signed on as a regular medical officer.[158]

For the other CMCs the inspiration to contribute their skills in a different setting to the traditional practice of medicine was also evident, each under unique circumstances. For one, the dream of a medical career almost proved stillborn due to seemingly insurmountable socio-economic hurdles: "Affordability was a problem. Dad was a clerk for Singapore Telecommunication. He had five extra mouths to feed plus mum. We were not rich. I went through school winning awards. I was hoping that even though there was no scholarship for medical schools I could get the Singapore Finance Scholarship for top undergraduate students in university."[159]

This situation prompted contingency plans if medical school fees proved beyond reach—but those plans eventually proved unnecessary. Even then, it was the twin factors of paltry NS allowances and the opportunities in military medicine that proved decisive:

> "If I did not enter medicine I would be a scientist, something with a research bent in my career, but I never figured I would join the SAF. Why did I sign on? Frankly speaking, I needed the money. NS pay was really quite low compared to Regular. <grins> Actually for one year I had placed a down payment on an HUDC flat. I was not yet married. I got married to my wife-to-be in NS. Second, there was a SAF hospital at Changi, so I decided why not do medicine in the SAF? I could commence postgraduate studies quite quickly. After two years I could go back to the hospital to complete training."[160]

Another CMC was inclined to military service and explored possibilities after completing his medical degree. Although more lucrative paths existed, he stayed true to his interests in both medicine and the military:

> "I intended to serve for six or 12 years to live out the career goal to be a surgeon. But being a military surgeon you had the challenges of maintaining currency. Being qualified is no issue, but maintaining currency is difficult. [Specialization A] was an important area. The SAF saw a need in the area of [specialization A] and I could do both. There was an opportunity to grow something."[161]

---

[158] Ng Yih Yng and Lionel Cheng, "In Remembrance: Wong Yue Sie (1960-2010)", *Singapore Medical Association News* (June 2010): 12–3.

[159] Interview No. 20.

[160] Interview No. 20. HUDC is the acronym for Housing and Urban Development Company, which was responsible for constructing affordable housing for middle-income citizens during the 1970s and 1980s.

[161] Interview No. 18.

A third CMC considered the possibility of regular service when he resumed NS after medical studies and housemanship. For him the motivator was the satisfaction of practising medicine in an environment beyond the clinic or hospital:

> "During MOCC our course commander was co-opted into [overseas] ops (operations). It highlighted medicine beyond the clinic. Medicine in an international context was about adventure and the ability to do things in a larger perspective. I was motivated by the chance to do something different. It was exciting and less conventional. Was it about 'duty, honour, country'? <pause> Perhaps it was more a sense of self-fulfilment. It was not about material gain. Definitely not about money. It was about satisfaction, the ability to achieve more than a 'standard doctor'. It was a different, less conventional path but one where I could also succeed in achieving something with my career ... I soon disrupted for my three (years at hospital) plus three (in the SAF), but it became 17. <laughs> With time I realized the original motivation was to go and see the world and do something different. I asked CMC for the opportunity and was the third MO deployed (on a specific overseas mission). It was something beyond the usual clinical and hospital rotation. I wanted to do some international work."[162]

One thing is certain regardless of the men's motivations. These men probably had the least to gain in material terms by joining the SAF compared to those who came in as top students on scholarships or were skilled military leaders who made the most of opportunities. As CMCs they collectively pushed the capability frontier of the SAFMC, which has matured into an operationally experienced formation second to none in the SAF.

3.3.4 Technology

The fourth primary motivation for a segment of military elites is working with military technology. The SAF's unending quest to harness technology as a force multiplier has been a constant feature of its metamorphosis from infancy through to the present 3G manifestation. Deviation from this path is unlikely, and the journey to leverage the technological edge to address both realized and potential threats will continue. This is hardly surprising given that "[a]rmed forces naturally look to improved means of fighting not only to increase their ability to weaken and hurt the enemy, but also to reduce the risks to their own personnel".[163] The constant stream of new and exciting tech-based projects has become a fixture in

---

[162] Interview No. 23.

[163] Hugh Smith, "What Costs Will Democracies Bear? A Review of Popular Theories of Casualty Aversion", *Armed Forces & Society* 31, 4 (Summer 2005): 491.

the SAF. One positive outcome is that those involved—from frontline operators to engineering support—are constantly faced with challenging projects from fielding and integrating new platforms, to extending equipment lifespan through maintenance and upgrading, and innovation to adapt off-the-shelf technology. The military is the one place where aircraft do not simply fly or ships simply sail. Many are also armed, armoured and advanced war machines by design.

The officers who cited technology as a primary motivation were mostly inclined towards platform-centric vocations such as engineering and combat vocations across the navy and air force. In the army, this motivation was most evident for armour, artillery, combat engineer and signals vocationalists. The primary reasons for this were abilities in the physical sciences and an inherent interest and curiosity about technology. These factors converged nicely for one general: "I chose the air force based on a process of elimination. I was in NCC Air, and so I had an affinity for the service. The air force is also platform-centric, which provides the excitement of working with cutting-edge technology. But I was open to all. If I was channelled to the navy I would have given it my best all the same."[164]

Another general deconstructed the logic behind his choice of vocations in the following manner:

> "Before, the air force was well established; and with my technical background I thought I would fit in well as an engineering officer. Infantry, well, if they posted me there I supposed I would have to sweat it out. Artillery, they also told me it was not too bad because you need to be able to calculate. There was another choice. Combat engineer, especially the bridging engineers. If I had a choice I would like to have served in something equivalent to the British Corps of Royal Electrical and Mechanical Engineers (REME), and the second choice would be artillery … After commissioning I made the grade as an officer. There was a new dimension in the air force. In the back of my mind I thought that if the Singapore Air Defence Command (SADC, as the RSAF was then known) could be like RAF then it would be a good organization to be in and flying was more technical and hands on. It was academic and practical like engineering. It all flows together in that you study the theory then you do it practically. It reinforces the idea that it was something worth pursuing. If I remained in the army it was about serving your duty and not so much about interest. The air force provided the opportunity and my interest was a match, so that was the key. At that point in time, 'duty, honour, country' was a catchword. Whether it was … there was a bit of that."[165]

---

[164] Interview No. 02.

[165] Interview No. 24.

A third general viewed technology beyond the immediate technical aspects and focused on its utilization to accomplish a mission as a team:

"My ambition growing up? I was fascinated with planes and saw myself as a pilot or engineer in the military. It was a noble career of defending Singapore. Looking at planes in the sky it conveys a sense of the high-end technology associated with flying. The design and construction of the aircraft, the sophistication required of the pilot, [air traffic] controllers and engineers. It was the ability to meet the mission, vision and outcome in a purposeful manner. It was fascinating. The combination of teamwork required from air control, technicians and pilots. It conveys teamwork and sophistication with a purpose in mind. The pilot had to handle six degrees of motion while taking into consideration weather, wind conditions, the machine which can break down, the target which is the mission, and the challenges posed by the enemy. Individually as well as a team you plan ahead, to bring force to bear to meet the objective in a deliberate manner. As a student I saw a plane flying through clouds during a thunderstorm, and it reminded me of the challenges in life. You need a route and you go through rough weather to reach the end point. This is life. So I said one day I must be up there flying it or on the ground maintaining it. I must be part of the team."[166]

While technology was a primary motivation, it was sometimes aided by other factors. One scholarship recipient who took engineering was funnelled into the career from his technological interest coupled with the prevailing economic conditions, and an outstanding bond with the public service. It helped that the air force proved a perfect fit:

"At that time in 1986 there was a recession. Rumours circulated that the PSC was releasing Malaysian scholars because they did not have jobs for them. There was an economic depression. It weighed on my mind of where PSC could put me. That was the tone of the time, but it was not a major factor for me. The other factor was my own interest in aviation. I was a science nerd but also interested in aircraft. I entertained being a pilot until I wore glasses. I was posted to an air base, and in the control tower seeing aircraft take off and landing was a lot of fun. I could see the air force is different from the army in one sense. It is involved in real operations. Flying. Everyone is professional in their job. The business of flying is professional. The pilots, technicians, (and) controllers. That impressed me. The nature of army is preparing for something that may or may not happen. Whether you train well or not, who knows? So you do all kinds of rubbish things. You put in resources to train and train. In the air force launching an aircraft is real. At the back of my mind it was something I could look at."[167]

---

[166] Interview No. 14.

[167] Interview No. 21.

Another officer described his family of four, comprising parents and one younger sibling, as "modest" but strongly contemplated employment to contribute financially to the family. This consideration was all the more urgent in light of his mechanic father's impending retirement. The SAF met this need and the officer's long-standing technological interests:

> "In my earlier days, in Primary School, I already had a fascination with all things mechanical. At that time it was F1 and fast cars. Back then being an engineer was the cool thing, especially in mechanical engineering. In secondary school, I spent quite a lot of time on aero-modelling, and from planes to tanks. It was also during this time that I developed an interest in military history. This battle, that battle, who won. I became fixated on armoured vehicles, but I did not think about a career in the military. Since I had to be in the military anyway I thought I could work with equipment I had fascination for. I signed up in BMT. It was a five-year contract which was a salary for a good five years when people were bumming around for two-and-a-half years (of NS). I thought a better script would be for university studies to be included, and so the bond was extended. It was not a bad job because it was interesting and challenging."[168]

An interest in technology did not restrict one to only "hands-on" engineering. The flexibility of engineering and the physical sciences had multifaceted military applications. Officers with tertiary qualifications took such disciplines in overwhelming proportions until the mid-1990s. One example is BG (RET) Lee Fook Sun (SAFOS 1975), who was intrigued by engineering and spent time "[p]laying with radios, amplifiers, oscillators, modulators and transmitters" at an early age.[169] As an engineering science undergraduate at Oxford he already envisaged that "You can do a lot with a basic tank. Make it a recovery vehicle or convert it to an Armoured Personnel Carrier. I would certainly like to do a bit of innovation on my own—but all this in good time."[170] His technical ability served him well as an armour officer, and he later applied related concepts to the intelligence field, where large information sets were mined efficiently.[171]

---

[168] Interview No. 22.

[169] Pan Zhengxiang, "Interview with Mr Lee Fook Sun", *National Engineers Day 2011* (Institute of Engineers Singapore), www.ies.org.sg/ned/intweb/leefooksun.html, accessed 28 May 2014.

[170] "Fourteen 'Firsts' from Crowd of SAF Scholars", *Pioneer* (Sept. 1975): 6–7.

[171] Ibid.

3.3.5 Interest in the Military

The final primary motivation is the attraction of the military itself. Officers in this category are in the minority, as other military elites cited the other four primary motivations more frequently. This is not surprising considering the lack of, or limited, ambitions and information on possibilities they had while growing up between the 1950s and 1970s. Even those who cited the military as a reason for signing on did not ground their decisions on a knowledge of what a military career entailed. What held more significance was what they had seen in their adolescence coupled with vicarious experiences.

One general was born in China amidst the tumultuous period of the "Great Leap Forward", and the subsequent famine forced his mother's relocation to Singapore in 1960 with her two boys. His early exposure to the People's Liberation Army (PLA) and Singapore seeded a penchant for uniformed service, while ECAs entertained his curiosity. He explained:

> "Growing up in China I admired the PLA soldiers and so had the ambition to be an army officer. Then I saw the air shows and glamour of the pilot in Singapore. I was so impressed by the Hawker Hunter when I first saw it at an air show in Changi Air Base—the 'Blue Node' of Hunters flying at low altitude struck a deep impression. At age 12 I joined NCC Air and later the air cadets. On Saturdays we would meet at Ghim Seng School with those from other schools. I also flew gliders during my [junior college] years because I was too young to take the private pilot licence course with the Junior Flying Club. I was motivated to join the air force because of my love of military stuff and the romantic ideals and experience of aviation. There was no question of joining SIA. I was fully set on the air force only."[172]

It was the sea that caught the attention of another officer. This admiral lost his father barely into his teenage years, which forced his mother to juggle part-time work to provide for her two boys. He was also exposed to the possibilities of a naval career through vicarious experiences:

> "When I was 15 or 16 I wanted to join the navy. The primary motivating factor came from documentaries. This was reinforced by two secondary reasons. The first was the image projected through the bearing of naval personnel in public. I used to catch the bus from the front of my place, and there would be navy personnel dressed very smartly in their uniform. I saw the 'Marlin' formation insignia on their sleeves and knew I wanted to wear it one day. The second reason was my uncle's sharing about ships and his travels. Those were lasting impressions that motivated me to join the navy. That said, I wanted to try military life first, so I served as an NSF. I would be one year behind my peers, but it was OK. I had to ensure I

---

[172] Interview No. 08.

could take the regimentation … I could take the regimentation in the army, and so I decided to sign on. Furthermore, the pay looked quite OK. The recruitment tagline was 'join the navy, see the world', which meant travelling and voyages. The benefits and career progression were also attractive."[173]

While the scholarship proved a primary motivation for many scholar-officers, it would be erroneous to think none had an interest in military service. Although the scholarship was instrumental in their decision to sign on, there were those who were also attracted by the promise of challenges and adventure. BG (RET) then-LTA Chua Chwee Koh (SAFOS 1982) said: "I was interested in the army even before my enlistment into service. The military environment toughens you up. You learn to lead men. More importantly, it is not a routine job, there are many challenges to face."[174] RADM2 (NS) Joseph Leong Weng Keong (SAFOS 1990) described himself as "a restless young man who craved a sense of adventure and the challenge of mastering a variety of professional disciplines".[175] Former CDF (2015–18) LG (NS) Perry Lim Cheng Yeow (SAFOS 1991) was drawn to a career that demanded both brains and brawn. As an OCT he revealed: "I prefer to be in the infantry where I can manage men as well as plan their exercises. I like the tough infantry life; it suits me."[176]

3.4 Secondary Motivation

The primary motivations of scholarships, employment opportunities, interest in the military, and an attraction to atypical medical work and cutting-edge technologies were necessary and sufficient for military elites to join the SAF. This section continues by looking at secondary motivations: salary, fly, the chance to go to the sea, "escape" conscription in the army. Lastly we consider family's influence on the choice of a military career. These considerations were insufficient on their own. They must instead be paired with at least one primary motivation for regular military service. Most of these factors are likely to be found in other militaries, perhaps with the exception of the army serving as a recruitment tool for the other services.

---

[173] Interview No. 04.

[174] "Educational Opportunities and a Challenging Career", *Pioneer* (Oct. 1986): 2.

[175] Gabriel Ong, "Charging the FLEET Forward, Onward and Upward", *Navy News* 6 (2010): 16–7.

[176] "SAF Scholars", *Pioneer* (Nov. 1991): 32.

3.4.1 Salary

Setting the salary scale for the SAF Officer Corps is a sensitive issue. Salaries must be high enough to compensate for the rigours of military life, address the relatively short SAF career, and reward consistent performers. As Huntington reasoned, remuneration must be "continuing and sufficient" for officers to focus on their profession and not worry about making ends meet.[177] That said, salaries cannot reach a level where they become the primary reason for regular service and turn the SAF into a quasi-mercenary outfit. This concern is reasonable, and Moskos observed that intense competition and increasing pressure to secure manpower had forced the US military to adopt market principles.[178] This phenomenon is applicable also to Singapore, where soldiering was once frowned upon, competition for talent is strong, and conscription has proven to be double-edged.[179] On one hand, conscription slowly eradicated the stigma associated with the profession of arms. On the other, every Singaporean son is obligated to wear the uniform, and so career personnel are not accorded due societal respect because they are not necessarily viewed as exclusive or set apart in any way.

Although salary expectations were not a primary motivation, they still mattered in the overall package that the SAF career offered, and few could say otherwise. For the scholarship recipients this was secondary because the biggest lure was education at prestigious foreign universities and/or military academies. Salaries and maintenance allowances were bonuses that sweetened the scholarship package. Salary was also a secondary motivation for non-scholars, because the SAF offered the best opportunity for employment at that point in time. This reason explains why most non-graduates signed on only towards the middle to end of their NS obligations. If salary was a primary motivation, they would in all likelihood have opted for regular service much earlier. Non-SAF scholarship graduates were enticed with the opportunity to pursue an avenue of interest, but compensation expectations had to be commensurate with their education level. Although the SAF salary scale was attractive in the 1960s, it soon proved

---

[177] Huntington, *The Soldier and the State*, p. 15.

[178] Charles C. Moskos, "The Emergent Military: Civil, Traditional, or Plural?" *Pacific Sociological Review* 16, 2 (Apr. 1973): 271, 276; Charles C. Moskos, "From Institution to Occupation: Trends in Military Organization", *Armed Forces & Society* 4, 1 (Nov. 1977): 42–4; Charles C. Moskos, "Institutional/Occupational Trends in Armed Forces: An Update", *Armed Forces & Society* 12, 3 (Spring 1986): 380–1.

[179] Tay Lim Heng, "The Regular Military Career: From Profession to Occupation?" *Pointer* 17, 2 (Apr.–June 1991): 96–7; Aaron Chia Eng Seng, "Are We Military Professionals or Professionals in the Military?" *Pointer* 23, 2 (Apr.–June 1997): 56; Tan, "Singapore: Civil-Military Fusion", p. 289.

inadequate and remained attractive only to those with an O-level education. A general contextualized this in another way:

> "I mentioned pay is low but still attractive enough for a single person. No family, no children. It was about feeding yourself and having enough to give some to your parents. SAF provided lodging, food, and at that time you can still afford a small car. I paid two thousand, which I don't think you can get today. <laughs> It was easier in those days. <laughs> So it was adequate. We were placed on the pension scheme, but when you joined the SADC it was a fresh contract. I went in with my eyes open. It was [a 12-year contract] at once. I did not look too far. It looked exciting, but I did not think too far."[180]

An admiral sacrificed making more in the private sector, but this was partially offset by compensation for graduates who then formed a minority among naval officers:

> "In the late '70s the SAF pay was shitty compared to other sectors. I could get more outside than as a Regular. In those days, the navy also had a lot of COs who were lieutenants. There was no annual promotion. Captains and majors were rare. Only a few went for the promotion interview, and I heard it was not exactly a good experience. Not all who went got promoted. The officer pay was also pegged to O-levels. Graduates had some sort of education allowance, but the overall pay was lousy. When I decided to sign on there was a combat graduate scheme. There was the promise of a promotion to Captain if I did well. But it was only verbally communicated to me. If I had more than a second-class upper honours degree, I would get Captain in 31 months of joining. In those days there were not so many captains. A captain's pay was not a big deal compared to outside but better than the O- or A-level pay scale. This scheme was OK as it mitigated the (remuneration) situation."[181]

The failure to recruit enough officers prompted the drastic salary revision of 1982. For some, salary was a significant motivator due to financial considerations for an overseas education or housing. Yet salary remained secondary because the primary motivation was the work and opportunities available in the armed forces. As one general revealed:

> "My initial thoughts were to complete the initial three-year contract and head overseas to further my studies. The other point was at the end of the (subsequent) six-year contract, but there were two considerations due to the high opportunity cost in terms of skills and salary. First, I was still hoping for SAF sponsorship for higher studies, but it did not occur. Second, I made the difficult and bold decision to purchase a terrace house.

---

[180] Interview No. 24.

[181] Interview No. 15.

> It was a heavy investment of $500,000 at that time. Money was not an issue at any other time in my career except this period as a Lieutenant/ Captain."[182]

Salary was a secondary motivation to sign on and served as an attractive addition either as part of a scholarship package or to a meaningful and stable career for those with non-tertiary education. Yet, there were also those who signed on despite the lower compensation package compared to what they would command in the private sector. The 1982 salary revision and constant updates have since ensured that officers are now remunerated in line with Huntington's reason of adequacy to keep officers focused on their duties. Whether such high salaries have crossed, or will cross, the Rubicon between secondary and primary motivations for the military elites of tomorrow remains to be seen.

3.4.2 Flying

The attraction of flying featured prominently in the lives of a third of the flag officers interviewed, but this childhood ambition would go unfulfilled for many. Pilot traineeship required stringent physical standards for height, reach and eyesight in the first decade and a half of the air force, and this shattered many dreams. One non-pilot air force general said, "I did not get to fly in the air force. Body, physical dimensions mattered to fit into the Hunter or Skyhawk, and I did not fit those dimensions."[183]

An army general recollected:

> "Growing up, I had the ambition to be a pilot. This lasted right until I completed junior college and enlisted for NS. I always marvelled at people who can fly. To me flying a plane is awesome. I had great respect for them. This was also due in part to the status and influence by television shows. After I enlisted I approached the possibility of a flying career with the RSAF, but in those days the standard was 6-6 and no less. I was 6-9 or 6-12, and so that dream was out."[184]

And an admiral recalled, "I had two ambitions while growing up. The first was to be a pilot, either in the air force or commercial, but this lasted until I became myopic in primary three."[185]

For those who made the cut as RSAF pilots, an overwhelming majority had shown an interest in flying early in life while some had been exposed to the possibility late into their teenage years. Before Singapore's independence, such

---

[182] Interview No. 06.

[183] Interview No. 14.

[184] Interview No. 06.

[185] Interview No. 18.

interests came by exposure to the RAF but without any avenues for realization. For one of the early pilots the seed was sown in school:

> "I was also a lot more hands on. We walked at Bukit Timah Hill with neighbours, walked to Pierce Reservoir and camped out there as well. I was involved in a lot of outdoor activities. Bukit Panjang government high school was two to three miles from home where I joined the Scouts. The [class] teacher was very good. Lessons were conducted outdoors for science and nature studies. We went outside to see how things actually are. We also went to Tengah Air Base because one of the teachers, Mrs Boswell, brought us there to swim. You saw the squadrons and it kindled a subconscious interest in the RAF of how professional they were in their work. In those days you didn't know what type of aircraft you saw. It was just a lot of noise, people running around, base security and the organization. Even as a 14-, 15-year-old you could see that they were well organized. People were working in harmony. People looked satisfied. There were amenities on base, welfare, and the family setting. The family unit was contained within the base. As a kid something like that impressed you, but it never triggered [that] it was a possible profession."[186]

This changed with the establishment of the air force and affiliated organizations. Some entertained their desire to fly through books, aero-modelling, and participation in NCC and the JFC.[187] For BG (RET) Jek Kian Yee (SAFOS 1983), model airplanes gave way to NCC (Air) because "[f]lying is a thrilling experience, it's something which few have a chance to experience. It's such a rare opportunity and I would not want to miss it."[188] Another individual destined for the skies was BG (RET) Charles Sih Seah Wee. His father flew a Cessna, and their common love for planes translated into time spent plane-watching at Changi Airport. Sih furthered this interest through biographies, journals and magazines, and earned his Private Pilot Licence (PPL) with the JFC before he could drive.[189] Former CDF (2013–15) LG (RET) Ng Chee Meng also flew with the JFC in junior college and earned his PPL before NS because "being a pilot is a job that you enjoy".[190]

---

[186] Interview No. 24.

[187] The Junior Flying Club was established in 1971 and subsequently renamed the Singapore Youth Flying Club. Interest in taking to the skies was so great that the first JFC flying course in 1973 had 1,800 applications, of which 42 eventually earned the private pilot's licence. See "Top Student Pilots", *Pioneer* (Feb. 1973): 11; and "Creating Pilots: The SYFC Wings and Awards Ceremony", *Air Force News* 106 (July 2008): 11.

[188] "Soldier Scholar", *Pioneer* (Sept. 1982): 27.

[189] Low Mei Mei, "Move over Airforce, Here Comes the Real McCoy", *Straits Times*, 8 May 1988, p. 2.

[190] "Gateway to Rocky Mountain High", *Pioneer* (Mar. 1988): 15.

Although many aspired to fly, there were no guarantees of making the cut as an RSAF pilot even if one held a PPL. Low graduation rates attested to the stringent competency requirements and the fact that flying was very much a matter of "you either have it or you don't".[191] The air force was thus hard pressed to recruit intelligent individuals with the necessary attributes to make the cut as pilots coupled with the character and cerebral capacity to lead at higher echelons. Potential pilots were courted with a contract that eliminated the dilemma of choosing between flying or tertiary education and packaged them in a symbiotic manner. One SAF general recalled his experiences:

> "I did not have any particular ambition. I was too preoccupied doing what I enjoyed. No long-term view. It's not like growing up I already mapped out what I wanted to do. In the '80s I believe parents would like their children to get a degree and professional recognition. Engineering, accountancy. It was going to be one of those, but flying came along and Junior Flying Club opened up. Signing up to be an air force pilot was a convolution of various factors. One, I was interested in flying and I also received encouragement from my parents. Two, there was the university cadet pilot scholarship scheme which provided tertiary education and meant my parents did not have to pay any money for my education. <smiles, pauses> Three, the air force was expanding and there was a lot of publicity in the papers. And finally, people said pilots made good money. <laughs> Incidentally, I was not attracted or influenced by the image of pilots. I also did not attend air shows or spend time reading (about the air force). I had no time as I was too busy pursuing my interests in sports. <laughs> I applied (to the air force) before completing my A's. I can't recall if I proactively pursued it or if I responded to a letter. I did not call up CMPB. I think it was because of Junior Flying Club then the letter came and I applied and met them (the recruiters). The conditions were also attractive. There was a one-to-one exchange where one day in flight school was considered one day of NS should you be unsuccessful. I thought 'what the heck' and I did not have to do BMT. <laughs> That is incidental reasoning. <laughs> My first payslip was $520 and I thought 'Wow, this is fantastic.' <laughs> But the primary aim was flying. After applying, the rest was up to the air force evaluation system. I mean, I was blessed with good eyesight, good genes and physical dimensions. I met the prerequisites. <smiles> From there I was pushed along. I did not dictate the tempo, but wherever I was I did my best. I am one of those who feel things will happen if you do your best, and they usually do. I was not looking for reward. The terms were straightforward: a 12-year bond with emplacement on pensionable service until 50. I did not see the bond as an exit point. Then again, if I felt I had to exit for any reason I had the confidence I could 'make it' elsewhere outside."[192]

---

[191] Interview No. 25.

[192] Interview No. 16.

Flying eventually came into the picture for pilots whose primary motivation was the scholarship even if they had never thought seriously about it. Consider the example of former CAF (2001–06) MG (RET) Rocky Lim (SAFOS 1977):

> "I did not come from a well-to-do family. All I wanted was to go to university and have a good career. It has certainly been an eventful and rewarding career, all thanks to the defence ministry. I had no real aspirations to fly, but since I was physically fit for the job, I accepted the challenge and soon fell in love with it. I started with the A4 and subsequently, with the F16 fighter jet. There is no greater thrill than to get out of the office and fly. When you are in the air, there are no distractions. You are free and focused to kill your adversary. It is a great get away."[193]

3.4.3 The Sea

Flying in the air force was an attractive option from the onset, but the same could not be said of sailing the world with the navy. The early pioneers were cobbled together from various sources. Aside from earning their keep, in the words of Singapore's first navy chief LTC (RET) Jaswant Singh Gill: "The main driving force was to protect Singapore and be independent of our colonial masters so that we could chart out our own destiny."[194] Despite the pioneers' intestinal fortitude, limited budgetary and strategic considerations relegated the navy to third fiddle among the services with the sole duty of coastal defence. The procurement of naval assets paled in priority compared to raising an army battalion or the more visually apparent and appealing squadron of planes. Shortages in the quantity and quality of manpower and equipment became painfully apparent against the backdrop of operational requirements. One admiral recalled:

> "In the 1970s, when the navy was in its infancy, we got people from all over the place. Civil service, merchant navy, some former Malaysian navy, from the army. In 1975 there was Operation Thunderstorm to handle the Vietnamese refugee situation, and the navy could not cope. It was not really a navy then but a motley crew who tried to hold things together in a period of adversity. After 1975 there was increased patrolling in the straits to keep them out. The problem was we had very poor night vision capabilities then. You literally had to pull alongside [refugee vessels] to identify them. A lot of them (refugees) slipped through at night. There were also other problems. A harbour launch list at Brani [Naval Base] was an indicator to the higher up of things not running properly. This equipment problem is linked to the strategic view and use of the navy for coastal defence purposes only. Most of the budget went to the air force

---

[193] Tan, *100 Inspiring Rafflesians 1823–2003*, p. 127.

[194] Yeo Kei Seen, "The First Decade (1967–1966): Humble Beginnings", *Navy News* 2 (2007): 6.

and army. The navy had high ops tempo but very little new capabilities. The people were just working a lot. We wanted to beef up the fighting capabilities, but it was difficult to ask for resources because of the perceived strategic contribution from the navy. Was the money better spent on a ship or a squadron of jets? Potential aggressor naval capabilities at that time were also not so great."[195]

Naval personnel then held relatively low ranks with an LTC at the helm, an LTA commanded a ship, while a corporal served as coxswain and chief radar plotter.[196] It was little wonder that COL (RET) Peter Ho Hak Ean (SAFOS 1973), a naval officer whose post-SAF career included service as PS (Defence) from 2000 to 2004, depicted the RSN as a "demoralised, down-and-out outfit" even in the 1980s.[197]

Beyond the issue of budget, the importance of morale in the navy and indeed the wider SAF depended on the senior civilian leadership.[198] An admiral contextualized the situation and explained why this was so:

> "One of the political leaders implied the navy should put a gun on a barge and tow it with a tug and on another occasion similarly opined that since the Japanese came on bicycles and crossed rivers on wooden bridges there was no need to procure expensive and modern bridging equipment. Now, what would junior officers think if they heard this? So morale was low, and it was not a place you would want to be. There were hardly any chances for overseas courses. Perhaps India. The ops tempo was high, and your family did not know when you would return (from sea patrols). It did not help that we did not have many qualified watch-keepers. Comfort on the ships was also minimal. Toilets were converted to keep equipment. Officers bunked seven to eight a cabin. <pause> You can do this for a few years but not for 20. Then there was the issue with food. There was a trial to replace fresh rations prepared by naval chefs with catered pre-prepared food like those served on airlines. It failed after a three-month trial. <laughs>"[199]

---

[195] Interview No. 15.

[196] "Ahoy There Mates!" *Pioneer* (July 1972): 22–6.

[197] Chew and Tan, *Creating the Technology Edge*, p. 160.

[198] See, for example, Oral History Centre, National Archives of Singapore, interview with Lim Siong Guan for "The Civil Service—A Retrospection" project, Accession No: 003060, Reel 5 of 14, pp. 63–4; Oral History Centre, National Archives of Singapore, interview with COL (RET) Ramachandran Menon for "The Civil Service—A Retrospection" project, Accession No: 003250, Reel 11 of 17, pp. 238–40; and *A Maritime Force for a Maritime Nation: Celebrating 50 Years of the Navy* (Singapore: Straits Times Press, 2017), pp. 50–3.

[199] Interview No. 15.

It is perhaps not surprising that the navy was not attractive except to true-blue "sea dogs" and those for whom it was a rice bowl. SAFOS officers from the early batches were channelled into the navy, not by choice but to make up for small numbers of graduate officers who chose to be there. The first SAFOS naval officer LTC (RET) Tan Kian Chew (SAFOS 1972) had never been to sea but reasoned he "was looking for something adventurous".[200] In the next batch, two SAFOS officers were channelled to the navy and their pioneering work paved the way for the RSN's development. Deputy Prime Minister (DPM) and former CNV (1991–92) RADM1 (RET) Teo Chee Hean (SAFOS 1973) revealed that as a COL "The idea of sitting behind a desk doing paperwork didn't appeal to me. I wanted something more attractive and the SAF offered the variety I was looking for ... I was asked to give the Navy a try and found I like it."[201]

More specifically, Teo and another colleague reported to the Istana (the Presidential Palace), where PM Lee told them in no uncertain terms: "Young men, I would like you to give the Navy a try. You will give the Navy a try, won't you?"[202] There was only one possible answer.

Beyond the low priority and low morale of the navy, scholar-officers—who were then small in number—were deployed to areas deemed more important and pressing to defence development. This soon changed, as one admiral observed:

> "Scholars were assigned to the navy. It was hardly a choice they had. They were a strategic asset and had to be assigned around the SAF. Some of them justified a greater role for the navy that threats came from all directions. How about the projection of SAF forces? Singapore is also surrounded by sea. How could we safeguard our territorial integrity like Pedra Branca? We were outgunned by some others ... The police craft was only deployed in local waters. The possibility of a blockade is also high if the navy is weak. Even then the acquisition of mine hunters was problematic because they were single-use and expensive. But on the whole the role of the navy became more obvious. In the late 1980s things started to change. Things improved, it became a more credible outfit, and more scholars joined."[203]

The groundwork laid by those early SAFOS naval officers proved instrumental in lifting the RSN's profile, as another admiral noted:

> "When I got to HQ (headquarters) and saw the larger issues the Ministry of Defence already saw the importance of the navy. Teo Chee Hean and

---

[200] Felix Siew, "SEAsons in the Sun", *Pioneer* (May 2002).

[201] "Uniform Life", *Special Life! Soldier, Scholar and Leader (Straits Times)*, 18 Mar. 1991, p. 4.

[202] Susanna Kulatissa, "Lessons from Lee Kuan Yew: What Teo Chee Hean Learnt from Singapore's First Prime Minister", Channel NewsAsia, 23 Mar. 2016.

[203] Interview No. 15.

> Peter Ho got navy prominence and a larger slice of the defence budget
> and initiated various projects. In [the plans department] the main project
> was to upgrade the missile gunboats. We had to argue piece-meal, system
> by system like missiles, electronics. Each upgrade had to be justified in
> context and arguments made from the beginning from where the system
> fits into the platform, the platform within the navy, and the navy within
> the SAF's mission."[204]

From then onward the recognition of the navy's importance in maintaining
Singapore's territorial integrity and keeping its sea lines of communication
(SLOC) open have ensured it is well funded. Today, those looking to serve in
a close-knit family of professionals flock to the RSN, which has successfully
attracted around a third of SAFOS recipients.

3.4.4 *"Escaping" the Army Life*

In earlier sections some of the interview participants indicated their desire to
avoid conscript service in the army as a factor in their decision to sign on with
the RSAF or RSN. This trend continued with others, and some common reasons
surfaced. First, there was a strong desire to utilize skills in the engineering or
maritime-related disciplines. Second, the professional manpower required to
master sophisticated air and naval platforms meant they would be serving with
other Regulars who wanted to be there, as opposed to conscripts in the army who
were fulfilling a statutory requirement. Third, the competencies required of day-
to-day naval and air operations are conspicuous. Shortcomings invariably result
in accidents and, at worst, the unnecessary loss of life. Finally, the army career is
not for everyone as it is "less than comfortable". For these individuals, the line "I
don't want to live an army life" from a popular army cadence proved more than
tongue in cheek. The army's loss was very much to be the RSN and RSAF's gain.

BG (RET) Gary Yeo, a mechanical engineering graduate from Singapore
Polytechnic and member of the First Batch, reasoned that army "life was too
regimented ... I think an air force career is much more professional. We are
disciplined, but we are required to use more brain than brawn."[205] Yeo was one
of four graduates from the pioneering batch of six Singaporean pilot trainees
sent to Yorkshire in 1968 and became the first local Qualified Flying Instructor
(QFI) when the others were British and Australian.[206] For another officer it was
a push from the army and a pull from the navy. The prospects of a scholarship

---

[204] Interview No. 17.

[205] Lim Suan Kooi, "The Most Exciting ... Most Exacting ...", *Straits Times*, 9 Aug. 1971,
p. 15.

[206] "Six to Be Trained as Jet Pilots", *Straits Times*, 6 Aug. 1968, p. 14.

also outweighed the litany of problems that plagued the navy back then. He said in retrospect: "The advertisement was for the navy. It was out of the blue and not a conscientious choice. If it was for air force I would also apply. You know, the army is not all that comfortable but I was prepared to struggle through the two-and-a-half years if I was not successful. If no scholarship I would just carry on with NS and decide what to do after."[207]

Although the navy was a well-established and well-known entity by the mid-1990s, the less than appealing army life also resonated with RADM1 (NS) Harris Chan Weng Yip. The first SAFOS officer to command an international task force at sea outlined his motivation:

> "Actually, it was a little bit of a coincidence of fate! I wanted to take up the SAF Overseas Scholarship, so I needed to decide which of the three services to choose. I wasn't too taken by army life, and with my spectacles … I would not be able to be a pilot. These, plus the fact that the Navy Recruitment Centre was the first to talk to my platoon [at OCS], made me sign on with the Navy."[208]

For another general things were not so straightforward, but conscription in the army proved less than appealing. He tried to engineer his way to better things, but events did not unfold as planned. Medicine's loss was the RSAF's eventual gain:

> "In OCS things did not make much sense, so I tried to [disrupt and become] a doctor. I was a straight 'A' student so I could be anything I wanted. Those who had applied for medical studies were disrupted from NS and were attached to hospitals, but only a selected number was actually admitted to medical school. This whole medical disruption issue was quite a farce. They (those responsible for this scheme) must have realized it was really disruptive for the people involved and also for MINDEF. We had to return to the Army and initially we were going to become corporals, but after a couple of days we were sent back to OCS. Some of us grumbled and bitched about it. The next year, they did selection first and only disrupted those who had been accepted. Later (when we were about to finish OCS) they told us 'you are not graduating' as we had missed two months on disruption. We went for an additional course before we got commissioned. We were a funny (an odd) group. I guess it messed up some of our lives. There was a tight quota for medicine, so today we are short of doctors. Then the prevailing view was that doctors and lawyers generate business for themselves."[209]

---

[207] Interview No. 17.

[208] Young Yi Yong, "Mission Success First Time, Every Time: A Chat with the Commander of the Maritime Security Task Force", *Navy News* 2 (2012): 27.

[209] Interview No. 21.

The prospects of two to three years as a conscript in the army proved less than appealing for a segment of the military elites. This was a secondary motivation for them to join the navy or air force and one that surfaced frequently enough to warrant its inclusion as a factor for regular service.

3.4.5 Family

Parents play an important role in the career choices of their children, and this holds greater significant due to the onerous nature of a military career.[210] Furthermore, those who sign on are young and impressionable, and the SAF would in all likelihood be their first full-time employer, one that is incredibly inelastic in recruiting.[211] The defence force of any state seldom recruits personnel from other militaries in the way a company in any other industry would. Promotions are almost exclusively from within the ranks.[212] Singapore, during the period when most of the interview participants grew up, had strong familial roots; this meant children were not left to their own devices. Parental views after all were the main expression of negative societal views of the profession of arms. This proved double-edged, with objections in the early days giving way to encouragement, all the more as the military career gained greater acceptance—with scholarships playing no small part.

One officer who joined the armed forces in pre-independent Singapore faced parental concerns over how far his career could go:

> "My parents and relatives asked me: 'What can you become?' Remember at that time there was only one battalion—1 SIR. The CO was a British LTC, and all the Majors were British. I thought I could be a Major one day. You get a Land Rover to send you home. <laughs> At that time there was no scope beyond LTC which was the CO. There was no 2 SIR yet. <smiles>"[213]

For another officer who joined in the early days of independence, it was the stigma attached to the military profession that drew objections:

---

[210] Jennifer Lee Gibson, Brian K. Griepentrog and Sean M. Marsh, "Parental Influence on Youth Propensity to Join the Military", *Journal of Vocational Behavior* 70, 3 (2007): 525–41.

[211] The entry age of officers is usually capped at 25 years and in some cases up to 27 years for university graduates.

[212] There are some exceptions; examples include the colonial armies of the British Empire and in the present day the close relationship between the defence forces of Australia, Britain and New Zealand.

[213] Interview No. 19.

"I would say at that time Singapore was a young country and national education was not quite there so you did not see much of it. It is more a personal motivation to join. For better prospects [and a better] future. I won't say that 'duty, honour, country' was not important. Remember that there was resistance from old folks about the military. My dad, even though he fought the Japanese in China, and my relatives were resistant. It was seen as a crap thing where only the bad went to the army. For me, I saw the opportunity to help Singapore by moulding or building something that is necessary. The education sector did not need much help, and how much could I help? You also think 'I am a part of history.' Whether I am glorified or not did not matter, but I did lasting and important things for the army, for Singapore."[214]

BG (RET) Leong Yue Kheong's father was a World War II veteran with service in the British Army's REME Corps. He recalled how his decision to sign on drew mixed reactions at home despite his having received a merit award as one of the top graduating officer cadets in 1976: "My mother was quite upset. She asked me what was so great about an Army career. Perhaps, as one married to a soldier mechanic, she was not sanguine about the Army. And after that there was a quarrel between my dad and mum. I felt very bad to have started the argument."[215]

Parental concerns remained even with the introduction of military scholarships. Liu Tsun Kie (SAFOS 1971), a President's Scholar who left the army as a MAJ, revealed: "At first, my mother was rather surprised and she raised strong objections to me giving up the Colombo Plan Scholarship to take up the SAF Scholarship but she had to give way to my personal convictions."[216] LG (RET) Lim Chuan Poh recalled a similar situation:

"I can remember my mother's disappointment when I told her I have switched from Overseas Merit Scholarship to the SAF Overseas Scholarship ... Around the time I was making that decision, about three months into my National Service, I asked myself a very simple question. Who are the people who have made that decision before? And the list of names was obviously very impressive. I must say I had faith in these people and in their having made a very good and conscious decision. I decided if it was good enough for them, surely it must be good enough for me."[217]

---

[214] Interview No. 27.

[215] *40/40: 40 Years & 40 Stories of National Service* (Singapore: Landmark Books, 2007), pp. 100–4.

[216] "When Scholars Become Officers", *Straits Times*, 15 Oct. 1971, p. 18.

[217] "Army's New Chief: The Man Himself", *Army News* (June 1998): 5.

By the mid-1990s, parental concerns were still evident at times. Wong Kock Sum, the mother of then-OCT now BG (NS) Ong Tze-Ch'in (SAFOS 1994), admitted: "At first I was taken aback that he wanted the scholarship and objected quite strongly. I was afraid that the army training would be very tough."[218] Such concerns were assuaged at the SAFOS Tea Session, where conversations with scholar-officers in attendance provided assurances that Ong "had made the right choice".[219] This example highlights the importance of recruitment information sessions and why no effort was spared in wooing potential scholar-officers.

Even if one's family could afford tertiary education, the thought of a son signing up as a Regular after studies seemed like a waste of resources with the opportunity costs of "better" career prospects elsewhere. This was especially glaring for one general whose family was relatively well off:

> "My parents asked me: 'Are you sure you want to sign on?' <laughs> Well, it was a contract for six years, so if things don't work I had a way out. I would finish six years and then decide, but the pension was offered in the sixth year. The thoughts of signing on were seeded in OCS. The initiative to sign on took place in OCS, and within a couple of months of being posted to a [manoeuvre] battalion I signed on."[220]

Other officers also experienced parental concerns, as one could expect, but the prestige and benefits of a scholarship, even if non-SAFOS, more than made up for it. Like so many in the past and also the present, the opportunity to study at a prestigious university or military academy overseas would remain a pipe dream if not for a scholarship: "My parents were OK with the scholarship. My mother said: 'You are going away? No way!' <laughs> It was a motherly reaction. There were no real objections. In some ways they were glad I got a scholarship so there was no need to fund my education."[221]

Apart from individual gain, some parents also saw a scholarship as a way to break free of the socio-economic trap faced by families of that generation. Without a scholarship one might very well be obligated to find employment to supplement the family income at the opportunity cost of realizing one's potential as a military leader. As one general said: "My parents were quite happy and supportive as it was a scholarship. My older siblings had to forgo university after secondary school or pre-university to contribute to the family."[222]

---

[218] "The SAF Overseas Scholarship", *Pioneer* (Oct. 1994): 14.

[219] Ibid.

[220] Interview No. 23.

[221] Interview No. 17.

[222] Interview No. 14.

A career in the armed forces has normalized over time, with the stigma seemingly consigned to the pages of history. At times the normalization process commenced with immediate family members who had a direct influence on career decisions. Examples of this included sons who followed the paths of their fathers into uniformed service.[223] One such second-generation officer is BG (RET) Bernard Richard Tan Kok Kiang (SAFOS 1985), who as an undergraduate cited his father, LTC (RET) Albert Tan Yang Wah, and the scholarship as motivating factors: "My dad is someone I look to with admiration, and I feel that I must continue a tradition that he started … The scholarship is attractive in terms of benefits like full officer's salary, educational and challenging career opportunities but it is not a piece of cake."[224]

Then there were cases of siblings who entered regular service and joined the ranks of the military elite. Lee Hsien Loong and Lee Hsien Yang both made BG, as did Chin Siat Yoon and Chin Chow Yoon. The most conspicuous set is certainly the Ng brothers, with former CNV (2011–14) RADM2 (NS) Ng Chee Peng following his elder brothers former CAF (2006–09) MG (RET) Ng Chee Khern (SAFOS 1985) and LG (RET) Ng Chee Meng into the SAF. As a 2LT in the RSN, he reasoned "that the best way to contribute to the nation is to work for the security and defence of the nation as this will provide a safe haven for political, social and economic prosperity".[225] He added two decades later: "Having joined the National Cadet Corp while in school and with brothers choosing the military path, a career in the SAF was a natural choice."[226]

The role played by parents and siblings constitutes a secondary motivation to join the SAF. Some candidates received parental support, especially when they secured a scholarship. Yet others faced concerns over their future, the rigours of military life, and questions over whether they had carefully considered their choices. Parental objections invariably gave way as parents acquiesced to their sons' decisions. With the passing of time, following in the footsteps of parents and siblings to join the military has become an added motivational factor.

---

[223] The number and proportion of intergenerational (parent-child, uncle-nephew, siblings, etc.) families within the officer corps and among scholar-officers are unknown but present. For anecdotal evidence, see Timothy Lo, ed., *Onwards and Upwards: Celebrating 40 Years of the Navy* (Singapore: SNP Editions, 2007), pp. 147–8; and "More than One Generation of RSAF Airmen in the Family", *Air Force News* 107 (Sept. 2008): 15.

[224] "Educational Opportunities and a Challenging Career", *Pioneer* (Oct. 1986): 2. LTC (RET) Albert Tan graduated from FMC in 1962 and held key appointments such as CO 3 SIR, COMD 4 SAB, ACGS (Personnel) and ACGS (Intelligence).

[225] "Cream of the Crop", *Pioneer* (Nov. 1989): 4–5.

[226] Lee Kwok Hao, "A Man Who Walks the Talk", *Navy News* 3 (2011): 31–3.

3.5 Summary

The establishment of SAFTI and the introduction of conscription provided the SAF with a desperately needed indigenous self-sustaining pipeline of commissioned officers. The defence establishment benefited from the services of all eligible males, even though not all conscripts wore the uniform willingly. This proved beneficial because without NS an overwhelming proportion of military elites would have never considered a military career in light of their ambitions (or lack of) and the dearth of information about the SAF career and organization. The "best and brightest" from the general pool of National Servicemen were enticed to accept scholarships, which proved to be a primary motivation. Military elites who did not receive military scholarships signed on because the SAF offered the best of the available options. Some needed a job, others did not want to "waste" their time as conscripts, and others sought to leverage their educational background and interests. These factors were bolstered by opportunities that only the military could offer, including the practice of medicine "beyond a patient and four walls" for MOs, to the lure of high-tech machines in the platform-centric RSN and RSAF. More secondary for some were salary considerations, parental concerns, the attractions of flying or sea-voyaging, the desire to avoid the army.

The combination of primary and secondary motivations made the military career very attractive to the young men who would one day become Singapore's military elite. It was also clear that the quixotic Huntingtonian ideal had proven elusive for most. This is not surprising given the initial lowly status of a military career, the belated campaign to foster belief in the construct of Singapore as a home, and the fact that the SAF has often operated beyond the public's consciousness. As COL (RET) Tan Swee Bock, former Head Air Manpower (2005–09), reflected in his contribution to the SAF's official Golden Jubilee publication:

> "I recall some colleagues advising me to recruit only those who are joining for duty, honour and country. I said I certainly preferred to do that too, but it would not be realistic to set such an expectation for all our school leavers in a peaceful Singapore. I believe the responsibility lies with the professionals in the SAF, particularly the leaders, to imbue in our recruits the right values and a sense of purpose in serving our nation."[227]

Realities show that some values are more "right" than others, and the purpose of serving the nation is sometimes not as clear as it ought to be.

---

[227] *SAF 50: Giving Strength to Our Nation: The SAF and Its People* (Singapore: Ministry of Defence, 2015), p. 77.

CHAPTER 4

Commitment to Military Service

"The military leader must embrace his duty as a military professional and not perceive his role as merely a job or an occupation. Only then will his leadership position transcend self-interest in favour of the higher good—the primacy of the security and defence of our nation ... As a military professional, you are not driven by economic and materialistic gain, nor are you bound by the contractual terms of the market place. You lead as the professional with competence, courage and care for the people under your charge."[1]

> — LG (RET) Winston Choo Wee Leong
> Chief of Defence Force (1974–92)

4.1 Introduction

What turns a job into a career? This chapter examines the reasons conveyed by the flag officers and specifically asks "Why were they committed to stay on?" Academic literature suggests three typologies of commitment, and these were utilized as sensitizing concepts during interviews. Affirmative commitment arises from a desire to maintain employment for reasons based on personal goals and values, benefits and rewards, the lack of a better alternative, and interpersonal and organizational attachments. Continuance commitment is grounded in the future economic cost of not maintaining employment in addition to the time and effort already invested in an organization. Finally, there is normative commitment from an obligation (e.g., bonds, contracts) to maintain employment. These typologies are neither ossified nor mutually exclusive, and changes during the course of employment are certainly possible. The defence force is unique in that those in service can attribute their choices to a "calling" (not unlike religious ministry). Here career experiences are specific to the profession of arms.

---

[1] Matthew Neo, "Building Engaging and Adaptive Leaders", *Cyberpioneer*, 9 Feb. 2015.

This chapter has three sections. The first explores the wider context of SAF officer retention and why the interview participants considered leaving active duty. This provides a background with which to compare and contrast reasons for why they stayed. The second section covers elements of transactional commitment (egotistic/micro-centric), which vary in importance according to individuals and are manifested in obligations to stay in service, remuneration, and career progression. The final section is on the convergence towards transformational commitment (altruistic/macro-centric), illustrated by the military elites staying on because of the camaraderie, their dedication to the profession of arms, and the sacred mission apportioned to the SAF. Coverage extends to episodes where officers faced personal danger or challenges that highlighted instances of commitment beyond simply staying in uniform in times of peace.

4.2   The Challenges of Retention

SAF officer retention figures, as with all "sensitive" data in Singapore, are extremely rare, only revealed during episodes of candour. In 1998 the attrition rates for non-pilot officers after the first contract (usually six years) was two-thirds.[2] This took place against the backdrop of 4,000–5,000 officers within the more than 20,000-strong pool of Regulars.[3] Officers who leave the SAF invariably re-enter the civilian world for the simple reason that Singapore, like many other countries, has only one defence force where one can render uniformed military service.[4] Even those who remain in MINDEF or affiliated entities such as the various intelligence divisions or the vast military industrial

---

[2] "Factsheet: Dr Tony Tan's Announcement"; "SAF Pay 'Not Competitive Enough'", *Straits Times*, 5 July 1997, p. 39.

[3] Miller, "New SAF Rewards Package", p. 3; Jermyn Chow, "SAF Adds a New Rank: Senior Lt-Col", *Straits Times*, 27 Oct. 2009, p. 4; Jermyn Chow, "SAF to Recruit More Women", *Sunday Times*, 21 July 2013, p. 1; Jermyn Chow, "Soaring from Fledging to Aerial Fighting Force", *Straits Times*, 17 Feb. 2014; Chan Luo Er, "SAF Promotes First Female to Brigadier-General Rank", Channel NewsAsia, 26 June 2015. Another source places the figure at 5,000. Yip Kin Cheng, "The Professional Soldier: Organisational and Occupational Commitment of Regular Officers in the Singapore Army", honours thesis, National University of Singapore, 2002, p. 31. The size of the civil service in 2016 was 143,000-strong. Irene Tham, "Internet Surfing Devices Sought for Public Servants", *Straits Times*, 16 Nov. 2016.

[4] The rise of private military contractors obfuscates this in some way but remains a non-issue within the Singapore context. Certain responsibilities within the SAF have been outsourced to civilian contractors such as Singapore Technologies (maintenance, logistics), Singapore Food Industries (catering) and various transportation companies.

complex do so almost exclusively as civilians.[5] Unlike other professions, where one can leave an organization to join another with the same job description, Singapore's military professionals usually do not have this option.[6] The rare exceptions are limited to pilots, doctors, engineers, or AOs who can return to the AS for secondments to other government ministries. Others who seek change from the military life or the general focus of work despite periodic posting rotations must simply resign.[7] For example, former Cabinet Minister Lim Hng Khiang (SAFOS 1973) left active service as an LTC after 15 years. He reasoned: "I needed a change. The idea of staying 30 years in the SAF was neither realistic nor desirable."[8]

4.2.1 Hurdles to Retention

It comes as no surprise that officers leave active service due to an array of reasons just as there are various motivational factors to join the military. The six broad and sometimes overlapping reasons contained in this subsection were gleaned from the author's personal observations over two decades: opportunities on the "outside"; opportunists exhausting the benefits of regular service; the relationship between society and the profession of arms;

---

[5] It is possible for officers to leave uniformed service and remain serving in MINDEF as defence executive officers. Civilians also fill the majority of billets in the external (Security and Intelligence Division, Ministry of Defence) and domestic (Internal Security Department, Ministry of Home Affairs) intelligence apparatus.

[6] This is most significant for combat officers as Private Military Companies are almost non-existent in Singapore. Furthermore, the majority of SAF officers lack the operationally relevant experiences sought by international firms. This leaves a handful of private security firms, with Certis CISCO the most notable among them. Not all SAF officers face this challenge: pilots, engineers and MOs arguably possess the most transferrable skills and experiences. In 2003 the RSAF established three pipelines for pilots to transfer smoothly to Singapore Airlines (SIA) and its subsidiary SilkAir: (1) RSAF-SIA Junior Scheme for pilots between 32 and 39 years of age who have completed the 12-year Minimum Term of Service (MTS); (2) RSAF-SIA Senior Scheme for pilots who serve beyond the 12-year MTS and are below 41.5 years of age in the case of helicopter pilots or 43.5 in the case of fighter and transport pilots; (3) RSAF-SilkAir Scheme for pilots who serve beyond the 12-year MTS and are between 43.5 and 45 years of age in the case of helicopter pilots and 43.5 to 50 years of age in the case of fighter and transport pilots. "A New Career Transition Scheme for RSAF Pilots", *Air Force News* 84 (Jan. 2003): 16.

[7] Examples of secondments include Perry Lim to the Ministry of Education (2006–08) and Melvyn Ong to the Ministry of Social and Family Development (2012–14).

[8] Ng Kai Chee Wah, "Chance of a Lifetime", *Special Life! Soldier, Scholar and Leader (Straits Times)*, 18 Mar. 1991, p. 2.

meritocracy and its discontents; disillusionment and cynicism; and other unique "miscellaneous" factors.[9]

The first and most common category is the lure of seemingly better opportunities on the outside. This reason manifests itself in various forms: a non-exhaustive list includes financial gain, change in pace or lifestyle, exposure to another industry, following "real" interests or "true calling", seeking more specific and relevant skills, and the possibility of a lifelong career which is impossible in the SAF. These reasons, perhaps with the exception of the last, are also applicable to other professions and become more enticing when juxtaposed against the perception that the military environment limits cognitive growth and creativity and stifles entrepreneurial possibilities. Take the case of COL (VOL) Mohamed Ismail S/O Abdul Gafoor, incumbent COMD 12 SIB (a reserve infantry brigade) and CEO of Singapore's largest real estate company, PropNex, who left the SAF after 13 years as a Regular:

> "It is not that I don't love the army. In fact, I'm still serving as a Brigade Commander, I'm a Colonel in the armed forces. I enjoy the army duty and the work and the responsibility and the challenges. But what dawned on me as I asked the question was this—Will I be a General one day? Is this what I want? Somehow, there was a softer voice telling me, 'Maybe you will not be.' It is not that I'm not being optimistic about it, but the fact is I wasn't a scholar. I was just a rank-and-file officer. Then I said, 'What else can I do?' There was a deep desire within me to be an entrepreneur and do something that could make a difference. And that's why I threw in the towel, I quit, and that was a very tough decision to make, because I left at the age of 32. Today I'm 52; twenty years ago. It was a very tough decision, but I made up my mind to say, 'Let me try. I do not want to regret later.' That's why I walked out."[10]

Even scholar-officers with their high profile and career advantages appeared in this category. One dual SAFOS-PS recipient reasoned: "When I went to the Ministry of Finance after my SAF stint, I had a 20 percent cut in salary. I have no regrets at leaving, since I wanted to have some private sector experience rather than one of a generalist."[11] Similarly, former submariner MAJ (NS) Tan Gim Chong (SAFOS 1992) left the RSN for a career in wealth management because "[he] felt the urge to explore other opportunities on land. Influence from

---

[9] Based on author's conversations with (ex-)Regular officers between 1997 and 2013.

[10] Bharati Jagdish, "Property Cooling Measures Need to Ensure a 'Fair Fall': PropNex", Channel NewsAsia, 21 Nov. 2015.

[11] Gerry De Silva, "The Bright Young Bond-Busters", *Straits Times*, 4 Dec. 1988, p. 16.

friends in the industry gave [him] insight to the banking world and it sparked [his] interest."[12]

The second category consists of opportunists who were never really interested in a military career but optimized their extraction of front-loaded benefits in terms of education opportunities, relatively handsome starting salaries, and valuable network connections within Singapore and afar. Their motivation for military service was purely contractual at best and a zero-sum transaction at worst. Superiors commonly depicted such clock-watching officers as "lazy" and "disinterested".[13] It was not out of the question for such Regulars to be habitually absent from their units.[14] The responsibilities of higher office, assuming they got there, would eventually unmask their intentions—hopefully before any real damage was done.

The third category comes from the perception that the military profession did not—and still does not—hold a prestigious place in society and even among active service personnel. Among the three services, this is most striking in the conscript-dominated army. Army recruitment slogans over the years have included "A Career That Demands Respect", "Our Army—Ready, Decisive, Respected", and —most recently in 2016—"Army Ready, Soldier Strong".[15] The last bears an uncanny resemblance to the US Army's "Army Strong" branding campaign (2006–15). The word "respect" has surfaced time and again. As BG (NS) Ong Tze-Ch'in, then a COL and Assistant Chief of General Staff (ACGS) for Plans (ACGS [Plans]), reasoned: "Just because the Army is Ready and Decisive does not mean it will be Respected, so we must respect the sacrifices that our soldiers have made in serving the country. In doing that, they will then respect themselves as soldiers of the Army."[16]

The demand to be respected seems unfulfilled for various reasons. The tyranny of peace means the SAF has rarely been called upon to defend citizens in a direct manner. The only such occasions are probably the Laju Ferry hijacking

---

[12] Jeremy Au Yong, "Hottest Job in Town: Private Bankers", *Straits Times*, 16 Apr. 2006.

[13] Several interviewees, including COL-grade officers, levelled such adjectives against scholar-officers under their charge.

[14] Sandra Davie, "PM Lee's Son in NS Reprimanded by SAF", *AsiaOne*, 13 July 2007; Selina Lum, "SAF Officer Cited in E-mail by PM's Son Fined", *Straits Times*, 9 Aug. 2007.

[15] "A Career That Commands Respect", *Singapore Monitor*, 13 Dec. 1982, p. 5; "The Army: A Career That Commands Respect", *Straits Times*, 4 Mar. 1990, p. 13; "A Warning from the SAF", *Straits Times*, 11 Apr. 1998, p. 38; Glen Choo, "Ready, Decisive, Respected: What Does It Mean to You?" *Army News* 196 (Jan. 2012): 2–3; "Our Army: Ready, Decisive, Respected", *Army News* 198 (Mar. 2012): 6–7.

[16] Bjorn Teo, "Project 300: Updating Commanders on Key Events and Developments", *Army News* 206 (Dec. 2012): 4.

(1974), Operation Thunderbolt to free hijacked SIA flight SQ117 (1991), and Operation Crimson Angel to evacuate Singaporeans and PRs from unrest in Cambodia (1993). Details of these operations remain shrouded in secrecy, and only a select few involved know what truly transpired. As a result, society at large often relegates the brave actions to a historical footnote at best. Those interested in the stories grasp at morsels of information only to find frustration and eventually join the disinterested masses. Furthermore, conscription is applicable to almost all males, and in a superficial sense an NS officer, especially in the army, can climb all the way to COL (NS) while holding a civilian career. The gulf between appointments apportioned to NS and Regular officers at senior levels may be wide, but this is also irrelevant to the average citizen. Conscripts also serve in almost every area of the SAF, with few exceptions such as pilots and sensitive billets within special operations, intelligence, and signals.

The fourth category comes from discontent with meritocracy despite ubiquitous proclamations of performance-based advancements. This issue is two-dimensional. First, there were structural concerns in days past that appointment and rank ceilings disadvantaged certain vocations for advancement. These included non-pilots in the RSAF before pathways were created for air defence and weapon systems officers to make BG. For example, Tang Kok Fai (SAFOS 1977) left as an LTC because his career path "reached a plateau" after tours as head of the air plans and intelligence departments.[17] An invisible ceiling was once seen to cap commandos at the rank of LTC, but six red berets have since made BG. At present, the terminal rank for naval engineers and submariners seems to be COL/ME7 and reflects the highest appointments currently attainable.

The other manifestation of this challenge comes from individual perceptions of a career ceiling. It is common to hear education level and scholarship status cited as factors and, with decreasing frequency, the sensitive issues of race, religion and cliques (factions). This flows on to the belief that the organization is unfair in terms of performance appraisals and career potential, which invariably impact promotions and postings. Some Regulars continue to harbour parochial and anachronistic expectations of time-based promotions even though performance and potential replaced seniority as key factors more than three decades ago. Another gripe arises from individuals who perceive that they are better than the system—namely, the structure, processes, and people who run it—recognizes. They fault the system for allowing them to fall behind peers within the same cohort or get leapfrogged by those junior in rank and/or appointment. Resignation is the only face-saving measure.

---

[17] "A High-Flying Career", *Special Life! Soldier, Scholar and Leader (Straits Times)*, 18 Mar. 1991, p. 2.

Individual perception extends also to postings, which are sources of excitement but also create tension and disappointment that spur officers to leave active service. Some question the need to serve an appointment (usually junior) twice when the first is deemed "unofficial". Others have their romantic ideals of officership shattered by seemingly mundane desk-bound staff appointments. Then there are those who cite broken promises of a particular posting that never materialized. Such incidents are invariably career-changing setbacks for the more ambitious officers, especially those who missed out on all-important command assignments. This situation is worsened when a perceived lesser candidate in terms of experience or ability is given the prized appointment that one was eying. In unique circumstances individuals have resigned because they did not receive command of a specific unit or sought to avoid serving under a particular superior officer. On extremely rare occasions, officers have attributed resignations to unfairness over being made a scapegoat in incidents beyond their control.

The fifth category contains individuals overwhelmed by disillusionment and cynicism. The intense pressure to recruit has proliferated "brochures and advertisements [that] can sugar-coat many aspects" of the military career.[18] Those in the targeted age bracket continue to be overwhelmingly young and impressionable. Their parents are potentially no wiser. Some become disillusioned when realities set in and the romanticism and heroism portrayed in recruitment campaigns fade while the seeds of "this is not what I signed up for" germinate. This can occur as early as their undergraduate studies, especially when a strong economy offers a gamut of career opportunities. As one general said:

> "If I ever considered leaving it was in university when you see the opportunities classmates had to pursue other occupations. There were fleeting moments where I wondered if I had made the right decision. But once I graduated and got back to the air force it did not matter. [For seven years] it was pretty much a carefree career. I was just following a timetable consisting of Flight School and then university. <smiles>"[19]

Others find themselves trapped in a "stifling bureaucracy" despite an early inclination for a military career. Moving from a ground unit to a large formation HQ or MINDEF can lead to culture shock. At times this is made unbearable by the ubiquitous office politics and occasional condescending attitudes and prima donna antics of more senior officers. Even scholar-officers have been caught in this bind: "scholar-on-scholar" incidents have accounted for, or at the very least

---

[18] "Nothing Less Than the Best for Our Nation", *Scholarship Guide*, 17 Feb. 2009, scholarshipguide.wordpress.com/2009/02/17/nothing-less-than-the-best-for-our-nation, accessed 28 May 2014.

[19] Interview No. 16.

hastened, some leaving service due to undue mental stress. At times in the past, as one general recalled, "Scholars were given bad reports by their formation chiefs so that they could be kept within the formation".[20]

Disillusionment and cynicism also surfaced after poor performance and failure to meet expected standards. Doubts over the future of one's military career became inevitable. The most glaring examples are of commanders who fail to pass muster at unit evaluations or fail to exercise command responsibility. Disciplinary issues ranging from lapses in following procedure (e.g., tenders from suppliers) and questions of integrity to civil offences such as alcohol and traffic violations frequently prove detrimental. The slap on the wrist or blotch on the disciplinary record may not warrant discharge from service, but they obviously prove too much for some people. Next, there have been cases of burnout prevalent in units with hectic and sustained training tempos or due to "stand-by fatigue" in various high-readiness units. Such stressors on repeated tours are a sure recipe for resignation. The greatest concern, however, is over those who resign because of changes in culture or training standards that they deem unacceptable, encapsulated in the notion "this is not the SAF I joined". It is not known whether this is a matter of individual perception and expectation or a reflection of a greater malaise that plagues the defence establishment. Hearsay is certainly rife, but details remain sketchy at best.

Finally, there are miscellaneous reasons for leaving. Some incidents seem *sui generis*, as this admiral opined:

> "Exodus of personnel comes from various sources. Policies. From scholars. There was an incident when scholars from the army were parachuted in who did not understand navy culture which created massive morale problems. Even simple things such as food. Food is a basic morale booster on the ship. There was a three-month trial of pre-packed food by SATS (a catering company), the same type as the catered meals served on SIA flights but it could not replace the taste of fresh rations and skill of our navy chefs. It was not surprising the trial 'failed'."[21]

Other incidents include physical injuries suffered early on before mandatory ground tours are cleared to allow career continuation as staff officers. There are those who leave once the adventure is over—usually after battalion, ship or squadron command, the apex of directly leading and influencing soldiers, sailors and airmen under their charge. Then there are those who due to the very nature of a military career have to resign when they emigrate because of marriage and/ or in search of a better future overseas.

---

[20] Interview No. 28.

[21] Interview No. 04.

4.2.2 Why the Military Elites Considered Leaving

What were the circumstances and reasons for which around half of the interview participants considered leaving the SAF early? The emergent categories pointed to the negative side of people, career progression, bond completion, concerns with overstaying, and personal ambitions. One category is excluded as it has already been alluded to in the previous chapter: the more highly educated (and then-junior) officers were enticed by more appropriate compensation expectations outside the military prior to the salary revision of 1982. The other half of the interview participants indicated that they never considered leaving active duty before retirement. This was best encapsulated by one who simply said: "I never considered leaving. I never saw the reason to once I saw the larger purpose and saw the part of my role in the SAF."[22]

The importance of people in any organization is undeniable. This is even more so for the military in light of its sacred and possibly violent mission. It is people who give the SAF strength and motivate others to join its ranks as Regulars. On the other hand, people also contribute to manpower woes, forcing service personnel to not join the SAF full time or making those in regular service want to leave. One officer was a self-proclaimed maverick and emphatically concluded his interview saying: "You cannot fault me for doing my job, but you can fault me for being an arsehole."[23] Perhaps it was not surprising that he considered leaving, because his character and style often did not sit well with others. Towards the end of his career fatigue had also set in. When asked whether he ever considered leaving service prematurely he mused:

> "When I was an instructor at SAFTI my company 2IC (second-in-command) and I had <pause> let us say we had 'differences'. Maybe he did not like my style of doing things. So I got charged, and my Lieutenant-to-Captain promotion was delayed. I was one of the last in my batch to get promoted, and some of them came to show off their Captain rank and asked me to salute them. B*******. I told them to f*** themselves … When I was finally promoted to Captain, I tell you when it was time to collect promotion certificate from the brigade commander at a parade I was playing billiard in the Officers' Mess. The guy (he was playing against) was trying to get my money (wager), and I was not going to let him. The brigade commander was Colonel [X], a real terror. He walked into the mess and asked: 'Where were you?' Then he gave me the (promotion) cert[ificate] and 14 extra duties. <laughs> I didn't care because I was prepared to leave anytime. [Then] when I was commander (of a unit) I wanted to resign. I went to see [the commandant] (his superior). It was

---

[22] Interview No. 21.

[23] Interview No. 26.

all [Officer Y's] fault, the b******. He was deputy commandant and came to my office to say the windows are dirty. I was always in the field with the training troops. Where do I find time to do area cleaning? He said the office must be spick and span at all times. So I hijacked a platoon of officer cadets to clean the office. Anyway [the commandant] refused my resignation. I said OK but tell [Officer Y] to lay off. When I got promoted to Lieutenant Colonel, [the commandant] said: 'You don't go and *hum tum* (Malay for "hit") [Officer Y]!' <laughs> ... [Finally], [t]hey also gave me the appointment of [formation commander]. Must deal with reservists. Headache. <palms forehead> I wanted to quit. I was tired and very stressed out ... I wanted to quit, and I had reached the end of the road. I submitted my resignation, and [the CDF] suddenly became very nice to me. He rejected the resignation. He said take three weeks leave. When I came back I told him the same thing, so he said take three months more. <laughs> [The service chief] complained that I spoke directly to CDF. I told him to stay out of it; if not, he'd get hurt. I didn't care. I was leaving anyway. [A politician] invited me and my wife to dinner ... He asked me why I wanted to leave. I told him very frankly ... I am a non-scholar ... I [also] told him to keep the army young. Don't ever end up looking like [another country] where you have a 70-year old general looking like Mickey Mouse. And people like me were jamming up the system for the scholars coming up."[24]

For a second officer, his initiative was not taken too lightly and his career almost ended prematurely at a time when pagers (not to mention mobile phones) were yet to appear on the scene:

"I was charged and fined $200 (around two weeks' wages). I was fed up and decided to leave. In those days we have the Hokkien platoon (segregation of soldiers based on language of communication). One of my soldiers got married, but the battalion was in confinement. I was looking for the CO, but he could not be found, so I released the platoon mates for the wedding. CO found out later and decided to charge me. On Friday that week I was charged by the brigade commander, who never asked [for my] reason. The whole situation was stupid, and I did not want to be part of the organization. On Saturday I demanded to see CO OPC. On Monday I was posted out to the training department under Colonel [T]. He told me that I should not leave. <grins> I subsequently became part of the first batch of Wranglers and was soon promoted to Captain."[25]

---

[24] Interview No. 26.

[25] Interview No. 13.

A third officer considered leaving mid-career within three different contexts, two of which illustrate some of the darker encounters in military life:

> "I thought of leaving the SAF three times. The first was at age 32 or 34 to do a PhD in Operations Research (OR). As you know, Singaporeans often look at the name of the university more than the actual course. I was asked to consider [an American university known for OR], but it was a 'no name' university so I stayed. The next was when my mum had a stroke. I am very close to her. The [formation chief] did not allow me to go and see her, so I told him that he could keep the job. He wanted to charge me but never got round to it. I think my godfather and fairy godmother looked after me. <grins> This incident made me ensure that it would never happen to another soldier in the SAF. When I was a battalion CO one of the [subordinate] commanders did not allow his soldier to go and see his dying father. I made sure it did not happen. <shakes head> The last was when I was a weapon staff officer I also wanted to leave. It was over the production of [a weapon] … [due to certain technical details] I said you (manufacturers) can be at the arms show but you will not have the export licence. The [manufacturers] wanted to market the weapon and sell it, so some people tried to implicate me and put me out of the picture. I was investigated for allegedly 'cosying up' to defence contractors. You know you do your best and yet people want to screw you and get you out of the equation."[26]

The final example is from an officer who contemplated leaving the SAF most frequently among all the interviewees. He cited three of his more negative experiences:

> "I had serious thoughts of leaving twice a year on average. There were some incidences [*sic*] that pushed me to the very edge of leaving, and it always revolved around people. The first incident took place when I was 2LT. There was a toxic culture where I was subjected to mental abuse and the treatment I received was disparaging, totally demeaning as an officer. The conduct of certain officers who were more senior was questionable. The second was in [year X] nearing the end of my initial [Y-]year contract. The HR policy offered pensionable service to captains, but 'someone at the top' deemed promotions were taking place too fast, so some of us lieutenants were delayed in promotion to Captain. So instead of pension we were offered a three-year contract. Anyhow I stayed on, got promoted to Captain in [year X+1] and got pensionable service. The third was [a superior] who I think was bipolar and had serious issues. He made me think of leaving service twice a day! I thought then I would not climb any further and my career was probably over."[27]

---

[26] Interview No. 28.

[27] Interview No. 04.

This officer related how a new posting and subsequent superiors—all of whom became military elites in due course—"resurrected" his career through trust in his judgement and abilities. A career he thought was over instead moved from strength to strength and culminated in flag rank.

The experiences of some officers at the hands of others proved instrumental in their thoughts of resigning, but this was not always the case. The SAF is not littered with crazy people. A career that was not moving as planned was at times a good enough reason to question one's role in the military, especially when realistic peer comparisons were made. For one non-scholar-officer, a new posting indicated a halt in career progression when he was tasked with the same job but in a different setting. He explained:

> "I was then shoved to [Y] Division as [an Assistant Principal Staff Officer (PSO)]. I was taking over my ex-OC (company commander, his ex-superior) when I was a PC. By then I was age 29, and I saw my career not going anywhere. You needed to attend SCSC to be promoted, and if you miss it, at that time by age 33, then that's it. I already did [Battalion PSO] tour for three years. There was no progression, and so I asked if that was the life I wanted. Perhaps it was time to leave and learn something else. So I prepared my resignation letter for the [branch head] who was [officer L]. Sometimes I wonder what would have happened if I did not do this and simply continued as an [Assistant PSO]. <smiles> [Officer L] asked me: 'What will make you not leave?' Being young I wanted to do what I liked to do, so I said: 'I wanted to be S3 (operations officer)' because I like ops. They must have thought I was stupid since I already completed a [comparable] staff tour, and for three years, why would I want to do another one? I was willing to move laterally, but that did not happen."[28]

This officer eventually received another posting because of his proven abilities coupled with the branch head's recognition of his potential, and the willingness of the division HQ to release him without citing the omnipresent "manpower shortage" or "unit requirements" clichés. As for scholar-officers, a case in point is provided by former CDF (2003–07) LG (RET) Ng Yat Chung (SAFOS 1980), who felt hard done by as a CPT when he was posted to a logistics billet after his battery command tour while peers received seemingly more prestigious appointments. His disappointment should not come as a surprise given the sentiment that "[t]he transport of food and ammunition was an important activity but hardly glamorous", something likely to resonate with ambitious officers in first-class militaries, both past and present.[29] Yet the episode proved

---

[28] Interview No. 05.

[29] Heinz Guderian, *Achtung—Panzer! The Development of Tank Warfare*, transl. Christopher Duffy, intro. and notes by Paul Harris (London: Cassell, 1999), p. 9.

a blessing in disguise, as LG (RET) Ng reflected: "Logistics in those days was considered the backwater of the Army. It was such a blow—that was the only time I considered quitting the SAF ... It turned out to be one of the best postings and learning experiences I had. Because you get into the innards of the Army and learn what it really takes to keep the Army going."[30]

The third occasion on which some military elites considered leaving was at the completion of their bond or Minimum Term of Service (MTS). None of them counted down to this point of their career, but it allowed individuals to take stock of career progression, the fit and satisfaction with military life, and future opportunities within and beyond the SAF. There were certainly options for most if they seriously contemplated leaving early to mid-career. One officer made contingency plans to address future options rather than preparations to leave: "It was clear that I wanted to do well while serving my bond in my work for the nation. I made a decision in [year X] to start [a postgraduate degree] because in three years' time I have to decide whether to stay or leave (the SAF). I had the options of staying in uniform, the civil service, or going to the private sector. I needed to plan with alternatives."[31]

One interesting point to note is that among the flag officers interviewed, besides those who considered leaving because of financial considerations before 1982, it was those with the most transferable skills who considered leaving at the completion of their bonds. The most notable were pilots and doctors. One considered leaving to continue his love of flying, a point not lost on other pilots: "At some point after the 12-year bond was up I thought of moving to SIA because I wanted to fly. I could not see any other way up except out. The air force was pretty much a fighter pilot's world. I stayed on because a good friend counselled me. Then postgraduate opportunity came and with it a five-year bond. <smiles>"[32]

Such considerations arose because the flying hours clocked by air force pilots usually tapered off after squadron command and gradually decreased as one climbed the hierarchy from LTC onward. It dawned on LG (RET) Ng Chee Meng that any pilot in the operational fighter squadrons had a shelf life. The former CDF realized: "It was time to really seriously look at how to give back in terms of policy-making, and (use) the ground experiences that I had garnered to be the most effective commander that I could be."[33]

---

[30] Ng et al., *Called to Lead*, p. 94.

[31] Interview No. 14.

[32] Interview No. 25.

[33] Koh Eng Beng, "Bidding Farewell to the SAF", *Cyberpioneer*, 4 Sept. 2015.

Similarly, another RSAF general explained: "Flying has its limits as you climb. There are other responsibilities to handle and other skills to develop. The desire to only want to fly has to be moderated. For those who only want to fly as a career the space and opportunity has to be created. That's the only way to continue to fly late into the career."[34] Flying at senior ranks is about maintaining currency and keeping in touch with flying squadrons, as former CAFs related. For example, BG (RET) Michael Teo Eng Cheng tried to "fly twice a week, or at least 10 hours a month".[35] LG (RET) then-BG Bey Soo Khiang similarly flew "once a week" and visited the squadrons "to get a feel of the ground".[36]

While some of the CMCs were set on a full career in the SAF, others, like their non-medical counterparts, used the bond as markers to weigh alternatives. One MO explained his goals:

> "When I signed on it was pensionable. I thought after the bond, when the training is over, I thought I would leave and go back to private practice, traditional medicine. There was a five-year bond for postgraduate studies. I thought it was a point to consider after the bond, but I was given better and better challenges. I would say I was one of the pioneers in [a specialized field of military medicine]. I was able to practise [specialized military] medicine for a good ten years after graduation in [year X] to set up [a specialized medical centre in the SAF]."[37]

Another MO explained:

> "I intended to serve for six or 12 years to live out the career goal to be a surgeon. But being a military surgeon you had the challenges to maintain currency. Being qualified is no issue, but maintaining currency in skills is difficult. [Medical specialization Y] was also an important area. The SAF saw a need in the area of [the said specialization], and I could do both. There was an opportunity to grow something. If I apportioned my career into three parts it would look like this. <draws a diagram> After first six, I was offered a job in MOH but CMC offered me an important job. After second six, I had options in NUH (National University Hospital) and NUS but CMC asked me to help him establish certain things. After these 12 years I was quite sure I was going to stay on until the end (retirement)."[38]

---

[34] Interview No. 16.

[35] "Yes Sir, It's a Dream and Love That Got 2 to the Top", *Straits Times*, 1 Nov. 1985, p. 11.

[36] "Meet SAF's Four New Generals", *Straits Times*, 27 June 1992, p. 26.

[37] Interview No. 20.

[38] Interview No. 18.

A third echoed:

> "In hospital I had no regrets [about signing on]. It was just to cross the different milestones. My life was structured by events. I had to complete my training in three years, so the preoccupation was to pass exams. No thoughts of regret or 'wrong' choice. I was under the impression of being able to do both military and [medical specialization Z]. I intended to finish six years first then decide if I should stay on. I was offered the pension in the sixth year."[39]

The fourth category of flag officers who considered leaving questioned whether they had overstayed their welcome in the armed forces. One officer was concerned with the maturing pipeline of scholar-officers who appeared in increasing numbers among the senior ranks and appointments. He was prepared to make way for others but, like an obedient soldier, continued as long as his services were required:

> "In [year X] before I went [overseas for a SAF-sponsored course] I thought that upon my return to Singapore it would be a good time to leave the SAF. I went to see [the defence minister] about it, and he said, 'I just became defence minister, how can you leave?' <smiles> So I remained, but mentally I was prepared to leave anytime after [the course]. You have all the young scholars moving up. They are more restless and ambitious. I didn't want to come to the office one day and see a bucket in front of my door waiting for me to kick it."[40]

Another general weighed options beyond the SAF and in light of opportunities to continue adding value to the organization:

> "I considered leaving, but this was the pull from the outside and not a push from the inside (the SAF). I did ask myself if I was overstaying my welcome. I felt that there were interesting prospects out of uniform and I might even be doing better. But I also felt that I was still needed and I could contribute, and this contribution was enough to offset the pull. In fact, if I wanted to leave my family would be concerned and ask: 'Are you sure?' <laughs>"[41]

The fifth and final category included officers who considered leaving because of personal ambitions that could be fulfilled only beyond the confines of military service. One harboured the long-standing ambition to experience living overseas, but circumstances dictated otherwise:

---

[39] Interview No. 23.

[40] Interview No. 19.

[41] Interview No. 22.

"I was thinking of migrating to gain wider experience of living overseas and thought [an English-speaking country] looked quite good. A week after submitting my resignation I went for medical check-up and MSD also reminded me of the OSA (Official Secrets Act). It was around this time that the [said country's] economy took a downturn, and so I withdrew my resignation. I thought my career *liao* (Hokkien for 'finished') already, so I commenced applying for jobs. I applied to a shipping company, but they told me: 'You have a career in the army so you better stay on.' <smiles> Eventually my career continued, and I went to [Staff College] where I graduated as one of the top students and received my desire for command. Yes, I was also surprised my career was not impacted in any adverse manner. <grins>"[42]

For a second officer his ambition was to continue a lifelong dedication in leadership and learning but without the confines of rank and hierarchy. In some ways this was an extension of his motivation for a military career, which was to make a difference in the lives of conscripts who did not want to be in uniform. Policy changes also intervened in a career that proved fortuitous:

"I considered leaving because my belief is in leading beyond [the association with one's] rank and not because I did not like the SAF. If I stayed on in the SAF anything I did had rank attached to it. I had the desire to lead without rank, to lead by who I am, to be among equals. [Accepting] the postgraduate study award carried with it a five-year bond, which meant more of rank. But I thought 'stay on and see' [what unfolds]. Besides, there were still NSFs around, so my work was not done. The next time I considered leaving was when I was 44. The retirement age then was 45, so I thought: 'Why wait until then?' I informed [CDF], but he told me the policy was changing to 47 and asked if I could stay because there was a gap [in the succession of senior officers]. There were no promises made to me of future appointments. I stayed on and it became 'NS' for once. <smiles>"[43]

All the flag officers invariably did not leave the SAF before reaching retirement despite having thoughts of doing so. A few were undoubtedly prevented by human or economic intervention. Often it was fleeting disillusionment—not something that pushed them to take the step of actually starting work in another organization.

4.3 Transactional Commitment

If the interview participants considered leaving the SAF but stopped short, or if they never considered leaving, there must have been reasons for it. This

---

[42] Interview No. 11.

[43] Interview No. 07.

section places the spotlight on transactional commitment, which is grounded in egoism, where the individual is the ultimate beneficiary of his goals and actions.[44] Sensitizing concepts indicate that transactional commitment occurs for various reasons. An officer remained on active duty because he or she had contextual obligations (normative commitment) to fulfil in return for the SAF's investment in professional development through training, education, and experiences at various stages of any career. Then there are other transactional reasons, such as remuneration, career progression, and opportunity costs associated with leaving the military, such as lower salary, fewer benefits and barriers to entry (i.e., esoteric knowledge and experiences) for other industries. It must be stressed that an outstanding bond or MTS, salary and career progression are not automatic indicators of transactional commitment because they can be correlated with, but not necessarily be the cause of, an officer staying on. The following subsections and examples illustrate such complexities.

4.3.1 Obligation

Every Regular officer has a normative commitment to the SAF through bonded service for scholarships (SAF or PSC transferred to the SAF) and/or an MTS. The period of commitment varies depending on the scholarship, training award, course(s) attended and vocation.[45] The lengths of contractual service are invariably extended (unless served concurrently) depending on the additional military course(s) attended, postgraduate studies, specific postings, and receipt of a meritorious promotion.[46] While details differ, these practices are certainly not unique to the SAF and are common practice in other militaries.

The interview participants took their initial obligations in one of two ways. The first came from the broad view that it was non-negotiable and must be

---

[44] C. Daniel Batson, *The Altruism Question: Toward a Social-Psychological Answer* (Hillsdale: Lawrence Erlbaum Associates, 1991), pp. 8–9; Bruce J. Avolioa and Edwin E. Locke, "Contrasting Different Philosophies of Leader Motivation: Altruism versus Egoism", *Leadership Quarterly* 13, 2 (2002): 171; C. Daniel Batson, Nadia Ahmad and E.L. Stocks, "Four Forms of Prosocial Motivation: Egoism, Altruism, Collectivism, and Principlism", in *Social Motivation*, ed. David Dunning (New York and Hove: Psychology Press, 2011), p. 106.

[45] Scholarship recipients who are not qualified pilots serve a six-year bond, while qualified pilots (rotary or fixed-wing) serve theirs within an MTS of 12 years.

[46] A non-graduate is commissioned a 2LT and forwarded to LTA a year later, after which promotions are merit based. A non-medical graduate with a university degree recognized by MINDEF is commissioned an LTA and forwarded to CPT 18 months later followed by merit-based promotions. A combat MO is commissioned a CPT and forwarded to MAJ upon completion of postgraduate/specialized medical studies followed by merit-based promotion. A service (non-combat) MO is commissioned an LTA and is usually a National Serviceman.

fulfilled, that it was a period to find the necessary fit for a career in the military. Some explanations were straightforward. One general quipped: "No matter what, I would have served out my bond because I could not afford to break it."[47] Another simply said: "At signing on, an eight-year bond was attached so just try it (military life)."[48] For others, a combination of factors shaped their circumstances. Most of these officers signed on at a time when Singapore was in transition from a colonial port to an industrialized city-state. They often did not have the option of breaking the bond or incurring financial penalties for not meeting associated MTS, due to their lower-middle socio-economic background. They could ill afford to "buy out" the bond, and salaries received frequently financed household expenses.

One general reflected on the scholarship benefits that enticed him to join the SAF in the first place and underlined the bond as a "trial" period:

> "The bond was for eight years. For me breaking bond was never an issue or a possibility. My allowance went to subsidizing the family, so I could not afford to do so even if I wanted to. <grins> My elder brother could have probably received university education, but my father suggested that he work to help support the family. This initial eight years was bonded, but it also gave me a sense of military life and what the career entails. I wanted to do a good job in any case. Some liked it (military life) and some did not."[49]

Another general who was also primarily attracted by the scholarship viewed the bond as an opportunity to fulfil the ambition to fly:

> "In my second year I joined the university air squadron, but as a foreigner you have lower priority [compared to the locals] and so [I] ended up sitting around and doing nothing much. But I started flying during the [university] vacation. Every summer I was at Changi Air Base flying. I was actually offered a [doctoral] research scholarship at [the same university], but I knew I had to come back. I could not fight the government. <laughs> I also could not afford to [break the bond] because my salary went into supporting the family. I was also looking forward to fly. <laughs>"[50]

For a third general it was a simple case of fulfilling the bond before taking stock of whether to remain in service:

> "The initial contract was for 12 years with a bond of eight. I wanted to complete the bond first and then see (progress and options). In fact, while

---

[47] Interview No. 11.

[48] Interview No. 12.

[49] Interview No. 10.

[50] Interview No. 25.

> I was still at university my undergraduate supervisor enticed me to take up [doctoral] studies in medical engineering. The area of research was related to the heart. But as you know, the SAF then had a very strict policy on postgraduate studies."[51]

The offers for postgraduate research opportunities that these officers received upon completion of their undergraduate studies at reputable universities bore testament to their high academic standards, but the offers were invariably turned down. In fact, this precedent was set by Lee Hsien Loong after he completed an honours degree in mathematics and a diploma in computing. He declined an offer for further research work in mathematics and told Cambridge University: "No, thank you, I've got to go back. This is my country and my obligation and I do not want to be elsewhere where my contribution doesn't make much of a difference."[52]

The initial obligation was a non-issue from a second vantage point. Although there were contractual terms and moral obligations to be met, they were peripheral because officers wanted to serve—not because they were obliged or needed to be in service. This does not imply that they never considered leaving the SAF short of retirement, but they started off quite set on staying beyond the bonded period, possibly to the point of retirement. One admiral explained: "The terms and conditions were an eight-year bond for the scholarship and emplacement on pensionable service. I was prepared for a full career, to serve until retirement. You could say the bond was of no consequence and that the eight years were irrelevant to me."[53]

Another interview participant was not placed on pension initially, but he acknowledged: "The contract at that time was for seven years, but I was mentally prepared for life."[54] MG (RET) Ng Chee Khern, who saw himself as an accountant if not a fighter pilot, framed his commitment in moral terms: "If I had gone out to be a private citizen after my bond was up, I would have felt guilty. In truth, I would have deprived someone else of the opportunities I got."[55]

Bonds and MTSs did not exist only in the initial stages of a career; others invariably followed as an officer developed professionally and ascended the ranks. Take this individual's experience: "I had an eight-year bond to January

---

[51] Interview No. 02.

[52] See interview with Béla Bollobás in Y.K. Leong, "Béla Bollobás: Graphs Extremal and Random", *Imprints* (Institute for Mathematical Sciences, NUS) (11 Sept. 2007): 21; and Han et al., *Lee Kuan Yew*, pp. 76–7.

[53] Interview No. 17.

[54] Interview No. 04.

[55] Lynn Lee, "All the President's Men and Women", *Straits Times*, 17 Aug. 2007, p. 30.

[year X]. When I took the [master's degree at a prestigious foreign university] there was an additional three years. It should have been an additional five, but there was a rule then which stated an individual cannot be bonded to the civil service for more than 11 years. Therefore the bond was an additional three and not five. <laughs>"[56]

Extended bonds and MTS's were quite the norm for military elites whose careers progressed more rapidly that their peers' in order for them to make one-star and above within the prevailing age of retirement. This meant checking off on merit-based promotions, milestone courses, command and senior staff appointments, postgraduate studies, and perhaps time at War College. Each milestone signalled an officer's progress and his services appreciated in return for a mandatory extended period of service. This is still the case and illustrates how the defence establishment retains talented officers independent of their individual convictions. Most important, bonds and MTS's provide an effective means of keeping well-performing individuals on active service until retirement. One officer recalled his decision to stay on: "… my bond was extended after attendance at various courses, and later we were offered pensionable service. Finally we switched to the SAVER scheme, and that was when I decided to stay until retirement."[57]

Another officer talked about the system's effectiveness in retaining his services: "The lifestyle worked with me, but you don't think [you would stay] 25 years. <laughs> Four, five years maybe, but after the postgraduate studies I was sure I would stay until retirement. The upgrading opportunities at university were very important for staying in the SAF. The bonds were also reasonable, so I had no issue."[58]

The bond was not always a clearly delineated matter of staying on in uniform. Proven abilities attracted attention in much the same way as brilliant undergraduates. As one CMC recalled: "I received offers to return to the public health service, even a proposal to buy out the bond. I did well (for postgraduate studies) and was advised that I should pursue a career as [a civilian medical specialist]. It was put to me before the end of the day, but I rejected such offers because I wanted to fulfil the bond and did not want to be a bond-breaker."[59]

It can be concluded that normative commitment based on obligations in the SAF is manifested through the contractual practice and extension of bonds and MTS's. Yet, there were also instances where an officer felt obligated to remain

---

[56] Interview No. 14.

[57] Interview No. 02.

[58] Interview No. 22.

[59] Interview No. 23.

due to a moral conviction based on the SAF's investment in his professional development. Then there are the cases where obligations proved superfluous as the commitment to remain on active service was neither contractually nor morally based.

4.3.2 Remuneration

In chapter 3 it was revealed that salary was a secondary motivation for the military elites to join the SAF. The reasons cited included the need to contribute to household expenditures; the desire for a salary instead of subsistence allowance during two to three years of NS; the intention to save for planned expenditure such as education and housing; and starting SAF salaries being better than the private sector, especially for those with lower formal education. In this subsection, remuneration was not frequently cited as a reason to stay on. In fact, salary was a source of anxiety for graduate officers who were paid less handsomely than their scholar-officer counterparts. The 1982 salary revision and subsequent periodic reviews allayed concerns over remuneration, yet salary was not a reason for commitment to the SAF. It simply eliminated monetary reasons for leaving. This is not to say remuneration was unimportant. It was more a reflection of salaries having met daily needs (and more) so that officers could freely focus on their role as military professionals.

This was not simply a matter of paying lip service that "money did not matter". A commercial pilot made twice as much as an air force pilot before the pay revision of 1982.[60] One general overcame this challenge and focused instead on the "rich" reward of commanding a fighter squadron and the familial sense of belonging:

> "As CO all the [squadron] personnel were on base. Married personnel had their quarters, and singles lived in the mess. At the squadron functions everyone and their family members joined in, so it was truly 'family' in the sense of the word. When there was a recall we just moved from quarters to the flight line and we were fully functional, operational very quickly. Nobody complained, and it was a good atmosphere. There was the sense of belonging and a sense of concern among squadron members. The sense of camaraderie. But the pay was still not attractive. <laughs> For me, if the present factor (current state) plus the 'taste' factor (intangible rewards) is greater than the future pay I could get from outside the air force then I should stay. The bottom line is that pay must meet needs, first as a single then for the family. A positive organizational structure draws commitment

---

[60] Lim, "The Most Exciting … Most Exacting …", p. 15.

from you to stay and do well. You could look forward to promotion, recognition such as medals, and of course a pay rise. <laughs>"[61]

An admiral expressed similar concerns:

"There was a possibility of leaving in [year Z], but in 1982 there was a salary revision which helped a lot. After 1982 pay was no longer an issue, and my thoughts of leaving dissipated. It was a matter of 'see what happens'. Before that the navy was underpaid and overworked. No annual promotions, and you had to take a promotion exam before you could be shortlisted for the promotion interview. [In fact] I was actually told by HR admin[istration] that the combat graduate scheme was no longer in force. I went to MINDEF general orders to prove my case and saw that it was still in force! So I went for a promotion interview chaired by (then-CDF) Winston Choo. I received my Captain which meant less disparity of pay and there were also not so many Captains in those days."[62]

While these officers tolerated low wages they were perhaps the exception rather than the norm. The increasing attrition rates among Regular officers before 1982 were exacerbated by low recruitment numbers. Appealing to values and professionalism is one thing. Pragmatism kicked in as Singapore developed economically and the standard of living improved. It was not surprising that the 1982 revision ensured SAF salaries were competitive with private sector offerings.[63] This was especially notable for officers with the most transferable and specialized skills yet low in supply such as pilots and MOs. One general continued:

"The 1982 pay revision came about in the air force because we were expanding very rapidly adding aircraft, helicopters and were training more pilots. But it was insufficient because people leave for SIA so we needed to see how we could retain them. The pay revision allowed us to retain experienced guys, and we looked to match SIA if possible. Besides the increase in rank pay there were also command allowances, and some specialized allowances depending on the aircraft you flew."[64]

Salary revision was not the panacea to competition from SIA. External consultants also raised uneasy questions, and the HAYS Job Evaluation Method in particular established the relative importance of jobs within an organization.[65] In one

---

[61] Interview No. 24.

[62] Interview No. 15.

[63] "Air Force Pilots Get More Pay", *Pioneer* (Dec. 1992): 15.

[64] Interview No. 24.

[65] Tan Cheong Hin and Lim Lay Ching, "Potential Appraisal: The Shell Appraisal System", NTU School of Accountancy and Business Working Paper Series, No. 29 (1993), p. 20.

instance it was "asked how can the squadron CO only be a major when he was in charge of assets worth millions?"[66] Officer ranks were soon commensurate with appointments, and salaries better matched responsibilities.

As for doctors, they needed to be compensated well enough to forgo more lucrative opportunities but not at a level where money became the reason to remain on active service. One CMC explained how salaries for MOs were formulated:

> "Technically MOs are paid two ranks up. Although you are not promoted in rank you are also not slowed in salary. There is corporate cohort comparison with your peers in medical school. But you could not compare with some of the surgeons, so there is some sacrifice there. And while you cannot get surgeon's pay SAF also makes sure you won't be the last among peers; if not it will be hard or impossible to attract and retain doctors. The salary is still reasonably good but most importantly you must be able to say: 'Hey, you can serve your country.'"[67]

Another CMC added:

> "SAF pay is comfortable. Comparable to MOH. The SAF salary attracts a 10 to 20 per cent premium, so for a $3,000 start (in the 1990s) you are looking at least $300 more. Doctors at hospitals also receive allowances, so the pay is comparable. Of course, depending on speciality and grade the hospitals can be higher. The SAF pays you well enough to let you focus on the job, to set up a family. Let me say the pay is comfortable but not an avenue where you will be rich."[68]

For non-MOs the prevailing view was that salary was not a reason to stay on but it was "continuing and sufficient", which eliminated the need to leave for greener financial pastures.[69] A general expressed gratitude "that MINDEF's remuneration framework recognizes the onerous nature of the military career. It was good to have but not the main concern."[70] Another echoed: "Salary is important but not a major consideration (of whether to stay on). The SAF pays you very well, so there is no need to think of it. There is no need to think of bread and butter issues. In fact, there is enough spare cash for cohesion activities."[71]

Yet another MO who made general/admiral, after taking into account the consistent salary revisions, even considered the pay scale relatively unattractive:

---

[66] Interview No. 24.

[67] Interview No. 20.

[68] Interview No. 18.

[69] Huntington, *The Soldier and the State*, p. 15.

[70] Interview No. 14.

[71] Interview No. 05.

"Salary SAF-wise it is not a plus. Compared to my peers [in the private sector] I could be earning more, but I do it because I love the job. There are always new changes. Furthermore, breaking the comfort zone is designed into the job."[72]

This is not to say that empirical evidence refuted the existence of a comfortable and consistently increasing income from morphing into a basis for staying on active duty. It certainly does happen, as one officer said: "Married with kids you think about the long-term future and also your commitment on the house."[73] With few exceptions, the opportunity cost of leaving the SAF invariably results in a pay cut, perhaps even starting from scratch, as a military career is unlikely to provide the requisite experience for higher-paying industries. This is unless one is hand-picked and parachuted into GLCs or ministries. This chain of thought lends credence to the countervailing view to leave the SAF once service obligations are met and enter another industry (and increasingly overseas) while one is still marketable. The initial decrease in salary would prove insignificant in the long run. Leaving early also means avoiding the disadvantage of mandatory mid-life retirement in the 40s and transition into a second career. This decision, however, is often made on the basis of career progression.

4.3.3 Progression

The overwhelming majority of interview participants indicated that remuneration after 1982 was a secondary reason at best for their career commitment. The significance of this point is best viewed in relation to expectations of career progression. This is in no way unrealistic or unique to the military in light of keen societal competition and the need to keep up appearances and be seen as making progress. As 1WO (RET) Mohammed Saleh Bin Amir Khan Surattee, former Sergeant Major of the School of Naval Training and later RSM of the RSN, observed back in 1983: "... youngsters today are an impatient lot ... They want almost instant promotions and rewards ... Most young people today dream of working only in air-conditioned comfort."[74]

The rank structures for the SAF Officer Corps, the Warrant Officers and Specialists (WOSPEC) Corps—as the NCOs have been known since the early 1990s—and the Military Domain Experts Scheme (MDES) have expanded at different junctures to address the general need for conspicuous progression. In 1992 MINDEF added five ranks to the then four-rank WOSPEC structure, which afforded "greater [career] mobility and, indirectly, attract[ed] more people

---

[72] Interview No. 07.

[73] Interview No. 10.

[74] "Wives on Voyages with Husbands", *Navy News* (May 1983): 4.

to join" the SAF amidst decreasing birth rates and increasing competition for manpower.[75] The tenth and 11th WOSPEC ranks were added in 2009 and 2012 respectively.[76] The nine-tier officer rank structure expanded to ten in 2010 with the introduction of the SLTC rank after the retirement age was raised in 2009.[77]

The MDES, established in 2010 to operate in parallel with the officer and WOSPEC corps, also had to accommodate the need for conspicuous rank progression. The MDES ranks from ME1 to ME8 correspond to an eight-tier hierarchy spread over a career designed with possible retirement at age 60.[78] For graduate Military Experts, there are only five ranks (ME4 to ME8 albeit with multiple grades within each) to the apex of the MDES structure. This means relatively long periods between visible promotions in rank. The simple solution came in March 2013, when enhanced name tags were introduced indicating the rank, grade and name of the Military Expert.[79] This means a promotion in grade is now accompanied with a conspicuous change in name tag. The need to be seen to progress is not unique to the SAF—slow rates of promotion had adverse effects also on the retention of AOs in the AS, which necessitated the implementation of faster promotions and more pay grades.[80]

The interview participants measured their career progression in a few ways. The first came through estimated time norms congruent with one's education level. This proved unreliable as progress was relative and measured differently depending on the era. In the 1960s to early-1980s, making MAJ was an achievement in itself, as was the case of LTC to the mid-1990s, and since then

---

[75] The ranks of Sergeant (SGT), Staff Sergeant (SSG), Warrant Officer Class Two (WO2) and Warrant Officer Class One (WO1) were expanded to nine: Third Sergeant (3SG), Second Sergeant (2SG), First Sergeant (1SG), SSG, Master Sergeant (MSG), Second Warrant Officer (2WO), First Warrant Officer (1WO), Master Warrant Officer (MWO) and Senior Warrant Officer (SWO). See "New Professional Corps of WOs and Corps of Specialists", *Pioneer* (Mar. 1992): 21–5.

[76] The rank of Third Warrant Officer (3WO) was introduced in 2009 and Chief Warrant Officer (CWO) in 2012. See Glen Choo, Bjorn Teo and Shawn Tay, "Warrant Officer Corps Reaches New Heights", *Army News* 201 (June 2012): 12–5.

[77] Ian Cheong, "The New SAF Career Schemes: Meeting Future Challenges Today", *Army News* 165 (Apr.–May 2009): 6.

[78] The MDES rank structure runs from Military Expert 1 (ME1) to ME8 (one-star equivalent), with university graduates commencing at ME4.

[79] Lim Wei Liang, "Enhanced Name-Tag Presentation Ceremony for Army Engineers", *Army News* 212 (June 2013): 5.

[80] David Seth Jones, "Recent Reforms in Singapore's Administrative Elite: Responding to the Challenges of a Rapidly Changing Economy and Society", *Asian Journal of Political Science* 10, 2 (Dec. 2002): 80–1.

it has been making COL. A second yardstick was to make relative comparisons with peers within a commissioning cohort or batch of scholarship recipients (if applicable), as one officer revealed: "I stayed on in the SAF based on a relative comparison of how I was doing. Am I progressing relative to my batch of scholars? I mean, there was an expectation to move (up the ranks). Towards the end of my initial period of service I was progressing. The second fastest (in my batch)."[81]

Others made comparisons with peers:

> "In 1987 you look at your contemporaries outside (of the SAF) and you are not doing so badly. You were doing interesting things. In 1989 there was the Pedra Branca and the refugee issues. I had autonomy in running operations. HQ ran operations, and the fleet was more focused on training. I was happy and took things one step at a time. If I was stagnant for several years then the issue of leaving would have featured. In the 1980s being a LTC was good. In the 1990s as a COL was OK."[82]

Not progressing to a respectable level based on realistic expectations would certainly have raised the question of whether the military was a suitable career. This was especially so for scholar-officers who could serve in other government ministries or pursue a private sector career. This might seem self-serving, but a majority of the military elites were not preoccupied with progress because their performances ensured their timely progress. For others, progress was a non-issue because they never thought that they would better mid-level expectations.

Transactional commitment arises when the individual officer is the ultimate beneficiary of his goals and actions. Such commitment within the military context usually takes the form of service obligation(s), salary and career progression. These were often secondary considerations for the flag officers to remain on active duty. When an officer accepted a scholarship, training course, promotion or appointment, he was aware of the service obligations. For those who were focused on monetary compensation, the military would pale in comparison to for-profit industries. Promotions were important albeit secondary considerations in the career commitment of generals and admirals. The simple explanation is that their performance and estimated potential resulted in an acceptable pace of career progression. Yet such views are placed at risk with the proliferation of fast promotions and high salaries to entice and retain personnel. The normalization of this practice risks turning the privileges of the military elite into entitlements for the rank and file. A one-star who once headed a personnel department said:

> "One important question is to ask if the younger generation is resilient in matters such as promotion and salary. The SAF pays a comparatively

---

[81] Interview No. 02.

[82] Interview No. 15.

competitive salary to compensate the serviceman for the unique skill sets in the profession and the shorter career. But some are not contented. They want to have the cake and eat it and then eat another piece. If the organization starts to pander to such people then we must ask: 'Are we retaining the right people?'"[83]

The "right" people who ascended into the Aristocracy of Armed Talent proved resilient in transactional considerations but were anchored by their stronger transformational commitment to the profession.

4.4 Transformational Commitment

Transactional commitment is centred on egoism, and for the military elites this was a mix of service obligation, remuneration and career progression. Such factors proved secondary in many instances because they were insufficient on their own to keep the officers in service and perform at the highest levels until retirement. They needed to transit towards transformational commitment by finding reasons to stay in service for altruistic purposes—to serve a greater good and maximize the welfare of others. The next two subsections cover these factors, namely, the camaraderie with peers, superiors and subordinates; the military profession; and the sacred mission of the SAF. The third subsection follows with examples of dangers and challenges faced by certain flag officers during their respective careers.

4.4.1 The People

Fellow service personnel are crucial in establishing commitment to a military career. The people referred to by the interviewees were comrades-in-arms who started out as soldiers, sailors, airmen, fellow officers and superiors in the battalion, ship or squadron. This circle invariably expanded as the military elites climbed the ranks; but the underlying theme that surfaced, albeit under different contexts, was their genuine care and concern for those under their charge and a willingness to learn from those around them. It is people who are the soul and heart of the military, and this differentiates them from the machines they operate. One general underlined the importance of people using an example from his tour as a brigade commander:

> "When I was at [a prestigious university] I asked [MINDEF] for a two-year tour. Before me, people looked at brigade command as a stepping stone. I told my superiors that two years would allow me to know the trade. To be a commander you must be on the ground. You need to learn and be able

---

[83] Interview No. 06.

to relate to people, especially the warrant officers and specialists. During the brigade exercises, I got to relate and learn in two aspects. First, to fight combined arms you need to learn about manoeuvre. If you are humble, you get to learn a lot. Second, it also allows you to learn about people and for people to know about you. People get to believe in you. You also know who knows their stuff because you observe and not only rely on hearsay. You get to see who the *jia jua* (Hokkien slang indicating 'skiving') kings are. Being close to people on the ground is vital for those who command. It is only this that will ensure people will follow you when the button is pushed in the time of crisis."[84]

Another general had a philosophical approach to people within his concept of leadership:

"Listen, especially at exit interviews, because that is when people will say everything, or they will say nothing about the tour. That is why we must always be 'Mission first, People always'. Leadership is tempered by previous experiences and extrapolated to make decisions. It is not something which can be taught. How do you make people do things themselves because they want to? [At times] I have an attitude problem because I just say it. I also trust my people because they return hundred-fold. I use people well, but I don't manipulate people. Also, don't be opportunistic. One measurement is when people leave. Do you behave differently toward them because you were only interested in what they can give? Give opportunity to people and also provide a safety net (to avoid detrimental failure) to develop competency, compliance and a calling [for the profession]. If they are in the wrong field you must transform their mindset, but at the core they must remain an individual and keep their own identity."[85]

A third officer contextualized the role people played in service commitment after he reneged on an original plan to continue studies. He looked forward to remuneration and promotions, but these proved secondary:

"Above all, I did not leave because there was still a sense of purpose. I was doing something useful which was bigger than me. For the rest of my career there were certainly disappointments along the way, but not to the point of 'throwing paper' (colloquial expression for 'resigning'). I had certain obligations to the organization and the men under me, both Regulars and NSmen. They looked up to [me] for leadership. I had to be there for them when chips are down and when odds are not in our favour. So I need to be there for the men. It says a lot if you thrown in the towel for the 'not so right' reasons. If you have the right values and reasons for joining the SAF they will endear and endure. Hold true to them and you

---

[84] Interview No. 10.

[85] Interview No. 28.

will press on. I also asked myself if the organization treated me well and the answer was 'it did'."[86]

A fourth officer stressed the urgency and seriousness of the military profession, its values, and the SAF's reason for being. He gave an example from his CO tour of how he inculcated a sense of mission and a familial sense of belonging into the battalion from day one:

> "To me, military life is about buddies, friends, going through shit together. As a PC I learned the importance of caring for your men. Going back to the unit is like returning to family ... I like to work with people, to develop people. I liked command not because of the authority but because I wanted to make a difference. I stayed in the SAF because it was a Profession-of-Arms, not just a career. I was preparing to send people into harm's way. It was really clear. It was a commitment to be mission ready. The values system is also important. It is something I live by. The core values were formulated in 1986 and [promulgated] SAF-wide in 1996, but I have been living them all these while. It was already internalized. Singing 'duty, honour, country' in OCS inculcated these core values. As CO I gave the first day to the companies. Section commanders had the morning, platoon commanders in the afternoon, and OCs in the evening. The next morning there would be a parade and then I will gather the whole battalion. I would remind them of the Japanese occupation and my message was clear. 'You do not want others to defend what is ours.' You do not want others to do it."[87]

The practice of senior officer cadets at OCS drilling "duty, honour, country"—a line made famous by Douglas MacArthur's farewell speech at West Point—into the minds of junior OCTs was widespread by the mid-1970s.[88] It evidently proved effective in the case of the officer cited above. Mantras aside, working with people to achieve mission success was challenging but gave great joy to commanders at all ranks:

> "I thoroughly enjoyed my career. There were tremendous challenges in meeting the military's mission. There were plans and technology to see through to initial capability and the task of developing officers and men. The camaraderie of the people you serve with and the pride and passion that comes with the job. You had to imbue pride in people and to develop and encourage passion."[89]

---

[86] Interview No. 06.

[87] Interview No. 05.

[88] "From Start: A New Way of Life", *Pioneer* (Oct. 1975): 22–3.

[89] Interview No. 14.

While one reason to stay in the armed forces is the people, it can at times lead to heartbreak. This is epitomized by peacetime fatalities. A general related his experience working with subordinate armoured units:

> "Tank overturned and people die. I got walloped by one mother. The toughest thing is going to the home and telling the mother and father. They are traumatized. It is a traumatic experience for everyone. The worst is when people lose life. There was this incident when [a serviceman] drowned in Area D (a designated live-fire area). [Officer Y] was the CO. People were worried about [officer Y] and whether he would get into trouble but not about the victim. The body was not washed, still full of mud and the parents were coming. So I said: 'Come on lah this is someone's son.' <shakes head>"[90]

Another highlighted the dangers inherent in an organization entrusted to fight and win the nation's conflicts, yet said this was never an excuse for fatalities:

> "We train hard and realistically and because of this the possibility of negative consequences are there. As commander [of an armoured brigade] a tank overturned and fortunately there were no casualties. On another occasion I remember a soldier being hospitalized for pneumonia while on an overseas exercise and he almost did not make it. You don't want anything to befall your men. Their families do not look at causes. They only know [their loved one] died under your watch, so whoever you bring out for training your must also bring them home safely."[91]

More recently, BG (RET) Lim Teck Yin reflected on the loss of three soldiers from his company during a night heli-rappelling exercise at Peirce Reservoir on 16 July 1990. The helicopter co-pilot released the ropes prematurely, before ascertaining that the commandos had reached the ground, which caused them to plunge 26 metres to the ground.[92] Lim disclosed in a November 2017 interview with Channel NewsAsia that the incident left an ineffaceable sense of guilt and was the "darkest moment" of his three decades (1980–2011) of active service:

> "It is one thing to know that we put our lives on the line every day but a totally different thing to have to manage that loss … One of the soldiers we lost was actually not scheduled on that exercise. One of the other soldiers fell ill that day and I asked this soldier to join in. He could have

---

[90] Interview No. 26.

[91] Interview No. 06.

[92] "3 Soldiers Die during Training", *Straits Times*, 18 July 1990, p. 1; "Military Funeral for Commando", *Straits Times*, 19 July 1990, p. 3; "Commandos Resume Helicopter Rappelling", *Pioneer* (Aug. 1990): 15; "Death of 3 Commandos: RSAF Pilot Fined $8,000", *Straits Times*, 22 Nov. 1990, p. 2; "Pilot Who Caused 3 Deaths Discharged from SAF", *Straits Times*, 7 Dec. 1990, p. 2.

avoided the whole thing if I hadn't done that. But what can I do? We have to move on."[93]

The possibility of fatalities has wide-ranging repercussions for the SAF and impacts society's trust in the armed forces. For these reasons it has been continually stressed that every serviceman—and not just commanders—must be responsible for and have a vested interest in those they serve with. A former service chief highlighted the need to "Mitigate risk. My personal observation is that accident rates are very low during exercises, but it occurs more frequently in day-to-day situations. During exercises, people are focused and 'on the ball' but once 'end-ex' (end of exercise), yes, once *pang kang* (Hokkien for 'finish work') is declared all hell breaks loose. <frowns>"[94]

This does not mean making training safer by making it less realistic. That, after all, would not mitigate but simply transfer risk, as a former division commander (DIV COMD) opined: "We lose heart when we say 'exercise play' only. If standards decrease, it is a slippery road. There must be no compromise on standards. We must always take the view that we are training people to save their lives. Do it well and do it once."[95]

For the military elites, this translated into taking on personal responsibility for those under their charge. Another former formation chief explained this in detail within the context of military professionalism. His unwavering stance on training was clear:

> "I was lucky not to have suffered fatalities during training. But I made myself lucky. I prepared the training safety officers to make sure they knew their roles. They had to sit for tests. It was my responsibility to ensure the safety team knew what they were to do. Check the risks and minimize it. They must know the rationale behind what we do. This takes time and commitment. There is a need to institutionalize it. People do it well because of seriousness and not because their heads are on the chopping block. Training must never be made safer by making it easier. Good training simulates a wartime environment and also increases the confidence level of those involved. Training is the main duty of a peacetime army. And you train for war. That is the driving force. You must always ask: 'What is sacrosanct? What is fundamental? Are you preparing the army, and is this followed by enforcement?' There must always be

[93] Bharati Jagdish, "On the Record: Lim Teck Yin, CEO of SportSG", Channel NewsAsia, 3 Dec. 2017.

[94] Interview No. 25.

[95] Interview No. 28.

clear expectations and enforcement. As a leader you must always take responsibility by being there."[96]

This focus on safe yet realistic training was once implicitly subsumed under the SAF Core Values of "Leadership", "Professionalism" and "Care for Soldier". The continuation and increasing sociopolitical costs of service-related deaths, however, prompted the SAF to strengthen the message of commitment to people through the explicit institution of "Safety" as the eighth core value in 2013.[97] Singaporeans can be confident that the SAF will not soften training standards in any way so as to undermine its very reason for being.

While flag officers lead at the very highest levels of the SAF, they were also once followers and beneficiaries of people-centred officers of an earlier generation. At times, as noted in the previous chapter, their superiors proved instrumental in motivating subordinates to sign on. More often than not, this was due to examples set through actions that were remembered fondly and considered worthy of emulation. Grandiose lip service certainly has no place and only calls an individual's intention (even integrity) into question. The reasons and circumstances varied but invariably converged on the themes of genuine care and concern for those under their charge, and a dedication to the military profession indirectly inspired officers' commitment to stay on in the SAF. One air force general recalled the impression created when he met the DGS as a 2LT:

> "I was inspired by [LG (RET)] Winston Choo. He was one of the three on the [scholarship] interview panel. The other was COL (later BG) Tan Chin Tiong and one other person. They asked why I wanted to take up the [scholarship]. I looked up to Winston for his professionalism as an officer. He was firm but had a heart for people. He knew people by name regardless of rank. He has a genuine interest in them. He was also leading and moulding a professional armed forces."[98]

In the early years of the SAF it was not only Singaporean officers who made a difference—the organization benefited from the experiences of foreign consultants. It depended on the consultants' willingness to teach and share and whether locals were willing to learn from them. A one-star recalled an earlier tour at Staff College:

---

[96] Interview No. 09.

[97] The SAF Core Values are Loyalty to Country, Leadership, Discipline, Professionalism, Fighting Spirit, Ethics, Care for Soldiers, Safety. Charles Eu, "Giving Safety Top Priority in Our Army", *Army News* 207 (Jan. 2013): 18–9; Jotham Yeo, "Safety: An Army Core Value", *Army News* 211 (May 2013): 6–7.

[98] Interview No. 14.

"Singapore [had] no experience, so advisers came depending on [country of origin] to work with the various services. I was fortunate to meet some real battle-hardened officers. You speak with them, question them, [and] ask them for the logic behind why they do things. Their experiences rubbed off on me. I was also lucky this German General [Siegfried] Schulz was around. He came to help and was also at SCSC. Every day he would come and talk, so I learned the German way of thinking. I got along well with Schulz. I found him more passionate about working in the military than Singaporeans. He had a 'Singapore is me' passion and not merely acting like a paid consultant."[99]

As time passed, locally commissioned officers replaced the retired military elites from the early years and foreign consultants concluding their tenures. The key was the continuity in people-orientation and consistency in seeking to improve various facets of the SAF. A former head of training cited a COA who paid attention to detail and went out of his way to match words and deeds:

"[MG (RET)] Lim Neo Chian is a man of principles. He once said: 'Gandhi is my idol.' <smiles> He changed the two-sided division exercises from once every two to once every three years. This was because holding a two-sided division exercise literally paralyzed the army (before the computerization of war games). He is a true leader by example. He cared for soldiers in practical ways. One was through the upgrading of camps. In the 1960s the camps were an upgrade for many soldiers. You had a bed with a pillow. But by the 1990s it was actually a downgrade. He upgraded the camps and improved camp life. He always led by example."[100]

Others remembered a former CDF for his willingness to right the wrongs he perceived to have plagued and prevented the uniformed services from moving in the right direction. One army general with first-hand experience shared: "The moral fabric of the SAF is very important. It was [LG (RET)] Bey Soo Khiang who took a stand to ensure there were no camps (factionalism) and favours (cronyism)."[101] An RSAF general who benefited from improvements in training, education and experiences recalled:

"[LG (RET)] Bey Soo Khiang wanted a more rounded development of pilots and not just flying. This was because people only stayed in the base and flew. How can an OC or CO [not possess experience in] staff work? No staff writing, no exposure to people across the other vocations and services. You cannot wait until [Staff College] to get to know people and to be exposed to staff work. Staff work provides exposure to other people. It is about a well-rounded development. But it can also be stifling and it

---

[99] Interview No. 27.

[100] Interview No. 09.

[101] Interview No. 13.

should not be taken to extreme to force people into it, especially those who are cut out differently. What is essential is a balance to keep people happy and motivated."[102]

Beyond raising morale and making tough and unpopular decisions, those who inspired commitment were often teachers willing to invest in the next generation of officers by imparting skills, experiences and knowledge. They were not merely well liked but valued substance over style. One general known for his humble demeanour explained:

> "It is important to be able to work with people. Along the way you do the best you can and always learn so that you can get wiser. Learn about the systems in place, and be aware of how the organization operates. I learned a great deal from [BG (RET)] Law Chwee Kiat. He had a good planning system that was rational. He also liked to test and teach his subordinates, and I learned a lot from him. I also learned from peers, different individuals who also made general. On the whole the environment in the SAF fosters learning, but this also depends on who you work with. Under some bosses you are more 'fearful' because they are temperamental."[103]

In the SAF, however, just like in any other organization, the bad is interspersed with the good. While there were those who inspired, there were also those with questionable intentions. One officer lamented: "Some people you work for are 'bad' people who betray you after you work your butt off."[104] Another griped:

> "You meet 'bad' commanders. I felt weary dealing with them, but you cannot influence that. Just be professional and focus on the job. Along the way you also meet others who stand in the way. There was a controller on exercise who created a lot of problems. Logical criticism is one thing, but childish behaviour is just not acceptable. But I also learned not to take things personally."[105]

As the SAF seeks to consolidate its much hyped transformation into a 3G SAF, one former CDF cautioned emphatically: "I always remember one G: the man with the gun. Train him well. You will not win with technology alone but only if the man with the gun is holding ground."[106] While some might criticize this chain of thought as parochial and anachronistic in terms of modern warfare, it is best seen as highlighting the importance of people in defence and how people elicit commitment from those who lead them.

---

[102] Interview No. 16.

[103] Interview No. 11.

[104] Interview No. 28.

[105] Interview No. 09.

[106] Interview No. 19.

4.4.2 Profession and Mission

The importance of people in securing the commitment of the military elite and indeed the wider SAF cannot be overstated. This factor is important also in other occupations but takes on added significance in light of the military profession and the mission of the armed forces. A commitment to the profession of arms is not merely the personal mastery of technical skills and maintaining competence. In the eyes of the flag officers, it was about having found purpose and meaning in the military's mission and taking personal responsibility for it. The mission of national defence is sacred and unique to the armed forces, even though other organs of state also contribute to the overall scheme of national security. This subsection covers the factors that led to the realization of what it takes to be a military professional and what made—and continues to make—the mission important.

The first realization is that it takes time to become a professional and view oneself in that light. It is not merely a matter of donning the uniform and clocking time in appointments. What matter most are the contributions one makes and the changes one effects to improve the organization. This applies to both followers and leaders. One general started out as an artillery officer who simply sought to change the small things:

> "Initially it was not about 'duty, honour, country'. But things started to pick up. I developed an interest in the organization. I also felt strongly about the stupid things done in the SAF at the time. For example, the battery prof[iciency] test was more about procedure than substance. When delivering orders the test was concerned with 'Whether the people were seated?' and 'Did the commander speak loud enough?' It was nuts! You could pass [the test] but cannot deliver fire on target and on time … Because there was no doctrinal manual instructing us what to do there was opportunity for improvement and change. As a battery commander the template was small and so there could only be incremental change. As formation Head GS (General Staff) there would be better opportunities to make changes. But why bother? Who the hell knows? It is surely not to impress the [SAF] General Staff. It boils down to ownership and professionalism. The only way was to speak the truth to the senior commanders. They needed to know. We needed truthful reflection if we really wanted to be a first-class artillery force. Professionalism calls and demands that you have the knowledge and experience to recognize problems and be willing to do something about it. But the question is: 'Are officers willing to do this and risk not getting promoted?' I did this because I saw that a part of the SAF's capabilities were in my hands. It is also about interest in the next level (subordinates). To be a role model and inculcate in the next echelon the values and standards. Once there is a break in this cycle there is a problem. It is hard to measure, but you

can see it occurring. I always asked myself: 'Can I be party to making the organization worse off?'"[107]

The second officer, a military engineer, highlighted his gradual transformation from being a professional in the military into a military professional:

"It was not clear to me I would be there (in the SAF) for life. I had no plans beyond the fact I was an engineer and it was an interesting job. I did not think of the six years (bond). I would do it as long as it is meaningful and fulfilling. I had an idea what it would be like and it would not be a mistake. I did not see it as long term or six years. I will cross the bridge when I get to it. After five years I was placed on pensionable scheme, but I did not have any goals of where I would be in the organization ... It started off as an engineer looking for something to do. Somewhere along the way you are part of a larger enterprise with implications for the country. I joined because it looked like fun. I thought of myself as an engineer first, (service) officer second. Later it was (service) officer first and then engineer. In the mid-'90s I started to get involved in (service) exercises, doctrine and the big picture. How does the (service) defend Singapore and execute a war? I came to understand what my role was. Beyond branch head it is a different job, and once you reach the Colonel level you operate at an international level."[108]

Another officer echoed how the initial adventure gave way to a larger contribution:

"Earlier in my career it was a mixture of interest, fun, fulfilment and also making a contribution. In those years I could feel I was making a contribution. Consistently I could make a difference. I had something to offer and could always have ideas that were better than those around me. I felt needed, and I contributed. There was a lot to be done. Can things improve, can I lead, can I help to make changes? Yes. Things can be done better, and the organization is open to change. Can I contribute to the change movement? Yes I can, and I can do so leading. At all times I felt I had a role."[109]

The second factor is the importance of the armed forces' mission, which is both challenging and unique. Within the Singaporean context, this encompasses a range of activities—from maintaining its technological edge in the region to reviewing organizational structure, updating plans and doctrine to ensure relevance, implementing new initiatives, and overcoming the evident geographical and increasingly demographic constraints. This has been the preoccupation since the early years, as pointed out by a general:

---

[107] Interview No. 09.

[108] Interview No. 21.

[109] Interview No. 22.

"There were many things to do. Overseas training in Brunei, Taiwan, Australia. We reorganized the SAF Headquarters. Dr Goh was fascinated with how the Japanese High Command and German General Staff system operated. We had General Siegfried Schulz, who advised us on combined arms training. These were the new challenges while I was in [MINDEF], such as implementing the General Staff system and also combined arms and even joint capabilities. We had to make sure the given resources translated into capabilities. Dr Goh was always on the lookout to maximize resources. For example, National Day Parade organization was an opportunity to train combined arms coordination. We also used SIA to fly us [overseas] to test the ability to project troops. He also made great use of *Pioneer* magazine. There were lots of photos to attract readers. As a NS army it was also important to have soldiers in a happy mood for the parents to see. There was also a lot of coverage on the superior weapon capabilities we possessed: an indirect form of deterrence."[110]

Over time this has continued. One officer who served during the nascent manifestations of the Joint Staff (JS) emphasized:

"I believe it was a profession and not just a job. Today this belief, this value, might not be there. The structure was not very close in those days in the sense when we signed up it was a lifelong commitment until retirement. Today you have a two-career system, so you plan and need to migrate to a second career. But when I signed up the thinking was 'I am a professional soldier' and that the career will look after me when I retire. I enjoyed army life. It was good for me in the sense it drew out my full potential. It offered me an opportunity to think. I built a lot of things for the SAF but I cannot talk about them, I cannot say. Designed some of the exercises. One day DJOPD (Director Joint Operations and Planning Directorate) asked me to build this war-gaming capacity for the SAF. So I think, analyze, then present to HQ. I also had to change uniform for the SAF. It was challenging because we were going to reflect a citizen's army with no class distinction, no brass, but some of the older officers who were used to such things got my blood. <grins> In some ways I got a little bit more (out of the career) than my comrades."[111]

The seemingly simple task of changing uniforms might seem trivial to some, but another general, then a staff officer, showed much gusto and epitomized giving one's best no matter how mundane the task might seem: "Change the uniform to reflect the citizen's army. We got rid of the belt for generals, the gold trim belt which costs £2,000, yes, £2,000 because of the gold thread. The spurs worn by

---

[110] Interview No. 03.

[111] Interview No. 27.

armour also had to go. I told them we had no horses nor tradition of that (in the SAF) so what for you need spurs? <laughs>"[112]

An admiral reiterated the importance of people for his commitment to the navy and added the professional, operational and future planning factors:

"You find that you can achieve certain things [while serving in the SAF]. Some things you cannot do outside. The people in the navy are a good bunch. It is a close-knit community where there is mutual support. The work is also meaningful and fulfilling. There is also the aspect of professional interest. It was not merely a job, it was a career. In the latter you strive to master the domain you are in. At an early age I received exposure to higher headquarters, and this helped in developing domain expertise not just at the tactical level but also higher levels. There were also real operations which you could describe as a 'Mexican standoff'. <nods> As a branch head and subsequently as head of naval plans I had to argue and justify for the missile corvette. It was an exciting time. The navy was also in a build-up phase and expanding from being a coastal navy. At the later part of my career it was with the frigate and LST (Landing Ship Tank) programmes. My career coincided with exciting times. <smiles>"[113]

Similarly, an air force general explained:

"There were exit points and options along the way. But I stayed on for some reasons. I was involved in challenging tasks that were interesting and kept me occupied. I was lucky in time and place. There were enough things to do. From [year X] onwards the air force embarked on a series of cutting-edge and secretive programmes. We were operating under budget constraints, so we focused on urgent areas. It was something new. Building a new air base. Then there was setting up of [formation Y] with conceptual inputs and involvement from joint, the three services, and intelligence. This was followed with work on the ideas and concepts for [formation Y], the structural and operational aspects. In all these projects you had to ensure the air force was not only no worse off but better than before. We envisaged how we would fight in war and then engineered backward. It was a major transition. I was fortunate enough to be in the right time and right place, which kept me going. Implementing new, interesting concepts. They were paradigm shifts in what we were doing. There was no time to do other things <smile>."[114]

---

[112] Interview No. 28. The Indian Army supposedly sold Singapore 80 or more "cavalry horses for the proposed Singapore presidential bodyguard" in 1967. "S'pore Briefed on Indian Offer of Aid", *Straits Times*, 25 June 1967, p. 7.

[113] Interview No. 15.

[114] Interview No. 16.

In the medical field, a CMC explained what kept him going:

> "It is the mission. I was fortunate to be in the SAF when it was growing; to be part of a transformation. You cannot take it from me. It is something that is my luck or good fortune. Few have the honour and opportunity to experience. It also showed that my work and my life mattered ... I was fortunate to start new things that I would not be able to do outside (of the SAF). Outside it would be four walls and one-to-one with the patient but I would not get the helicopter view and be able to influence bigger things and implement initiatives such as research in the SAF, sports medicine with PT and Sports branch covering IPPT (the annual Individual Physical Proficiency Test), obese platoon, myopia, electronic medical reports, paramedic course with the Justice Institute in British Columbia for our Emergency Medical Technicians. I was a prime mover. I thought I'd take leadership to build a career in sports medicine. If I had done so, I would build medical groups and leverage on the fitness movement and medical screening. But then the chance to put the SAF Medical Corps on an operational footing came. It was prophetic because we had to deploy. My aim was to make sure the MO could stand tall among the military profession. In those days infantry officers thought we were 'half-past-six' (colloquial expression for 'incompetent' or 'shoddy') soldiers. Doctors were not part of the planning and subordinate to the logistics officer. My personal mission was to put the SAF Medical Corps on an operational footing which included trauma medicine, paramedic course, and for everyone to take a serious approach towards medical exercises. I ensured Division Medical Officers became active in planning independent of the logistics plan. The Division Commander must know it is his lifeline and must make full use of his medical officer."[115]

The military mission is important, yet it is often lost on society at large because of the peace that Singapore has enjoyed since independence. The mission can also be lost on officers, who are at times shielded from the larger picture. The impetus to take training seriously has at times suffered since conflict(s) usually seem so far from Singapore. That is unless one experiences it first-hand like MG (RET) Ravinder Singh—one of the first scholar-officers deployed on an overseas mission—who recalled:

> "In 1991, as a young captain, I was deployed to Kuwait as a UN (United Nations) Military Observer. When we flew into Kuwait city, it had just been liberated from Iraq. I vividly remember landing at the airport which had been destroyed by the war. The city was destroyed, homes were pillaged and many lives lost. Even though they wanted to protect their families and friends, young Kuwaiti men could do nothing because they were not trained, not equipped and not organized. That was a poignant reminder for me. If I don't do my part for Singapore now, there would be

---

[115] Interview No. 20. See also "Audit of Paramedic Training", *MEDLink* (July 2005): 6–7.

no second chance. I realized then, that serving in the Army was not just a job but it was a sacred duty, to protect our country and our way of life."[116]

The deployment developed General Ravinder as a professional military officer, but such operational experiences on land are increasingly restricted to a niche group of Regulars.[117]

The third factor is that the interview participants felt valued and recognized by the SAF as corporate members of the profession, which in turn deepened and amplified their commitment to the military's mission. Value and recognition was most evident by the responsibilities entrusted to them by superiors. Their performances and established reputations led to greater appointments and opportunities. For one officer this was instrumental in his service commitment, which offset the days of poorer salary conditions: "Did I consider leaving? No, because, I would say, due to the responsibility. The career was not just about reward but also recognition and responsibility. My contributions were valued, and I could feel it. I did not want to leave, but the pay outside was very attractive. <laughs> I was rewarded in other ways."[118]

Another recollected finding meaning in his role during the junior years of his career. This epiphany was reinforced through recognition from his superior:

> "During my stint in [unit J], my CO then [officer K] appreciated what I did. Towards the end of my [X]-year contract he told me that he'd get me promoted to Captain if I signed another contract. For a non-graduate to reach Captain within four years after Lieutenant was fast. Most importantly, I liked what I was doing. I found a purpose in what I was doing. The years in [unit J] had an influence on me. I was looking at assigning resources to units, career planning for Regulars. It was something meaningful."[119]

A third officer continued this line of thought with examples from later in his career, an accumulation of mutual investment between him and the SAF:

> "I think I became more restless but never to the point of looking for jobs outside. Partly because the SAF was kind to me. They found value in me, and I was given challenging jobs. As [head of] plans I had a budget to

---

[116] "Service with Distinction", Public Service Commission Scholarships, www.pscscholarships. gov.sg/content/pscsch/default/ourscholars/eminent_scholars/servicewithdistinction.html, accessed 28 May 2014.

[117] Samuel Chan Ling Wei, "Strategic Gains Without the Strategic Corporal: The Singapore Armed Forces in Afghanistan (2007–13)", in *The Strategic Corporal Re-Visited: Challenges for Combatants in Twenty-First Century Warfare*, ed. David W. Lovell and Deane-Peter Baker (Cape Town: UCT Press, 2017), pp. 147–71.

[118] Interview No. 24.

[119] Interview No. 06.

look after and decide on what to spend, to procure, the structure of the SAF and how to introduce new equipment. It was a very respectable job. Those were good years as [head of] plans. There were of course trying times, but this is part and parcel of the appointment. On the whole [it was] very satisfying. [Head of operations] was more complex but also enjoyable. Such appointments and the SAF's willingness to invest in you makes you stay on. They also sent me to [a prestigious university overseas for postgraduate studies]. The desire to go to the private sector was also not strong enough to get me to leave. In [year X] I decided to stay for the long term until I had to return to the Admin Service. I had invested so much time, [Y] years, and if I leave the SAF I would be giving up on this investment. For me to do so I would need to start another career, and this would not be maximizing the [Y]-year investment in the SAF where I spent time and energy, having learned about it, networked and also gained credibility. It would be wasteful to do so. At this mark I was also near the top of the echelon where I could really contribute. Every year that I go on I could contribute more. The thought of leaving never came."[120]

The factors of patience, challenges and recognition cited by the preceding officer are not mutually exclusive. In fact, it would be an exception rather than the norm for the military elites not to cite a combination of the three. Explicit expressions of patriotism—which in local parlance is referred to using Douglas MacArthur's famous "duty, honour, country"—seemed conspicuously absent.[121] Only a handful of officers cited patriotism as their motivation to sign on and commitment to stay on. The reasons given included the fact that Singapore was forced into nationhood and national identity had to be painstakingly forged over time, and that Singapore—as one of them put it—was not a "rah rah, flag waving society" (i.e., not known for explicit expressions of patriotism except on National Day).[122] Peace has given Singapore the luxury of deploying the SAF on operations of choice rather than necessity. Furthermore, almost any occupation can be for "duty, honour, country" in view of Singapore's Total Defence concept based on civil, economic, military, psychological and social pillars.[123]

---

[120] Interview No. 10.

[121] American General Douglas MacArthur's famous speech to the Corps of Cadets at the United States Military Academy, West Point, 12 May 1962.

[122] Interview No. 11.

[123] Deck, "Singapore: Comprehensive Security", pp. 247–69; Ron Matthews and Nellie Zhang Yan, "Small Country 'Total Defence': A Case Study of Singapore", *Defence Studies* 7, 3 (Sept. 2007): 376–95.

For most of the military elites, the overriding reasons were simply a commitment to the profession and the mission entrusted to the armed forces. One general enthused:

> "I stayed; I was committed to the profession. I was also trying out new things, seeing personally how we could solve problems. Coming up with new systems, making it work, improving things. Being with people, looking after them. It was fun. I loved the outdoors. I enjoyed my life in the field. To be truthful I never thought it was for 'duty, honour, country'. Perhaps I should have, but I did not. I loved the outdoors, I could shoot, I was physically fit. I also happened to have the same interests as my bosses. Some people saw this as 'carrying balls' or being in 'their camp', but this was not the case. [A senior general] liked to swim and jog, but I hated swimming and jogging so I told him I would be his safety officer. <grins>"[124]

Another general, after a moment of reflection, said:

> "To me I did not see it as a job because flying was like a hobby. I always felt this pre-match tension to do well on every flight, and so the intensity and competitive streak came naturally. Through the [SAF scholarship] I received a good education in [a Western country] where I also won other prizes and scholarships. Further on I had the opportunity to attend the prestigious [foreign Staff College] at [a Western country] and also SAF sponsorship for postgraduate education at [a Western university]. Each course carried a bond, but to me it never mattered because I did not intend to leave. I never thought of leaving once. My motivation and commitment to the RSAF are one in the same. I love the military, I love flying, and in fact today I still work with the air force as the [senior civilian] in [a defence-affiliated institute]. I got to BG based on hard work, good opportunities, and love for the profession."[125]

Even when patriotism was cited as a factor for commitment, it was centred on the people and the mission, as an admiral reasoned:

> "First was the type of work. This is not to say the quality of lifestyle is bad. The work is about the mission, the people, and 'duty, honour, country'. Second, the lifestyle at work, but this is separate from family life. My brother was a Regular and so was my brother-in-law, but we don't talk about work. Does it (military service) run in the family? Yes, you can say it does, but not much from conversing with them. Does the uniform matter? You look smart, but I did not get married in my number one (ceremonial) uniform. <laughs> I am proud of the uniform, but I did not don the uniform … It was a response to organizational needs, and I could also match my strength and abilities. The result was a good match

---

[124] Interview No. 26.

[125] Interview No. 08.

and alignment, which led to an environment which was fun and where I could contribute positively. It was a response to a calling, but there is always a need to assess [whether it is a good match] … I cannot comment on the current generation, but mine had a call of mission and purpose."[126]

For most of the military elites, commitment was a matter of dedicated service until retirement. For a handful, their commitment was tested and they showed their resolve under trying circumstances.

4.4.3 Close Calls

The nature of military service in preparing individuals for war means those in uniform are frequently exposed to the hazards of the profession. Within the SAF such incidents occur almost exclusively in times of peace and frequently as a result of man and/or machine. This section does not highlight an exhaustive overview of equipment failure or account for the broad—albeit infrequent—array of accidents. The purpose is to provide instances where the officers involved remained committed to active service even after harrowing incidents that held the possibility of disability and even death.

The Old Guard of 1 SIR certainly encountered such possibilities as they deployed to Sabah during *Konfrontasi* and were employed in traditional infantry roles. Patrols were frequent to deny infiltrators any sanctuary or freedom of action. Within the battalion "[t]here was a tremendous spirit of camaraderie and sense of purpose in the unit at that time, in the face of great odds and danger".[127] Like many of the early pioneers, the expectation of seeing combat was high; and both LG (RET) Winston Choo and BG (RET) Patrick Sim came under fire during the tour. Life on the line started with excitement but soon gave way to monotonous routines. That was until the first shot was fired in anger: "We were prepared, and the tension was real. <pause> Fear was to be expected … We are all human. During the first contact, when enemy bullets fly all around you. Wow boy, it brings a new meaning to life."[128]

Another *Konfrontasi* veteran, WO1 (RET) See Koon Swee, former Chief Medical Orderly at Pulau Brani Naval Base, said quite simply: "The bullets do not distinguish between a medic and a rifleman."[129]

---

[126] Interview No. 18.

[127] Surinder Kaur, "A Soldier-Diplomat: LT GEN Choo Leaves the SAF", *Pioneer* (June 1992): 1–3.

[128] Interview No. 01.

[129] Dominic Nathan, "SAF Pays a Special Tribute to Its Pioneers", *Straits Times*, 21 Nov. 1989, p. 24.

A fine line separated life and death in this cat-and-mouse game in the jungle, and the two veterans remembered close calls:

> "It was a challenging time. We were there for real. The battalion organized patrols into Indonesian territory to find out exactly where the enemy was. The KKO or *Korps Komando Operasi* (Indonesian Marines). It was an interesting time, and 1 SIR lived a charmed life. Six months on Sebatik and one month on Sabah before we were rotated. A Malaysian regiment took over on Sebatik, and the patrol boat I used before got shot up. That is why I say we lived a charmed life. When we got back to Singapore we were deployed to Kota Tinggi, where a platoon from 2 SIR was ambushed suffering fatalities."[130]

In another incident, BG (RET) Patrick Sim recalled:

> "While we were with COL (then-CPT) John Morrice in this protection game ... I think the enemy must have spotted my platoon base ... because later when we moved to another hill ... the place where I was came under heavy mortar fire from the Indonesian side. I remember while we were on the OP hill (where the observation post was sited), when the bombs started falling, my feeling was 'Gosh! How lucky we were!'"[131]

Soldiers were trained to put their life on the line, but there was also great relief for troops returning to Singapore. Since then, the only other general officer to have possibly engaged an adversary is BG (RET) Lam Shiu Tong, who was a member of Operation Thunderbolt to free hijacked SIA flight SQ117 on 26 and 27 March 1991.[132]

In times of peace the hazards of military duty usually arise from accidents as a result of equipment failure; carelessness due to fatigue, ignorance or even phlegmatism; unfamiliar or challenging terrain; and inclement weather. This lethal mix can prove deadly in any vocation but perhaps none more so than flying, especially until the late 1980s, when the RSAF commenced its relatively impressive safety record. On 2 August 1971, BG (RET) then-CPT Gary Yeo, a QFI and his trainee pilot OCT Ng Kwang Ngen ejected safely when their BAC-167 Strikemaster developed engine trouble and crashed in South Johore,

---

[130] Interview No. 19.

[131] "The Story of One", *Pioneer* (Jan. 1978): 21.

[132] "SAF Commandos Storm Hijacked Plane", *Pioneer* (Apr. 1991): 3; *Defining Moments: Our Army Experience: Shaping Lives and Beliefs* (Singapore: Ministry of Defence, 2004), pp. 32–6.

Malaysia.[133] On 3 January 1973 former CAF (1995-8) MG (RET) then-LTA Goh Yong Siang experienced engine troubles on his Hunter aircraft during a naval exercise. The loss of engine thrust provided him with a flying altitude of only 3,500 feet as he made for Changi Air Base, where he "carried out a successful flame-out approach and landed without further damage to the aircraft".[134]

Other generals also experienced close calls. Another former QFI revealed: "I was also involved in an accident. I was with a trainee and took over the aircraft quite late, so the nose wheel hit the ground and the propeller got whacked. If you take over too soon the trainee does not get the flight experience. Too late and this could happen."[135]

The dangers inherent in flying were ever present and could strike irrespective of experience and rank, as another testified:

> "I experienced a flame-out over the South China Sea just as my CO tour was concluding. I managed to relight the engine and returned to base. There was inclement weather condition just as I was coming in to land. It was a thunderstorm and raining very heavily. The controller changed the runway but did not lower the landing net on this re-routed runway. Visibility was poor so the controller must have missed it, and I only saw it when I was landing—so I did a 'grasshopper' [jump] over the net. When I got out of the aircraft my legs were trembling. <laughs>"[136]

While these officers survived, others fell in the line of duty. Most notably, two SAFOS officers lost their lives under tragic circumstances. A "misadventure" over the Straits of Johor on 25 July 1985 claimed the life of 25-year-old dual SAFOS-PS (1979) recipient CPT Seah Boon Thong. His single-engine A-4 Skyhawk aircraft lost power after "a snapped hydraulic pressure line" started a fire and crashed three seconds after take-off. Seah ejected from the cockpit, but the traumatic experience sent him into shock and he subsequently drowned in "murky waters".[137] This occurred in a July–August period when the RSAF lost

---

[133] "Two SADC Pilots Saved after Jet Crash", *Straits Times*, 3 Aug. 1971, p. 1. One of the Martin Baker MK PB4 ejection seats was subsequently placed in the air force museum marking the first pilot ejection in RSAF history. The other seat was allegedly kept by the Malaysian Armed Forces. Kalpana Rae Naidu, "Journey to the Past", *Pioneer* (Oct. 1991): 19–21; Oral History Centre interview with COL (RET) Ramachandran Menon for "The Civil Service—A Retrospection" project, Accession No: 003250, Reel 10 of 17, p. 211.

[134] "Good Show", *Pioneer* (Apr. 1973): 12.

[135] Interview No. 25.

[136] Interview No. 24.

[137] "Search Goes on for Missing Pilot", *Straits Times*, 27 July 1985, p. 9; Charmaine Chan, "Pilot Seen Struggling in Sea after Mishap", *Straits Times*, 20 May 1986, p. 9; "Drowned Pilot in Shock after Ejecting from Plane", *Straits Times*, 27 May 1986, p. 10.

three A-4s to crashes in quick succession, leading to a temporary grounding of the aircraft.[138] A total of five Skyhawks were eventually lost during the "A-4 Crisis" of 1985 due to the "severe degradation of airworthiness".[139] Six years later, on 16 August 1991, CPT Edmund Ying Jat Mun (SAFOS 1986), 24, drowned and CPT James Poon Kok Seng, 28, succumbed to head injuries during a "misadventure" over Poyan Reservoir in the Lim Chu Kang area of northwestern Singapore. The AS332M Super Puma helicopter piloted by Ying crashed and flipped as it was "negotiating a turn over the reservoir ... during a routine low-terrain tactical flight exercise".[140] Only trainee crewman Panneerselvam Thangarju survived.

In the army, accidents manifested themselves in various ways, from the hazards of driving in unfamiliar locations or over vast distances overseas, to tanks and jeeps flipping over, mortar base plates sinking after heavy rain so that rounds landed outside the safety template during live-fire exercises, and so on. Merely travelling in vehicles could prove hazardous, as several generals experienced. For one of them:

> "In ROC (Republic of China) there was a landslide and the rovers (Jeeps) could not get across. We also could not reverse all the way out, so we had to go forward. We were in a convoy of six vehicles. With the vehicle scraping the other side there was only about 30cm between the vehicle and a steep drop. So I drove all six across with one person guiding me. It was close, but I was the commander so lead by example. <grins>"[141]

Another cited familiarity of training in Singapore but experienced a freak incident:

> "I was also lucky because during one exercise in Lentor the Land Rover we (CO, OC, two signallers and a diver) were travelling in overturned and rolled into water. Fortunately the Rover ended upright; if not, there would have been five fatalities because we were in chest-high water. We got out, checked equipment, another vehicle came over, and we continued with the exercise."[142]

---

[138] "Skyhawks Grounded for Thorough Checks", *Straits Times*, 31 Aug. 1985, p. 14; "RSAF Skyhawks Flying Again", *Straits Times*, 12 Sept. 1985, p. 10.

[139] Speech by COL Cheng Siak Kian, Head Air Plans, titled "Towards the 3rd Generation RSAF" at the RSAF 17th NSmen Seminar, Air Force School Auditorium, 23 Mar. 2007; Adrian Chan, *Leading in the Third Generation SAF* (Singapore: *Pointer: Journal of the Singapore Armed Forces*, 2012), p. 34.

[140] "Misadventure Verdict on Deaths of Two Pilots", *Straits Times*, 25 June 1993, p. 26.

[141] Interview No. 26.

[142] Interview No. 05.

While those officers avoided injury, other incidents proved less forgiving. In the late 1980s one general, then a MAJ, suffered injuries with lingering physical effects while attending a foreign CSC. Similarly, in 1994 BG (RET) Yeo See Peng, then a 28-year-old MAJ with the 1st Commando Battalion, "suffered head injuries and a fractured left wrist" when a vehicle he was in overturned during a training exercise in Thailand.[143] Then there were close calls involving live ammunition that sometimes ended with a loss of life. BG (RET) then-CPT Lee Hsien Loong was training in ROC when a stray artillery round fell into a village.[144] BG (RET) then-CPT Lee Hsien Yang was on another exercise in Taiwan when a sentry to the bunker he was in succumbed to wounds from a bullet ricochet.[145] In 1986, BG (RET) then-CPT Pang Hee Hon (SAFOS 1979) was a battery commander when a gunner came into possession of a rifle grenade during training. For unknown reasons the grenade was taken into an armoured personnel carrier, where it detonated killing the gunner and injuring four others.[146]

Two other generals interviewed also suffered life-threatening injuries, which sheds light on their commitment yet raises the question of when officers must say "no" without apologies. The first questioned the risks he took while in service and in the context of seemingly fit and healthy men—both military and civilian—who succumbed to sudden cardiac arrest while exercising:

> "In retrospect I ask if commanders in the SAF are over-committed in leading their men. After suffering a heart attack in March [year Z] I reflected on two incidences. The first was as [battalion CO] and completing the 40km march with piles. The second was as [brigade commander] and running the Army Half Marathon when I was feverish. I ask myself: 'Was I foolish?' Perhaps. But I reasoned that I was building a team. This is the predicament. Did I overdo it? If something really happens to you; 'how'? So I always say consider your family aspects. The organization cannot do more than, or replace, your family. So as commanders, we must have the moral courage to say we cannot do it when we are physically under the weather. We always ask the men if anyone is not feeling well. This must extend to leaders at all levels including our own self."[147]

---

[143] "Two SAF Men Hurt in Thailand Accident", *Straits Times*, 23 Nov. 1994, p. 22. 1SG Lim Ah Han, who was travelling with Yeo, suffered head and lung injuries and was aero-evacuated to Singapore, where he died three days after the accident (22 Nov. 1993).

[144] Oral History Centre, National Archives of Singapore, interview with COL (RET) Goh Lye Choon for "The Civil Service—A Retrospection" project, Accession No: 003275, Reel 12 of 17 (2008), p. 262.

[145] Ibid.

[146] "Court Told of Trip into Grenade Launching Area", *Straits Times*, 20 Sept. 1987, p. 13.

[147] Interview No. 06.

The second officer suffered a physical injury mid-career and decided not to risk worsening the ailment even though it would adversely affect his prospects for progression. He carefully deliberated his options as such:

> "After my [postgraduate studies] I was designated the next Commander [of unit X]. Then COA [officer Y] told the doctors they better ensure that I could continue in the SAF. The medical examination was all clear. On Friday I received a call informing me that COA wanted a review so the Change of Command was delayed. I immediately rang CARMO (Chief Army MO) and queried why there was a change of heart after I cleared the medical. COA had asked if the [said appointment at unit X] will lead to a deterioration of my condition and the medical opinion was that it could. On that Saturday I told myself I can do it so why should there be any doubt? But on Sunday after some reflection I asked what I wanted to do in life. I wanted the ability to walk when I am 50 and for the rest of my life. If anything will impede that then it will not be on my list [of things] to do. On Monday I told COA I would not like to be Commander [of unit X]. His reply was that he could not guarantee me a Colonel-grade appointment anymore. I was medically downgraded to [a lower medical classification] and no longer required to take IPPT. I was mentally prepared to remain at Lieutenant Colonel for the remainder of my career."[148]

While the majority of challenges faced by the military elite were hazards inherent to the profession of arms, there were those who overcame obstacles that would have forced others to resign. Some gripes, such as "unreasonable" superiors, "office politics" and "micromanagement", are not unique to the military. In fact, the military has the advantage of periodic posting rotations that (hopefully) negate such issues. Two flag officers remained committed despite adverse circumstances, which bore testament to their strength of character. The first officer, in perhaps the only incident of its kind, had his commitment challenged in a way that would question anyone's definition of fairness:

> "I was initially administered as a SAFOS, but this was eventually revised. Someone in the administration department must have just 'copy and paste' the terms and condition of the SAFOS. The name of the scholarship also sounded very similar. I mean I went through [initial officer training and university], and in the initial years MINDEF was probably confused and thought I was SAFOS. <laughs> But I did not get the monthly meetings with minister and someone probably checked the record and noticed my name was not on the SAFOS list. The apologies came later and there was a salary clawback. After the clarification and revision there was also a revised career trajectory. That being said, I was given an administrative backdate for my promotion to Captain, which offset, compensated the

---

[148] Interview No. 07.

amount of money I had to pay back. To a lesser officer it would be a bone of contention, but for me it did not generate any ill will. I accepted the explanation. We all make mistakes, and steps were taken to make the best of the situation. It was only fair that it be sorted out. Whether the backdating of my Captain helped in my subsequent promotions I do not know, but logically it could have had a flow-on effect. <smiles>"[149]

For BG (RET) Ishak Bin Ismail, the first ethnically Malay officer to ascend into Singapore's military elite, self-doubt surfaced over whether accolades received early in his career were based on merit or affirmative action. It was the former, but as he recalled this was not always apparent:

"I only questioned the SAF once, and this was at the end of Company Tactics Course (CTC). The Chief Instructor (CI) told me I was the top student, and I remembered the conversation we had. I said: 'Can I ask you a question? Did the SAF have to stoop so low as to put a Malay officer as the top student to prove something?' The CI riposted saying: 'Don't you dare question my system. You are who you are. Race is not a consideration. But I understand. People will tell you it is because you are Malay. It will not stop. But ask yourself, can the people around you agree you are there (the top student)?' I wondered about this, and I got confirmation less than two hours later. In the course souvenir magazine I was given the course nickname 'ideal top student' by my peers. They agreed even though they did not know I was top. Those around have a sense of who you are. My quiet confidence was firm again. As a battalion S3 I topped BTC (Battalion Tactics Course). I saw the same CI from CTC and he said: 'Don't you dare ask me the same question.' <laughs> I was the third army officer to top both CTC and BTC. My confidence continued to develop as did my desire to contribute and give back to the SAF. It did not matter where my career ended. I became the first Malay officer to command an active infantry battalion in modern times and to attend an overseas command and staff course. I knew it was not because I was Malay."[150]

4.5 Summary

There were many reasons for officers to leave the military service. Some of the officers with higher levels of education cited uncompetitive salaries, which

---

[149] Interview No. 17. For other examples of administrative frustrations experienced by regular officers, see Yip Kin Cheng, "The Professional Soldier: Organisational and Occupational Commitment of Regular Officers in the Singapore Army", honours thesis, National University of Singapore, 2002, p. 49.

[150] Interview with BG Ishak Bin Ismail. Permission for open attribution received 28 May 2014.

prompted the drastic 1982 revision. Yet other themes have endured, such as seizing opportunities beyond the SAF, exhausting front-loaded benefits, societal lack of respect for the profession of arms, discontentment with meritocracy, falling into disillusionment and cynicism, and other varied and personal reasons. Flag officers considered leaving on similar lines but did not do so, and their reasons for remaining on active service fell into two categories. The first consisted of transactional commitment in the form of obligations, remuneration and progression. The bond or MTS was to be fulfilled, and they were contractually obligated to stay. Yet for others this was not the case, as they were set on a long-term commitment to the military career. In the same way, remuneration and progression were also important but secondary reasons for the interview participants to stay on. While the importance of transactional commitment differed among the military elites, there was a convergence towards transformational commitment based on the importance attached to the people they served with, their dedication to the military profession, and the sacred mission apportioned to the armed forces. Although the SAF has been a military at peace, its undertaking to prepare for war has invariably involved risks with the unintended consequences of disability and even death.

CHAPTER 5

The Ascension Process

"The nation that will insist on drawing a broad line of demarcation between the fighting man and the thinking man is liable to find its fighting done by fools and its thinking done by cowards."[1]

— Lieutenant-General Sir William Francis Butler (1838–1910)

5.1 Introduction

The annals of the SAF indicate that no officer has risen to the rank of General or Admiral outside of regular service. The rare exceptions took place in the early days of independence and have not been repeated since. This chapter addresses the processes instituted to govern officer progression in terms of rank. Ascending any rank hierarchy is possible through various factors, including cronyism and patronage, merit using absolute or relative measures, visibility to superiors who determine postings and promotions, and luck. These are certainly applicable to the military organization. Empirical evidence from the SAF indicates that ascension comes from cookie-cutter careers performed well but at the higher levels requires innovation, discretion, political skills above and beyond technical competency, and being in the right place when opportunities arise. This four-section chapter commences with processes initiated in the early SAF and the organization's evolution towards contemporary practices. The second and third sections cover the 4P's of performance, potential, promotions, and postings, all of which are necessary to reach the apex of rank hierarchy. The final section looks at intangibles that gave the military elites an edge over the remainder of the SAF Officer Corps.

---

[1] Volker Franke, *Preparing for Peace: Military Identity, Value Orientations, and Professional Military Education* (Westport and London: Praeger, 1999), p. 39.

5.1.1 *The Star and Some Parameters*

The SAF has long been thrifty in the promotion of its generals and admirals, for various reasons. At the beginning it was the dearth of qualified professional officers in tandem with the conscious initiative to ensure the primacy of civilian oversight and control. Although Singaporeans scoff at the possibility of a *coup d'état* today, the 1960s were quite different. Frequent reminders came from the immediate region and farther afield in Latin America, Africa and the Middle East. The Defence Council (DEFCO) was established with the PM at the helm and serves as the chief defence body. High-level defence-related political decisions are made by this council and implemented through policies involving the relevant ministries such as defence, home affairs and foreign affairs.[2] The AFC (initially called the Army Board) forms a second tier of civilian oversight with a focus on the general running of the defence establishment. The AFC at its formation in 1972 comprised the PS, Second PS, and the four DIR's of "General Staff, Manpower, Logistics and Security and Intelligence".[3] The DGS was the only uniformed officer among the six. At present the AFC comprises political appointees, civilian bureaucrats, and the most senior SAF officers in the CDF, service chiefs, and Chief of Staff – Joint Staff (COS-JS). All council members are recommended by the Council of Presidential Advisers, approved by the President, and tabled before Parliament.

The civilian leadership has held such primacy over the military that they effectively ran the SAF for a good number of years. One general who was summoned to DEFCO recalled that in the early years the council was made up of

> "the PM, the Defence Minister, the Foreign Minister, and others when they are needed. The Secretary of DEFCO is the Permanent Secretary (Defence). The CDF comes to DEFCO as and when uniform representation is required. MINDEF did not have very strong representation. I was very conscious of civilian supremacy over the military. Lots of decisions were made by Dr Goh. It was a one-man show. The SAF did not have to fight for money. The SAF and its officer corps had not reached a stage of maturity. The Permanent Secretary was above the CDF (in seniority) for a long time. But there exists the danger of decisions being taken without professional inputs."[4]

Indeed, this was seen to be the case as a declassified memo from the British High Commission in Singapore to London in 1974 read:

---

[2] Chia Poteik, "Lee to MPs: Keep Your Hands Clean", *Straits Times*, 24 Feb. 1977, p. 7.

[3] "Six Top Defence Men for Forces Council", *Straits Times*, 15 June 1972, p. 5.

[4] Interview No. 19.

A great deal of the credit belongs to Dr. Goh who characteristically read voluminously on military subject and on occasions has confounded his expatriate advisers and visiting officers with his knowledge of a particular subject. However, he is fascinated by technology and many of the short comings of the SAF are also due to Dr. Goh's lack of military experience and understanding of the complex support organisation necessary to turn men and equipment into an effective fighting machine. Dominated as they are by Dr. Goh and civilian officials, the SAF have been afforded little chance to develop an officer cadre or truly professional expertize [sic].[5]

An attached report by the British defence adviser further noted: "The Director General Staff (a one-star officer) is the senior uniformed Singaporean who exercises some command and operational control functions direct from the Ministry of Defence. However, he has no operational HQ nor is he wholly responsible for the work of his staff officers."[6]

It took until the late 1970s and early 1980s for this deficiency to be addressed with the creation of the GS and subsequently the JS. Even then, a retired foreign military officer and consultant noted that the "SAF, in terms of generals is understaffed. It was under-promoting officers. He (the consultant) also recommended that the SAF increase salaries by 25% and that the [army's] divisions should be mixed in terms of active and NS [personnel]."[7] Such actions eventuated in a slow and cautious manner. Those who wore one or more stars had to carry the rank and fulfil the responsibilities of leadership over the subordinate team. It is never a reflection of administrative function or arithmetic where three or more colonels always report to a one-star. A BG or RADM1 at the helm reflects that a combat formation has achieved requisite operational capabilities and highlights the critical role fulfilled by a specific staff department, or that a diplomatic mission holds great relevance and importance to Singapore. Defence ministers also consciously avoid a "top heavy" structure, and many have approved the bestowment of a star out of necessity rather than luxury or aesthetics.

---

[5] Memo from S. Falle at the British High Commission, Tanglin Circus, Singapore 10, dated 18 Mar. 1974, reference 10/41A, and originally classified Confidential (Covering Secret: UK Eyes: Bravo), declassified 2005, to C.W. Squire Esq. MVO, South-East Asian Department, Foreign & Commonwealth Office, London SW1, pp. 2–3.

[6] "Singapore Armed Forces Military Capability", report by Defence Adviser, British High Commission Singapore Part I, originally classified Secret (UK Eyes Bravo), declassified 2005, p. 8. Report was attached to the above-mentioned memo from S. Falle at the British High Commission in Singapore.

[7] Interview No. 03.

5.1.2 Counting Stars

The regular SAF Officer Corps is a small community, and not all appointment holders receive the corresponding rank. Legislation governing the rank structure allows for the four-star rank of General (GEN) or Admiral (ADM), but the current structure has a three-star (LG/VADM) CDF with three two-star (MG/RADM2) service chiefs. Ranks are cautiously pegged to reflect the SAF's capabilities and organizational structure to prevent the organization from turning into a laughing stock. As Defence Minister Yeo Ning Hong explained in 1994: "The SAF has reached the stage of its full capabilities such that it is possible for us to have the chief of services attain the established ranks of Major-Generals."[8] The other senior officers are DIR Military Intelligence (DMI), who is dual-hatted as Chief Command, Control, Communications, Computers and Intelligence (C4I) Community, and the four Chief of Staff (COS) billets at the respective joint- and service-levels. As of 2018 there are up to 42 one-star and above billets, but the actual numbers of active military elites are lower (Appendix C). There are four reasons for this. First, a handful of appointments are hybrid in nature in the sense that they are held by either military officers or senior civil servants. Second, certain appointments are often dual-hatted, others are held concurrently on an ad hoc basis, and some even go unfilled at times. These are the straightforward reasons.

The third reason is the deliberate attempt to place a cap on the number of stars at any one time. As one interviewee explained: "The one-star reflects privilege and opportunity. It is capped to prevent brass-creep."[9] This follows on to the fourth reason that an officer frequently, but not always, enters a one-star and above billet while holding one rank lower. For example, an incoming DIV COMD is usually a COL who is promoted to BG in the course of the tour subject to satisfactory performance. That said, there are no guarantees that an individual in a one-star appointment will actually receive the rank, and this has evoked differing opinions. One former member of the elite nucleus propounded:

> "I am an advocate that once you sit in the appointment, you should get the rank. I mean, if you put a Colonel to do a one-star job what are you saying to the world? That you are not confident in the individual you put there? It speaks of the system. If there is a steep trajectory like in the early days it is OK. But as the organization matures it should be OK to bestow the accompanying rank. [That being said] [t]he general rank should be given to a person who needs it to command, and not a staffer

---

[8] "How Officers Move up the Ranks", *Straits Times*, 29 June 1994, p. 3.

[9] Interview No. 18.

(staff officer). If he is a staffer on the way to a command appointment then that is different."[10]

Another member of the elite nucleus explained:

"There is a line of reasoning that if you are not a commander then there is no need for a star because brass "creep" dilutes the value of the rank. This view arises from the need to distinguish those who have the capability as a commander and did not get the chance to earn the star versus those who are not seen as good commanders and still get a star (from non-command appointments)."[11]

These views, while valid, have remained personal opinions as realities indicate officers enter the military elite though command, staff, or a mixture of both lines. These routes are equally valid, as it was once reasoned: "The leaders in the field at all levels are the hearts of the SAF, while the staff officers are the minds of the SAF."[12] Then there is the added impetus to ensure the possibility of earning the star through the staff route to retain scholar-officers not suitable for command but who could still contribute their intellect to defence requirements. "The SAF is what it is today because of its ability to bring in the best and the brightest minds amongst our young people into service," reflected LG (RET) Winston Choo in 2000. "You have some scholars who make very good soldiers, you get some scholars who make very good staff officers, the most important thing is to look at the man and try to fit him into what he does best."[13] Similarly, LG (RET) then-COL Lim Chuan Poh observed: "Most scholars are naturally inclined towards staff work but you require additional qualities to command men. You need to be comfortable dealing with people of diverse backgrounds, to work under extreme pressure and to be exemplary in the way you conduct yourself."[14]

Finally, it is timely to point out the existence of military elites who at one time were authorized to wear temporary ranks—or "local" ranks in SAF parlance and denoted with an "L/" before the rank abbreviation—while serving on multinational operations overseas. These practices have invariably led certain uninformed observers to view such actions as demotions rather than reversions. The use of local general and admiral ranks has involved selected senior officers serving on UN field missions, as the Defence Attaché at the Singapore Embassy in Washington (DA Washington), and at the helm of the multinational anti-

---

[10] Interview No. 25.

[11] Interview No. 15.

[12] "Let Us Find Hearts and Minds of SAF", p. 10.

[13] "Celebrating 30 Years of SAF Overseas Scholarships", *Army News* 62 (May 2000): 4.

[14] "Ready for Any Mission", *Straits Times (Scholarship Special)*, 7 Mar. 1997, p. 15.

piracy Combined Task Force 151 (CTF-151). This feature of the SAF is further examined in chapter 7.

5.2 Dr Goh and the Early SAF

The early growth of the SAF was made possible through the hard work of trailblazing pioneers and the numerous collective discussions that peppered the political echelons. Dr Goh was the key architect who played a part in almost every facet of the SAF, including promotions. His frequent visits to camps and bases and interactions with people there allowed him to know a good proportion of regular officers on a personal basis. Dhoraisingam Samuel worked with Goh in the defence and education ministries and provided this first-hand account:

> Dr [Goh's] direct contact with individual officers had another advantage. On one promotion exercise when the interviewing board submitted their recommendations to Dr [Goh] for his approval, the file was sent to me after Dr [Goh] had gone through the promotion list. Dr [Goh] had deleted some of the names of officers as he had personally known them and not fit for promotion [*sic*]. If Dr [Goh] through his personal contact found a capable officer, he would assign additional responsibilities to him and even promote him.[15]

Such additional responsibilities gave an officer visibility but could also prove to be a double-edged sword, as one general recalled:

> "One day I received a call and was told to report to Dr Goh's office. I was a Lieutenant Colonel then. Dr Goh wanted to showcase the SAF to the people of Singapore ... it was an opportunity, but my head was also on the chopping block. I came up with detailed suggestions and Dr Goh critiqued them. He asked questions and could tell if you put thought and effort into it ... one had to be confident ... In the end the displays turned out well and Dr Goh was happy."[16]

Besides meeting Goh's standards and expectations, it was also essential to decipher his actions. He frequently bypassed the chain of command and went straight to the source of any issue that caught his attention.[17] A staff paper submitted for Goh's approval passed muster if it returned marked with a "G", but "two circles" or his full name indicated failure.[18]

---

[15] Dhoraisingam, *Working for Dr. Goh Keng Swee*, p. 57.

[16] Interview No. 01.

[17] Desker and Kwa, *Goh Keng Swee*, pp. 92, 97, 100, 107; Oral History Centre, National Archives of Singapore, interview with COL (RET) John Morrice for "The Civil Service—A Retrospection" project, Accession No: 003306, Reel 10 of 13 (2008) pp. 270–1.

[18] Desker and Kwa, *Goh Keng Swee*, pp. 93, 98, 104.

Despite such eccentricities Dr Goh kept a lookout for good people to build and lead the SAF. He cast the net beyond the pool of professional military men and counted AOs such as Kirpa Ram Vij and Tan Chin Tiong, who were seconded to the SAF as uniformed officers, or capable civilian administrators such as Philip Yeo.[19] Goh also handpicked LG (RET) Winston Choo, who recalled how the news was delivered to him:

> "One day I was at the Command and Staff College at Fort Canning, Dr. Goh called me up and mapped out my entire military career for me. He said I was going to be given command of 4 SIR. I was to go to the Command and General Staff College in the US because I was going to be Director of General Staff. I was only about 30 years old then. I pointed out that if I became DGS so soon, my career would be very short because I wondered for how long I could remain as DGS. He told me not to worry, to just go and do it. As it turned out, I survived for 18 years as Chief."[20]

It must also be highlighted that talent on its own merits was insufficient for Goh, who took a no-nonsense approach. He held high expectations of senior officers, for the stakes were clear. Another general opined:

> "Dr Goh was a mentor to anyone he felt had talent. He nurtured those who did well. He was also merciless when it came to the question of upholding character and integrity. For example, COL [X] was demoted to LTC for not being completely truthful to Dr Goh. Dr Goh was sharp and saw through it. <pause> Dr Goh was preparing the SAF to be ready for war in those early days. Confrontation, riots, the Malaysian years, all made it clear to us that we would have to manage Malaysia and Indonesia one day. We were in danger. It was more vivid to us then. In later years this has not become so, but you must never belief it won't happen. The moment you do it will happen."[21]

While the SAF was fortunate to have leaders like Dr Goh in its formative years, there were no guarantees that others who followed would be equally selfless. Furthermore, no matter how objectively Goh approached personnel issues, they were still personal and subjective. A retired COL once quipped: "The thing about Goh Keng Swee, when he likes you, he likes you. That's the trouble."[22] A more

---

[19] In an official publication Philip Yeo was depicted as "Dr. Goh Keng Swee's protégé, technology buff and Permanent Secretary of MINDEF", See Chew and Tan, *Creating the Technology Edge*, p. 8.

[20] Desker and Kwa, *Goh Keng Swee*, p. 92.

[21] Interview No. 03.

[22] Oral History Centre, National Archives of Singapore, interview with COL (RET) Goh Lye Choon for "The Civil Service—A Retrospection" project, Accession No: 003275, Reel 17 of 17 (2008) p. 382.

objective system was required to guard against possible favouritism arising from cleavages within the officer corps and curtail any personality cults in personnel promotions.[23] Furthermore, the SAF Officer Corps had grown too large for any one individual to know its members personally and manage promotion and succession planning. Such concerns were also prevalent across the civil service.[24] Promotion systems across the uniformed and civil service had to be transparent, as then-Second Minister for Defence Teo Chee Hean reasoned: "… if you don't have rules and systems in place, but a very personalised system for promoting, moving and promoting people, you may well demoralise good people in the public service, who may feel that their opportunities for advancement are determined by factors other than merit."[25]

5.2.1 Project Wrangler

Despite Dr Goh's centrality in the promotion of senior officers in the early days, it was certainly not done on a whim. Project Wrangler was initiated under his watch in February 1974 as a pipeline to identify, test and groom regular officers deemed to have senior leadership potential. To consider the initiative as "a scholarship and leadership program for serving officers", as Barr claims, is erroneous because the project covers both scholars and non-scholars.[26] The rationale behind the project was rather simple:

> "The SAF needed brainpower to make a difference. This is an expensive initiative because it takes away brainpower from other institutions, ministries. The Wrangler scheme was established to shortlist and narrow down the list of individual officers to be monitored. Dr Goh himself chaired the Wrangler project. Those on the scheme were given exposure to special projects and mentors. The scheme was designed to get bright people into the system and advance them quicker than others. Some Wranglers are more inclined toward staff work, others command, some both staff and command."[27]

---

[23] For anecdotal evidence of perceived favouritism, see Yip Kin Cheng, "The Professional Soldier: Organisational and Occupational Commitment of Regular Officers in the Singapore Army", honours thesis, National University of Singapore, 2002, p. 34.

[24] Tan and Lim, "Potential Appraisal", p. 8.

[25] Warren Fernandez, *Without Fear or Favour: 50 Years of Singapore's Public Service Commission* (Singapore: Times Media for the Public Service Commission, 2001), p. 19.

[26] Barr, *Ruling Elite of Singapore*, p. 92.

[27] Interview No. 19.

Those who made the cut as Wranglers ascended the SAF's hierarchy along command and/or staff appointments and received promotions "regardless of age or seniority".[28] The term "Wrangler" was allegedly adopted from Cambridge University, and, perhaps coincidentally, Lee Hsien Loong was the only Wrangler in the sense of the pronoun from the inception of SAFOS in 1971 until the project was officially revealed in 1981.[29] The critical nature of identifying and grooming those with potential to lead at the highest echelons was taken very seriously. The Wrangler Committee provided civilian oversight and included senior defence bureaucrats and the military's elite nucleus.[30] An SAF officer needed to meet at least one of the following conditions to become a Wrangler: he had to be a returning scholar-officer, have an undergraduate degree with good honours, place in the top 15 per cent of advanced combat training courses, graduate from a foreign military academy, or receive recommendations through a superior's "Merit List".[31]

While the initiatives of Project Wrangler seemed sound in terms of objectives, practice fell short on a number of accounts; this was the situation also with promotions in the wider SAF.[32] First, Wranglers were often judged solely on performance in current positions and not in tandem with their potential to hold higher appointments. Second, recommendations by superiors were subjective and varied according to individuals. This impacted the final point, which was the selection, development and continual assessment of Wranglers. As a former CO OPC admitted: "Some officers who entered the Wrangler list on

---

[28] Paul Jensen, "Getting the Best Brains into SAF", *Straits Times*, 7 Sept. 1981, p. 1; Paul Jacob and Ronnie Wai, "PROJECT WRANGLER: What It's All About …", *Straits Times*, 7 Sept. 1981, p. 1; *Manpower Policies Affecting the SAF Officer*, p. 10.

[29] The name Wrangler is bestowed on undergraduate students who complete the mathematical tripos at Cambridge with first-class honours. The "senior wrangler" is the *primus inter pares*. See John Gascoigne, "Mathematics and Meritocracy: The Emergence of the Cambridge Mathematical Tripos", *Social Studies of Science* 14, 4 (Nov. 1984): 547–84; and "Hsien Loong Gets His Honours Degree", *Straits Times*, 22 June 1974, p. 7. Twenty-three of the 76 SAFOS recipients between 1971 and 1981 studied at Cambridge when Project Wrangler was revealed. Twenty took engineering, and one read economics. The only two who studied mathematics were Lee Hsien Loong, a Wrangler in 1974, and Lim Chuan Poh, who in 1981 was a second-year undergraduate.

[30] Senior civilian representation initially comprised the Minister for Defence, Second Minister for Defence, Minister of State (Defence), Permanent Secretaries of Defence, Deputy Secretaries of Defence, and Director Manpower. The military was represented by the CGS and DCGS.

[31] Jacob and Wai, "PROJECT WRANGLER: What It's All About …", p. 1; *Manpower Policies Affecting the SAF Officer*, p. 14.

[32] "New Look Wrangler to Better Spot Talent in SAF", *Straits Times*, 5 Apr. 1982, p. 11.

the basis of their scholastic achievements did not subsequently prove themselves in performance."[33]

The changes to manpower policies in 1982 led to several revisions of the Wrangler scheme. University and foreign military academy graduates continued to be automatically included as "provisional Wranglers", the top graduates of advanced courses were included on a case-by-case basis, while superiors' "Merit Lists" were replaced by a Promotion Recommendation Board (PRB) at different levels.[34] Psychological testing was also introduced to weed out those with "psychopathological problems".[35] Specific details invariably changed as the SAF evolved, but Project Wrangler has remained true to its core focus of identifying and grooming the top 10 per cent to 15 per cent of the SAF Officer Corps, essentially officers with the potential to make COL and above by retirement.[36] It is perhaps not surprising that the SAF subscribes to the Pareto Principle, according to which "80% of the effort involved must be concentrated on the top 20% of staff members".[37]

Finally, this initiative had a divisive effect on the officer corps between those who had a bright future and those who felt a ceiling was placed on their careers because they were not Wranglers. Edwin Lee, author of *Singapore: The Unexpected Nation*, reasoned:

> Many of their brother officers who were not chosen, would have been disappointed by the scholarship schemes, and Project Wrangler, and felt that the future belonged, not to them, but to the scholar-officers and the 'Wranglers' ... Meritocracy in the SAF had its less happy side. The search and grooming of scholar-officers inevitably led to a class distinction between them and the others. These others, many of who were capable and experienced, could not accept the fact that academic qualifications should count for so much in the Profession-of-Arms ... Their discontent, which NSmen knew of, with varying degrees of empathy, could be detrimental to nation-building as a by-product of NS.[38]

The career progressions of Wranglers were once directly managed by a committee chaired by the defence minister. The present day-to-day running of the project and career management of those in the rank of COL and above has been delegated to OPC with an active-duty LTC/SLTC (usually from the army) at

---

[33] Ibid.

[34] *Manpower Policies Affecting the SAF Officer*, p. 14.

[35] Ibid.

[36] Ibid., pp. 14–5.

[37] Tan and Lim, "Potential Appraisal", p. 18.

[38] Lee, *Singapore: The Unexpected Nation*, pp. 289, 292–3.

the helm. Civilian oversight of this crucial personnel pool is maintained with OPC placed under the jurisdiction of DIR Manpower, who is subordinate to the Deputy Secretary (DS) for Administration. Both senior civilian appointments reside within MINDEF's Defence Management Group (DMG).[39] This is not surprising: Janowitz identified oversight of manpower issues, specifically promotions, as "a crucial lever of civilian control".[40] In addition, approvals for decisions and actions beyond the norm lie solely with senior civilian bureaucrats and the political appointees on the recommendation of senior military officers.[41] Non-Wranglers—officers likely to retire in the ranks of SLTC and below—have their careers managed by personnel management branches or centres within the respective services, such as the Army Officers Management Centre (AOMC) under G1 Army (the army's personnel department).

5.2.2 *Officer Appraisal until 1982*

From the early days of the SAF until the manpower revisions of 1982, an officer's promotion was based on meeting two to four requirements.[42] The first was the specified "time in rank" norm (which was shorter for Wranglers) before one was considered eligible for promotion. The second requirement, applicable only to lieutenants and captains, was to pass the respective LTA-to-CPT and CPT-to-MAJ exam. These promotion exams were implemented to confirm that junior officers possessed baseline competencies but certainly disadvantaged officers in

---

[39] OPC was first established to manage the careers of all Regular officers but later focused solely on the crème de la crème of the SAF Officer Corps due to manpower growth. OPC works closely with the SAF Recruitment Centre to publicize the SAFOS and SMS at publicity events. The selection of SAFOS recipients falls under the Public Service Commission (PSC), which also administers other top-tier government scholarships to ensure synergy in the management of Singapore's talent pool. Ivan Heng, "SAF Training Awards", *Pioneer* (Oct. 1985): 4–5; Oral History Centre, National Archives of Singapore, interview with COL (RET) Ramachandran Menon for "The Civil Service—A Retrospection" project, Accession No: 003250, Reel 11 of 17 (2007), p. 236.

[40] Janowitz, *Professional Soldier*, p. 353.

[41] This group included the Director Manpower Policy Division under MINDEF's Defence Management Group, Deputy Secretary (Administration) in charge of the Defence Management Group, the Permanent Secretaries in MINDEF, and various political appointments such as Minister of State (Defence), Senior Minister of State (Defence), Second Minister for Defence and Minister for Defence. Advice can be sourced from the CDF, the service chiefs and the Director Military Security Department.

[42] *Manpower Policies Affecting the SAF Officer*, p. 6; "Finer Points and Aim of Scheme Explained", *Straits Times*, 5 Apr. 1982, p. 11; "Promotion Exercise '83", *Navy News* (Aug. 1983): 3.

more hectic appointments.[43] Such practices predated Singapore's independence, as one general who served during *Konfrontasi* remembered: "I took the promotion exam while in Sabah on operations. We would fly to Kuching for our exams on civilian aircraft with our weapons. It was quite normal then. <laughs>"[44] Third, junior officers attended a promotion interview and required the interview panel's approval for promotion. Majors and above were considered for promotion in absentia. Promotion interviews proved subjective and even perfunctory at times. Still, performance and the ability to impress proved all-important, as a one-star recounted:

> "In the earlier days it (the promotion system) was a lot more subjective. The promotion interview was chaired by Perm[anent] Sec[retary] and CDF. I remember entering the room and the panel were seated up there, literally, on an elevated stage. It was for junior officers eligible for Lieutenant and Captain promotions. I thought it was awkward. Did they know me or what I did based on a few minutes of interaction or from the piece of paper in front of them?"[45]

The final requirement was a rather vague assessment made by an officer's immediate superior and whether the unit recommended the officer for promotion. This annual Staff Confidential Report (SCR) was forwarded to the formation commander for endorsement and, where applicable, a promotion recommendation made. The SCR also proved subjective because immediate superiors differed in expectations and standards so that strictness or leniency and not necessarily an officer's performance often determined assessment grades.[46] COL (RET) Ramachandran Menon, a former ACGS (Personnel) in the late-1970s, recollected the practice:

> The annual performance ranking up till then (the revisions of 1982) had been identical to the standard government format that ultimately provided only a vague summary of how an officer had performed the preceding year. It was then left to the Officers' Personnel Centre to review previous records and attempt to shortlist the individual deserving of promotion, depending as much on the assessor as the assessed.[47]

---

[43] For example, the LTA-to-CPT promotion exams for army officers were administered by SATO and covered tactics and map reading. The CPT-to-MAJ promotion exam was administered by the Military History Branch at the Command and Staff College. "SATO— More than Just a School for Captains", *Pioneer* (Jan. 1977): 20–2; "Where History Isn't Bunk", *Pioneer* (Feb. 1977): 8–9.

[44] Interview No. 19.

[45] Interview No. 17.

[46] *Manpower Policies Affecting the SAF Officer*, p. 6.

[47] Menon, *One of a Kind*, pp. 340–1.

Superiors were at times too lax in their assessments, with detrimental effects. Dr Goh openly rebuked senior officers at the 1973 promotion ceremony:

> … when your subordinate officer is found to be inadequate, you should not hesitate to give him an unfavourable assessment in your annual confidence report … As matters stand, virtually all commanders in the SAF are reluctant to give a frank report on weak officers under their command. The result is that the annual confidential reporting system is virtually useless.[48]

Other superiors also made promotion recommendations without accounting for an officer's potential to meet the demands and responsibilities of the next higher rank.[49] This placed the SAF at risk of fulfilling the Peter Principle, whereby officers climbed the hierarchy until they reached a level of incompetence. This was certainly not what the SAF wanted or needed.

5.2.3 The Shell System

Such problems were not confined solely to the SAF as the civil service expanded in size. There was general discomfort with a system where "promotions and appraisals were decided subjectively by bosses based solely on their own perception and understanding of the employees".[50] There was also a pressing need for succession planning, meaning those with potential had to be identified early. The best solution, so it seemed, came from the cutthroat world of business, as LKY explained:

> "Shell Oil, the multinational, once gave me the idea for the term 'helicopter quality'. In other words, you can see a problem in total and you can zero in on the detail, which you have to see to solve, and zoom on it. That's called helicopter quality. Now, if you are too low, your helicopter quality is too low, you do not see the whole picture nor can your zoom be powerful."[51]

The then-PM was so impressed that he dispatched a six-member delegation of civil servants in 1982 to study the appraisal system first-hand at the company's registered office in London.[52] Royal Dutch Shell (hereafter Shell) ranked

---

[48] Goh Keng Swee, *The Practice of Economic Growth* (Singapore: Federal Publications, 1977), p. 232.

[49] *Manpower Policies Affecting the SAF Officer*, p. 6.

[50] Tan and Lim, "Potential Appraisal", pp. 8–9.

[51] Plate, *Conversations with Lee Kuan Yew*, p. 68.

[52] Fernandez, *Without Fear or Favour*, pp. 43, 120. The six-member team that visited Shell's head office in London from 1 to 18 February 1982 was led by Joseph Yuvaraj Manuel Pillay and comprised Lee Ek Tieng, Wong Hung Khim, Koh Cher Siang, Lim Siong Guan and Er Kwong Wah. Shell would also provide "pointers on the art of scenario planning" for MINDEF later, in 1991.

the performances of executives within the same seniority and estimated an employee's Current Estimated Potential (CEP)—the highest job that could be held comfortably in the organization by age 45—on an annual basis.[53] Some others defined CEP as the highest rank (and concomitant appointment) that an officer could "hold comfortably" and "handle competently" before retirement assuming unlimited opportunities.[54]

While performance specifics varied across different roles, CEP was matched against four common qualities encapsulated in the acronym HAIR. "Helicopter vision" was the ability to both see details and contextualize within the big picture. "Analytical power" framed how well one turned complicated problems into workable and thoroughly examined segments. "Imagination" was an individual's perception in uncovering possible alternative and non-obvious solutions. "Reality" came with the interpretation of information grounded in reality and intuition leading to feasible solutions.[55] CEP based on these HAIR qualities was adopted as a tool to identify and nurture talented individuals (i.e., those with high CEP) across the civil service and in GLCs.[56] This was also the case for the SAF, with slight modifications. Such qualities were openly championed for those who aspired to important postings in the then newly created (1983) Joint Operations and Planning Directorate (JOPD).[57] Revisions to the CEP yardsticks were made over time to include "helicopter" and "whole person" dimensions, namely, intellectual qualities, results orientation, and

[53] Menon, *One of a Kind*, pp. 340–1.

[54] "How Officers Move up the Ranks", p. 2; Presentation on "Human Capital Development in the Singapore Civil Service" by Lim Soo Hoon, Permanent Secretary (Public Service Division), at the 11th Malaysian Civil Service Conference, 21–22 Aug. 2006, unpan1.un.org/intradoc/groups/public/documents/apcity/unpan028179.pdf (no longer available); Jon S.T. Quah, *Public Administration Singapore Style* (Singapore: Talisman Publishing, 2010), p. 80.

[55] *Manpower Policies Affecting the SAF Officer*, pp. 10–4; Ronnie Wai, "No Quotas when Promoting Officers", *Straits Times*, 29 June 1983, p. 14; Tan and Lim, "Potential Appraisal", pp. 4–5; "How Officers Move up the Ranks", p. 2.

[56] Oral History Centre, National Archives of Singapore, interview with Lim Siong Guan for "The Civil Service—A Retrospection" project, Accession No: 003060, Reel 5 of 14, pp. 73–5; Tan and Lim, "Potential Appraisal", p. 1; Lian Tian Tse, "Application of Logistic Regression and Survival Analysis to the Study of CEP, Manpower Performance and Attrition", master's thesis, US Naval Postgraduate School, 1993; David Seth Jones, "Recent Reforms in Singapore's Administrative Elite: Responding to the Challenges of a Rapidly Changing Economy and Society", *Asian Journal of Political Science* 10, 2 (Dec. 2002): 70–93.

[57] "Joint Armed Forces Team Will Be Set Up", *Straits Times*, 16 Apr. 1983, p. 1; "SAF Should Be the Concern of Every Singaporean", *Straits Times*, 16 Apr. 1983, p. 14.

leadership qualities.[58] The civil service currently utilizes the AIM (Analytical and intellectual capacity, Influence and collaboration, and Motivation for excellence) principles for CEP and augmented appraisals with a 360-degree feedback for leaders.[59]

5.2.4 Officer Appraisal after 1982

The SAF instituted new manpower policies in 1982 predicated on Shell's practices modified to reflect the SAF's unique circumstances and practices. Concurrent changes to the salary schemes were made to attract and retain officers. The promotion system also underwent key changes to make it more robust. "Time in rank" requirements were eradicated and obviously benefited high-flying officers. Eleven were made COL in 1982; ten of them would receive further promotions in due time.[60] Flexibility was built into the promotion exams, which were renamed the General Military Knowledge Exams (GMKE). Officers with hectic schedules were no longer penalized when it came to receiving the next promotion, but passing the exams was still mandatory for further promotions. The GMKE were in due course superseded by a formal tri-service course prior to attendance at CSC.[61]

---

[58] Lim, "Human Capital Development in the Singapore Civil Service"; "The Truth about Performance Management", *Challenge: Public Service for the 21st Century* (Oct. 2006), www.challenge.gov.sg/magazines/archive/2006_10/staff/staff.html (no longer available). Shell's revised attributes are: Capacity, Achievement and Relationships (CAR). Kim E. Ferrarie, "Processes to Assess Leadership Potential Keep Shell's Talent Pipeline Full", *Journal of Organisational Excellence* 24, 3 (Summer 2005): 17–22.

[59] "Written Reply to Parliamentary Question on CEP and 360 Degree Feedback in the Civil Service", *Public Service Division*, 15 Aug. 2016.

[60] The 1982 promotion list to COL included Boey Tak Hap, Chin Chow Yoon, Chin Siat Yoon, Patrick Choy, Lee Hsien Loong, Lee Seng Kong, James Leo, Sin Boon Wah, Michael Teo, Colin Theseira and Gary Yeo. "Promotion: Ranks and Responsibilities", *Pioneer* (Aug. 1982): 6. All except COL (RET) Lee Seng Kong were subsequently promoted to BG/RADM1.

[61] The five-week Joint Junior Staff Course (JJSC) was first held on 7 June 1989 for cross-service learning and networking, and in preparation for appointments in MINDEF. The Tri-Service Course superseded the GMKE and JJSC in October 1998 with 43 courses conducted until its re-establishment in May 2006 as a week-long SAF Staff Officers' Course covering non-operational staff work plus a four-week Tri-Service Warfighter Course (TSWC) covering SAF joint operations. *Manpower Policies Affecting the SAF Officer*, p. 8; "First Joint Junior Staff Course", *Pioneer* (July 1989): 42; "SAFTI MI Scores Another World First for Tri-Service Training", *Army News* (Oct. 1998): 2; "Tri-Service Warfighter Course (TSWC)", *SAFTI Link* (2006): 7; *SAFTI 50*, pp. 89–90.

The greatest emphasis and changes came with the appraisal and promotion system.[62] The SCR—since superseded by the Annual Feedback Report (AFR) and Performance Management Report (PMR)—required inputs from people beyond the immediate superior and co-opted the relevant hierarchy for collective assessment. CEP assessments also replaced the commander's recommendation list.[63] Since 1982 the SAF's appraisal system has been manifested as the Annual Ranking Exercise, which generates merit lists of all officers across the same rank and is based on the twin yardsticks of performance ("realized past success or failure") and potential ("anticipated future success or failure").[64] An officer's first CEP is made two years after enlistment and subsequently revised annually. It is adjusted if required and determines the path and pace of an individual's rank ascension assuming realized performances coincide with projections.[65]

5.3   Performance and Potential

Performance does not mean merely checking off various key performance indicators but is a holistic assessment of an officer. In 1983 it was underlined that the hallmarks of "a good officer are commitment and leadership: Character, discipline, compassion and guts built on brains".[66] A decade later it was highlighted that Singapore and the SAF demanded "qualities such as organization ability, reaction under stress, team work, responsibility and discipline" from officers.[67] In 2011 LKY reiterated that "[t]alent, therefore takes in not only raw academic or professional success, but also the fuzzier concept of having the 'right' personality and outlook. Integrity and honesty are vital."[68] The latter qualities were emphasized by the late President Devan Nair, who explained: "brains alone are not enough, for crooks also have good brains. Which is why qualities of character and motivation are equally important."[69]

While the qualities of sound character are necessary, they are insufficient on their own merits. BG (RET) then-MAJ Chin Phei Chen, a former CO OPC,

---

[62] Paul Jensen, "Getting the Best Brains into SAF", *Straits Times*, 7 Sept. 1981, p. 1.

[63] "New Look Wrangler to Better Spot Talent in SAF", p. 11.

[64] "Towards a Dynamic, Thinking Man's Army", *Straits Times*, 27 May 1982, p. 10; "Teamwork among Rank and File a Success: Chok Tong", *Straits Times*, 28 June 1985, p. 15; Tan and Lim, "Potential Appraisal", pp. 2–3.

[65] "How Officers Move up the Ranks", p. 2.

[66] Wai, "No Quotas when Promoting Officers", p. 14.

[67] "How Officers Move up the Ranks", p. 2.

[68] Han et al., *Lee Kuan Yew*, p. 100.

[69] "What Price Our High-Achievers?" *Straits Times*, 2 July 1982, p. 16.

noted: "Some officers may have the impression that promotion is based solely on potential. In reality, both potential and performance are equally important."[70] Another general with experience in personnel issues further explained: "Ranking takes place within all officers of the same rank and is based on performance and CEP. If an officer is outside the formation, a formation ranking is also made for checking purposes. Performance determines an officer's promotion prospects and CEP the speed of promotion. To be promoted you need both."[71]

An officer who had a high CEP but did not perform was considered "deadwood" and should, in practice, remain at the present rank.[72] It was also highlighted that "whether a serviceman is actually promoted is his ability to perform and excel in his work".[73] This is certainly true early in the military career, but CEP becomes increasingly ossified in later years. It is the officer who performs, possesses a high CEP, and is deemed to be of irreproachable character that has the highest likelihood of entering the military elite.

The performance and CEP of every active-duty SAF officer, both Regular and NSF, is reviewed annually. Superiors appraise subordinates on key indicators stipulated at the start of an assessment period with a grade of A (superior performance) to E (failure).[74] While character may not improve grades, any flaws are certainly detrimental. Peer appraisals are frequently utilized as an indicator of character. An individual's CEP is stipulated in the form of a specified rank. Performance reports are revealed to officers, with avenues for grievances and recourse over disagreements. CEP, however, remains the purview of assessment panels only because it is subjective and could affect morale.[75] It must be handled carefully, as one officer observed:

> "CEP is not an exact science. It is subjective and dependent on who (superior) fights for who (subordinate). The ranking committee must 'pen it down' (document the decisions and reasons). I had to make sure that you don't have to be an SAF scholar to advance but you have to be a Wrangler to be seen to be better than the others."[76]

The issue of subjectivity is further compounded as it is easy to forget that CEP is only a current estimation. Appraisals from subsequent postings are cross-

---

[70] "How Officers Move up the Ranks", p. 2.

[71] Interview No. 11.

[72] Hin and Lim, "Potential Appraisal", p. 16.

[73] "Promotion Exercise '83", *Navy News* (Aug. 1983), p. 3.

[74] "Who Gets Promoted and How?" *Straits Times*, 29 June 1994, p. 2.

[75] Tan and Lim, "Potential Appraisal", p. 16; Interview No. 19.

[76] Interview No. 19.

checked for accuracy in CEP projections, and consistency provides confirmation. Furthermore, as one service chief explained: "CEP has both staff and command tracks. At the junior level if your CEP is two to three grades above current rank it is a good sign that you are promotable."[77] Each appraisee has a reporting officer who is usually the direct superior and a countersigning officer with knowledge of the appraised. For example, in an air force squadron "[f]or an engineering officer, the CO writes a report and the base S4 (logistics officer) countersigns. For the pilot officer, the OC writes the report and the CO countersigns."[78]

In the pre-1982 appraisal system this would be the end of it, with the SCR submitted to the formation HQ for processing and a promotions list generated after the necessary interviews and exams were completed. After 1982, however, the AFR and PMR are forwarded up the chain of command for panel deliberation over performance grade and CEP, the merger of subordinate ranking lists, and consensus must be achieved before collective approval is given. This is a key gatekeeping feature built in to avoid the corruption of the system by individuals or groups to reward acolytes and purge rivals.[79] The first panel takes place at the unit (battalion, ship or squadron) level with the CO as chairman. After this panel reaches consensus on the various appraisals, the latter are forwarded to the next higher HQ where applicable. An admiral illustrated the practice in the navy: "The first level of ranking is at the ship and then merged at the squadron level. Here the squadron commander and COs will decide. Then it moves on to the flotilla and fleet. It is all subjective, but new postings will check for consistency. Different vocations will be ranked separately up until LTC, where it is merged across formations."[80]

The basis for this is simple, as other flag officers reasoned. The first explained:

> "There is structure in the ranking appraisal in that it aims to forge consensus on whether people are good. It is not something that is privately decided and is as elaborate a process and as fair as you can get. The majors ranked the captains, lieutenant colonels ranked the majors, the colonels the lieutenant colonels, and so on. In terms of appointments the OCs provide feedback to the COs, and the CO level is the first level of consensus. You start this process at different levels in September–October each year. By January–February the next year all ranking is consolidated at [service HQ] and then submitted to the CDF Board."[81]

---

[77] Interview No. 15.

[78] Interview No. 24.

[79] Lee, *Defect or Defend*, p. 40.

[80] Interview No. 15.

[81] Interview No. 16.

A second officer reiterated:

> "Both performance ranking and CEP are decided by a panel of people. For example, captains are judged by a panel of COs and brigade commanders who have exposure to other captains not in their direct chain of command. If changes are made to the ranking and CEP list there must always be an explanation why it was so. The panel acts as the check and balance and must be satisfied with the explanations given. The system fails if this is not the case and it is a case of collective failure."[82]

A third officer said:

> "Problems arise when individuals change ranking without explanation, or if the argument put forward is not convincing it is also a problem. Changes can occur if processes fail or if you think you have 'higher wisdom' than others. But there must always be an explanation of the basis for making changes. It must be stated and convincing. If you are powerful and the ranking committee members are part of your clique, then you can do what you want. The SAF has a system and the institution remembers. Therefore stories and myths exist."[83]

It is difficult to ascertain whether there has been a collective failure in ranking exercises. Disconcerting whispers occasionally circulate citing widespread disillusionment after changes are made to performance ranking within a formation. The resignation of Regulars en masse from a formation is supposedly tangible evidence, but precise information is unavailable and approximations have proven elusive at best.

The Annual Ranking Exercise is made more tedious because the assessed officers are not privy to these closed-door panels; nor are the conversations or initiatives through which consensus is forged a matter of open information. The SAF, however, is not alone in this challenge. An observer of civilian firms noted that "performance appraisal has aroused more controversy than most human resource management practices" but also concluded that "[t]he Singaporean civil service is openly meritocratic, and boasts no pretence towards representativeness".[84] Also, since the armed services operate on a non-profit basis, "[t]he measures of performance are not so clear and objective. In for-profit organizations there is a bottom line to meet."[85] These issues are compounded by individual perceptions. One interview participant reasoned that "[t]he politics of envy happens in

---

[82] Interview No. 12.

[83] Interview No. 15.

[84] Sarah Vallance, "Performance Appraisal in Singapore, Thailand and the Philippines: A Cultural Perspective", *Australian Journal of Public Administration* 58, 3 (Dec. 1999): 78, 83.

[85] Interview No. 15.

all organizations. People get upset over it."[86] "Ranking is difficult to compare because it is not so black and white," explained another. "Was the individual a marginal candidate? Is the CEP for a given appointment higher? What are the circumstances of the specific case? The problem is that people will see what they want to see."[87] A third added:

> "[In] ranking there must be a common understanding that you are not just fighting for officers, to place them in positions for reward. It is never about carrying the flag. You fight for your people by beginning with their well-being in mind, by training them and holding them to high standards. You mentor, push and develop them. Then ask: 'Do the people around agree with the ranking?' And remember the starting point of ranking is from the first to the last day of the ranking period. The whole period and not just when it comes to submitting the ranking report. But one human flaw is that people always think they are better than what they are."[88]

Finally, a fourth participant opined: "Those who lag behind in promotions and postings tend to feel the system is unfair. Not all will agree, and a meritocratic system does not seek to please everyone. If it does, then the system is not meritocratic anymore."[89]

The notion of fairness is debatable, and it is essential to view the system for what it is and not what one thinks it should be. Several common practices were built into the appraisal system for it to remain credible. The SAF apportions performance grades according to a standardized bell-curve distribution to account for relatively lenient and stringent assessors.[90] This controls the numbers of officers promoted annually, but adequate discretionary flexibility is built in to ensure well-performing officers are not penalized by statistics. As for CEP, logic dictates that officers on Project Wrangler have been assessed to be of "COL and above" calibre. Non-Wranglers could realistically expect CEPs in the range of CPT to SLTC. In the early stages of the uniformed career there is room for variation. However, CEP converges with reality once the career event horizon is crossed and becomes increasingly ossified when an officer reaches the age range of 34 to 36, the rank of senior MAJ, and completes CSC. Finally, fairness comes with the soft skills of superiors who show care and concern for their subordinates'

---

[86] Interview No. 26.

[87] Interview No. 15.

[88] Interview No. 09.

[89] Interview No. 23.

[90] On average the top 10 per cent receive A's, the next 20 per cent B's, the middle 40 per cent C's, and the lowest 30 per cent D's and E's.

careers. Very simply, "[i]f you want family values you must show concern to invest in a guy, and be a father figure".[91]

Open and frank communication remains key in handling the sensitive issues of performance appraisal and potential estimation, as a DIV COMD reasoned:

> "To prevent the perception of 'unfairness', there must be rapport and communication with your subordinates at all levels. You must stay connected and really know your people. Know how they are beyond the confines of the camp, get to know their family. Care and concern is for all ranks including the officers and not just the men. It must be genuine and there from the start. If you only start communicating when people write resignation letters then it is too late."[92]

Another air force general reiterated this point and emphasized the importance of setting clear expectations:

> "I want to identify potential as early as I can. Ranking starts at the start of the year and not at the end. Yardsticks must be made known so that you can justify the ranking. It is easier to give higher grades to those who are more 'senior', but I give projects to test and make the yardsticks known. These are above the normal job scope. Everyone does their job, but where is the premium? Performance bonus is given for performances exceeding expectations. Because everyone works hard you get 13th month (salary bonus), but now we are talking not just about working hard. Communication with your people is very important. They need to know that if they don't work hard they can expect a C. So the key is to communicate early and also truthfully. They need to earn their performance grade, and it will never come on a silver platter. You also need to remind people where they stand along the way. There is no right or wrong, but it is useless to tell people only at the end. I place a premium on exceeding tasks, leadership, initiative, and drive to meet objectives. As a CO, for example, you want to judge your flight commanders on leadership, ability to translate your intent and guidance into tangible actions. I look out for these attributes. If I need to step in and sort things out then you know your performance can start with a D. I compare the A grade against a set of attributes for growth, efficiency and effectiveness. I mean, our people are all qualified and have brains, so I look for independent and fearless decision making. Think, rationalize, and go with it! Further up, you want your COs to decide, stand by their decisions, and be responsible for all consequences. Regardless of vocation, including engineers. But officers like that are not in abundance, therefore ranking is quite easy for me. <laughs>"[93]

---

[91] Interview No. 24.

[92] Interview No. 06.

[93] Interview No. 16.

Equity in performance appraisal and potential estimation are subjected to checks and balances essential to maintaining a robust system. These are never easy exercises, as various interview participants attested. One highlighted the perennial challenge of finding a good fit for officers to serve in a capacity commensurate with their abilities and personal ambitions:

> "Potential can be judged by a person's (reporting officer) experience. The aim of the ranking exercise is to distinguish between the top, middle and bottom. Limited potential does not mean an officer is no good. It is about finding the correct fit. If an officer is given a job beyond his abilities, all will suffer. The organization, the officer, and the people around him. Once potential is reached the officer can still contribute. But this is a tough issue, and leaders at all levels are responsible for challenging their people and exposing them to demanding jobs."[94]

Another interviewee underlined the twin responsibilities of representation on a ranking panel—championing the justified interests of subordinates and possessing sound reasons for performance grades:

> "How do you apportion the performance grade? There is a ratio. The pain of ranking is in the pressure. A ratio is needed if you want system discipline, because there are lenient and strict leaders. A ratio is used to normalize across the different leaders. Some argue it is too rigid, but the SAF works on the philosophy that if there is a good candidate then the superior will have to carry the staff through. At the ranking committee discussions the members must also agree or disagree with stated reasons."[95]

Another explained further:

> "Any responsible commander will push people up, but there exists quotas for performance rankings. There will be give and take as there is a need to balance the cohort within a bell curve. There are checks in the system to ensure quotas for promotion. It is a rigid structure, but there is spare 'bandwidth' at ranking boards for arbitration. There is also a need to justify A's as well as D's."[96]

Unscrupulous officers who practise favouritism and cronyism do not hesitate to exploit the subjective nature of performance gradings and CEP assessments. This is why stringent and tedious measures are essential to protect the integrity of the Annual Ranking Exercise. One general highlighted these realities and stressed the need for awareness and inclusiveness for the system to work:

---

[94] Interview No. 25.

[95] Interview No. 18.

[96] Interview No. 23.

"You cannot prevent cronyism and cliques. It happens and will happen. I maintained an open door policy so that a private soldier could come in and see me. If you're good, you're good. It is those you do not get along with where I consciously work at so as not to unconsciously penalize him … I also look out that in the ranking process you break up the cliques. You know people are fighting for some people. If something is amiss it is up to you to step in. You must also declare your interest. You cannot eradicate this from occurring, but you need to be conscious that is exists. You must not be guilty of doing all this. You must break it up because it affects morale. A clique is a sign of insecurity … Bickering among officers exist based on individual personality. This is a nature of military relationships. Professional jealousy exists and will always exist. If two generals cannot get along can you afford to remove them both?"[97]

Another explained the need to tread carefully in such matters:

"Bickering among the top brass and cultivation of cliques are unhealthy. When I was [a member of the elite nucleus] I broke the cliques. While we must plan for succession I advocated the view we do not have the depth nor are we fortunate enough to select one and remove the others. The challenge is how to manage and not let it become adversarial. That's where you hear out views of [subordinate commanders] and use channels to hear ground sentiment. People are always looking [at the actions of senior leaders]. The important thing is to be inclusive. Include people from cliques and respect them for who they are."[98]

Two Singaporean academics cited four further possible shortcomings of the ascension system. First is the halo effect, where appraisers "allow one overwhelming characteristic of the appraisee to affect their assessment" and overshadow other attributes.[99] Second, the leniency or strictness effect occurs when an appraisal panel is "excessively lenient" and at other times "excessively strict", which benefits or penalizes the appraisees.[100] Third, the central tendency effect "is the reluctance of the appraisers to rate people at the extreme ends of the scale" because they do not know the appraised officer adequately.[101] Finally, interpersonal bias occurs "where appraisers have great personal preference or dislike for the appraisee which will have tremendous effect on the appraisee's ratings".[102]

---

[97] Interview No. 19.

[98] Interview No. 25.

[99] Tan and Lim, "Potential Appraisal", p. 22.

[100] Ibid.

[101] Ibid., p. 23.

[102] Ibid., p. 22.

Perhaps there is no greater influence on CEP than an individual officer's level of education. Education starts off as a proxy for potential in the first two to three years of an officer's career before realized performances and superiors' assessments are supposed to take precedence.[103] In 1981, Goh Chok Tong rationalized:

> "A graduate is not synonymous with a good officer and a non-graduate an average officer. Given the social and economic conditions today, a university degree is a fair first indication of brain, but that is about all. There are other qualities required of a good officer besides a good academic record—character, commitment and leadership. Leadership is the most problematical. It is more inborn than nurtured."[104]

First PS (Defence) Lim Siong Guan reiterated a year later: "… we don't see ourselves constrained by whether the officer is a graduate or not, because by the time you come to this (senior) level, either you have proved it in your performance or you have not. And it's potential you must be able to see, not from your degree but from performance and the kind of thinking you put into various issues and so forth."[105]

This was exactly how Project Wrangler was envisaged, but as COL (RET) Menon observed:

> The CEP not only provided the standing of the officer among his peers, but also underwrote his career planning by OPC. The Shell system resolved the arbitrary issues that had plagued the traditional performance reporting, giving a sense of purpose to the charting of career paths in a very large organization, and forcing assessors to make hard comparative choices. But with the best of intentions, an assessor could not help being influenced by the educational qualifications of the assessed, thereby favouring the higher educated and those with prestigious scholarships. It tended to maroon the less qualified officer in the lower stratum.[106]

Several interview participants proffered similar views and remarked on the undue influence of education on an officer's career trajectory. One general from the earlier years noted:

> "Dr Goh was not just for brains but also fighters, as long as the latter could command. Over the years the focus has been on brains. The SAFOS was to entice the best brains with the benefits of tertiary education overseas and full pay. To accommodate the scholars OCS was shortened. It was eventually cut from 14 to 10 months. People soon saw the SAF scholarship as a stepping stone for something greater. Eventually certain

---

[103] Interview No. 25.

[104] "Let Us Find Hearts and Minds of SAF", p. 10.

[105] Fong and Wai, "Top Officers Given Exposure", p. 1.

[106] Menon, *One of a Kind*, pp. 340–1.

elements crept in. COs might be hesitant to take action against scholars because of their 'halo' where they are predestined to rise to high positions. That being said, many who get there do deserve it."[107]

This view was reinforced by another interviewee: "I feel that today it is largely academic qualifications that are used to base your CEP. There is a need to look at the overall picture. Are academic credentials the only criteria? When we first started off maybe it is OK."[108] Even grades within degrees have at times proven significant: "Whether an officer is scheme B (pass or merit degree) or C (good honours degree) should not determine CEP, but it has happened. CEP is very subjective and is usually capped at two grades up."[109]

The primacy of education was noted also in a 1993 study by a MINDEF civilian official at the US Naval Postgraduate School: he concluded that higher education levels predicted higher CEP.[110] On the whole, an officer's education was not sufficient on its own to affect performance assessments but those with lower education levels were disadvantaged as it affected CEP and subsequently capped promotion prospects.[111]

The possibility of negative influences on appraisals obliged the military establishment to improve the robustness of the system. The way forward was to reach confirmation on decisions through consensus by involving different panels further up the hierarchy to minimize "prejudice, bias, human error and allow more room for fair and honest analysis".[112] Several practices were strictly enforced. First, at least two members of the panel were required to possess first-hand knowledge of the appraised officer, in order to prevent assessments grounded on hearsay. Second, the appraisal panel had to be large enough to avoid positive and negative biases. Finally, members had an equal say as they worked towards consensus but the final decision rested with the panel chairperson. While these practices might seem simplistic on paper, realities told a different story, especially in the early 1980s during their nascent implementation. It boiled down to ensuring that the appraised officer's performance and not the specific

---

[107] Interview No. 03.

[108] Interview No. 24.

[109] Interview No. 11.

[110] Lian, "Application of Logistic Regression and Survival Analysis to the Study of CEP, Manpower Performance and Attrition", p. 47.

[111] S.R. Nathan with Timothy Auger, *An Unexpected Journey: Path to the Presidency* (Singapore: Editions Didier Millet, 2011), p. 195.

[112] "Promotion Exercise '83", *Navy News* (Aug. 1983): 3; "Who Gets Promoted and How?" p. 2; Tan and Lim, "Potential Appraisal", p. 9.

vocation mattered most. An air force general recalled one particularly heated discussion:

> "Within [formation K] there was individual unit ranking, and this is followed by a cross unit ranking for comparison. The Shell CEP system was implemented in 1984. It was not easy to assess CEP. It took time for people to accept it. At the ranking board you try to hear everybody's views. I believe that in every organization there exists a spread of talent which follows a bell curve. Who is better relative to each other. So ranking is not a given conclusion. As [the formation commander] I approved rankings for LTC downward. Of course the unit COs always provided inputs. For colonels it was collectively done by Head Air Manpower, CAF and [the formation commander]. Then in a ranking forum we need to do cross-ranking. Once I represented [formation K] when I was a Major and the rest were LTC and Colonel. I was quite vocal. My officers (from a specific vocation) had to be ranked higher. The chairman thought I was overly vocal. He did not agree and asked me to leave the room. But this is a fair process, so he eventually asked me to come back. <laughs>"[113]

Another admiral experienced similar teething problems, where competing superiors vied for their subordinates to be recognized:

> "Post-1982 it (the appraisal system) was a big improvement. In the early days of implementation it would take a long time. We would start at eight in the morning, and chief said we're not leaving until the list is done. We often went past 2359 (midnight). This revision was painful initially because we spent hours arguing, especially when two commanders would 'fight for' (rank) one candidate. How could we merge different vocations? The system forces judgement in that all officers of a particular rank were on one single ranking list but forcing different vocations into a list is quite artificial. Therefore there are separate lists for different vocations. This matches reality, and the ranking order made better sense. After the ranking list is completed the Ranking Authority decides on the quota of promotions. The initial implementation was quite painful, but it was a learning process."[114]

Even as the practice entered its third decade one air force general saw that it was unavoidable to find

> "… conflicting opinions during ranking. You must say 'why' you have a particular view of an individual, but eventually there must be a degree of consensus. If you're too predictable it might not be a good thing. As one chairing a ranking exercise you learn to accommodate the various views, but at the end you must have consensus. This expectation is high, and sometimes you give benefit of doubt to an individual. At other times

---

[113] Interview No. 14.

[114] Interview No. 17.

you assess the individual for another year. At the ranking board the more support there is for you (the appraisee) the better. But what does the ranking board chairman or the service chief see? You (the appraisee) must be visible. For the commander, he must also know a spectrum of people. By nature I mix around people of different vocations, different hierarchies. The more you (the appraiser) mix around the better for them (the appraisees)."[115]

In time, officers were not only ranked within the unit or formation in which they were assessed. Officers also had their performance assessed and compared with others of the same rank and vocation under the purview of a Senior Specialist Staff Officer (SSSO) who ensured the vocation was not unfairly favoured or penalized across MINDEF and SAF. Such practices were especially important for vocations such as MOs and engineers, who were sometimes treated more as professionals in the military rather than specialized military professionals. Interview participants who served as SSSO for such vocations indicated vocation-specific disadvantages had been rooted out and ranking boards were certainly not perfunctory exercises carried out in an extempore fashion. An engineering officer explained:

> "I always come away with condition that the boards and board chairman must agree on the ranking. I never felt engineers were disadvantaged because the organization recognizes context-based contributions. I was never swayed by backgrounds and allegiances. This is a non-issue because the strength of the SAF system is that it is able to see beyond identity cliques. For the SAF to be successful there must be something for everybody in any vocation to contribute. The question is always whether we are putting good people into places with the budget and opportunities. If we cannot find good candidates, then you must look at the talent distribution. If you still continue to fail in finding good people then it is a failure of people management."[116]

One CMC referred to the specifics of the medical community:

> "Only recently MOs are classified as combat officers. In my time we were called service officers. There was an issue with ranking all the time. The fighting generals get ranking, but do they have the ops experience? In terms of ranking the MOs are not at the top but also not at the bottom. Commanders make a fair assessment because once doctors can understand the operational imperative they can contribute. You might never be COA but you are also not disadvantaged."[117]

---

[115] Interview No. 16.

[116] Interview No. 22.

[117] Interview No. 20.

Another CMC remarked:

> "In medical corps there is less protégé grooming because it is more homogeneous. All MOs have a common educational background. Promotions are based purely on performance as well as whether an individual has the intention to stay. For those more inclined towards medical work rather than military operations, it will show up. MOs have been graded at the top of formations outside the medical corps, better than officers in their own parent formation. So there is no disadvantage for MOs."[118]

One general confidently concluded that "[i]n the ranking board no vocations lose out. As a commander the more people you know the better so that you can contribute by making recommendations. There are many points for contact and observations such as exercises and meetings."[119]

To minimize the probability of a fluke assessment, or one that blindsides collective panels higher up, officers who are promoted also require consistent annual performance grades (usually two consecutive grades of B or higher), a CEP higher than the current rank held, and at times even hold an appointment commensurate with the next rank. Consistency is crucial as it creates an impression of an officer and determines whether he or she can be entrusted with greater responsibility. Yet it is not always about superiors, as one former service chief noted:

> "Peer and subordinate perceptions are really important. Can he carry the ground when making decisions? Are people willing to go to war with them? Some manage up by 'carrying balls', but appointments are usually a choice between two or three candidates and not just one. There are also important questions to be answered. Are people willing to work for them? In times of conflict can they make difficult decisions objectively? Do they possess the strong 'X-factor' to be strong operationally?"[120]

Despite a relatively robust and improved assessment system, there are officers who have attempted to game performance and potentials evaluations with the sole focus on climbing the rank hierarchy. This is not a new development but a perennial challenge for the SAF, as a retired service chief lamented: "Careerism or career creep is the result of competing social forces at work. That is why values inculcation is very important. It gives you a value compass to navigate without which you have individuals arguing over performance bonus, asking why they don't receive medals, etc."[121]

---

[118] Interview No. 23.

[119] Interview No. 16.

[120] Interview No. 15.

[121] Interview No. 25.

At times this turned adversarial, as then-CPT Choy Yong Kong (SAFOS 2004) observed:

> Currently, the SAF's performance evaluation process is strongly top-down with superiors ranking their subordinates annually based on their perceived performance. This process prompts the subordinates' behaviour to align themselves strongly with their superiors, sometimes at the cost of their adjacent units and their own people. Also, the expectations the superior has can be prescriptive—to get what he wants done—with no regard for feedback from the ground. The incentive model is inconsistent with the desired behaviours in an adaptive organization.[122]

To address such issues the Annual Ranking Exercise has expanded somewhat for Regulars. In 2006 the SAF initiated 360-degree Multisource Leadership Feedback (from the superiors, peers and subordinates of officers with a rank of MAJ and above).[123] In 2011 this was extended to officers after completion of company command and serves to highlight their positive and negative behavioural traits.[124] The actual benefits, outcomes and efficacy of these recent initiatives are unknown, in the public domain at least.

5.4 Promotions and Postings

At the completion of the appraisal and ranking boards, uniformed officers deemed deserving of promotions in rank and/or grade are shortlisted and approved through a three-tier structure. The first is the PRB, which ranks officers from subordinate units and determines whether an individual is "strongly recommended", "recommended" or "not recommended" for promotion. The Promotion Council (PC), the second tier, is the checking mechanism that investigates the veracity of PRB recommendations where required (e.g., by conducting random interviews). The PC-approved list is then submitted to the final tier, the Promotion Authority (PA), which signs off on the final ranking of officers.[125] DXOs are promoted separately under MINDEF Personnel Board A and those from SID under MINDEF Personnel Board B.

---

[122] Choy Yong Kong, "Forcing Strategic Evolution: The SAF as an Adaptive Organization", *Pointer* 38, 1 (2012): 38.

[123] Kim-Yin Chan, Ping-Tzeun Chua, Kok-Yee Ng, Jeffrey C. Kennedy, Soon Ang, Christine Koh, Regena Ramaya and Sukhmohinder Singh, "Development of a Multisource Leadership Feedback Instrument for the SAF", presentation at the 49th International Military Testing Association Conference, Gold Coast, 8–12 Oct. 2007.

[124] Tan, "Ready, Relevant and Decisive": 7.

[125] "Finer Points and Aim of Scheme Explained", *Straits Times*, 5 Apr. 1982, p. 11.

The Promotion Authority (PA) has varied according to the rank of promotion. In 1981 they were the First PS (Defence) for promotions to CPT, Minister of State (Defence) to MAJ, and Minister for Defence for LTC and above.[126] As the SAF Officer Corps expanded and the ranks corresponding to various appointments increased (e.g., a unit CO from MAJ to LTC, a brigade commander from LTC to COL), such roles were devolved to lower echelons. For example, in 1994 the PAs were the respective service chiefs or DS (Administration) for promotions to CPT, CDF or PS (Defence Development) to MAJ, PS (Defence) to LTC, and Minister for Defence for COL and above.[127] These tiered approvals are not mere exercises where necessary signatures are simply added and forwarded annually. The seriousness is relayed by the fact that some officers recommended for promotion have been rejected since the days of Dr Goh. A member of the elite nucleus noted:

> "The reason why an officer is blocked [from promotion] is based on feedback and inconsistency. This eliminates those who are 'gaming' the system. You look at performance consistency. For example if all along an individual gets 'C' and then suddenly 'B' it could be a ploy to push for promotion. You need to be consistent if not wait for another year's assessment."[128]

Another officer admitted:

> "Yes, I have had recommendations for appointments and promotions blocked. The impression that the senior civilians and senior officers have of an individual can be a real barrier, an obstruction to promoting the individual. I had to explain it to the minister who understood why [officer L] should be promoted. You can say this is fighting for your people."[129]

Yet one must be careful to view such incidents as exceptions rather than the norm. Decisions to correct perceived mistakes must be explained and documented. The system in place is otherwise allowed to run its course. Moreover, the small community of Regulars means that capable officers are known to superiors, peers and subordinates. A reputation forged on consistently high performance serves as a prelude to future promotions and postings. A former ACGS explained: "There is a talent base so there are no sudden appearances. You know who is and who is not making it. When a name is mentioned consistently, it floats up and gets

---

[126] *Manpower Policies Affecting the SAF Officer*, pp. 7–8.

[127] "Who Gets Promoted and How?" p. 2.

[128] Interview No. 25.

[129] Interview No. 24.

noticed. It is never a single point of decision. There is also the question 'is a guy due yet' (for promotion or postings)?"[130]

Another former SSSO concurred:

> "In any organization you deal with people you need to motivate and reward the right people. There must be a right fit through succession planning by placing a square peg in a square hole. Who to go for courses overseas? Posting, planning. The current system is good but subjective in the sense of how you apply and manage it. The top 10 per cent of officers are visible to the superiors and their counterparts (of the superior)."[131]

At present, all promotions to COL and above are recommended by the elite nucleus, seconded by senior defence bureaucrats, and approved by the political echelon. The appointments of the CDF and service chiefs rest with the president based on recommendations from the PM. These procedures are reflections of the administrative structure. A former service chief reasoned: "At that level you must be seen to carry the rank. Military ability and intelligence are all necessary. Character is also scrutinized because they don't want an ex-general or admiral getting into problems."[132] This is hardly surprising since Singapore as a whole does not take too kindly to any opprobrium from its public officials, much less those at the apex of the military apparatus.

Promotions are inextricably linked to postings, and vice versa. One feature of the SAF career, like many other first-class militaries, is the constant rotation of appointments among command, staff and instruction. Postings are also subjected to collective panel decisions to minimize subjectivity and safeguard against unsavoury practices. An army general explained:

> "OPC is under MINDEF, AOMC by the Army. There is power to recommend [officers to appointments], but OPC will sit down with the COA. The committee system is chaired by the Perm[anent] Sec[retary]. There are checks and balances to ensure the 'old boys network' does not predominate. Collective inputs are given to make a collective decision. The recommendation is not based on a cliquish decision."[133]

Another general revealed: "I heard of the existence of factionalism, but I never encountered it in any personal capacity. I would say it is a minor part of the SAF. Favouritism is natural. It is not a conscious thing, but it is a fact. Therefore, there

---

[130] Interview No. 22.

[131] Interview No. 09.

[132] Interview No. 15.

[133] Interview No. 10.

must be a collective assessment. You can never run away from it. Higher-ups have a different view of people."[134]

A third officer agreed and highlighted that cronyism died out rather quickly with non-performance:

> "Postings and promotions are a collective decision. Therefore, it is difficult to have cronies. At the same time the system is as objective as it can be. Commanders can have their 'blue-eyed boy' whom they groom and prepare well so that they will be given a particular posting. But he still needs to prove himself. The importance of ranking and posting is that there must be communication and consistency in its implementation. If this is not the case people will get disillusioned. The system must be followed and any deviation explained. Postings are not always neat."[135]

In practice, nominees for an appointment are shortlisted when they meet prerequisites in terms of experience, past performance(s), and completion of necessary preparatory course(s) where applicable. In the early days this was not necessarily the case, due to a shortage of qualified officers. Such were the responses when some older members of the military elite were asked how they received postings. "Frankly speaking, there were only two of us of that vintage," admitted one officer. "There was no one else to compare with. So you see, I ended up serving at every level of leadership. There was no one else around. The rest were junior."[136] Similarly, another air force general acknowledged: "There was nobody else in [the service] HQ, so I got recommended by the [foreign military advisers]. Although I would rather be in the squadron the timing was right (to move). Lots of the expat officers were going home, so we needed locals to be there to take over."[137]

Such reasons became increasingly anachronistic as the SAF grew and panel consensus became the norm. Command appointments in particular were subjected to the most intense scrutiny, and credentials were scrutinized *de novo* if two equal candidates presented themselves. One army general cited the appointment of battalion and brigade commanders as an example:

> "The SAF system shortlists and identifies potential candidates based on criteria such as experience of relevant tours and grades on courses and assessments. When you meet the criteria for battalion CO, OPC and AOMC will line up the list. COA will deliberate with the division commanders and ACGS Pers[onnel]. For brigade commanders AOMC is

---

[134] Interview No. 12.

[135] Interview No. 11.

[136] Interview No. 20.

[137] Interview No. 24.

not involved. For the selection of division commanders, COA, CDF and MINDEF are involved. The strength of the SAF is also one that there are more potential candidates than available appointments so not all will get it. Those who do are selected based on the system and a collective decision and not based on any one individual. This is also the same for the annual appraisal and ranking board. It is always a collective decision."[138]

Another general explained much the same but also highlighted the use of command interviews in the appointment process and pointed out that commanders were often restricted in their choice of subordinates: "An appointment is based on whether an officer is course qualified, and prior experiences and performances. There are also command interviews. At one stage the PS, CDF and Director JOPD sat on the interview panel. There are proper processes and authorities in place. Formation always gets to suggest but higher authority determines the final outcome."[139]

Posting orders, like promotions, are never simple cases of rubber-stamping and signing off. This is especially significant for command appointments and key staff and instructional billets. Not surprisingly, recommendations have been turned back, as one commander reasoned:

> "When I have somebody who works for me, I want to know this person well. How he thinks, his motivation. If I am comfortable, carry on. For not so important appointments I am flexible. But I have rejected one or two individuals who were pushed up for CO that I did not agree with. They were, how can you say, 'not quite there'. They had to show they could do it. Yes, you need to empower your people, but in a critical job you are responsible. If you don't accept, I will explain to you. I have a system to listen (to grievances) but not keep on listening and not move on."[140]

The importance of placing only the most able officers in command billets was emphasized also by an admiral:

> "In the navy going out (to sea) it is always on ops, exercises, and there are plenty of opportunities for evaluation by the squadron commander, and higher up by the task group, flotilla, and fleet commanders. The foreign exercise commanders are also able to ascertain the quality of our leaders and if we're short we won't get invited to, let alone command, large-scale multilateral exercises."[141]

---

[138] Interview No. 06.

[139] Interview No. 11.

[140] Interview No. 27.

[141] Interview No. 15.

Although processes are in place for promotions and postings, various facets of the system have remained subjective. Not all officers shortlisted for the more prestigious (usually command) appointments have an equal probability of selection. This is especially so for the all-important CO appointments of active warfighting units, which often serve to separate the best from the rest. Officers from three categories seem most favoured. First are the scholar-officers: "SAF scholars—by virtue of being 'better officers'—are given the 'pick of the better positions available' among the many 'interesting and challenging' SAF jobs."[142] Those who perform can expect the system to ensure their ascension at an accelerated pace, with the fastest among them in line for double promotions.[143] This perceived advantage unsurprisingly makes non-scholars "unhappy with the number of rapid shifts and promotions".[144] Such sentiments are misplaced at times because the second category, the Wranglers, are also systematically favoured when it comes to postings. With a CEP of COL and above it is always in the SAF's best interest to test and retain quality officers to lead the SAF of tomorrow. Finally, non-scholar and non-Wrangler officers can even the odds by being visible to those sitting on posting panels.[145] This is possible through the recognition of consistent high performances and the willingness of superiors to fight for the subordinate's career progression and recognition.

5.5   Intangibles

An officer's ascension is not necessarily the deterministic outcome of a system where performance appraisals and estimated potential influence promotions and postings in the larger scheme of things. There are four categories that may be considered intangibles. The scholarship one obtains, natural talent for the military profession, an ability to proactively manage one's career, and a "godfather" willing to fight for worthwhile officers all play a role. These intangibles are not a matter of luck, which would otherwise connote that behaviour and outcome are mutually exclusive.

---

[142] Loh Chee Kong, "3 Released in 9 Years", *TODAY*, 14 Apr. 2009, p. 6.

[143] "Chief of Navy Promoted to Rear Admiral (Two-Star)", *Pioneer* (Aug. 1995): 24; "Three Generals Promoted", *Straits Times*, 30 June 1999, p. 1.

[144] Patrick Smith and Philip Bowring, "The Citizen Soldier: Singapore Stresses Security as an Arm of Nation-Building", *Far Eastern Economic Review* 119, 2 (13 Jan. 1983): 27.

[145] The emphasis on being visible was theorized in a study of US Navy admirals. David W. Moore and B. Thomas Trout, "Military Advancement: The Visibility Theory of Promotion", *American Political Science Review* 72, 2 (June 1978): 452–68.

5.5.1 *The Scholarship*

Scholarships are an intrinsic component of the SAF's recruitment effort. The SAFOS in particular has been—and remains—instrumental in grooming recipients for service at the apex of the military establishment. LTC (RET) Dominic Ng (SAFOS 1972) underlined: "The fact that you're a scholar makes you visible, always. And it is a big advantage because it gets you more projects and better appointments."[146] Other officers have highlighted the opportunities afforded by the scholarship and its indispensable role in their eventual appointment as CDF. "I don't imagine that I would get to do such jobs if I was not an SAF Scholar," reflected LG (RET) Bey Soo Khiang (SAFOS 1974).[147] LG (RET) Lim Chuan Poh similarly revealed that "One of the high points in his career was receiving the SAF Overseas Scholarship, without which, he said, his present career might not have been possible. He said an SAF overseas scholar will fly high in his career as long as the scholar can sustain it."[148]

An SAFOS provides three-and-a-half advantages to its beneficiaries. The three most obvious are tertiary education at renowned universities in the United States and United Kingdom, a comparatively high starting salary, and challenging postings throughout a specially managed career not afforded to other SAF officers. SAFOS scholars are routinely found in key departments within the labyrinths of MINDEF-SAF such as manpower, plans, joint transformation, communication and information systems, future systems and technology, and the Defence Policy Office (DPO). Billets in intelligence and operations come only with experience and demonstrated ability. Then there are the seemingly exclusive advantages such as exposure to senior defence officials, mentoring by SAFOS seniors, the dual-career option of joining the AS, and possible inclusion in key by-invitation circles such as the Pyramid Club. Consider the following blog entry by COL then-CPT Chua Jin Kiat (SAFOS 1998) in October 2003:

> Today, Saturday, was pretty different though. I actually had class this morning, but I was excused from lessons as I had to go meet someone. He is COL Chan Chun Sing, [Commander] 10 SIB, 1988 SAFOS/ [President Scholar], the BEST SAFOS ever. Such a well respected figure, and Chief of Army one day in the future. I had to go see him because CO OPC wanted him to coach me for my PSC Admin[istrative] Service interview, which is happening sometime in November. I guess I don't really care if I get it or not, but the [important] thing is that I [am] not just representing myself, but also the organisation. It was a very fruitful

---

[146] "Going Places", *Special Life! Soldier, Scholar and Leader (Straits Times)*, 18 Mar. 1991, p. 4.

[147] Susan Tsang, "Finding a Few Good Men", *Straits Times*, 15 Feb. 1998, p. 4.

[148] "SAF Faces Competition for Talent", *Straits Times*, 30 June 1999, p. 22.

session, my first ever interaction with the great man, someone whom I have heard so many stories of but never talked to myself. So much to learn from him. Interesting takeaway: in 1992, when he just came back from his studies, he was also 5 SIR Bravo PC 6. My predecessor from 10 years ago. I would be proud to follow in his footsteps man. PC to a Brigade Commander in 12 years. Unbelievable.[149]

Visibility and access to the most senior civilian officials and military officers come through periodic meetings and additional roles such as private secretary. In the words of one RSAF general:

> "SAFOS has its attached advantages. You get noticed and are provided with many opportunities to prove yourself. You become very visible but you are also under constant scrutiny. We often had lunch meetings with the Perm[anent] Sec[retary] or Minister with others from cohorts within comparable seniority. But it is a double-edged sword. It becomes apparent to everyone if you do not have what it takes. So the impression of the importance of SAFOS is sometimes created and inflated. For the non-SAFOS there is less visibility but they will also climb so long as they make the most of opportunities. At the higher levels the scholarship one obtained becomes immaterial. The question is: 'Can you do the job?'"[150]

BG (RET) then-COL Tay Lim Heng echoed: "The route of advancement planned for SAF scholars will of course put you in challenging positions at a young age. But if you don't perform, you just won't move up."[151] LG (RET) then-COL Desmond Kuek reiterated that the scholarship opened the first door but "beyond this, what happens and how far you go very much depends on you."[152]

A common expectation is that scholar-officers must perform to high expectations, but those who underperform are not simply discarded and left derelict—not when "disproportionate resources and investments" have been ploughed into SAFOS and SMS recipients.[153] The remaining "half" advantage is the "second bite" of the ascension cherry afforded to scholar-officers. "Scholars are given more opportunities and the benefit of doubt," remarked one general who once handled manpower matters. "The system is now in place to test them to see if they do well or fail. Unless there is a better system we will stick with Shell."[154] Another said: "In shades of grey, scholars get a second chance and are given the

---

[149] Entry at http://renjie.diaryland.com/031025_52.html. The blogger's identity is revealed at http://renjie.diaryland.com/030515_81.html and http://renjie.diaryland.com/030602_39.html (no longer available).

[150] Interview No. 02.

[151] "No Easy Climb", *Straits Times*, 15 Feb. 1998, p. 4.

[152] "It's about Serving the Country, Guarding Our Future", *Straits Times*, 7 Feb. 1999, p. 4.

[153] Glen Choo, "Attracting the Best and Brightest", *Army News* 192 (Sept. 2011): 8.

[154] Interview No. 11.

benefit of doubt. The issue is whether a scholar gets command of a premier unit when a 'better' commander exists, especially if the 'better' commander may not have the CEP and so the scholar gets the appointment."[155]

These second chances afford some scholar-officers prized command billets when their prior performances suggest otherwise. Such seemingly unmerited and systematic "favours" lie at the root of consternation and friction between officers of different educational backgrounds. This was especially noteworthy when the scholarships were first implemented. One army general noted:

> "Some scholars were pushed ahead of their time. The system pushed them because they were scholars. There were those who were good in theory but practically f*****. Some also got cocky. [Officer J] (a scholar) was playful, lazy, and not interested in the military but very smart. He spent half his life on the phone watching the stock market. In one two-sided brigade exercise [officer K] (a non-graduate) won big time over [officer J]. I had to stop the exercise before it became a massacre."[156]

Another expressed the same concerns using slightly different adjectives:

> "Some of the scholars are real scholarly type—nerdy—and good planners. But when you don't have people there is a danger of pushing the wrong type of people to be implementers. You cannot have a 'staffer' who does not come from the ground. You need the empathy, the understanding of the people, the ability to read the groundswell. Policy can be theoretically sound but absolutely impractical."[157]

A third officer highlighted some specific problems encountered by scholar-officers on an accelerated ascension pathway:

> "I am not sure if this is a systematic or selection problem. Scholars are smart, but is it merely academic smart? The question is whether they are also leaders and commanders. Some are uncomfortable in command, and in planning they are less than able. If tours are short, there is inadequate exposure. You will not be able to earn respect of the men and carry command. Command is not about being a decision maker; that is a manager. A commander has to be seen. You need to have presence. You need to do it (lead by example). Listen. Make constructive suggestions."[158]

In light of such problems, one must not conclude that the SAF has fallen into the trap foreseen by William Francis Butler, whose quote appears at the beginning of this chapter. Empirical figures highlight two important points (Table 5.1). First, SAFOS officers are a minority (68 of 170, or 40 per cent)

---

[155] Interview No. 15.

[156] Interview No. 26.

[157] Interview No. 25.

[158] Interview No. 05.

within the military elite despite their specially tailored careers. This figure rises slightly (68 of 158, or 43.04 per cent) if statistics are adjusted to account for 12 officers—five from the early SAF and seven MOs—whose careers or vocations are not comparable with SAFOS officers. Second, even though SAFOS recipients account for the majority of two- and three-star officers, almost two-thirds of individuals with the highest authorized rank of one-star were non-SAFOS officers. This clearly shows that an officer did not need to be a SAFOS recipient to enter the military elite but that the elite nucleus was dominated by presumably the crème de la crème of SAFOS officers. The scholarship may afford recipients a choice of vocations, but standards are certainly not compromised. SAFOS recipients accounted for two-fifths of most vocations among the 170 flag officers but were skewed in notable others (Appendix D). They had low representations in vocations where absolute standards were critical (e.g., fighter pilot, commando) or those where ascension pathways into the military elite were limited (e.g., signals, logistics, engineering). On the other hand, they dominated the more cerebral-intensive vocations (e.g., naval combat officer, and Command, Control, and Communications [C3]).

Table 5.1. Proportion of SAFOS officers within the military elite (1965–2018)

Rank Tier	Raw			Adjusted		
	Total	SAFOS	SAFOS as % of Total	Total	SAFOS	SAFOS as % of Total
Officers authorized to wear one star and above	170	68	40.00%	158	68	43.04%
Officers with the highest authorized rank of one star	140	49	35.00%	129	49	37.98%
Officers authorized to wear two stars and above	30	19	63.33%	29	19	65.52%
Officers with the highest authorized rank of two stars	20	12	60.00%	20	12	60.00%
Officers authorized to wear three stars	10	7	70.00%	9	7	77.78%

The empirical data above elucidates the advantages and limitations of the SAFOS within officer ascension. SAFOS officers are by no means guaranteed entry into the military elite even if they are placed on a well-planned and accelerated career pathway towards senior leadership. Tertiary education is insufficient on its own for ascension, yet it would seem to be an indispensible feature of the Aristocracy of Armed Talent where close to 95 per cent (160 of 170) completed a degree or more at some time during their career. The SAFOS scheme is further examined in chapter 7.

5.5.2 Natural Talent

If someone was not a scholar-officer with a specially managed career path, the odds could be evened by their sheer abilities as a military officer. For one fighter pilot: "I was fortunate that I could fly. I reached CAT-A (operations category A) status and accumulated more than [Y] thousand hours flying [various aircraft] during my career."[159] An armour officer recalled likewise: "I had good hands-on skill. I could drive, shoot, and I like the outdoors, and much of it came rather naturally to me."[160] Finally, an infantry officer said: "I never thought I was inferior to anybody. I thought I was the best in tactics. I was also blessed with a keen sense of navigation and terrain. I could find my way around while on overseas exercises and at night with no difficulties."[161]

Beyond mastering technical skills one had to be mentally strong and confident in one's abilities to compete with the scholars while avoiding the pitfalls of factions:

> "I never consider myself a 'farmer'. I disliked the word. You are what you are. If you label yourself you will be affected. This classification is quite clear but unhelpful. Does this mean a scholar will be promoted if he does not rock the boat? And are a farmer's contributions any less? I never bother about promotion or increment upgrades. Don't try to control something you cannot. What can you control? Only your own behaviour and performance competency. Focus first on these and just let the system recognize it. Don't 'carry balls' and be non-aligned."[162]

The ability to focus on what was important while disregarding distractions proved critical. Frequently this meant mastering vocational tradecraft and the development of essential soft skills:

---

[159] Interview No. 08.

[160] Interview No. 26.

[161] Interview No. 13.

[162] Interview No. 09.

"Three things were very important in my 20s and 30s. First, I had to be a domain expert in [my vocation] and to be the best and be on top of the trade. Second, the ability to make good decisions based on the summation of education, experience, and the ability to apply myself to a problem and get the best solution. Third are people skills, the ability to motivate, coerce, and persuade ... Fortune favours the brave and those who are prepared."[163]

Finally, it was critical to "[n]ever antagonize your boss and make him lose face," said one general as he delved into the past:

"You can win the battle but lose the war. [A superior] used to make a decision in public and declare it to everyone, but I had to bring him to the back room and explain why it cannot be done. To save face I told him that at the next meeting I would bring up a point. He would then scold me and ask why I never brought it up before and this will be the reason for him to reverse the decision. <grins> I was also COS (Chief of Staff) for [a general-rank scholar-officer] on exercise and did planning for him. Outside in public I gave him respect, but one-on-one I gave it to him."[164]

In addition to excellent technical skills and mental toughness one required a measure of common sense in public and an uncommon measure of conviction in private.

5.5.3 Managing Your Career

Although natural talent and abilities helped, it was essential to take proactive measures to be visible, to seize opportunities when billets became available, and to ensure the appropriate boxes for ascension were ticked off. One general reasoned that each officer was responsible for his own career:

"After [a tour at a manpower department] I realized that you needed to do your own career development. You need to be proactive and not simply rely on someone else to do it for you. You must know your strengths and interests. You may not always get what you want, but you must take proactive actions. Do your part. If what you desire does not happen you know at very least that you did your part. People are always busy, therefore there is no harm asking."[165]

Asking never guaranteed a favourable outcome, and one had to be prepared to soldier on in case of any eventuality. "I don't ask for postings frequently," replied

---

[163] Interview No. 28.

[164] Interview No. 26.

[165] Interview No. 11.

one general as he recalled requests for posting, "On the two occasions that I did, I did not get my wishes. <laughs>"[166]

For others who were more successful in this endeavour, the reality differed according to individual circumstances. The common denominator was being proactive in seeking billets that provided exposure to new challenges and skill sets. At times it helped that one had a supportive superior who was genuinely concerned enough to offer good advice:

> "During my term as CO I had a discussion with my brigade commander [Colonel S], after which I opted for a posting in MINDEF. While it would be challenging as it was my first pure MINDEF staff job, I knew that I had to be exposed to the wider organization and not be 'safe' within the confines of [my parent formation]. [Officer T] (who later made general) was my boss. I was appointed a branch head and got into [the specifics of the appointment]. It was great."[167]

Furthermore, while scholar-officers were specially groomed by the organization, those without that advantage had to seize opportunities. At times it involved a career-wagering risk, as one pilot reflected:

> "When I was in [an air base] in [year X] I engineered my way to a staff tour. I felt that I already achieved a CAT-B and so I should move on instead of staying put, and I did not want to be stuck not really doing anything productive. It was [LG (RET)] Bey Soo Khiang who initiated the requirement of staff tours between CATs to develop a more holistic air force officer. So, I had finished achieving what was required of me and I wanted to move on. For me I needed to build something from scratch. Once I have completed a task, that's it. I get restless. I did not want to waste time. I needed new challenges. The posting orders came out, and the CO was on leave. You could say I was driven by conviction and abilities. I was not afraid of getting marked, and I did not toe the line. If I get a D grade then so be it. In the senior ranks I recalled saying: 'Sack sack lah' (colloquial phrase meaning 'If I got the sack then so be it'). I don't get weighed down by what others think. Think for yourself. I have [the] courage and conviction to act. You just have to be prepared for the consequences. The worst thing that could happen is you get sacked. This is not to say you can be casual or frivolous. Think and then act. If you consider what other people think you'll get encumbered and cannot act. Focus on the big picture. An attitude like that removes shackles. It allows you to be free to act on convictions and not act based on what others think, or the ranking you might get. So it went from 'I want to go' to 'I am going' <laughs>. If you want opportunities you must ask for them."[168]

---

[166] Interview No. 23.

[167] Interview No. 06.

[168] Interview No. 16.

5.5.4 *The "Godfather"*

Finally, there is the influential proverbial "godfather" (at times in the plural) who has stepped in to correct the temporarily wayward ascension trajectories of future military elites. This is not necessarily an indicator of cronyism, for the officers they aided already had the talent in terms of performance and potential. It could, however, indicate patronage if there was a relationship predicated on the understanding of loyalty in exchange for favouritism. The success of patronage depends on personalism, which is "the degree to which decision making and coercive power is concentrated in the hands of one person".[169] A high degree of personalism is illustrated through actions such as deciding on military matters without input from the armed forces or overruling the top brass, promoting certain officers with disregard for norms and standards, and cleansing the officer corps of those who have grown too powerful, who harbour political ambitions, or who simply disagree with the person in power.[170] However, as discussed in previous sections, an officer requires the collective agreement of superiors from three tiers to ascend to the apex of the rank structure. If all three tiers are in agreement, then chances are it reflects an intersection of ability and opportunity rather than favour and personalism.

Such checks and balances minimize patronage. For the interview participants their godfathers remained anonymous, and at times the interviewees hinted at the possibility of luck. Said a general who preferred the mud in the field to the confines of an office:

> "I was fortunate to get promoted because I worked well on projects. I was able to show that things could be done. It is not rocket science. It is a matter of whether you want to do it or not. If you only adhere to all the rules and regulations you get caught in a box. Some did not want me to get promoted. In one year my ranking was last among all the colonels. <grins> I was blessed with good luck. I could have been sacked a few times. Looking back I came to a realization and attribute my motivation to my dad and wife ... It was my dad and wife who put me straight in life. I promised my dad that I would make something out of life. When I was promoted to [one-star] I went missing for three days. I went to my dad's grave and put flowers on it. He would have been proud. <tears>"[171]

A second general remained intransigent by conviction and chose the harder "right" by standing his ground over the easier "wrong" of being a yes-man:

---

[169] Lee, *Defect or Defend*, p. 38.

[170] Ibid., pp. 41–2.

[171] Interview No. 26.

"I did not think what rank I would achieve. In those days there was a sense of purpose, a sense of urgency because Singapore was just independent. The first few batches at SAFTI really contributed a lot to the SAF in terms of the systems, but they were also prepared to put their life on the line. Fortunately it was never called for. I was outspoken and had strong views and rationalised how things should be done. This led to arguments with bosses who did not like me but I didn't give a damn. I am not sure how my career did not get 'killed' along the way. <grins> It must have been the foreign consultants who gave me good reports. <laughs>"[172]

Finally, a general who "placed the mission first and his soldiers always" admitted:

"When I first signed on I did not know if I would make Major or LTC. I never dreamt of reaching Colonel or BG. Today, you need to have the CEP and education plays a big part. I was fortunate as they looked at me in a different light. I was an ops guy, a ground guy who made things happen. To rise in the ranks you must have the opportunity and do a good job at it. It is when people will give you more important jobs to do. At any opportunity you must also teach and groom the next generation. Nurturing. That's why I am close to a lot of people."[173]

Who are these godfathers? Processes in place point to individuals along the hierarchy who had a hand in promotions and postings. They included immediate superiors, representatives on panels seeking consensus, and even foreign consultants in the early SAF. Even though not every member of the military elite was a scholar-officer, each one of them was certainly a Wrangler and visible to the upper echelons of senior military officers and civilian bureaucrats. While the exact identities of the godfathers have remained a mystery, their actions certainly benefited a segment of those who would one day wear one or more stars.

5.6 Summary

This chapter commenced with four sensitizing concepts that could explain officer ascension: cronyism and patronage, merit (performance and potential), visibility to those who determine postings and promotions, and luck. Each has certainly played a part in shaping officer ascension in the SAF. The ascension process commenced with merit cloaked in terms of personalized performance appraisals and seniority. Such practices gave way to a multi-collective effort implemented in 1982 based on the Shell system. Consensus was required on the twin yardsticks of performance subjected to a standardized bell curve, and estimated potential was usually capped at two ranks up for junior officers. The

---

[172] Interview No. 13.

[173] Interview No. 05.

merit list in turn determined an officer's promotion and posting possibilities. The current ascension process is still subjective, without absolute standards, and remains susceptible to human interference. Nevertheless, it is an improvement on prior practices and is the best available at this time.

The need for collective agreements highlights the challenges of cronyism and patronage. The former is rare because non-performance, while possible at the lower ranks, is easily flagged to have a detrimental impact on performance, promotions and postings. The latter is possible based on the patron's blue-eyed boy having both performance and potential, and then consensus from the patron's peers and superiors on promotions and postings. The challenge faced by the military elite has been to break such cliques while fully utilizing and developing an officer's potential. This is not a matter of personal vendetta but recognition that any factionalism threatens the ascension process and indeed the quality and integrity of the SAF Officer Corps. If left unchecked, a patron could eventually have undue influence—perhaps even control—over committee panels charged with collective oversight over the 4P's. Decisions could then be passed with minimal resistance. This would, of course, represent a complete failure of leadership, a gross travesty of moral courage, and a grave violation of integrity at the individual level.

The issue of visibility does not commence at the senior ranks but with entry into Project Wrangler. This scheme comprises scholar-officers who by the nature of their status are considered better than the rest until proven otherwise and beyond the benefit of doubt. Non-scholar-officers have to prove themselves to a standard that warrants their inclusion as Wranglers. Visibility is a double-edged sword for all officers. It serves to advance the careers of those who perform, but the spotlight invariably proves too glaring for others. Some non-scholars consider themselves lucky to enter the Aristocracy of Armed Talent, but their skills and abilities often eclipse their shortcomings. Their rightful place in the profession of arms is confirmed by a consensus of their seniors. Perhaps it is only the scholar-officers who are less than able and still become military elites who are truly the lucky ones.

CHAPTER 6

The Ascension Structure

"The shaping of a general, like the making of a soldier, is a complex process involving both heredity and environment. It is a process that defies definition or consistent pattern. Like the miracle of man, it can be examined but never analyzed."[1]

— Hanson W. Baldwin

6.1 Introduction

The processes that enable an officer to ascend the SAF's rank hierarchy are encapsulated in the 4P's of performance, potential, promotions and postings. These processes do not take place in a vacuum, and a holistic approach to ascension must include the organizational structure unique to the armed forces under examination. This situates the ascension processes (the software) within the skeletal structure (the hardware) that determines the pyramidal rank distribution of the SAF Officer Corps. There are no theories for structural specifics, which is unsurprising. There is, after all, no common definition for military elites nor norms as to which appointments are held by flag officers. Although modern defence establishments share structural similarities, their respective organizational specifics are unique. The most straightforward examination of any ascension structure is to identify well-trodden or cookie-cutter pathways if they exist.

It is essential to contextualize the physical structure of Singapore's military establishment. The local installations where military personnel carry out their work are numerous yet in very close geographical proximity. This is a given since the main island of Singapore has a north-south measurement of some 20-odd kilometres and twice the distance on the east-west axis. Military camps and bases are sprinkled across the island despite such restrictions. The army's manoeuvre division HQs are located in Jurong (3 DIV), Mandai (6 DIV), Selarang (9 DIV), Sembawang (21 DIV), Sungei Gedong (25 DIV) and

---

[1] Quoted in Aubrey S. Newman, *What Are Generals Made Of?* (Novato: Presidio Press, 1987), p. 4.

Clementi (2 PDF). Manned flying assets are spread across air bases at Tengah, Paya Lebar, Changi and Sembawang. The navy divides its platforms between naval bases at Tuas and Changi. MINDEF and the SAF HQ are located at Bukit Gombak, SAFTI MI at Jurong, and the Basic Military Training Centre on the offshore island of Pulau Tekong.

Small detachments are on fixed-term postings at the various Singapore-leased or foreign-operated training facilities overseas. Others are overseas to integrate new equipment into the SAF's arsenal and/or for training purposes. Any such inconveniences invariably attract handsome monetary compensation and other tangible benefits. Deployments encompass both expeditionary and domestic operations but rarely place uniformed personnel in harm's way. On the whole, any change in posting is rarely a large disruption and military families can hardly speak of, or complain about, an itinerant lifestyle—to include changes in home address, school and spousal employment—found in the militaries of larger countries. This chapter proceeds within this context. The first of its five sections covers SAF officer development in broad terms from commissioning through to attendance at CSC. This is followed by post-Staff College ascension pathways through the three services and in the MINDEF-SAF echelon.

6.2   Pre-commissioning to Command and Staff College

The first step for ascension into the upper echelons of the SAF is clearing necessary milestones. SAF officers spend their junior years from pre-commissioning until CSC learning and sharpening their vocation-specific tradecraft, absorbing military education, and honing the acumen essential in the profession of arms. This period consists of rotation between tours at operational units—namely, the army battalion, navy ship, or air force squadron—and staff and/or instructional billets interspersed with a multitude of developmental courses. Dr Goh explained that this has been the norm for military officers, as "this is the means whereby they achieve professional competence. I refer to the practice of successful military courses at various levels and covering tactical, staff, and technical and operational subjects. The military profession resorts to courses to a far greater degree than any other profession I know of."[2]

The training, education and experiences culminate in CSC—though it seems not to have been mandatory for MOs and engineering officers in days past—and prepare an officer for the first true test of command as a unit CO. The overall practice is similar to most first-class militaries around the world, with the

---

[2] "Creating a Military Elite", *Pioneer* (June 1972): 13–4.

possible exception being the compressed time frame given the lower mandatory age of retirement in the SAF.

The path to an officer's commission consists of enlistment, BMT as a REC, and completion of a pre-commissioning course as an Officer Cadet Trainee (OCT) in the army and air force, as an Midshipman in the navy, or an MDES trainee among the three services.[3] In the late 1960s and early 1970s, a potential army OCT would have first completed the section leader course and served as a section commander in a battalion before being nominated for an Officer Cadet Course (OCC). Over the years SAF officers have attended OCCs locally and a few selected Regulars been given the opportunity to attend the finest institutions of military leadership overseas. The majority of scholar-officers received the SAFOS, the OTA (Academic) or SMS as OCTs and MIDs. Most were also commissioned at the respective scholarship presentation ceremonies prior to the completion of their OCCs. The shortened and short-lived Standard Military Course (SMC) was introduced to commission scholar-officers with their peers upon completing the newly designed syllabus.[4] The corresponding duration of the OCC decreased from 13 months (more for those in support arms) to 38 weeks.[5] This time frame allowed scholar-officers to meet the British academic calendar for undergraduate studies. Yet it soon became apparent that the nine-month SMC was too "short by any standards" to provide adequate preparation for commissioned service. SAFTI ran 11 SMCs between 1974 and 1980.[6] The majority of scholar-officers since then have

---

[3] BMT was initially conducted at SAFTI and the respective infantry battalions until the establishment of the School of Basic Military Training (SBMT) at Nee Soon Camp on 1 December 1971 and the Infantry Training Depot (ITD) on Pulau Tekong on 1 January 1976. On 1 December 1991 the BMT system was reorganized into three schools, each affiliated with an active infantry brigade. SBMT devolved into the 3rd Brigade Training School (3 BTS) and 7 BTS, while ITD became 2 BTS. This gave way in 1999 to the current arrangement with the Basic Military Training Centre (BMTC) responsible for all non-unit specific (e.g., armour, commando, combat engineer and artillery) BMT. CMPB moved from Dempsey Road to its current premises at Depot Road in 1989. "Last Enlistment at Dempsey Road", *Pioneer* (Apr. 1989): 22–3; "Brigade Training Schools to Conduct BMT", *Pioneer* (Nov. 1991): 18–9; "Brigade Training Schools Take Over from SBMT", *Pioneer* (Feb. 1992): 26; "Better through Basics", *Pioneer* (Mar. 1992): 13.

[4] "Is the SM Course Good or Bad for Officer-Cadets?" *Pioneer* (June 1975): 6–9.

[5] The SMC comprised a 19-week junior term for recruit and section leader training, and a 19-week senior term covering platoon commander training. Trainees who performed well at the then-School of Section Leaders could cross over and join the SMC in the senior term.

[6] From 1975 onwards the SMCs catered to officer cadets from "all-arms" (instead of just the infantry) during the junior term. "Keep Up the Traditions: Dr. Yeoh", *Straits Times*, 13 June 1975, p. 10; "A Proud Day for Sword of Honour Winners", *Straits Times*, 17 Oct. 1979, p. 10.

received their commission mid-OCC and completed their training only after university studies.[7]

Pre-commissioning training after the SMC-era reverted to nine weeks of BMT or initial military training (IMT) followed by specific-to-service and specific-to-arms training at SAFTI and various training schools.[8] The 39-week Infantry OCC at SAFTI ran between 1980 and 1990. The first tri-service 42-week OCC commenced in 1990 and lasted until March 2005, when the course duration was reduced to 38 weeks thanks to improved learning technologies and in line with the shortening of NS from 30 to 24 months with effect from December 2004.[9] Freshly commissioned army officers and non-flying air force officers are usually most employable in their primary roles requiring only on-the-job experience.[10] This is not a matter of them being better than their counterparts in the RSN or pilots in the RSAF. It is, rather, a matter of standardizing the length of all pre-commissioning courses for the respective officers to "keep pace in terms of rank and accompanying endowments more than to mark the end of their training".[11]

Naval officers first received indigenous pre-commissioning training at the Midshipman School in Sembawang in 1974. The MIDs received IMT followed by a 43-week course that included a two-month Midshipman Sea Training Deployment (MSTD) voyage.[12] Newly minted naval officers continued their training at the RSN Fleet as Additional Officers (AO)—known today by the

---

[7] In Singapore they would most often join the "professional term" of an OCC, which covers specific-to-arms training. A likely alternative for scholar-officers is to complete a "basic officers' course" in the United States.

[8] "SAF Combat Officers Command Men, Resources and a Top Salary (SAF Advertisement)", *Straits Times*, 20 Mar. 1980, p. 10.

[9] The 42-week pre-commissioning course consisted of an 11-week tri-service term, an eight-week service term (specific-to-service), and a 23-week professional term (specific-to-arms). "Officer Training Goes Tri-Service", *Pioneer* (Nov. 1990): 12–3; "Towards a Leaner, More Capable 3rd Generation SAF", *Army News* 108 (May–June 2004): 8; "Officer Cadet School: New 38-week Officer Cadet Course", *SAFTI Link* (2006): 12; *SAFTI 50*, p. 62. The current pre-commissioning terms vary according to service between an initial two-week Common Leadership Module and the final three-week Joint Term. Army cadets face a 12-week Service Term and 21-week Professional Term. Navy midshipmen have an 11-week Foundational Term, 11-week Advanced Term and 12-week Internship Term. Air Force cadets undertake a seven-week Service Term and 26-week Professional Term.

[10] Some officers are required to undertake additional qualification (e.g., commando and guards), skills-specific (e.g., scout, sniper, intelligence, rigger), or confidence (e.g., Ranger) courses.

[11] "The Young Men & the Sea", *Pioneer* (Jan. 1982): 10.

[12] Ibid., pp. 9–11.

equally endearing term Officer Under Training (OUT)—for practical experiences in seamanship. This formative period was interspersed with certificates and exams, which have since been replaced by contemporary training courses in navigation, and taking charge of a ship at sea and safe harbour. Only then did a naval officer hold shipboard appointments congruent with more advanced seamanship in communications, weaponry and specialized maritime warfare.

The first milestone for a pilot is the successful completion of the "wings" course, which marks entry into the flying fraternity. Early RSAF pilots were fully trained by the RAF in the UK. Basic and advanced flight training are presently conducted by the RSAF in Singapore and detachments in Australia and France. Passing the basic course is no mean feat regardless of era, as attrition rates are high. As one general reminisced:

> "My two and half years in the UK were challenging, fun, lots of flying and the fear of failure. I had no one to look to, so see how the instructors do it. You keep diligent and try to simulate. I would simulate mechanically with equipment in my room. I would hold a broomstick in one hand and another for throttle. So next morning when you fly you know what to do. There were no simulators in those days. Perhaps only a link trainer. You have to make sure you are prepared and not cold when you step into the cockpit. You really don't have much time to get used to it, and everything seems alien if you are not comfortable. You could also get claustrophobia, and you need presence of mind. You have to be on the ball. My mind was 'I'm here', and it was challenging enough to succeed. I liked it and wanted to do it well. I was the first batch of Singaporean pilots, and sometimes you see your friends in the course not making it. It's tough with only 11 of 25 earning the coveted RAF wings."[13]

His experiences were not unique, as another interviewee admitted: "I was not very confident in earning my 'wings'. Flying, whether you can make it or not, is very much touch and go. There are a lot of imponderables. In my batch we started with 20 but only six graduated, so it is not easy. I was best overall because I was also good in ground school with theory and such, but I was not the hottest in terms of flying."[14]

The graduation rates from those classes were fairly consistent with other cohorts at the RSAF's Flying Training School during the mid-1970s: 6 of 22 in the 10th course, 9 of 27 in the 11th, and 9 of 26 in the 12th.[15] It is understood that contemporary graduation rates have improved from the 30 per cent average

---

[13] Interview No. 24.

[14] Interview No. 25.

[15] "Two Top Performances", *Pioneer* (Oct. 1975): 6–7; "Top of the Wings Parade", *Pioneer* (Mar. 1976): 7; "Nine 12th FTS Course Pilots Get Their Wings", *Pioneer* (Oct. 1976): 22.

with the implementation of more stringent tests, such as the Computerised Aptitude Selection System, before a pilot trainee can progress to the flying phase of training. The development of an RSAF pilot continues after the wings course with a lead-in or conversion course in one of three flying streams—fighter, transport and helicopter—at an operational squadron locally, a training squadron overseas usually in partnership with the US Air Force (fighter, transport) and Army National Guard (helicopter), or a course with foreign air forces.

The SAF's primary preoccupation in its first decade of existence was with growth in terms of manpower and infrastructure. Standards in training and doctrine came from foreign advisers or were copied wholesale before being adapted to local conditions and expectations. The Career Planning Branch was established only in 1975 under the purview of OPC, which was then responsible for the career administration of all regular SAF officers. A year later MINDEF issued a general order for officers to rotate among command, staff and instructional appointments at durations of two, three and three years respectively.[16] Wranglers and eventual flag officers invariably bucked such prescriptions because their steeper career trajectory necessitated shorter tours and often skipped instructional billets to meet the prevailing retirement age. Such "high fliers" also completed relatively short tours in prime appointments to prevent personality cults and enable upward mobility within the SAF Officer Corps. One general remarked:

> "To rise through the ranks you need to have a good combination of ground and staff experiences. Ground tours with the troops so that you know what is going on. Staff tours help you understand the mechanics of decision making. These are also key activities that are seen in exercises. The only critique is that in a deep organization how do you compress the tours into a 25-year career? You end up with a lot of appointments that are touch and go. It is also difficult to let people leapfrog because how do you have a meaningful career and postings and still make a 25-year timeline work?"[17]

As a result, most military elites rotated between command and staff tours with limited instructional tours—if at all. Some served as QFIs during the formative years of the RSAF when there was a shortage of local instructors. Army generals' instructional tours usually involved training OCTs.

Various milestone courses had to be checked off. Until the 1980s there was only one milestone course, namely, the service-specific "advanced" course. Such a course prepared army officers to serve as company commanders and

---

[16] "Off to a Good Start", *Pioneer* (Aug. 1976): 7–9.

[17] Interview No. 22.

battalion or brigade deputy PSOs. Naval officers functioned as shipboard Principal Warfare Officers or even assumed junior command of a patrol craft or vessel. Air force officers could lead as flight commanders (equivalent of army company commanders). With the evolution of operational complexities, officers are required to complete "intermediate", "tri-service" and "advanced" courses specific to service and vocation prior to attending CSC.[18]

An officer usually in the rank of MAJ is deemed ready for attendance at a local or foreign CSC after completing prerequisite courses and junior tours.[19] Staff College is a necessity for further promotion at this stage of the career, and non-attendance is a sure sign of career stagnation. CSC is not merely a gateway to higher-level appointments but necessary for the first true test of command. The premium placed on leading an active unit is further emphasized by service-specific pre-command preparation courses.[20] After CSC the only remaining and mandatory course conducted locally is the Senior Commanders Program, which comprises mainly colonels.[21] A handful of them are further nominated for attendance at a foreign War College. It is also common for the SAF to invest in quality officers through sponsored postgraduate studies at civilian universities. Those selected for top institutions overseas know they have been earmarked for greater things. The next four subsections examine the post-CSC ascension pathways to one-star and above billets across the different services and at the MINDEF-SAF level.

6.3 Army

The Singapore Army was commanded directly by the defence chief from early independence until the 1988 reorganization made the army a separate service. The path towards generalship was limited and reflected the nascent capabilities of the armed forces. From 1966 to 1978 there was usually only one general, who

---

[18] For the evolution of intermediate courses for officers of the respective services, see *SAFTI 50*, pp. 82–93.

[19] For the evolution of the CSC in Singapore, see *SAFTI 50*, pp. 94–107.

[20] For example, in 2003 the biannual Battalion Commanders' Course was launched to prepare COs leading active and NS battalions in terms of command, responsibilities and professional knowledge. A similar course is conducted for brigade commanders. The Navy also holds a Command Preparation Program for designated ship COs. Jonathan Chan, "Gearing Up Our Battalion Commanders", *Army News* 192 (Sept. 2011): 9.

[21] The first Senior Commanders' Course ran between 6 October and 21 November 1980 for officers in the ranks of MAJ and LTC. Subsequent courses lasted between five and seven weeks. Attendees at contemporary courses have usually completed brigade (or equivalent) command and hold the rank of COL.

was also the SAF's top officer. In 1976 the post of DGS was renamed CGS, and in July 1978 it was bestowed a second star as MG. This paved the way for the concurrent creation of the DCGS position, which lasted from 1978 to 1986 and during which time two of the three appointees made BG. It was late in this period when the nascent manifestations of the JS took distinct shape and opened up more flag rank billets. Officers were first promoted to BG as Chief of Staff of the General Staff (COS-GS) in 1984, DJOPD in 1984, and Director Joint Intelligence Directorate (DJID) in 1986. Indeed, the army's primacy was clear as nine of the first ten SAF officers to make one-star between 1965 and 1987 wore olive green fatigues, with five from command and four in staff appointments.[22]

By 1988 the SAF had reached sufficient maturity and was restructured into a tri-service defence force. On 1 July (SAF Day) that year the two-star CGS was replaced by the three-star CDF. The growing size and operational capabilities of the army, navy and air force further justified the appointment of a DCGS (Army) to prepare and command land forces. This move allowed the CDF to concentrate on leading the SAF with functional assistance from the JS and subordinate component commanders in the form of three two-star service chiefs. The General Staff departments were subsumed under Army HQ and their work coordinated by the Chief of Staff–General Staff (COS-GS). On 1 May 1990 the DCGS (Army) was renamed COA, but the General Staff retained its nomenclature and in effect functions as the Army Staff.[23] From 1988 to 2018 another 85 army officers joined the general ranks, with 59 receiving their star as DIV COMD (or equivalent) and one as the Deputy Force Commander of a UN observer mission (Appendix E). Three of the remaining 25 were CMC, as there is no one-star billet in the army for MOs. Another 19 army officers earned their rank on the GS, JS or other Joint-level formations. An additional three officers were engaged in further studies or on secondment.

The specific division and date of command proved crucial for the earliest officers who made BG as DIV COMD. This was because these commanders earned their stars in a staggered manner beginning with 3 DIV in 1990 followed by 21 DIV (1991), 9 DIV (1993), 6 DIV (1995), 25 DIV (1998), 2 PDF

---

[22] Command: (1) BG Thomas Campbell, COMD SIB (1965); (2) BG Kirpa Ram Vij, DGS (1972); (3) BG Winston Choo, DGS (1976); (4) L/BG Patrick Sim, COMD 3 DIV (1978); and (5) BG Tan Chin Tiong, DCGS (1980). Staff: (1) BG Lee Hsien Loong, DJOPD/COS-GS (1984); (2) BG Chin Siat Yoon, DJID (1986); (3) BG Ng Jui Ping, COS-GS/ACGS (Ops) (1986); and (4) BG Boey Tak Hap, COS-GS/ACGS (Ops) (1987). The tenth officer was BG Michael Teo, COMD RSAF (1987).

[23] "New SAF Post", *Straits Times*, 1 July 1988, p. 17. In a similar manner the SAF refers to either the defence force as a whole or only the army. There is no "Republic of Singapore Army", unlike the RSN and RSAF.

(2002), and most recently the division-sized Combat Service Support Command (CSSCOM) in 2013 and the SAF C4 Command in 2018.[24] Certain officers from the First Batch who were the earliest to hold division command invariably missed out on making BG altogether. One could say these were cases of being in the right place at the wrong time because the respective divisions had not achieved full operational capabilities.[25] Since then only three DIV COMDs have not made BG. This is elaborated more fully in the next chapter.

The dates of a DIV COMD first making BG reflect the relative importance and capabilities of the respective divisions in the army. For example, 3 DIV has the greatest number of active sub-units and possesses the most advanced equipment, which are reflected in its motto—"Foremost and Utmost".[26] The division can also be considered the "Scholar's division" due to its long lineage of scholar-officers at the helm and where seven of 13 army chiefs held division command.[27] Another example is 2 PDF, which was once considered a second-line and in days past perhaps even a second-rate formation responsible for homeland defence.[28] Such operations have taken on greater importance in the post-September 11 environment, even though the division-sized outfit has long deployed and employed soldiers for the protection of installations. 2 PDF is today the Island Defence Task Force (IDTF) within Singapore's inter-agency approach to homeland security, and its status is on par with any of the army's

---

[24] The only COMD of the now-defunct 1 PDF (1985–2004) promoted to BG was Lim Kim Lye in 1998; he led the formation from 1996 to 2000.

[25] They included COL (RET) Chan Jwee Kay, COMD 6 DIV (1980–86); COL (RET) Kwan Yue Yeong, COMD 3 DIV (1982–84) and later in 1991 as COMD 25 DIV; and COL (RET) Quek Koh Eng, COMD 6 DIV (1990–93).

[26] 3 DIV was formed in 1976 and became the first fully active division with three infantry brigades (2, 3 and 7 SIB). It became the first combined arms division in 1991 and remained fully manned by active units until 1995, when the army's divisions were reorganized into mixed active and NS units. As the SAF transformed under the 3G concept, 3 DIV became "the first networked Division in the Army" and was also the first equipped with the "digitised Division Command Post". At present 3 DIV retains the greatest number of subordinate active-duty combat units among the army's divisions. "First Combined Arms Division", *Pioneer* (May 1991): 4–5; "Towards a Networked Division", *Army News* 147 (Oct.–Nov. 2007), p. 6; "Moving 3 Div Forward as a Team", *Army News* 150 (Jan.–Feb. 2008), p. 2; Jared Yeo, "Tiger Family Gets New Commander: BG Lim Helms 3 DIV", *Army News* 189 (June 2011), p. 3; "3 DIV Turns 40", *Army News* 205 (Nov. 2012): 18–9.

[27] COMD 3 DIV who became COA: (1) COL Boey Tak Hap (1984–86); (2) BG Ng Jui Ping (1986–89); (3) BG Lim Neo Chian (1991–92); (4) BG Han Eng Juan (1992–95); (5) BG Ng Yat Chung (1996–98); (6) BG Desmond Kuek (1998–2000); and (7) BG Perry Lim (2011–13).

[28] "PDF: A Second Line of Defence", *National Pioneer* (Nov. 1970): 10–1.

manoeuvre divisions.[29] The most conspicuous evidence of this has come in the form of high-profile visits to the formation by politicians and the fact that BG Terry Siow Meng Meng (SAFOS 1990) became the first scholar-officer appointed COMD 2 PDF (2014–16).

The first important step for generals who ascend through command is to overcome the scarcity of active battalions. The number of such units has grown from two infantry battalions in 1965 to at least 18 combat and 14 combat support battalions as of 2018.[30] These figures mean the majority of regular officers will miss this career highlight, having satisfaction only in command of NS (i.e., non-full-time reservist) units should the opportunity arise. Combat officers appointed CO of combat battalions may not necessarily be from the same vocation and are subjected to caveats.[31] They are usually ineligible to lead combat support battalions as they lack the specialized skills and relevant experiences. It is the norm for combat service officers to lead battalions congruent with their specific vocation, with rare exceptions.[32]

Battalion command provides the first true test of leading and moulding a self-contained unit both in the field and in camp. The appointment is prized, visible, and closely scrutinized by superiors, peers and subordinates. Stringent prerequisites and intense competition from the high demand and low supply of such billets mean very few COs fail to discharge their duties and exercise

---

[29] Soldiers were deployed at various oil refineries on Pulau Bukom (Shell), Pulau Merlimau (Singapore Petroleum) and Pulau Ayer Chawan (Esso) after the 1974 "Bukom Bombings". 2 PDF also has elite Guards battalions under command. Yeong Wai Cheong, "Military Protection for Oil Refineries", *Pioneer* (Mar. 1974): 19.

[30] The 18 active combat units comprise the SOF (all-regular special operations unit of unknown size), ADF (all-regular, multi-mission capable, and high-readiness unit with five companies), Commando Regular Force (all-regular commando unit of unknown size), six infantry (light/motorized) for manoeuvre operations, one infantry for protection of key civilian installations, one infantry (regimental police) for defence of SAF installations, one commando, two guards, and four armoured (three mechanized and one tank) battalions. The active combat support units consist of four artillery (one radar and three fires), five combat engineer (one each of field, bridging, EOD, armoured and CBRE), and at least five C4I/signals battalions.

[31] The combat vocations comprise infantry, armour, commando and guards. As a rule of thumb any combat officer who has held company command and completed CSC can command an infantry battalion. Infantry and armour officers normally complete the Guards Conversion Course before command of a Guards battalion. Non-armour officers can command an armoured battalion subject to prerequisites stipulated by HQ Armour. Only a Ranger-qualified commando officer can command a commando battalion.

[32] BG (RET) Mark Tan Ming Yiak, a combat engineer, was CO 3 SIR (1998–2000).

command responsibility.[33] Supply was further tightened after 2010 with the move to lengthen the tenure of active battalion COs from one to two (or more) years. Key staff appointments at formation, army and MINDEF levels invariably await post-battalion command for officers earmarked for greater things. Appointments such as Head Personnel Development Branch in G1 Army, Head Force Plans in G5 Army, Head of the RSAF's Office of Strategy, Deputy DIR (Personnel Policy) within the Manpower Policy Division of MINDEF's Defence Management Group, Head Force Transformation Office in Joint Plans and Transformation Department (JPTD), and Army Attaché at the Singapore Embassy in Jakarta seem almost exclusive to SAFOS officers. Training or instructional roles beyond staff billets within the confines of G6 Army are rare for those on an accelerated path. The completion of battalion command is also an opportune period for postgraduate studies.

The next key appointment is command of an active brigade or specialized group. There are at present five combat brigades, one combat support brigade and six combat support groups. In contrast, there was one under-strength infantry brigade at independence. Each combat brigade has an established lineage of more than 30 years and is subordinate to one of the army's divisions or formations.[34] The history of the only combat support brigade in the form of 3 Division Artillery (3 DIV ARTY) is very similar.[35] The six combat support groups were established as army- and SAF-level assets.[36] The caveats on vocation compatibility applicable to battalions apply generally to the brigades and groups but are less stringent for the SIBs. Active brigade command provides colonels

---

[33] Some have failed battalion proficiency tests conducted by the Army Training and Evaluation Centre or by the respective combat support formations. There were also two instances of failure in leadership when the respective battalions were disqualified from the annual Best Unit Competition for questionable conduct amounting to "cheating".

[34] The five active combat brigades include the light infantry 2 SIB (active since 1968), the motorized 3 SIB (1969), the mechanized 4 SAB (1970), the heliborne 7 SIB (1975) and the mechanized 8 SAB (1980). 10 SIB was an active light infantry brigade from 1995 until the mid-2000s, while 1 SIB was active in the early days of independence and again for a very brief period in the early-2010s.

[35] 3 DIV ARTY was formed in April 1976. In November 1980 the brigade was placed under the command of HQ Singapore Artillery. In March 1991 it was transferred to 3 DIV, which was inaugurated as a Combined Arms Division.

[36] The active combat support groups are as follows: (1) Army Combat Engineer Group (ARMCEG) is an army-level asset (1994); (2) Chemical, Biological, Radiological and Explosives Defence Group is an SAF-level asset (2005); (3) Army Command Systems Group is an army-level signals unit; (4) C4 Operations Group is an SAF-level C4 unit; (5) Imagery Support Group (ISG) is an SAF-level intelligence unit (2000); (6) Cyber Defence Group is an SAF-level cyber operations unit (2017).

with first-hand experiences and deeper understanding of divisional and army operating templates, and command exposure to SAF-wide manoeuvres. It also allows colonels to mentor subordinate battalion commanders and ensure the brigade HQ remains operationally ready amidst periodic technological and doctrinal changes. This advantage stands in contrast to peers who command NS brigades on a concurrent, often secondary, basis.

The juncture of brigade command poses several implications for officer ascension. First, the organizational structure—and most certainly the segment dealing with the field component of the SAF—has long favoured the progression of combat (infantry, armour, commando, guards) and to some extent combat support (artillery, combat engineers) officers from active battalion to active brigade command. This situation was partially alleviated for combat engineers when the brigade-sized Army Combat Engineer Group (ARMCEG) was created in 1994. Second, the imbalance faced by combat support vocations obliged the army to channel them into command of an active SIB, or appointment as formation chief in lieu, before they progressed to division command.[37] Third, for many years the organizational structure disadvantaged signal officers most among all the combat and combat support vocations. The nature of their specialization in providing critical communications capabilities often limited their practical exposure to manoeuvre warfare. Ascension through the signals battalions and Signals formation (now called Signals and Command Systems) does not yield division command. This forced signal officers in the past to either transfer to a combat vocation or take command of an active combat brigade and compete for opportunities as DIV COMD. LG (RET) Winston Choo, COL (RET) Michael Low Oon Hoe and MG (RET) Ravinder Singh are the only active signals battalion COs tapped for active infantry brigade and subsequently division command.

The appointments after relinquishing brigade command establish a pecking order among all colonels and indicate the likelihood of leading a division. Colonels have rarely been promoted to BG while holding staff appointments at the army level since the 1988 reorganization. The post of COS-GS is either

---

[37] Combat support officers who led active infantry brigades en route to division command include: (1) LG (RET) Ng Jui Ping, artillery, 3 SIB (1978–79) and 3 DIV (1986–89); (2) MG (RET) Lim Neo Chian, combat engineer, 3 SIB (1989–91) and 3 DIV (1991–92); (3) LG (RET) Ng Yat Chung, artillery, 3 SIB (1994–95) and 3 DIV (1996–98); (4) BG (RET) Tay Lim Heng, artillery, 3 SIB (1995–96) and 6 DIV (1999–2002); (5) MG (RET) Ravinder Singh, signals, 2 SIB (1998–2000) and 6 DIV (2006–07); (6) BG (RET) Tan Yih San, combat engineer, 2 SIB (2001–03) and 3 DIV (2005–08); (7) BG (RET) Mark Tan, combat engineer, 3 SIB (2006–07) and 3 DIV (2009–11); and (8) BG Dinesh Vasu Dash, artillery, 3 SIB (2013–14) and 2 PDF (2016–present).

held concurrently with or after division command. The second-most senior staff appointment as ACGS for Operations (ACGS [Ops]) was once held by colonels after brigade command en route to a division.[38] The role was redesignated a post-division command billet in 2009 and is now held by a one-star, like counterparts in the RSN and RSAF. The role of Director Joint Operations (DJO) on the JS, and the third-most senior army appointment as COMD Army Training and Doctrine Command (TRADOC), both followed similar evolutionary paths and are held post-division command.

Army officers responsible for plans at the GS and JS have historically been, and presently are, the closest certainties for division command. Other billets with competitive probabilities include the respective ACGS for manpower, intelligence and training, and Head National Service Affairs Department (NSAD). Other less frequently travelled routes include Commandant (COMDT) GKSCSC, COMD OCS, Chief Artillery Officer, Chief Engineer Officer, and department heads from Joint Intelligence Directorate (JID)/Military Intelligence Organization (MIO).[39] Postgraduate study (if not taken earlier) interspersed within this post-brigade career stage is a positive indicator, although the significance of attendance at a foreign War College is increasingly opaque. The army usually nominates a DIV COMD from this pool of highly visible officers.[40] It must be highlighted that while these are the cookie-cutter pathways, there are alternatives—albeit rare. First, one can hold active brigade command without commanding an active battalion.[41] Second, one can hold division command without command of an active brigade or active equivalent.[42] Third, it is possible

---

[38] Ng Jui Ping (1986) and Boey Tak Hap (1987) were both promoted to BG while ACGS (Ops), but the rank was for the concurrent appointment of COS-GS. In 2007 Philip Lim was promoted to BG while ACGS (Ops) but relinquished the appointment five days later to command 25 DIV.

[39] All formation chiefs are non dual-hatted except for COMD 21 DIV/Chief Guards Officer (since October 1994), COMD 25 DIV/Chief Armour Officer (since June 1998), and COMD 9 DIV/Chief Infantry Officer (since August 2004).

[40] The SAF has lost some officers from this talent pool. COL Ha Weng Kong, then-COMDT SCSC, passed away from cancer at the age of 42 on 12 December 1986. He was CO 7 SIR, COMD 4 SAB, Chief Armour Officer, and ACGS (Personnel). COL Bernard Tan, then-ACGS (Personnel), passed away at the age of 39 after suffering a heart attack during the RSN Biathlon on 26 March 2006. The graduate from RMC Sandhurst was CO 3 Guards and COMD 7 SIB.

[41] BG Siew Kum Wong commanded the active 4 SAB (2009–12) without command of an active armoured battalion. Similarly, COL (RET) Tan Kian Heong was CO 441 SAR (1997–2002), an NS battalion, and later COMD 4 SAB (2006–08).

[42] BG (RET) Ishak Ismail was COMD 12 SIB and COMD 6 DIV (2008–11), and BG (RET) Chiang Hock Woon was COMD 76 SIB and COMD 9 DIV (2013–16).

to progress directly from active brigade to active division command.[43] It must be reiterated that these are exceptions rather than the norm.

The effect of organizational structure on officer ascension into the military elite is best illustrated by the impact of operational requirements and changing threats. For example, army logistics and engineering officers once seemed capped at the rank-ceiling of COL. They could command one of numerous combat service support (CSS) units—transport, maintenance, supply, engineering, ammunition—and proceed on to a brigade-sized CSS formation, a divisional support command (DISCOM) or the Army Logistics Command.[44] The most senior staff appointments were the plans departments at the respective CSS formations and logistics billets on the GS and JS. It was at the latter where two officers made BG as Head Joint Logistics (HJL).[45] This practice was ephemeral as it proved inefficient to run logistics as a joint command in the same way as the medical corps. G4 Army (the GS department for logistics) and the CSS formations were instead integrated and reorganized as the division-sized CSSCOM in 2006.[46] The formation's capabilities and importance to the army warranted the officer at its helm—a logistician, engineer or any army officer with specialization in logistics—to be a BG/ME8.[47] Although this seems to be the pinnacle command appointment for army logistics and engineering officers, the army has shown flexibility in opening up other pathways traditionally held by combat officers. The most prominent have been the appointments of BG Ngien Hoon Ping (SAFOS 1988), a logistics officer, as DJO and ME7 Chow Wai Yein, an engineering officer, as COS 3 DIV.[48]

---

[43] MG (RET) Lim Neo Chian from 3 SIB to 3 DIV (1991); LG (RET) Lim Chuan Poh from 10 SIB to 9 DIV (1996); and BG Siew Kum Wong from 4 SAB to 25 DIV (2012).

[44] CSS units include army maintenance bases, logistics bases, transport battalions, ammunition bases, and CSS battalions. CSS formations included Maintenance and Engineering, Supply, Transport, and the SAF Ammunition Command.

[45] Pang Hee Hon made BG in 2000 while HJL (2000–04); Philip Lim made BG in 2005 as HJL (2005–07). Officers appointed HJL since remained in the rank of COL.

[46] The formations and units under CSSCOM include Maintenance and Engineering Support, Supply, Transport, Army Medical Services, Army Logistics Training Institute, and the SAF Ammunition Command. See "Combat Service Support Command", *Army News*, Special Supplement #5 (Jan. 2011): 2.

[47] The first and second commanders of CSSCOM were logistics officers. The third COMD CSSCOM (since 2014) BG Lam Sheau Kai is an artillery officer who specializes in logistics. He was formerly Chief Supply Officer (2009–11), COMD 9 DISCOM, and HJL (2011–14).

[48] ME7 Chow held appointments such as CO 6 DSMB, Branch Head in HQ Maintenance and Engineering Support, Deputy Chief Maintenance and Engineering Officer, COMD 3 DISCOM, and COMD Army Logistics Training Institute.

The significance of cyber threats has also widened the career scope and advancement potential of signals officers as the vocation takes on added importance within the highly networked defence ecosystem. Signals officers' initial groundwork led to the creation of the Cyber Defence Operations Hub under HQ Signals and Command Systems in 2013. This was replaced by the Defence Cyber Organisation (DCO) in March 2017. The organization's status among MINDEF-level outfits is self-evident given the Defence Cyber Chief at the helm holds DS-equivalent seniority.[49] The early DCO structure comprises the Cyber Security Division, Policy and Plans Directorate, and Cyber Security Inspectorate. The three formations with a targeted aggregate strength of 1,300 by 2027 are situated within MINDEF.[50]

The DCO also provides policy and development inputs to the Cyber Defence Group (CDG). The CDG and the C4 Operations Group (C4OG) are both brigade-level units with established strengths of 1,300 and 700 personnel respectively under the SAF C4 Command (a division-sized formation), which is part of the C4I Community.[51] Signals officers dominate the hierarchy, and the vocation is primed to share benefits with qualified civilian associates and specialist counterparts from the RSAF and RSN. Singapore was considered "lucky" to be spared the worst of the cyber attacks in 2017, and luck is certainly not a strategy in the government's playbook.[52] The DCO and SAF C4 Command will share the limelight and stand ready to support the national-level Cyber

---

[49] BG (RET) David Koh became the inaugural Defence Cyber Chief on 1 April 2017. At that point he was also DS (Technology) MINDEF, DS (Special Projects) MINDEF, and CE CSA. He relinquished the DS (Technology) portfolio to RADM1 Frederick Chew in late 2017.

[50] (1) The Cyber Security Division has operational responsibility for the cyber security of all defence-related organizations; (2) the Policy and Plans Directorate is responsible for developing cyber defence capabilities; and (3) the Cyber Security Inspectorate ensures defence-related organizations adhere to requirements and conduct regular "red team" exercises. The Cyber Defence Group is responsible for the SAF's cyber security and comprises the Security Monitoring Unit, the Incident Response and Audit Unit, and the Cyber Defence Test and Evaluation Centre. See "Fact Sheet: Next Gen SAF's New Cyber Command to Combat Growing Cyber Threat", MINDEF, 3 Mar. 2017; Kenneth Cheng, "New SAF Unit to Battle Cyber Threats", *TODAY*, 3 Mar. 2017; and Adrian Lim, "Parliament: Mindef Sets Up New Cyber Command to Beef Up Defence against Cyber Attacks", *Straits Times*, 3 Mar. 2017.

[51] "Factsheet: SAF C4 Command Integrates C4 and Cyber Defence Capabilities", MINDEF, 30 June 2017. The SAF C4 Command was inaugurated on 15 November 2017 with COL Percival Goh Beng Ngan at the helm and SLTC Andrew Wan Wei Chung and SLTC Yeo Lip Khoon as commanders of C4OG and CDG respectively.

[52] Lee Li Ying, "'We Were Just Lucky': Cybersecurity Chief on Attacks in Singapore in 2017", Channel NewsAsia, 17 Dec. 2017.

Security Agency (CSA) of Singapore as the digital realm expands its stranglehold on everyday reality.[53]

6.4 Navy

Thirty-one naval officers have had the honour to serve as admirals in the RSN: 26 naval combat officers, three naval MOs who served as the CMC, and two naval engineers (Appendix F).[54] The majority of combat officers first wore the rank of RADM1 holding RSN appointments, with 15 from command and four on the Naval Staff (NS). Two of the remaining seven earned their first star on MINDEF-SAF billets, and five from three-month command tours of CTF-151.[55] The first admiral's star was first bestowed in 1988 and unsurprisingly went to the CNV. Subsequent promotions to RADM1 were allocated to the Chief of Staff–Naval Staff (COS-NS) in 1994, Head Naval Operations (NHO) in 1994, Fleet COMD in 1995, and COMD Maritime Security Task Force (MSTF) in 2009. Nine admirals would also go on to wear a second star, with eight in the capacity as CNV (first in 1994) and one as DMI (2013). These admiral billets reflect the navy's growth from a modest fleet of three ships—*Singapura*, *Panglima* and *Bedok*—and "89 mobilised personnel and 278 volunteer officers and men" to a modern and professional outfit.[56] The mission template has also expanded from mere coastal constabulary duties in the early days. Today, Singapore's maritime interests are protected by an RSN capable of multidimensional warfare, and this has in turn allowed participation in and even leadership of combined exercises and operations abroad.[57]

In earlier chapters it was noted that the navy played third fiddle to the army and air force for close to 25 years. In addition to its sister services receiving

---

[53] The CSA was formed in 2015 under the PMO with daily operations overseen by the Ministry of Communications and Information.

[54] Naval combat officers serve on surface (strike or specialized warfare) platforms, on submarines, or as divers. There are no naval aviators in the RSN because all manned aircraft fall under the ambit of the RSAF. Two air force squadrons currently support RSN Fleet operations. 121 SQN operates Fokker-50 maritime patrol aircraft, and 123 SQN deploys one Sikorsky S-70B Seahawk helicopter on each *Formidable*-class frigate when put to sea.

[55] Command of CTF-151 by RSN officers: (1) L/RADM1 Bernard Miranda (20 Jan.–20 Apr. 2010); (2) L/RADM1 Harris Chan (31 Mar.–30 June 2011); (3) L/RADM1 Giam Hock Koon (7 Mar.–6 June 2013); (4) L/RADM1 Ken Cheong (31 Mar.–30 June 2016); (5) L/RADM1 Saw Shi Tat (28 June–27 Sept. 2018).

[56] "Defending Ourselves", *Straits Times*, 5 June 1968, p. 10; "Back Paddle", *Navy News* 4 (2005): 14; Lo, *Onwards and Upwards*, pp. 14–7.

[57] Lo, *Onwards and Upwards*, p. 11.

priority in funding and technical development, the RSN lacked sufficient and appropriate manpower. The outfit was cobbled together by a motley crew of enthusiastic volunteers before a professional naval officer corps matured. The early navy chiefs were certainly cut from the same cloth. LTC (RET) Jaswant Singh Gill juggled teaching during the day and evenings training to earn his 1951 commission into the Malayan Royal Naval Volunteer Reserve.[58] He entered full-time service with the Royal Malaysian Navy (RMN) in 1964 during *Konfrontasi* and was subsequently entrusted to lead Singapore's infant navy.[59] The late COL (RET) James Aeria was also a teacher who spent "seven years with the Singapore Division of the Royal Naval Reserve as a volunteer officer" before his secondment to the RMN in 1963.[60] Aeria charted the future of the navy in 1968 and subsequently served at its helm from 1970 to 1975.[61]

The late COL (RET) Khoo Eng Ann succeeded Aeria as chief (1975–78) and joined the RSN in September 1974 at age 47 after a 27-year career with the Taiwanese Navy.[62] The shortage of qualified naval officers in the 1980s even required the transfer of two SAFOS officers from the army to fill senior naval appointments.[63] Manpower limitations also resulted in the unusual ascension pathways of the first two CNVs. RADM1 (RET) James Leo, who succeeded Khoo in 1985, was a naval engineering officer, in contrast to other CNVs who were naval combat officers. His unique career path included command of the Naval Technical Training School and a Naval Maintenance Base, and key staff billets such as Head Naval Engineering, HNL, and Chief Staff Officer (likely equivalent to present-day COS-NS). Succeeding Leo in 1991 was the inaugural SAFOS recipient appointed CNV RADM1 (RET) Teo Chee Hean. His initial years were spent stationed at the RSN Fleet, which culminated in his becoming a ship's executive officer. A long decade (1981–91) was then spent in key staff appointments on the NS and JS interspersed with a year each at the US Naval

---

[58] Sarah Hardy, *30th Anniversary: Onwards and Upwards* (Singapore: Republic of Singapore Navy, 1997), p. 20.

[59] "First in Honours-Roll Meets CNV", *Navy News* 1 (2007), p. 12.

[60] Lim, "Full Steam Ahead for the Future", p. 2.

[61] "First Navy Chief of Singapore Dies", *Straits Times*, 26 Apr. 1994, p. 17.

[62] "Anchors Aweigh for Navy Chief", *Straits Times*, 3 Mar. 1985, p. 14; "Adieu, Comd RSN", *Pioneer* (Apr. 1985): 24.

[63] LTC Ho Meng Kit (SAFOS 1975), an infantry officer, was HNP, while LTC Lim Chong Kiat (SAFOS 1975), an artillery officer, was HNO.

War College and Harvard University.[64] In many ways Teo's first senior command was of the RSN and a matter of circumstance over design. The navy of the late 1970s to the mid-1980s had the difficult choice of either grooming the limited number of SAFOS officers through fleet appointments, or utilizing them in staff billets to address the challenges facing the naval service. It chose the latter.

From 1992 onwards, the starting point of ascension for naval combat officers into admiralship has been the essential post-CSC command of a naval vessel. The appointment as CO of a Republic of Singapore Ship (RSS) and command at sea are undoubtedly the highlights of any naval combat officer's career. This is the first true test of command ability, and the CO is responsible for everything that happens on and to the ship whether at port or at sea, and independent of higher-ranking individuals (civilian or military) on board. The ships commanded by those on the path to admiral are not simply any vessel in the RSN fleet but are always the most advanced and powerful surface warships (no submariner has yet made one-star) of a particular era. In the early days these were the patrol craft, patrol boat and minesweeper, but they gave way to cutting-edge strike platforms such as the *SeaWolf*-class Missile Gun Boats (MGBs) from the latter's commissioning in 1975 until the introduction of the *Victory*-class Missile Corvette (MCV) in 1988. The MCVs were in turn overshadowed in prestige and capability by the arrival of the *Formidable*-class Stealth Frigates from 2007 onward. The scarcity of such command billets is very clear, with only six vessels in each class under 185 SQN and 188 SQN.[65] An admiral's post-CO tour could include a second tour in command of another ship from the same or more advanced class, key staff billets on the NS or JS, and often a period of postgraduate studies.

The next milestone in the ascension of 20 of the 26 naval combat officers is SQN or equivalent command. These units usually comprise six platforms for a strike squadron, or four ships for a support squadron. A squadron CO might not command a ship, but the mission is critical in mentoring the individual ship COs and has responsibility for the warfighting capabilities of an entire class of platforms. A squadron CO is also experienced enough to lead a task group of two or more ships configured to meet specific mission objectives. Yet one must be mindful that not all squadrons hold the same prestige within the RSN, as 19

---

[64] After service in the RSN Fleet, Teo was HNP (1981–82), a student at the US Naval War College (1982–83), Head Joint Plans Management Department in JOPD (1983–86), a Master in Public Administration candidate at Harvard University (1986–87), HNO (1987–88), COS-NS (1987–88), DJOPD (1988–91), Deputy CNV (1990–91), and CNV (1991–92).

[65] 185 SQN (established in 1975) housed six MGBs until they were decommissioned in 2008 and replaced by the frigates. 188 SQN (established in 1987) has six MCVs.

of the 20 admirals led either 185 or 188 SQN. Only one officer helmed 191 SQN, which operates the *Endurance*-class Landing Ship Tanks (multipurpose transport ships).

After squadron command, officers often returned to the familiar pattern of key staff billets on the NS or JS or entered postgraduate studies (if not done earlier) or attendance at a Naval War College. The navy's growth in terms of assets and manpower over time necessitated the formation of an additional hierarchical layer. In 1992 the RSN Fleet's strike and support assets were placed under the First and Third Flotillas respectively. Eleven of the 20 admirals who commanded a strike SQN also led the First Flotilla (1 FLOT), frequently overlapping with their SQN command tour. The primacy of ascension through billets on strike platforms and higher HQs is undeniable. Nine of the last 14 (1995–2018) Fleet COMDs also helmed 1 FLOT.[66] As of SAF Day 2018, only one COMD 3 FLOT experienced admiralship, and even he was once CO of a strike vessel.[67] In a similar manner, the navy's elite Naval Diving Unit (NDU), formerly on par with an SQN but since upgraded to the same status as a FLOT, was the route taken by only one admiral.[68]

Twenty-four of the 26 naval combat officers who earned their first star between 1991 and 2018 did so in one of four appointments. RADM1 (RET) Teo Chee Hean and RADM2 (RET) Kwek Siew Jin were the first in the capacity as CNV. As the navy grew, another nine entrusted to oversee the navy's tri-dimensional naval warfare capabilities as the Fleet COMD received their certificates of promotion. The fleet was for a long while the navy's only subordinate command billet in which admiralship was attained.[69] This obliged certain officers to make admiral as HNO instead of Fleet COMD. This is usually the case when two or

---

[66] The exceptions include RADM1 (RET) Tan Kai Hoe, the 20th COMD (2006–07), RADM1 Timothy Lo, the 24th COMD (2012–14), and RADM1 Lew Chuen Hong, the 25th COMD (2014–16), who bypassed FLOT command. The 18th COMD (2003–04), COL (RET) James Soon was COMD 3 FLOT.

[67] L/RADM1 (RET) Bernard Miranda was CO RSS *Sea Wolf* (1996–99), an MGB in 185 SQN. He was subsequently CO RSS *Persistence* (1999–2002), COMD 191 SQN (2004–06) and COMD 3 FLOT (2006–09).

[68] The SAF Diving Centre was formed in 1971 and renamed the NDU in 1975. The formation currently consists of the Frogman School, Underwater Demolition Group (underwater obstacle clearance), Clearance Diving Group (de-mining operations), and Special Warfare Group, which forms the naval special warfare component of the Special Operations Task Force (SOTF). RADM1 (RET) Tan Wee Beng was CO NDU (2000–03).

[69] The RSN Fleet was established in 1971 and at present houses surface strike platforms (185 SQN and 188 SQN) under 1 FLOT, support vessels (191 SQN and 192/193 SQN) under 3 FLOT, submarines (171 SQN), and fixed- (121 SQN) and rotary-wing (123 SQN) aircraft from the RSAF.

more officers converge on the apex of the RSN while billets corresponding to their seniority are unavailable on the NS and JS. Fleet command tour lengths have lasted 18 months or longer in order to be meaningful and beneficial—rather than perfunctory—to both the RSN and the appointment holder. The logjam at this juncture of the RSN hierarchy necessitated the creation of a second ascension pathway equivalent to fleet command.

The amalgamation of operational necessity and organizational structure redesign resulted in the 2009 reestablishment of Coastal Command (COSCOM)—once seemingly the poor cousin of the fleet—as the MSTF to work in partnership with the Police Coast Guard and the Maritime Port Authority to safeguard Singapore's territorial waters.[70] COMD COSCOM was a senior COL's billet, with several former commanders having held the same squadron and flotilla commands as their fleet counterparts who made admiral. COMD MSTF is a one-star billet, and though its first three admirals were short on squadron or flotilla command, they possessed other experiences commensurate with the formation's mission to safeguard Singapore's territorial integrity and keep the critical SLOC open. Subsequent COMD MSTFs have career profiles virtually indistinguishable from those of their Fleet COMD counterparts. Finally, command of the anti-piracy CTF-151 in the Arabian Gulf allowed five colonels to make L/RADM1 with three given the subsequent opportunity to earn their ranks permanently.[71]

These trends highlight three important characteristics in the ascension and profile of RSN admirals. First, their command experiences are usually rooted in the strike community where they served in all-important roles as ship and squadron CO. The majority then went on to flotilla and fleet command. Second, for the few who earned their stars as staff officers this was more a reflection of demand over supply in command billets rather than ability. Finally, despite a second ascension route through MSTF, it would seem that officers from non-surface strike communities such as 3 FLOT, NDU and the submarine services are at a distinct disadvantage. Only two officers from these specialized communities have made RADM1. History seems particularly unkind to officers from 3 FLOT who have knocked on the door of admiralship. James Soon Peng Hock made Fleet COMD but retired as a COL. Bernard Miranda was deemed competent for

---

[70] The MSTF currently includes *Fearless*-class patrol vessels (182 SQN), inter-agency accompanying sea security teams (180 SQN) and *Bedok*-class Mine Countermeasure Vehicles (194 SQN). Eight *Independence*-class Littoral Mission Vessels are scheduled to replace the 12 patrol vessels by 2020.

[71] (1) Harris Chan, COMD MSTF (2012); (2) Giam Hock Koon, COMD MSTF (2014); and (3) Ken Cheong, Fleet COMD (2017).

command of CTF-151 as L/RADM1, but no billets were available back home for him to earn a permanent promotion. It is little wonder that SAFOS naval officers tend to shun this community and it seems only COL (NS) Richard Lim Kai-Chuan (SAFOS 1994) ascended the ranks with the flotilla.[72]

It is clear that the majority of RSN admirals are naval combat officers and there is a ceiling for their brethren in the engineering and logistics community. RADM1 (RET) James Leo proved capable but was nevertheless an outlier in the appointment as CNV. The only other naval engineer to make RADM1 was Jway Ching Hua in 2000 while Head Naval Logistics (HNL). This aberration could be attributed to a cap on the number of admirals in the RSN even though HNL is a designated one-star billet on paper.[73] There are three plausible reasons for this practice. First, naval logistics and related engineering requirements are apportioned between the Naval Logistics Department (NLD) led by HNL and the Naval Logistics Command (NALCOM) headed by COMD NALCOM. Both officers hold the rank of COL or ME7. NLD focuses on the "longer-term strategic plans, policies and governance" to meet logistical requirements.[74] NALCOM, on the other hand, is responsible for the current maintenance and logistical support for RSS platforms at sea or berthed at Tuas and Changi naval bases.

Next, in 2011 both NLD and NALCOM were brought under the umbrella of the Naval Logistics Organisation (NLO) without a single officer at its helm because NLO acts as an interface to streamline logistics processes and not as a command HQ.[75] Finally, the naval logistics and engineering community is small (~500, including civilian staff) relative to the size of army logistics (division-size with multiple independent brigade-size support commands and battalions) and the delineation between success and failure is also less obvious than air

---

[72] COL (NS) Richard Lim was appointed CO RSS *Endurance* (2006–08) upon completion of the US Marine Corps CSC in Quantico (2005–06). He was later Deputy CO 191 SQN (2008–10); Head Project Capstone Office in the Naval Plans Department (2010–11); CO 191 SQN (2011–13); Head Naval Personnel (2013–15); COMD 3 FLOT (2015–17); and Head RSN Strategic Redesign (2016–17).

[73] The RSN seems to have a cap of one RADM2 allocated to the CNV and four other RADM1, usually COS-NS, HNO, Fleet COMD, and COMD MSTF. This cap excludes admirals serving in MINDEF-SAF appointments.

[74] Ong Hong Tat, "New Structure for Better Naval Logistics", *Cyberpioneer*, 15 Nov. 2011; Lee Kwok Hao, "A Better NLO for a Stronger Navy", *Navy News* 1 (2012): 18–9.

[75] Lee, "A Better NLO for a Stronger Navy": 18–9.

logistics (~4,000, including civilian personnel).[76] For such reasons it is unlikely that a naval engineer will make ME8 unless an additional star is allocated to the navy or the overarching appointment of DIR NLO is created.

6.5   Air Force

The CAF was first promoted to BG in 1987, and 44 other RSAF officers have joined him since (Appendix G). Twenty-five of the 45 (56 per cent) air force generals wore pilot's wings: 19 were from the fighter community, three from transport squadrons, and three flew helicopters. Fourteen of the 20 non-flyers were Air Warfare Officers (AWOs), with nine responsible for C3 systems and five for ground-based air defence (GBAD). The remaining six generals possessed specialized skills including five air engineering officers (AEOs) and one aviation MO.[77] Thirty air force generals wore their first star holding RSAF appointments, with the remaining 15 holding MINDEF-SAF billets. No unmanned aerial vehicle (UAV) pilot has made BG so far due to the vocation's relative youth. This will invariably change with time as the SAF leverages on technological advancements and increases operational reliance on unmanned platforms.

The ascension pathway for pilots until the 2007 RSAF reorganization usually followed the template of command at squadron and air base, followed by a one-star staff appointment on the Air Staff (AS) or JS. As with counterparts in the sister services, these key ascension appointments were frequently interspersed with staff billets at the RSAF and/or SAF HQ and a period of postgraduate studies and/or attendance at an Air War College. After the 2007 reorganization Operational Commands have replaced the air bases in importance for career ascension. An additional subordinate echelon of groups was also created within each command. Each group is responsible for three or more squadrons and is to the RSAF as brigades are to the army and squadrons are to the RSN. The

---

[76] Ibid., p. 19; "Defence Technology Community", Defence Science and Technology Agency, www.dsta.gov.sg/scholarship-student-outreach/defence-technology-community, accessed 28 May 2014.

[77] The Air Warfare Officers (AWOs) were initially called Air Operations and Communications Officers and Air Defence Artillery Officers. They were renamed Weapons Systems Officers (WSO) specializing in command, control and coordination (C3) and air defence artillery (ADA) respectively. The latest changes in nomenclature include renaming ADA as Ground-Based Air Defence (GBAD). On 28 August 2009 the WSO (C3) and WSO (ADA) vocations were renamed AWO (C3) and AWO (GBAD) respectively. Other AWO vocations include AWO (Radar) and AWO (C3 – Aerodrome/PAR). The "WSO" designation is still in use for WSO (Fighter). "ADOC 3rd Anniversary Celebrations", *Air Force News* 112 (Dec. 2009): 43; "RCGC/RGDI 01/13", *Air Force News* 125 (2013): 26.

only difference, it seems, is that pilots on their way to BG often bypass group command, although this observation could prove flawed given the relatively short existence of the squadron-group-Operational Command structure. Twenty of the 25 pilots who made general held both command of a flying squadron and an air base and/or Operational Command. Of the other five, one held squadron command twice in the embryonic RSAF, while two SAFOS pilot officers had no open records of command at squadron level but subsequently helmed an air base each. The final two officers had no record of command in any of the open-source literature examined.

The flying fraternity seems to have a flat post-CSC command ascension pathway from squadron to air base or Operational Command. Yet one must be cognizant of the resources and time required to improve a pilot's CAT rating, which reflects both ability and responsibility.[78] The rationale was rather simple, as one general explained:

> "CAT-A is the pinnacle of the flying profession. You want to be there if you aspire to be OC (flight commander) and CO. Otherwise you cannot lead as a pilot if you don't have CAT-A. As a pilot, you need CAT-A to be credible. It is one requirement for the profession, leadership and command. But without CAT-A, it does not mean you cannot be a good officer or leader because you can follow the staff line. CAT-A is not the be all and end all. As a commander I also pushed people to develop other aspects and not just to aspire towards being CAT-A. For example the ability to interact and communicate with people is very important, especially from the flying point of view."[79]

This had implications for the military elites, especially when the relatively short SAF careers—two years longer on average for pilots—are taken into account. Some were appointed as staff officers at the opportunity cost of flying with the squadron. It was a simple case of prioritizing needs and allocating resources, because:

> "There is no perfect system. In the '90s the air force was expanding. There was no structured career route in place as this took years to develop. Furthermore, with a short career do you have time to do that (structured route)? Today with a proper structure there are better HR mechanisms in place. The priority in the early days was to produce, to churn out pilots. Now we are more HR focused. If you want someone to be Chief [of Air Force] can he be taken through all the appointments (pilot, flight lead, OC, CO)? Remember that developing a pilot takes time. Each CAT

---

[78] The CAT status was initially based on UK standards for fighter pilots and Australian standards for transport pilots until the RSAF developed its own template.

[79] Interview No. 16.

takes anywhere from nine to 12 months to attain. So that's already four years at very least to reach CAT-A. So there is not always the luxury to let them take all the appointments. The RSAF is also small. Is an OC appointment available? It becomes a matter of time and space, one of duration versus availability (of an appointment). Is the RSAF a factory for churning out OCs or are we preparing a war-fighting unit (with experienced personnel)?"[80]

For pilots who made flag rank, the first test of command came at the helm of a squadron according to aircraft of expertise. These were scarce billets, much like their counterparts in the army and navy. The first operational fighter squadron was established in 1970, and the fighter community reached a peak of seven operational squadrons based in Singapore at several periods in RSAF history (1990–97, 2000–03, 2004–05) before the current status of six.[81] A further two fighter detachments are based in the continental United States for training purposes. The scarcity of CO appointments is exacerbated by the competitiveness within the fighter community, leading one interviewee to depict them as "a mafia" in a "dog-eat-dog world".[82] The transport community comprises four squadrons, each with specialized aircraft and roles.[83] After squadron command, the COs vied for command of an air base that housed fixed-wing aircraft: Tengah (TAB), Paya Lebar (PLAB) and Changi (CAB), which are located in the west, central and east of Singapore respectively. For members of the smaller rotary-wing fraternity, their ascension commenced at one of five operational squadrons and one operational detachment stationed at the sole helicopter air base, Sembawang Air Base (SBAB), in the north of Singapore.[84]

---

[80] Interview No. 16.

[81] Variants of the F-74 Hawker Hunter, A-4 Skyhawk, F-5 Tiger, F-16 Falcon and F-15 Eagle were operated at various times by 140 SQN (since 1970), 141 SQN (1972–81, 1990–2005), 142 (1974–2005, 2016–present), 143 (1975–97, 2000–present), 144 SQN (since 1979), 145 SQN (1984–2003, 2004–present), and 149 SQN (since 1985). Sean Yang Shunxiong, ed., *Air Combat Command: Poised and Deadly* (Singapore: Air Combat Command, Republic of Singapore Air Force, 2009), pp. 100–4, 105–12, 113–7.

[82] Interview No. 16.

[83] 111 SQN (G550-AEW and formerly E-2C Hawkeye) provides airborne early warning; 112 SQN (KC-135R Stratotanker) extends the RSAF's operational endurance through air-to-air refuelling capabilities; 121 SQN (Fokker-50 and formerly SH-7 Skyvan) supports naval operations with maritime patrol aircraft; and 122 SQN (C-130 Hercules) provides army operations with transport and aerial delivery options.

[84] 120 SQN (AH-64D Apache, formerly Bell 212, UH-1H, and Aerospatiale SA 316B Alouette III); 123 SQN (S-70B Seahawk, formerly AS-550 Fennec, AS-350 Ecureuil, UH-1B); 125 SQN (AS-332M Super Puma for SAR); 126 SQN (AS-332M Super Puma); 127 SQN (CH-47 Chinook); and Peace Support Operations Detachment.

Most air base commanders served in the rank of COL even though the appointment was ostensibly pegged at one-star. Only three commanders at TAB bucked this trend: two were promoted en route to serve as DA Washington, while the third made BG shortly before assuming command.[85] A fourth officer was somewhat of an aberration as he commanded the same air base twice and earned his star in a staff billet between both tours.[86] The reason air base commanders frequently remained as colonels came down to operational continuity:

> "In terms of established rank, a division commander in the army and the base commander in the air force are both one-star, but they are not seen as equivalent. But within the 3G air force concept the newly established Operational Commands are similar to the army divisions and the navy task group. In the past the base commander played a more supporting role in the sense that what you do in peace is not what you do in war. The Operational Commands now ensure that the commander in peace is also the commander in war. You are given a stake in plans, in decision making, in ensuring the concept and execution are similar. So with the new command structure you could say it is more deserving of a one-star and the appointments will be seen different across the SAF."[87]

The first two pilots to make general did so as commander and deputy commander of the RSAF in 1987 and 1989 respectively. Between that time and prior to the 2007 RSAF reorganization, most of the pilot generals received their first star as Chief of Staff–Air Staff (COS-AS) (1992); Head Air Operations (HAO) (1997); or in JS appointments, namely, DA Washington and DJO.

Six of the 14 AWO generals first wore the rank of BG as commander of the now-defunct Air Defence Systems Division (ADSD), which was reflagged as the present Air Defence and Operations Command (ADOC). Seven others were promoted in AS and JS billets, and one at MINDEF en route to an atypical air base command. Eleven AWOs would spend a portion of their generalship in command, with ten following the well-trodden squadron-brigade-division/Operational Command path. This is similar to an army division, but AWOs are concentrated in three specialized subordinate brigades and a variety of active

---

[85] Loh Kok Hua made BG (1999) as COMD TAB (1998–99), and Richard Lim was promoted in 2004 in the same capacity (2001–05). Both generals were en route to their final active-duty appointment as DA Washington. Gary Ang made BG (2005) while serving as DIR (Policy) DPO, four days before assuming command of TAB (2005–07).

[86] Wong Huat Sern made BG (2004) as HJO (2004–06) and was COMD SBAB (1999–2003, 2006–08).

[87] Interview No. 16.

battalions.[88] Those who made BG usually did so in either the Air Defence Brigade (ADB) or the Air Force Systems Brigade (AFSB). The only AWO to buck the cookie-cutter command route was BG (RET) Gary Ang, who mirrored a pilot as CO 111 SQN (airborne early-warning) and COMD TAB.[89]

Air Engineering Officers (AEOs) comprise the third group of military elites within the RSAF. The first AEO made BG in a MINDEF billet, but since 2001 the next four have earned their star (or equivalent) as HAL.[90] This billet has the longest continuation of appointees promoted to BG/ME8 among the four heads of logistics at the service and joint levels.[91] This highlights the critical importance of engineering and logistics as part of air force capabilities. The RSAF was once plagued by flying accidents as a result of shortcomings in engineering support and pilot error. This reached crisis point in the 1980s, when five A-4 fighter/ ground-attack aircraft were lost. The first HAL to make one-star, BG (RET) Lim Yeow Beng, then a CPT and staff officer in the Air Logistics Department (ALD), recalled the harsh lessons learned:

> "There was an urgent need to investigate and find out the root causes of the accidents. On the other hand, we also had to update the operators on the findings and recovery actions, so as to help restore confidence in the A-4 fleet in the aftermath. In fact, one of the key lessons learnt was the need for close integration between operations and logistics, not only in a crisis like this, but in day-to-day operations too."[92]

---

[88] (1) Air Defence Brigade (with 160, 163, 165 SQN) for medium-range surface-to-air defence coverage over Singapore; (2) Air Force Systems Brigade (with 200, 202, 203 SQN), which acts as the "eyes and ears" of the RSAF; (3) the Divisional Air Defence Artillery Brigade (with 3, 6, 9, 18 and other reserve battalions) provides a short-range surface-to-air defence coverage for the army's divisions. Augustine Khoo, ed., *ADSD: 20 Years of Integrated Air Defence Operations* (Singapore: Air Defence Systems Division, 1999); "Heritage, Heartware and Hardware", *Air Force News* 94 (2005): 16.

[89] "14th Commander for Tengah Air Base", *Air Force News* 95 (2005): 26.

[90] Wesley D'Aranjo made BG in 1992 while DS (Technology) at MINDEF (1991–97). His early tours were spent as an engineering officer at the Air Defence Radar Unit (formerly Bukit Gombak Radar Station) and later on the E-2C Hawkeye induction team. He was also Deputy HAL (Electronics and Weapons) and then DIR DMO (1987–91).

[91] The four heads of logistics at the service and joint levels are one-star billets, but the RSAF's logistics head has received the commensurate rank since 2001. Only Jway Ching Hua made RADM1 (2000) as HNL, while Pang Hee Hon and Philip Lim made BG as HJL in 2000 and 2005 respectively. Tan Peng Kuan (2013) and Lam Sheau Kai (2015) earned their star as COMD CSSCOM in charge of army logistics.

[92] Leow Meng Fai, *Super Skyhawks: The RSAF A-4 Story* (Singapore: Tengah Air Base, Republic of Singapore Air Force, 2006), p. 46.

The crucial role played by air engineering and logistics was by no means less than those who took to the skies. In fact, the lives of the latter literally depended on the quality of the former. The drive for quality at the expense of quantity proved difficult but necessary:

> While the technical cause of the Skyhawk crashes was the ageing J65 engine, a key lesson learnt was in logistics management. One of the concerns was the inadequacy of maintenance competence and supervision, attributed to the dilution of skilled manpower in a period of expanding [organizational structure] and operational demands. Depth of skill was inadequate, and the quality control system was stretched.[93]

Since then, Air Engineering and Logistics (AEL) units with their comparatively large numbers of engineers and technicians vis-à-vis the army and navy have ensured the airworthiness of all RSAF aircraft. Defects have been minimized to the point that non-engineering factors such as pilot error and nature (e.g., birds, lightning) are the most probable cause(s) of accidents today.

The AEO ascension pathway towards the vocation's pinnacle rank of BG/ME8 is the flattest and narrowest of all RSAF vocations. This was certainly the case before the 2007 reorganization. The various junior engineering billets supporting the squadrons at air bases to staff appointments across the sections and branches of ALD converged in the all-important post of CO Air Logistics Squadron (ALS) at an air base.[94] The importance of TAB to the RSAF was further highlighted as it was where three of the first four HAL who made BG served their respective ALS tours.[95] The next post after ALS command was one of four Deputy HAL appointments, with each responsible for a specialization in aviation engineering and air logistics. These posts have grown to the current six as the RSAF assets have become more diverse and technologically complex.[96] A successor to the incumbent HAL is normally selected from one of the deputies.

The 2007 RSAF reorganization into five Operational Commands strengthened the warfighting capabilities of the RSAF and also redesigned the cookie-cutter pathways of ascension towards generalship for pilots, AWOs and AEOs. The first

---

[93] *At the Leading Edge: 30 Years of RSAF Logistics* (Singapore: Times Editions for the Ministry of Defence, 1999), p. 185.

[94] Other units such as the former ADSD and Tactical Air Support Command (TASC), which was the predecessor of today's UC, also received support from their dedicated ALS.

[95] BG (RET) Lim Yeow Beng, CO ALS TAB (1991–93); BG (RET) Tsoi Mun Heng, CO ALS SBAB (1998–2001); ME8 (RET) Lee Ling Wee, CO ALS TAB (2004–06); and ME8 Francis Cheong, CO ALS TAB (2006–07).

[96] The six Deputy HALs are responsible for: (1) Planning and Control; (2) Engineering; (3) Electronics and Weapons; (4) Systems; (5) Material; and (6) Aircraft.

test of squadron command remains quintessential, but ascension now seems to include leading specialist groups and Operational Commands that correspond roughly in size and seniority to the army's brigade and division, and the navy's squadron/flotilla and fleet. Current practices indicate four of the five commands are billets for promotion to BG.

The first is ADOC, which forms part of the SAF High Readiness Core (HRC) responsible for operations in times of peace and "ensures the development and operational readiness of the command and control and ground-based air defence units of the RSAF".[97] The key functions provided by ADB and AFSB have been retained despite the metamorphosis of ADSD and various changes in nomenclature.[98] Their importance for the ascension of AWOs has remained intact and been bolstered by the addition of a third group within ADOC.[99] However, unlike ADSD, both pilots and AWOs have commanded ADOC, the net result of which invalidates any vocational monopoly on the appointment.

The Air Combat Command (ACC) is the sharp edge of the RSAF, with fixed-wing assets under the Fighter Group (fixed-wing fighter aircraft) and Transport Group (fixed-wing transport aircraft). Thus far only fighter pilots have led ACC, which is responsible for the SAF's ability to conduct integrated air combat operations.[100] Although air base command has faded in importance for pilot ascension, the four bases comprise the centrepiece of the Air Power Generation Command (APGC), which sustains the RSAF's ability to fight through the launch, recovery and turnaround of aircraft. The flying squadrons at each air base are supported by an Air Engineering and Logistics Group (AELG) with three specialized squadrons in logistics, engineering and maintenance. The importance of the AELGs at air bases and certain Operational Commands for AEOs remains to be seen but is very likely to form a necessary post-squadron command billet for the future. Both pilots and AWOs have helmed APGC, but given the nature of its mission there is nothing that precludes AEOs from earning the rank of ME8 in this appointment.

---

[97] "Organisational Restructuring: The New RSAF Commands", *Air Force News* 107 (Special Issue 2008), p. 11.

[98] Air Surveillance and Control Group (ASCG) with 200, 202 and 203 SQN superseded the former Air Force Systems Brigade (AFSB). Air Defence Group (ADG) succeeded the Air Defence Brigade (ADB).

[99] The Air Operations Control Group (AOCG) was formerly the Air Force Operations Group (AFOG).

[100] "Organisational Restructuring", p. 11.

The remaining two commands are tasked with raising, training and sustaining sub-units that are allocated to other SAF units during operations. Participation Command (PC) supports the army and navy with rotary-wing aircraft (Helicopter Group) capable of transport, scout and attack missions; mobile command posts (Tactical Air Support Group); and short-range air defence coverage (Divisional Air Defence Group) for the army's divisions. Two of the first three officers appointed COMD PC were helicopter pilots, but it is still too early to determine whether the vocation, with its inherent advantages, is favoured over fixed-wing pilots and AWOs.

Finally, UAV Command (UC) oversees the capability development and operational readiness of the SAF's UAV programme.[101] UAVs are now a ubiquitous part of the SAF, but initial attempts to introduce such platforms into the RSAF faced strong resistance in an earlier era when fighter pilots dominated the helm. A former PS at MINDEF was even obliged to develop UAV capabilities separately under the JS, and "[i]t was only when a more enlightened [CAF] took over that he took back the entire set-up that had been built in the [JS]".[102] UC maintains three brigade-sized groups to support joint operations, but it would not be surprising if planners are moving beyond the intelligence-centric mission template to cover strike, logistical and extended C3 missions.[103] The command seems destined to remain as an appointment for senior colonels in the near future unless additional flag ranks are allocated to the RSAF. The command is nevertheless important to the future development and operational capabilities of the SAF. The significance of the COMD UC billet into the upper echelons of the RSAF is also clear, with the first four commanders making BG before retirement. Even though the commanders since the 2007 reorganization have been pilots, it is only a matter of time before UAV pilots—especially with the career maturation of SAFOS officers—come to the fore.[104]

---

[101] Ibid.; Wayne Tan, "Persistent Surveillance: The New Heron 1 UAV", *Air Force News* 122 (2012): 8–9.

[102] Danson Cheong, "Militaries Can Gain from Tech, 'but Must Overcome Resistance'", *Straits Times*, 4 June 2017.

[103] The publicly disclosed groups are: (1) UAV Group comprising 116 SQN (Hermes-450), 119 SQN (Heron 1) and 128 SQN (Searcher); (2) Imagery Exploitation Group overseeing 129 SQN (imagery exploitation operations air) and 138 SQN (imagery exploitation operations land); and (3) 1 Air Engineering and Logistics Group (1 AELG) with 801 SQN and 811 SQN.

[104] At least three SAFOS recipients on active duty are trained as UAV pilots: (1) Timothy Ang (SAFOS 2002); (2) John Nehemiah Samuel (2005); and (3) Seah Jun Hao (2010). CPT (NS) Ren Jinfeng (2006) departed active service in 2016 upon completion of the six-year bond.

There are early indicators that more senior billets are beginning to be vocation-free, which should allow officers to reach the apex of the RSAF irrespective of their technical specialization. Fighter pilots no longer hold a monopoly; one general explained:

> "When you are the top guy you don't have all the expertise. Even within the ranks of pilots. There are specializations within the fighter, transport and helicopter communities. Leadership is about understanding the organization, the people, and asking questions to everyone to make sure things are done properly. You must be prepared to learn and listen. Be humble. War plans are already in place with specialized staff in place to assist, so there is no need to be so fixated with a certain vocation to be Chief [of Air Force]. Certain vocations need to break the mentality of the 'ruling class'. Just because you are paid more it does not mean you are more important. It simply reflects the function of supply and demand. It does not mean you have the right to promotion. With this, the question became: 'If we have or were allocated a certain number of stars, who do we give it to?'"[105]

In fact, given the current trends in UAV development one should not be surprised if pilots (in the traditional sense) become redundant before their AWO and AEO counterparts.

How has the 2007 reorganization impacted the ascension pathways to generalship? First, there are four Operational Commands—ADOC, ACC, APGC and PC—for pilots to make BG in a command billet. Previously this was only possible as CAF or COMD TAB, as most pilots made general in staff billets on the AS or JS. Second, with COMD ADOC opened to both flyers and non-flyers, the latter seemed to have lost the only command billet they once monopolized as COMD ADSD. However, AWOs need not worry as closer inspection reveals that their vocations have increasing broken appointments long-dominated by pilots. For example, COL (RET) Soh Poh Theen (SAFOS 1984) was the first non-pilot and AWO (C3) appointed CO of a flying squadron when he led 111 SQN (1995–96).[106] BG Tan Meng Dui (SAFOS 1986) bucked the trend of pilots serving as HAO when he held the post for nine months in 2007. MG Hoo Cher Mou broke through another ceiling when he was the first non-flyer appointed CAF in 2013. The RSAF tapped BG Gan Siow Huang as

---

[105] Interview No. 25.

[106] Goh Yong Kiat, *The Cutting Edge of the Air Force: Tengah Air Base: A Pictorial History 1939–2001* (Singapore: Tengah Air Base, Republic of Singapore Air Force, 2001), p. 68. Since then several other AWO (C3) such as COL (RET) Soh Poh Theen (1995–96), BG (RET) Gary Ang (1997–98) and COL (NS) Tan Ying Kiat (2005–06) have commanded 111 SQN.

COMD APGC in 2016, the second Operational Command after ADOC with an AWO at the helm.

Finally, the reorganization has impacted those responsible for keeping all the RSAF's mechanical assets in top condition. The structure of APGC as a "force generator" has enhanced the importance and billets available for AEOs, and their command ceiling is no longer the ALS. Their command route now commences with a specialized squadron (i.e., ground logistics, operational maintenance, specialist maintenance) and then progresses to an AELG that oversees these squadrons at an air base. AEOs have been appointed Deputy COMD at air bases and one Deputy HAL was even given the top job.[107] The apex of the AEO hierarchy is still the ME8 (MDES equivalent of BG/RADM1) billet of Head Air Engineering and Logistics (HAEL) Organization, as HAL has been known since October 2012. While it is early days yet, there are no rational reasons to prevent the appointment of an AEO with demonstrated operational acumen as COMD APGC.

6.6 MINDEF-SAF

Key appointments at the MINDEF-SAF level offer a fourth avenue after the three services to enter the military elite. It is at this echelon that eight of the first ten flag officers earned their first star between 1965 and 1987. This took place before the army became a separate service in 1988 with a COA instead of the CDF at the helm. Since then, 35 officers (18 army, two navy and 15 air force) and the seven MOs (one air force, three army, and three navy) have joined the esteemed list. There are notable differences between MINDEF and SAF billets. First, MINDEF appointments are usually held by civilians, but hybrid positions can be filled by either civilian or military personnel. They work in administration, policy, technology and cyber defence, with jurisdiction apportioned between the PS (Defence) (PS [D]) and PS (Defence Development) (PS [DD]). SAF-level billets, in contrast, fall under the ambit of the CDF and deal with the warfighting capabilities of the SAF. The permanent secretaries and CDF are all accountable to political appointees in charge of the defence portfolio. Second, some unique billets have dual MINDEF-SAF reporting lines, most notably the COS-JS and the Future Systems and Technology Architect

---

[107] For example, ME6 Andy Chiang was Deputy COMD TAB and ME6 Stewart Ng Siew Loon was Deputy COMD PLAB. ME8 Francis Cheong was appointed HAEL in 2013 and promoted to his present rank in 2015. He was Deputy CO ALS CAB (2006); CO ALS TAB (2006–07); Deputy HAL (Planning and Control) (2007); Deputy HAL (Engineering) (2007–11); COMD SBAB (2011–13); and Head Ops Development Group in HQ APGC (2011–13).

(FSTA). This deliberate design reinforces civilian oversight and, by extension, societal control over the armed forces.

6.6.1 SAF-Level Billets

The CDF stands at the apex of all SAF appointments both military and civilian. He is assisted by the COS-JS, who coordinates the principal staff functions at the SAF-level. The COS-JS is the fifth-most senior military officer, trailing only the three-star CDF and two-star service chiefs. This was most conspicuous albeit poignant during the lying-in-state of founding PM Lee Kuan Yew, where the five were the first set of officers to carry out vigil guard duties.[108] Four other one-star billets external to the JS also report to the CDF, namely, the DMI/Chief C4I who oversees intelligence and is the sixth-most senior SAF officer, the FSTA, COMDT SAFTI MI, and the CMC who is equivalent to the chief MO or surgeon general.

The Joint Staff (JS) supports the CDF, who leads the SAF as an institution and exercises command over forces in the field. The staff of specialist departments synergize additional assets placed under the CDF's direct control in times of emergency which otherwise remain under peacetime administration and training of the respective services. The concept of the JS came to fruition when MINDEF went public with the JOPD in 1983 and JID in 1984.[109] JOPD's subordinate departments—the Joint Plans Department (JPD), Joint Operations Department (JOD), and Joint Communications and Electronics Department (JCED)—followed suit in 1986.[110] The Joint Manpower Department (JMPD) and Joint Logistics Department (JLD) rounded out the five main departments of the JS. The directors of JOPD and JID started out as one-star billets, while the subordinate department heads were officers in the rank of LTC and COL. This changed over time as the SAF successfully eliminated the isolation between services. The ranks of appointment holders today reflect both the levels of responsibilities and joint capabilities attained. The established ranks for DJOPD and DJID are set at two-star, which essentially places them on par with the service chiefs—but only two officers have actually worn a second star

---

[108] LG Ng Chee Meng (CDF), MG Lim Cheng Yeow, Perry (COA), RADM2 Lai Chung Han (CNV), MG Hoo Cher Mou (CAF) and BG Chia Choon Hoong (COS-JS) performed the first vigil guard duties on 25 March 2015 from 0945hrs to 1015hrs.

[109] "SAF Should Be the Concern of Every Singaporean", *Straits Times*, 16 Apr. 1983, p. 14.

[110] "JOPD: Playing a Key Role", *Pioneer* (June 1987): 19; Sherlyn Quek, "SAF Joint Staff Celebrates 25 Years and Beyond", *Cyberpioneer*, 18 Sept. 2008.

in those appointments.[111] Three officers made BG as DJOPD after the 1988 reorganization of the army as a separate service, and since 1995 the appointment is a post-one-star billet.

The role of DJID has a more storied evolution from establishment until its current manifestation as DMI in charge of MIO. There are two appointments among JID's various subordinate departments where officers have made flag rank. The first is DA Washington, although the associated rank has oscillated in seniority. For three officers it was a post-one-star billet, but another five first wore a star in the appointment, with four of them including the incumbent as L/BG.[112] The second appointment is the Military Adviser at the Permanent Mission of Singapore to the UN (MA UN). This proved ephemeral, with only one officer making BG in this capacity; and for his successor it was a third tour as a general.[113] Every officer appointed MA UN since 2007 has remained in the rank of COL.

In the last decade the importance of military intelligence has increased in tandem with the SAF's transformation and as part of an interagency approach to uncover potential threats from both state and non-state actors. This is most evident through the acquisition and reorganization of intelligence assets across the three services and the establishment of the Intelligence Officer as a vocation instead of a skill set that officers specialize in when required. The critical role played by the intelligence community was further highlighted by two significant promotions. One officer appointed Head Joint Intelligence (HJI) was promoted to ME8 in 2013, while another made BG in the role of Deputy Chief C4I (Intelligence) in 2016.[114] It remains to be seen whether these rank-appointment relationships are transient or remain a permanent fixture.

---

[111] (1) Ng Yat Chung made MG (1999) as DJOPD/COS-JS (1998–2000) and later became COA (2000–03) and CDF (2003–07); and (2) Joseph Leong made RADM2 (2013) as DMI/Chief C4I (2012–14) before his appointment as DIR SID in 2014.

[112] (1) Sin Boon Wah (1997–2000) made BG (1993) as COMD 9 DIV; (2) Loh Kok Wah (2000–02) made BG (1999) as COMD TAB; (3) Voon Tse-Chow (2002–05) made BG (2002) as DA Washington; (4) Richard Lim (2005–08) made BG (2004) as COMD TAB; (5) Cheng Siak Kian (2008–11) made L/BG (2008) and BG (2010) as DA Washington; (6) Tan Chee Wee (2011–13) made L/BG as (2012) DA Washington and BG (2014) as DIR (Policy) DPO; (7) Leong Kum Wah (2013–16) made L/BG (2013) as DA Washington and retired as COL or L/BG; and (8) Tan Boon Kim made L/BG (2016) as the incumbent DA Washington.

[113] Yap Ong Heng was promoted to BG (2000) as MA UN (1999–2004). His successor, Leong Yue Kheong, made BG (1999) as COMD 9 DIV (1998–2000) and subsequently completed tours as COMD TRADOC (2000–04) and MA UN (2004–07).

[114] Lau Cher Loon made ME8 (2013) as HJI, while Ng Chad-Son made BG (2016) as Deputy Chief C4I (Intelligence).

Certain departments of the JS also offer opportunities for flag rank.[115] Five officers were forwarded to BG as Head Joint Operations (HJO), later renamed DJO, with responsibility for writing joint doctrine and executing joint operations across a spectrum of missions.[116] HJO commenced as a "pre-brigade/squadron command" staff appointment (1986–90) but soon evolved into an officers' "pre-division/air base/fleet command" (1990–2003). The role of DJO has since been apportioned to generals and admirals after successful leadership of a division, fleet or Operational Command. The post of Head Joint Communications and Information Systems (HJCIS) joined the list of one-star billets in 2006. The role is a critical part of the 3G SAF's central nervous system and facilitates inter-service communication and information sharing.[117] Three army signals officers made BG as HJCIS before the role was superseded by COMD SAF C4 Command in 2017.

The other heads of department on the JS have largely remained as colonels, but there have been exceptions. Two officers earned their first star as Head Joint Planning and Transformation (HJPT) with planning responsibilities for budget allocation, infrastructure (organizational and physical), and manpower requirements for the SAF.[118] This seems somewhat of an aberration given the roles of HJP and HJPT have long been "pre-division/air base/fleet/Operational Command" billets and the HJPT's since 2010 have remained in the rank of COL. Similarly, only one Head Joint Manpower (HJMP) was promoted to BG in the history of the JMPD, which oversees personnel matters at the SAF level. This particular case is discussed more fully in chapter 7. Two army officers made BG at the helm of the Joint Logistics Department (JLD) between 2000 and 2007 while addressing the logistical requirements at the SAF level. Their respective promotions took place during an initiative to restructure JLD from a staff department into a tri-service command. However, realities indicated the optimal solution was for the individual services to run their own logistics and for JLD to utilize such expertise when required. Since 2007, the HJL has remained

---

[115] The hierarchy in terms of staff billets is: (1) staff officer; (2) section; (3) branch; (4) department/office; (5) directorate/staff/office.

[116] (1) Chua Chwee Koh made BG (2001) as HJO (1998–2001) en route to COMD 21 DIV/ CGO 53 days later on 23 August 2001; (2) Ng Chee Khern made BG (2003) as HJO (2003–04); (3) Wong Huat Sern made BG (2004) as HJO (2004–06); (4) Ng Chee Meng made BG (2008) as DJO (2006–09); and (5) Ngien Hoon Ping made BG (2011) as DJO (2010–13).

[117] The main components of the JCISD were the IT Infrastructure Office, C4 Plans Group and C4 Operations Group.

[118] (1) Ravinder Singh made BG (2004) as HJPT (2004–05) and assumed command of 6 DIV 18 months later, on 6 January 2006; and (2) Joseph Leong made RADM1 (2008) as HJPT (2007–09) and assumed command of the RSN Fleet 17 months later, on 4 December 2009.

a COL and at times juggled the concurrent appointment as commander of a DISCOM in a role accountable to a DIV COMD.

There are two other one-star billets at the SAF level external to the JS and independent of the respective services. The first is COMDT SAFTI MI, a post-one-star appointment established in 1994 with responsibility for all formal military leadership development in Singapore ranging from sergeants to colonels. A posting to SAFTI MI beyond a brief tour as a PC training cadets in OCS, or a short stint en route to another appointment, once indicated that an army officer was not going to make BG. This holds true for naval and air force officers, but there are indications that from time to time a deliberate effort was made to infuse high-calibre individuals from the army into the SAFTI environment.[119] Most of them would go on to earn their star first beyond the institute, and only one officer was promoted to BG as COMDT SCSC.[120]

The second billet is exclusive to MOs, and seven distinguished doctors have made one-star, with the first in 1994. This is the sole one-star billet for MOs and reflects the importance of the SAFMC—arguably the SAF's most decorated and operationally experienced formation—despite its small numbers relative to many other formations. The CMC does not command the SAFMC as a field force because the majority of its units are decentralized in support of the respective services. That said, the CMC is still responsible for tri-service units at the SAF level and is the adviser to the CDF on all medical issues. The pathway to CMC begins with the completion of a recognized medical degree, houseman attachment at a government hospital, and pre-commissioning MOCC, which focuses primarily on preparing NSF doctors for service in the army's various and numerous medical units.[121] Regular MOs in the early days had a less structured path given the embryonic stage of organizational development; manpower directives were hardly in place. This is not surprising since the SAFMC, initially

---

[119] Army officers having held significant appointments at SAFTI/SAFTI MI include: Kirpa Ram Vij, DIR SAFTI (1966–68); Tan Chin Tiong, CO OCS (1974); Patrick Sim, DIR SCSC (1975–78); Chin Chow Yoon, DS and later CI in SCSC (1978–79); Colin Theseira, COMD SATO (1978–80); Law Chwee Kiat, CO OCS (1980–81); Lim Kah Kee, COMDT SCSC (1995–2000); Chan Wing Kai, OC in OCS (1996–97) and COMDT SCSC (2007–09); Ishak Bin Ismail, CI (1998–2000) and later COMD AOAS/SAS (2003–05); Lim Teck Yin, COMDT SCSC (2003–07); Chiang Hock Woon, COMD OCS (2007–11); and Chua Boon Keat, COMD OCS (2011–13).

[120] Lim Kah Kee made BG (2000) as COMDT SCSC (1995–2000) en route to COMD 3 DIV four months later, on 18 October 2000.

[121] "The Making of the SAF Doctor", *Pioneer* (Dec. 1988): 30–3. This includes, but is not restricted to, the Battalion Casualty Station (BCS), which supports a battalion; a medical company for a brigade; and a Combat Support Hospital (CSH) for a division. MOs also serve as brigade and division staff officers.

named the SAF Medical Services, started off as an independent department under MINDEF's manpower division.[122] The early pioneers built expertise from scratch in areas relevant to the respective services and the military profession in general. Regular MOs were, however, very few and engaged in lengthy tours and concurrent appointments, and some held almost every appointment available.

Various initiatives were implemented to attract more doctors into the military career. The MO Career Scheme was introduced in 1986 through a six-year contract in a "3+3" format. The first three were on supernumerary secondment to MOH to master a selected specialization. The next three years were in uniformed service, although these junior MOs (usually in the rank of MAJ) also spent two days weekly at hospitals to maintain currency or as part-time university lecturers.[123] The Advanced MO's Course was implemented in 1988 to further develop the MOs' military role "to plan and command medical support for large scale operations and to coordinate this with other arms of the SAF".[124] In 1991 attachments to MOH on a 3+3 format were extended to MOs who opted for a second six-year contract allowing them to become full-fledged specialists (usually in the rank of LTC) with salaries commensurate with peers in the public medical sector.[125]

The LMS was later introduced somewhat belatedly, with recipients bonded for 12 years' service in return. This alleviated the manpower crunch to a degree through the steady pipeline of regular MOs in the ranks of CPT to LTC. As one CMC explained:

> "The SAF awards six to eight LMS scholarships annually. For a six-year cycle, that would be 36 to 48 officers. Over 12 years, around 60 to 80. Around half of each cycle will be on basic and advance specialist training. The program for the first 12 years is very structured, with progression through various job grades and appointments. There is no prescribed path, no cookie-cutter <smiles>, for advancement on the military side of things. There is flexibility to align individuals to work of significance depending on ability, vacancies, competency and manning requirements. Every individual is managed due to the small number [of regular MOs] ... There is no specialization bias, but certain specialized training helps to prepare an officer for the job because there are inherent advantages.

---

[122] "Medical Services' Mixed Bag of Miracles", *Pioneer* (May 1976): 6.

[123] Specialists in oral surgery, psychiatry, occupational medicine and aviation medicine were also part-time lecturers at NUS. "Operational Medical Unit", *Pioneer* (Jan. 1989): 8–11; "SAF Medical Professionals", *Pioneer* (Feb. 1989): 28–9.

[124] "SAF Doctors: Grooming for Command", *Pioneer* (Aug. 1989): 54.

[125] An enhanced specialist allowance for these specialists (in the rank of "senior" MAJs and above) was also introduced, ranging from $570 to $2,600 to reflect market rates. "Specialist SAF Doctors", *Pioneer* (May 1991): 21.

> For example, if an individual specializes in, say, public health, he or she would be better for an appointment dealing with public health. Someone with a background as a surgeon may not have the exposure. The key issue is to find job match in terms of core competency and organizational needs. Sure, if you are intelligent you can overcome the challenges. The question is also whether you are willing to learn new tricks and draw on the background of past experiences."[126]

Certain appointments indicate an MO had checked the right boxes for ascension, although there are no cookie-cutter pathways into the upper echelons of the SAFMC. Examples include the army's Soldier Performance Centre, the Naval Underwater Medical Centre, the Aeromedical Centre, and certain SAF-level medical units such as the Medical Classification Centre at CMPB, the inter-ministry Military Medicine Institute, and the SAF Medical Training Institute (formerly School of Military Medicine). There are also important staff appointments such as Head GS Branch of the medical HQ at the respective service and SAF levels, and the two now-defunct Senior MO (Healthcare) billets. Once these were successfully completed it was essential to become the chief MO for one of the services, from which one of the three would be selected as CMC.

6.6.2 MINDEF-Level Billets

The political appointees at the apex of MINDEF have been civilians, and only four were former career officers.[127] Similarly, the PS (D) and PS (DD) appointments have been held exclusively by civilian bureaucrats, and only four were former SAF regular officers.[128] SAF-level appointments normally trace their way upwards to the CDF, while MINDEF billets often lead to the PS (DD), PS (D) and at times even directly to the Minister of Defence. Few appointments such as COS-JS and FSTA have dual-reporting lines within both the SAF and

---

[126] Interview No. 18. Each CMC has a different specialization thus far: (1) BG (RET) (Dr) Lim Meng Kin (Aviation Medicine) (1986–95); (2) BG (RET) (Dr) Lionel Lee (Sports Medicine) (1995–2001); (3) BG (RET) (Dr) Wong Yue Sie (Orthopaedics) (2001–06); (4) RADM1 (RET) (Dr) John Wong (Psychiatry) (2006–09); (5) BG (RET) (Dr) Benjamin Seet (Ophthalmology) (2009–11); (6) RADM1 (RET) (Dr) Kang Wee Lee (Ear, Nose, and Throat) (2011–15); (7) RADM 1 (Dr) Tang Kong Choong (Anaesthesiology) (since 2015).

[127] (1) Lee Hsien Loong was Political Secretary (Defence) (1984), MOS (Defence) (1984–87) and Second Minister (Services) for Defence (1987–90); (2) Teo Chee Hean was MOS (Defence), Second Minister for Defence and Minister for Defence (2003–11); (3) Chan Chun Sing was Senior MOS (2012–13) and later Second Minister for Defence (2013–15); and (4) Lui Tuck Yew was Second Minister for Defence (2015).

[128] (1) Peter Ho Hak Ean was PS (DD) (1995–2000) and PS (D) (2000–04); (2) Tan Kim Siew was PS (DD) (2003–12); (3) Ng Chee Khern was PS (DD) (2014–17); and (4) Neo Kian Hong was PS (DD) (2017–18).

MINDEF hierarchy. The MINDEF appointments held by military elites are usually hybrid in nature, with the sole exception of DIR MSD.

The most senior hybrid post is DIR SID, who is responsible for the collection, processing and analysis of external intelligence. The division remains extremely secretive but is known to cooperate closely with neighbouring and Anglosphere intelligence agencies.[129] The main HQ is presently housed on the MINDEF grounds at Bukit Gombak for reasons of technological, logistical and administrative expediency. DIR SID reported directly to the Minister of Defence in days past, but the streamlining of Singapore's security apparatus could have altered this arrangement.[130] It is not beyond question for the division's current operational purview to fall under the Coordinating Minister for Security or the Prime Minister's Office (PMO). BG (RET) Choi Shing Kwok (SAFOS 1978) was the first uniformed officer to hold this billet in 1995 and made BG in the same capacity a year later. He retired from the SAF mid-tenure and later relinquished the appointment as a civilian. His successor, BG (RET) Chee Wee Kiong (SAFOS 1982), held the directorship as a post-one-star billet and subsequently as a civilian.[131] MG (RET) Ng Chee Khern was next in the hot seat, having retired from the SAF in 2009 before becoming Senior Deputy DIR (2010) and later DIR (2010–14) SID. Incumbent DIR RADM2 (NS) Joseph Leong took a similar path after retirement from active service in 2014.[132]

The echelons below the PS (D) and PS (DD) are anchored by four DS appointments. Three of the long-standing appointments were formed in the mid-1980s and over the years have evolved to handle the defence establishment's increasingly complex tasks and structure.[133] DS (Administration) has always

---

[129] Yap Chuin Wei, "Examining the World's Second-Oldest Profession", *Straits Times*, 19 May 2001; Philip Dorling, "Singapore, South Korea Revealed as Five Eyes Spying Partners", *Sydney Morning Herald*, 25 Nov. 2013; Murray Hunter, "Is Singapore Western Intelligence's 6th Eye?" *Asia Sentinel*, 9 Dec. 2013.

[130] Chew and Tan, *Creating the Technology Edge*, p. 16.

[131] Chee Wee Kiong served as COS (2004–05) and subsequently DIR SID (2005–10). He made BG (2000) as COMD ADSD (2000–02) and was later COS-AS (2001–04) and DJOPD (2003–04).

[132] Presentation slides for "National Junior College Career Talk 2015" uploaded to *Prezi* by Eileen Cheng on 5 Mar. 2015, https://prezi.com/dsd8oq1qjlpp/mindefsaf/, accessed 18 Mar. 2015.

[133] The Deputy Secretary (DS) appointments in MINDEF have continually evolved. Starting from one billet it grew to four billets in the early 1980s with DS (Air Force), DS (Development and Engineering), DS (Finance and Administration), and DS (Resources Management). In 1986 this was reorganized into Senior DS (Technology), DS (Personnel and Policy), DS (Development), and DS (Policy). "New Jobs for 4 Deputy Secretaries at Mindef", *Straits Times*, 15 Feb. 1986, p. 32.

been a civilian who heads the DMG and provides oversight for personnel and financial matters in MINDEF and the SAF.[134] Subordinate DMG functions include OPC (currently headed by a SLTC), which manages the careers of scholar-officers, Wranglers, and officers in the rank of COL and above. DS (Technology) leads the Defence Technology and Resource Office (DTRO), which develops Singapore's military capabilities by leveraging on the indigenous defence technology community and various foreign partnerships.[135] Only one officer made BG as DS (Technology), although other military elites have held the role either as a post-one-star billet in transition towards retirement, or as a civilian.[136] Two officers also served as DIR Defence Industry and Systems Office (DISO), a subordinate office of DTRO, as a post-one-star billet.[137] Both DS (Administration) and DS (Technology) report directly to PS (DD).

DS (Policy) heads MINDEF's Defence Policy Group (DPG), and only one officer made BG in that capacity, although others have held the appointment as post-one-star billets.[138] Four officers also received their first star leading sub-units within DPG. Two were at the helm of the DPO, which translates political

---

[134] The Defence Management Group includes the Manpower Division, Professional Services (Defence Psychology Department, SAF Counselling Centre, and Centre for Heritage Services), MINDEF Scholarship Centre, Defence Finance Organization, MINDEF Information Systems Division, Legal Services and Internal Audit Department.

[135] The Defence Technology Community consists of the Defence Science and Technology Agency (DSTA), DSO National Laboratories, Centre for Strategic Infocomm Technologies (CSIT), and the SAF logistics and engineering departments at service- and joint-levels. The DRTO oversees the Defence Industry and Systems Office, Industry Group, Systems Group, and Shared Services Management Department.

[136] Wesley D'Aranjo made BG (1992) as DS (Technology) MINDEF (1991–97). RADM2 (RET) Richard Lim was CNV (1996–99) and later DS (Technology) (2000–04); MG (RET) Ravinder Singh was COS-JS (2007–09) before serving as DS (Technology) (2009–11) and later recalled to active service as COA (2011–14); BG (RET) Tan Meng Dui was DMI (2008–11) before DS (Technology) (2011–14); BG (RET) David Koh was DIR MSD (2006–14) and then DS (Technology) (2014–17); and RADM1 Frederick Chew was DJO (2016–17) before assuming the DS (Technology) portfolio in 2017.

[137] Tsoi Mun Heng was DIR DISO (June 2007 to January 2009) and made BG (2006) as HAL (2003–07). Tan Peng Kuan was DIR DISO (May 2014 to September 2015) and made BG (2013) as COMD CSSCOM (2010–14).

[138] The Defence Policy Group includes the Defence Policy Office, Information Directorate, Public Communications Directorate and Nexus (responsible for National Education). Uniformed officers appointed DS (Policy) include the following: (1) Tan Yong Soon made BG (1993) while serving as DS (Policy) (1992–95); (2) Gary Ang made BG (2005), served in this capacity on active service (2008–11) and relinquished the role as a civilian in 2012; and (3) Lai Chung Han made RADM1 (2011) as the Fleet COMD (2011–12) and was later DS (Policy) (2012–14).

decisions into tangible actions via policies concerning Singapore's defence interests and relations.[139] DIR (Policy) DPO is a hybrid post and over the last decade has been held by officers of various seniorities.[140] The post-one-star appointment of Group Chief (Policy & Strategy) DPG was created in 2017, and this should stabilize DIR (Policy) DPO as a senior COL's appointment. The fourth and most recent position of DS (Special Projects) was created in 2015. The longevity of this appointment is unknown, as the "Special Projects" moniker seemingly refers to the creation of the CSA, DCO and SAF C4 Command. It remains to be seen whether the post will be merged into the Defence Cyber Chief appointment. The post-one-star role of DIR Cyber Policy and Plans Directorate was created in 2018 to make the DCO more robust. Both DS (Policy) and DS (Special Projects) report directly to PS (D).

Aside from the four DS's there are two other one-star positions at the MINDEF echelon. The FSTA heads the Future Systems and Technology Directorate (FSTD), which was inaugurated in February 2003 and is a post-one-star billet. FSTD, as the name suggests, is responsible for the research and development of advanced technological systems for the SAF with funding of up to 1 per cent of the annual defence budget. The directorate is staffed by both military officers drawn from the three services and civilians with technical expertise. The hybrid nature of the FSTA role was unveiled in 2017, when MINDEF's Chief Defence Scientist and veteran of the defence technology community Quek Gim Pew was tapped for the appointment. Finally, three officers made BG as DIR MSD although the role has also been held as a post-one-star billet.[141] The fact that the billet has been held by a BG since 1996 indicates the importance placed on counter-espionage initiatives and non-physical security of MINDEF and SAF installations and personnel.

---

[139] Gary Ang made BG (2005) as DIR (Policy) DPO en route to COMD TAB; and Ng Chee Peng made RADM1 (2007) as DIR (Policy) DPO in 2007, six months prior to assuming command of the RSN Fleet.

[140] DIR (Policy) DPO over the last decade (2007–17): Philip Ong Wee Kiat (2007–08); COL Lai Chung Han (2008–11); BG Cheng Siak Kian (2011–14), who made L/BG (2008) and BG (2010) while serving as DA Washington (2008–11); BG Tan Chee Wee (2014–15), who made L/BG (2012) as DA Washington (2011–13) and then BG (2014) as DIR (Policy) DPO; COL Kelvin Fan Sui Siong (2015–7); and COL Aaron Beng Yaocheng (since 2017).

[141] Lee Fook Sun, Jek Kian Yee and Paul Chew made BG as DIR MSD in 1996, 2000 and 2015 respectively. David Koh made BG (2006) as HJCIS (2004–06) before he assumed the appointment (2006–14).

6.7 Summary

Officer ascension refers to both the processes that allow officers to progress in rank and the underlying structure that determines the distribution of the rank hierarchy. From 1965 to 1977 the SAF usually had one active-duty one-star officer at the helm. This deliberate act elucidated the nascent state of military capabilities and a political leadership conscious of ensuring civilian primacy over the military. The community of active military elites expanded slowly as the SAF matured with key developments such as the creation of the JS (early 1980s) and a separate army HQ (1988). The number of flag officers is a reflection of the respective formations' warfighting capabilities, the critical role played by staff departments, and the importance of a specific diplomatic mission overseas.

Ascension pathways have been etched into the structure, and while some seem well trodden others have proven ephemeral, even *sui generis*, as the importance and responsibilities of specific billets evolve. For the army general the established path of battalion, brigade and division command seems set to continue. For the admiral this means captaincy of a ship followed possibly by command of squadrons, flotillas and eventually the RSN Fleet. The 2009 restructuring of COSCOM into MSTF has provided a second fleet-level opportunity for admiralship. The pathway for air force generals hinged very much on their vocations, but this dependency is slowly fading in importance. Prior to the RSAF's 2007 restructuring into Operational Commands, the requisite pathway for pilots normally included squadron (usually fighter) and air base command; but unlike army and navy counterparts, their first star usually came in a staff billet. Similarly, Air Engineering Officers—the only engineering vocation in the SAF that has consistently made one-star—ascended through squadron command followed by staff billets. On the other hand, the pathway for Air Warfare Officers (both GBAD and C3) covered squadron and brigade and culminated in command of the Air Defence and Systems Division. The Operational Commands altered the ascension paths, and four of the five have offered generalships to pilots. Air Engineering Officers also have a wider variety of billets, including logistics group and air base command. Air Warfare Officers may have conceded monopoly over the ADSD, but the vocation has pushed new frontiers in appointments traditionally dominated by pilots.

The MINDEF-SAF level has afforded opportunities for a third of the military elite beyond the confines of their own service. It is only at the SAF level where MOs earn their star in the capacity of CMC. It is also as Head Joint Communications and Information Systems, which was superseded by COMD SAF C4 Command, where army signals officers have an appointment to their distinct advantage. In other posts such as Head Joint Plans and Transformation it is anyone's guess whether the appointee will actually receive a star. Other officers have also earned their first stars in hybrid MINDEF posts that are held by either military officers or civilian bureaucrats. In some cases promotions have proven *sui generis*, and there seems to be a conscious attempt to ensure that the star is a reflection of abilities in the profession of arms and not a mere reward for administrative competence.

CHAPTER 7

Scholars and Stars by Numbers and Cases

"It is said of leaders that some are born great, some achieve greatness and some have greatness thrust upon them. But in Singapore, such things are not left to chance."[1]

— *The Straits Times*

7.1 Introduction

The keys to ascending the SAF Officer Corps are performance and potential, which in turn dictate postings and promotions. The organizational structure is also of great importance as it provides the necessary pathways and appointments towards the upper echelons and into the military elite. Personnel recruitment and movement may seem to take place in a deterministic and even uniform manner at times, but history indicates otherwise. This chapter covers three of the more conspicuous areas unique to Singapore's military establishment. The first is a closer examination of the SAFOS to elucidate significant quantitative and historical points of interest. The scheme has been trumped as a success, is a subtopic of books on politics and governance in Singapore, and serves as a discussion point for various Internet forums. Yet, empirical evidence can be used to paint any picture depending on the point of view. The second area highlights outliers in the conferral of flag ranks through unique career pathways, bestowment of temporary "local" ranks for operational duty overseas, those bypassed for promotion despite holding established flag appointments, and on the flip side aberrations in the promotion of one-star officers. The third area focuses specifically on the transition of a one-star into the elite nucleus, an inner sanctum within the military elite, as one of three service chiefs. The *primus inter pares* will emerge from among the three to be the SAF's number one officer and lead as the CDF.

---

[1] Cherian George, "Groomed", *Straits Times*, 9 Aug. 1993, p. 4.

7.2   A Closer Look at the SAFOS

Several former SAFOS recipients have heralded the scholarship initiative as "a proven source of the best talent for the defence of Singapore" and depicted scholar-officers as a "national resource".[2] Proponents further adduce the successes in attracting the best and brightest and their service in the highest echelons of MINDEF and the SAF as reasons for the scholarship's longevity and continued existence. Ardent critics, on the other hand, decry an elitist scheme that selects future military leaders on teenage potential and ushers them into the top brass barring any catastrophic career failures. This leads to a belief in some quarters that opportunities to ascend are not equal and, *ceteris paribus*, the scholar will also be selected in order to justify the seemingly excessive investment in the individual.

Empirical evidence from the SAFOS community sheds light on the scheme and serves as one proxy to gauge the manpower quality factor in the SAF. The latter undertaking is subjective and at times impossible even for established foreign forces. For example, an article in the *Royal United Services Institute Journal* notes that "since the British Army monitors only its quantitative losses in manpower, it simply has no feel for how much of its quality has left prematurely".[3] The SAFOS sample size is small, yet enough time has passed and adequate data exist for various pictures to emerge. This is in contrast to other metrics such as the exit of specialized military personnel with easily transferable skill sets—such as pilots, doctors and engineers—for which information lies beyond the realm of open sources.

7.2.1 *Elite Schools and Institutions*

An appropriate starting point is the secondary (pre-university) institutions from which 332 students were awarded the SAFOS between 1971 and 2018. Among the 332 were 70 dual SAFOS-PS recipients, and the initiative has produced 68 flag officers to date from the 1971 to 1998 cohorts. The data have four clear features (Table 7.1). The first is the conspicuous dominance of Raffles Institution, with its alumni bagging 144 scholarships—almost 44 per cent of the total. This is no small feat considering this lion's share is greater than the 138 recipients from the next four institutions combined. The institution also leads in terms of dual SAFOS-PS recipients: its 25 recipients outpace runner-up Hwa Chong (17) by a factor of 1.5 and three times as many recipients as third-placed National

---

[2] Geraldine Yeo, "Without Peer", *Straits Times*, 9 Mar. 2003, p. 2; Nicholas Yong, "Six Join Ranks of 'National Resource' with SAF Overseas Scholarship", *Straits Times*, 12 Aug. 2009.

[3] Patrick Little, "Lessons Unlearned", *RUSI Journal* 143, 3 (June 2009): 14.

(eight). Four in ten (29 of 68) of the SAFOS officers within the military elite are Rafflesians. Next, the consistent proportions of former Raffles (two-fifths) and Hwa Chong (one-fifth) students—the institutions with greatest numbers of recipients—across the SAFOS, SAFOS-PS and SAFOS flag officer categories indicate that secondary institution of origin neither favours nor hinders their rank ascensions.

The third feature indicates the existence of elite secondary institutions within Singapore's education system. Raffles, Hwa Chong and National account for three-quarters of the recipients of the nation's second-most prestigious scholarship. The proportion rises to nine in ten if Anglo-Chinese, Victoria and Temasek are included to round out the top six schools. Finally, the SAFOS flag officer ascension rate is approximately one-in-three, with 68 of the 197 scholars from 1971 to 1998 making BG/RADM1 and above by the conclusion of 2018. Hwa Chong paced the schools in this conversion metric, accounting for 13 flag officers from its 31 scholar-officers (41.94 per cent). It would seem that the ratio of one flag officer emerging from every three SAFOS awarded is acceptable to the defence establishment judging by the longevity of the scheme. The greater concern for defence planners is whether internal expectations—from evolving social and moral norms to the voluntary attrition rates of scholars—are currently met and whether the scholarship will address future needs.

7.2.2 SAFOS Retention, Attrition and Flag Officer Ascension Rates

There are two plausible scenarios, *ceteris paribus*, where the scholarship could fail to address future needs. Both are concerned with diminishing rate of returns but for different groups of officers. One scenario is that the SAFOS has outlived its usefulness in attracting the best talent given rising education levels and the fact that a military career is no longer frowned upon. Perpetuating this initiative becomes detrimental to recruitment and retention efforts when non-scholar-officers—whether NSF, NSmen or Regulars—shun a uniformed career due to perceived biases favouring scholar-officers for reasons (scholastic, sporting and leadership achievements) that are increasingly invalid in contemporary Singapore. In this scenario the defence establishment continues to award the SAFOS and SMS annually at the expense of junior officer (2LT to CPT) recruitment and the even greater challenge of retaining officers in the middle tier (senior CPT to SLTC) who are ambitious, experienced and capable. The problem with this scenario is that it is completely hypothetical as there are no open sources available to either support or deny its existence. Even the defence establishment may have trouble finding empirical evidence to test this hypothesis. It is also unlikely that individuals were specifically asked whether the scholarship schemes

Table 7.1. Distribution of SAFOS recipients and flag officers among secondary education institutions (1971–2018)

Secondary Institution	SAFOS Awarded	% of All SAFOS	SAFOS-PS Awarded	% of All SAFOS-PS	SAFOS Flag Officers	% of All SAFOS Flag Officers	SAFOS Awarded (1971–1998)	Flag Officer % from SAFOS Awarded
Raffles	144	43.37%	25	35.71%	29	42.65%	79	36.71%
Hwa Chong	68	20.48%	17	24.29%	13	19.12%	31	41.94%
National	34	10.24%	8	11.43%	9	13.24%	28	32.14%
Victoria	19	5.72%	2	2.86%	3	4.41%	9	33.33%
Anglo-Chinese	17	5.12%	4	5.71%	6	8.82%	17	35.29%
Temasek	15	4.52%	2	2.86%	3	4.41%	14	21.43%
Catholic	9	2.71%	5	7.14%	1	1.47%	8	12.50%
Anglo-Chinese (Independent)	7	2.11%	1	1.43%	–	–	–	–
St Joseph's	6	1.81%	4	5.71%	2	2.94%	5	40.00%
River Valley High	3	0.90%	1	1.43%	–	–	–	–
NUS High	2	0.60%	–	–	–	–	–	–
Nanyang	2	0.60%	–	–	1	1.47%	1	100.00%
St Andrew's	1	0.30%	–	–	–	–	1	0%
Pioneer	1	0.30%	1	1.43%	–	–	–	–
Unknown	4	1.20%	–	–	1	1.47%	4	25.00%
TOTAL	332	100%	70	100.0%	68	100%	197	34.52%

and scholar-officers were reasons for their avoidance of regular service or for leaving active service.

A second scenario where the SAFOS fails to meet future needs is when recipients do not ascend to the apex of the armed forces as expected. There are those who fail to meet the high expectations despite investments in their professional development through education, training and experiences. Then there are those who depart active service before realizing their career potential. A look at the 197 SAFOS invested in by the state between 1971 and 1998 provides some insight into the retention and ascension of cohorts that have passed the 20-year mark since they received the scholarship (Appendix H). Raw figures indicate that 108 officers (54.82 per cent) served until retirement having either rendered 20 or more years of active service, or reached the ranks of COL and above. Within this category, 68 (62.96 per cent) become flag officers while 37 of the remaining 40 made COL or ME7 in line with their status as Wranglers. The percentage of those who served until retirement rises slightly to 56.25 per cent (108 of 192) if figures are adjusted to exclude the three who were transferred to the SPF and two who perished on active duty. The flip side is that 43.75 per cent (84 of 192) of the SAFOS recipients departed the SAF in their early to late career, a period ranging from six to 19 years on active service, in the ranks of CPT to SLTC. These figures provide rough retention and ascension rates of the SAFOS scheme, although they are by no means indicative of the cohorts from 1999 and after.

One pressing area of concern for defence planners is the retention of scholars. Some scholars may find that the transition from the military, in terms of industry-specific experiences sought by the private sector, becomes more challenging with each passing year. Furthermore, the perceived rigidity of the civil service in terms of career structure and a conservative approach to risk and reward may not appeal to those with an entrepreneurial streak. Certain cracks have already appeared within the junior SAFOS ranks, although the repercussions in terms of succession planning will only be known later. History indicates that almost every SAFOS cohort from 1971 to 1998 has produced at least one flag officer, but the 1996 cohort was the first to buck the trend. The seven recipients should have been in the ranks of SLTC to BG/RADM1 at the 20-year career mark, but all resigned between the 12th and 15th years of active service (Table 7.2). In light of this precedent, all eyes are on subsequent batches. The 2001 cohort has four of eight recipients on active service; three left as MAJ and one as CPT (all in 2011 after ten years of service). The 2002 cohort has two of six remaining, with four having left as MAJ (after ten to 11 years of service). It is unknown whether such figures are alarming to the defence establishment, and much will depend on the future career performances and decisions of the remaining SAFOS recipients.

Table 7.2. Service lengths and post-SAF career destinations of 1996 SAFOS recipients

Name	Vocation	Rank	Left SAF	Career Destination (sector)
Choy Dawen	WSO (C3)	MAJ	2008	Management (GLC)
Goh Meng Kiat	WSO (GBAD)	MAJ	2008	Finance (private)
Khoo Teng Lip	Armour	MAJ	2008	Finance (private)
James Lee Tze Wei	Naval Combat Officer	MAJ	2008	Management (GLC)
Lien Choong Luen	Commando	MAJ	2010	Consultancy (private)
Kelvin Lim Wee Khoon	Naval Combat Officer	LTC	2011	Management (public)
Frederick Teo Li-Wei	Infantry	LTC	2010	Consultancy (private)

The retention and attrition of SAFOS officers of a specific vocation is another gauge of manpower quality within individual formations. Empirical data indicate significant early to mid-career departures at various junctures within the signals and armour formations. A chronological list of the former begins with COL Lai Seck Khui (SAFOS 1971), who served for 28 years and was the SAF's fourth Chief Signals Officer (1982–87). The next officer with such active-duty longevity is former HJCIS (2013–16) BG Milton Ong Ann Kiat (SAFOS 1992). There were 12 other SAFOS recipients between Lai and Ong who commenced their careers as signals officer. Four opted for re-vocation as guards, armour or intelligence officers. Seven of the remaining eight departed mid-career in the ranks of MAJ and LTC, while BG George Yeo was seconded to the RSAF after only three years in the army. One strong reason for the attrition is the limited ascension pathway towards generalship before the creation of the HJCIS billet. Other possible explanations include the lure of careers beyond the SAF, especially in the telecommunications industry, and that the vocation is not the most visible and requires much toiling in obscurity.

While the limited ascension pathway towards flag rank is a plausible reason in the case of signals officers, it does not hold any weight in the more recent early- to mid-career departures from the armour formation. Generals from the armour formation are represented on the Rolls of Honour for every army division including the defunct 1 PDF. Yet only four of the 13 SAFOS recipients between 1989 and 2005 remained on active service at the end of 2017 (Table 7.3). Seven of the nine who left did so early, before the highly anticipated career highlight of commanding an active mechanized battalion in the form of an Armoured Battle Group (ABG) comprising over 600 personnel and 60 vehicles, or the highly vaunted main battle tank battalion. A rather unusual cluster of four departed in 2011. These figures stand in stark contrast to the 16 officers between 1971 and 1988, 11 of whom served to retirement, with eight making BG and above. There is a need to caution that figures presented for the armour vocation do not indicate any causality among the officers' respective decisions to leave active service, nor do they indicate a wider exodus of officers from the formation. What is clear is that the formation lost a good number of its SAFOS officers for reasons that may or may not be known to the defence establishment, but certainly reasons that lie beyond the remit of open-source information.

Table 7.3. Service status of SAFOS recipients (1989–2005) in the armour vocation at the end of 2017

SAFOS Year	Name	Last/ Latest Rank on Active Service	Last Year of Active Service	Active Unit Command
1989	Tay Han Chong	MAJ	2000	–
1992	Dominic Ow El Gene	LTC	2007	40 SAR
1995	Ng Chia Yong	LTC	2011	48 SAR
1996	Khoo Teng Lip	MAJ	2008	–
1997	Chang Yi-Chian	MAJ	2010	–
1998	Frederick Choo Wei Yee	COL	–	42 SAR, 8 SAB
1999	Jason See Chong Wei	COL	–	41 SAR, 4 SAB
2000	Nigel Chan Kwong Lee	MAJ	2011	–
2000	Lin Maoyu	MAJ	2011	–
2001	Ryan Tan Jian Yuan	MAJ	2011	–
2003	Cai Dexian	SLTC	–	48 SAR
2004	He Ruijie	CPT	2015	–
2005	Chong Shi Hao	MAJ	–	–

7.2.3 *The SAFOS Edge*

The final examination in this section deals with the significance of the SAFOS in the careers of the military elite. There are various metrics of interest from a statistical point of view, but open-source information is too limited to make a comprehensive enquiry. It is, however, possible to form three relatively complete pictures from the constructed empirical data. These include the estimated age in the year of wearing the first star, the years of active flag officership, and age in the year of retirement. There is also adequate information to present the sole case of a recipient who was later stripped of the scholarship. Inter- and intra-cohort comparisons underline the opportunity costs for an academically gifted individual who was once deemed to have as much potential as his cohort peers.

The relative youth of its military leaders is a known feature of the SAF.[4] Tim Huxley observed the widely held belief that

> SAF regular officers in command and staff positions are generally decidedly young and inexperienced compared with their western counterparts ... Moreover, observers from the other armed forces sometimes question SAF officers' commitment to their military careers, particularly in the case of SAF scholars, who sometimes appear to be "marking time" before moving into more powerful or lucrative civilian posts.[5]

Some of the more extreme examples skew the overall picture. It is true that PM Lee Hsien Loong made COL in 1982 aged 30 and retired as a BG in 1984 with the record of being the youngest member of Singapore's military elite. It is also true that LG (RET) Lim Chuan Poh earned his third star in 2001 while serving as CDF aged 39. On the other hand, few hear of the officers who reached the pinnacle of the SAF Officer Corps in their mid- to late-40s after 25 or more years of service.

The estimated statistical parameters certainly do not dispute the relative youth of Singapore's military elite (Table 7.4). The mean, or average, age of SAF officers wearing flag rank is 41.52 years ($\sigma = 3.39$). The advantage of the scholarship is clear, with deserving SAFOS officers receiving their promotion to BG/RADM1 at an average age almost five years younger than their non-SAFOS counterparts. The frequency distribution along the age spectrum further illustrates the bifurcation between SAFOS and non-SAFOS flag officers (Graph 7.1). These

---

[4] Derek Da Cunha, "Sociological Aspects of the Singapore Armed Forces", *Armed Forces & Society* 25, 3 (Spring 1999): 466; Huxley, *Defending the Lion City*, p. 252; Sean P. Walsh, "The Roar of the Lion City: Ethnicity, Gender, and Culture in the Singapore Armed Forces", *Armed Forces & Society* 33, 2 (Jan. 2007): 267.

[5] Huxley, *Defending the Lion City*, p. 252.

parameters provide clarity to the long-suspected albeit unsurprisingly compact career and steeper ascension trajectory of SAFOS officers.

Table 7.4. Estimated age (years) in year of first star (N=170)

	SAFOS	Non-SAFOS	Total
Number of officers	68	102	170
Mean (μ)	38.71	43.39	41.52
Standard deviation (σ)	2.30	2.63	3.39
Median	38.50	44	41
Mode	38	44	44
Youngest	32	35	32
Oldest	47	49	49

Graph 7.1. Frequency distribution of estimated age (years) in year of first star (N=170)

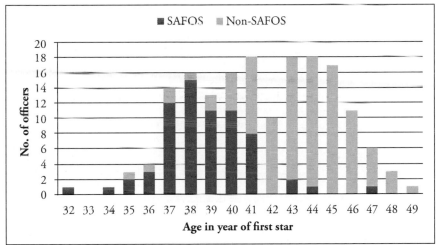

The second picture of interest is the years of active flag officership. Evidence suggests that the 135 who by mid-2018 had retired from service rendered slightly more than four years of active duty as flag officers on average (Table 7.5). Several outliers were clearly visible in the frequency histogram, with LG (RET) Winston Choo the most notable, having spent 16 of his 18 years as defence chief in the general ranks (Graph 7.2). At the other end of the spectrum are some who resigned shortly after earning a star to answer their calling to politics, a fact addressed later in the chapter. SAFOS officers usually spend a year longer (μ = 4.98, σ = 2.40) in flag rank than their non-SAFOS peers (μ = 3.81, σ = 2.37). There are two reasons for this. First, a number of non-SAFOS officers earned their first star in penultimate or terminal career appointments. These include army division command, RSAF Operational Commands, respective service heads of logistics, CMC, DA Washington, and DCGS in the early SAF. Second, the careers of a segment of SAFOS officers are extended with the group's domination of post-one-star billets such as COS-JS (formerly DJOPD), DMI (formerly DJID), DJO (formerly HJO), FSTA (formerly FSA), DIR SID, and the more senior positions of COA and CNV.

Table 7.5. Years of active flag officership (N=135)

	SAFOS	Non-SAFOS	Total
Number of officers	54	81	135
Mean (μ)	4.98	3.81	4.28
Standard deviation (σ)	2.40	2.36	2.44
Median	5	3	4
Mode	6	2	2
Shortest	0	1	0
Longest	11	16	16

Graph 7.2. Frequency distribution of years of active flag officership (N=135)

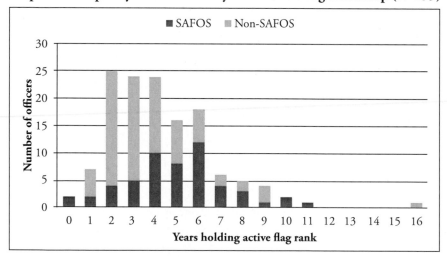

Statistics reiterate that it is usual for SAFOS officers (μ = 4.41, σ = 2.09) to spend more time in flag rank than non-SAFOS (μ = 3.40, σ = 1.76) officers even after accounting for members of the elite nucleus (Table 7.6). On the other hand, SAFOS (μ = 6.24, σ = 2.61) and non-SAFOS (μ = 6.00, σ = 3.70) defence and service chiefs seem to have more equal tenures. There is, however, greater variation within the non-SAFOS officers in the elite nucleus given unique entries from the early SAF and transitional junctures. These include long (Winston Choo, 16 years) and short tenures (Kirpa Ram Vij and Thomas Campbell, two years each), the British rank and appointment system (Campbell made brigadier as a brigade commander), and those service chief billets that were upgraded from COL to one-star (namely, CNV James Leo and CAF Michael Teo).

Table 7.6. Years of active flag officership accounting for defence and service chiefs (N=135)

	Non-Elite Nucleus			Elite Nucleus (DGS, CGS, CDF & Service Chiefs)		
	SAFOS	Non-SAFOS	Total	SAFOS	Non-SAFOS	Total
Number of officers	37	68	105	17	13	30
Mean (μ)	4.41	3.40	3.75	6.24	6.00	6.13
Standard deviation (σ)	2.09	1.76	1.94	2.61	3.70	3.07
Median	4	3	3	6	5	6
Mode	6	2	2	6	5	6
Shortest	0	1	0	1	2	1
Longest	9	9	9	11	16	16

The third picture of interest is the estimated age of retirement from active service (Table 7.7). It probably comes as no surprise that SAFOS officers (μ = 43.20, σ = 3.39) leave at a younger age vis-à-vis their peers (μ = 47.33, σ = 2.59). The official retirement age of officers has oscillated between 42 (under the 23-year route of advancement for COLs and above) and 50 (current employment scheme), which has truncated and stretched careers where necessary. The distribution of retirement age for non-SAFOS is closely grouped in the range of mid-40s to early 50s. This would be even more apparent if some of the early military leaders were excluded from the population (Graph 7.3).

Table 7.7. Estimated age (years) in year of retirement from active service (N=135)

	SAFOS	Non-SAFOS	Total
Number of officers	54	81	135
Mean (μ)	43.20	47.33	45.68
Standard deviation (σ)	3.39	2.59	3.56
Median	44	47	46
Mode	44	46	44
Youngest	32	38	32
Oldest	50	52	52

Graph 7.3. Frequency distribution of estimated age (years) in year of leaving active service (N=135)

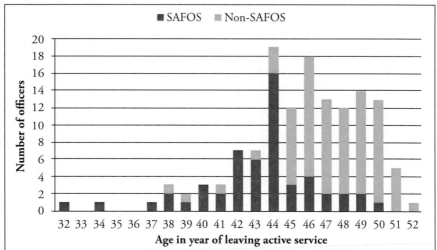

There are various reasons for the great variability within the SAFOS segment. There is poaching from the political arena, but the more pressing need is to deploy selected scholars elsewhere in government vis-à-vis the need of the political echelon to poach scholars for politics. This is especially pressing for the most suitable AOs who have another 15 to 20 years to serve at the highest echelons as PS at a ministry and Chief Executive Officer (CEO) of a government-affiliated institution and GLC. Yet, this managed early career transition is not applied equally across the board. There are those who leave shortly after earning their star, most notably army DIV COMDs. Some recognize that any further delay will diminish their prospects in the private sector. Others are simply satisfied at having reached the pinnacle of their profession. There are also the ambitious ones who drop out once their hopes of making service chief or higher are dashed, usually with the announcement of an anointed successor. Sometimes it is a combination of the preceding reasons.

There are, of course, those who leave once they meet the retirement age or once there are no further appointments to hold. Then there are those at the other end of the spectrum who render longer than usual service. For example, BG (RET) Wong Huat Sern enlisted for NS in December 1981, joined the RSAF on 10 May 1982, received the SAFOS in 1983, and retired from active service on 1 March 2013.[6] The helicopter pilot made BG at 41 and served for another nine years, the longest period of active service for a one-star officer. RADM1 (RET) Tan Wee Beng (SAFOS 1986), former CO NDU and inaugural COMD MSTF, earned his rank aged 44 and concluded active duty as COS-NS five years later. Most recently L/BG Tan Boon Kim (SAFOS 1988) received his star at age 47 upon assuming his duties as the SAF's 11th DA Washington.

It has been observed that the top brass have their post-career transitions "managed in a more structured and systematic" manner.[7] Empirical data support this claim, and three telling aspects become apparent from a cursory examination of the civilian positions held by retired military elites (Appendix A). First, the majority transit to the kaleidoscope of government ministries, associated statutory boards or GLCs. For AOs this is simply a matter of continuing their public service under the AS scheme. Non-AOs accepted into government service are transitioned into roles commensurate with their military seniority. The norm is for former CDFs and service chiefs to be parachuted in at the PS, President or CEO level. Second, while most of the top brass transition into government or related entities, this is by no means a realization of the theoretical military-administrative state. The presence of ex-military officers in positions of public administration is indubitable. What remains unknown is how much power and influence they wield over policy and the strength of their affiliation or loyalty, if any, to the armed forces.

Finally, after officers leave service the privilege of military rank becomes immaterial and their success boils down to their expectations, character, acumen, performance and networks as well as circumstances. There are those who have made seamless transitions to the public and/or private sectors, with their contributions recorded in the open domain. Some seem to have vanished

---

[6] "Change-of-Command for Sembawang Air Base", *Air Force News* 100 (Jan. 2007): 28; "Tribute to BG Wong Huat Sern", *Air Force News* 124 (2013): 38.

[7] Goh Chin Lian, "Army Man Taking Over as Defence Force Chief", *Straits Times*, 7 Feb. 2003, p. 4.

completely from the public eye. A few have struggled in obscurity to adapt beyond the military environment in terms of personality, leadership styles, industry-specific experiences and performances. Their records are also open news. Such setbacks are often exceptions rather than the norm, and any breaches of discipline through personal indiscretions an even greater rarity.

The matter of discipline is consistently emphasized in relation to the SAF, and SAFOS recipients are not immune to the consequences of unbecoming conduct. The number of recipients from 1971 to 2018 is listed at 332, but news releases often place official figures at one fewer due to the case of Jacques Wei-Ren Erasmus. The Raffles alumnus received the SAFOS-PS in 1999 but ran into problems at the University of California, Berkeley, where he elected to study nuclear engineering. The undergraduate reportedly "joined a fraternity house and smoked, drank and gambled liberally … (and eventually) stopped going to classes altogether".[8] MINDEF's generous gesture in reaching out to a wayward scholar proved limited, as Erasmus did not manage to raise his grades. He was eventually stripped of both scholarships but was saved from having to repay $355,000 in costs and instead received an LSA to study physics at the National University of Singapore.

This is a *sui generis* case of an individual who in 1999 was identified as having as much potential for senior military leadership as his SAFOS batchmates. Comparisons of the individuals' subsequent career trajectories provide insights into the advantages of the scholarship among officers once deemed equal. It must be acknowledged that Erasmus has stayed true to his interest in a military career and has remained on active duty notwithstanding the embarrassment of losing the SAFOS-PS. The infantry officer was the Distinguished Graduate at the 28th Tri-Service Warfighter Course (2013) and graduated from the 46th Command and Staff Course (2015) in Singapore. These are certainly commendable accolades of an above-average Regular, but they pale in comparison to the achievements of the other 1999 SAFOS recipients. All eight were LTC or above, and almost all had completed their CO tours when Erasmus made MAJ in 2014 (Table 7.8).

From another vantage point it is also clear that all the army officers from the 2005 SAFOS cohort—Chong Shi Hao (armour), Robert Khoon Liat Colflesh (commando), Edwin Lee Wen Jun (artillery) and Mikail Kalimuddin (artillery)—received their promotions to MAJ that same year. This provides a rough estimate of losing the SAFOS measured by "time to MAJ" of approximately six years. Losing the scholarship resulted in a reassessment of Erasmus' inclusion

---

[8] Ng Shing Yi, "The School of Second Chances: A President's Scholar Who Lost His Award Speaks Out", *TODAY*, 6 Sept. 2004, p. 2.

in the Wrangler program, which determines his career ceiling and, more immediately, whether the opportunity of active battalion command is even on the cards.

Table 7.8. Career stage of 1999 SAFOS recipients at the end of 2014

Rank and Name	Vocation	CSC	CO Tour
SLTC Lau Boon Ping	Pilot (Heli)	USA (2011–12)	126 SQN (2012–14)
L/COL Lee Yi-Jin[9]	Artillery	USA (2009–10)	21 SA (2010–12)
LTC James Low Wei Min	Combat Engineer	Singapore (2011)	30 SCE (2012–13)
LTC Jason See Chong Wei	Armour	UK (2011)	41 SAR (2013–15)
SLTC Tan Yueh Phern	Intelligence	Australia (2009)	11 C4I Bn (2012–13)
LTC Andrew Wan Wei Chung	Signals	Australia (2010)	10 C4I Bn (2011–12)
LTC Amos Yeo Tze Kuan	AWO (C3)	Australia (2011)	203 SQN (2012–14)
SLTC Yong Wei Hsiung	Naval Officer	USA (2010–11)	*Unknown*

7.3   Outliers in the Aristocracy of Armed Talent

The finer points of performance and potential that determine postings and promotions, as well as the organizational structure that facilitates ascension towards flag rank were covered in previous chapters. Norms have surfaced and expectations formed over time, but outliers exist—cases of unparalleled career advancements likely never to be repeated in the annals of SAF history. The bestowment and rescission of "local" ranks are likely to continue, although their scale and visibility will depend on specific operations. Some officers will have the opportunity to earn their rank permanently, while others will face reversion and perhaps fade quietly into retirement. There have also been instances of officers bypassed for promotion despite holding established one-star appointments, for

---

[9] Lee Yi-Jin was promoted to SLTC (2014) but wore the L/COL rank while serving as the Army Attaché at the Singapore Embassy in Jakarta (2013–16). He was promoted to COL in 2016 while COMD 3 SIB (2016–17).

reasons that remain elusive. On the flip side there have been those who received early promotions in COL billets, while one general even seemed to move laterally. These are not the only outliers, but they are the most prominent to date.

7.3.1 Unique Career Advancements

The careers of Thomas Campbell, Patrick Sim, Winston Choo, Kirpa Ram Vij and Tan Chin Tiong are special among the SAF's generals and have been addressed in some detail. A small number of flag officers were also unique, having ascended the rank hierarchy purely through staff work with scant records of command if at all. At the other end are those who held the distinction of multiple command tours within the respective services at the division, air base and fleet levels. Yet it is the military career of PM Lee Hsien Loong that has drawn the most interest from domestic and foreign observers alike, for different reasons. For some it was because of what he accomplished from the time he enlisted in 1970 until he left active service in 1984, a career unlikely to be repeated in the annals of Singapore's military history. Then there are those such as Michael Barr, who forged a career as an ardent critic of Singapore politics. The Australian academic hinted at something other than merit for Lee's ascension through the army: "I have no precise knowledge of the operation of favouritism during his military career, so we can only speculate about the importance of his family name in his rapid and comfortable rise through the ranks, risking not much more injury than a paper cut."[10]

It is worthwhile to recap Lee Hsien Loong's military service record for readers to reach a more informed conclusion and form an independent view of the individual as an SAF officer. Lee's selection for the President's Scholarship in 1970 and SAFOS a year later are clear indicators of his cognitive abilities. Anything less would throw a scholarship system in its infancy into disrepute. His brilliance in mathematics as an undergraduate at Cambridge University is unquestionable, as he completed the syllabus with first class honours in two instead of the usual three years. He then stayed on for a Diploma in Computer Science to meet stringent residency requirements at the university.[11] His early military experiences, like those of other SAFOS recipients, were enhanced during term breaks through an attachment with the British Army's 1st Royal Tank Regiment as an observer for a live-firing exercise in Canada. He also

---

[10] Michael D. Barr, "Beyond Technocracy: The Culture of Elite Governance in Lee Hsien Loong's Singapore", *Asian Studies Review* 30, 1 (Mar. 2006): 12–3.

[11] "It's Back to the Military for SAF Scholars", *Pioneer* (Sept. 1973): 3; "Why Top Student Chun Wei Opted for a Career in SAF", *Straits Times*, 16 Mar. 1976, p. 24.

experienced regimental life with the Queen's Dragoon Guard during a summer camp in Yorkshire, northern England, which he described as "more of a holiday than anything else".[12] After graduating from Cambridge in 1974, Lee politely declined the offer of graduate studies in mathematics to fulfil his bond with the SAF. He completed junior artillery officer training with the US Army at Fort Sill before ascending the hierarchy within a decade. His junior tours included battery command in the 20th Battalion, Singapore Artillery (20 SA), with MAJ Ng Jui Ping as CO, and as S4 of 3 SIB commanded by LTC Syed Hashim Bin Aljoffery. From 1978 to 1980 Lee was in the United States, where he attended the US Army CGSC and subsequently earned a Master of Public Administration at Harvard University.

Upon his return to Singapore in the second half of 1980, MAJ Lee commanded 23 SA within the artillery formation helmed by COL Chan Jwee Kay and later in the year attended the First SAF Senior Commanders' Course. A commemorative book celebrating the centenary of Singapore Artillery in 1988 captured Lee's tangible contributions during his tenure with the gunners: "During his service with the artillery, Brig-Gen Lee was instrumental in modernising the Artillery and was personally involved in the development of several significant projects such as the HP-41CV hand held calculators, the TPQ-36 Artillery locating radars and the Position Azimuth Determining System."[13]

After relinquishing battalion command, the newly promoted LTC Lee was appointed ACGS (Ops) on 1 July 1981 and in that capacity held responsibility for directing SAF-level operations.[14] The retirement of DCGS BG Tan Chin Tiong from the SAF the following year witnessed the apportionment of duties between COL Mancharan Singh Gill, 48, and the newly promoted COL Lee Hsien Loong, 30. Both men reported to then-CGS MG Winston Choo.[15] Lee retained the ACGS (Ops) portfolio and on 1 July 1982 concurrently held the newly created post of COS-GS to coordinate the staff work of the six General Staff departments.[16] Gill took on the DCGS title as the SAF's number two and worked "mainly with the troops on the ground".[17]

On 29 January 1983, elements of the SAF—including foreign military personnel—were mobilized when the oil-drilling ship *Eniwetok* severed cables

---

[12] "It's Back to the Military for SAF Scholars", p. 3.

[13] *Singapore Artillery 100th Anniversary: 1888–1988* (Singapore: HQ Singapore Artillery and Public Affairs Department, Ministry of Defence, 1988), p. 128.

[14] "Pips & Crests", *Pioneer* (Aug. 1981): 8.

[15] "Promotion: Ranks and Responsibilities", *Pioneer* (Aug. 1982): 6.

[16] "Changes in the General Staff", *Straits Times*, 17 Sept. 1982, p. 1.

[17] Fong and Wai, "Top Officers Given Exposure", p. 1.

linking Sentosa and Singapore. Two cable cars plunged into the sea below, killing seven. Thirteen passengers were left stranded in four cabins dangling precariously 60 metres above water until they were rescued by units under Lee's direction.[18] He relinquished the appointment of ACGS (Ops) shortly after and became the inaugural DJOPD as the SAF took nascent steps towards achieving operational synergy between the three services. In August 1983, Lee's services were recognized when he became the fourth recipient of the Public Administration Medal (Military) (Gold). The accompanying citation of the then-highest military decoration bestowed on SAF officers read:

> "His rise to the rank of Colonel on 1 July 1982 was due to a consistently high level of performance. When he was logistics officer of an infantry brigade, he improved the logistics management of that formation. When he was commander of a field artillery battalion, he introduced new doctrines and tactical concepts for that arm of the service. More recently, he led and directed the joint operations planning team to formulate long-term strategic plans and develop land force doctrine, particularly combined arms doctrines."[19]

On 1 July 1984 Lee was promoted to BG aged 32; he holds the record for youngest general in SAF history. He resigned from the SAF shortly after and was given a farewell parade at Khatib Camp on 19 September, two days before officially leaving active duty.[20] He relinquished the appointment of COS-GS to ACGS (Ops) COL Ng Jui Ping, while Director of Special Projects Organization COL Lui Pao Chuen became acting DJOPD.[21] Lee was officially announced as the Political Secretary to then-Defence Minister Goh Chok Tong on 21 September.[22] He was unveiled the day after as a PAP candidate at the 1984 General Election.[23]

---

[18] "Salute to the Heroes", *Straits Times*, 10 Feb. 1983, p. 11; "A Job Well Done", *Pioneer* (Mar. 1983): 2–7.

[19] "Gold Medals to Four Leading Civil Servants", *Straits Times*, 19 Nov. 1983, p. 7.

[20] Benny Ortega, "Brig-Gen Lee Will Leave SAF on Friday", *Singapore Monitor*, 19 Sept. 1984, p. 1; Robert Conceicao, "Farewell to Arms", *Singapore Monitor*, 20 Sept. 1984, p. 4; "Navy Says Farewell", *Navy News* (Oct. 1984), p. 3.

[21] "Farewell to the SAF", *Straits Times*, 20 Sept. 1984, p. 1.

[22] "Statement from the Prime Minister's Office", *Singapore Government Press Release*, Release No. 42/Sept (02-4/84/09/21), 21 Sept. 1984.

[23] "233 SAF Officers to Be Promoted", *Straits Times*, 29 June 1984, p. 1; "Brig-Gen Lee Appointed Political Secretary", *Straits Times*, 22 Sept. 1984, p. 1; "What Makes the General Run", *Straits Times*, 23 Sept. 1984, p. 15; Lee Kim Chew, "It's Door-to-Door on the Campaign Trail in Teck Ghee", *Straits Times*, 24 Sept. 1984, p. 13; "The General Marches in by a Large Majority", *Straits Times*, 23 Dec. 1984, p. 5.

Lee's 83-day generalship raised eyebrows among those who bothered with such matters. Even fewer were willing to publicly question this short generalship beyond passing banter, and in more recent times through occasional anonymous comments online. Only Joshua Benjamin Jeyaretnam sought a parliamentary inquiry after Lee hung up his uniform soon after becoming the sixth general in SAF history. The sole opposition MP questioned the numbers of SAF officers bypassed for promotion and whether the SAF knew in advance of Lee's intention to enter politics. The most visible officer bypassed for promotion, if this was ever the case, was Mancharan Singh Gill, whose predecessors as DCGS—Patrick Sim (1979–80) and Tan Chin Tiong (1980–82)—both made BG during their respective tenures. Gill retired in August 1986 as a COL and during his four-year tour as DCGS was surpassed in rank by three officers holding ostensibly more junior staff appointments: Lee Hsien Loong (DJOPD/COS-GS) in 1984, and Ng Jui Ping (COS-GS/ACGS [Ops]) and Chin Siat Yoon (DJID) in 1986.[24]

Jeyaretnam suggested Lee's promotion was politically motivated despite MINDEF's professed merit-based reasons. He rescinded the claim when First DPM Dr Goh made clear that he (Jeyaretnam) "would be sued for libel if he repeated his suggestion without the protection of parliamentary privilege".[25] Perhaps the missing piece in the debate over Lee's conspicuous rise to the top of the SAF can be identified only with the benefit of hindsight. At Singapore's Golden Jubilee one could appreciate that he was an officer well ahead of his time, one with the "second generation" technological, organizational and doctrinal foresight to aid in the SAF's transition from the "first generation" era. This would not have been immediately clear in the mid-1980s and certainly not to traditionalists within the SAF Officer Corps preoccupied with the fact that Lee skipped the crucial tests of brigade and division command. Even then, the reason(s) for Mancharan Singh Gill to mark time in the rank of COL remains elusive and is unlikely to be identified. For those beyond the military realm, the fuss was not over ranks but more a question of whether a career military officer should enter politics. Critics were swiftly silenced by the Teck Ghee constituency (formed from parts of the Chong Boon and Ang Mo Kio electorates), which approved of Lee's candidacy with 80.4 per cent of its votes on Election Day 1984.[26]

---

[24] "Changes at the Top after Brig-Gen Lee's Resignation", *Straits Times*, 28 Oct. 1984, p. 17; "SAF Promotes 273 of Its Best Senior Officers", *Straits Times*, 1 July 1986, p. 10.

[25] "How the SAF Decides on Promotions", *Straits Times*, 20 Oct. 1984, p. 15.

[26] "Tinker, Tailor, Soldier—and Newsmaker", *Straits Times*, 24 Sept. 1984, p. 1.

What Lee Hsien Loong's career did for the SAF and Singapore was to normalize rapid promotions for the crème of each SAFOS cohort and pave the way for selected and willing officers to enter the political arena. Singapore and the SAF did not have long to wait, as former Foreign Minister George Yeo became the second career officer to enter politics. The 1973 SAFOS-PS recipient studied engineering at Cambridge University and spent three years in the army (1976–79) as a signals officer. This was followed swiftly with a secondment to the RSAF as Head Weapons Systems Branch (1979–81) in the Air Plans Department and subsequently as Head Air Plans (1981–83). The next port of call for the 29-year-old LTC was Harvard Business School, where he completed a Master of Business Administration. Yeo was instrumental in the formation of the Air Staff, and it was fitting that he became the inaugural COS-AS (1985–87) upon his return to Singapore. He had become the second most senior officer in the RSAF at age 31. Early the following year he added the responsibility of DJOPD (1986–88) to his portfolio and made COL. Yeo received his promotion to BG on 1 July 1988 and within 43 days—on 12 August 1988—had his farewell parade. He entered politics a month later as "both Mr Goh Chok Tong and BG Lee were very persuasive".[27] Even then, Yeo reportedly had "to forgo his pension of $80,000 and pay $60,000 in liquidated damages for breaking his bond to the SAF".[28]

Lee Hsien Loong and George Yeo hold the distinctions of being the SAF's youngest generals at the ages of 32 and 34 respectively. Both saw fleeting generalships as they sought and made successful transitions to elected office. Other career officers would follow in time and become Cabinet ministers, but at a different pace (Appendix I). Lim Hng Khiang (SAFOS 1973), Lim Swee Say (SAFOS 1973) and Lui Tuck Yew (SAFOS 1980) entered the political arena only after leaving active duty and spending a few years in the civil service and affiliated institutions. They are exceptions to the norm as the recruitment of high-level political candidates from the SAF has usually taken place directly from the ranks of active-duty uniformed officers. Teo Chee Hean turned over command of the navy in December 1992 after 18 months at the helm to contest a by-election with

---

[27] Paul Jacob, "New Body to Look After SAF's Materials Needs", *Straits Times*, 15 Feb. 1986, p. 13; "Winston Choo Is Singapore's First Three-Star General", *Straits Times*, 1 July 1988, p. 1; Mathew Yap, "BG Yeo Silent on His Plans in Politics", *Straits Times*, 13 Aug. 1988, p. 20; "SAF Bids Farewell to BG Yeo", *Pioneer* (Sept. 1988): 17; "4 New MPs Made Ministers of State", *Straits Times*, 11 Sept. 1988, p. 2. Yeo indicated that the alternative to politics would be to serve "the remaining year of his SAF bond and then move into the civil service or do trade and finance in the private sector". Bertha Henson, "From Sky-Blue to White-and-White: The General Goes Campaigning", *Straits Times*, 31 Aug. 1988, p. 17.

[28] "PAP MPs Make Big Sacrifices when They Enter Politics: PM", *Straits Times*, 15 Aug. 1988, p. 12.

then-PM Goh Chok Tong. His departure paved the way and perhaps proved fortuitous for the very experienced Kwek Siew Jin to lead the RSN (1992–96). Kwek made RADM1 in 1993 and in 1995 became the first two-star CNV.

In 2011 two high-flying generals were poached from the army. MG Chan Chun Sing relinquished command of the army 12 months into a usual three-year term. The impact of his decision was amplified by the concurrent departure of BG Tan Chuan-Jin, who could very well have succeeded Chan as COA. This forced MINDEF to make its first ever reserve-to-active recall of BG (NS) Ravinder Singh in March 2011 to fill the leadership void. BG Mark Tan Ming Yiak took on the full-time appointments of Future Systems Architect (2011–13) and COMDT SAFTI MI (2011–12) on a concurrent basis. The rotation of general officers to accommodate the departure of then-CDF LG Ng Chee Meng for politics in 2015 was slightly less disruptive, but the cascading effects were still evident. Ng handed the reins of the SAF some seven months prematurely to MG Perry Lim in August. Lim in turn handed over command of the army to BG Melvyn Ong Su Kiat (SAFOS 1994) after 17 months in the role. Ong similarly relinquished command of 21 DIV after only 14 months. Defence planners are certainly cognizant of the possibility for the PAP to recruit from the military elite at every GE as long as there are worthy and willing candidates.

7.3.2 Local Stars, No Stars, Special Stars

The question of who is deemed worthy of making general or admiral, and whether they remain so is contentious at times. Wearing one or more stars is no guarantee that the epaulettes will remain. This is most significant on overseas postings at UN field missions, the Singapore Embassy in Washington, and CTF-151, where local ranks are sometimes used at the general and admiral levels. The rank held by an SAF officer designated to hold one of those appointments is supposedly inadequate. A higher rank is therefore required for an SAF officer to be accorded the necessary respect. Wearing a local rank does not guarantee any opportunities to earn a permanent promotion. There is also the possible need for officers with a local rank to explain the practice to foreign counterparts. Perhaps the only certainty is that wearers should beware.

Troop contributions to UN Peacekeeping Operations (UNPKO) have raised Singapore's profile within the "Parliament of Men". Yet, it is ironic that the two who have held the most senior UNPKO field appointments among SAF officers had to accept a reversion of rank when they returned from their year-long tours. The first was COL (RET) Yeo Cheng Ann, an infantry officer who commanded 2 SIR and 2 SIB in a career interspersed with various staff tours in intelligence and operations. In October 1993 he was appointed COS and Deputy

Force Commander of the UN Iraq-Kuwait Observation Mission (UNIKOM) reporting to BG Vigar Aabrek of Norway (Acting Chief Military Observer) and later MG Krishna Narayan Singh Thapa of Nepal (Chief Military Observer and subsequently Force Commander).[29] Yeo was introduced to the UN General Assembly as a BG and wore the rank for the duration of his tour as part of Operation Blue Torch. He reverted to COL upon his return to Singapore in November 1994 and served as SAF's sixth Chief Infantry Officer (CIO) and then COS 3 DIV until his retirement.

History would repeat itself almost a decade later with BG (RET) Eric Tan Huck Gim. The artillery officer with a background in both intelligence and operations was CO 20 SA, COMD 3 DIV ARTY, and Chief Artillery Officer. He received a second star as L/MG in 2002 while COMD 9 DIV (2000–02) and in August that year assumed the appointment of Force Commander, UN Mission of Support in East Timor (UNMISET), from LG Winai Phattiyakul of Thailand. Tan was introduced to the UN General Assembly as an MG and wore the rank for the duration of his tour as part of Operation Blue Heron.[30] He was in the spotlight more than COL (RET) Yeo thanks to the publicity surrounding his appointment. Social media further magnified the UNMISET campaign since it coincided with Singapore's inaugural deployment of a rifle platoon and subsequently a reinforced rifle company of peacekeepers. MG Tan relinquished command of UNMISET's military component to LG Khairuddin Bin Mat Yusof of Malaysia in August 2003. Two months later he assumed duties as the fourth COMDT SAFTI MI, a post he held until September 2005, and he retired as a BG after 31 years of distinguished active service.

The utilization of local ranks for temporary use on specific international billets may be an accepted practice within the SAF, but among international partners it is viewed as a demotion despite the sterling services rendered. The argument for such practices is to ensure the SAF officers are accorded respect in a rank commensurate with the accompanying appointment. Yet the resulting burden of explanation, reputation or embarrassment, if any, is placed squarely on the shoulders of the respective officers. The practice of using local flag ranks has continued for officers serving as DA Washington and COMD CTF-151 (Table 7.9). What has changed is that the majority of officers experience only short-term reversion to COL upon their return to Singapore, and prior to postings where they retire in the local rank or receive permanent promotions to BG/RADM1.

---

[29] Report of the Secretary-General on the United Nations Iraq-Kuwait Observation Mission (for the period 1 Oct. 1993–31 Mar. 1994), No. S/1994/388, 4 Apr. 1994.

[30] *Year Book of the United Nations 2003* (New York: United Nations Publications, 2005), pp. 370, 1561.

The SAF does not flinch at the prolonged use of local ranks in the international arena even if the practice might seem alien to some foreign observers. Opinion will remain divided over whether the officer in question should be allowed to keep the local rank and retire, be given the opportunity for a permanent promotion, or perhaps decline the rank altogether.[31]

Table 7.9. Use of local flag ranks and subsequent promotions to BG/RADM1

Year	Rank and Name	Appointment	Promotion to BG/RADM1
1978	L/BG Patrick Sim Hak Kng	COMD 3 DIV	1979
2008	L/BG Cheng Siak Kian	DA Washington	2010
2010	L/RADM1 Bernard Donald Miranda	COMD CTF-151	Retired as L/RADM1
2011	L/RADM1 Harris Chan Weng Yip	COMD CTF-151	2012
2012	L/BG Tan Chee Wee	DA Washington	2014
2013	L/RADM1 Giam Hock Koon	COMD CTF-151	2014
2013	L/BG Ken Leong Kum Wah	DA Washington	Retired as L/BG
2016	L/RADM1 Ken Cheong Kwok Chien	COMD CTF-151	2017
2016	L/BG Tan Boon Kim	DA Washington	Incumbent
2018	L/RADM1 Saw Shi Tat	COMD CTF-151	*Unknown*

What seems certain to raise eyebrows within the military establishment is when COLs are bypassed for promotion in billets where officers have long made one-star. Such occurrences have sent ripples through the ranks of Regulars, with questions over performance and ability at best, or malfeasance and opprobrium at worst. The SAF expects its officers to conduct themselves with propriety, and there is zero tolerance for wayward behaviour regardless of scholarship status and rank. Disciplinary action is never hushed up, in order to avoid cliques from protecting their own and corrupting the military justice system. The cases involving former CARMO Low Wye Mun, SAFOS recipient Frederick Teo and SMS recipient Phua Poh Sim are clear warnings to the SAF Officer

---

[31] It is said that LTC (RET) Gwee Peng Hong commanded 1 SIR from 17 October 1977 to 6 November 1978 in the rank of CPT after he declined a "promotion" to L/MAJ.

Corps.[32] What is one to make of senior officers, especially field commanders, who are bypassed for promotion? The absence of any public explanation means that verdicts remain outstanding. The only possible certainty is that being good enough for an appointment does not necessarily mean one is good enough for the accompanying rank.

Consider the cases of COL (RET) Michael Low (SAFOS 1976) and COL (NS) Wong Yu Han (SAFOS 1991). Both scholars are the only officers to have completed a division command tour and not been promoted since the respective DIV COMDs made BG. Low's command record included the 3rd Signals Battalion (3 SIG), 7 SIB, and as the third COMD 21 DIV from 26 October 1995 to 11 September 1997. He then became ACGS (Logistics) before retiring in 1999. His predecessors as COMD 21 DIV—Colin Theseira (1991–93) and Low Yee Kah (1993–95)—made BG, as have successive commanders with the exception of COL (RET) Nelson Yau Thian Hock, who resigned from active duty mid-tour in 2012 citing personal reasons. Details remain unknown, but Yau's name was replaced swiftly on the Singapore Army webpage while other key appointments remained glaringly outdated.[33] Nevertheless, Yau would always be held in high regard for his commitment to the Guards formation, where he held the highly coveted commands of 1 Guards and 7 SIB.

The case of COL (NS) Wong Yu Han is recent and even more conspicuous under the glare of social media. He was CO 2 SIR, COMD 2 SIB, and ACGS (Training)—where he was bestowed the Public Administration Medal (Silver) (Military) in 2012—before taking the helm as the 15th COMD 6 DIV from 16 August 2013 to 12 June 2015. Wong bears the unenviable distinction of being

---

[32] COL (Dr) Low was tried in a subordinate military court for making sexual advances to a married female civilian subordinate between April and July 1998 and again on 4 January 1999. He pleaded guilty to two charges of disgraceful conduct and was demoted in rank to MAJ and reportedly lost $324,000 in retirement benefits. LTC Teo was court-martialled and fined $6,000 for "inappropriate behaviour" towards a female civilian subordinate. He read Politics, Philosophy and Economics at the University of Oxford (1996–99) before postgraduate studies in International Relations at the London School of Economics (2000). CPT Phua was sentenced to 16 weeks jail in 2011 for divulging confidential information in 2008 to Richard Yow Wah, a defence contractor, in return for $53,100 in loans to pay off gambling debts. He graduated with a mechanical engineering degree from Imperial College (2001) and subsequently earned postgraduate degrees in operational research from the University of Cambridge (2002) and computer science from the US Naval Postgraduate School (2007).

[33] "About Us > Organization Structure", MINDEF, www.mindef.gov.sg/imindef_websites/ atozlistings/army/About_US/Org_Structure.html (page updated). The webpage also listed Chief Armour Officer as BG Benedict Lim (instead of COL Siew Kum Wong), ACGS (Intelligence) as COL Lawrence Teh Yew Kiat (COL Steven Seng Wei San), ACGS (Plans) as COL Milton Ong Ann Kiat (COL Ong Tze-Ch'in), and ACGS (Training) as COL Ng Wai Kit (COL Wong Yu Han).

the first officer on the Cobra Division's Roll of Honour to relinquish command and retire as a COL since Stephen Wong Kong Yip became the inaugural COMD 6 DIV to make BG in 1995. This fact must have been even more caustic as COL (NS) Wong turned over command amidst the media frenzy associated with the first female general officer in SAF history, some 20 days before the annual 1 July promotion ceremony. The contrasts in career fortunes could not be clearer than in his role as adviser to the 2015 NDP Executive Committee chaired by COMD 21 DIV BG Melvyn Ong. Ong was announced shortly after as the next COA, having edged out other worthy contenders—namely, COS-JS BG Chia Choon Hoong (SAFOS 1991) and COMD 3 DIV BG Ong Tze-Ch'in—to the army's top post.

Over in the navy, the only conspicuous case of a senior officer not receiving a star was COL (RET) James Soon. His higher command and staff billets included CO NDU, COMD 3 FLOT and Head Naval Plans. He served as the 18th Fleet COMD from 14 February 2003 to 21 June 2004. The first Fleet COMD forwarded to RADM1 was Larry Loon Leong Yoon in 1995, and since then only Soon and Ronnie Tay (SAFOS 1982) did not make the rank in the same capacity. Tay, who took command of the fleet in 1999 at age 36, would go on to receive his first star as HNO in 2001 and a second as the RSN's sixth CNV (2003–07) in 2004. Soon, on the other hand, relinquished command of the RSN Fleet and was immediately tapped for a civilian role as Head of the Defence Technology Office at the Singapore Embassy in Washington.[34]

History indicates that COL (RET) Soon is the only non-scholar-officer to have helmed the RSN Fleet between 1995 and 2018, while the others were either SAFOS (ten) or SMS (two) recipients. He was also the only one who ascended the ranks through both the NDU and 3 FLOT. These factors are in all likelihood a matter of correlation and not causality, as Soon was deemed the best candidate to be Fleet COMD and not merely an acting commander for 16 months. Yet it could prove difficult to dissuade ambitious naval officers of the scholarship factor, or that service in 3 FLOT was in no way detrimental for attaining admiralship. Any factitious claims that there were "too many" admirals for Soon to be promoted are also unsubstantiated. In 2002, there were five active-duty admirals.[35] On 1 July 2003—Soon's only opportunity to make RADM1—there were only three active-duty admirals following the retirements of HNL RADM1 Jway Ching Hua in late 2002 and CNV RADM2 Lui Tuck

---

[34] "New Command Helming the Fleet", *Navy News* 3 (2004): 6.

[35] RADM2 Lui Tuck Yew (CNV), RADM1 Ong Hung Eng, Simon (COMDT SAFTI MI), RADM1 Jway Ching Hua (HNL), RADM1 Ronnie Tay (HNO/COS-NS) and RADM1 Sim Gim Guan (Fleet COMD).

Yew in early 2003.[36] An alternative, albeit equally weak, explanation is that Soon was caught in a career dead end as there was simply no billet commensurate with seniority available after fleet command. An extended tenure at the fleet was unlikely given then-COL Chew Men Leong needed to take the cookie-cutter path of Fleet COMD, NHO and COS-NS before arriving at CNV (2007–11). Are any of these reasons adequate for denying Soon an admiral's star? He was evidently good enough to be given the command but not the rank.

There is a third area that draws attention to the promotion system in addition to the rescission of local ranks and the non-promotion of colonels in well-established flag appointments. This occurs when colonels are promoted to one-star and in effect hold a rank higher than expected for the incumbent appointment(s) held, or for the appointment(s) scheduled in the near future. There are several examples of colonels receiving an "early" promotion en route to their flag billets (Table 7.10). This practice is historically rare, but rarer still is a one-star who seems to move from one COL billet to another.

The SAF marked a first in Singapore's military history by promoting COL Gan Siow Huang, a 1993 SMS recipient, to BG on 1 July 2015. The occasion was heralded as a conspicuous demonstration of the unbounded career possibilities for women in the military. It was also fitting that the main races, the main religions and both genders could claim at least one member in the Aristocracy of Armed Talent on Singapore's Golden Jubilee 40 days later. Yet the outstanding question that was never openly raised is which appointment warranted the promotion. This is assuming that the SAF does not use a promotion in rank as a reward, because that is what medals and salary increments are for. A rank reflects the importance of an appointment, the weight of responsibilities, and the abilities of the associated unit.

To date, no HJMP (Gan's final appointment in the rank of COL) or Head Air Intelligence (HAI) (Gan's first appointment as BG) has been a one-star officer. There are, however, three possible and not necessarily mutually exclusive explanations as to why the rank was bestowed. First, Gan's concurrent—albeit amorphous and seemingly newly created—appointment as DIR Special Projects (DIR [SP]) could command the seniority. The creation of the DS (Special Projects) billet in 2015, held concurrently by then-DS (Technology) BG (RET) David Koh, suggests the "Special Projects" community was most likely concerned with the development of the SAF's cyber defence and C4I capabilities. This likelihood is extrapolated from Koh's three-decade-long experience as an army signals officer and Gan's vocation as an AWO (C3). The second, less likely, explanation is that the HAI is now a *de facto* one-star billet and widens the ascension pathway for

---

[36] RADM1 Ronnie Tay (CNV), RADM1 Simon Ong (COMDT SAFTI MI) and RADM1 Sim Gim Guan (HNO).

RSAF officers towards flag rank. If so, this would mark a first for the intelligence department of any of the three services.

Table 7.10. Officers promoted to BG/RADM1/ME8 in a COL billet en route to a one-star appointment

Year	Name	COL Appointment	One-Star Appointment
1989	BG Gary Yeo	Deputy COMD RSAF (1986–89); COS-AS (1987–89)	On course (UK) (1989–90); DJID (1990–93)
1992	BG Bey Soo Khiang	COS-AS (1992)	CAF (1992–95)
1992	BG Chin Chow Yoon	Head SAFTI MI Development Project (1991–94)	COMDT SAFTI MI (1994–96)
2000	BG Lim Kah Kee	COMDT SCSC (1995–2000)	COMD 3 DIV (2000–03)
2001	BG Chua Chwee Koh	HJO (1998–2001)	COMD 21 DIV/CGO (2001–04)
2004	BG Goh Kee Nguan	On course (USA) (2003–04)	COMD 21 DIV/CGO (2004–07)
2004	BG Ravinder Singh	HJPT (2004–05)	COMD 6 DIV (2006–07)
2005	BG Tan Meng Dui	Head Air Training (2003–5)	COMD ADSD/ADOC (2005–07)
2007	BG Philip Lim	ACGS (Ops) (2004–07)	COMD 25 DIV/CAO (2007–09)
2007	BG Tan Chuan-Jin	On studies (Singapore) (2007–08)	COMD 3 DIV (2008–09)
2008	RADM1 Joseph Leong	HJPT (2007-9)	Fleet COMD (2009–11)
2013	ME8 Lau Cher Loon[37]	HJI (2011–14)	Deputy Chief C4I (Intelligence) (2014–15)
2018	BG David Neo Chin Wee	On secondment (Singapore) (2016–18)	COMD 3 DIV (2018–present)

---

[37] No appointment holder has made BG/RADM1/ME8 as HJI with the exception of Lau Cher Loon. The second Deputy Chief C4I (Intelligence) to wear one-star is BG Ng Chad-Son.

The third and final possibility is that a BG sitting in the appointment of HAI or DIR (SP) will prove to be a one-off occurrence. The possibility is rare but not without precedent. Lim Kim Lye is the only COMD 1 PDF to make BG (1998) and Jway Ching Hua the only HNL thus far forwarded to RADM1 (2000). The only glaring difference is that 1 PDF was a division-sized formation, while HNL is established as a one-star billet but one where incumbents are likely to remain as COL/ME7. Whether the three explanations possess any merit is unknown, and time will eventually provide some answers. What is certain is that the promotion was not a ruse to recruit more women into the armed services or simply to coincide with the Golden Jubilee celebrations. That would only insult Gan's capabilities as a professional military officer and, of even great concern, cheapen the elusive rank and weaken the notion of merit-based ascension. In any event, BG Gan subsequently received an established one-star posting as COMD APGC on 5 October 2016.

7.4 The Elite Nucleus

The elite nucleus consists of Singapore's most senior uniformed military officers in the three-star CDF and the three two-star service chiefs. These appointments are made by the President of Singapore on the advice of the Prime Minister and are responsible for the SAF's present operational readiness and future defence capabilities. Each of the four is tri-hatted as guardian of the SAF and its constituent services as an institution, a component commander of the field force, and a diplomat in uniform. The CDF has always been selected from the three service chiefs and is Singapore's most senior uniformed officer (Appendix J). In times of war he serves as the overall military commander accountable to the elected leadership and ultimately the President, who is the Commander-in-Chief. In times of peace the CDF oversees the whole SAF but does not exercise direct command over subordinate units. The day-to-day running of the military is left to the service chiefs, the COS-JS who oversees the departmental functions of the Joint Staff, the DMI/Chief C4I who runs the military intelligence apparatus, and other members of the Joint Staff Conference. The CDF has assets of the SAF HRC under direct command in emergencies and in the event of war.

Members of the elite nucleus are also gatekeepers and collectively determine who enters the highest echelons of the military establishment. No COL/ME7 makes BG/RADM1/ME8 without their recommendation and approval, which is countersigned by senior bureaucrats and political appointees. It was noted earlier that SAFOS officers were in the minority among one-stars but they formed the majority among two- and three-stars. This is the end result of selecting the best among the pool of one-stars, and it reflects a scheme that favours recipients who have realized their potential when it comes to choosing among equals. Yet it must be highlighted that at such senior levels what matters most are the appointments held, the performance displayed to instil all-around confidence within the defence force, and the contenders for and the availability of billets. This section is concerned with those who have served as the COA, CNV or CAF.

7.4.1 Chief of Army

The post of a one-star DCGS (Army) was created in 1988 to command the army and allow the CGS to focus solely on leading the tri-service SAF. The DGCS (Army) was renamed COA in May 1990 as the SAF reached a level of operational maturity and made MG for the first time in July 1991. The General Staff, which provided staff expertise at the SAF level, was relocated to address army-level staff requirements. In times of peace the COA works with Senior Specialist Staff Officers who serve as formation chiefs and provide advice on arms-specific matters. The various formations are responsible in varying degrees for the training of junior (section, platoon and company/battery) commanders, doctrine, unit evaluations, acquisition and integration, and generating active and maintaining reserve units to meet operational requirements. The COA also ensures the six- to seven-division army maintains an acceptable degree of operational readiness as the designated land component commander in the event of war.

Thirteen officers have had the honour to serve as COA (Appendix K). Their ascensions towards the office of COA began with successful command of a division (Table 7.11). It would seem that 3 DIV was initially the path of choice given that it was the first Combined Arms Division (CAD) formed on 21 March 1991 and manned with active units.[38] The most technologically advanced division in the SAF still counts the highest number of active brigades and battalions, even after the CADs (3, 6 and 9 DIVs) were reorganized on 1 January 1995 with a mix of active and reserve units. It would seem 9 DIV emerged as a comparable command to 3 DIV with three future COAs formerly at the helm, two of whom would go on to became CDF. The appointment of COAs from 6 and 21 DIVs were correlated with resignations of high-profile generals to contest General Elections in 2011 and 2015 respectively. There is nothing to suggest any shortcomings with these divisions in relation to others.

---

[38] "First Combined Arms Division", *Pioneer* (May 1991): 4–5.

Table 7.11. Appointments and duration between division command and appointment as COA

Rank and Name	Appointments from DIV COMD to COA	End of DIV Command to COA (days)	Other Possible Contenders for COA
BG Boey Tak Hap	3 DIV, ACGS (Ops), COS-GS	688	BG Ng Jui Ping
MG Ng Jui Ping	3 DIV, DJID	430	Nil
MG Lim Neo Chian	3 DIV, COS-GS	93	BG Lee Hsien Yang, BG Patrick Choy
MG Han Eng Juan	3 DIV, COS-GS	99	BG Patrick Choy, BG Sin Boon Wah
MG Lim Chuan Poh	9 DIV, COS-GS	20	BG Ng Yat Chung, BG Law Chwee Kiat
MG Ng Yat Chung	3 DIV, DJOPD, COS-JS	673	BG Ong Boon Hwee
MG Desmond Kuek	3 DIV, DJID, COS-GS	891	BG Tay Lim Heng, BG Leong Yue Kheong, BG Chua Chwee Koh
MG Neo Kian Hong	9 DIV, COMD TRADOC, DJOPD, COS-JS	1,007	BG Bernard Tan
MG Chan Chun Sing	9 DIV/CIO, COS-JS	428	BG Tan Yih San, BG Tan Chuan-Jin, BG Philip Lim Chern Tjunn
MG Ravinder Singh	6 DIV, COS-JS [DS (Tech) as a civilian]	1,429[39]	BG Tung Yui Fai, BG Mark Tan Ming Yiak
MG Perry Lim	3 DIV, COS-GS	197	BG Mark Tan Ming Yiak, BG Chia Choon Hoong
MG Melvyn Ong	21 DIV/CGO	1	BG Chia Choon Hoong, BG Ong Tze-Ch'in
BG Goh Si Hou	6 DIV	8	BG Ong Tze-Ch'in BG Mark Tan Ken-Li BG Ng Ying Thong

[39] The figure includes first retirement in early 2009, when he served as a civilian DS (Technology) until recalled to active service to command the army on 25 March 2011.

After DIV command there seem to be two divergent routes towards COA, and the actual path followed depends on the succession schedule. The first is almost exclusively through DJOPD/COS-JS (presently COS-JS) or the intelligence equivalent as DJID (presently DMI/Chief C4I). The former coordinates the manpower (J1), operations (J3), logistics (J4), plans and transformation (J5/J7), and communications and information systems (J6) functions of the JS. The latter focuses on the collection, analysis, fusion and dissemination of intelligence products for the SAF and, when required, partakes in information sharing with other security agencies. The second route is from DIV COMD to COA, with most using the COS-GS billet as a stepping stone. Their role as the army's number two officer either overlaps with division command or is held in a standalone and often-transient manner. Generals Lim Neo Chian, Han Eng Juan, Lim Chuan Poh and Perry Lim followed this sequence designed to ensure smooth leadership renewal. In fact, two of them went from command of brigade to division to army in rapid succession: MG (RET) Lim Neo Chian went from 3 SIB to 3 DIV, while LG (RET) Lim Chuan Poh did the same at 10 SIB and 9 DIV. The most recent COAs—Generals Melvyn Ong and Goh Si Hou—skipped intermediate appointments altogether, going from DIV COMD straight on to command of the army in 2015 and 2018 respectively.

7.4.2 Chief of Navy

The navy, unlike the army, has always had its own commander who reports directly to the defence chief. The men at the helm since 5 May 1967 have led a service that was at different times known as the Singapore Naval Volunteer Force, Sea Defence Command, Maritime Command, and finally the RSN. The navy chief held the designation of Commander until May 1990, when the present CNV title was established. He was first promoted to one-star Commodore in 1988, and in 1994 the nomenclature changed to Rear-Admiral (One-Star). In 1995 the CNV was forwarded to the current rank of RADM2. In times of peace the CNV oversees the administration, training, routine operations, and future plans of the RSN. In times of war the CNV is the designated naval component commander. Subordinate units are configured to operate at the Task Group or larger Task Force levels, and expectedly with additional units mainly in the form of air and intelligence assets. The CNV is assisted by the COS-NS, who coordinates the work of the Naval Staff. Reporting to the HQ RSN echelons in peacetime are three key formations capable of kinetic operations, namely, the RSN Fleet, MSTF and NDU.

Fifteen officers have had the opportunity to lead the navy, with ten in the capacity of CNV (Appendix L). It was noted in chapter 6 that the first two navy chiefs had unique careers, and since then the path to CNV has become fairly consistent, commencing with fleet command for most (Table 7.12). RADM2 (RET) Richard Lim Cherng Yih is the only exception, although he did hold ship and squadron command in addition to significant (in terms of duration and importance) staff tours in intelligence and operations. Subsequent CNVs usually took a mix of key appointments such as HNO, COS-NS or DJOPD/ COS-JS post-fleet command. There have been two exceptions. First, RADM2 (RET) Lui Tuck Yew (SAFOS 1980) had the shortest interval between command of the fleet and the RSN due to posting bottlenecks. This prompted a reversal in posting orders so that he completed a year as HNO and another at the US Naval Command College prior to fleet command. Second, RADM2 (NS) Lai Chung Han (SAFOS 1992) entirely skipped senior billets on the Naval Staff and instead held the hybrid post of DS (Policy) in MINDEF. His closest competitor in the 2014 CNV race, RADM2 (NS) Joseph Leong, had a similar experience having been tapped as DMI/Chief C4I after leaving the fleet. This would indicate a surplus in talent among admirals vis-à-vis the available billets more than a deliberate shift in officer development. In fact, there were eight active-duty admirals on 1 July 2016, the most at any one time in RSN history.[40]

7.4.3 Chief of Air Force

The air force chief, like his navy counterpart, held the Commander designation of the Singapore Air Defence Command and subsequently the RSAF. He was first promoted to BG in 1987, bestowed the CAF title in May 1990, and forwarded to the current rank of MG in 1994. In times of peace, the CAF has jurisdiction over all RSAF units and oversees every aspect of the service and its future plans. The rare exceptions include units under operational control of other services, and training squadrons based overseas. In times of war the CAF is the air component commander with the sole purpose of achieving air supremacy or, at the very least, air superiority to enable land and naval forces to operate unimpeded by opposing air power. The CAF is assisted by the COS-AS, who directs the dedicated departments of the Air Staff.

The history of Singapore's air force chief is differentiated from the other services in two aspects. First, the air force did not exist at independence and was created from scratch, even though existing British infrastructure and surplus equipment eased the burden. Second, the dearth of indigenous leadership and

---

[40] (1) RADM2 Lai Chung Han (CNV), (2) RADM1 Jackson Chia (COS-NS), (3) RADM1 Harris Chan Weng Yip (FSTA), (4) RADM1 Timothy Lo Khee Shik (HNO), (5) RADM1 Giam Hock Koon (COMDT SAFTI MI), (6) RADM1 Frederick Chew Chih Chiang (COMD MSTF), (7) RADM1 Lew Chuen Hong (Fleet COMD), and (8) RADM1 (Dr) Tang Kong Choong (CMC).

Table 7.12. Appointments and duration between fleet command and appointment as CNV

Rank and Name	Appointments from Fleet COMD to CNV	End of Fleet Command to CNV (days)	Other Possible Contenders for CNV
RADM1 James Leo	HNL, Chief Staff Officer HQ RSN, Deputy COMD RSN	N/A (naval engineer)	COL Lee Seng Kong
RADM1 Teo Chee Hean	HNO, COS-NS, DJOPD	Nil	COL Lee Seng Kong, COL Kwek Siew Jin
RADM2 Kwek Siew Jin	Fleet COMD, HNO, COS-NS	838	COL Richard Lim
RADM2 Richard Lim	HNO, COS-NS, DJOPD	Nil	RADM1 Larry Loon
RADM2 Lui Tuck Yew	Fleet COMD, Deputy CNV	112	RADM1 Larry Loon
RADM2 Ronnie Tay	Fleet COMD, HNO, COS-NS	842	RADM 1 Simon Ong Hung Eng, RADM1 Sim Gim Guan
RADM2 Chew Men Leong	Fleet COMD, HNO, COS-NS	583	RADM1 Tan Kai Hoe
RADM2 Ng Chee Peng	Fleet COMD, COS-NS, COS-JS	481	RADM1 Tay Kian Seng, RADM1 Tan Wee Beng
RADM2 Lai Chung Han	Fleet COMD, DS (Policy) MINDEF	718	RADM2 Joseph Leong
RADM1 Lew Chuen Hong	Fleet COMD, COS-NS	309	RADM1 Frederick Chew Chih Chiang, RADM1 Timothy Lo Khee Shik

expertise resulted in Singapore's nascent air force being led by army officers "press-ganged into transferring" and by ex-RAF, RAAF and ROCAF officers on loan or contract service.[41] It was only in the 1980s that two Singaporeans—BG (RET) Michael Teo (1980–82, 1984–92) and BG (RET) Gary Yeo (1982–4), both of

---

[41] Langer, *From the Spitfire Cockpit to the Cabinet Office*, pp. 206, 210–2.

whom impressed the foreign officers based on flying and leadership merit—took turns at the helm (Appendix M).[42]

Nine officers have led the RSAF as CAF. Eight of them are pilots (six fighter, two transport) and one an AWO (C3). Seven of the nine also have open-source records of having completed an operational squadron CO tour, which is the first test of command potential. The established starting point on the journey towards CAF, however, began with command of an air base and more recently— after the 2007 RSAF reorganization—that of the Operational Command. These formations are to the air force as divisions are to the army, and the RSN Fleet and MSTF to the navy. Certain commands are also favoured from which the CAF ascends in much the same way as counterparts in sister services. PLAB and TAB were long considered more esteemed commands thanks to the concentration of RSAF strike assets at the respective locations. It was only in early 2004 that CAB reached prestige parity when an eight-year extension of its eastern sector was completed.[43] An established hierarchy has also emerged from the five Operational Commands. ACC may be the sharp end of the RSAF, but ADOC holds the greatest importance in peacetime as the Air Defence Task Force (ADTF), which is part of the SAF HRC.

The path from air base or Operational Command towards CAF is very similar to that of the CNV in the RSN (Table 7.13). HAO, COS-AS and DJOPD/ COS-JS are all well-worn billets taken by the respective CAFs. A few are also appointed DJO, which has traditionally been apportioned between army and air force officers. There have been three exceptions to the norm, but these were never without valid reasons. The first CAF, BG (RET) Michael Teo, went from squadron command—140 SQN (1975–77) followed by 144 SQN (1979–80)— to HAO at a time when the RSAF hierarchy was much flatter. There was also a need for local officers to relieve foreign loan and contract officers holding billets equivalent to the present-day HAO and CAF. Next, LG (RET) Bey Soo Khiang had the shortest interval from air base command to CAF. However, it should be noted that he headed the intelligence and operations departments on the Air Staff separated by a year at Harvard University prior to becoming COMD PLAB. Finally, MG Mervyn Tan Wei Ming may not have held operations or COS appointments on either the Air or Joint Staff, but this was evidently not an obstacle. On the contrary, his confirmation as CAF—together with RADM2 (NS) Joseph Leong as DIR SID—further emphasized the newfound importance of the DMI/Chief C4I appointment on the path to higher appointments.

---

[42] Ibid., p. 214.

[43] 145 SQN operating the dual-seat F-16 Block 52+ multirole fighter was relocated from TAB to CAB (East) and joined transport squadrons operating from CAB (West). "Changi Air Base Spreads Its East Wing", *Air Force News* 91 (Jan. 2005): 10.

Table 7.13. Appointments and duration between air base/operational command and appointment as CAF

Rank and Name	Appointments from Air Base/ Operational Command to CAF	End of Air Base/ Operational Command to CAF (days)	Other Possible Contenders for CAF
BG Michael Teo	HAO, Deputy COMD RSAF	N/A	COL Gary Yeo
MG Bey Soo Khiang	COMD PLAB, COS-AS	[63, 92] between 63 and 92 days, exact date unknown	BG Gary Yeo
MG Goh Yong Siang	COMD PLAB, HAO, COS-AS, DJOPD	[1339, 1369]	Nil
MG Raymund Ng Teck Heng	COMD TAB, HAO, COS-AS	[427, 456]	BG Yam Ah Mee (non-pilot)
MG Rocky Lim Kim Choon	COMD TAB, HAO, COS-AS	[1067, 1096]	BG Loh Kok Hua, BG Voon Tse-Chow, BG Jimmy Khoo Siew Kim (non-pilot)
MG Ng Chee Khern	COMD TAB, HAO, DJO, DJOPD, COS-AS	1835	BG Chee Wee Kiong (non-pilot), BG Richard Lim Keng Yong, BG Charles Sih, BG Wong Huat Sern
MG Ng Chee Meng	COMD CAB, DJO, Deputy CAF	1162	BG Wong Huat Sern, BG Tan Meng Dui (non-pilot), BG Hoo Cher Mou (non-pilot), BG Richard Christopher Pereira
MG Hoo Cher Mou	COMD ADOC, COS-AS, COS-JS	1702	BG Lim Yeong Kiat, BG Neo Hong Keat, BG Sarbjit Singh S/O Tahil Singh
MG Mervyn Tan	COMD ADOC, DMI/Chief C4I	767	BG Lim Tuang Liang, BG Kelvin Khong Boon Leong

7.5   Summary

Three conspicuous aspects unique to Singapore's military establishment have been covered in this chapter. The status of Raffles, Hwa Chong and National as the elite schools was cemented with their having produced the majority of SAFOS recipients to date. Data from the first 25 years of the highly touted scheme indicate that more than half of the officers serve out a 20-year or longer career, and one-third of all recipients go on to wear at least one star. Yet there are no guarantees the scholarship will be perpetuated if future needs are not met. This could occur due to a failure to attract the best talent given the rising trend of education levels in society coupled with the acceptance of the military career as a noble undertaking. Favouring scholarship recipients over non-scholars who perceive themselves as being no less capable will only exacerbate the twin issues of recruitment and retention. The scheme is also threatened internally when recipients do not meet high expectations or when they leave active duty early. The cohorts of 1996, 2001 and 2002 have witnessed a premature thinning of their ranks. The signals and armour formations have similarly experienced spates of early- to mid-career departures of their SAFOS officers.

The differences between SAFOS and non-SAFOS recipients within the flag ranks are evident where empirical evidence is accessible. The average age of officers entering the military elite is slightly over 41.5 (SAFOS 38.71, non-SAFOS 43.39), and they render another 4.28 years of active service (SAFOS 4.98, non-SAFOS 3.81). Service lengths for members of the elite nucleus as CDF and service chiefs are virtually identical on average (SAFOS 6.24, non-SAFOS 6.00). The average age of retirement from active service is 43.20 years for SAFOS and 47.33 years for their counterparts. The majority join the government and affiliated entities after leaving service, but this does not necessarily imply a military-administrative state. Their power over policymaking is unknown, and their continued affiliation and loyalty are not explicitly observable. Their post-military successes, on the other hand, are in the open domain; and military rank is quickly immaterial in public administration and even more so in business. Finally, the case of Jacques Erasmus highlights the cost of losing the premier scholarship. In 2014, his fellow recipients from the 1999 batch had completed CSC and almost all their respective CO tours. Erasmus received the rank of MAJ that year, which was the same time as the army officers from the 2005 cohort.

There have also been several notable outliers within the Aristocracy of Armed Talent. The first was none other than PM Lee Hsien Loong, who set the pace for scholar ascension and the transition of career officers into politics. Former Foreign Minister George Yeo's military career and entry into politics mimicked Lee's stellar career. Subsequently, SAFOS recipients in Cabinet were drawn directly from active service ranks or from government-affiliated bodies. In 2015 Ng Chee Meng became the first non-SAFOS recipient to accept the ruling party's invitation to run for office. There were also other notable outliers aside from those recruited into politics. COL (RET) Yeo Cheng Ann and BG (RET) Eric Tan served their tours on UNPKO as L/BG and L/MG respectively before retiring in their permanent ranks. COL (RET) Michael Low, COL (RET) James Soon and COL (NS) Wong Yu Han all completed tours in long-established one-star appointments either as DIV COMD or Fleet COMD but never received a promotion—for unknown reasons—prior to leaving active service. Finally, BG Gan Siow Huang became the first female officer to join the military elite, although the appointment(s) that initially warranted the promotion seems inconspicuous. Nevertheless, she currently holds an established one-star command appointment.

The final section examined the ascension of a one-star into the elite nucleus as a service chief. Each service has unique starting points, but these are not entirely deterministic in nature. The COA usually commenced with command of 3 or 9 DIV, although 6 and 21 DIV can now be counted in the mix. The CNV has been a naval combat officer who commanded surface strike platforms through 1 FLOT and then the RSN Fleet itself. The CAF has usually been a pilot who helmed PLAB, TAB, or recently CAB. After the 2007 RSAF restructuring it would seem that command of ADOC or ACC is a prime appointment for any potential CAF. There are indicators of who is likely to become a future service chief after relinquishing command of the army division, navy fleet or air force air base/Operational Command. These include heading operations departments and/or serving as COS at either the respective service HQs or on the JS. It is rare, but not improbable, for the DMI (formerly DJID) to make service chief. In sum, certain trends have developed over the last five decades regarding SAF officers and those who ultimately became generals and admirals. Yet there are unexplained exceptions, which will hopefully have no detrimental effect on the morale of the SAF Officer Corps or the avowed practice of meritocracy.

CHAPTER 8

Character Determines Destiny

"Their generation was not as well-educated, poorer in material riches, and yet their sense of kinship and honour surpasses the highest standards …"[1]

— *NS is …*

8.1 Introduction

The military elites featured in the preceding chapters commenced their careers with the armed forces in colonial Singapore, and during the growing years of an independent nation. For a long while the profession of arms was not well accepted as a career for decent men—and certainly no place for women. The country was less prosperous, the population was less educated though not necessarily less intelligent, and social norms differed. The fact that Singapore has evolved is by no means peculiar. It is the mix of conspicuous and surreptitious challenges that are of immediate importance for defence planners as they seek to maintain a strong and credible defence force. High-tech weaponry can be purchased, training spaces negotiated, and de facto alliances forged, but the heart and soul necessary for a true commitment to defence must be won over time and again with each passing generation.

This chapter offers some of the challenges in securing quality manpower for defence purposes as Singapore moves beyond the various Golden Jubilee markers along its journey of nationhood. The commitment to defence remains a perennial struggle based on the eclectic mix of peace, materialism, meritocracy and individualism that has come to characterize modern Singapore. The challenges are compounded by the ostensible effects of emigration, immigration, trends in general health among potential recruits, decreasing birth rates, and the concerted effort to recruit more women into the defence force. The defence establishment strives to minimize negative side effects and remain cognizant that the solutions of today can become the problems of tomorrow. There are no easy solutions on the road ahead.

---

[1] *NS Is …* (Singapore: Ministry of Defence, 2012), p. 51.

8.2 The Changing Social Character

The "heart-ware" dimension is the crux of C2D, and in the ideal scenario all of society would be wholeheartedly committed to defence. NS would be more than a perfunctory rite of passage; it would be viewed as a first job taken seriously in both word and deed. NSFs would be give their best during their two years of full-time service, and there would be more volunteers than billets available for the most demanding vocations. As NSmen they would carry the same fortitude and determination to their yearly ICTs. Those who volunteered for overseas missions would be taken seriously and never viewed as a nuisance. Malingering, insubordination and the like would be relegated to the pages of the dictionary. Recruitment targets for Regulars would never fall short, and there would be no need to emphasize benefits. Service status (i.e., Regular, NSF or NSmen) would be a mere formality as everybody would be viewed and treated as one. Society in return would show its gratitude through simple yet meaningful gestures so that heraldry and monetary incentives paled in comparison. There are those who personify such ideals, but the different shades of reality have pitched a myriad of challenges that erode C2D.

8.2.1 Peace and Progress

Singapore was a colonial outpost, strategic naval base, and trading port of the British empire for 140 years. Decolonization after World War II came with the responsibility and concomitant problems of self-rule in 1957, namely, "those relating to unemployment, inadequate housing, security, survival and nation-building".[2] Social discord predicated on race and religion was real and threatened the possibility of a harmonious multicultural society. Secret societies undermined the rule of law. The country also needed infrastructure to improve living conditions, optimize the use of scarce economic resources (land, labour and capital), and attract foreign capital and expertise to develop the local workforce.[3] The way forward was export-oriented industrialization to diversify what Singapore could offer and for it to remain relevant, because Singapore needed the world

---

[2] Chong Li Choy, "Durable Stability with Prosperity and Legitimacy: Perceptual Leadership in Singapore", in *Durable Stability in Southeast Asia*, ed. Kusama Snitwongse and Sukhumbhand Paribatra (Singapore: Institute of Southeast Asian Studies, 1987), p. 174.

[3] Initiatives include the HDB in February 1960 to address public housing issues, PA in July 1960, EDB in August 1961 to diversify the economy and attract foreign investment, PUB and PSA in 1963, Singapore Family Planning and Population Board in January 1966, DBS and the JTC in 1968, and the Urban Redevelopment Authority in April 1974. See Quah, "Singapore: Towards a National Identity": 210.

but not necessarily vice versa.[4] Foreign multinationals were courted because the local business scene comprised small enterprises incomparable to "Hong Kong's cosmopolitan entrepreneurs" and without the necessary technological and managerial skills necessary to industrialize successfully on a global scale.[5]

However, it was not a free for all, as the government possessed "regulatory powers it used to ensure that the companies that came to Singapore remained good corporate citizens".[6] Swiftness and efficiency became hallmarks of the Singapore brand, which allowed basic housing objectives and employment through industrialization to be achieved by the late 1970s.[7] Relative peace and the Republic's expanding military capabilities placed "national survival and security" far from the thoughts of citizens, who were free to focus on "the needs for greater prosperity and better living".[8] As then-MG Winston Choo observed:

> "… if most Singaporeans are still hazy about the SAF's rank structure, 'despite the fact that we have had national service for fourteen years and nearly every family has some military connection, this largely reflects Singapore's good fortune in that military affairs have not had to be at the forefront of our people's daily concern'."[9]

Such complacency is tolerated in times of peace, but any form of armed conflict will meet with less forgiveness.

By the 1980s Singapore's transformation into an industrialized city was nearly complete. Full employment was achieved, and the population was well housed in government and private accommodations with high levels of homeownership. Public services delivered high standards of health care, education and transportation. In a short two decades, "Singapore had been transformed from an Asian port city of coolies and *taukehs* [businessmen/bosses] to a global metropolis inhabited by an affluent middle class and a fully industrialized and reasonably well-paid working class".[10] The focus and challenge shifted towards greater "happiness, prosperity and progress" once basic necessities were not only

---

[4] Chua Beng Huat, "The Cultural Logic of a Capitalist Single-Party State, Singapore", *Postcolonial Studies* 13, 4 (2010): 342; Lee, *Singapore: The Unexpected Nation*, pp. 649–51.

[5] Vogel, *Four Little Dragons*, pp. 77–8.

[6] Ibid.

[7] Peter van Ham, "The Rise of the Brand State: The Postmodern Politics of Image and Reputation", *Foreign Affairs* 80, 5 (2001): 2–6.

[8] Chong, "Durable Stability with Prosperity and Legitimacy", p. 174; Ooi, *In Lieu of Ideology*, pp. 128, 134.

[9] "First Three Reservist Majors Made Lt-Cols", *Straits Times*, 30 June 1981, p. 7.

[10] Trocki, *Singapore*, p. 147.

met but increasingly surpassed.[11] The impressive progress was due in no small part to the PAP's vision and ability to steady the ship through the turbulent era. In the process Singapore effectively became a "guardian state" where the government acts as the "trustee of the people" and acts in the best long-term interest of the state.[12]

Social engineering was undertaken with urgency to direct social norms. Since 1959 more than 200 national campaigns have been held to educate and guide the population's attitudes towards social issues such as courtesy, hygiene, illicit drugs, family planning and language usage.[13] According to one explanation, the PAP

> continues to see itself as motivated by a confident pragmatism, quite sure of its ability to engage successful in whatever social engineering it deems necessary. Through the exercise of effective—some would say ruthless—governmental and party authority, Singapore's leadership believes itself capable of acting efficaciously, in social science terms, as an independent variable; that is, it feels itself capable of manipulating the political, social and economic environments in a direction consonant with its vision of what Singapore ought to become.[14]

Success in the first two decades, however, laid the foundations for other issues in the years that followed. At the very least, what were once considered privileges soon turned into entitlements and were readily taken for granted. Back in 1983 LKY already voiced his concern for "the young people—they are growing up taking for granted safety and prosperity. How will they learn to run lean?"[15]

Perhaps the younger generations had no intention to run lean. To deal with this the economy would have to retool, reorganize and continue expanding. Singapore courted global companies in the mid-1980s to relocate "in order to develop the city into an international business hub, serving countries within

[11] Chong, "Durable Stability with Prosperity and Legitimacy", pp. 174, 179.

[12] Leonard C. Sebastian, "The Logic of the Guardian State: Governance in Singapore's Development Experience", *Southeast Asian Affairs* (1997): 282.

[13] *Campaign City: Life in Posters*, exhibition held at the National Library Board, 9 Jan.–7 July 2013; Quah, "Singapore: Towards a National Identity": 207–19. For example, the proliferation of illicit drugs across Singapore peaked in 1978, when 32,000 were arrested on drug-related offences. Political will and tough laws (including the death penalty) reversed, but did not eliminate, the scourge of drugs. Ivan Fernandez, "Frank and Sober Picture of Drug Problems in the SAF", *Straits Times*, 25 Apr. 1981, p. 14.

[14] Stanley S. Bedlington, "Ethnicity and the Armed Forces in Singapore", in *Ethnicity and the Military in Asia*, ed. DeWitt C. Ellinwood and Cynthia H. Enloe (New Brunswick: Transaction Books, 1981), p. 243.

[15] "The Only Way to Survive", *Straits Times*, 7 Apr. 1983, p. 14.

and beyond the Southeast Asian region" and stay ahead of competitors.[16] Light manufacturing industries that absorbed unemployment by "exploiting labour cost advantages" to attract foreign firms gave way to globally competitive high-end operations in manufacturing goods (e.g., telecommunications, pharmaceuticals, electronics and chemicals) and services (e.g., finance, communications, refined petroleum and logistics).[17]

By the 1990s Singapore proactively ventured abroad instead of merely attracting investors, spearheaded by GLCs—under the umbrella of Temasek Holdings and the Government Investment Corporation of Singapore—to reap the rewards of being a world-class city and "one of the key nodes in the global economy".[18] Singapore's economic scorecard showed an impressive 8.6 per cent annual growth and a concomitant increase in gross national income from US$1 billion to US$86 billion between 1965 and 1995.[19] The questions of chronic unemployment and underdevelopment were addressed swiftly within two generations. By 2015 Singapore's GDP had broken US$300 billion and the nation had one of the highest per capita rates globally. Singapore had done very well for itself, or so it would seem on the surface.

8.2.2 Materialism

The cyclical relationship between economic success and the lure of materialism is undeniable, and deep-seated issues with implications for the civil service soon emerged. While public sector employment entails economic sacrifices in certain countries, the same cannot be said of Singapore today. Any "sacrifices" made are compensated for, and indicators of this abound. The pragmatic step has always been to ensure salaries remain competitive in order to hire and retain. In 1989 there was a startling outflow of top bureaucrats from the AS,

---

[16] Henry Wai-Chung Yeung and Kris Olds, "Singapore's Global Reach: Situating the City-State in the Global Economy", *International Journal of Urban Sciences* 2, 1 (1998): 33.

[17] Andrea Goldstein and Pavida Pananond, "Singapore Inc. Goes Shopping Abroad: Profits and Pitfalls", *Journal of Contemporary Asia* 38, 3 (Aug. 2008): 418; Linda Low, "Singapore Inc.: A Success Story", *South African Journal of International Affairs* 10, 7 (Summer 2003): 49; Garry Rodan, "Singapore: Emerging Tensions in the 'Dictatorship of the Middle Class'", *Pacific Review* 5, 4 (Jan. 1992): 371.

[18] Other reasons include remaining competitive, decreasing vulnerability to sharp economic downturns, pitching its expertise as a springboard for those looking to the Asia-Pacific, and the rewards of integration with high-growth economies. Rodan, "Singapore", p. 371; Yeung and Olds, "Singapore's Global Reach": 33, 39–40; Low, "Singapore Inc.", p. 50; Goldstein and Pananond, "Singapore Inc. Goes Shopping Abroad", pp. 420, 422.

[19] Kishore Mahbubani, *The New Asian Hemisphere: The Irresistible Shift of Global Power to the East* (New York: PublicAffairs, 2008), p. 54.

and reportedly "[m]any of those who have resigned have complained, among other things, that promotions came too little and too late. The most successful of those who left the Service are earning 40 per cent to 100 per cent more than their contemporaries who stayed ... Able civil servants are opting out and are not being replaced fast enough."[20]

The civil service gave in by pegging salaries to the private sector, which translated to a rise of 7 per cent to 20 per cent depending on seniority, in addition to "end-of-year variable bonus; introduction of discretionary performance bonus, and faster promotions for deserving officers".[21] Career diplomat and inaugural Dean of the LKY School of Public Policy Kishore Mahbubani added: "To get the best to serve as AOs, the Singapore government tries to pay the most senior AOs almost as much as the private sector ... It's a small price to pay if a country wants to progress and succeed in a far more competitive global environment"[22] In 1994 it became necessary to introduce the formula of pegging ministerial salaries to 80 per cent of the top earners in six professions and businesses in Singapore. This was seen as a small price to attract competent individuals and ensure they did not lose out on material rewards, but million-dollar salaries for ministers also became a bugbear at several elections.

The same market expectations are embedded in the social consciousness. LKY captured the changing environment and challenges of governing in a 1992 address to the PAP cadre:

> "Success and a sense of security have brought about a very different mood in Singapore ... Now there's peace and plenty. We have got substantial savings and reserves. Why not spend more? Costs of living are going up, my salary should go up, but prices should not go up. So we have this querulous mood ... Singapore has become too comfortable—MRT, good buses and taxis, big comfortable homes, secure social environment, parks and recreational activities ... Singaporeans are preoccupied with minor aches and little itches."[23]

---

[20] "Flow of Talent into the Service Has Not Been Maintained", *Straits Times*, 18 Mar. 1989, p. 16.

[21] Ibid.

[22] Mahbubani, *The New Asian Hemisphere*, p. 73.

[23] Edited excerpt from a speech delivered by Lee Kuan Yew to the PAP cadre at a conference in November 1992. Reproduced in "So You Think We've Arrived?" *The Sunday Times*, 3 Jan. 1993, pp. 1, 6–7.

That same year society was seen to be over-reliant on domestic helpers—or "maids" as they are known in local parlance—from neighbouring countries such as Indonesia and the Philippines, resulting in a Maid Dependency Syndrome.[24]

In 2002 it was felt that such illusory comforts had disconnected Singaporeans from realities beyond the city-state's borders. A segment of the citizenry became "[c]omplaining, unmotivated, unrealistic, and dependent on handouts and welfare".[25] The "Singapore Dream" was conveniently encapsulated in the 5C's of "cash, credit card, car, condominium and country club membership". Another "C" in the form of conscription was certainly not part of the dream but tolerated as an inconvenient part of the material chase. General Elections were at times a spectacle of who could sustain the ever-growing, voracious and seemingly insatiable epicurean appetites. One local academic reasoned that since only one party had "performance legitimacy" many "continue to vote for the PAP at every subsequent general election, despite being fully aware of its less-than-democratic ways".[26] Other observers have further posited that Singaporeans will remain apolitical, even apathetic, so long as their perceived—and perhaps increasingly unrealistic—expectations are met.[27] After all, many seem to "look to the government not only as pilot, priest and pal, but as Santa Claus too".[28] The ability to deliver economic growth, the rule of law, and security has kept the PAP in power since 1959 (Appendix N).

Economic progress through industrialization and education, and the associated rewards of prosperity drew more women into the workforce.[29] Fewer families could depend solely on one income, leading to the decline of "housewife" as an occupation and its permanence an increasingly rarity. More women entering the workforce, coupled with personal aspirations and changing values, correlated with a decreasing total fertility rate that has fallen short of replacement levels since 1976.[30] Singlehood and divorce rates have also increased

---

[24] "Lucky Singapore Women", *Straits Times*, 11 Sept. 1992, p. 10.

[25] "PM Goh: Are You a Stayer or Quitter?" *Straits Times*, 19 Aug. 2002, p. 1.

[26] Chua, "Cultural Logic of a Capitalist Single-Party State": 338; "PM Goh", p. 1; Sim and Print, "Citizenship Education in Singapore": 706.

[27] Sim and Print, "Citizenship Education in Singapore", p. 706; Tan Ern Ser, "Reality Check Needed for S'poreans with Unrealistic Expectations", *TODAY*, 12 Aug. 2016.

[28] "Nation of Self-Reliant People Needed", *Straits Times*, 19 Aug. 2002, p. H5.

[29] Trocki, *Singapore*, p. 147.

[30] "Tackle Emigration Rationally, Says PM", *Straits Times*, 21 Aug. 1989, p. 1; Joseph B. Tamney, *The Struggle over Singapore's Soul: Western Modernization and Asian Culture* (Berlin: de Gruyter, 1996), pp. 117–43; Peggy Teo, Elspeth Graham, Brenda S.A. Yeoh and Susan Levy, "Values, Change and Inter-generational Ties between Two Generations of Women in Singapore", *Ageing & Society* 23, 3 (May 2003): 327–47.

compared to years past. In many ways it seems marriage and children are hurdles to materialistic pursuits.[31] Even the *New York Times* chimed in, saying "[t]he focus in Singapore is not to enjoy life, but to keep score: in school, in jobs, in income … Many see getting attached as an impediment to this."[32] Perhaps the most extreme mark of materialism is that "social escort agencies are seeing a bigger supply of Singaporeans willing to join the trade … money is the biggest lure, but gifts from clients such as designer handbags, meals at swanky restaurants and sometimes even paid holidays are other attractions."[33]

In 2015 the Chief Executive (CE) of the Singapore International Chamber of Commerce, Victor Mills, decried the "absolute nonsense" of Singapore's obsession with materialism mixed with a cocktail of "overfussiness" and "sense of entitlement". The naturalized Singaporean continued:

> "But it's the unintended consequence of the fantastic economic success which we have enjoyed. In our headlong rush for more money, a lot of values seem to have been lost. The ability to communicate with anybody else is less evident, and people now, generally, want to interact only with people of their own perceived social group. So we're now a more stratified and polarised society, which is why you hear people longing for the return of the *kampung* spirit."[34]

The perceived loss of the Singaporean soul (be it real or constructed) is not necessarily surprising since Singaporeans have been fed the pill of economic success since independence. The city-state has positioned itself as a global centre for wealth management and a safe haven for the global rich to safekeep their wealth.[35] Furthermore, Singapore is geographically ideal for the rich from countries with high taxes in the Pacific Rim, the *nouveau riche* from China and India, and investors globally as the "economic centre of gravity" shifts to Asia.[36] The Lion City had the world's highest GDP per capita in 2010 and by some estimates will still hold top spot in 2050.[37]

---

[31] Norman P. Li, Amy J.Y. Lim, Tsai Ming-Hong and O. Jiaqing, "Too Materialistic to Get Married and Have Children?" *PLoS ONE* (May 2015), pp. 1–12.

[32] David Brooks, "The Age of Possibility", *New York Times*, 15 Nov. 2012.

[33] Leonard Lim, Tham Yuen-C. and Bryna Sim, "What Lures Women to Become Social Escorts", *Straits Times*, 21 Apr. 2012, p. 12.

[34] Walter Sim, "Singaporeans Have Misplaced Sense of Entitlement, Says SICC Head Victor Mills", *Straits Times*, 26 Jan. 2015.

[35] Yoolim Lee, "Where Millionaires Stash It Away", *International Herald Tribune*, 23 Mar. 2006.

[36] Frank Knight Research, *The Wealth Report 2012: A Global Perspective on Prime Property and Wealth* (Citigroup, 2012), p. 8.

[37] Ibid., pp. 11–3.

8.2.3 Meritocracy and Its Discontents

Meritocracy was introduced by the British in 1951 for local applicants to the civil service.[38] Individual performance, rather than family ties or wealth, was the determinant of recognition and reward so that "[t]he best man gets the job".[39] At the entry level, "best" is equated with a word that has become cliché: talent. Explicit definitions vary and encompass a variety of skills, but in Singapore "the bottom line, to put it bluntly, is brains".[40] For this reason a premium is placed on education, and the key metric in the form of examination results determines the pecking order for a kaleidoscope of scholarships and career options. Incumbent DPM Tharman Shanmugaratnam explained Singapore's brand of meritocracy in his former capacity as Minister of Education during an official visit to the United States:

> "We both have meritocracies. Yours is a talent meritocracy, ours is an exam meritocracy. We know how to train people to take exams. You know how to use people's talents to the fullest. Both are important, but there are some parts of the intellect that we are not able to test well—like creativity, curiosity, a sense of adventure, ambition. Most of all, America has a culture of learning that challenges conventional wisdom, even if it means challenging authority. These are the areas where Singapore must learn from America."[41]

Examinations have distilled successive cohorts of students in the crucible that is Singapore's education system.[42] Streaming occurs at an early age in primary school, and though this has been relaxed somewhat the system is still designed to discriminate and separate the best from the rest. Additional resources are then directed to draw out their full potential. As Harvard don Ezra Vogel observed: "During the colonial period, those who had performed best in school exams were admitted to Singapore's elite school, Raffles, and then went to England for further training, with the expectation that they would return and serve the government."[43] This trend has continued to the present, with Singapore's talent centred in top schools such as Raffles and Hwa Chong. These institutions'

---

[38] Quah, *Public Administration Singapore Style*, p. 210.

[39] Josey, *Lee Kuan Yew*, pp. 209–10; "A Govt That Does Not Abandon the Ship: By Lee", *Straits Times*, 23 Dec. 1976, p. 14; "What Makes for Strong Defence", *Straits Times*, 3 May 1984, p. 16.

[40] "Talent: Real Issue Is How to Net the Right Ones", *Straits Times*, 16 Mar. 1989, p. 15.

[41] Fareed Zakaria, "We All Have a Lot to Learn", *Newsweek*, 8 Jan. 2006; Fareed Zakaria, "A Global Education for a Global Age", *Yale Daily News*, 3 Apr. 2012, http://www.yaledailynews. com/news/2012/apr/03/zakaria-a-global-education-for-a-global-age.

[42] Chua, "Cultural Logic of a Capitalist Single-Party State": 347–8.

[43] Vogel, *Four Little Dragons*, pp. 78–9.

reputations are held in such high esteem globally that graduating students utilize school-issued diplomas for university applications even before the official release of A-level results.[44]

Educational excellence lies at the foundation of Singapore's meritocracy, but this seemingly one-track focus has saddled students and their families with an acknowledged social cost. The government's Singapore 21 Committee presented the stark truth of the education environment at the turn of the millennium:

> Students are constantly reminded to excel academically. While not a bad thing itself, stress comes from not knowing how to respond. In recent years, the pressure is extending downward, even to the kindergartens. Extra-curricular activities, ideally a way to de-stress, are viewed by some students as additional work. Parents add to the stress when they pressure their children into taking up ECA not to their inclination.[45]

The Australian academic Carl Trocki's observations were also very much in sync:

> Lee Kuan Yew's belief that Singapore should be a meritocracy saw greater stress on testing regimes. Those Singaporeans who hoped to advance their children's career prospects had to embrace these opportunities, regardless of the conditions imposed by the government. The limited number of places in tertiary institutes meant that competition for places in (university) was extremely fierce. Even by the beginning of the twenty-first century, when there were more universities, successful entrance was still open only to those who had run the gauntlet of IQ, achievement and suitability tests that screened and streamed the students throughout their academic careers. By 2000, it was necessary for a toddler to enter the right preschool, so that they could be prepared for kindergarten, gain entrance into the right primary school and thereby qualify for the best secondary school.[46]

The Singaporean sociologist Chua Beng Huat additionally accounted for the high price paid by families as a whole:

> School-going children are subjected to the pressures of a highly competitive public education system. In line with the ideology of meritocracy, there are no private elite schools for local students, although there are elite public schools to which the best achievers in national examinations are sent. Students live not only with anxiety about their own academic performance, but also with their parents' fear of having a child who fails academically—and the future which that failure implies.

---

[44] Stacey Chia, "Varsity Entry, Thanks to Raffles, Hwa Chong Diplomas", *Straits Times*, 1 Mar. 2012, p. 10.

[45] Singapore 21 Committee, *Singapore 21: Together, We Make the Difference* (Singapore: Public Service Division, Government of Singapore, 1999), p. 18.

[46] Trocki, *Singapore*, p. 152.

> When the children are able, the imagined and real costs of educating
> them for success are an additional source of tension. Young parents readily
> admit that accepting their own children unconditionally is much easier
> said than done.[47]

Finally, Chong Siow Ann, Vice-Chairman of the Medical Board (Research) at
the Institute of Mental Health in Singapore, reiterated:

> With growing affluence and with most couples having fewer children, the
> latter have become the most precious of all possessions and, in tandem,
> parenting has become a very deliberate, self-conscious and angst-riven
> activity … To a certain extent, some parents may feel hapless as their
> children, being compelled as they were in a meritocratic elitist society
> where—so goes the popular narrative—the best chance of material success
> in later life is attaining the requisite academic credentials earlier in life.[48]

The game is rather straightforward, with education the basis of Singapore's
social Darwinism. Shortly after independence "education became a tool for
sorting the elite from the rest, reproducing the social division of labour and the
social order that serves the interests of the elite".[49] It is therefore not surprising
that Gary Rodan confidently declared: "There is probably no other place in
the world where formal qualifications represent as much economic or social
capital."[50] Indeed, by Singapore's Golden Jubilee, students relied not only on
individual brilliance but also their parents—who were likely to be "affluent
and well-educated"—to guide their entry into the very top schools.[51] As the
principal of Raffles explained in 2015, the institution had become "a 'middle-
class' school that now largely caters to the affluent segment of the population … it
'can no longer afford the comfortable illusion that [Raffles] is truly representative
of Singapore'".[52]

Questions of non-academic achievements have proven secondary within
the academic game simply because "[t]he stark reality is that schools and
principals in Singapore are still largely judged by pupils' performance in national
examinations".[53] Christopher Tremewan saw that "the ideological impact of early

---

[47] Chua, "Cultural Logic of a Capitalist Single-Party State": 343.

[48] Chong Siow Ann, "Tiger Mums, Helicopter Parents and Modern Child-Rearing Angst",
Straits Times, 20 Aug. 2016.

[49] Jasmine B.-Y. Sim, "The Burden of Responsibility: Elite Students' Understandings of Civic
Participation in Singapore", *Educational Review* 64, 2 (May 2012): 199.

[50] Rodan, "Singapore: Emerging Tensions in the 'Dictatorship of the Middle Class'": 373.

[51] Amelia Teng, "A Hard Look at Averting Elitism", *Straits Times*, 5 Aug. 2015.

[52] Amelia Teng, "RI Now a 'Middle-Class' School", *Straits Times*, 4 Aug. 2015.

[53] Joy Chew Oon Ai, "Civics and Moral Education in Singapore: Lessons for Citizenship
Education?" *Journal of Moral Education* 27, 4 (1998): 519.

streaming was to heighten the sense of competition at all levels of education and to increase the fear of failure".[54] This fear, known colloquially as *kiasu* (literally "afraid to lose" in Hokkien), arises because most get only one bite of the limited cherry. Second chances are rare thanks to "an unforgiving society" and "a culture of risk aversion".[55] One tabloid piece even claimed that "[w]hen life is on the skids in Singapore, nobody wants to know your name ... failure is like an infectious disease".[56] Such educational pressure fosters competition but over time has also spawned a segment of "talents" who blend self-centredness with hubris. Yet who could blame them for this conditioning? After all, it was performance that mattered, and they performed.

There have been calls for the education system to widen the definition of merit. As Kenneth Paul Tan explained in the *Washington Post*:

> Today, the Singaporean idea of meritocracy is criticized for entrenching structural limits on mobility; for its overly narrow idea of merit and success; and for an increasingly self-regarding elite that seems too interested in staying in power and that citizens perceive as arrogant and unresponsive to their needs.
>
> There has, however, been some attempt to re-balance meritocracy, bringing the egalitarian considerations back by introducing redistributive policies in a cautious shift to the left, partly no doubt in reaction to strong signals of popular displeasure in the general elections of 2011. A "compassionate," "inclusive" and "lifelong" meritocracy has found its way onto the government's agenda, including changes to its "pressure cooker educational system," criticized for streaming students into pathways that determine their life prospects at a very early age.[57]

Such changes may well prove to be slow and tedious, if at all possible; it was noted in late 2017 that "[d]ecades of an excessive fixation on grades and educational streaming have left a seemingly indelible mark on the Singapore psyche. Also, it's believed the fixation on grades was, in some part, perpetuated by the Government so much so that its attempts at a paradigm shift are met with scepticism."[58] Perhaps this is not surprising since academic results remain the clearest metric for success and key spokes in the wheel of meritocracy.

---

[54] Christopher Tremewan, *The Political Economy of Social Control in Singapore* (New York: St. Martin's Press, 1994), p. 122.

[55] Singapore 21 Committee, *Singapore 21*, p. 19.

[56] Elisia Yeo, "Price of Failure", *TODAY*, 23 Sept. 2003, p. 1.

[57] Kenneth Paul Tan, "How Singapore Is Fixing Its Meritocracy", *Washington Post*, 16 Apr. 2015.

[58] Bharati Jagdish, "Are We Still Missing the Point of Education?" Channel NewsAsia, 11 Nov. 2017.

8.2.4 What Matters: I or We?

Certain social commentators have painted a rather negative picture of Singaporean society given the broad trend of materialism and selective meritocratic hubris. One attributes the runaway lure of material success to "the comparatively poor standard of social behaviour amongst Singaporeans … [which] had not kept pace with the [economic] transformation … [so] that Singaporeans generally were self-centred and ill-mannered".[59] Another sees economic success as the medium that perpetuates the materialistic and apolitical citizenry with "a general mindset to defer to the government".[60] Even neighbouring states seem to take the same macro-view of the country's graces at times. Joseph Liow pointed out that during the 1997 Asian Financial Crisis:

> Singapore's economic success since independence has mostly been met with negative responses from the region. Indeed, political leaders from neighbouring countries regularly opine that Singapore's wealth has brought with it "arrogance" and "conceit". At the height of the regional financial crisis, former Malaysian Prime Minister Dr Mahathir Mohamad accused Singapore of adopting a "beggar thy neighbour" policy towards its immediate regional locale, while Indonesian leaders blamed Singapore for "harbouring" economic criminals and taking advantage of Indonesia's economic weakness by encouraging the relocation of investments and Indonesian wealth to the city-state.[61]

Perhaps the phenomenon that best epitomizes the scourge of micro-level self-centredness is recipients breaking the bonds that accompany government scholarships. The scholarship avenue was once the only means for academically gifted students to earn a university degree. Over time more and more families came to afford local, and increasingly overseas, education.[62] By the late 1990s there was a growing concern that scholarships had turned from state-sponsored privileges into mere "symbols of success" and "trophies and passports to a comfortable career" for a segment of recipients.[63] At worst, scholarships had

---

[59] Quinton Clements, "A Gracious Society: The Engineering of a New National Goal in Singapore", *History and Anthropology* 11, 2–3 (1999): 257, 259, 265.

[60] Sim and Print, "Citizenship Education in Singapore": 706.

[61] Joseph Chinyong Liow, "Confronting the Weight of History: Singapore and Key Neighbours", in *Impressions of the Goh Chok Tong Years in Singapore*, ed. Bridget Welsh, James Chin, Arun Mahizhnan and Tan Tarn How (Singapore: NUS Press, 2009), p. 145.

[62] "Flow of Talent into the Service Has Not Been Maintained", *Straits Times*, 18 Mar. 1989, p. 16.

[63] Lydia Lim, "What's Next along the Scholarship Trail?" *Straits Times*, 22 July 2000, p. 74; Chua, "Cultural Logic of a Capitalist Single-Party State": 341.

become tickets into the "caste of social prestige".[64] The crux of the saga was the tussle between those who viewed scholarships as mere contracts that could be broken with financial penalties versus those who were adamant that recipients had a social obligation to honour the attached bond.[65] In an alarming survey of 30 scholarship recipients in 2000, 25 said they had no issues with breaking the bond, with 11 of the 25 even admitting they had no intention of completing their own bonds.[66] Their reasons included the need to broaden horizons in a "new economy" and maximize their "prime" years; that the "scholar" tag and networking contacts were more valuable than scholarship benefits; and two out of three had the financial means to cover the costs associated with breaking the bond. In a separate incident, one PSC scholar who read economics at MIT broke his bond because failure to make the AS ranks as an AO placed him in a "slower [career] trajectory".[67]

The ensuing uproar was swift. Scholarship providers resorted to "naming and shaming" in an attempt to deter future bond breakers.[68] A former head of the Teachers College even opined:

---

[64] "Is Being 'Able' or Being 'Proper' of More Value in Business?" *Daily Princetonian*, 23 Feb. 1967, p. 6; Joe Haggerty, "Students Who Spurn the Lure of Money", *Straits Times*, 11 Nov. 1967, p. 10.

[65] Susan Leong, "I'll Tell a Bond-Breaker to His Face He Is Wrong", *Straits Times*, 31 July 2000, p. 3.

[66] Josephine Chew, "We'll Break Bonds, Say 11 Scholarship Holders", *Straits Times*, 9 July 2000, p. 1; Josephine Chew, "Scholarship Not Simply a Commercial Contract", *Straits Times*, 9 July 2000, p. 2.

[67] Lydia Lim, "He Broke Bond, but Puts His Name to It", *Straits Times*, 22 July 2000, p. 74.

[68] Dual President and Colombo Plan Scholar Hsieh Tsun-Yan is reportedly the first bond-breaker (1978). He studied mechanical engineering at the University of Alberta in Canada, rejected an offer to join the Administrative Service after completing NS, and instead served in the Public Works Department. Hsieh secured a place at business school, and when the PSC rejected his application for deferment to study he bought out his remaining bond ($27,000) and took his MBA at Harvard. He joined McKinsey Consulting in 1980, eventually become its first chairman for Asia. Zakir Hussain, "Still Adamant That Scholarship Holders Serve Their Bonds", *Straits Times*, 24 July 2008, p. H4; Lynn Lee, "The Return of the Original Bond-Breaker", *Straits Times*, 17 Aug. 2007, p. 31; Susan Long, "What It Takes to Succeed Globally", *Straits Times*, 1 Feb. 2013, p. A25; Geraldine Yeo and Pearl Lee, "Bond Busters: Smart or Selfish?" *Straits Times*, 17 Aug. 1997, p. 3; "NCB Fair in Dealing with Bond-Breaker", *Straits Times*, 12 Mar. 1998, p. 34; "NCB Names Bond Breaker at Stanford", *Straits Times*, 26 Mar. 1999, p. 3; "EDB Names Second Bond-Breaker This Year", *Straits Times*, 26 Nov. 1999, p. 81; "Scholar Breaks Bond", *Straits Times*, 3 June 2000, p. 64; "EDB Names Another Bond-Breaker", *Straits Times*, 27 Oct. 2001, p. H7.

"Our elitist horde of talented scholars have smooth-sailing careers after graduating from renowned British and American universities. But looking at the increasing number of bond breakers in recent years we have to ask: Is this elitist educational system producing a problematic by-effect? Are top students who lack a sense of sacrifice worthy of our nurture?"[69]

The press also vilified bond breakers, who "smacked strongly of individualism and careerism", but acknowledged they were merely "a by-product of a system that places tremendous emphasis on material success".[70] The whole saga even led to one of the rare public disagreements between political heavyweights. Former Defence Minister and later President Dr Tony Tan went so far as to suggest that "government scholarships be scrapped and replaced with study loans", an idea swiftly countered by then-PM Goh Chok Tong and then-DPM Lee Hsien Loong.[71] By 2004 bond breakers were supposedly fewer in number, and future cases were to be handled privately on individual merits.[72] This makes sense since "naming and shaming" commenced as a deterrent. Should the trend persist, a redefined normality will emerge where bond breaking is seen as acceptable because others have done it. Yet in 2006 some companies reported that scholarships were not paying off, due to bond breaking, scholars not measuring up to expectations, the prima donna attitude of some, and competition from bond-free scholarships.[73]

The general issue of self-centredness can be attributed to how society is conditioned to perceive the notion of success and the associated costs of being considered successful:

> ... Singapore became rich too quickly. Success was framed only in terms of economic utility. Their parents came to judge personal success exclusively by income and possessions.
>
> Notions of societal inclusiveness, compassion for the disadvantaged, considerateness, community involvement and patriotism (except in a superficial way) do not cloud their universe ... Well-educated middle-class parents have themselves sharpened the migratory instincts of their smart children studying abroad ... Now, if more and more Singaporeans who launch their careers abroad have every intention of returning some day, the nation need have no worry. But if bright sparks handed scholarships worth the value of an apartment say they might break the bond and return

---

[69] "When Brightness Falls", *Straits Times*, 30 Mar. 1998, p. 8.

[70] Lim, "What's Next along the Scholarship Trail?" p. 74.

[71] Ibid., p. 75.

[72] Tracy Quek, "No More Shaming of Bond-Breakers", *Straits Times*, 1 Aug. 2004, p. 17.

[73] Nur Dianah Suhaimi, "Scholarship Blues", *Sunday Times*, 17 Sept. 2006, p. 8.

the money after collecting an elite degree (and taking foreign citizenship), it is going to be one hard battle for hearts and minds.[74]

In 2008 a Singaporean don extrapolated this trend in tandem with global competition and concluded: "According to these sorts of arguments, it is no longer reasonable for contemporary Singapore to expect its talented citizens to choose politics and government as a career out of a sense of passion and altruism, since the opportunity costs of such a choice will continue to rise."[75]

This challenge was ostensibly less severe within the SAF: it was reported that only "three officers were released prematurely from their bonds" between 2000 and 2009.[76] The three were certainly not the only ones dissatisfied with uniformed service.[77] The SAF is not immune from the pervasive tendency of the current generation to ask "What is in it for me?" One senior officer commented:

> "How different are our younger generations of Regulars? Their reasons for joining may fundamentally be similar—a mix of ideals and pragmatism, though they tend to have higher expectations and aspirations. The pioneers were generally contented to have a stable career to support their families, while potential Regulars today ask about career schemes, vocations, scholarships and overseas training. Some of them, including their parents, are even concerned about career transition beyond the SAF, even before they sign up. Talking about aspirations, a pre-enlistee considering an SAF career actually asked me how long one would take to become a Service Chief! I doubt our pioneers who did eventually become Service Chiefs or CDF ever thought that far and, even if some did, would probably have refrained from asking such a question. This change is not for the better or worse; it is just different. Each generation will have its own set of aspirations and challenges, so the SAF will have to continue to innovate and adapt in order to recruit and retain high-quality Regulars."[78]

---

[74] "Angst of a Nation", *Straits Times*, 20 Aug. 2002, p. 10.

[75] Kenneth Paul Tan, "Meritocracy and Elitism in a Global City: Ideological Shifts in Singapore", *International Political Science Review* 29, 1 (Jan. 2008): 18–9.

[76] Loh Chee Kong, "3 Released in 9 Years", *TODAY*, 14 Apr. 2009, p. 6; "SAF Bond: 3 Officers Given Early Release since 2000", *Straits Times*, 14 Apr. 2009, p. 31.

[77] The most extreme and conspicuous case came with the suicide of 27-year-old CPT (Dr) Allan Ooi Seng Teik. The Regular MO went Absent Without Official Leave (AWOL) on 15 October 2008, and his body was discovered under the Westgate Bridge in Melbourne, Australia, on 3 March 2009. The late CPT (Dr) Ooi allegedly listed his grievances about the job scope and bonded service to the SAF. "Absent Doc Found Dead", *Straits Times*, 6 Mar. 2009, p. 1; "Singaporean Doctor Found Dead in Melbourne", *Straits Times*, 6 Mar. 2009, p. 8.

[78] *SAF 50: Giving Strength to Our Nation: The SAF and Its People* (Singapore: Ministry of Defence, 2015), p. 77.

Bond breaking aside, the overarching spectre of perceived self-centredness manifests itself in various forms. The PM in 2012 alluded to the rise of "turf-guarding" in neighbourhoods against "unwanted developments" (e.g., nursing homes, hostels for foreign labourers) or the NIMBY (Not In My Backyard) syndrome in land-scarce Singapore.[79] The Graciousness Index released by the Singapore Kindness Movement also dropped to its lowest point in 2013 but rebounded slightly thereafter.[80] Such characteristics are not uniform across society as there are always individuals and groups committed to making Singapore a better place.[81] Yet the status quo will likely remain in the foreseeable future. It will take drastic changes in the social milieu and not simply education campaigns or news reports for a paradigm shift from "I" to "We".

8.3   Emigration and Migration

Despite its impressive economic progress, Singapore has suffered from a brain drain. As far back as the 1970s LKY attributed this to the mobility of an educated English-speaking Singaporean and the lure of the West:

> "Let us acknowledge the fact that a high-level trained manpower, particularly in the English-speaking world, is an international commodity. It crosses caste barriers, national barriers, and seeks returns which are higher probably in North America or Western Europe ... I think it is for us to find mixed incentives, appeal to loyalty, satisfaction of positions of command. They would help to keep the best brains within a country, while allowing a marginal fringe to go out to seek wider experience and to return."[82]

By the late 1980s, Singapore's founding PM labelled those who emigrated for materialistic reasons as "washouts" but concurrently recognized that the nation was losing talent.[83] This was most notable "among the young, English-educated, high-income Singaporeans".[84] Cabinet ministers attempted to deter others by

---

[79] Li Xueying, "PM Lee Flags Two Worrying Trends in Singapore", *Straits Times*, 5 Apr. 2012.

[80] Priscilla Goy and Cheng Jingjie, "Graciousness in Singapore Hits Five-Year Low: Survey", *Straits Times*, 10 Apr. 2013, pp. 2–3.

[81] Walter Sim, "Singaporeans See Virtues Like Compassion in Themselves but View Society as Materialistic", *Straits Times*, 23 July 2015; Daryl Chin, "The Importance of Being Awe-Inspiring", *Straits Times*, 31 July 2016; Tang See Kit, "Good Businesses: Meet the Entrepreneurs Who Want to Make Singapore a Better Place", Channel NewsAsia, 27 Dec. 2017.

[82] Josey, *Lee Kuan Yew*, p. 88.

[83] "Tackle Emigration Rationally, Says PM", p. 1.

[84] Rodan, "Singapore: Emerging Tensions in the 'Dictatorship of the Middle Class'": 376.

citing a kaleidoscope of reasons against emigrating to the West.[85] In 2002 the new term "quitters" was used to describe "fair weather Singaporeans" who had "no sense of belonging" and when things got rough would "run at the drop of a hat".[86] However, over time quitters began to take on the negative connotation of "those who emigrated or went abroad to work".[87] Name calling to any degree did not help, and LKY further conceded in 2008: "The brain drain is pretty serious, our brain drain, losing them ... According to the people who give up their citizenship and take out their savings, their pension funds, we're losing about, at the top end, 1,000 a year ... It will grow because I think the numbers are growing."[88]

Emigration data released in 2012 indicated some 1,200 Singaporeans renouncing their citizenship annually, some 300 of whom were naturalized citizens who exploited the Singapore branding as a stepping stone for a smoother transfer elsewhere.[89] It seems that NS and the associated opportunity costs were just one among the plethora of reasons for emigrating.[90] Patchy official figures indicate NS evasion has been relatively low, with an average annual default rate of 0.50 per cent to 0.67 per cent (2001–05) and a threefold increase to between 1.58 per cent and 2.11 per cent (2006–11), assuming an annual intake of between 15,000 and 20,000 conscripts (Table 8.1). It was further revealed that

---

[85] "Tackle Emigration Rationally, Says PM", p. 1; "Nation-Building 'Requires Passion and Conviction'", *Straits Times*, 21 Aug. 1989, p. 16. Reasons cited: (1) Quality of life in Singapore was not inferior to the West, and Singapore was not plagued by "racial discrimination, drugs, promiscuity, and crime"; (2) older emigrants faced isolation, and "old-age security" was not well catered for in the West; (3) Asians in the West faced invisible glass ceilings; children risked street muggings and exposure to violence and immorality; (4) the average émigré student in the West will not have the same opportunities as the average student in Singapore; and (5) problems marrying Asians and alienation arising from difficulties assimilating into a white community.

[86] "PM Goh: Are You a Stayer or Quitter?" p. 1.

[87] "Govt and People Moving Apart, Warn MPs", *Straits Times*, 2 Oct. 2002, p. 3.

[88] "Transcript of Minister Mentor Lee Kuan Yew's Interview with Arnaud De Borchgrave of UPI on 2 February 2008 at Istana", http://www.straitstimes.com/STI/STIMEDIA/pdf/20080213/transcript.pdf; "1,000 S'poreans Give Up Citizenship Each Year", *Straits Times*, 21 July 2008.

[89] Amanda Tan and Tay Suan Chiang, "300 New Citizens Give Up Their Status Each Year", *Straits Times*, 2 Mar. 2012, p. C14.

[90] "Do not want your son/s to serve National Service" is listed as a reason for emigrating. See point 24 of the "Singapore Police Force Certificate of Clearance (COC)".

in addition to defaulters around 500 men were exempted annually between 2011 and 2014 due to mental health issues.[91]

Table 8.1. National Service defaulters (2001–05, 2006–11)[92]

Year(s)	Citizens	Permanent Residents	Total
2001–05 total	*Unknown*	*Unknown*	~500
2006	254	99	353
2007	235	353	588
2008	259	36	295
2009	174	27	201
2010	148	56	204
2011	181	78	259
2006–11 total	1,251	649	1,900
2001–05 average	*Unknown*	*Unknown*	~100
2006–11 average	208.50	108.17	316.67
2001–05, 2006–11 average	*Unknown*	*Unknown*	218.18

Defaulting on NS is no small matter, with sentences reflecting the seriousness of the charge. Official figures indicate the courts convicted 185 defaulters between 1986 and 2006: 43 were jailed, 140 were fined (35 were subsequently jailed for defaulting on their fines), and two were imprisoned for other offences. After the sentences were carried out the 185 were reassessed for their suitability to complete NS. In the end 127 enlisted, two repeated the offence of defaulting, 33 were exempted on grounds that would have not have required them to serve in the first place, and 23 were above the age limit or had become foreign citizens.[93] More recent figures indicate that around 12 per cent of the 100 or so who defaulted annually between 2001 and 2005 were charged and convicted according to the merits of the respective cases. It became evident that the increase

---

[91] Rachel Au-Yong, "2% Exempted from NS Annually over Mental Health", *Straits Times*, 30 May 2014, p. 8.

[92] Monica Kotwani, "More NS Defaulters in 2011 than in 2010: Ng Eng Hen", Channel NewsAsia, 15 Oct. 2012; "Written Reply by Minister for Defence Dr Ng Eng Hen to Parliamentary Question on National Service Defaulters", *MINDEF*, 15 Oct. 2012, https://www.mindef.gov.sg/imindef/press_room/official_releases/nr/2012/oct/15oct12_nr.html, accessed 7 Nov. 2016; Calvin Yang and Dominic Teo, "Contrasting Reactions to Jailing of NS Defaulter", *Straits Times*, 14 Feb. 2016.

[93] "Ministerial Statement on National Service Defaulters by Minister for Defence Teo Chee Hean", *MINDEF*, 16 Jan. 2006, https://www.mindef.gov.sg/imindef/press_room/official_releases/nr/2006/jan/16jan06_nr.html, accessed 7 Nov. 2016.

in defaulters had to be curbed even though no official figures of convictions were released for 2006 onwards. Public outcry over seemingly lenient sentences (fines rather than jail) in prominent cases prompted Supreme Court of Singapore Justice Chan Seng Onn to set clear sentencing guidelines in 2016. A year later, the High Court was obliged to set new and harsher sentencing benchmarks on imprisonment terms after prosecution appeals against earlier penalties levied on three NS defaulters.[94]

It is not possible to give a specific reason why Singaporeans seek to emigrate. The crux of the matter is whether Singapore is a home or merely a "hotel" with a revolving door to the world. The sense of belonging is sometimes found wanting beyond the tangible material benefits. Until the early 1990s some leaders recognized that Singapore was "a place to which one temporarily migrated in order to accumulate savings rather than an ideal state to which one owed ultimate allegiance".[95] This was a problem that had to be addressed urgently in order to surmount the tide of pessimism. In 1997 the government mooted the concept of "Active Citizenship" where citizens would "contribute their ideas, time and energy to build a better Singapore" and in the process "strengthen their sense of ownership and belonging to Singapore".[96] There are no illusions that such initiatives within a setting of peace and prosperity will be a trans-generational effort.

In 2012 the messages of ownership and belonging "for Singapore to endure and succeed in the long term" still resonated strongly.[97] Surveys, if in any way accurate and representative, highlighted why this was necessary. In 2002, three quarters of students "were pessimistic about the country's future" while "two in 10 adults polled considered leaving Singapore".[98] In 2006, it was reported that "53 per cent of Singaporean teens would consider emigration".[99] A 2010 Gallup study portended that 374,000 Singaporean adults would like to leave

[94] "High Court Sets Out New Sentencing Framework for NS Defaulters", Channel NewsAsia, 25 July 2017.

[95] LG (RET) Winston Choo and COL (RET) James Aeria quoted in Peled, *A Question of Loyalty*, p. 93.

[96] Points 15 and 16 of speech by DPM Lee Hsien Loong at the Administrative Service Dinner and Promotion Ceremony, Mandarin Hotel, 29 Mar. 1999, http://www.singapore21.org.sg/speeches_290399.html (no longer available).

[97] "Engaging Students and Their Teachers on the Importance of Defence", *MINDEF News Releases*, 25 May 2012.

[98] "PM Goh: Are You a Stayer or Quitter?" p. 1; "2 in 10 S'poreans Have Thought of Leaving: Survey", *Straits Times*, 31 Aug. 2002, p. 6.

[99] Quoted in "Interview with DPM Wong Kan Seng, Minister-in-Charge of Population Issues", 16 Aug. 2006, https://www.ica.gov.sg/downloads/Interview.pdf, accessed 1 Nov. 2016.

the country but 8.3 million foreigners would gladly replace them.[100] In 2012, 56 per cent of the 2,000-odd surveyed indicated they would emigrate if they had a choice.[101] These figures certainly have a potential negative impact on defence. As Singapore's first DPM (1965–68) Dr Toh Chin Chye reasoned, the most important ingredient for a successful army "was the soldier's belief—his faith in his unit, confidence in the future, and abiding faith in the cause of his country".[102]

The number of Singaporean passport holders resident overseas grew steadily from 172,000 (2007) to 180,000 (2012) and in 2016 stood at 213,400.[103] This represents some 6 per cent of Singaporeans, and the global diaspora is large enough to establish "280 Singapore clubs in 120 cities worldwide".[104] The Singapore International Foundation was established in 1991 "to facilitate contact with and between Singaporeans abroad" and allow them to keep in touch with their country of birth.[105] The Overseas Singaporean Unit organizes an annual Singapore Day in cities with a significant Singaporean population—New York City (2007), Melbourne (2008, 2017), London (2009, 2014, 2018), Shanghai (2011, 2015), Brooklyn (2012), Sydney (2013) and San Francisco (2016)—and the omnipresent MINDEF booth is ready to "reach out to parents with sons eligible for NS, and update overseas NSmen … on the latest developments in the SAF".[106] In addition, Singaporeans overseas have their own networks to keep abreast of general developments back home. For those who have put down roots permanently in another country they now call home, news from Singapore is often the topic of conversation and at times a validation of their decision to migrate. One simple gauge of the country's collective pride and self-worth is represented by the population of locals at the highest echelons of the business elite and within the intelligentsia. These are the clearest indicators for any state and certainly no different for Singaporeans whether local or abroad.

---

[100] Neli Esipova, Julie Ray and Rajesh Srinivasan, *The World's Potential Migrants: Who They Are, Where They Want to Go, and Why It Matters* (Washington, DC: Gallup, 2010), p. 4.

[101] "More than Half of S'poreans Would Migrate if Given a Choice: Survey", *AsiaOne*, 9 Oct. 2012.

[102] "Arms and the Men in the Army: By Dr Toh", *Straits Times*, 20 Sept. 1967, p. 11.

[103] Tessa Wong, "Do More to Help Foreigners Adjust: DPM Teo", *Straits Times*, 29 Apr. 2012, p. 4; Charissa Yong, "Study to Find Out Mindsets of Overseas Singaporeans", *Straits Times*, 16 May 2017; Leong Chan Hoong, "More Singaporeans Going Abroad, but Are No Less Singaporean for It", Channel NewsAsia, 2 Sept. 2017.

[104] Wong, "Do More to Help Foreigners Adjust", p. 4.

[105] Rodan, "Singapore: Emerging Tensions in the 'Dictatorship of the Middle Class'": 373.

[106] Angelina Chung and Sheena Tan, "Little Red Dot in the Big Apple", *Cyberpioneer*, 8 June 2012.

If those who emigrated were not well rooted and had the means to do so, what prompted them to take the leap? Christopher Tremewan attributes the cost of economic success as being too much for some, and they are pushed into emigration as the only option available:

> Escape as a form of dissent reflects the realisation of the middle class either that their or their children's chances of joining the capitalist class were minimal or that the rewards were not worth the effort … They were escaping the classification system altogether. Mass emigration indicated, among other things, a breakdown in the meritocratic educational practice and ideology. There was no choice in Singapore that they wished to choose.[107]

Others emigrate due to the lure of new opportunities and second chances in countries that they perceive would afford them a better future in terms of employment, education and quality of life. Those who perceive restrictions on liberty invariably cite "one-party repression; detention without trial; the suppression of the trade union movement, student movement, and intellectual freedom; and control of the press".[108] Some contemplate a future where they cannot afford to retire and where ageism is a clear and present issue.[109] Indeed, senior citizens are at times made to feel that growing old is a problem as they are tagged with seemingly benign yet subliminally derogatory terms such as "Silver Tsunami" and "Grey Brigade". Others decry the government's decision to open integrated resorts with their casino centrepieces and see the spate of unrelated high-profile scandals as signs that the country's moral compass—something they once took pride in—has become faulty.

Then there are those who believe the country has been sold out by liberal immigration policies and an open economy designed to stem the brain drain and attract "foreign talents" to keep Singapore economically competitive. For these individuals, their quality of life has been compromised by the opening of the immigration floodgates and policies perceived to favour foreigners over sons of the land. Their empirical evidence is based on physical stresses on infrastructure, housing and transportation, which have heightened tensions between Singaporeans and foreigners. Would one be hard pressed to find locals in certain occupations and senior management either by design or circumstance?

---

[107] Christopher Tremewan, *The Political Economy of Social Control in Singapore* (New York: St. Martin's Press, 1994), p. 123.

[108] C.J. W.-L. Wee, "'Asian Values', Singapore, and the Third Way: Re-Working Individualism and Collectivism", *Sojourn: Journal of Social Issues in Southeast Asia* 14, 2 (Oct. 1999): 346.

[109] Yaw A. Debrah, "Tackling Age Discrimination in Employment in Singapore", *International Journal of Human Resource Management* 7, 4 (1996): 813–31.

The perceived cheapening of citizenship as a recruitment tool, "a tradable asset that official agents of the state can flexibly barter", worsens perceptions.[110] From Olympians to the rich and famous, the red passport and pink IC have been issued to those whose wealth may reside within the republic but whose hearts may not.[111] Despite promises to keep Singaporeans at the core, various population projection figures—such as 6.9 million by 2030 and 10 million by 2100—have drawn more flack than ameliorated concerns.[112]

Beyond bread-and-butter issues, one must also question the related impact (if any) on national, cultural and religious identity. Singaporean don Edwin Lee identified the conundrum despite the government's best intentions:

> Globalization came with another social cost. It made possible the emigration of large numbers of Singaporeans, and necessitated the influx of foreign talent, partly to compensate for the loss of the former. However, this would lead to a divide between citizens and foreigners in Singapore, in addition to the divide between the rich and the poor … In the case of Singapore globalization had taken by storm a country that was not yet a nation, or a country with only a short history of nation building to date … Thanks to globalization Singapore rose from a third-world to first-world economy in one generation, market values were paramount, success was conceived in monetary terms and no other way, people were extremely stressed, anxious, and unsmiling. Somewhat belatedly, the government initiated communitarian values. But the government's depiction of the Asian virtue of community before self was a construct that had no real basis in the nation's short history.[113]

Perhaps it should come as no surprise that Singapore remains a country seeking to answer an age-old question: "Who are you?"[114]

---

[110] Ayelet Shachar, "Picking Winners: Olympic Citizenship and the Global Race for Talent", *Yale Law Journal* 120, 8 (June 2011): 2095.

[111] Ibid.: 2088–139.

[112] Prime Minister's Office, *A Sustainable Population for a Dynamic Singapore: Population White Paper* (Singapore: National Population and Talent Division, Jan. 2013); Janice Heng, "Look ahead to 10 Million People by 2100?" *Straits Times*, 28 Apr. 2013, p. 14.

[113] Lee, *Singapore: The Unexpected Nation*, pp. 649–51.

[114] Lin Yanqin, "National Day Special 2016: Wanted—A National Identity for Singapore", *TODAY*, 8 Aug. 2016.

8.4 Human Capital: Declining Quality amidst Decreasing Quantity?

The question of C2D is further complicated by the human capital that is essential for maintaining a credible defence force. The concern in Singapore's context is with the concurrent decline in the quality of health amidst decreasing birth rates. Singapore's national health risks have made the epidemiologic transition from tuberculosis, pneumonia, diarrhoea and infections of newborns in 1950 to cancer, heart disease, cerebro-vascular disease, pneumonia and accidents some six decades later.[115] These trends mirror lifestyles in general thanks to the successful economic transition, the subsequent affluence, and the stress with keeping up appearances. The greatest health concerns with regard to the impact on defence capabilities have been maintaining physical fitness while tackling the scourge of obesity, and the overall deterioration of ocular health within the pool of service personnel.

The obesity rate among schoolchildren caused much alarm as early as the 1980s, as it climbed steadily from 5.4 per cent (1980) to 8.8 per cent (1985), 10.4 per cent (1989) and 13.2 per cent (1990).[116] This trend necessitated the creation of the SAF Physical Performance Centre in October 1984 to address the issue of overweight/obese and unfit servicemen.[117] In 1989 further doubts surfaced over the physical fitness of recruits as obesity was still on the increase.[118] From 1 January 1991 obese recruits underwent a five-month BMT (instead of three months), which was credited with producing "healthier, fitter, and capable" soldiers.[119] Future conscripts were enticed to keep fit with the reward of a one-month reduction in the overall duration of full-time NS.[120]

Speaking on the need for a healthy lifestyle campaign, then-DPM Lee Hsien Loong explained the concern and impact on the SAF: "It is difficult for national servicemen to maintain their physical fitness after their ROD (completion of

---

[115] Lim Meng Kin, "Aging Asia: A Perspective from Singapore", presentation at Aging Asia: Economic and Social Implications of Rapid Demographic Change in China, Japan, and Korea Conference, Stanford University, 26 Feb. 2009, iis-db.stanford.edu/evnts/5501/Lim. pdf, accessed 28 May 2014.

[116] "First Batch of Fat Recruits Doing Fine", *Straits Times*, 14 Mar. 1991, p. 24; "Many Singaporeans Not Fit, Says Report", *Straits Times*, 27 Nov. 1991, p. 13.

[117] "SAF Plan for Fitter, Stronger Soldiers", *Straits Times*, 27 July 1985, p. 15.

[118] "No Softies Here", *Straits Times*, 14 Sept. 1989, p. 2.

[119] "Combating Obesity", *Pioneer* (Sept. 1990): 18; "SAF Fights the Flab", *Pioneer* (Feb. 1991): 30–2; Walter Fernandez, "The 5 Month Saga …", *Pioneer* (June 1991): 15–25; "Successful Fight against Obesity", *Pioneer* (Dec. 1991): 12.

[120] "Shorter NS for Fit Recruits", *Pioneer* (May 1991): 22–3.

full-time NS) ... Every year, 400 combat-fit reservists become non combat-fit due to obesity ... many Singapore children, long before they are called up at age 18, have already become obese."[121]

The reasons for increasing obesity were perhaps best captured in the reflections of a Singaporean growing up in the "poor" 1950s and 1960s, when obesity was rare:

> ... basically due to our active lifestyles and humble diets. Without television or the personal computer, our leisure hours were mostly spent outdoors. As for food, we seldom ate meat, which was more expensive than vegetables. *Char siew* (roast pork), which is such a common dish nowadays, was considered a luxury dish for those who came from the less well-to-do families. Chicken was another luxury available only on festive or special occasions like birthdays. Usually, the birthday boy or girl would get to eat the drumstick. Birthday parties and birthday cakes were Western traditions that my generation, especially those from rural backgrounds, never practised.[122]

Tackling obesity is necessary but insufficient for addressing the perennial question of physical fitness.[123] The pre-enlistment screening of volunteers for the PDF in 1966 already uncovered "that many from urban areas were physically unfit for military training".[124] An exasperated LKY further decried during a speech at Tanjong Pagar Community Centre that: "It is not only the middle-aged who are not physically fit. Young people, including secondary school students have also been found to be in poor physical condition."[125] At a later passing out parade of soldiers who were sons of "farmers and rural folks", the then-PM quipped: "Rural people in all countries make excellent soldiers, and I am sure these are no exception."[126] The problem is that Singapore no longer has any rural folk to speak of. In fact, the press has continued to take periodic pot-shots at the lifestyle of its city slickers. One broadsheet asked, following the death of a National Serviceman:

> Is the physical regimen in our armed forces too tough for our boys? Singaporeans in recent years have shown greater interest in sports and physical fitness. But a large proportion of our youth is apparently still less

---

[121] "Think Healthy, Stay Fit", *Pioneer* (Aug. 1991): 8.

[122] Lam Chun See, *Good Morning Yesterday: Growing Up in Singapore in the 1950s and 1960s* (Singapore: Hoshin Consulting, 2012), pp. 54–5.

[123] "They Are Swift and Deadly", *Singapore Monitor*, 6 Oct. 1984, p. 4.

[124] "Lee: The Unfit City Dwellers", *Straits Times*, 13 Mar. 1966, p. 3.

[125] Ibid.; "Lee: The Rural Lad Makes a Good Soldier", *Straits Times*, 1 Jan. 1967, p. 4.

[126] "Lee: The Rural Lad Makes a Good Soldier", p. 4.

than rugged. Possibly this is a consequence of high-rise city living and the inadequacy of sports facilities. The emphasis on academic achievements could also be a disincentive to participate in sports and other physical pursuits. In any case, the latest deaths and previous fatalities in the army are indicators that at least a few of our youths are not fit enough for the army but somehow have been drafted into it.[127]

That was written in 1979. Some three decades later there was a sense of *déjà vu* when the same paper touched a raw nerve by asking: "Are the younger generation of Singaporeans growing up less physically rugged than their fathers? Is the obsession with the Internet and computer games leading to a generation who exercise only their fingers and are not as fit as they should be?"[128]

On SAF Day 2016 Lucy Toh, a member of the Advisory Council on Community Relations in Defence (ACCORD), highlighted the question of physical fitness "with more youngsters eating unwisely and living a sedentary life".[129] The principal of St Andrew's Secondary School reiterated that "[a] strong defence is the cornerstone of Singapore's peace and security, but may not be on the minds of most".[130]

Any attempts to deflect such shortcomings by lauding the higher education levels of today's servicemen are superficial and partial to reported statistics. In 2009 approximately half of the "more than 20,000 new enlistees each year" failed to meet the minimum physical fitness standards expected.[131] The *Straits Times* further reported in 2015 that "[t]he most recent figures given in 2010 by the Ministry of Defence showed that the test is failed by half of the 116,000 NSmen who take it every year".[132] This test is none other than the IPPT, which is the most basic gauge of physical fitness. It is not to be confused with measures of combat fitness usually involving physical tests with combat equipment, such as the standard and advanced obstacle courses, route and fast marches, and overseas field exercises of extended duration.

The consistent 50 per cent failure rate for physical fitness is problematic, but the *Straits Times*' journalistic licence could be even greater cause for alarm. In 2012 Dr Ng Eng Hen revealed, in response to a parliamentary question, that

---

[127] "How Rugged an Army?" *Straits Times*, 5 Jan. 1979, p. 16.

[128] Jamie Ee Wen Wei, "Are the Youth of Today Less Rugged?" *Straits Times*, 15 June 2008, p. 3.

[129] Lucy Toh, "Support of All Is Vital for a Strong SAF", *TODAY*, 1 July 2016.

[130] Ibid.

[131] Nicholas Yong, "Prepping Unfit NSmen", *Straits Times*, 12 Feb. 2009.

[132] Jermyn Chow, "SAF Shelves Boot Camp Plans for IPPT Defaulters", *Straits Times*, 13 June 2015.

"about 116,000 SAF personnel take the IPPT annually".[133] It is fair to assume that the astute defence minister would not confuse the categories of servicemen within his portfolio and "SAF personnel" includes Regulars, NSFs and NSmen. There are two possible interpretations of the figure of 116,000. It could mean that only 33 per cent to 39 per cent of the oft-flaunted total mobilized strength of 300,000 to 350,000 are fit and healthy enough to take the most basic measure of fitness in the form of the IPPT. The alternate explanation is that not all eligible NSmen are called up for annual training, which renders a portion of the SAF a mere "paper" or "phantom" force. Both interpretations and the spectrum in between are not particularly flattering but provide crucial insights into the state of NS human resource challenges.

Aside from the issues of physical fitness and obesity, there is the question of ocular health. This is nowhere more apparent than in elite units, where near-perfect vision was once required. The first to relinquish this standard were the Singapore Guards, who in the past stipulated a maximum of 6/9 (shortsightedness of 75 degrees) for entry into the fraternity of heliborne infantry.[134] Next to feel the effects were the SAF Commandos with the use of prescription glasses (not ballistic shields, goggles or sunglasses) increasing among the ranks of conscript operators.[135] This challenge was far-reaching as the RSAF was forced to make concessions in order to arrest the shrinking pool of pilot trainees. The stringent 6/6 (perfect eyesight) standard of 1965 was revised to 6/9 in 1983 and 6/24 (100 degrees) in 1986.[136] Recruitment revisions in 2000 changed the "eyesight criterion for pilot applicants from 0-100 degrees per eye correctable to 6/6, with no colour blindness, to 0-300 degrees. In line with different operational demands, candidates with eyesight of up to 150 degrees can be streamed into

---

[133] "Reply by Minister for Defence Dr Ng Eng Hen to Parliamentary Question on IPPT and Cardiac Events", *MINDEF News Releases*, 17 Feb. 2012, https://www.mindef.gov.sg/oms/imindef/press_room/official_releases/ps/2012/17feb12_ps.html.

[134] The requirements to be a Guardsman at one time included: PES A medical status (i.e., deployable to all combat vocations), minimum height of 1.57m, minimum weight of 54kg, 6/9 eyesight, no criminal record, and at least Secondary 1 education. "SAF Display '81", *Pioneer* (Sept. 1981): 28; Edwin Pang, "Guardsmen: Ready to Strike", *Pioneer* (June 1989): 7–19; "SAF Guardsmen Get New Tab", *Straits Times*, 24 June 1989, p. 18; Malcolm Tay, "The Singapore Guards: Ready to Strike", *Pioneer* (July 2007): 23.

[135] See, for example, Jonathan Chan, "A Unique and Priceless Experience", *Army News* 191 (Aug. 2011): 10.

[136] Salma Khalik, "Air Force Relaxes Eyesight Rule", *Straits Times*, 16 Dec. 1986, p. 40; "RSAF Revises Eyesight Requirement", *Pioneer* (Jan. 1987): 15; "RSAF Pilots Say Lenses Are Easy on the Eye", *Straits Times*, 26 Sept. 1989, p. 24; "More Than Meets the Eye", *Pioneer* (Sept. 1989): 6.

flying fighter aircraft and helicopters, and those with more than 150 degrees into flying Transport aircraft."[137]

Also in 2000, a study indicated that 34 per cent of Singaporean children were shortsighted.[138] By 2014 it was noted that only 10 per cent of the 20,000-strong pool of NS recruits met RSAF requirements, with myopia affecting eight in ten.[139] It is little wonder that Singapore is crowned the myopia capital of the world, a somewhat ironic twist in its frequent quests to top national rankings. It would seem that the NDU is the only outfit to preserve the requirement for perfect vision given the unforgiving hazards of underwater operations. Only time will tell whether this obstacle proves insurmountable and how detrimental flow-on effects are to manning levels in the SAF.[140]

Aside from the issues of obesity, physical fitness and eyesight, the defence establishment is faced with the unique characteristics of the "Strawberry Generation". Like the fruit, these conscripts allegedly look good but are easily bruised. It is unknown whether they require more benefits than generations past or whether welfare was forced upon them. Parents today have more access to their sons' NS journeys than ever before. Fresh recruits at BMT can expect welcome gift packs on arrival that include a personalized EZ-Link (transport debit) card.[141] Each recruit has two buddies, with one assigned and one of personal choice.[142] Letters from family and loved ones are *sine qua non* during the weeklong field camps, which have led to recruits tearing from seeing their "mother's handwritten message" or from hearing a motivational speech.[143] A Parent Engagement Program keeps parents informed of their sons' progress on a weekly basis throughout BMT. It does not stop there: OCS also has a Home

---

[137] "New Entry Requirements for Aspiring Pilots", *Air Force News* 76 (Jan. 2001): 16.

[138] David Boey, "What Fewer Babies May Mean for SAF Planners", *Straits Times*, 17 Dec. 2003, p. 16.

[139] Jermyn Chow, "Soaring from Fledging to Aerial Fighting Force", *Straits Times*, 17 Feb. 2014.

[140] Benjamin Seet, Tien Yin Wong, Donald T.H. Tan, Seang Mei Saw, Vivian Balakrishnan, Lionel K.H. Lee and Arthur S.M. Lim, "Myopia in Singapore: Taking a Public Health Approach", *British Journal of Ophthalmology* 85, 5 (2001): 521–6.

[141] *My Son, the NSman: What Parents Should Know about NS* (Singapore: Central Manpower Base, MINDEF, 2007), p. 53; *Recruit's Handbook: A Guide through Basic Military Training* (Singapore: Central Manpower Base, MINDEF, 2007), p. 44.

[142] *My Son, the NSman*, p. 28; *Recruit's Handbook*, p. 34.

[143] "Recruits, You've Got Mail!" *Army News* 147 (Oct. –Nov. 2007), p. 2; Hedi Khoo, "His 'Tough Talk' Makes Them Cry", *New Paper*, 6 Sept. 2010.

Visitation Programme to keep parents abreast of training.[144] The Facebook pages of training schools are easily the most current of all SAF social media platforms to avoid the swift ire of overzealous folks should updates be delayed.

The top brass has adapted to the new generation of conscripts in the quest to elicit a strong response in terms of C2D. In 2011, then-COA MG Ravinder Singh stated, "In the past year, 357 NSFs chose to extend their service. This is about two percent or 1 in every 50. To me, this is a testament to our soldiers' dedication and a reflection of the Army's success in engaging them."[145] A year later, then-CDF LG Neo Kian Hong visited the Combat Engineers formation and praised conscript trainees attending a leadership course: "I salute you because your mere presence here symbolises your commitment and willingness to serve our country. It is very important for each of you, as commanders, to engage your soldiers and build a common sense of commitment and purpose."[146] Cynics invariably highlight that 49 of every 50 NSFs do not extend their service, and that conscripts wear the uniform not by choice but by law. Yet it is clear that morsels of optimism and praise are necessities in the context of peace, rising opportunity costs associated with conscription, and the limitations placed on where and how NSFs and NSmen can serve.

The latest improvement in terms of C2D allows conscripts to express an interest in certain vocations subject to organization requirements from 2017 onwards. Such initiatives were not required in days past but have today become the norm and, in due course, perhaps necessities. Service personnel today enjoy better food, field rations, personal equipment and benefits (notwithstanding the now defunct pension system) than ever before.[147] It is uncertain how such developments will impact operational capabilities, as these NSFs form the backbone of tomorrow's SAF as NSmen. One anecdotal measure is the deployment and employment of citizen-soldiers who volunteer for actual operations (and not mere exercises) where the stakes are real. Unfortunately, this metric indicates that the "Strawberry" moniker could very well be warranted

---

[144] Chia Han Sheng, "Home Support for Officer Cadets", *Army News* 154 (May–June 2008): 4.

[145] Jonathan Chan, "Every Soldier a Leader", *Army News* 190 (July 2011): 3.

[146] Bjorn Teo, "CDF Visits Engineer Formation", *Army News* 205 (Nov. 2012): 5.

[147] Dominic Nathan, "These Boots Are Made for Soldiering … in Singapore", *Straits Times*, 10 Oct. 1993, p. 23; "Gearing Up!" *Army News* 107 (Apr.–May 2004): 4–5; "Tracing the Hands That Feed Us", *Army News* 108 (May–June 2004): 6; "The Rationale for Our Rations", *Army News* 109 (June–July 2004): 6; Jonathan Chan, "Exercise in Greater Comfort", *Army News* 179 (Aug. 2010): 10; Ling Wei Chao, "Feeding Our Army! Providing Quality Meals and Services", *Army News* 193 (Oct. 2011): 3.

given the most recent SAF deployments to Afghanistan and Iraq where National Servicemen were a near non-feature.

If the quality of human capital was not enough of a concern for defence planners, then the declining quantity certainly is. The latter situation began with policies designed to arrest high birth rates in the lean economic years of early independence. The Singapore Family Planning and Population Board Bill passed on 1 January 1966 aimed "to direct and execute a five-year family planning project to reduce the present birth-rate by half".[148] In actual numbers this meant cutting the live birth rate from 30,000 to 20,000 and with the mortality rate of 5,000 resulted in a "manageable" net growth of 15,000 per annum.[149] The strategic approach was encapsulated in the "Stop at Two" campaign launched in 1971.[150] Parents with more than two children faced the prospects of a reduction in tax benefits, an increase in delivery fees, higher school fees for children of higher birth order, a limit on paid maternity leave, and negative effects in terms of primary school admission and subsidized housing.[151] Sterilization incentives were also implemented for those in the lower socio-economic group.[152] The targeted reduction in birth rate was met in 1973, but, like a runaway train, Singapore has experienced under-replacement since 1976.[153] In 1986 a new pronatal policy was implemented, captured in the slogans "At least Two" and "Three or More" if parents could afford it.[154] Yet there were also subliminal nuances in the message, with the educated and affluent encouraged to have more children while the less educated and poorer were discouraged.[155]

Socio-economic developments discussed earlier countered efforts to arrest dwindling birth rates. Indeed, an analysis on societal stability and durability by Chong Li Choy remains as relevant today as it was three decades ago. The

---

[148] "Birth Control Bill Passed", *Straits Times*, 2 Jan. 1966, p. 3.

[149] "Planned Families", *Straits Times*, 3 Jan. 1966, p. 8.

[150] Lim Keak Cheng, "Post-Independence Population Planning and Social Development in Singapore", *GeoJournal* 18, 2 (Mar. 1989): 166; Wan Fook Kee and Margaret Loh, "Singapore", *Studies in Family Planning* 5, 5 (May 1974): 163.

[151] Wan and Loh, "Singapore": 163–5; Peggy Teo, "Population Planning and Change in Singapore", *Population and Environment* 16, 3 (Jan. 1995): 243.

[152] Lim, "Post-Independence Population Planning and Social Development": 170.

[153] "Interview with DPM Wong Kan Seng, Minister-in-Charge of Population Issues", 16 Aug. 2006, https://www.ica.gov.sg/downloads/Interview.pdf, accessed 1 Nov. 2016.

[154] Lim, "Post-Independence Population Planning and Social Development": 171; Peggy Teo, "Population Planning and Change in Singapore", *Population and Environment* 16, 3 (Jan. 1995): 239.

[155] Kuldip Singh, Yoke Fai Fong and S.S. Ratnam, "A Reversal of Fertility Trends in Singapore", *Journal of Biological Social Science* 23, 1 (Jan. 1991): 74.

Singaporean professor in Switzerland knew where the difficulties in arresting fertility trends lay:

> This is due to the very successful family planning programme in Singapore. Not only have Singaporeans kept to the slogan of "stop at two" in their procreation pattern, but they have even come to the point where the population is no longer replacing itself. This is particularly so among Singaporeans who are more highly educated and economically better off. This has grave social and economic consequences for Singapore. Socially, those who are best able to support their children and to provide the best environment to nurture them are not producing enough children.[156]

The repercussions of such a trend are clear. The government of Singapore once projected a minimum of 50,000 live births annually "to sustain economic, defence and other national needs".[157] For defence this translates to roughly 25,000 conscripts annually, but actual intakes have displayed stochastic behaviour. A figure of 16,000 annually was cited at the turn of the millennium.[158] Figures from MINDEF publications placed average annual recruit numbers at 19,100 (1990–2005), 24,300 (2006–15) and 20,600 (2016–30).[159] The *Straits Times* chimed in with "[a]bout 21,000 males enlisted for national service in 2011. But given the declining birth rate, the number is expected to shrink to about 15,000 a year in future."[160] This is consistent with MINDEF, which is "already looking into how to deal with an impending manpower crunch, even though it will only happen 10 to 20 years down the road. The SAF is expecting a 20 percent drop in the number of conscripts by 2030."[161] If population trends remain unchanged, the annual intake of male recruits could be halved to between 10,000 and 12,500 by 2065.[162]

The SAF has proactively increased female participation in defence to compensate for the personnel deficit. The question of extending NS to women was mooted when the conscription question was first raised. The topic continues

---

[156] Chong, "Durable Stability with Prosperity and Legitimacy", pp. 179–80.

[157] Boey, "What Fewer Babies May Mean for SAF Planners", p. 16.

[158] C.S.C. Cheok, Y.G. Ang, W.M. Chew and H.Y. Tan, "Adjusting to Military Life: Servicemen with Problems Coping and Their Outcomes", *Singapore Medical Journal* 41, 5 (May 2000): 219.

[159] Keith Lin, "Full-time NS Cut by Six Months", *Pioneer* (July 2004): 9.

[160] Chow, "SAF to Recruit More Women", p. 1.

[161] Koh Eng Beng, "Strengths That Bind", *Cyberpioneer*, 2 July 2015.

[162] "Number of Women Recruits in SAF Doubled in 2014", *Straits Times*, 11 Feb. 2016.

to surface intermittently but has never come to fruition.[163] Three women were commissioned in 1967, and the first female OCC that targeted active-duty NCOs at SAFTI took place only in 1972. By 1976 there were only 13 officers among the 1,000-odd female uniformed personnel when an OCC to commission female logistics and manpower officers took place.[164] Beyond the SAF the PSC only increased the number of scholarship spots for women in the mid-1970s even though women have always been part of the civil service and the armed forces. In 1975 then-President Benjamin Sheares declared: "Meritocracy will be applied equally to women."[165]

Female Regulars have since broken various ceilings over the years in the male-dominated arena. At present there are over 1,500 women in combat vocations, and their numbers are increasingly steadily.[166] The SAF's short-term recruitment goal is to add another 500 by 2018 and eventually double the number of female combatants to 3,000.[167] This publicly stated goal will certainly be met and even exceeded. This is how things are done the Singapore way. Recruitment numbers in recent years have averaged 60 to 70 annually, with a third receiving education awards and scholarships tenable at polytechnics and universities.[168] The dedicated recruitment campaign kicked into overdrive and yielded a bumper crop of another 140 female Regulars in 2015.[169] That was, coincidentally, the same year that the SAF made history with its first female general. In 2016 an unprecedented 20 of the record 47 top-tier defence scholarships (SAFOS, SMS, DMS and SAFES) awarded went to females. The intangible and long-term impact of increasing female participation in defence remains to be seen. The worst-case scenario would be an exodus of male non-scholar-officers should

163 See "Woman Doctors' Views on NS Proposal", *Straits Times*, 19 Mar. 1976, p. 8; Philip Lee, "Women, This Is Your National Service", *Straits Times*, 10 Apr. 1983, p. 1; "The Straits Times Says Women's Real NS Role", *Straits Times*, 12 Dec. 1983, p. 18; "Why Women Should Do NS", *Straits Times*, 18 Dec. 1983, p. 21; "NS for Women? Not Yet", *Straits Times*, 5 Aug. 1991, p. 20; Mathew Pereira, "Reporting for Duty at the Front Line?" *Straits Times*, 23 Aug. 1992, p. 8; "45% of Women Say 'Yes' to NS", *TODAY*, 6 Mar. 2004, p. 3; "NS for Women? Yet Another Nay", *Straits Times*, 16 Mar. 2004, p. 4; Elgin Toh, "NS for Women a Hot Topic among Youths at Singapore Conversation", *Straits Times*, 11 May 2013; Jermyn Chow, "Let Women Choose to Do NS, Says Female Focus Group", *Straits Times*, 24 July 2013.

164 "New SAF Scheme to Train More Woman Officers", *Straits Times*, 20 June 1976, p. 7.

165 "PSC Will Pick More Girls for Oxford, Cambridge", *Straits Times*, 2 July 1975, p. 24.

166 Chan Luo Er, "SAF Promotes First Female to Brigadier-General Rank", Channel NewsAsia, 26 June 2015.

167 Chow, "SAF to Recruit More Women", p. 1.

168 Jermyn Chow, "Ready for Take-off, Madam General", *Straits Times*, 2 July 2015.

169 "Number of Women Recruits in SAF Doubled in 2014".

they perceive gender, in addition to scholarship status, to be a significant factor in promotions and postings. At present the only clarity is that society as a whole seems unfazed at best, or indifferent at worst, over the initiative. After all, armed conflict in defence of Singapore is unfathomable to most, and for many the spectre of terrorism is an afterthought realized only on television screens. The profession of arms seems destined to remain no different from any other occupation, and the ideals proffered by philosophers and consummate practitioners will long remain esoteric.

8.5   Summary

Singapore has made great economic progress in the last five decades. Postcolonial industrialization and a favourable investment climate have added to the city-state's strategic location as a transportation hub. The subsequent economic diversification has ensured that the country, while physically constrained, remains relevant on the global stage. The SAF has played its role as a silent sentinel, which has allowed society to enjoy the fruits of relative peace and prosperity. Yet the social changes along the relatively short journey of nationhood have ensured that each generation faces a different set of challenges from the one before. At times these are the result of yesterday's solutions, which seemed ingenious at the time but are certainly less so under present conditions. This will long be the conundrum facing those who govern and the governed.

The peace and progress enjoyed in Singapore have greatly benefited the local population. The conditions faced at independence have been consigned to history, and today much is taken for granted as privileges increasingly become entitlements. Materialism is a clear and present spectre, which has necessitated the alignment of remuneration for senior bureaucrats and politicians with the private sector. Such an alignment should not be equated with individual greed; rather, it is a reflection of a society that often equates tangible wealth with success. This is most telling as the cost of living rises and the divide separating rich and poor becomes more pronounced. Meritocracy built on educational excellence has served Singapore well, but the associated stress and social costs have increasingly bred discontentment. Students do not jump over educational hurdles alone; their families often share the same intimidating stresses, especially at major milestones in order to reach an educational goal (streaming, PSLE, A-Levels, etc.). There have been calls for a wider definition of meritocracy, but any changes will likely be slow in the shadow of an education-oriented system. Adding to the woes of materialism and the discontentment with meritocracy is the scourge of self-centredness. This was most evident in the breaking of bonds by a segment of government scholarship recipients. Career, rather than public service, was their motivation, yet this is simply a reflection of the socio-economic milieu in which they were conditioned.

There are those who have emigrated as the only means to escape the seemingly endless grind in Singapore. The law-abiding and educated English-speaking population faces few hurdles in transitioning to life overseas. Families with sons factor the opportunity costs of NS in their calculations. Official statistics for the period 2001 to 2011 indicate an increase in NS defaulter rates, which have remained low at less than 2.1 per cent. That said, enough prominent cases of default have taken place for concerned authorities to set sentencing guidelines. Some emigrants cite pessimistic factors such as a superficial sense of belonging, the quest for a better future, suppression of certain freedoms, faltering moral standards, and the seemingly unchecked influx of migrants as reasons to leave the city-state.

Emigration is certainly a concern for defence planners, but the more specific challenge is to address the declining quality and decreasing quantity of raw human capital. Ensuring that service personnel, especially National Servicemen, are physically fit while tackling the scourge of obesity is a perennial challenge. Obesity reflects the changing and more affluent lifestyles compared to earlier generations. The overall deterioration in ocular health has further shrunk the available manpower pool and forced the guards, commandos and even air force to relax their stringent entry requirements. The recent generation of servicemen may be the most educated in SAF history, but they have also been labelled as soft in physical and emotional terms. The problem is exacerbated by dwindling fertility rates, which have fallen short of replacement levels over the last four decades. Smaller families mean each child is more precious than before. The defence establishment has in turn proactively recruited female personnel to offset these deficiencies. The impact of increased female participation in defence will not be known for some time. Then again, it may never be known and could well fade into insignificance in the larger scheme of challenges facing Singapore.

CHAPTER 9

The Aristocracy of Armed Talent

"I should like to end as I begin, by exhorting Singaporeans to take more interest in the history of their country—its founding, development and progress. They will then realize the magnitude of the problems that have had to be faced, and the great achievements that have been accomplished."[1]

— Dr Goh Keng Swee (1918–2010)
Deputy Prime Minister (1973–84)

The honour of leading in uniform at the highest levels of the Ministry of Defence and the Singapore Armed Forces is bestowed on a very select few. Only 170 SAF officers wore the ranks of BG/RADM1/ME8 and above from independence in 1965 until 2018. Another six colonels— Andrew Lim Heng Tiew (COMD 9 DIV/CIO), Seah Poh Yeen (COMD MSTF), Seet Uei Lim (COMD 21 DIV/ CGO), Leung Shing Tai (COMD 6 DIV), Ho Kum Luen (COMD ACC) and Terry Tan Koon Woo (COMD CSSCOM)—are poised to join the Aristocracy of Armed Talent in due time. The common characteristics of the exclusive few are undoubtedly an irreproachable character, cognitive intelligence, competency and devotion to the profession of arms, strategic foresight, diplomatic acumen, and political trustworthiness. The sum of these traits is necessary to imbue confidence in peers and subordinates and to secure the trust of civilian defence bureaucrats and political appointees. An even more exclusive few are selected as members of the elite nucleus as service chiefs and CDF and entrusted to provide strategic direction for the defence establishment.

Several lines of inquiry were undertaken to paint a portrait of the military's top brass. Why were they motivated to sign on as Regulars? Why were they committed to staying on in the SAF? How did they ascend the rank hierarchy in terms of processes and organizational structure? The lived realities of 28

---

[1] Excerpts from speech delivered by Dr Goh Keng Swee, Deputy Prime Minister and Minister for Education, at the opening of the "150 Years of Development" Exhibition, Elizabeth Walk, 1 Aug. 1969. Reproduced in Goh Keng Swee, *The Economics of Modernization* (Singapore: Federal Publications, 1995), p. 146.

retired generals and admirals supported by an exhaustive survey of open-source literature provide the necessary insights. The assembled empirical data afford a deeper examination of the SAF Overseas Scholarship and several outliers among the military elites. Finally, the changing social character has thrown up a myriad of challenges that shrink the available personnel pool from which to produce the leaders of today and tomorrow. The conclusions drawn may be limited by the availability of information and difficulty in accessing certain open sources. Nevertheless, this book drew inspiration from *The Professional Soldier: A Social and Political Portrait* by Janowitz and represents the most detailed current account of the military elite in Singapore.

Motivation

Motivation to join the military is a story that began before Singapore achieved self-governance as a British colony and subsequently independence from Malaysia. For the SAF's pioneering generals, their common reasons were grounded in a hardy upbringing where the outdoors and the playground were one and the same. The military appealed to the sense of adventure, and the uniform spoke of regimental discipline—even though a stigma was generally attached to the profession of arms. Most were simply seeking to make the most of what life and their individual situations offered. BG (RET) Thomas Campbell joined the Straits Settlement Volunteer Force in 1940, when Britain was already at war in Europe. He would pay the price of uniformed service when Singapore fell on 15 February 1942. Forced labour on the railway of death in Siam gave way to incarceration at Singapore's infamous Changi Prison. Campbell later sought an officer's commission, having seen the horrors of war. For BG (RET) Patrick Sim and LG (RET) Winston Choo the opportunity to train at a foreign military college was an extension of school days divided between books, sports and uniformed activities. Both would see combat as junior officers when the 1st Battalion, Singapore Infantry Regiment, was deployed to Pulau Sebatik during *Konfrontasi*. These three are the only SAF generals ever to have faced a shot fired in anger.

Singapore's independence in 1965 unexpectedly delivered nationhood. The city-state had no hinterland, and its only natural resources were its strategic location along the Malacca Straits and the people within its borders. This meant Singapore would not be ignored, but the population sometimes had more that divided than united them. Defence was overshadowed by the greater economic concerns of employment, industrialization and foreign investment. That changed with the accelerated British withdrawal from Singapore. Against this backdrop, Singapore's defence architect, Dr Goh Keng Swee, made three key decisions together with PM Lee Kuan Yew. First, he personally tapped Administrative Officers who were not merely graduates but also had the brawn and necessary character for secondment from the civil service to the SAF as regular officers. They were not promised any reward except to answer the nation's call, serve a pressing need, and entertain an innate interest for uniformed service. BG (RET) Kirpa Ram Vij (commissioned as a part-time volunteer in 1960) and BG (RET) Tan Chin Tiong (commissioned as a National Serviceman in 1968) both cut their teeth under Goh's relentless crucible of testing appointments and received their due rewards before returning to the Administrative Service.

Goh's second decision was the creation of SAFTI, where Vij played an instrumental role in turning plans for an indigenous cradle of the SAF Officer Corps into reality. The institute, which has become synonymous with training excellence today, accepted the first cohort of trainees within ten months of independence; and 117 were commissioned as officers on 16 July 1967. The famed all-Regular First Batch laid the foundations of excellence and proved instrumental in the expansion, development and modernization of the SAF. LG (RET) Ng Jui Ping, BG (RET) Gary Yeo, BG (RET) Patrick Choy, BG (RET) Colin Theseira and BG (RET) Chin Chow Yoon would emerge as the highest-ranking among their trailblazing peers. Few had clear-cut ambitions, and the prospects of a military career were both intriguing and unknown. Some of these generals were motivated by the prospect of doing something new and more interesting than their pre-military occupations (most notably teaching), the competitive starting salaries, and the physical fitness demanded by the rigours of military life. One cited the desire to repay the bursary he had received for his education and took on the challenges necessary to earn status as a commissioned officer. Regardless of their individual motivations to sign on, nothing quite prepared the officers for the mental and physical challenges that lay ahead when they walked through the front gates of SAFTI on 1 June 1966.

The third of Goh's decisions was the implementation of National Service in a stepwise manner. The first 848 men reported for full-time NS in August 1967 with 3 and 4 SIR, after which civil servants and then university graduates followed suit. Early teething problems included the small core of Regular cadre, infrastructure limitations, a shoestring budget, and administrative uncertainty over NS eligibility. The latter was clarified by legislation in 1970 for the universal conscription of all eligible males born on or after 1 January 1949. NS has since become a central feature in the career decisions of the military elites. Conscription obligated them to wear the uniform, but an overwhelming majority never actively pursued a career in the SAF until they were motivated to do so at various junctures. The lived experiences gleaned from their interviews suggested a dichotomy of motivation into primary and secondary categories. The former included factors that were necessary and sufficient to sign on, while the latter were necessary but insufficient reasons.

The first of the five primary motivations was the host of military scholarships and awards designed to attract the "best and brightest" from the annual crop of conscripts. The scholar-officers who received the SAF Overseas Scholarship (now known as the SAF Scholarship), and also those bestowed the Overseas Training Award (Graduating) (presently called the SAF Merit Scholarship), were educated at the best British and US universities on a full salary, generous allowances and other attractive benefits. It was an opportunity to head overseas and live independently, with an education and remuneration package that would otherwise be beyond reach for the majority. The SAF was seen as the best employment opportunity at that point in time for those who did not receive a military scholarship. They had already gained some military experience and in all cases had performed well as conscripts. Most of these officers signed on only towards the end of their NS, while others were non-military scholarship recipients and graduates who chose to serve their bond in the SAF. In the case of medical officers, their motivation was not grounded in scholarships or employment opportunities but in an atypical medical career. More lucrative pathways lay elsewhere, but the SAF afforded them an avenue to practise medicine in an unconventional and increasingly international environment beyond "four walls and a patient". The SAF also attracted engineers and officers in platform-centric vocations keen to gain technical competence and work on cutting-edge technology. Finally, there were the few among the military elite who harboured a genuine interest in the military seeded through a variety of vicarious experiences from an early age. The SAF presented the perfect environment for them to realize their boyhood dreams.

The first of five secondary motivations was the salary, which was attractive to the majority. For scholar-officers the salaries and allowances alleviated their families' financial needs. The SAF pay met the needs of non-graduates and was competitive compared to other options available. Medical officers would not earn a surgeon's pay, but remuneration was pegged to a respectable level that reflected the challenging nature of uniformed service. Those with higher education levels, namely non-military scholars and non-medical graduates, were the most disadvantaged. Dismal recruitment and retention figures eventually led to a correction of this issue, with the drastic salary revisions of 1982. Salaries since then have been pegged to the civil service and private sector, with a premium for the arduous and relatively short military career.

The second motivation was flying. This was cited as a childhood ambition for quite a number of officers, but few actually made the cut as military pilots.

In fact, there was no certainty of earning one's wings, and all simply started out entertaining the possibility and took their best shot if given the chance.

In contrast to flying, the motivation for a naval career was not as straightforward given the RSN's initial low priority among the three services. Some of the early admirals took up a scholarship offered by the navy, others sought to utilize their maritime-related skills and education, and some of the early scholar-officers were simply channelled into the service. As time passed, the strategic importance of the navy in ensuring that sea lines of communication remained open became apparent. A strong familial sense among members and the frequent deployment of assets on expeditionary operations afar created new motivations for naval service. The SAF also benefited from those who wanted to escape conscription because of the less than appealing conditions in the army, the paltry NS allowances that paled in comparison to a Regular's salary, and a more fruitful utilization of 24 to 30 months of their lives. Finally, the family served as a secondary motivation when encouragement and approval was given for the choice to sign on. This was not always forthcoming in the earlier days due to the stigma and tough life associated with a military career. It is less of a concern today, as the SAF career has become a known commodity.

Commitment

SAF officers are motivated by various factors to sign on, but history indicates that only around a third remain on active service beyond the initial Minimum Term of Service. There are different reasons for leaving active duty: the lure of opportunities beyond the SAF, the exhaustion of front-loaded benefits, a society that did not and perhaps still does not accord the profession of arms with adequate respect, discontentment with the practice of meritocracy, disillusionment and cynicism, and factors unique to individual circumstances. Half of the interview participants considered leaving but decided otherwise for reasons similar to those who never considered leaving. Their reasons for staying on were a combination of transactional and transformational commitment.

Transactional commitment is grounded in egotistical considerations, where the individual is the ultimate beneficiary of his or her goals and actions. The first form of this commitment is the legal or contractual obligation to remain in service. This is usually in the form of an initial bond or a Minimum Term of Service. These terms varied but were around eight (subsequently revised to six) years for scholar-officers, six for non-scholars and medical officers, and 12 for pilots. Such obligations were invariably extended with attendance at additional military courses, postgraduate studies, specific postings, and receipt of a meritorious promotion. This remains the best way for the SAF to ensure a sound return on investment, and officers who break such contracts are liable for stiff financial penalties. Remuneration also elicited transactional commitment, but it was a reason to stay on in its own right. The military today pays its officers well enough to ensure their families are taken care of and allow them to concentrate fully on the tasks at hand. In fact, some officers even considered the SAF salary to be less than what they could earn in a civilian capacity. The reason that remuneration proved a non-factor for these officers is attributed to career satisfaction and progression. Some made comparisons with peers, while others had an idea of where they should be within the rank hierarchy by a certain age.

While the interview participants indicated varying degrees of transactional commitment, they invariably converged towards transformational commitment. This form of commitment is anchored in altruistic reasons that seek to benefit and maximize the welfare of others. The first factor was the people they worked with and was grounded in the familial setting and established camaraderie with subordinates, peers and superiors. Commitment to remain on active duty was about playing their part and not disappointing those who depended on them during peacetime and ultimately for operations if the need ever arose. This is a crucial dimension of commitment if the military is to be operationally ready and maintain its combat effectiveness. Yet it is disappointing, albeit expected, that a few interview participants found reciprocity wanting at times. While the people were important, they shared centre stage with commitment to the military profession and the concomitant importance of the sacred mission apportioned to the armed forces. Within the former, the military elites saw it as their personal responsibility as leaders and subject matter experts to maintain the high standards demanded of the profession of arms in Singapore. Commitment to the mission was intertwined with people and the profession and was more than just having something new and exciting to do. Commitment was in varying degrees based on the importance of the tasks assigned, the sense of self-fulfilment, and ensuring that at the very least the defence establishment was no worse off under their watch.

There were instances where commitment was stretched beyond simply remaining on active service. These usually came in the form of hazards inherent to the military career and environment. While three of the early generals saw direct combat, most of the risks to life and limb since then have occurred during training incidents or from overexertion when pushing physical limits. Such is the price of realistic training and leadership by example. It must be highlighted that categories that surfaced for the motivation to sign on and the commitment to stay on revealed by the interview participants are not necessarily different from those in the rank of COL/ME7 and below. Their lived experiences could in fact be even more limited than the much larger pool of non-flag ranks.

Ascension

Career motivation and commitment explain why officers join and remain in Singapore's defence establishment. The key processes of performance appraisals and potential estimation, on the other hand, determine promotions and postings. The associated organizational structure supports the rank hierarchy and provides the pathways for officer ascension to take place. The processes that governed the careers of officers in the early SAF were plagued with problems. Appraisals were frequently determined by personality, localized unit conditions, and rather vague guidelines. Potential was often an afterthought given the premium placed on performance. Promotions were not automatically warranted upon completion of the necessary paperwork but also included exams and promotion interviews for junior officers. There was also the time-in-rank requirement applicable to most across the hierarchy. One saving grace was Goh's tireless effort to get to know many officers, and he personally approved promotion lists at the higher echelons. Yet as the SAF manpower pool grew, the risks associated with individual-centric processes became evident. Officers would lose faith in a frail system if the unscrupulous succeeded in perpetuating cronyism and patronage through cliques.

The military establishment's quest to strengthen the ascension processes led to the adaptation of modified practices from Shell Oil in 1982. Every officer since then has been assessed annually for realized performance matched against a list of key performance indicators, and the anticipated potential of an individual gauged against a list of characteristics. The measurements of performance and potential are subjective to some extent, but they are an improvement on pre-1982 practices. Performance grades are subjected to a standardized bell curve to account for strict and lenient assessors but with adequate flexibility to reward deserving officers. Processes have been made more robust through a series of checks and balances that require consensus from various panels and different levels of superiors. Processes that govern promotions and postings have also been strengthened and streamlined before recommendations are approved by higher echelons. Promotions are no longer bounded by time norms, exams are woven into milestone courses, and ranks are today bestowed on officers who perform consistently well and have the potential to serve at the rank. Posting considerations commence with a list of shortlisted officers who meet the prerequisites of prior experiences, relevant courses, potential estimation, superior's recommendations, and intangibles such as character and temperament. Those tapped for command billets starting with the army battalion, navy ship, and air force squadron and upward come even under greater scrutiny.

Realities do not always turn out neatly even though the guidelines for ascension are stipulated. Consensus remains a cornerstone requirement, and this practice is only as effective as the panel members' knowledge of the subordinates being appraised. Any shortcomings have ripple effects. Attributes such as education level, the scholarship received, and whether one was a Wrangler can all exert undue influence and overshadow a holistic view of the appraisee. This could force panels into adopting strict or lenient postures while others simply group officers they do not know safely at the centre of the ranking list. The effect of positive or negative biases can also be amplified due to the absence of opposing views. At worst, collective failure is possible should rankings be altered unilaterally without adequate explanation or queries by panel members bent on appeasing the panel chairperson. Whether this has ever occurred is unknown.

Promotions and postings have at times generated similar controversies. Some scholar-officers hold command despite earlier indicators contrary to expectations. They have been given the benefit of the doubt and second chances. At other times an officer with a higher estimated career potential is given posting preference over a seemingly more capable officer albeit one with a lower estimated career potential. Greater scrutiny becomes even more crucial at the highest echelons. Promotions to colonel and above and related appointments are recommended by the elite nucleus, seconded by senior defence bureaucrats, and approved at the political echelon. Even at this senior level it must be recognized that the billets held by colonels vary in importance, prestige and visibility. Even NSmen can climb to such lofty heights as deputy squadron commanders, brigade commanders, and division Chief of Staff. In contrast, every general and admiral reflects not only technical competency and the importance of an appointment, but also the distinct blend of military professionalism, critical responsibility, impeccable character, diplomatic acumen and political trustworthiness.

Ascension into the Aristocracy of Armed Talent is not only determined by administrative processes but is also a function of the organizational structure in place. The appointments in which officers earn their first star have devolved from the defence chief to service chief and are now made up by various key command and staff positions across the SAF and at MINDEF. The numbers of military elites reflect the maturity of the armed forces through the operational capabilities of key formations, the roles of vital staff departments, and the relevance and importance of a bilateral relationship. Premium is placed on command and staff tours at the expense of instructional roles. The development of SAF officers commences with pre-commissioning training, and junior tours provide a thorough grounding in vocational tradecraft. Command and Staff College is the gateway for senior officership and prepares the crème de la crème of the SAF Officer Corps for command of a battalion, ship or squadron. Those who perform well can expect further rotations between command and staff appointments interspersed with postgraduate studies and perhaps attendance at War College. It would seem cookie-cutter templates have been established across the services. This means multiple battalion-brigade-division command routes for combat and combat support officers in the army. Combat service support officers are more limited, with CSS Command their sole command billet for generalship. Fortunes have changed for signals officers with the gradual widening of ascension pathways beyond the formation to include the JCISD and now the SAF C4 Command. For naval officers the milestone commands usually comprise a ship-squadron-flotilla route followed by either the RSN Fleet or the MSTF. The variation for air force officers seems much greater depending on vocation. Pilots once sought to complete the flatter squadron-air base command, while those in C3 and GBAD mirrored the army template of squadron-brigade-division. The 2007 reorganization has brought a more consistent template across the vocations, with squadron-group-Operational Command the likely norm. Naturally, there are exceptions to such established pathways.

The organizational structure seems to advantage certain vocations while others remain restricted by their respective specializations. The vocational composition of the military elite is skewed towards combat (infantry, armour, commando, guards) and combat support (artillery, combat engineer) officers in the army, pilots (especially fighter) and AWO (C3) in the RSAF, and naval combat officers specialized in surface strike warfare in the RSN. These vocations have inherent advantages given their greater ascension routes and appointments in which officers can earn their first star. In contrast, other vocations such as engineers, logisticians, medical officers and army signals officers are seemingly disadvantaged by the intense competition and an organizational structural that offers very few appointments (if any) where they can make one-star. Whether this will change depends on the invariable need to reorganize to meet future requirements.

Scholars and Stars

One unique facet of the defence establishment that warrants frequent scrutiny (behind closed doors at least) is the scholarship system. The SAF Overseas Scholarship was designed to entice the best and brightest within the annual cohort of school leavers to a career in uniform. This scheme is pitched as a passport to success with an accelerated ascension pathway, and its recipients—with the majority being alumni of Raffles and Hwa Chong—are depicted as a national resource. The aura surrounding these scholars is undeniable given the mix of recruitment advertisements, selective examples, and certain overgeneralized academic proclamations that only perpetuate tales of success. Empirical evidence from the 197 SAFOS awarded from 1971 to 1998 indicates 108 officers reached the ranks of COL/ME7 and above, with 68 wearing one or more stars. This means one general or admiral emerged from the ranks of every three SAFOS awarded. The 68 SAFOS flag officers represented two-fifths of Singapore's military elite, but their numbers were not uniformly distributed across the vocations. This fact makes clear that one does not need the SAFOS to earn a star but the best among these scholar-officers have come to dominate the elite nucleus as service chiefs and ultimately as the CDF.

Success stories of the SAFOS scheme are trumpeted, while the scheme's shortcomings are less conspicuous. Every SAFOS cohort from 1971 to 1995 produced at least one flag officer, but the 1996 batch became the first to buck the trend: all the scholars from that year departed active service mid-career. The ranks of the batches of 2001 and 2002 are also perilously thin. It remains to be seen whether they too will meet with active-duty extinction, although statistics may have already provided early assurance to the remaining officers of their place as generals and admirals. There were also episodes of a perceived exodus of SAFOS recipients from the signals and armour formations. The former was once plagued by limited ascension opportunities, which resulted in departures from active duty or obliged the more ambitious to seek revocation. This is no longer the case, with signals officers today being forerunners for prime positions in the SAF C4 Command, MIO, and C4I Community. The case of the armour formation is more recent and somewhat more puzzling given the vocation's rank mobility and uncapped possibilities. The reasons nine of the 13 armour officers from the SAFOS cohorts of 1989 to 2005 resigned in the ranks of CPT to LTC remain unknown.

The edge that SAFOS affords to its recipients is clear despite any shortcomings with the scheme thus far. The benefits go beyond the world-class education, salary and allowances, networking opportunities, closely managed career pathways, and possibility of a dual-career in the Administrative Service. For those who turn potential into reality, this means earning their first star some five years earlier than their non-SAFOS counterparts. Their tenures as one-stars are also longer by a year on average, although scholarship status is inconsequential for two- and three-star members of the elite nucleus. As a result of their accelerated careers, it is not surprising that SAFOS flag officers conclude their active service some 4.5 years younger than non-SAFOS officers. Their transition to post-SAF careers seem managed for them, with the majority moving to positions in the government and affiliated entities. This is where privilege from the military ends; subsequent success depends very much on the individual. The sole case of an individual being stripped of the premier military scholarship further illustrates some of the inherent advantages. Attendance at CSC comes four to six years earlier and promotion to MAJ six years faster for SAFOS recipients vis-à-vis other above-average officers.

Appointments, flag rank and ascension trajectory may seem deterministic, but there are outliers. The pioneering members of the military elite were formed from the ranks of volunteers (Thomas Campbell), the Old Guard of the SIR (Patrick Sim, Winston Choo), and Administrative Officers (Kirpa Ram Vij, Tan Chin Tiong) on secondment to the SAF. All had unique careers shaped by the challenging socio-economic and evolving geopolitical environment of the time. Attempts were made to establish norms, but changes to them would continue to arise time and again. Lee Hsien Loong and George Yeo are the youngest to have made BG—at age 32 and 34 respectively—and departed active service within 83 and 43 days of their promotions to enter the political arena. Yeo Cheng Ann and Tan Huck Gim, two highly respected field commanders, were asked to represent Singapore at the highest echelons of United Nations peacekeeping operations. Both earned distinction for Singapore and the SAF on their respective tours of duty, and they were bestowed a higher rank albeit on a temporary basis (i.e., a local rank). However, the local rank was rescinded and they reverted to their original ranks. They were not demoted, but outsiders would not know that. Then there are those in established one-star billets who were never forwarded to the next rank and instead bypassed for promotion. Michael Low and Wong Yu Han completed their respective division command tours, while James Soon was the RSN Fleet Commander. All three retired as colonels, and the reasons why the star eluded them will probably never be known. On the flip side it seems Gan Siow Huang made BG while ostensibly moving from one colonel appointment into another. It is speculated that the role of Director (Special Projects) and its associated responsibilities warranted the rank. The only certainty is that gender and the concomitant publicity for recruitment efforts were not factors in Gan's promotion: that would have denigrated both the rank and the individual. In any case, Gan moved on to an established general's appointment as COMD APGC.

A select few from among the one-stars emerge periodically to form the elite nucleus and provide strategic direction for the various services and the SAF as a whole. The 13 officers who have served as Chief of Army indicate that division command is mandatory before hitting a fork in the ascension pathway. One route takes the future COA through the most senior one-star tours as DJOPD/COS-JS or DJID. The second is an ephemeral stop as COS-GS to observe the army from the vantage point as its number two soldier. Over in the naval services, seven of the ten who had the privilege to lead as Chief of Navy commenced their ascension as Fleet Commander. This was usually followed by a structured mix of staff billets as HNO, COS-NS or DJOPD/COS-JS. The ascension pathway for the nine men at the helm of the RSAF as the Chief of Air Force commenced with command of an airbase and, since the 2007 reorganization, an Operational Command. This is frequently followed by senior staff appointments such as HAO, DJO, COS-AS, DJOPD/COS-JS and, more recently, DMI/Chief C4I. Succession planning normally affords MINDEF-SAF the luxury of selecting its service chiefs from a pool of quality one-star candidates. In a more calibrated manner, one emerges from among the three service chiefs as the *primus inter pares* and becomes Singapore's top military officer as the three-star Chief of Defence Force.

Changing Character

The military establishment has weathered a host of manpower challenges over the years. Responsible leadership and a good dose of patience were necessary to stop the rejection of the military as a career with its relatively low education levels, comparatively harsh training methods, and questionable discipline and morale. All this took place against the backdrop of a city-state seeking to find relevance by ensuring its place in the region and modernizing rapidly to make a mark on the global stage. Singapore succeeded in many ways within a short period, but certain solutions to the problems of yesteryear pose challenges to contemporary and future defence requirements. The "tyranny of peace" continues to challenge society's commitment to defence because national security is far removed from the daily concerns of the city-state's inhabitants. Economic success through industrialization and a hunger for material well-being made the country rich. Yet materialism also made it necessary for the civil service, including the security services, and political echelons to peg salaries to the private sector. The sacrifices of a military career must be adequately compensated in order to retain the very best talent. Beyond such an oxymoron, there are those who decry the loss of the Singapore soul (loss of community spirit, multiple tears in the social fabric, and self-centredness) in the quest for material riches, which, as in many other countries, serves to widen the gap between rich and poor. Others simply could not care less. As long as wants are met, everything is in excellent order for the elites who govern and the governed masses. Or so it seems.

Meritocracy with its foundation in educational excellence has served as a foundational pillar in Singapore's development. The crucible is designed simply to separate the best from the rest. Disproportionate resources are then spent to groom selected individuals in the quest to turn identified potential into lived reality. This critical aspect of social Darwinism has come under criticism for its narrow focus but remains the key concern of most parents. Change will come very slowly as long as the Pavlovian mindset of pegging success to scholastic achievements and subsequent material abundance maintains social primacy. The challenge is compounded by a segment of elite scholars who place individual pursuits above the nation. For them it is all about entry into a caste of social prestige. The associated bonds prove to be mere financial contracts that can be made and broken without any social obligation. Financial penalties and public castigation via naming and shaming for breaking bonds are no longer a deterrent, not in the shadow of perceived opportunity costs on the global stage in the digital age.

The broad challenges of materialism and meritocracy for defence are further compounded by the demographic threats of emigration, migration, health trends among potential recruits, and decreasing birth rates. Emigration and migration are double-edged swords. Singapore stands to gain greatly if its citizens venture overseas, broaden their horizons, and return with essential skills. The question is always whether they will return and whether they will be welcomed. In a similar fashion, Singapore gains from skilled migrants and transitory workers. It remains to be seen whether these groups will gain the critical mass to have an impact on the nation's identity in national, cultural and religious terms. In the case of minted citizens it becomes a question of loyalty and whether Singapore is home or a mere stepping stone for an easier transition elsewhere.

Amidst the quest of turning "us and them" into a collective "we" lies the deleterious twin effects of health trends among potential recruits and decreasing birth rates. Obesity due to affluence and its influence on diets and lifestyles, lingering questions over physical fitness, the plague of deteriorating ocular health, and the perceived Strawberry Generation do not help with the defence situation. The four-decade-long general trend of decreasing birth rates shrinks an already small population even further. If one likens the manpower pool to the proverbial candle, then it is currently burning from both ends, slowed only by the perceived panacea of advanced technology.

The effort to recruit more women into the defence force has gained traction to arrest the tide of decreasing quality and quantity of available servicemen. The goal to double the number of female combatants from 1,500 to 3,000 will be met given the high-level backing and generous recruitment enticements. Furthermore, the low possibility of deployment in harm's way and geographical limitations in postings make the uniformed career attractive for Singapore's daughters today. One key concern is how male non-scholar-officers will take this initiative given they are already up against male scholar-officers. Any perception of gender bias in promotions and postings is currently the clearest latent fault line.

There are those who will take umbrage at this study, from those who believe that all is well with the armed forces to those who believe that only a well made-up and glossy—even if fictitious—image should be presented. The latter would like the SAF to be a citizens' army, but those who fill its ranks should not question or only know about the institution in selective terms. Transparency is a threat to them, perhaps one greater than any identifiable enemy at the gate, and not a source of strength or an avenue of accountability. Then again, transparency and accountability in the armed forces have always been the privilege of a select few, with the exception of parliamentary questions. Society at large is ignorant of military affairs. National Education has socially engineered a sense of patriotism, and "duty, honour, country" has entrenched itself in the lexicon of the SAF. The difficulty in times of peace is differentiating between style and substance, words and deeds.

The lived realities of retired military elites captured in this book have elucidated the challenges faced, crises weathered, and conditions endured from past years. The quixotic Huntingtonian ideal of military service as a sacred duty with sacrifices may have proven elusive, and for most it was the amalgamation of Moskosian institutional and occupational characteristics. The candid lived realities captured in this volume reveal frailties that made military elites human and identify various drivers that allowed and aided their career mobility. These leaders also ensured that enough quality individuals were retained to succeed them and eventually constitute the present Aristocracy of Armed Talent. Whether the top brass of the future will possess the same motivation, commitment, passion and conviction as their predecessors is unknown. The only certainty seems to be the evolving character of each generation and the need to win their commitment to defence time and again. The battle for the hearts, minds and souls of tomorrow's leaders is unquestionably the greatest challenge faced by Singapore's military elites today.

Appendix A

Year of authorization to wear BG/RADM1/ME8 and post-SAF career (1965–2018)

S/N	Year of First Star	Rank and Name	Appointment when Promoted	Estimated Year of Birth	Age in Year of First Star	SAFOS	Year of Leaving SAF	Years in Flag Rank	Post-SAF Career or Current Active-Duty Military Appointment
1	1965	BG Thomas James Duncan Campbell	COMD Singapore Brigade	1922	43	–	1971	6	Principal, St. Stephen's School (1971–73); emigrated to Perth (1973); passed away on 20 October 1989
2	1972	BG Kirpa Ram Vij	DGS	1935	37	–	1974	2	DS Ministry of National Development (MND) (1974–75); Ambassador to Egypt (1975–79); DIR, Civil Service Institute/DS in Ministry of Science and Technology (1979–81); Executive Chairman, Neptune Agencies (1991); General Manager (GM), Neptune Orient Lines (1981–95); CEO Gateway-Distriparks; Vice President (VP), Indian Education Trust

S/N	Year of First Star	Rank and Name	Appointment when Promoted	Estimated Year of Birth	Age in Year of First Star	SAFOS Year	Year of Leaving SAF	Years in Flag Rank	Post-SAF Career or Current Active-Duty Military Appointment
3	1976	BG Winston Choo Wee Leong [retired as LG]	DGS	1941	35	–	1992	16	Deputy Chairman, Central Provident Fund Board/Chairman, Chartered Industries of Singapore (1992–94); High Commissioner to Australia (1994–97); Chairman, Singapore Red Cross Society (1996–2008); High Commissioner (Non-Resident) to Papua New Guinea (2000–06); Ambassador (Non-Resident) to Israel (since 2006); Chairman, Metro Holdings (since July 2007); Honorary President, Boys Brigade Singapore (since February 2012)
4	1978	L/BG Patrick Sim Hak Kng [retired as BG]	COMD 3 DIV	1936	42	–	1981	3	Stockbroker; Executive DIR, Singapore Association for the Blind; GM, Serangoon Country Club; passed away on 23 June 2017
5	1980	BG Tan Chin Tiong	DCGS	1944	36	–	1982	2	2PS (1982–85) and later PS MHA (1985–93) Chairman, CISCO (1986); PS MOF (1993–95); PS MITA (1995–97); PS MFA (1997–2004);

(cont'd overleaf)

Appendix A *(cont'd)*

S/N	Year of First Star	Rank and Name	Appointment when Promoted	Estimated Year of Birth	Age in Year of First Star	SAFOS Year	Year of Leaving SAF	Years in Flag Rank	Post-SAF Career or Current Active-Duty Military Appointment
									Ambassador to Japan (2004–12); DIR (2012–18) and Senior Adviser (since January 2018), ISEAS; Ambassador-at-Large MFA (since March 2012)
6	1984	BG Lee Hsien Loong	DJOPD/COS-GS	1952	32	1971	1984	0	Political Secretary (Defence) (1984); Member of Parliament (since 1984); MOS for Trade and Industry, and Defence (1984–87); Second Minister (Services) for Defence (1987–90); Minister for Trade and Industry (1987–92); DPM (1990–2004); Chairman, MAS (1998–2004); Minister for Finance (2001–07); Secretary-General, People's Action Party (since 2004); Prime Minister (since 2004); Chairman, Government of Singapore Investment Corporation (since June 2011)

S/N	Year of First Star	Rank and Name	Appointment when Promoted	Estimated Year of Birth	Age in Year of First Star	SAFOS Year	Year of Leaving SAF	Years in Flag Rank	Post-SAF Career or Current Active-Duty Military Appointment
7	1986	BG Chin Siat Yoon	DJID	1949	37	–	1995	9	Ambassador to Thailand (1990–94); Singapore Trade Representative to Taiwan (1995–96); Ambassador to Germany (1996–97); Ambassador to China (1998–2012); Ambassador to Japan (2012–17)
8	1986	BG Ng Jui Ping [retired as LG]	COS-GS/ ACGS (Ops)	1948	38	–	1995	9	Deputy Chairman, CPF Board (1995–96); Chairman, Chartered Industries of Singapore (1995–96); Executive Chairman, August Kennedy Consultancy (1995–98); Chairman, ST Automotive (1996); Chairman, Ordnance Development & Engineering of Singapore (1996); CEO and Group Chairman, Horizon Education and Technologies Ltd. (1999–2004); Founder, August Asia Consulting (2004); VP, Football Association of Singapore

(cont'd overleaf)

Appendix A *(cont'd)*

S/N	Year of First Star	Rank and Name	Appointment when Promoted	Estimated Year of Birth	Age in Year of First Star	SAFOS Year	Year Leaving SAF	Years in Flag Rank	Post-SAF Career or Current Active-Duty Military Appointment
9	1987	BG Boey Tak Hap	COS-GS/ ACGS (Ops)	1952	35	1971	1990	3	Deputy CE (Finance & Planning) (1990–95) and later CEO (1995), Public Utilities Board; President and CEO, Singapore Power (1995–2001); President and CEO, SMRT Corp (2002); Non-executive Chairman, Jurong Engineering (2003)
10	1987	BG Michael Teo Eng Cheng	COMD RSAF	1947	40	–	1992	5	High Commissioner to New Zealand (1994–96); Ambassador to South Korea (1996–2001); High Commissioner to the UK (2002–11); High Commissioner to Australia (2011–14)
11	1988	RADM1 James Leo Chin Lian	COMD RSN	1946	42	–	1991	3	Executive DIR, Port of Singapore Authority (1991–95); Chairman, Chartered Industries of Singapore (1991–95); Executive Chairman, Singapore Shipbuilding Engineering (renamed ST Shipbuilding and Engineering) (1995–97)

S/N	Year of First Star	Rank and Name	Appointment when Promoted	Estimated Year of Birth	Age in Year of First Star	SAFOS Year	Year of Leaving SAF	Years in Flag Rank	Post-SAF Career or Current Active-Duty Military Appointment
12	1988	BG George Yeo Yong Boon	DJOPD	1954	34	1973	1988	0	Member of Parliament (1988–2011); MOS for Finance and Foreign Affairs (1988–90); Senior MOS for Foreign Affairs (1990–91); Acting Minister (1990–91) and later Minister for Information and the Arts (1991–99); Second Minister for Foreign Affairs (1991–94); Chairman, Young PAP (1991–2000); Minister for Health (1994–97); Second Minister (1997–99) and later Minister for Trade and Industry (1999–2004); Minister for Foreign Affairs (2004–11); Vice Chairman (since January 2012) and later Executive DIR (since November 2013), Kerry Group (HK) (part of Kuok Group in Hong Kong and China)
13	1989	BG Gary Yeo Ping Yong	Deputy COMD RSAF/ COS-AS	1946	43	–	1993	4	Deputy President, Singapore Aerospace (1993)

(cont'd overleaf)

Appendix A *(cont'd)*

S/N	Year of First Star	Rank and Name	Appointment when Promoted	Estimated Year of Birth	Age in Year of First Star	SAFOS Year	Year of Leaving SAF	Years in Flag Rank	Post-SAF Career or Current Active-Duty Military Appointment
14	1990	BG Patrick Choy Choong Tow	COMD 3 DIV	1947	43	–	1996	6	Ambassador to Myanmar (1996–99); Senior VP/DIR (International Marketing), ST Kinetics (2000); Executive VP (Strategic Marketing), ST Kinetics/Executive VP (International Marketing), ST Engineering; Executive VP/Chief Marketing Officer, ST Land Systems; Executive VP (Strategic Programs), ST Engineering
15	1991	BG Lim Neo Chian [retired as MG]	COMD 3 DIV	1952	39	1972	1995	4	CEO (1995–98) and later Chairman (1998–2002), JTC (later renamed Ascendas); CEO, China-Singapore Suzhou Industrial Park (1998–2000); Deputy Chairman and CEO, ST Engineering (2001–02); CE and Deputy Chairman, Singapore Tourism Board (2002–09); Vice Chairman, Singapore Red Cross (2001–11); Executive DIR (2011–13) and CEO (2011–13), Singbridge International; Deputy Chairman, Agri-Food and Veterinary Authority Board

S/N	Year of First Star	Rank and Name	Appointment when Promoted	Estimated Year of Birth	Age in Year of First Star	SAFOS Year	Year of Leaving SAF	Years in Flag Rank	Post-SAF Career or Current Active-Duty Military Appointment
16	1991	RADM1 Teo Chee Hean	CNV	1954	37	1973	1992	1	Member of Parliament (since 1992); MOS for Finance, Communications and Defence; Minister for the Environment and Second Minister for Defence (1996); Minister for Education and Second Minister for Defence (1997); Minister for Defence (2003–11); Minister for Home Affairs (2011–15); Minister-in-Charge of the Civil Service (2003–18); DPM (since April 2009); Coordinating Minister for National Security (since May 2011)
17	1991	BG Colin George Theseira	COMD 21 DIV/DIR NS Affairs	1945	46	–	1993	2	CEO, Tele-Medical Service; Chairman, Singapore Jet Boats
18	1992	BG Bey Soo Khiang [retired as LG]	COS-AS	1955	37	1974	2000	8	Senior Executive VP (Technical) and later Senior Executive VP for Operations & Planning and then Marketing & Corporate Services, SIA (2000–11); Vice Chairman, Raja Garuda Emas (EGM, formerly RGM International) (since March 2011)

(cont'd overleaf)

Appendix A (cont'd)

S/N	Year of First Star	Rank and Name	Appointment when Promoted	Estimated Year of Birth	Age in Year of First Star	SAFOS Year	Year of Leaving SAF	Years in Flag Rank	Post-SAF Career or Current Active-Duty Military Appointment
19	1992	BG Chin Chow Yoon	Head, SAFTI MI Development Project	1947	45	–	1996	4	Executive DIR, Singapore Discovery Centre (1996–2008); Chairman, Singapore Pools (2002–04); VP DIR of PT Bintan Resort Cakrawala (BRC)/ Chairman of Bintan Resort Ferries/ President of Bintan Resort Development Corporation/Executive Chairman of Island Leisure International
20	1992	BG Lee Hsien Yang	DJOPD/ COS-GS	1957	35	1976	1994	2	Executive VP (Local Services) (1994–95) and later President and Group CEO, SingTel (1995–2007); Non-Executive DIR (2007–13) and Chairman (2007–13), Fraser & Neave; Chairman, CAAS (2009–18); Special Adviser, General Atlantic, and Chairman, General Atlantic Singapore Fund
21	1992	BG Wesley Gerard D'Aranjo	DS (Technology), MINDEF	1954	38	1972	1998	6	Managing DIR, Beth-El (Asia); Chairman, Worldwide Education Services Group

S/N	Year of First Star	Rank and Name	Appointment when Promoted	Estimated Year of Birth	Age in Year of First Star	SAFOS Year	Year of Leaving SAF	Years in Flag Rank	Post-SAF Career or Current Active-Duty Military Appointment
22	1993	BG Han Eng Juan [retired as MG]	COMD 3 DIV	1954	39	1973	1998	5	CE Land Transport Authority (LTA) (1998–2003)
23	1993	RADM1 Kwek Siew Jin [retired as RADM2]	CNV	1950	43	–	1996	3	MD and President, Singapore Mass Rapid Transit (SMRT) (1996–2001); Chairman, Students Care Service (1996–2006); President, Singapore Power (2002–04); Chairman, National Volunteer & Philanthropy Centre (2005–07); President, Singapore Dragon Boat Association; VP (2004–06) and later President (2006–12), National Council of Social Service; Deputy Chairman, Board of Directors, Stroke Support Station
24	1993	BG Sin Boon Wah	COMD 9 DIV	1952	41	1971	2000	7	Deputy CE (Strategic Development), DSTA (2000–09)

(cont'd overleaf)

Appendix A *(cont'd)*

S/N	Year of First Star	Rank and Name	Appointment when Promoted	Estimated Year of Birth	Age in Year of First Star	SAFOS Year	Year of Leaving SAF	Years in Flag Rank	Post-SAF Career or Current Active-Duty Military Appointment
25	1993	BG Tan Yong Soon	DS (Policy) MINDEF	1955	38	1974	1995	2	PPS to PM (1995–97); DS (Revenue) (1997–98) and later DS (Policy) (1998–2001), MOF; CEO, Urban Redevelopment Authority (2001–03); PS MEWR (2004–10); PS (National Climate Change), National Climate Change Secretariat in PMO (2010–02)
26	1993	L/BG Yeo Cheng Ann [retired as COL]	Deputy Force COMD/COS UNIKOM	1949	44	–	1999	1 (1993–4)	DIR (Vehicle and Transit Licensing Division), LTA (1999–2001)
27	1994	BG Goh Yong Siang [retired as MG]	DJOPD/ COS-AS	1951	43	–	1998	4	President, ST Engineering (USA) (1998–2000); Partner, Beta Capital Group LLC (2001); CEO, Patriot Air LLC (2001–03); VP (Technology) and DIR, Sponsor Investment (2003); Head, Strategic Relations (2006–13)/Co-Head, Organisation & Leadership (2010–3)/ Head, Australia & New Zealand Strategic Relations (2011–13)/Head, Indochina (2012–13), Temasek Holdings; Chairman, Stratagem Group

S/N	Year of First Star	Rank and Name	Appointment when Promoted	Estimated Year of Birth	Age in Year of First Star	SAFOS Year	Year of Leaving SAF	Years in Flag Rank	Post-SAF Career or Current Active-Duty Military Appointment
28	1994	RADM1 Richard Lim Cherng Yih [retired as RADM2]	HNO/COS-NS	1954	40	–	1999	5	DS (Technology), MINDEF (2000–04); Chief Information Officer, MINDEF; CEO DSTA (2002–07); Chairman, National Grid Steering Committee; Chairman, Board of Directors, ST Logistics; Adjunct Professor, School of Mechanical & Aerospace Engineering, College of Engineering, Nanyang Technological University (NTU); Deputy Chairman, LTA
29	1994	BG (Dr) Lim Meng Kin	CMC	1950	44	–	1995	1	Adjunct lecturer (1985–95) and later Adjunct Associate Professor (1995–99), NUS; DIR, Defence Medical Research Institute, DSO (1995–97); CEO, Health Corporation of Singapore (1997–99); Associate Professor of Health Policy and Management, Yong Loo Lin School of Medicine, NUS (1999–2013); Vice Chairman, Singapore Red Cross Society; Adjunct Professor, A*STAR (2008–13);

(cont'd overleaf)

Appendix A (cont'd)

S/N	Year of First Star	Rank and Name	Appointment when Promoted	Estimated Year of Birth	Age in Year of First Star	SAFOS Year	Year of Leaving SAF	Years in Flag Rank	Post-SAF Career or Current Active-Duty Military Appointment
30	1994	BG Low Yee Kah	COMD 21 DIV/CGO	1951	43	–	1995	1	DIR of Alumni Relations NUS (2010–13); passed away on 31 January 2013. Senior VP/GM, Unicorn International (1998) (international marketing subsidiary of Chartered Industries of Singapore); Senior VP (Marketing), ST Engineering; Senior VP (Defence Business), ST Engineering
31	1995	BG Law Chwee Kiat	COMD 9 DIV	1949	46	–	2000	5	Senior Research Fellow at IDSS-NTU (2000–03); DIR and Non-Executive Chairman of the Board, Linair Technologies Ltd. (2004–11)
32	1995	RADM1 Larry Loon Leong Yoon	Fleet COMD	1954	41	–	1999	4	President (Naval Business Group), ST Marine (1999–2007); Counsellor, Singapore High Commission in Bandar Seri Begawan; Counsellor, Singapore High Commission, Kuala Lumpur
33	1995	BG Stephen Wong Kong Yip	COMD 6 DIV	1951	44	–	2001	6	Engagement Committee Chairman, Sembawang Country Club

S/N	Year of First Star	Rank and Name	Appointment when Promoted	Estimated Year of Birth	Age in Year of First Star	SAFOS Year	Year Leaving SAF	Years in Flag Rank	Post-SAF Career or Current Active-Duty Military Appointment
34	1996	BG Choi Shing Kwok	DIR SID	1959	37	1978	2000	4	DIR SID, MINDEF (2000–05); PS MOT (2005–12); PS MEWR (2012–17); DIR, ISEAS (since January 2018)
35	1996	BG Lam Joon Khoi	COMD 3 DIV	1958	38	1978	1997	1	DS (Policy), Ministry of Education (MOE) (1997–98); DS (Services), MOF (1998–2002); CEO, National Environment Agency (2002–05); CEO, Singapore Land Authority (SLA) (2005–09); DS (Management), MEWR (2009–12); Secretary-General, Singapore Manufacturers' Federation (2012–18)
36	1996	BG Lee Fook Sun	DIR MSD	1956	40	1975	2000	4	President (Defence and International Business) (2000–05) and later Deputy President (Operations) and President (Defence Business), ST Electronics (2005–09); President, ST Electronics (2009–16); Deputy CEO and President (Defence Business), ST Engineering Group (2013–17); Chairman, Building and Construction Authority; DIR, SMRT Corporation

(cont'd overleaf)

Appendix A *(cont'd)*

S/N	Year of First Star	Rank and Name	Appointment when Promoted	Estimated Year of Birth	Age in Year of First Star	SAFOS Year	Year of Leaving SAF	Years in Flag Rank	Post-SAF Career or Current Active-Duty Military Appointment
37	1997	BG Lim Chuan Poh [retired as LG]	COMD 9 DIV	1961	36	1980	2003	6	2PS (2003) and later PS (2003–07) MOE; Deputy Chairman (2006–07) and later Chairman (since April 2007), A*STAR
38	1997	BG Raymund Ng Teck Heng [retired as MG]	HAO	1956	41	–	2001	4	Senior VP (Flight Operations), SIA (2001–06)
39	1997	BG Ng Yat Chung [retired as LG]	COMD 3 DIV	1961	36	1980	2007	10	Head, Energy and Resources/Co-Head of Australia and New Zealand/Co-Head of Strategy, Temasek Holdings (2007–11); Executive DIR and CEO Designate (2011) and later Group President and CEO, Neptune Orient Lines (2011–16) until sold to CMA CGM SA of France; Executive DIR (since July 2017) and CEO (since September 2017), Singapore Press Holdings

S/N	Year of First Star	Rank and Name	Appointment when Promoted	Estimated Year of Birth	Age in Year of First Star	SAFOS Year	Year of Leaving SAF	Years in Flag Rank	Post-SAF Career or Current Active-Duty Military Appointment
40	1997	BG Andrew Tan Kim Teck	COMD 6 DIV	1950	47	–	1999	2	GM, AETOS Security Management (2004–05); Founder/MD, Universal Maritime Solutions
41	1997	BG Yam Ah Mee	COMD ADSD/COS-AS	1957	40	–	1998	1	DS (Development) PSD (1998-2004); CEO and Dean, Civil Service College (1998–2004); DS (Sea & Air) MOT (2004–05); CE LTA (2005–10); CE DIR PA (2010–13); MD, Sembcorp Design and Construction (since April 2013)
42	1998	BG (Dr) Lionel Lee Kim Hock	CMC	1951	47	–	2001	3	DIR, Defence Medical Research Institute, DSTA (2001–03); Adjunct Associate Professor, Department of Physiology, NUS (2001–07); DIR, Defence Medical and Environmental Research Institute, DSO National Laboratories (2003–11); Adjunct Professor, Office of Research, Duke-NUS Graduate Medical School (2009–12); COO (2011–13) and later Professor and Executive Vice-Dean (Administration) (since April 2002),

(cont'd overleaf)

Appendix A *(cont'd)*

S/N	Year of First Star	Rank and Name	Appointment when Promoted	Estimated Year of Birth	Age in Year of First Star	SAFOS Year	Year of Leaving SAF	Years in Flag Rank	Post-SAF Career or Current Active-Duty Military Appointment
									Lee Kong Chian School of Medicine, NTU
43	1998	BG Lim Kim Lye	COMD 1 PDF	1951	47	–	2000	2	First VP and later Adviser, Singapore Shooting Association; Chairman Special Committee, Singapore Rifle Association
44	1998	BG Rocky Lim Kim Choon [retired as MG]	HAO	1958	40	1977	2006	8	Senior Deputy DIR-General, CAAS (2006–07) and later DIR General and CEO, CAAS (2007–09)
45	1998	RADM1 Lui Tuck Yew [retired as RADM2]	Fleet COMD	1961	37	1980	2003	5	CEO, Maritime and Port Authority of Singapore (2003–05) and concurrently DS (Land) MOT (2004–05); CEO, HDB (2005–06); Member of Parliament (2006–15); MOS, MOE (2006–08); Senior MOS, MOE and MICA (2008–09); Acting Minister (2009–10) and later Minister (2010–11) for Information, Communications and the Arts; Second Minister for

Foreign Affairs (2011–12); Minister for Transport (2011–15); Second Minister for Defence (2015); Ambassador to Japan (since July 2017)

S/N	Year of First Star	Rank and Name	Appointment when Promoted	Estimated Year of Birth	Age in Year of First Star	SAFOS Year	Year of Leaving SAF	Years in Flag Rank	Post-SAF Career or Current Active-Duty Military Appointment
46	1998	BG Ong Boon Hwee	COMD 25 DIV/CAO	1956	42	–	2002	4	MD (Strategic Relations & Projects), Temasek Holdings/CEO, Temasek Management Services (2002–07); COO, Singapore Power Ltd (2007–11); MD, Beyond Horizon Consulting /Co-owner, Stratton Management Company; CEO, Stewardship Asia Centre (Temasek Management Services)
47	1999	BG Jimmy Khoo Siew Kim	COMD ADSD	1962	37	1981	2007	8	MD (Australian Investments), Singapore Power Ltd; Deputy MD (Planning and Strategy), SP PowerGrid (subsidiary of Singapore Power Group); Head (Business Ventures) and Senior VP, Singapore Power; MD, Singapore District Cooling

(cont'd overleaf)

Appendix A (*cont'd*)

S/N	Year of First Star	Rank and Name	Appointment when Promoted	Estimated Year of Birth	Age in Year of First Star	SAFOS Year	Year of Leaving SAF	Years in Flag Rank	Post-SAF Career or Current Active-Duty Military Appointment
48	1999	BG Desmond Kuek Bak Chye [retired as LG]	COMD 3 DIV	1963	36	1982	2010	11	PS and later Senior Adviser, MEWR (2010–12); President and CEO, SMRT (2012–18)
49	1999	BG Lawrence Leong Yue Kheong	COMD 9 DIV	1955	44	–	2007	8	Counsellor at the Singapore Permanent Mission to the UN (2007); DIR F1 Project, Singapore Tourism Board (2007–09); Assistant CE (International Group and Corporate Development Group), Singapore Tourism Board
50	1999	BG Loh Kok Hua	COMD TAB	1955	44	–	2002	3	Chief Operations Analyst, DSO National Laboratories; Adjunct Associate Professor, School of Mechanical and Aerospace Engineering, NTU; VP (windsurfing), Singapore Sailing Executive Committee; Deputy President, Singapore Sailing Federation

S/N	Year of First Star	Rank and Name	Appointment when Promoted	Estimated Year of Birth	Age in Year of First Star	SAFOS Year	Year of Leaving SAF	Years in Flag Rank	Post-SAF Career or Current Active-Duty Military Appointment
51	1999	BG Philip Su Poon Ghee	COMD 21 DIV/CGO	1955	44	–	2001	2	Acting CEO, JTC (2001–10); Executive DIR (Retail Business Group), Far East Organization (since 2010)
52	1999	RADM1 Simon Ong Hung Eng	HNO	1954	45	–	2003	4	Deputy CEO/Commissioner of Lands (Lands Operations Group, and Land Information & Corporate Group) and later Deputy CEO (GeoSpatial & Corporate) and Controller of Residential Property, Singapore Land Authority, MINLAW
53	2000	BG Chee Wee Kiong	COMD ADSD	1963	37	1982	2007	7	DIR SID, MINDEF (2007–10); 2PS (2010–13) and later PS (since June 2013), MFA
54	2000	BG Jek Kian Yee	DIR MSD	1963	37	1983	2006	6	Unknown
55	2000	RADM1 Jway Ching Hua	HNL	1954	46	–	2002	2	Senior VP/GM, Chartered Ammunition Industries (2002); Senior VP (Land Systems & Solutions), ST Kinetics; Senior VP/GM, Advanced Material Engineering (ST Engineering);

(contd overleaf)

Appendix A *(cont'd)*

Senior VP (Projects), Engineering and Operations Division, ST Marine

S/N	Year of First Star	Rank and Name	Appointment when Promoted	Estimated Year of Birth	Age in First Star	SAFOS Year	Year of Leaving SAF	Years in Flag Rank	Post-SAF Career or Current Active-Duty Military Appointment
56	2000	BG Lim Kah Kee	COMDT SCSC	1954	46	–	2003	3	Unknown
57	2000	BG Pang Hee Hon	HJL/ACGS (Log)	1960	40	1979	2004	4	Deputy President (Operations), ST Electronics (Info-Software Systems) (2005–09); CEO, Keppel Telecommunications & Transportation (2010–14); Chairman, eGov Chapter, Singapore IT Federation; CEO Keppel Logistics (2012–14); Founder and MD, Veritas Global Healthcare (since July 2014); Assistant CEO (Special Projects), Crescendas (since September 2016)

S/N	Year of First Star	Rank and Name	Appointment when Promoted	Estimated Year of Birth	Age in Year of First Star	SAFOS Year	Year of Leaving SAF	Years in Flag Rank	Post-SAF Career or Current Active-Duty Military Appointment
58	2000	BG Tay Lim Heng	COMD 6 DIV/DIR N5 Affairs	1963	37	1982	2005	5	CE MPA (2005–09); DS (Development), MND (2009–10); Executive DIR (2010) and Deputy CEO (2010) and later CEO (2011–13), Keppel Integrated Engineering; Executive DIR (Sustainable Development), Keppel Group; MD (Waste-to-Energy), Keppel Infrastructure and MD, Keppel Seghers; DIR (Group Risk & Compliance), Keppel Corporation (2016); CEO, Sino-Singapore Tianjin Eco-City Investment and Development (since October 2016)
59	2000	BG Yap Ong Heng	Military Adviser UN	1960	40	1979	2004	4	Counsellor at the Singapore Permanent Mission to the UN (2004); DS MINLAW (2004–09); DIR-General, CAAS (2009–15); Senior Adviser, Ministry of Transport

(cont'd overleaf)

Appendix A *(cont'd)*

S/N	Year of First Star	Rank and Name	Appointment when Promoted	Estimated Year of Birth	Age in Year of First Star	SAFOS Year	Year of Leaving SAF	Years in Flag Rank	Post-SAF Career or Current Active-Duty Military Appointment
60	2001	BG Chua Chwee Koh	HJO	1963	38	1982	2004	3	COO and later CE (Integrated Services), Certis CISCO Security
61	2001	BG Lim Yeow Beng	HAL	1958	43	–	2003	2	Executive VP (Projects) and Group DIR (Government Business), SembCorp Logistics Group (renamed Toll Asia) (2003–07); President and CEO, ST Logistics/President, PLEXIS Services (ST Logistics [USA]) (2007–14); DIR of Government Business Group, Toll Global Logistics
62	2001	RADM1 Sim Gim Guan	Fleet COMD	1964	37	1983	2006	5	Senior DIR (Information & Corporate Management) (2006–07), DS (Information & Corporate Management) (2007–12) and later DS (Industry & Information) (2012–13), Ministry of Communications and Information); CEO, National Council of Social Service (since November 2013)

S/N	Year of First Star	Rank and Name	Appointment when Promoted	Estimated Year of Birth	Age in Year of First Star	SAFOS Year	Year of Leaving SAF	Years in Flag Rank	Post-SAF Career or Current Active-Duty Military Appointment
63	2001	BG Eric Tan Huck Gim [L/MG (2002–3); retired as BG]	COMD 9 DIV	1955	45	–	2006	5	DIR (Administration), LKYSPP-NUS (2005–06); Deputy Special Representative for the Secretary-General in Timor Leste (2006–07); COO, Singapore 2010 Youth Olympic Games Organising Committee; DIR, National Archives of Singapore; MD of Facilities Management, Singapore Sports Hub, UGL services and Premas Operations; Deputy DIR (Special Projects), Emerging Markets Division, and later DIR (Institutional Development), Amaravati Partnership Office, Ministry of Trade and Industry
64	2001	RADM1 Ronnie Tay [retired as RADM2]	HNO	1963	38	1982	2007	6	CEO, Infocomm Development Authority of Singapore (IDA) (2007–13); CEO, National Environment Agency (NEA) (2013–18)

(cont'd overleaf)

Appendix A (cont'd)

S/N	Year of First Star	Rank and Name	Appointment when Promoted	Estimated Year of Birth	Age in Year of First Star	SAFOS Year	Year of Leaving SAF	Years in Flag Rank	Post-SAF Career or Current Active-Duty Military Appointment
65	2002	BG Chin Phei Chen	COMD 6 DIV	1960	42	–	2004	2	Counsellor, Singapore Embassy in Beijing, PRC (2005–10); Chief Corporate Officer, CapitaLand China Holdings (2011–13); CEO, Sino-Singapore Guangzhou Knowledge City Investment and Development (2013–15); MD, Corporate Strategic Relations and Regional GM for North China CapitaLand (since September 2015)
66	2002	BG Tay Swee Yee	COMD 2 PDF	1957	45	–	2005	3	CEO, Home Team Academy, MHA (2005–09); CEO, PAP Community Foundation Group (2009–15); Adviser (Communications & Partnerships), CSA; Co-Chair, Cyber Security Awareness Alliance
67	2002	BG Voon Tse-Chow	DA Washington	1957	45	–	2005	3	Executive VP (Mergers & Acquisitions) (since August 2005) and Acting COO (since April 2017), Vision Technologies Systems (ST Engineering)

S/N	Year of First Star	Rank and Name	Appointment when Promoted	Estimated Year of Birth	Age in Year of First Star	SAFOS Year	Year of Leaving SAF	Years in Flag Rank	Post-SAF Career or Current Active-Duty Military Appointment
68	2003	BG Loh Wai Keong	COMD 3 DIV	1965	38	1984	2005	2	DS (Trade) MTI (2005–07); Country Head (India), CapitaMalls Asia/MD (South Asia and South East Asia), CapitaLand Industrial & Logistics; Senior VP (Investments), CapitaLand Retail; Executive VP (Real Estate Development & Investment)/CEO (South East Asia), Ascendas; MD, GIC Real Estate and Co-Head Investments (Asia) and later MD Enterprise Strategy GIC
69	2003	BG Neo Kian Hong [retired as LG]	COMD 9 DIV	1964	39	1985	2013	10	PS (Education Development), MOE (2013–17); PS (Defence Development), MINDEF (2017–18), CEO SMRT (since August 2018)

(cont'd overleaf)

Appendix A *(cont'd)*

S/N	Year of First Star	Rank and Name	Appointment when Promoted	Estimated Year of Birth	Age in Year of First Star	SAFOS Year	Year of Leaving SAF	Years in Flag Rank	Post-SAF Career or Current Active-Duty Military Appointment
70	2003	BG Ng Chee Khern [retired as MG]	HJO	1965	38	1985	2009	6	Senior Deputy DIR (2010) and later DIR (2010–14), SID MINDEF; PS (Defence Development), MINDEF (2014–17); 2PS MOH (2014–16); PS (Smart Nation and Digital Development), PMO (since May 2017)
71	2003	BG Jimmy Tan Cheng Yaw	COMD ADSD	1962	41	1981	2009	6	DIR, SAF-NTU Academy
72	2003	BG Bernard Richard Tan Kok Kiang	COMD 25 DIV/CAO	1966	37	1985	2008	5	MD, Debt Capital Market, Global Financial Markets, DBS (Singapore) (2008); Acting Country Head, DBS Taiwan; President Commissioner of PT Bank DBS Indonesia (2011–14); President, Commercial Business Group ST Kinetics (2014–16); VP, Football Association of Singapore; Chief Marketing Officer, ST Engineering

S/N	Year of First Star	Rank and Name	Appointment when Promoted	Estimated Year of Birth	Age in Year of First Star	SAFOS Year	Year of Leaving SAF	Years in Flag Rank	Post-SAF Career or Current Active-Duty Military Appointment
73	2003	BG (Dr) Wong Yue Sie	CMC	1960	43	–	2006	3	COO and Chairman (Division of Ambulatory and Clinical Support Services), Singapore General Hospital (2006–10); COO, SingHealth (2006–10); CEO, Ren Ci Hospital (2008–09); passed away on 28 May 2010
74	2004	BG Goh Kee Nguan	On course (USA)	1960	44	–	2008	4	CEO, Singapore 2010 Youth Olympic Games Organising Committee (2008–10); COO, Cityneon Holdings (2011–13); Chairman, National Cadet Corps for 15th and 16th NCC Council (2011–16); CEO, Huttons Asia (since May 2013)
75	2004	BG Richard Lim Keng Yong	COMD TAB	1958	46	–	2008	4	Pilot (Captain), SilkAir

(cont'd overleaf)

Appendix A (cont'd)

S/N	Year of First Star	Rank and Name	Appointment when Promoted	Estimated Year of Birth	Age in Year of First Star	SAFOS Year	Year of Leaving SAF	Years in Flag Rank	Post-SAF Career or Current Active-Duty Military Appointment
76	2004	BG Ravinder Singh S/O Harchand Singh [retired as MG]	HJPT	1965	39	–	2009 2014	8 (2004–9) (2011–4)	DS (Technology), MINDEF (2009–11); Deputy President (Corporate & Market Development, ST Electronics (2014–15); President, ST Kinetics (2015–7); President, ST Electronics; President (Defence Business), ST Engineering
77	2004	BG Charles Sih Seah Wee	HAO	1962	42	–	2008	4	Divisional VP (Safety, Security and Environment), Singapore Airlines
78	2004	BG Wong Huat Sern	HJO	1963	41	1983	2013	9	DIR, Safety and Systems Review Directorate, MINDEF
79	2005	BG Gary Ang Aik Hwang	DIR (Policy) DPO	1967	38	1986	2011	6	DS (Policy), MINDEF (2011–12); DS (Trade), MTI (2012–13); DS (Management), MEWR (2013–14); MD (Strategic and Public Affairs), Temasek Holdings (since January 2014)

S/N	Year of First Star	Rank and Name	Appointment when Promoted	Estimated Year of Birth	Age in Year of First Star	SAFOS Year	Year of Leaving SAF	Years in Flag Rank	Post-SAF Career or Current Active-Duty Military Appointment
80	2005	RADM1 Chew Men Leong [retired as RADM2]	Fleet COMD	1967	38	1987	2011	6	CEO, Public Utilities Board (2011–14); CE, LTA (2014–16); President (Defence Business), ST Marine (since November 2016)
81	2005	BG Philip Lim Feng	HJL	1962	43	–	2007	2	COO and GM, Singapore Food Industries (2007–09); GM (August 2009) and later CEO (December 2009), Exploit Technologies (subsidiary of A*STAR)
82	2005	BG Hugh Reginald Lim U Yang	COMD 6 DIV	1965	40	1984	2009	4	DS, MINLAW (2009–12); DS (Community, Youth and Sports), Ministry of Culture, Community and Youth (2012–14); CEO, Building and Construction Authority
83	2005	BG Tan Meng Dui	HAT	1967	38	1986	2011	6	DS (Technology), MINDEF (2011–14); DS (Development), MND (2014–18); CEO, NEA (since October 2018)

(cont'd overleaf)

Appendix A *(cont'd)*

S/N	Year of First Star	Rank and Name	Appointment when Promoted	Estimated Year of Birth	Age in Year of First Star	SAFOS Year	Year of Leaving SAF	Years in Flag Rank	Post-SAF Career or Current Active-Duty Military Appointment
84	2005	BG Winston Toh Bee Chew	COMD 9 DIV/CIO	1960	45	–	2007	2	DIR, Defence Executive Services (2007); GM, ST Electronics (e-Services) and Senior VP, ST Electronics (2007–11); Deputy CEO (Operations Group), Singapore Workforce Development Agency (2011–15); President, SAF Veterans Association (since 2012); Senior VP (International Marketing), ST Engineering; Executive VP/Chief Marketing Officer, ST Kinetics (since May 2015)
85	2005	BG Wong Ann Chai	COMD 25 DIV/CAO	1967	38	1986	2007	2	MD (Equity Capital Markets), Global Financial Markets, DBS (2007–10); Executive DIR, Investment Banking Division, Nomura (2010–11); CEO, Mahogany Global Advisers (2012–13); CEO and Managing Partner, Elie Vevey Capital (since 2013); Adjunct Professor, Nanyang Business School, NTU (since August 2011); Co-founder and MD, NanoSun

S/N	Year of First Star	Rank and Name	Appointment when Promoted	Estimated Year of Birth	Age in Year of First Star	SAFOS Year	Year of Leaving SAF	Years in Flag Rank	Post-SAF Career or Current Active-Duty Military Appointment
86	2006	BG Lowrence Chua	COMD 2 PDF	1960	46	–	2008	2	Executive DIR, Singapore Discovery Centre (since April 2008)
87	2006	BG David Koh Tee Hian	HJCIS	1965	41	–	2014	8	DS (Technology), MINDEF (2014–17); DS (Special Projects), MINDEF (since 2015); CE, CSA (since 2015); Defence Cyber Chief, MINDEF (since 2017)
88	2006	RADM1 Tan Kai Hoe	Fleet COMD	1966	40	1985	2009	3	Deputy CEO (Entrepreneurship & Innovation/Quality & Standards) (2009–13) and later CEO (2013–15), SPRING Singapore; President & CEO, Accuron Technologies (since August 2015)
89	2006	BG Tan Yih San	COMD 3 DIV	1966	40	1985	2011	5	CEO, Intellectual Property Office of Singapore (2011–16); MD, Candela Reach Capital
90	2006	BG Tsoi Mun Heng	HAL	1961	45	–	2009	3	DIR, Defence Industry & Systems Office, MINDEF (2009–11); DIR, Energy Innovation Challenge Directorate, National Research Foundation (2011–13); Senior DIR,

(cont'd overleaf)

Appendix A *(cont'd)*

S/N	Year of First Star	Rank and Name	Appointment when Promoted	Estimated Year of Birth	Age in Year of First Star	SAFOS Year	Year of Leaving SAF	Years in Flag Rank	Post-SAF Career or Current Active-Duty Military Appointment
91	2007	BG Chan Chun Sing [retired as MG]	COMD 9 DIV	1969	38	1988	2011	4	Academic Analysis & Planning Division and later VP (Planning) and Chair Campus Development Task Force, Singapore Institute of Technology Member of Parliament (since 2011); Acting Minister for Community Development, Youth and Sports (2011–12); MOS for Information, Communications and the Arts (2011–12); Acting Minister (2012–13) and later Minister (2013–15) for Social and Family Development; Senior MOS (2012–13) and later Second Minister for Defence (2013–15); Secretary-General (since April 2015), National Trades Union Congress; Minister in PMO (2015–18); Deputy Chairman, PA (since May 2015); Minister for Trade and Industry (since May 2018; Minister-in-charge of the Civil Service

S/N	Year of First Star	Rank and Name	Appointment when Promoted	Estimated Year of Birth	Age in Year of First Star	SAFOS Year	Year of Leaving SAF	Years in Flag Rank	Post-SAF Career or Current Active-Duty Military Appointment
92	2007	BG Hoo Cher Mou [retired as MG]	COMD ADOC	1966	41	–	2016	9	Unknown
93	2007	BG Philip Lim Chern Tjunn	ACGS (Ops)	1967	40	–	2010	3	COO, Singapore Food Industries (2010–13); Senior VP (Apron Services), Singapore Airport Terminal Service (2010–13); MD (South East Asia), OCS Group UK (2013); DIR, Advanced Systems at ST Dynamics, ST Engineering
94	2007	RADM1 Ng Chee Peng [retired as RADM2]	DIR (Policy) DPO	1970	37	1989	2014	7	DS (Special Projects), MOM (2014–15); CE, Central Provident Fund Board (since March 2015)
95	2007	BG Tan Chuan-Jin	On studies (Singapore)	1969	38	1989	2011	4	Member of Parliament (since June 2011); MOS (2011–12) and later Senior MOS (2012–13) for National Development; MOS (2011–12),

(cont'd overleaf)

Appendix A *(cont'd)*

S/N	Year of First Star	Rank and Name	Appointment when Promoted	Estimated Year of Birth	Age in Year of First Star	SAFOS Year	Year of Leaving SAF	Years in Flag Rank	Post-SAF Career or Current Active-Duty Military Appointment
									Acting Minister (2012–14) and later Minister (2014–15) for Manpower; Minister for Social and Family Development (2015–17); President, Singapore National Olympic Council (since July 2014); Speaker of Parliament (since 2017)
96	2007	RADM1 Tay Kian Seng	HNO	1967	40	1987	2010	3	DIR (Leadership & Organisation Development), SingHealth People Sector, MOH (2010–12); Founder and Principal Consultant, OpenSeed Consulting (since August 2010)
97	2007	RADM1 (Dr) John Wong Chee Meng	CMC	1963	44	–	2009	2	Senior Consultant, National University Health System (NUHS) Residency Program; Adjunct Associate Professor and Senior Consultant Psychiatrist, Department of Psychological Medicine (NUHS); Head of Department/ Associate Professor/Senior Consultant, Department of Psychological Medicine, Yong Loo Lin School of Medicine

S/N	Year of First Star	Rank and Name	Appointment when Promoted	Estimated Year of Birth	Age in Year of First Star	SAFOS Year	Year of Leaving SAF	Years in Flag Rank	Post-SAF Career or Current Active-Duty Military Appointment
98	2008	RADM1 Joseph Leong Weng Keong [retired as RADM2]	HJPT	1970	38	1990	2014	6	DIR, SID (since 2014)
99	2008	BG Lim Teck Yin	COMD 6 DIV	1962	46	–	2011	3	CEO, Singapore Sports Council (since April 2011) (renamed Sport Singapore in April 2014)
100	2008	BG Ng Chee Meng [retired as LG]	DJO	1968	40	–	2015	7	Member of Parliament (since 2015); Acting (2015–16) and later Minister (2016–18) for Education (Schools); Senior MOS (2015–16) and then Second Minister (2016–18) for Transport; Secretary-General National Trades Union Congress (since May 2018)

(cont'd overleaf)

Appendix A *(cont'd)*

S/N	Year of First Star	Rank and Name	Appointment when Promoted	Estimated Year of Birth	Age in Year of First Star	SAFOS Year	Year of Leaving SAF	Years in Flag Rank	Post-SAF Career or Current Active-Duty Military Appointment
101	2008	BG Teo Jing Siong	COMD 2 PDF	1963	45	–	2011	3	Deputy President (International Marketing/ Business Development) and later Deputy President (Defence Business and Business Development), ST Electronics (Info-Software Systems); Group DIR, Strategic Planning Office, Building and Construction Authority
102	2008	BG Tung Yui Fai	COMD 21 DIV/CGO	1964	44	–	2013	5	DIR NS Affairs, MINDEF (2013–16); Senior VP and later President (Defence Business Group), ST Kinetics (since February 2016)
103	2008	BG Richard Christopher Pereira	COMD ACC	1963	45	–	2011	3	DIR, Validus Engineers; DIR, BusHub Service; DIR, Gemini Travel; CEO, Aviation Topguns; DIR, Green Revolution
104	2008	L/BG Cheng Siak Kian [retired as BG]	DA Washington	1969	39	–	2015	7	Senior VP (Bus), SBS Transit (2015–16); CEO, ComfortDelGro Corporation in New South Wales, Australia (since December 2016)

S/N	Year of First Star	Rank and Name	Appointment when Promoted	Estimated Year of Birth	Age in Year of First Star	SAFOS Year	Year of Leaving SAF	Years in Flag Rank	Post-SAF Career or Current Active-Duty Military Appointment
105	2009	BG Ishak Bin Ismail	COMD 6 DIV	1963	46	–	2011	2	Senior VP/GM of ST Electronics (e-Services) (2011–12); CEO (Defence Services), CWT (2012–16); DIR Business Development (APAC), BAE Systems Hägglunds AB (since February 2017)
106	2009	BG Kwek Kok Kwong	COMD ADOC	1966	43	–	2012	3	Deputy CEO First Campus at NTUC First Campus; CEO, NTUC Learning Hub; Chairman, Singapore National Co-operative Federation (since September 2016)
107	2009	BG Lee Shiang Long	HJCIS	1966	43	–	2013	4	Deputy Executive DIR (2013–14) and later Executive DIR (2014–16), Institute for Infocomm Research (I2R), A*STAR; Deputy President and later President (Defence Business Group), ST Kinetics (2016–17); Deputy Chief Technology Officer, ST Engineering Group (2016–17); President, ST Kinetics (since April 2017)

(cont'd overleaf)

Appendix A *(cont'd)*

S/N	Year of First Star	Rank and Name	Appointment when Promoted	Estimated Year of Birth	Age in Year of First Star	SAFOS Year	Year of Leaving SAF	Years in Flag Rank	Post-SAF Career or Current Active-Duty Military Appointment
108	2009	BG (Dr) Benjamin Seet Hun Yew	CMC	1965	44	–	2011	2	Executive DIR, Biomedical Research Council, A*STAR (since August 2011)
109	2009	RADM1 Tan Wee Beng	COMD MSTF	1965	44	1986	2014	5	Group Director (Operations), Operations Cluster, Singapore Workforce Development Agency; Deputy CE, Skills Future Singapore
110	2010	BG Chan Wing Kai	COMD 21 DIV/CGO	1966	44	–	2016	6	Chairman, National Cadet Corps for 17th NCC Council (since January 2017); DIR at SEED Global Investment (since November 2017)
111	2010	RADM1 Jackson Chia	COMD MSTF	1969	41	–	2016	6	Unknown
112	2010	BG Lim Hock Yu	COMD 9 DIV/CIO	1965	45	–	2016	6	Deputy CE, PA (since April 2016)
113	2010	BG Ngien Hoon Ping	DJO	1969	41	1988	2013	3	DS (Performance) MOF (2013–16); CE, LTA (since November 2016)

S/N	Year of First Star	Rank and Name	Appointment when Promoted	Estimated Year of Birth	Age in Year of First Star	SAFOS Year	Year of Leaving SAF	Years in Flag Rank	Post-SAF Career or Current Active-Duty Military Appointment
114	2010	BG Mark Tan Ming Yiak	COMD 3 DIV	1968	42	–	2014	4	Pavilion Capital (a subsidiary of Temasek Holdings) (since September 2014)
115	2010	L/RADM1 Bernard Donald Miranda [retired as L/RADM1]	COMD CTF-151	1961	49	–	2011	1	DIR National Maritime Operations Group, National Maritime Security System, MINDEF (2011–15); DIR Corporate Services Division, Chief Information Officer, and Co-Chairman ASEAN Organising Secretariat – Economic Pillar, Ministry of Trade and Industry
116	2011	RADM1 Lai Chung Han [retired as RADM2]	Fleet COMD	1973	38	1992	2017	6	2PS (Education) (since June 2017); 2PS (Home Affairs) (since September 2017)
117	2011	BG Lam Shiu Tong	COMD 2 PDF	1965	46	–	2014	3	Senior DIR (DTZ), Event Support at Singapore Sports Hub (since 2014)

(cont'd overleaf)

Appendix A *(cont'd)*

S/N	Year of First Star	Rank and Name	Appointment when Promoted	Estimated Year of Birth	Age in Year of First Star	SAFOS Year	Year of Leaving SAF	Years in Flag Rank	Post-SAF Career or Current Active-Duty Military Appointment
118	2011	BG Benedict Lim	COMD 25 DIV/CAO	1968	43	–	2015	4	Group Chief, MINDEF Communications
119	2011	BG Perry Lim Cheng Yeow [retired as LG]	COMD 3 DIV	1972	39	1991	2018	7	Unknown
120	2011	BG Lim Yeong Kiat	COMD ACC	1966	45	–	2015	4	Unknown
121	2011	ME8 Lee Ling Wee	HAL	1966	45	–	2013	2	Senior VP, Maintenance & Engineering Division, SMRT Corp (2013); Executive VP (Trains), SMRT Corp (2013–14); MD and later CEO, SMRT Trains (since July 2014)
122	2011	BG Sarbjit Singh S/O Tahil Singh	COMD APGC	1964	47	–	2014	3	Executive VP (Defence Business), ST Aerospace

S/N	Year of First Star	Rank and Name	Appointment when Promoted	Estimated Year of Birth	Age in Year of First Star	SAFOS Year	Year of Leaving SAF	Years in Flag Rank	Post-SAF Career or Current Active-Duty Military Appointment
123	2011	BG Yeo See Peng	COMD 6 DIV	1966	45	–	2013	2	Senior VP (Fleet Services, Taxi Business), ComfortDelGro (2013–14); CEO, Swan Taxis (Subsidiary of Comfort DelGro) in Perth (2015–17); Head Bus Support Division, SBS Transit (since November 2017)
124	2011	L/RADM1 Harris Chan Weng Yip [retired as RADM1]	COMD CTF-151	1971	40	1990	2017	6	Deputy Chief Technology Officer and Chief Digital Officer, ST Engineering
125	2012	BG Chia Choon Hoong	COMD 9 DIV/CIO	1972	40	1991	2016	4	Pavilion Capital (since 2017)
126	2012	BG Neo Hong Keat	HAO	1967	45	–	2017	5	Executive VP (Corporate), ST Logistics
127	2012	BG Siew Kum Wong	COMD 25 DIV/CAO	1971	41	–	–	–	Active duty (COS-GS)

(cont'd overleaf)

Appendix A *(cont'd)*

S/N	Year of First Star	Rank and Name	Appointment when Promoted	Estimated Year of Birth	Age in Year of First Star	SAFOS Year	Year of Leaving SAF	Years in Flag Rank	Post-SAF Career or Current Active-Duty Military Appointment
128	2012	L/BG Tan Chee Wee (promoted to BG)	DA Washington	1974	38	1993	–	–	Active duty (DJO)
129	2013	RADM1 (Dr) Kang Wee Lee	CMC	1969	44	–	2015	2	COO, Sengkang Health; Consultant (ENT) at Sengkang Health and Singapore General Hospital; Consultant (Hyperbaric & Diving Medicine) at Singapore General Hospital
130	2013	ME8 Lau Cher Loon	HJI	1965	48	–	2015	2	DXO in MINDEF
131	2013	BG Lim Tuang Liang	COMD ACC	1972	41	1991	2018	5	Executive DIR, Research, Innovation and Enterprise Coordination Office, National Research Foundation, PMO (since 2018)
132	2013	RADM1 Timothy Lo Khee Shik	Fleet COMD	1971	42	–	–	–	Active duty (COS-NS)

S/N	Year of First Star	Rank and Name	Appointment when Promoted	Estimated Year of Birth	Age in Year of First Star	SAFOS Year	Year of Leaving SAF	Years in Flag Rank	Post-SAF Career or Current Active-Duty Military Appointment
133	2013	BG Desmond Tan Kok Ming	COMD 21 DIV/CGO	1970	43	–	2016	3	CE DIR, PA (since January 2017)
134	2013	BG Tan Peng Kuan	COMD CSSCOM	1969	44	–	2015	2	Senior VP and later Executive VP/Head (Singapore Business) and Head (International Business), ST Kinetics
135	2013	BG Mervyn Tan Wei Ming [promoted to MG]	COMD ADOC	1971	42	–	–	–	Active duty (CAF)
136	2013	L/RADM1 Giam Hock Koon [retired as RADM1]	COMD CTF-151	1968	45	–	2018	5	Unknown

(cont'd overleaf)

Appendix A *(cont'd)*

S/N	Year of First Star	Rank and Name	Appointment when Promoted	Estimated Year of Birth	Age in Year of First Star	SAFOS Year	Year of Leaving SAF	Years in Flag Rank	Post-SAF Career or Current Active-Duty Military Appointment
137	2013	L/BG Ken Leong Kum Wah [retired as L/BG]	DA Washington	1965	48	–	2016	3	Senior Strategic Adviser, FLiBE Energy in Alabama, USA; MD, Mursun (since June 2017)
138	2014	BG Chiang Hock Woon	COMD 9 DIV/CIO	1966	48	–	2016	2	Deputy CEO and Chief, Organization Strategy & Development Group, Sport Singapore (since 2016)
139	2014	BG Milton Ong Ann Kiat	HJCIS	1973	41	1992	–	–	Active duty (appointment unknown)
140	2014	BG Melvyn Ong Su Kiat [promoted to LG]	COMD 21 DIV/CGO	1975	39	1994	–	–	Active duty (CDF)
141	2014	BG Ong Tze-Ch'in	COMD 3 DIV	1975	39	1994	2018	4	Coordinating Divisional Director, Higher Education Group, MOE (2018)

S/N	Year of First Star	Rank and Name	Appointment when Promoted	Estimated Year of Birth	Age in Year of First Star	SAFOS Year	Year of Leaving SAF	Years in Flag Rank	Post-SAF Career or Current Active-Duty Military Appointment
142	2014	BG Terry Siow Meng Meng	COMD 2 PDF	1971	43	1990	–	–	Active duty (appointment unknown)
143	2015	ME8 Francis Cheong Han Kwok	HAEL	1970	45	–	–	–	Active duty (HAEL)
144	2015	RADM1 Frederick Chew Chih Chiang	COMD MSTF	1975	40	1994	–	–	Active duty (DS [Tech] MINDEF)
145	2015	BG Paul Chew	DIR MSD	1973	42	–	–	–	Active duty (DIR MSD)
146	2015	BG Gan Siow Huang	HJMP	1974	41	–	–	–	Active duty (COMD APGC)
147	2015	BG Kelvin Khong Boon Leong	COMD ACC	1976	39	1995	–	–	Active duty (COS-JS)

(cont'd overleaf)

Appendix A (*cont'd*)

S/N	Year of First Star	Rank and Name	Appointment when Promoted	Estimated Year of Birth	Age in Year of First Star	SAFOS Year	Year of Leaving SAF	Years in Flag Rank	Post-SAF Career or Current Active-Duty Military Appointment
148	2015	BG Lam Sheau Kai	COMD CSSCOM	1972	43	–	–	–	Active duty (appointment unknown)
149	2015	RADM1 Lew Chuen Hong [promoted to RADM2]	Fleet COMD	1976	39	1995	–	–	Active duty (CNV)
150	2015	BG Kenneth Liow Meng Kwee	COMD 25 DIV/CAO	1970	45	–	–	–	Active duty (COMD TRADOC)
151	2016	BG Chua Boon Keat	COMD 6 DIV	1972	44	–	–	–	Active duty (COMDT SAFTI MI)
152	2016	BG Alfred George Fox	COMD 3 DIV	1972	44	–	–	–	Active duty (appointment unknown)
153	2016	BG Ng Chad-Son	Deputy Chief C4I (Int)	1975	41	1994	–	–	Active duty (DMI/Chief C4I)

S/N	Year of First Star	Rank and Name	Appointment when Promoted	Estimated Year of Birth	Age in Year of First Star	SAFOS Year	Year of Leaving SAF	Years in Flag Rank	Post-SAF Career or Current Active-Duty Military Appointment
154	2016	BG Tommy Tan Ah Han	COMD ACC	1971	45	–	–	–	Active duty (COS-AS)
155	2016	BG Jonathan Tan Chin Kwang	COMD PC	1969	47	–	–	–	Active duty (COMD PC)
156	2016	RADM1 (Dr) Tang Kong Choong	CMC	1972	44	–	–	–	Active duty (CMC)
157	2016	L/RADM1 Ken Cheong Kwok Chien [promoted to RADM1]	COMD CTF-151	1973	43	1992	–	–	Active duty (HNO)

(cont'd overleaf)

Appendix A *(cont'd)*

S/N	Year of First Star	Rank and Name	Appointment when Promoted	Estimated Year of Birth	Age in Year of First Star	SAFOS Year	Year of Leaving SAF	Years in Flag Rank	Post-SAF Career or Current Active-Duty Military Appointment
158	2016	L/BG Tan Boon Kim	DA Washington	1969	47	1988	–	–	Active duty (DA Washington)
159	2017	RADM1 Alan Goh Kim Hua	COMD MSTF	1976	41	1995	–	–	Active duty (Group Chief [Policy & Strategy] DPG, MINDEF)
160	2017	BG Goh Si Hou	ACGS (Plans)/ COMD 6 DIV	1978	39	1997	–	–	Active duty (COA)
161	2017	BG Ng Ying Thong	COMD 9 DIV/CIO	1973	44	–	–	–	Active duty (ACGS [Ops])
162	2017	BG Mark Tan Ken-Li	COMD 21 DIV/CGO	1976	41	–	–	–	Active duty (DIR [Cyber Policy & Plans Directorate] DCO, MINDEF)
163	2018	L/RADM1 Saw Shi Tat	COMD CTF-151	1976	42	–	–	–	Active duty (COMD CTF-151)
164	2018	BG Dinesh Vasu Dash	COMD 2 PDF	1975	43	–	–	–	Active duty (COMD 2 PDF)
165	2018	BG Kelvin Fan Sui Siong	HAO	1979	39	1998	–	–	Active duty (HAO)

S/N	Year of First Star	Rank and Name	Appointment when Promoted	Estimated Year of Birth	Age in Year of First Star	SAFOS Year	Year Leaving SAF	Years in Flag Rank	Post-SAF Career or Current Active-Duty Military Appointment
166	2018	BG Gaurav Keerthi	COMD ADOC	1979	39	1998	–	–	Active duty (COMD ADOC)
167	2018	BG Percival Goh Beng Ngan	COMD SAF C4 Command	1972	46	–	–	–	Active duty (COMD SAF C4 Command)
168	2018	RADM1 Edwin Leong Wai Kwan	RSN Fleet COMD	1975	43	–	–	–	Active duty (RSN Fleet COMD)
169	2018	BG David Neo Chin Wee	On secondment (Singapore)	1977	41	–	–	–	Active duty (COMD 3 DIV)
170	2018	BG Yew Chee Leung	COMD 25 DIV/CAO	1977	41	–	–	–	Active duty (COMD 25 DIV/CAO)

Appendix B
The military elite by service and vocation (1965–2018)

Army (94)	Highest Rank Attained and Name
	1. BG (RET) Thomas James Duncan Campbell
	2. BG (RET) Patrick Sim Hak Kng
	3. BG (RET) Tan Chin Tiong
	4. BG (RET) Boey Tak Hap
	5. BG (RET) Chin Chow Yoon
	6. BG (RET) Tan Yong Soon
	7. COL (RET) Yeo Cheng Ann [L/BG (1993-94)]
	8. BG (RET) Law Chwee Kiat
	9. BG (RET) Stephen Wong Kong Yip
	10. LG (RET) Lim Chuan Poh
Infantry (21)	11. BG (RET) Lawrence Leong Yue Kheong
	12. BG (RET) Chua Chwee Koh
	13. BG (RET) Chin Phei Chen
	14. BG (RET) Loh Wai Keong
	15. MG (RET) Chan Chun Sing
	16. BG (RET) Ishak Bin Ismail
	17. BG (RET) Lim Hock Yu
	18. BG (NS) Chia Choon Hoong
	19. BG (NS) Desmond Tan Kok Ming
	20. LG Melvyn Ong Su Kiat
	21. BG Ng Ying Thong
	1. BG (RET) Patrick Choy Choong Tow
	2. BG (RET) Colin George Theseira
	3. BG (RET) Lee Hsien Yang
Armour (20)	4. MG (RET) Han Eng Juan
	5. BG (RET) Sin Boon Wah
	6. BG (RET) Lam Joon Khoi
	7. BG (RET) Lee Fook Sun

Army (94)	Highest Rank Attained and Name
Armour (20)	8. BG (RET) Lim Kim Lye
	9. BG (RET) Ong Boon Hwee
	10. LG (RET) Desmond Kuek Bak Chye
	11. BG (RET) Tay Swee Yee
	12. BG (RET) Bernard Richard Tan Kok Kiang
	13. BG (RET) Wong Ann Chai
	14. BG (RET) Lowrence Chua
	15. BG (RET) Benedict Lim
	16. BG Siew Kum Wong
	17. BG Kenneth Liow Meng Kwee
	18. BG Chua Boon Keat
	19. BG Alfred George Fox
	20. BG Yew Chee Leung
Artillery (14)	1. BG (RET) Kirpa Ram Vij
	2. BG (RET) Lee Hsien Loong
	3. LG (RET) Ng Jui Ping
	4. BG (RET) Low Yee Kah
	5. LG (RET) Ng Yat Chung
	6. BG (RET) Andrew Tan Kim Teck
	7. BG (RET) Philip Su Poon Ghee
	8. BG (RET) Pang Hee Hon
	9. BG (RET) Tay Lim Heng
	10. BG (RET) Eric Tan Huck Gim [L/MG (2002–03)]
	11. BG Terry Siow Meng Meng
	12. BG Lam Sheau Kai
	13. BG Goh Si Hou
	14. BG Dinesh Vasu Dash
Combat Engineer (9)	1. MG (RET) Lim Neo Chian
	2. BG (RET) Choi Shing Kwok
	3. BG (RET) Lim Kah Kee
	4. BG (RET) Hugh Reginald Lim U Yang
	5. BG (RET) Tan Yih San
	6. BG (RET) Teo Jing Siong
	7. BG (RET) Tung Yui Fai
	8. BG (RET) Mark Tan Ming Yiak
	9. BG (NS) Ong Tze-Ch'in

(cont'd overleaf)

Appendix B *(cont'd)*

Army (94)	Highest Rank Attained and Name
Guards (7)	1. LG (RET) Neo Kian Hong
	2. BG (RET) Goh Kee Nguan
	3. BG (RET) Winston Toh Bee Chew
	4. BG (RET) Tan Chuan-Jin
	5. BG (RET) Chan Wing Kai
	6. LG (NS) Perry Lim Cheng Yeow
	7. BG Tan Ken-Li, Mark
Signals (8)	1. LG (RET) Winston Choo Wee Leong
	2. BG (RET) George Yeo Yong Boon
	3. MG (RET) Ravinder Singh S/O Harchand Singh
	4. BG (RET) David Koh Tee Hian
	5. BG (RET) Lee Shiang Long
	6. BG Milton Ong Ann Kiat
	7. BG Ng Chad-Son
	8. BG Percival Goh Beng Ngan
Commando (6)	1. BG (RET) Philip Lim Chern Tjunn
	2. BG (RET) Lim Teck Yin
	3. BG (RET) Lam Shiu Tong
	4. BG (RET) Yeo See Peng
	5. BG (RET) Chiang Hock Woon
	6. BG David Neo Chin Wee
Engineering/ Logistics (4)	1. BG (RET) Chin Siat Yoon
	2. BG (RET) Philip Lim Feng
	3. BG (RET) Ngien Hoon Ping
	4. BG (RET) Tan Peng Kuan
Medical (3)	1. BG (RET) (Dr) Lionel Lee Kim Hock
	2. BG (RET) (Dr) Wong Yue Sie
	3. BG (RET) (Dr) Benjamin Seet Hun Yew
Intelligence (2)	1. ME8 (RET) Lau Cher Loon
	2. BG Paul Chew

Navy (31)	Highest Rank Attained and Name
	1. RADM1 (RET) Teo Chee Hean
	2. RADM2 (RET) Kwek Siew Jin
	3. RADM2 (RET) Richard Lim Cherng Yih
	4. RADM1 (RET) Larry Loon Leong Yoon
	5. RADM2 (RET) Lui Tuck Yew
	6. RADM1 (RET) Simon Ong Hung Eng
	7. RADM1 (RET) Sim Gim Guan
	8. RADM2 (RET) Ronnie Tay
	9. RADM2 (RET) Chew Men Leong
	10. RADM1 (RET) Tan Kai Hoe
	11. RADM2 (NS) Ng Chee Peng
	12. RADM1 (RET) Tay Kian Seng
Naval Combat	13. RADM2 (NS) Joseph Leong Weng Keong
Officer (26)	14. RADM1 (RET) Tan Wee Beng
	15. RADM1 (RET) Jackson Chia
	16. L/RADM1 (RET) Bernard Donald Miranda [L/RADM1 (2010-11)]
	17. RADM2 (NS) Lai Chung Han
	18. RADM1 (NS) Harris Chan Weng Yip [L/RADM1 (2011)]
	19. RADM1 Timothy Lo Khee Shik
	20. RADM1 (RET) Giam Hock Koon [L/RADM1 (2013)]
	21. RADM1 Frederick Chew Chih Chiang
	22. RADM2 Lew Chuen Hong
	23. RADM1 Ken Cheong Kwok Chien [L/RADM1 (2016)]
	24. RADM1 Alan Goh Kim Hua
	25. L/RADM1 Saw Shi Tat [L/RADM1 (2018)]
	26. RADM1 Edwin Leong Wai Kwan
Medical (3)	1. RADM1 (Dr) (RET) John Wong Chee Meng
	2. RADM1 (Dr) (RET) Kang Wee Lee
	3. RADM1 (Dr) Tang Kong Choong
Engineering/	1. RADM1 (RET) James Leo Chin Lian
Logistics (2)	2. RADM1 (RET) Jway Ching Hua

(cont'd overleaf)

Appendix B *(cont'd)*

Air Force (45)	Highest Rank Attained and Name	
Pilot (fighter) (19)	1.	BG (RET) Michael Teo Eng Cheng
	2.	BG (RET) Gary Yeo Ping Yong
	3.	MG (RET) Goh Yong Siang
	4.	MG (RET) Raymund Ng Teck Heng
	5.	MG (RET) Rocky Lim Kim Choon
	6.	BG (RET) Loh Kok Hua
	7.	BG (RET) Voon Tse-Chow
	8.	MG (RET) Ng Chee Khern
	9.	BG (RET) Richard Lim Keng Yong
	10.	BG (RET) Charles Sih Seah Wee
	11.	LG (RET) Ng Chee Meng
	12.	BG (RET) Richard Christopher Pereira
	13.	BG (RET) Lim Yeong Kiat
	14.	BG (RET) Sarbjit Singh S/O Tahil Singh
	15.	BG (RET) Neo Hong Keat
	16.	BG (NS) Lim Tuang Liang
	17.	L/BG (RET) Ken Leong Kum Wah [L/BG (2013-16)]
	18.	BG Kelvin Khong Boon Leong
	19.	BG Tommy Tan Ah Han
Pilot (transport) (3)	1.	LG (RET) Bey Soo Khiang
	2.	BG (RET) Jek Kian Yee
	3.	MG Mervyn Tan Wei Ming
Pilot (helicopter) (3)	1.	BG (RET) Wong Huat Sern
	2.	BG Jonathan Tan Chin Kwang
	3.	BG Gaurav Keerthi
AWO (GBAD) (5)	1.	BG (RET) Yam Ah Mee
	2.	BG (RET) Jimmy Khoo Siew Kim
	3.	BG (RET) Chee Wee Kiong
	4.	BG (RET) Cheng Siak Kian [L/BG (2008-10)]
	5.	BG Kelvin Fan Sui Siong
AWO (C3) (9)	1.	BG (RET) Yap Ong Heng
	2.	BG (RET) Jimmy Tan Cheng Yaw
	3.	BG (RET) Gary Ang Aik Hwang
	4.	BG (RET) Tan Meng Dui
	5.	MG (RET) Hoo Cher Mou
	6.	BG (RET) Kwek Kok Kwong
	7.	BG Tan Chee Wee [L/BG (2012-13, 2013-14)]

Air Force (45)	Highest Rank Attained and Name	
AWO (C3) (9)	8.	BG Gan Siow Huang
	9.	L/BG Tan Boon Kim [L/BG (2016–present)]
Medical (1)	1.	BG (RET) (Dr) Lim Meng Kin
Engineering (5)	1.	BG (RET) Wesley Gerard D'Aranjo
	2.	BG (RET) Lim Yeow Beng
	3.	BG (RET) Tsoi Mun Heng
	4.	ME8 (RET) Lee Ling Wee
	5.	ME8 Francis Cheong Han Kwok

Appendix C
One-star and above appointments in MINDEF and the SAF (c. 2018)

The following is a list of one-star appointments held by officers in the rank of Brigadier-General (BG), Rear-Admiral one-star (RADM1), or Military Expert 8 (ME8) and above. An asterisk (*) denotes that an appointment is usually held on a concurrent basis although there can always be exceptions.

- MINDEF hybrid billets (civilian or military) (5): 1) Deputy Secretary (Policy); 2) Deputy Secretary (Technology); 3) Director Security and Intelligence Division; 4) Future Systems and Technology Architect; 4) Director Defence Industry & Systems Office; 5) Group Chief MINDEF Communications.
- Aberrations in MINDEF hybrid billets (civilian or military) (2): 1) Director Defence Policy Office (four made BG/RADM1, usually held by COL); 2) Director National Service Affairs (formerly held on a concurrent basis by a BG, now held by a COL (RET)).
- SAF-level billets (12): 1) Chief of Defence Force (three-star); 2) Chief of Staff – Joint Staff; 3) Director Military Intelligence*; 4) Director Joint Operations; 5) Chief C4I (Command, Control, Communications, Computers and Intelligence)*; 6) Commandant SAFTI Military Institute; 7) Director Military Security Department; 8) Chief of Medical Corps; 9) Defence Attaché at the Singapore Embassy in Washington; 10) Head Joint Communications and Information Systems which has been superseded by Commander SAF C4 Command; 11) Group Chief (Policy & Strategy) Defence Policy Group; 12) Director (Cyber Plans & Policy Directorate) Defence Cyber Organisation.
- Aberrations in SAF-level billets (5): 1) Head Joint Logistics Department (only two BGs, now held by COL); 2) Military Adviser at the Permanent Mission of Singapore to the United Nations (only two BGs, now held by COL); 3) Head Joint Intelligence (once held by a ME8); 4) Director (Special Projects) (once held by a BG); 5) Deputy Chief C4I (Intelligence) (once held by a ME8 and subsequently a BG).

- Army billets (11): 1) Chief of Army (two-star); 2) Chief of Staff – General Staff; 3) Commander Training and Doctrine Command; 4) Assistant Chief of General Staff (Operations); 5) Commander 3rd Singapore Division; 6) Commander 6th Singapore Division; 7) Commander 9th Singapore Division/Chief Infantry Officer; 8) Commander 21st Singapore Division/Chief Guards Officer; 9) Commander 25th Division/Chief Armour Officer; 10) Commander 2nd Peoples Defence Force; 11) Commander Combat Service Support Command.
- Aberrations in Army billets (1): Commander 1st Peoples Defence Force (only one BG among its five commanders between 1985 and 2005; unit is now defunct).
- Navy billets (5): 1) Chief of Navy (two-star); 2) Chief of Staff – Naval Staff; 3) Head Naval Operations; 4) Fleet Commander; 5) Commander Maritime Security Task Force.
- Aberrations in one-star Navy billets (1): Head Naval Logistics (only one RADM1 at the helm since the department was formed).
- Air Force billets (8): 1) Chief of Air Force (two-star); 2) Chief of Staff – Air Staff; 3) Head Air Operations; 4) Commander Air Defence and Operations Command; 5) Commander Air Combat Command; 6) Commander Air Power Generation Command; 7) Commander Participation Command; 8) Head Air and Engineering Logistics.
- Aberrations in one-star Air Force billets (1): Commander Tengah Air Base (only three BGs since 1971, now held by COL).
- Possible aberrations in one-star Air Force billets (1): Head Air Intelligence (only one BG at the helm since the department was formed).

Appendix D
Distribution of SAFOS officers within the military elite (1965–2018)

Category	Raw Statistics			Adjusted Statistics		
	Total	SAFOS	SAFOS as % of total	Total	SAFOS	SAFOS as % of total
Flag officers	170	68	40.00%	158	68	43.04%
Army Officers	94	34	36.17%	86	34	39.53%
Infantry	21	8	38.10%	18	8	44.44%
Armour	20	8	40.00%	20	8	40.00%
Artillery	14	6	42.86%	13	6	46.15%
Combat Engineer	9	5	55.56%	9	5	55.56%
Signals	8	3	37.50%	7	3	42.86%
Guards	7	3	42.86%	7	3	42.86%
Commando	6	0	–	6	0	–
Engineering/Logistics	4	1	25.00%	4	1	25.00%
Medical	3	0	–	Incomparable with SAFOS		
Intelligence	2	0	–	2	0	–
Naval Officers	31	16	51.61%	28	16	57.14%
Naval Combat Officers	26	16	61.54%	26	16	61.54%
Medical	3	0	–	Incomparable with SAFOS		
Engineering/Logistics	2	0	–	2	0	–
Air Force Officers	45	18	40.00%	44	18	40.91%
Pilot (fighter)	19	4	21.05%	19	4	21.05%
Pilot (transport)	3	2	66.67%	3	2	66.67%

Category	Raw Statistics			Adjusted Statistics		
	Total	SAFOS	SAFOS as % of total	Total	SAFOS	SAFOS as % of total
Pilot (helicopter)	3	2	66.67%	3	2	66.67%
AWO (GBAD)	5	3	60.00%	5	3	60.00%
AWO (C3)	9	6	66.67%	9	6	66.67%
Medical	1	0	–	*Incomparable with SAFOS*		
Engineering/Logistics	5	1	20.00%	5	1	20.0%

Appendix E
Command appointments of generals in the Singapore Army (1965–2018)

S/N	Year Promoted	Rank and Name	Vocation	Battalion Command	Brigade Command	Division Command	Appointments held as one-star and above	Year Retired
1	1965	BG (RET) Thomas James Duncan Campbell	Infantry	1st Battalion; Singapore Volunteer Corps	Singapore Infantry Brigade; 1 SIB	N/A	COMD Singapore Infantry Brigade; DGS; COMDT SCSC	1971
2	1972	BG (RET) Kirpa Ram Vij	Artillery	–	3 SIB	N/A	DGS	1974
3	1976	LG (RET) Winston Choo Wee Leong	Signals	1 SAF Signals Bn; 4 SIR; 1 SIR	2 SIB	N/A	DGS; CGS; CDF	1992
4	1978	BG (RET) Patrick Sim Hak Kng	Infantry	10 PDF; 5 SIR	2 SIB; 3 SIB	6 DIV; 3 DIV	COMD 3 DIV; DCGS	1981
5	1980	BG (RET) Tan Chin Tiong	Infantry	4 SIR	–	–	DCGS; Ag CGS	1982
6	1984	BG (RET) Lee Hsien Loong	Artillery	23 SA	–	–	COS-GS; DJOPD	1984

S/N	Year Promoted	Rank and Name	Vocation	Battalion Command	Brigade Command	Division Command	Appointments held as one-star and above	Year Retired
7	1986	BG (RET) Chin Siat Yoon	Logistics	*Unknown*	*Unknown*	–	DJID; Seconded to MFA	1995
8	1986	LG (RET) Ng Jui Ping	Artillery	20 SA	3 SIB	3 DIV	COMD 3 DIV; DJID; COA; CDF	1995
9	1987	BG (RET) Boey Tak Hap	Infantry	3 SIR	*Unknown*	3 DIV	ACGS (Ops); COS-GS; DCGS (Army); COA	1990
10	1988	BG (RET) George Yeo Yong Boon	Signals	–	–	–	DJOPD	1988
11	1990	BG (RET) Patrick Choy Choong Tow	Armour	41 SAR	8 SAB (NS brigade); 4 SAB	3 DIV	COMD 3 DIV; COMD TRADOC; DJID	1996
12	1991	MG (RET) Lim Neo Chian	Combat Engineer	SAF Ammo Base	3 SIB	3 DIV	COMD 3 DIV; COS-GS; COA	1995
13	1991	BG (RET) Colin George Theseira	Armour	40 SAR	7 SIB	6 DIV; 21 DIV	DIR NS Affairs; COMD 21 DIV	1993
14	1992	BG (RET) Chin Chow Yoon	Armour	42 SAR	8 SAB (NS brigade); 3 SIB	9 DIV	COMD 9 DIV; Head SAFTI MI Development Project; COMDT SAFTI MI	1996

(cont'd overleaf)

Appendix E *(cont'd)*

S/N	Year Promoted	Rank and Name	Vocation	Battalion Command	Brigade Command	Division Command	Appointments held as one-star and above	Year Retired
15	1992	BG (RET) Lee Hsien Yang	Armour	46 SAR	2 SIB	–	COS-GS; DJOPD	1994
16	1993	MG (RET) Han Eng Juan	Armour	46 SAR	4 SAB	3 DIV	COMD 3 DIV; COS-GS; COA	1998
17	1993	BG (RET) Sin Boon Wah	Armour	*Unknown*	2 SIB	9 DIV	COMD 9 DIV; COMD TRADOC; DA Washington	2000
18	1993	BG (RET) Tan Yong Soon	Infantry	*Unknown*	*Unknown*	–	DS (Policy) MINDEF	1995
19	1993	COL (RET) Yeo Cheng Ann [L/BG (1993-94)]	Infantry	2 SIR	2 SIB	–	Deputy Force COMD/COS UNIKOM[1]	e. 1999
20	1994	BG (RET) Low Yee Kah	Artillery	22 SA	3 DIV ARTY	21 DIV	COMD 21 DIV/ CGO	1995
21	1995	BG (RET) Law Chwee Kiat	Infantry	6 SIR	7 SIB	9 DIV	COMD 9 DIV; COMD TRADOC	2000
22	1995	BG (RET) Stephen Wong Kong Yip	Infantry	3 SIR	2 SIB	6 DIV	COMD 6 DIV; COMDT SAFTI MI	2001

[1] Upon return to Singapore was appointed Chief Infantry Officer (CIO) and subsequently Chief of Staff (COS) 3 Division.

S/N	Year Promoted	Rank and Name	Vocation	Battalion Command	Brigade Command	Division Command	Appointments held as one-star and above	Year Retired
23	1996	BG (RET) Choi Shing Kwok	Combat Engineer	35 SCE	*Unknown*	–	DIR SID	2000
24	1996	BG (RET) Lam Joon Khoi	Armour	46 SAR	4 SAB	3 DIV	COMD 3 DIV; COS-GS; DJOPD	1997
25	1996	BG (RET) Lee Fook Sun	Armour	*Unknown*	*Unknown*	–	DIR MSD; DJID	2000
26	1997	LG (RET) Lim Chuan Poh	Infantry	3 SIR	10 SIB	9 DIV	COMD 9 DIV; COS-GS; COA; CDF	2003
27	1997	LG (RET) Ng Yat Chung	Artillery	21 SA	3 SIB	3 DIV	COMD 3 DIV; DJOPD; COS-JS; COA; CDF	2007
28	1997	BG (RET) Andrew Tan Kim Teck	Artillery	25 SA	3 DIV ARTY; 17 SIB (NS brigade)	6 DIV	COMD 6 DIV	1999
29	1998	BG (RET) (Dr) Lionel Lee Kim Hock	Medical	Medical Classification Centre; Physical Performance Centre	Army Medical Services	SAF Medical Corps	CMC; DIR DMRI at DSTA	2001

(cont'd overleaf)

Appendix E *(cont'd)*

S/N	Year Promoted	Rank and Name	Vocation	Battalion Command	Brigade Command	Division Command	Appointments held as one-star and above	Year Retired
30	1998	BG (RET) Lim Kim Lye	Armour	46 SAR	54 SAB (NS brigade); 56 SAB (NS brigade); 4 SAB	1 PDF	COMD 1 PDF	2000
31	1998	BG (RET) Ong Boon Hwee	Armour	42 SAR	4 SAB	25 DIV	COMD 25 DIV/ CAO	2002
32	1999	LG (RET) Desmond Kuek Bak Chye	Armour	41 SAR	4 SAB	3 DIV	COMD 3 DIV; DJID; COS-GS; COA; CDF; COMD 9 DIV; COMD TRADOC;	2010
33	1999	BG (RET) Lawrence Leong Yue Kheong	Infantry	4 SIR	7 SIB	9 DIV	MA at the Permanent Mission of Singapore to the UN	2007
34	1999	BG (RET) Philip Su Poon Ghee	Artillery	20 SA	3 DIV ARTY	21 DIV	COMD 21 DIV/ CGO	2001
35	2000	BG (RET) Lim Kah Kee	Combat Engineer	*Unknown*	Engineer Formation	3 DIV	COMDT SCSC; COMD 3 DIV	2003
36	2000	BG (RET) Pang Hee Hon	Artillery	*Unknown*	3 DIV ARTY	–	HJL	2004

S/N	Year Promoted	Rank and Name	Vocation	Battalion Command	Brigade Command	Division Command	Appointments held as one-star and above	Year Retired
37	2000	BG (RET) Tay Lim Heng	Artillery	20 SA	3 SIB	6 DIV	COMD 6 DIV; DIR NS Affairs; DJID	2005
38	2001	BG (RET) Chua Chwee Koh	Infantry	5 SIR	7 SIB	21 DIV	HJO; COMD 21 DIV/CGO	2004
39	2001	BG (RET) Eric Tan Huck Gim [L/MG (2002-03)]	Artillery	20 SA	3 DIV ARTY	9 DIV	COMD 9 DIV; Force COMD UNMISET; COMDT SAFTI MI	2005
40	2002	BG (RET) Chin Phei Chen	Infantry	5 SIR	2 SIB	6 DIV	COMD 6 DIV	2004
41	2002	BG (RET) Tay Swee Yee	Armour	42 SAR	54 SAB (NS brigade); 4 SAB	2 PDF	COMD 2 PDF	2005
42	2003	BG (RET) Loh Wai Keong	Infantry	1 SIR	2 SIB	3 DIV	COMD 3 DIV	2005
43	2003	LG (RET) Neo Kian Hong	Guards	1 GDS	7 SIB	9 DIV	COMD 9 DIV; COMD TRADOC, COS-JS; COA; CDF	2013
44	2003	BG (RET) Richard Tan Kok Kiang	Armour	40 SAR	4 SAB	25 DIV	COMD 25 DIV/ CAO; DMI	2008

(cont'd overleaf)

Appendix E *(cont'd)*

S/N	Year Promoted	Rank and Name	Vocation	Battalion Command	Brigade Command	Division Command	Appointments held as one-star and above	Year Retired
45	2003	BG (RET) (Dr) Wong Yue Sie	Medical	*Unknown*	Army Medical Services	SAF Medical Corps	CMC	2006
46	2004	BG (RET) Goh Kee Nguan	Guards	3 GDS	10 SIB	21 DIV	COMD 21 DIV/ CGO; COMD TRADOC	2008
47	2004	MG (RET) Ravinder Singh S/O Harchand Singh	Signals	3 SIG	2 SIB	6 DIV	HJPT; COMD 6 DIV; COS-JS; DS (Technology) MINDEF; COA	2009 (1st) 2014 (2nd)
48	2005	BG (RET) Philip Lim Feng	Military Engineer	GSMB	Maintenance and Engineering Formation	N/A	HJL; ACGS (Log)	2007
49	2005	BG (RET) Hugh Reginald Lim U Yang	Combat Engineer	35 SCE	Engineer Formation	6 DIV	COMD 6 DIV; COMD TRADOC; COS-GS	2009
50	2005	BG (RET) Winston Toh Bee Chew	Guards	3 GDS	7 SIB	9 DIV	COMD 9 DIV/CIO	2007
51	2005	BG (RET) Wong Ann Chai	Armour	40 SAR	8 SAB	25 DIV	COMD 25 DIV/ CAO	2007

S/N	Year Promoted	Rank and Name	Vocation	Battalion Command	Brigade Command	Division Command	Appointments held as one-star and above	Year Retired
52	2006	BG (RET) Lowrence Chua	Armour	40 SAR	54 SAB (NS brigade); 8 SAB	2 PDF	COMD 2 PDF	2008
53	2006	BG (RET) David Koh Tee Hian	Signals	3 SIG	Signals formation	-	HJCIS; DIR MSD	2014
54	2006	BG (RET) Tan Yih San	Combat Engineer	30 SCE	2 SIB	3 DIV	COMD 3 DIV; FSA	2011
55	2007	MG (RET) Chan Chun Sing	Infantry	2 SIR	10 SIB	9 DIV	9 DIV/CIO; COS-JS; COA	2011
							ACGS (Ops);	
56	2007	BG (RET) Philip Lim Chern Tjunn	Commando	1 SIR	4 SAB	25 DIV	COMD 25 DIV/ CAO; COS-GS	2010
57	2007	BG (RET) Tan Chuan-Jin	Guards	3 GDS	7 SIB	3 DIV	COMD 3 DIV; COMD TRADOC	2011
58	2008	BG (RET) Lim Teck Yin	Commando	46 SAR	4 SAB	6 DIV	COMD 6 DIV; DIR NS Affairs; COMD TRADOC; COMDT SAFTI MI	2011
59	2008	BG (RET) Teo Jing Siong	Combat Engineer	35 SCE	ARMCEG	2 PDF	COMD 2 PDF	2011

(cont'd overleaf)

Appendix E *(cont'd)*

S/N	Year Promoted	Rank and Name	Vocation	Battalion Command	Brigade Command	Division Command	Appointments held as one-star and above	Year Retired
60	2008	BG (RET) Tung Yui Fai	Combat Engineer	35 SCE	ARMCEG	21 DIV	COMD 21 DIV/ CGO; ACGS (Ops); COS-GS; DIR NS Affairs	2013
61	2009	BG (RET) Ishak Bin Ismail	Infantry	6 SIR	12 SIB (NS brigade)	6 DIV	COMD 6 DIV	2011
62	2009	BG (RET) Lee Shiang Long	Signals	3 SIG	Signals formation	–	HJCIS; Chief Information Officer MINDEF	2013
63	2009	BG (RET) (Dr) Benjamin Seet Hun Yew	Medical	Medical Classification Centre	Army Medical Services	SAF Medical Corps	CMC	2011
64	2010	BG (RET) Chan Wing Kai	Guards	1 SIR	2 SIB	21 DIV	COMD 21 DIV/ CGO; ACGS (Ops); COMD TRADOC; Ag COS-GS; COS-GS	2016
65	2010	BG (RET) Lim Hock Yu	Infantry	6 SIR	10 SIB	9 DIV	COMD 9 DIV; COMD TRADOC; COS-GS	2016

S/N	Year Promoted	Rank and Name	Vocation	Battalion Command	Brigade Command	Division Command	Appointments held as one-star and above	Year Retired
66	2010	BG (RET) Ngien Hoon Ping	Logistics	GSMB	Supply and Transport Formation	CSSCOM	DJO	2013
67	2010	BG (RET) Mark Tan Ming Yiak	Combat Engineer	3 SIR	3 SIB	3 DIV	COMD 3 DIV; COMDT SAFTI MI; FSA; COS-JS	2014
68	2011	BG (NS) Lam Shiu Tong	Commando	SOF; 3 SIR	2 SIB	2 PDF	COMD 2 PDF	2014
69	2011	BG (RET) Benedict Lim	Armour	40 SAR	8 SAB	25 DIV	COMD 25 DIV/CAO; COMDT SAFTI MI; Group Chief MINDEF Communications	2015
70	2011	LG (NS) Perry Lim Cheng Yeow	Guards	1 GDS	7 SIB	3 DIV	COMD 3 DIV; DIR NS Affairs; COS-GS; COA; CDF	2018
71	2011	BG (RET) Yeo See Peng	Commando	6 SIR	3 SIB	6 DIV	COMD 6 DIV	2013
72	2012	BG (NS) Chia Choon Hoong	Infantry	4 SIR	2 SIB	9 DIV	COMD 9 DIV/CIO; DJO; COS-JS	2016

(cont'd overleaf)

Appendix E *(cont'd)*

S/N	Year Promoted	Rank and Name	Vocation	Battalion Command	Brigade Command	Division Command	Appointments held as one-star and above	Year Retired
73	2012	BG Siew Kum Wong	Armour	*Unknown*	4 SAB	25 DIV	COMD 25 DIV/ CAO; ACGS (Ops); COMD TRADOC; COS-GS	
74	2013	ME8 (RET) Lau Cher Loon	Intelligence	*Unknown*	*Unknown*	–	Head Joint Intelligence; Deputy Chief C4I (Int)	2015
75	2013	BG (NS) Desmond Tan Kok Ming	Infantry	1 SIR	3 SIB	21 DIV	COMD 21 DIV/ CGO; DJO; COS-GS	2016
76	2013	BG (RET) Tan Peng Kuan	Logistics	1 TPT Bn	Supply Formation	CSSCOM	COMD CSSCOM; DIR DISO MINDEF	2015
77	2014	BG (RET) Chiang Hock Woon	Commando	1 CDO Bn	76 SIB (NS brigade)	9 DIV	COMD 9 DIV/CIO	2016
78	2014	BG Milton Ong Ann Kiat	Signals	3 SIG	ISG	–	HJCIS; *Unknown*	

S/N	Year Promoted	Rank and Name	Vocation	Battalion Command	Brigade Command	Division Command	Appointments held as one-star and above	Year Retired
79	2014	LG Melvyn Ong Su Kiat	Infantry	ADF[2]	7 SIB	21 DIV	COMD 21 DIV/ CGO; COA; CDF	
80	2014	BG (NS) Ong Tze-Chin	Combat Engineer	30 SCE	ARMCEG	3 DIV	COMD 3 DIV; DMI/Chief C4I COMD 2 PDF;	2018
81	2014	BG Terry Siow Meng Meng	Artillery	20 SA	3 DIV ARTY	2 PDF	ACGS (Ops); *Unknown*	
82	2015	BG Paul Chew	Intelligence	1 MI Bn	*Unknown* Supply Formation;	–	DIR MSD	
83	2015	BG Lam Sheau Kai	Artillery	23 SA	9 DISCOM (NS brigade)	CSSCOM	COMD CSSCOM	
84	2015	BG Kenneth Liow Meng Kwee	Armour	41 SAR	8 SAB	25 DIV	COMD 25 DIV/ CAO; COMD TRADOC	

(cont'd overleaf)

[2] The ADF was conceived as the Army Development Force under the 7th Singapore Infantry Brigade and subsequently renamed and publicly unveiled as the Army Deployment Force. The unit is also listed as '1 ADF' on official memorial decorations such as the Bernard Tan Cheow Han Challenge Trophy for years 2007, 2012, and 2013. Billets are filled by regulars with well performing enlisted personnel (PTE to CFC) eligible to "serve up to three contracts of either three-year or two-year terms" or cross over to the specialist (3SG to MSG) track. See "Passing on the Baton," *Army News*, Issue 144 (July-August 2007), p. 7; https://www.mindef.gov.sg/arc/our-careers-army-deployment-force.html.

Appendix E (*cont'd*)

S/N	Year Promoted	Rank and Name	Vocation	Battalion Command	Brigade Command	Division Command	Appointments held as one-star and above	Year Retired
85	2016	BG Chua Boon Keat	Armour	41 SAR	1 SIB	6 DIV	COMD 6 DIV; COMDT SAFTI MI	
86	2016	BG Alfred George Fox	Armour	46 SAR	8 SAB	3 DIV	COMD 3 DIV	
87	2016	BG Ng Chad-Son	Signals	8 SIG	C4 Operations Group	–	Deputy Chief C4I (Int); DMI/Chief C4I	
88	2017	BG Goh Si Hou	Artillery	20 SA	3 DIV ARTY 6 DIV	6 DIV	ACGS (Plans); COMD 6 DIV; COA	
89	2017	BG Ng Ying Thong	Infantry	4 SIR	3 SIB	9 DIV	COMD 9 DIV/CIO; ACGS (Ops)	
90	2017	BG Mark Tan Ken-Li	Guards	3 GDS	2 SIB	21 DIV	COMD 21 DIV/ CGO; DIR (Cyber Plans & Policy Directorate) DCO, MINDEF.	
91	2018	BG Dinesh Vasu Dash	Artillery	21 SA	3 SIB	2 PDF	COMD 2 PDF	
92	2018	BG Percival Goh Beng Ngan	Signals	3 SIG	Signals formation	SAF C4 Command	COMD SAF C4 Command	

S/N	Year Promoted	Rank and Name	Vocation	Battalion Command	Brigade Command	Division Command	Appointments held as one-star and above	Year Retired
93	2018	BG David Neo Chin Wee	Commando	1 GDS	2 SIB	3 DIV	Seconded to PA and MOH; COMD 3 DIV	
94	2018	BG Yew Chee Leung	Armour	41 SAR	4 SAB	25 DIV	COMD 25 DIV/ CAO	

Appendix F
Command appointments of admirals in the RSN (1988–2018)

S/N	Year Promoted	Rank and Name	Vocation	Ship Command	Squadron Command	Flotilla Command	Fleet-Level Command	Appointments Held as One-Star and Above	Year Retired
1	1988	RADM1 (RET) James Leo Chin Lian	Engineering	Naval Technical Training School; Naval Maintenance Base	N/A	N/A	N/A	CNV	1991
2	1991	RADM1 (RET) Teo Chee Hean	Combat	*Unknown*	*Unknown*	N/A	–	CNV	1992
3	1993	RADM2 (RET) Kwek Siew Jin	Combat	RSS Jupiter	*Unknown*	–	RSN Fleet	CNV	1996
4	1994	RADM2 (RET) Richard Lim Cherng Yih	Combat	RSS Daring	185 SQN	–	–	HNO; COS-NS; DJOPD; CNV	1999

S/N	Year Promoted	Rank and Name	Vocation	Ship Command	Squadron Command	Flotilla Command	Fleet-Level Command	Appointments Held as One-Star and Above	Year Retired
5	1995	RADM1 (RET) Larry Loon Leong Yoon	Combat	RSS Dauntless; RSS Sea Lion	188 SQN	1 FLOT	RSN Fleet	Fleet COMD; NHO; COS-NS	1999
6	1998	RADM2 (RET) Lui Tuck Yew	Combat	RSS Sea Hawk	185 SQN	1 FLOT	RSN Fleet	Fleet COMD; Deputy CNV; CNV	2003
7	1999	RADM1 (RET) Simon Ong Hung Eng	Combat	RSS Freedom; RSS Sea Lion; RSS Vigilance	185 SQN	–	–	HNO; COS-NS; COMDT SAFTI MI	2003
8	2000	RADM1 (RET) Jway Ching Hua	Engineering	Unknown	N/A	N/A	N/A	HNL	2002
9	2001	RADM1 (RET) Sim Gim Guan	Combat	RSS Sea Tiger	185 SQN	–	RSN Fleet	Fleet COMD; HNO; COS-NS	2006
10	2001	RADM2 (RET) Ronnie Tay	Combat	RSS Swift Warlord; RSS Sea Lion	188 SQN	1 FLOT	RSN Fleet	NHO; COS-NS; CNV	2007

(cont'd overleaf)

Appendix F *(cont'd)*

S/N	Year Promoted	Rank and Name	Vocation	Ship Command	Squadron Command	Flotilla Command	Fleet-Level Command	Appointments Held as One-Star and Above	Year Retired
11	2005	RADM2 (RET) Chew Men Leong	Combat	RSS Vigour	188 SQN	1 FLOT	RSN Fleet	Fleet COMD; HNO; COS-NS; CNV	2011
12	2006	RADM1 (RET) Tan Kai Hoe	Combat	RSS Swift Knight; RSS Valour	185 SQN	–	RSN Fleet	Fleet COMD; COS-NS; DIR (Policy) DPO; Fleet	2009
13	2007	RADM2 (NS) Ng Chee Peng	Combat	RSS Victory	188 SQN	1 FLOT	RSN Fleet	COMD; COS-NS; COS-JS; CNV	2014
14	2007	RADM1 (RET) Tay Kian Seng	Combat	RSS Victory; RSS Valour	188 SQN	1 FLOT	–	HNO; DJO	2010
15	2007	RADM1 (Dr) (RET) John Wong Chee Meng	Medical	Head, Psychological Care Centre; Head, Naval Medicine & Hyperbaric Centre	Military Medical Institute	Naval Medical Services	SAF Medical Corps	CMC	2009

S/N	Year Promoted	Rank and Name	Vocation	Ship Command	Squadron Command	Flotilla Command	Fleet-Level Command	Appointments Held as One-Star and Above	Year Retired
16	2008	RADM2 (NS) Joseph Leong Weng Keong	Combat	RSS Valour; RSS Vigilance	188 SQN	1 FLOT	RSN Fleet	HJPT; Fleet COMD; DMI/Chief C4I; DIR SID COMD	2014
17	2009	RADM1 (RET) Tan Wee Beng	Combat	Unknown	Unknown	NDU	MSTF	MSTF; HNO; COS-NS	2014
18	2010	L/RADM1 (RET) Bernard Donald Miranda (L/RADM1 [2010–11])	Combat	RSS Sovereignty; RSS Sea Wolf; RSS Persistence	191 SQN	3 FLOT	–	COMD CTF-151; DIR (Multi-National Operations) in CNV Office	2011
19	2010	RADM1 (RET) Jackson Chia	Combat	RSS Vigour; RSS Formidable	–	–	MSTF	COMD MSTF; HNO; COS-NS	2016

(cont'd overleaf)

Appendix F (cont'd)

S/N	Year Promoted	Rank and Name	Vocation	Ship Command	Squadron Command	Flotilla Command	Fleet-Level Command	Appointments Held as One-Star and Above	Year Retired
20	2011	RADM1 (NS) Harris Chan Weng Yip (L/RADM1 [2011–12])	Combat	RSS Vigilance; RSS Victory	—	—	MSTF	COMD CTF-151; COMD MSTF; FSTA	2017
21	2011	RADM2 (NS) Lai Chung Han	Combat	RSS Valiant	188 SQN	1 FLOT	RSN Fleet	Fleet COMD; DS (Policy) MINDEF; CNV	2017
22	2013	RADM1 (RET) Giam Hock Koon (L/RADM1 [2013])	Combat	RSS Vengeance; RSS Steadfast	185 SQN	1 FLOT	MSTF	COMD CTF-151; COMD MSTF; COMDT SAFTI MI; HNO	2018
23	2013	RADM1 (Dr) (RET) Kang Wee Lee	Medical	Unknown	Force Medical Protection Command	Naval Medical Services	SAF Medical Corps	CMC	2015

S/N	Year Promoted	Rank and Name	Vocation	Ship Command	Squadron Command	Flotilla Command	Fleet-Level Command	Appointments Held as One-Star and Above	Year Retired
24	2013	RADM1 Timothy Lo Khee Shik	Combat	RSS Justice; RSS Vigour	188 SQN	–	RSN Fleet	Fleet COMD; HNO; COS-NS	
25	2015	RADM1 Frederick Chew Chih Chiang	Combat	RSS Formidable	185 SQN	–	MSTF	COMD MSTF; DJO; DS (Technology)	
26	2015	RADM2 Lew Chuen Hong	Combat	RSS Vengeance	–	–	RSN Fleet	Fleet COMD; COS-NS; CNV	
27	2016	RADM1 Ken Cheong Kwok Chien (L/RADM1 [2016])	Combat	RSS Brave; RSS Valiant; RSS Stalwart	188 SQN; 185 SQN	1 FLOT	RSN Fleet	COMD CTF-151; Fleet COMD; HNO	
28	2016	RADM1 (Dr) Tang Kong Choong	Medical	Base Medical Squadron	Force Medical Protection Command	Naval Medical Services	SAF Medical Corps	CMC	

(cont'd overleaf)

Appendix F *(cont'd)*

S/N	Year Promoted	Rank and Name	Vocation	Ship Command	Squadron Command	Flotilla Command	Fleet-Level Command	Appointments Held as One-Star and Above	Year Retired
29	2017	RADM1 Alan Goh Kim Hua	Combat	RSS Vigour	188 SQN	–	MSTF	COMD MSTF; Group Chief (Policy & Strategy) DPG, MINDEF	
30	2018	L/RADM1 Saw Shi Tat (L/RADM1 [2018])	Combat	RSS Brave; RSS Steadfast	185 SQN	1 FLOT	–	COMD CTF-151	
31	2018	RADM1 Edwin Leong Wai Kwan	Combat	RSS Victory	188 SQN	–	RSN Fleet	Fleet COMD	

Appendix G
Command appointments of generals in the RSAF (1987–2018)

S/N	Year Promoted	Rank and Name	Vocation	Squadron Command	Brigade or Group	Air Base or Division	Operational Command	Appointments Held as One-Star and Above	Retirement
1	1987	BG (RET) Michael Teo Eng Cheng	Pilot (FTR)	140 SQN; 144 SQN	N/A	–	N/A	COMD RSAF; CAF	1992
2	1989	BG (RET) Gary Yeo Ping Yong	Pilot (FTR)	142 SQN	N/A	TAB	N/A	Deputy COMD RSAF; COS-AS; DJID	1993
3	1992	LG (RET) Bey Soo Khiang	Pilot (TPT)	–	N/A	PLAB	N/A	COS-AS; CAF; Acting CDF; CDF	2000
4	1992	BG (RET) Wesley Gerard D'Aranjo	Air Engineering Officer	*Unknown*	N/A	DMO	N/A	DS (Technology) MINDEF	1998
5	1994	MG (RET) Goh Yong Siang	Pilot (FTR)	140 SQN	N/A	PLAB	N/A	COS-AS; DJOPD; CAF	1998

(contd overleaf)

Appendix G *(cont'd)*

S/N	Year Promoted	Rank and Name	Vocation	Squadron Command	Brigade or Group	Air Base or Division	Operational Command	Appointments Held as One-Star and Above	Retirement
6	1994	BG (RET) (Dr) Lim Meng Kin	Medical	Head RSAF Aeromedical Centre; CO 3rd Medical Bn	N/A	SAF Medical Corps	N/A	CMC; DIR DMRI at DSO	1995
7	1997	MG (RET) Raymund Ng Teck Heng	Pilot (FTR)	145 SQN	N/A	TAB	N/A	HAO; COS-AS; CAF	2001
8	1997	BG (RET) Yam Ah Mee	AWO (GBAD)	165 SADA	SADA	ADSD	N/A	COS-AS; COMD ADSD	1998
9	1998	MG (RET) Rocky Lim Kim Choon	Pilot (FTR)	–	N/A	TAB	N/A	HAO; COS-AS; CAF	2006
10	1999	BG (RET) Jimmy Khoo Siew Kim	AWO (GBAD)	160 SADA	*Unknown*	ADSD	N/A	COMD ADSD; DJOPD; CIO MINDEF; FSA	2007
11	1999	BG (RET) Loh Kok Hua	Pilot (FTR)	140 SQN	N/A	PLAB; TAB	N/A	COMD TAB; DA Washington	2002

S/N	Year Promoted	Rank and Name	Vocation	Squadron Command	Brigade or Group	Air Base or Division	Operational Command	Appointments Held as One-Star and Above	Retirement
12	2000	BG (RET) Chee Wee Kiong	AWO (GBAD)	*Unknown*	ADB	ADSD	N/A	COMD ADSD; COS-AS; DJOPD; COS and later DIR SID	e. 2007
13	2000	BG (RET) Jek Kian Yee	Pilot (TPT)	*Unknown*	N/A	–	N/A	DIR MSD	2006
14	2000	BG (RET) Yap Ong Heng	AWO (C3)	*Unknown*	*Unknown*	*Unknown*	N/A	MA at the Permanent Mission of Singapore to the UN	2004
15	2001	BG (RET) Lim Yeow Beng	Air Engineering Officer	ALS TAB	N/A	N/A	N/A	HAL	2003
16	2002	BG (RET) Voon Tse-Chow	Pilot (FTR)	142 SQN	N/A	PLAB	N/A	DA Washington	2005
17	2003	MG (RET) Ng Chee Khern	Pilot (FTR)	149 SQN	N/A	TAB	N/A	HJO; DJOPD; COS-AS; CAF	2009

(cont'd overleaf)

Appendix G *(cont'd)*

S/N	Year Promoted	Rank and Name	Vocation	Squadron Command	Brigade or Group	Air Base or Division	Operational Command	Appointments Held as One-Star and Above	Retirement
18	2003	BG (RET) Jimmy Tan Cheng Yaw	AWO (GBAD); AWO (C3)	20X SQN	AFSB	ADSD	N/A	COMD ADSD; COMDT SAFTI MI	2009
19	2004	BG (RET) Richard Lim Keng Yong	Pilot (FTR)	140 SQN; Peace Carvin II	N/A	TAB	N/A	COMD TAB; DA Washington	2008
20	2004	BG (RET) Charles Sih Seah Wee	Pilot (FTR)	145 SQN	N/A	PLAB	N/A	HAO; COS-AS	2008
21	2004	BG (RET) Wong Huat Sern	Pilot (HELI)	120 SQN	N/A	SBAB	PC	HJO; COMD SBAB; COMD PC; COS-AS	2013
22	2005	BG (RET) Gary Ang Aik Hwang	AWO (C3)	111 SQN	–	TAB	–	DIR (Policy) DPO; COMD TAB; DS (Policy) MINDEF	2011

S/N	Year Promoted	Rank and Name	Vocation	Squadron Command	Brigade or Group	Air Base or Division	Operational Command	Appointments Held as One-Star and Above	Retirement
23	2005	BG (RET) Tan Meng Dui	AWO (C3)	20X SQN	ADB	ADSD	ADOC	HAT; COMD ADSD/ADOC; HAO; DMI; DS (Technology) MINDEF	2011
24	2006	BG (RET) Tsoi Mun Heng	Air Engineering Officer	ALS SBAB	N/A	N/A	N/A	HAL; DIR DISO MINDEF	2009
25	2007	MG (RET) Hoo Cher Mou	AWO (C3)	203 SQN	AFSB	N/A	ADOC	COMD ADOC; COS-AS; COS-JS; CAF	2016
26	2008	LG (RET) Ng Chee Meng	Pilot (FTR)	144 SQN	N/A	CAB	–	DJO; Deputy CAF; CAF; CDF	2015
27	2008	BG (RET) Richard Christopher Pereira	Pilot (FTR)	145 SQN	TASC	–	ACC	COMD ACC	2011

(cont'd overleaf)

Appendix G (*cont'd*)

S/N	Year Promoted	Rank and Name	Vocation	Squadron Command	Brigade or Group	Air Base or Division	Operational Command	Appointments Held as One-Star and Above	Retirement
28	2008	BG (RET) Cheng Siak Kian (L/BG [2008–10])	AWO (GBAD)	165 SQN	ADB	N/A	ADOC	DA Washington; DIR (Policy) DPO; COMD ADOC	2015
29	2009	BG (RET) Kwek Kok Kwong	AWO (C3)	20X SQN	AFOG, ASCG	N/A	ADOC	COMD ADOC	2012
30	2011	BG (RET) Lim Yeong Kiat	Pilot (FTR)	140 SQN	–	CAB	ACC	COMD ACC; COS-AS	2015
31	2011	ME8 (RET) Lee Ling Wee	Air Engineering Officer	ALS TAB	–	–	N/A	HAL	2013
32	2011	BG (RET) Sarbjit Singh S/O Tahil Singh	Pilot (FTR)	140 SQN	TASC	–	UC; APGC	COMD APGC	2014
33	2012	BG (RET) Neo Hong Keat	Pilot (FTR)	140 SQN	–	–	UC; APGC	HAO; COMD APGC; COS-AS	2017

S/N	Year Promoted	Rank and Name	Vocation	Squadron Command	Brigade or Group	Air Base or Division	Operational Command	Appointments Held as One-Star and Above	Retirement
34	2012	BG Tan Chee Wee (L/BG [2012–13, 2013–14])	AWO (C3)	203 SQN	–	N/A	ADOC	DA Washington; DIR (Policy) DPO; COMD ADOC; DJO	
35	2013	BG Lim Tuang Liang	Pilot (FTR)	145 SQN	–	–	UC; ACC	COMD ACC; HAO; COA-AS; COS-JS	2018
36	2013	MG Mervyn Tan Wei Ming	Pilot (TPT)	121 SQN	–	–	ADOC	COMD ADOC; DMI/Chief C4I; CAF	
37	2013	L/BG (RET) Ken Leong Kum Wah (L/BG [2013–16])	Pilot (FTR)	*Unknown*	–	–	–	DA Washington	2016
38	2015	ME8 Francis Cheong Han Kwok	Engineer	ALS TAB	–	SBAB	N/A	HAEL	

(cont'd overleaf)

Appendix G *(cont'd)*

S/N	Year Promoted	Rank and Name	Vocation	Squadron Command	Brigade or Group	Air Base or Division	Operational Command	Appointments Held as One-Star and Above	Retirement
39	2015	BG Gan Siow Huang	AWO (C3)	203 SQN	ASCG	–	APGC	HJMP; HAI; DIR (SP); COMD APGC	
40	2015	BG Kelvin Khong Boon Leong	Pilot (FTR)	149 SQN	–	–	ACC	COMD ACC; HAO; COS-AS; COS-JS	
41	2016	BG Tommy Tan Ah Han	Pilot (FTR)	145 SQN; Peace Carvin V	–	–	UC; ACC	COMD ACC; COS-AS	
42	2016	BG Jonathan Tan Chin Kwang	Pilot (HELI)	126 SQN; Peace Triton; 123 SQN	TASG	–	PC	COMD PC	
43	2016	L/BG Tan Boon Kim (L/BG [2013–present])	AWO (C3)	Unknown	–	–	–	DA Washington	
44	2018	BG Kelvin Fan Sui Siong	AWO (GBAD)	163 SQN	–	–	–	HAO	
45	2018	BG Gaurav Keerthi	Pilot (HELI)	127 SQN	–	–	ADOC	COMD ADOC; Chief Innovation Officer RSAF	

Appendix H
Estimated active service rank attainment of SAFOS batches (1971–98) by 2018

Year	Full Career (after 20 years or reaching COL/ME7 and above)		Left SAF Early (before 20 years)
	BG/RADM1/ME8 and Above	COL (unless stated)	LTC and Below
1971	Boey Tak Hap; Lee Hsien Loong; Sin Boon Wah	Lai Seck Khui	Liu Tsun Kie
1972	Lim Neo Chian; Wesley Gerard D'Aranjo	Soon Eng Boon	Chong San Chew; Choo Chun Wei; Chua Chin Kiat (transferred to SPF); Goh Liang Kwang (transferred to SPF); Richard Lim Koon Heng; Dominic Ng Ann Hoe; Pek Beng Choon; Tan Cheok Hoon; Tan Keng Hiang; Tan Kian Chew; Tsao Chieh; Wong Cheong Fook, David Cecil Vivian; Yong Choon Kong
1973	George Yeo Yong Boon; Teo Chee Hean; Han Eng Juan	Peter Ho Hak Ean; Tan Kim Siew	Khoo Boon Hui (transferred to SPF); Lim Hng Khiang; Lim Swee Say; Lim Teik Hock
1974	Bey Soo Khiang; Tan Yong Soon	–	Chew Leng Hock; James Kwa Boon Hwee; Leong Peng Kiong; Willie Tan Yoke Meng
1975	Lee Fook Sun	Ho Meng Kit	Lim Chong Kiat

(cont'd overleaf)

Appendix H *(cont'd)*

Year	Full Career (after 20 years or reaching COL/ME7 and above)		Left SAF Early (before 20 years)
	BG/RADM1/ME8 and Above	COL (unless stated)	LTC and Below
1976	Lee Hsien Yang	Michael Low Oon Hoe; Terence Siew Chee Kin	Gan Juay Kiat; Kee Teck Koon; Lee Hon Sun; Ed Ng Ee Peng; Tham Kui Seng
1977	Rocky Lim Kim Choon	–	John Kan Wei Seng; Lee Nyuk Sze; Ng Koh Wee; James Tan Ching Wen; Tang Kok Fai
1978	Choi Shing Kwok; Lam Joon Khoi	Lee Wai Mun	Philip Chua Wee Meng; Eng Heng Chiaw
1979	Pang Hee Hon; Yap Ong Heng	–	Eng Hung Chiaw; Ong Siang Hor; Steven Ong; Seah Boon Thong (perished on active service); Shae Toh Hock; Tay Hun Kiat; Tong Min Way
1980	Lim Chuan Poh; Ng Yat Chung; Lui Tuck Yew	–	Benny Goh Heng Heng
1981	Jimmy Khoo Siew Kim; Jimmy Tan Cheng Yaw	Poh Hee Kim	Cheong Kin Wah; Lu Cheng-Yang
1982	Desmond Kuek Bak Chye; Chee Wee Kiong; Tay Lim Heng; Chua Chwee Koh; Ronnie Tay	Goh Leong Huat	Paul Chong Kai Yew; Peter Gwee Choon Lin; Lim Boon Wee; Lim Ming Yan; Tan Sing Hock
1983	Jek Kian Yee; Sim Gim Guan; Wong Huat Sern	Cheong Keng Soon	Chai Chin Loon; Goh Kok Huat; Lee Kin Seng; Ng Chee Yuen; Poh Kwee Lin; David Tan Kim Hong; Wong Chen-Guan; William Yap Guan Hong

Year	Full Career (after 20 years or reaching COL/ME7 and above)		Left SAF Early (before 20 years)
	BG/RADM1/ME8 and Above	COL (unless stated)	LTC and Below
1984	Loh Wai Keong; Hugh Reginald Lim U Yang	Kenneth Kwok Fook Kay; Soh Poh Theen	Teo Kian Bin
1985	Neo Kian Hong; Ng Chee Khern; Bernard Richard Tan Kok Kiang; Tan Kai Hoe; Tan Yih San	Chng Ho Kiat; Tan Wei Ming; Toh Boh Kwee	Yoon Kam Choon
1986	Gary Ang Aik Hwang; Tan Meng Dui; Wong Ann Chai; Tan Wee Beng	Koh Peng Keng; Joshua Ho How Hoang (LTC)	Nicholas Chua Hwee Song; Neo Wei Ming; Edmund Ying Jat Mun (perished on active service)
1987	Chew Men Leong; Tay Kian Seng	Gerald Heng Mok Thye; Low Pat Chin; Gregory Thomas Tan Kheng Lee; Tay Kim Chiew	Spencer Phua Choon Kiat
1988	Chan Chun Sing; Ngien Hoon Ping; Tan Boon Kim (L/BG)	Seow Hwye Min; Woon Tai Shin	–
1989	Ng Chee Peng; Tan Chuan-Jin	Lee Seow Hiang	Tay Han Chong
1990	Harris Chan Weng Yip; Joseph Leong Weng Keong; Terry Siow Meng Meng	–	Kenny Lim Su Ann
1991	Chia Choon Hoong; Perry Lim Cheng Yeow; Lim Tuang Liang	Ang Heng; Wong Yu Han	–

(cont'd overleaf)

Appendix H *(cont'd)*

Year	Full Career (after 20 years or reaching COL/ME7 and above)		Left SAF Early (before 20 years)
	BG/RADM1/ME8 and Above	**COL (unless stated)**	**LTC and Below**
1992	Lai Chung Han; Milton Ong Ann Kiat; Ken Cheong Kwok Chien	Steven Seng Wei San	Brandon Murray Lee Thian Boon; Dominic Ow El Gene; Tan Gim Chong; Tan Yuh Cherng
1993	Tan Chee Wee	Ho Yung Peng; Lee Wee Lee (SLTC); Tan Ying Kiat	Kwek Ju-Hon; Lee Jek Suen
1994	Frederick Chew Chih Chiang; Melvyn Ong Su Kiat; Ong Tze-Ch'in; Ng Chad-Son	Richard Lim Kai-Chuan	–
1995	Kelvin Khong Boon Leong; Lew Chuen Hong; Alan Goh Kim Hua	Victor Huang Kuan Kai; Pang Tzer Yeu (SLTC)	Ng Chia Yong; Ng Sin Kian; Teo Cheng Hang
1996	–	–	Choy Dawen; Goh Meng Kiat; Khoo Teng Lip; James Lee Tze Wei; Lien Choong Luen; Kelvin Lim Wee Khoon; Frederick Teo Li-Wei
1997	Goh Si Hou	Ang Chee Wee; Tan Cheng Kwee	Chang Yi-Chian; Chua Lu-Fong; Teh Hua Fung
1998	Kelvin Fan Sui Siong; Gaurav Keerthi	Frederick Choo Wei Yee; Chua Jin Kiat; Ho Kum Luen; Kwan Hon Chuong	Adrian Choong Haw Chieh; Sim Kai; Alvin Teo Chin Wei; Teo Tse Hsiang
TOTAL	68	40	89

Note: Non-flag officers on active duty as of 1 July 2018 include COL Gerald Heng Mok Thye (Commander Maritime Training and Doctrine Command); COL Ho Yung Peng (Commander Paya Lebar Air Base); COL Victor Huang

Kuan Kai (Deputy Future Systems and Technology Architect [Concepts]/ Director Systems and Capability Group, FSTD); SLTC Pang Tzer Yeu (Director [Plans], Policy and Plans Directorate, DCO); COL Ang Chee Wee (former commander ISG, MIO); COL Tan Cheng Kwee (on secondment as Director, Strategic Planning, Research and Development Division at the Ministry of Social and Family Development); COL Frederick Choo Wei Yee (Head, Joint Plans and Transformation Department); COL Chua Jin Kiat (Assistant Chief of General Staff [Training]); COL Ho Kum Luen (Commander Air Command); and COL Kwan Hon Chuong (Director, National Maritime Operations Group, Singapore Maritime Crisis Centre, MINDEF).

Raw Figures:

Total number of SAFOS recipients (1971–98): 197

Percentage who made one-star and above: $\dfrac{68}{197} = 34.52\%$

Percentage who served until retirement or made COL and above:

$$\dfrac{68+40}{197} = \dfrac{108}{197} = 54.82\%$$

Percentage of flag officers among those who served until retirement:

$$\dfrac{68}{108} = 62.96\%$$

Adjusted Figures (accounting for the three officers transferred to the police force and the two who perished on active service):

Percentage who made one-star and above: $\dfrac{68}{192} = 35.42\%$

Percentage who served until retirement or made COL and above:

$$\dfrac{68 + 40}{192} = \dfrac{108}{192} = 56.25\%$$

Percentage of flag officers among those who served until retirement:

$$\dfrac{68}{108} = 62.96\%$$

Appendix I
Former regular SAF officers in the Cabinet (1984–2018)

Name	SAFOS Year	Left SAF	Terminal Rank	Last Appointment as a Regular in the SAF	Latest/Last Cabinet Appointment	Political Career
Lee Hsien Loong	1971	1984	BG	Chief of Staff of the General Staff (1982–84); Director Joint Operations and Planning Directorate (1983–84)	Prime Minister (since 2004)	1984–present
George Yeo Yong Boon	1973	1988	BG	Director Joint Operations and Planning Directorate (1986–88)	Minister for Foreign Affairs (2004–11)	1988–2011
Lim Hng Khiang	1973	1987	LTC	Director (Policy) Defence Policy Office, MINDEF (1986–87)	Minister for Trade and Industry (Trade) (2015–18)	1991–present
Teo Chee Hean	1973	1992	RADM1	Chief of Navy (1991–92)	Deputy Prime Minister (since 2009) and Coordinating Minister for National Security (since 2015)	1992–present
Lim Swee Say	1973	1984	MAJ	Head Information Engineering Centre, System and Computer Organisation, MINDEF (1982–84)	Minister for Manpower (2015–18)	1996–present

Name	SAFOS Year	Left SAF	Terminal Rank	Last Appointment as a Regular in the SAF	Latest/Last Cabinet Appointment	Political Career
Lui Tuck Yew	1980	2003	RADM2	Chief of Navy (1999–2003)	Minister for Transport (2011–15)	2006–15
Chan Chun Sing	1988	2011	MG	Chief of Army (2010–11)	Minister for Trade and Industry (since 2018)	2011–present
Tan Chuan-Jin	1989	2011	BG	Commander Army Training and Doctrine Command (2009–11)	Minister for Social and Family Development (2015–17)	2011–present
Ng Chee Meng	–	2015	LG	Chief of Defence Force (2013–15)	Secretary-General, National Trades Union Congress, Minister in PMO, Minister-in-Charge of the Civil Service (since 2018)	2015–present

Appendix J

Defence Chief roll of honour (1966–2018)
Director General Staff/Chief of the General Staff/Chief of Defence Force

Rank and Name	Service	Vocation	From	To	Initial Scholarship
ACP Tan Teck Khim	Police Force	Senior Police Officer	1966	July 1968	N/A
COL Kirpa Ram Vij	Army	Artillery	July 1968	Dec. 1968	N/A
BG Thomas James Duncan Campbell (Acting DGS)	Army	Infantry	Dec. 1968	Dec. 1969	N/A
BG Thomas James Duncan Campbell	Army	Infantry	Dec. 1969	Sept. 1970	N/A
BG Kirpa Ram Vij	Army	Artillery	Sept. 1970	May 1974	N/A
MG Winston Choo Wee Leong	Army	Signals	May 1974	1981	N/A
BG Tan Chin Tiong (Acting CGS)	Army	Infantry	1981	1982	N/A
LG Winston Choo Wee Leong	Army	Signals	1982	30 June 1992	N/A
LG Ng Jui Ping	Army	Artillery	1 July 1992	30 June 1995	N/A
LG Bey Soo Khiang	Air Force	Pilot (transport)	1 July 1995	31 Mar. 2000	SAFOS 1974
LG Lim Chuan Poh	Army	Infantry	1 Apr. 2000	27 Mar. 2003	SAFOS 1980
LG Ng Yat Chung	Army	Artillery	28 Mar. 2003	22 Mar. 2007	SAFOS 1980

Rank and Name	Service	Vocation	From	To	Initial Scholarship
LG Desmond Kuek Bak Chye	Army	Armour	23 Mar. 2007	31 Mar. 2010	SAFOS 1982
LG Neo Kian Hong	Army	Guards	1 Apr. 2010	26 Mar. 2013	SAFOS 1985
LG Ng Chee Meng	Air Force	Pilot (fighter)	27 Mar. 2013	17 Aug. 2015	MTA 1987
LG Perry Lim Cheng Yeow	Army	Guards	18 Aug. 2015	22 Mar. 2018	SAFOS 1991
LG Melvyn Ong Su Kiat	Army	Infantry	23 Mar. 2018	*Present*	SAFOS 1994

Appendix K

Army Chief roll of honour (1988–2018)
Deputy Chief of General Staff (Army)/Chief of Army

Rank and Name	Vocation	From	To	Tenure (days)	Initial Scholarship
BG Boey Tak Hap	Infantry	1 July 1988	31 Aug. 1990	791	SAFOS 1971
MG Ng Jui Ping	Artillery	1 Sept. 1990	30 June 1992	668	N/A
MG Lim Neo Chian	Combat Engineer	1 July 1992	30 Apr. 1995	1,033	SAFOS 1972
MG Han Eng Juan	Armour	1 May 1995	30 June 1998	1,156	SAFOS 1973
MG Lim Chuan Poh	Infantry	1 July 1998	30 Mar. 2000	638	SAFOS 1980
MG Ng Yat Chung	Artillery	31 Mar. 2000	26 Mar. 2003	1,090	SAFOS 1980
MG Desmond Kuek Bak Chye	Armour	27 Mar. 2003	19 Mar. 2007	1,453	SAFOS 1982
MG Neo Kian Hong	Guards	20 Mar. 2007	25 Mar. 2010	1,101	SAFOS 1985
MG Chan Chun Sing	Infantry	26 Mar. 2010	24 Mar. 2011	363	SAFOS 1988
MG Ravinder Singh S/O Harchand Singh	Signals	25 Mar. 2011	20 Mar. 2014	1,091	SMS 1983
MG Perry Lim Cheng Yeow	Guards	21 Mar. 2014	13 Aug. 2015	510	SAFOS 1991
MG Melvyn Ong Su Kiat	Infantry	14 Aug. 2015	20 Mar. 2018	950	SAFOS 1994
BG Goh Si Hou	Artillery	21 Mar. 2018	*Present*	*Incumbent*	SAFOS 1997

Appendix L

Navy Chief roll of honour (1966–2018)
Commander Singapore Naval Volunteer Force/Commander Maritime
Command/Commander Republic of Singapore Navy/Chief of Navy

Rank and Name	From	To	Tenure (days)	Initial Scholarship
LTC Jaswant Singh Gill	1 Oct. 1966	30 Dec. 1968	821	N/A
LTC Mohamed Bin Mohamed Salleh	31 Dec. 1968	31 July 1969	212	N/A
MAJ Geoffrey Vernon Dennis	1 Aug. 1969	31 Aug. 1970	395	N/A
COL James Aeria	1 Sept. 1970	8 Oct. 1975	1,863	N/A
COL Khoo Eng Ann	9 Oct. 1975	28 Feb. 1985	3,430	N/A
RADM1 James Leo Chin Lian	1 Mar. 1985	31 May 1991	2,282	N/A
RADM1 Teo Chee Hean	1 June 1991	7 Dec. 1992	555	SAFOS 1973
RADM2 Kwek Siew Jin	8 Dec. 1992	30 June 1996	1,300	~ LSA 1969 or 1970
RADM2 Richard Lim Cherng Yih	1 July 1996	30 June 1999	1,094	Colombo Plan 1972
RADM2 Lui Tuck Yew	1 July 1999	31 Mar. 2003	1,369	SAFOS 1980
RADM2 Ronnie Tay	1 Apr. 2003	30 Aug. 2007	1,612	SAFOS 1982
RADM2 Chew Men Leong	31 Aug. 2007	28 Mar. 2011	1,305	SAFOS 1987
RADM2 Ng Chee Peng	29 Mar. 2011	31 July 2014	1,220	SAFOS 1989
RADM2 Lai Chung Han	1 Aug. 2014	15 June 2017	1,050	SAFOS 1992
RADM2 Lew Chuen Hong	16 June 2017	*Present*	*Incumbent*	SAFOS 1995

Appendix M

Air Force Chief roll of honour (1970–2018)

Commander Singapore Air Defence Command/Director Air Staff RSAF/
Deputy Commander RSAF/Commander RSAF/Chief of Air Force

Rank and Name	Vocation	From	To	Tenure (days)	Initial Scholarship
LTC Ee Tean Chye	*Transferred from army*	15 Sept. 1970	31 May 1972	624	N/A
Air Commodore (~BG) John Francis Langer	*On loan service from the RAF*	4 Jan. 1973	23 Mar. 1975	808	N/A
Group Captain (~COL) William E. Kelly	*On loan service from the RAF*	24 Mar. 1975	30 Oct. 1975	220	N/A
Group Captain David John Rhodes	*On loan service from the RAF*	31 Oct. 1975	30 Aug. 1976	304	N/A
Group Captain Murray Alexander Turnbull	*On loan service from the RAAF*	1 Sept. 1976	20 May 1977	261	N/A
COL Liu Ching Chuan	*Contract retired ROCAF*	21 May 1977	31 May 1980	1,259	N/A
COL Michael Teo Eng Cheng	Pilot (fighter)	1 Nov. 1980	6 June 1982	582	N/A
COL Gary Yeo Ping Yong	Pilot (fighter)	7 June 1982	26 June 1984	750	N/A
BG Michael Teo Eng Cheng	Pilot (fighter)	27 June 1984	31 Aug. 1992	2987	N/A

Rank and Name	Vocation	From	To	Tenure (days)	Initial Scholarship
MG Bey Soo Khiang	Pilot (transport)	1 Sept. 1992	30 June 1995	1,032	SAFOS 1974
MG Goh Yong Siang	Pilot (fighter)	1 July 1995	30 June 1998	1,095	N/A
MG Raymund Ng Teck Heng	Pilot (fighter)	1 July 1998	31 Mar. 2001	1,004	OMS 1977
MG Rocky Lim Kim Choon	Pilot (fighter)	1 Apr. 2001	23 Mar. 2006	1,817	SAFOS 1977
MG Ng Chee Khern	Pilot (fighter)	24 Mar. 2006	9 Dec. 2009	1,356	SAFOS 1985
MG Ng Chee Meng	Pilot (fighter)	10 Dec. 2009	24 Mar. 2013	1,200	MTA 1987
MG Hoo Cher Mou	Air Warfare Officer (C3)	25 Mar. 2013	27 Mar. 2016	1,098	SMS 1985
MG Mervyn Tan Wei Ming	Pilot (transport)	28 Mar. 2016	*Present*	*Incumbent*	OTA 1992

Appendix N

Legislative Assembly (1959–65) and Parliamentary Elections (1965–2016) in Singapore

Election Year	Polling Day	Election Deposit	Eligible Voters	Voters in Contested Constituencies	% of All Eligible Voters	% of Contested Votes Won by PAP	Total Seats	Seats Won by PAP (seats held after by-election[s] if any)	Voter Turnout	%
1959	30 May	$500	586,098	586,098	100.0	54.1	51	43 (41)	527,919	90.1
1963	21 Sept.	$500	617,650	617,650	100.0	46.9	51	37 (50)	587,433	95.1
1968	13 Apr.	$500	759,367	84,883	11.2	86.7	58	58 (58)	77,952	91.8
1972	2 Sept.	$500	908,382	812,926	89.5	70.4	65	65	760,468	93.5
1976	23 Dec.	$1,200	1,095,817	857,297	78.2	74.1	69	69 (69)	815,130	95.1
1980	23 Dec.	$1,500	1,290,426	685,141	53.1	77.7	75	75 (74)	654,295	95.5
1984	22 Dec.	$1,500	1,495,389	944,624	63.2	64.8	79	77	903,499	95.6
1988	3 Sept.	$4,000	1,669,013	1,449,838	86.9	63.2	81	80	1,373,064	94.7
1991	31 Aug.	$6,000	1,692,384	847,716	50.1	61.0	81	77 (77)	805,593	95.0

Election Year	Polling Day	Election Deposit	Eligible Voters	Voters in Contested Constituencies	% of All Eligible Voters	% of Contested Votes Won by PAP	Total Seats	Seats Won by PAP (seats held after by-election[s] if any)	Voter Turnout	%
1997	2 Jan.	$8,000	1,881,011	765,332	40.7	65.0	83	81	734,000	95.9
2001	3 Nov.	$13,000	2,036,923	675,306	33.2	75.3	84	82	638,903	94.6
2006	6 May	$13,500	2,159,721	1,223,442	56.6	66.6	84	82	1,150,003	94.0
2011	7 May	$16,000	2,350,873	2,211,102	94.1	60.1	87	81 (80)	2,060,373	93.2
2015	11 Sept.	$14,500	2,462,926	2,462,926	100.0	69.9	89	83 (83)	2,307,746	93.7

Bibliography

Interviews

The interview participants are arranged in chronological order starting with the receipt of the first star, followed by highest rank attained, and then alphabetically by surname/name:

LG (RET) Choo Wee Leong, Winston (Army) – 1974

BG (RET) Sim Hak Kng, Patrick (Army) – 1978

BG (RET) Tan Chin Tiong (Army) – 1980

BG (RET) Yeo Ping Yong, Gary (RSAF) – 1989

BG (RET) Choy Choong Tow, Patrick (Army) – 1990

MG (RET) Lim Neo Chian (Army) – 1991

BG (RET) Colin George Theseira (Army) – 1991

LG (RET) Bey Soo Khiang (RSAF) – 1992

RADM2 (RET) Lim Cherng Yih, Richard (RSN) – 1994

BG (RET) Law Chwee Kiat (Army) – 1995

RADM1 (RET) Loon Leong Yoon, Larry (RSN) – 1995

BG (RET) Tan Kim Teck, Andrew (Army) – 1997

BG (RET) Yam Ah Mee (RSAF) – 1997

BG (RET) (Dr) Lee Kim Hock, Lionel (Army) – 1998

BG (RET) Loh Kok Hua (RSAF) – 1999

BG (RET) Su Poon Ghee, Philip (Army) – 1999

BG (RET) Chua Chwee Koh (Army) – 2001

BG (RET) Tan Cheng Yaw, Jimmy (RSAF) – 2003

BG (RET) Goh Kee Nguan (Army) – 2004

BG (RET) Lim Feng, Philip (Army) – 2005

BG (RET) Toh Bee Chew, Winston (Army) – 2005

BG (RET) Lowrence Chua (Army) – 2006

BG (RET) Tsoi Mun Heng (RSAF) – 2006

RADM1 (Dr) (RET) Wong Chee Meng, John (RSN) – 2007

BG (RET) Richard Christopher Pereira (RSAF) – 2008

BG (RET) Ishak Bin Ismail (Army) – 2009

BG (RET) (Dr) Seet Hun Yew, Benjamin (Army) – 2009

L/RADM1 (RET) Bernard Donald Miranda (RSN) – 2010

The following officers also provided invaluable insights into their careers with the SAF (by rank and then alphabetical order of surname):

COL (RET) Lim Teck Huat, Michael (Army)

COL (RET) Soh Guan Huat (RSN)

LTC (RET) Boon Hon Lin (Army)

LTC (RET) David Lee (RSN)

LTC (RET) Sng Seow Lian (Army)

Acknowledgement is also made of other ex-Regulars in the ranks of MAJ to COL who declined to be identified.

Oral History and Archival Records

Oral History Centre, National Archives of Singapore, interview with Lim Siong Guan for "The Civil Service: A Retrospection" project, Accession No: 003060 (14 reels).

Oral History Centre, National Archives of Singapore, interview with COL (RET) Ramachandran Menon for "The Civil Service: A Retrospection" project, Accession No: 003250 (17 reels).

Oral History Centre, National Archives of Singapore, interview with COL (RET) Goh Lye Choon for "The Civil Service: A Retrospection" project, Accession No: 003275 (17 reels).

Oral History Centre, National Archives of Singapore, interview with COL (RET) John Morrice for "The Civil Service: A Retrospection" project, Accession No: 003306 (13 reels).

Memo from S. Falle at the British High Commission, Tanglin Circus, Singapore 10, dated 18 Mar. 1974, reference 10/41A, and originally classified Confidential (Covering Secret: UK Eyes: Bravo), declassified 2005, to C.W. Squire Esq. MVO, South-East Asian Department, Foreign & Commonwealth Office, London SW1 (Kew Gardens, UK).

"Singapore Armed Forces Military Capability", report by Defence Adviser, British High Commission Singapore, Part I, originally classified Secret (UK Eyes Bravo), declassified 2005, attached to memo from S. Falle (Kew Gardens, UK).

Report of the Secretary-General on the United Nations Iraq-Kuwait Observation Mission (for the period 1 Oct. 1993–31 Mar. 1994), S/1994/388, 4 Apr. 1994, www.un.org/ Docs/s1994388.htm, accessed 28 May 2014.

Speeches

Speech by Dr Goh Keng Swee at a seminar on "Democracy and Communism" sponsored by the Ministry of Education for pre-university students at the Singapore

Conference Hall, 24–29 Apr. 1971. Reproduced in Goh Keng Swee, *The Economics of Modernization*. Singapore: Federal Publications, 1995, p. 146.

Speech by Dr Goh Keng Swee, Minister of Defence, at the Promotion Ceremony at MINDEF HQ, 2 May 1972. Reproduced in "Creating a Military Elite", *Pioneer* (June 1972): 13–4.

Speech by PM Lee Kuan Yew at the SAF Day Dinner, 1 Sept. 1981. Reproduced in "Ensuring Quality of Leadership in the Armed Forces", *Straits Times*, 7 Sept. 1981, p. 16.

Speech by Dr Goh Keng Swee at the Establishment Dinner, Mandarin Hotel, Singapore, 25 Sept. 1984. Reproduced in "Defence and the Establishment", *Pioneer: Journal of the Singapore Armed Forces* 11, 2 (Jan.–Mar 1985).

Speech by Minister of Defence Dr Yeo Ning Hong at the MINDEF Workplan Seminar, 26 Mar. 1994. Reported in "An SAF That Strives for Excellence", *Straits Times*, 1 July 1994, p. 4.

Speech by BG (NS) George Yeo, Minister for Information and the Arts, at the launch of SCCI publication "The Price of Peace", 21 June 1997. Inscription at the Bukit Chandu Memorial for the Malay Regiment, Singapore.

Speech by DPM Lee Hsien Loong at the Administrative Service Dinner and Promotion Ceremony, Mandarin Hotel, 29 Mar. 1999, http://www.singapore21.org.sg/speeches_290399.html.

Speech by Prime Minister Goh Chok Tong at the "35 Years of National Service Commemoration Dinner", 7 Sept. 2002, http://www.mindef.gov.sg/imindef/news_and_events/nr/2002/sep/07sep02_nr/07sep02_speech.html (no longer available).

Speech by RADM2 (RET) Kwek Siew Jin, president of the National Council of Social Service, at the Singapore Institute of Management University Convocation Ceremony, 7 Oct. 2011, www.ncss.gov.sg/About_NCSS/download_file.asp?speechid=121 (no longer available).

Speech by COL Cheng Siak Kian, Head Air Plans, titled "Towards The 3rd Generation RSAF", at the RSAF 17th NSmen Seminar, Air Force School Auditorium, 23 Mar. 2007, https://www.mindef.gov.sg/imindef/mindef_websites/atozlistings/air_force/news_events/events/events2007/AFNS2007.html (no longer available).

Speech by Minister for Defence Dr Ng Eng Hen at the MINDEF/SAF Scholarship Awards Ceremony, 29 July 2015, https://www.mindef.gov.sg/imindef/press_room/official_releases/sp/2015/29jul15_speech.html (7 Nov. 2016).

Speech by Chief of Army MG Desmond Kuek Bak Chye at the Chief of Army Change of Command Parade, 20 Mar. 2007.

Speech by Chief of Army MG Perry Lim Cheng Yeow at the Chief of Army Change of Command Parade, 14 Aug. 2015.

Speech by Chief of Defence Force LG Ng Chee Meng at the Chief of Defence Force Change of Command Parade, 18 Aug. 2015.

Speech by Chief of Air Force MG Hoo Cher Mou at the Chief of Air Force Change of Command Parade, 28 Mar. 2016.

Speech by Minister for Defence Dr Ng Eng Hen at the Committee of Supply Debate 2016, 8 Apr. 2016, https://www.mindef.gov.sg/imindef/press_room/official_releases/sp/2016/07apr16_speech1.html.

Speech by Minister for Defence Dr Ng Eng Hen at the Official Opening of the DSO Complex, 21 Apr. 2017, https://www.mindef.gov.sg/imindef/press_room/details.html?name=21apr17_speech&date=2017-04-21

Speech by Minister for Defence Dr Ng Eng Hen at the Committee of Supply Debate 2017, 3 Mar. 2017, https://www.mindef.gov.sg/imindef/press_room/details.html?name=03mar17_speech1&date=2017-03-03.

Talk by Bilahari Kausikan, Ambassador-at-Large at the Ministry of Foreign Affairs, titled "Why Small Countries Should Not Behave Like a Small Country" at the Singapore Platform for East-West Dialogue, 11 Oct. 2017, https://blogs.ntu.edu.sg/paralimes/2018/03/26/bilahari-smallcountries, accessed 4 Apr. 2018.

Presentations

Chan, Kim-Yin, Ping-Tzeun Chua, Kok-Yee Ng, Jeffrey C. Kennedy, Soon Ang, Christine Koh, Regena Ramaya and Sukhmohinder Singh. "Development of a Multisource Leadership Feedback Instrument for the SAF", presentation at the 49th International Military Testing Association Conference, Gold Coast, 8–12 Oct. 2007.

Lim, Meng Kin. "Aging Asia: A Perspective from Singapore", presentation at Aging Asia: Economic and Social Implications of Rapid Demographic Change in China, Japan, and Korea Conference, Stanford University, 26 Feb. 2009, iis-db.stanford.edu/cvnts/5501/Lim.pdf. accessed 28 May 2014.

Lim, Soo Hoon, permanent secretary (Public Service Division). "Human Capital Development in the Singapore Civil Service", presentation at the Eleventh Malaysian Civil Service Conference, 21–22 Aug. 2006, unpan1.un.org/intradoc/groups/public/documents/apcity/unpan028179.pdf (no longer available).

Soh, Star. "Applications of Psychology in HR and Training in a Conscript Army", presentation at the 46th International Military Testing Association Conference, Brussels, 26–28 Oct. 2004.

Tan, Charissa, Beng Chong Lim and Star Soh. "Understanding Attitudes towards National Defence and Military Service in Singapore", presentation at the 45th International Military Testing Association Conference, Pensacola, 3–6 Nov. 2003.

Willis, Don. "The Structure & Antecedents of Organisational Commitment in the Singapore Army", presentation at the 45th International Military Testing Association Conference, Pensacola, 3–6 Nov. 2003.

Museums and Exhibitions

Army Museum of Singapore, Jurong.

Campaign City: Life in Posters, exhibition at the National Library Board, 9 Jan.–7 July 2013.

Republic of Singapore Air Force Museum, Paya Lebar.

Republic of Singapore Navy Museum, Changi.

Government of Singapore and SAF Publications

Abisheganaden, John and Adrian Koh, eds. *Medical Corps: The Story of the SAF Medical Corps*. Singapore: HQ Medical Services, Singapore Armed Forces, 1992.

Boey, David. *Reaching Out: Operation Flying Eagle: SAF Humanitarian Assistance after the Tsunami*. Singapore: SNP Editions, 2005.

Chan, Adrian. *Leading in the Third Generation SAF*. Singapore: *Pointer: Journal of the Singapore Armed Forces*, 2012.

Chan, Gabriel Eng Han. *The Volunteer Corps: Contributions to Singapore's Internal Security and Defence (1854–1984)*, Supplement, *Pointer: Journal of the Singapore Armed Forces* (Nov. 1990).

Chan, Kim Yin, Sukhmohinder Singh, Regena Ramaya and Lim Kwee Hoon, eds. *Spirit and System: Leadership Development for a Third Generation SAF*. Singapore: Centre of Leadership Development, SAFTI Military Institute, 2005.

Chan, Samuel, Ho Shu Huang, Adrian Kuah and Bernard Loo. *Ready, Decisive, Respected: Chronicling Our Army's Overseas Operations (1970–2015)*. Singapore: Straits Times Press and Ministry of Defence, 2015.

Chew, Melanie and Bernard Tan Tiong Gie. *Creating the Technology Edge: DSO National Laboratories, Singapore 1972–2002*. Singapore: DSO National Laboratories, 2002.

Chiang, Mickey. *Fighting Fit: The Singapore Armed Forces*. Singapore: Times Editions, 1990.

———. *SAF and 30 Years of National Service*. Singapore: MINDEF Public Affairs, 1997.

Chong, Chun Hon, Christopher Cheok Cheng Soon and Ken Chiew Kia Sheng. *The SAF Medical Corps: Our Heritage, Our Pride, Our Commitment*. Singapore: HQ Medical Corps, Singapore Armed Forces, 2003.

Choo, Martin, ed. *The Singapore Armed Forces*. Singapore: Public Affairs Department, Ministry of Defence, 1980.

Goh, Kok Huat, ed. *In Service to Our Nation: The Temasek Brigade Story*. Singapore: Temasek Brigade (3rd Singapore Infantry Brigade), 1994.

Goh, Laurence Eng Yau, ed. *Together as One: 20 Years of 1 PDF History 1985–2004*. Singapore: 1st People's Defence Force Command, 2004.

Goh, Yong Kiat. *The Cutting Edge of the Air Force: Tengah Air Base: A Pictorial History 1939–2001*. Singapore: Tengah Air Base, Republic of Singapore Air Force, 2001.

Hardy, Sarah. *30th Anniversary: Onwards and Upwards*. Singapore: Republic of Singapore Navy, 1997.

Heng, Heok Theng, Foo Siang Yean and Sun You Ning, eds. *Defenders of Our Homeland: The 2 PDF Experience*. Singapore: 2 PDF Command, 2005.

Hoong, Bee Lok, ed. *Without Reserve: Commemorating 30 years of SAFRA*. Singapore: SAFRA National Service Association, 2002.

Khoo, Augustine, ed. *ADSD: 20 Years of Integrated Air Defence Operations*. Singapore: Air Defence Systems Division, 1999.

Koh, Boon Pin and Lee Geok Boi. *Shoulder to Shoulder: Our National Service Journal: Commemorating 35 Years of National Service*. Singapore: Ministry of Defence, 2002.

Lee, Bobby, ed. *The Black Berets: Training Transformation in Action*. Singapore: Armour Training Institute, 2006.

Leow, Meng Fai. *Super Skyhawks: The RSAF A-4 Story*. Singapore: Tengah Air Base, Republic of Singapore Air Force, 2006.

————, adviser. *Because We Are One: Changi Air Base*. Singapore: Changi Air Base, Republic of Singapore Air Force, 2007.

Lew, Esther, ed. *The Spirit of the Cobra: 6 Division Silver Jubilee*. Singapore: Headquarters 6 Division, 2001.

Lim, Chong Kiat, ed. *9th Singapore Division: Souvenir Magazine 1981*. Singapore: Headquarters 9 Division, 1981.

Lim, Kheng Sing, ed. *Singapore Combat Engineers celebrates XXV Anniversary, 1967–1992*. Singapore: Headquarters Singapore Combat Engineers, 1992.

Lim, Ming Yan, ed. *Distinction: A Profile of Pioneers*. Singapore: Second Singapore Infantry Brigade, 1993.

Liu, Gretchen. *The Air Force*. Singapore: Republic of Singapore Air Force, 1988.

Lo, Timothy, ed. *Onwards and Upwards: Celebrating 40 Years of the Navy*. Singapore: SNP Editions, 2007.

Low, Chin Min et al., eds. *Twenty Five Years of Flight Testing in the Republic of Singapore Air Force, 1986–2011*. Singapore: Flight Test Centre, Republic of Singapore Air Force, 2011.

Lui, Pao Chuen, ed. *Engineering Land Systems 50*. Singapore: Ministry of Defence, 2016.

Menon, Ramachandran. *To Command: The SAFTI Military Institute*. Singapore: HQ SAFTI Military Institute and Landmark Books, 1995.

————, ed. *One of a Kind: Remembering SAFTI's First Batch*. Singapore: SAFTI Military Institute, 2007.

————, ed. *One of a Kind: Remembering SAFTI's First Batch*. 2nd ed. Singapore: SAFTI Military Institute, 2015.

Nagpal, Ajit Singh, ed. *The Pioneers of SAFTI: Singapore Golden Jubilee*. Singapore: Innoprint & Gifts, 2015.

Ng, Wee Tiong, Christopher Cheok, Tan Peng Hui, Edwin Heng, Clive Tan and Enoch Tang. *The SAF Medical Corps: 40 Years of Operations*. Singapore: SAF Medical Corps Heritage Centre, 2007.

Ng, Zhi-Wen, Adrian Chan, Sukhmohinder Singh and Lim Teck Yin. *Called to Lead: A Reader for Aspiring SAF Leaders*. Singapore: *Pointer: Journal of the Singapore Armed Forces*, 2011.

Su, Poon Ghee, Ong Boon Hwee and Low Wye Mun, eds. *The Army's Commitment … Care of Soldiers*. Singapore: G1-Army, 1994.

Tan, Jason, ed. *Singapore Combat Engineers: Forty Years Anniversary*. Singapore: HQ Singapore Combat Engineers, 2007.

Tan, Wai Kee, chief ed. *1st SMC Magazine "C" Coy*. Singapore: OCS SAFTI, 1975.

Team PLAB: 25 Years of Readiness [Since 1981]. Singapore: Paya Lebar Air Base, Republic of Singapore Air Force, 2006.

Terh, Leslie. *Sons and Officers: Life at Prestigious Military College*. Singapore: Sea Sky Books Enterprise, 2000.

Wong, Chee Wai et al., eds. *SAFTI MI: 10th Anniversary 1995–2005*. Singapore: SAFTI Military Institute, 2005.

Woon, Tai Ho. *Partnering to Rebuild: Operation Blue Orchid: The Singapore Armed Forces Experience in Iraq*. Singapore: Ministry of Defence Public Affairs, 2010.

Yang, Shunxiong, Sean, ed. *Air Combat Command: Poised and Deadly*. Singapore: Air Combat Command, Republic of Singapore Air Force, 2009.

40/40: 40 Years & 40 Stories of National Service. Singapore: Landmark Books, 2007.

40 Years of the RSAF: Our People, Our Air Force. Singapore: Republic of Singapore Air Force, 2008.

A Maritime Force for a Maritime Nation: Celebrating 50 Years of the Navy. Singapore: Straits Times Press, 2017.

A Sustainable Population for a Dynamic Singapore: Population White Paper. Singapore: National Population and Talent Division, Prime Minister's Office, Jan. 2013.

At the Leading Edge: 30 Years of RSAF Logistics. Singapore: Published for the Ministry of Defence by Times Editions, 1999.

Defending Singapore in the 21st Century. Singapore: Ministry of Defence, 2000.

Defining Moments: Our Army Experience: Shaping Lives and Beliefs. Singapore: Ministry of Defence, 2004.

Lions in Defence: The 2 PDF Story: Commemorating 35 Years of Home Defence. Singapore: 2PDF Command Officers' Mess, 2000.

Manpower Policies Affecting the SAF Officer. The Pointer Special Issue. Singapore: Ministry of Defence, March 1982.

My Son, The NSman: What Parents Should Know about NS. Singapore: Central Manpower Base, MINDEF, 2007.

NS Is … Singapore: Ministry of Defence, 2012.

Our Army: Customs and Traditions. Singapore: Ministry of Defence, 2006.

Persistent & Precise: Ultimate AdVantage. Singapore: UAV Command, 2008.

Recruit's Handbook: A Guide through Basic Military Training. Singapore: Central Manpower Base, MINDEF, 2007.

Reflections on Leadership. Singapore: *Pointer: Journal of the Singapore Armed Forces*, 2009.

SAF 50: Giving Strength to Our Nation – The SAF and Its People. Singapore: Ministry of Defence, 2015.

SAFTI 50: Developing Leaders since 1966. Singapore: SAFTI Military Institute, 2016.

SAFTI Leadership Journal. Singapore: Centre for Leadership Development, SAFTI Military Institute, 2003.

SAFTI Silver Jubilee 1966–1991. Singapore: Ministry of Defence, 1991.

Singapore 21: Together, We Make the Difference. Singapore: Singapore 21 Committee, Public Service Division, Government of Singapore, 1999.

Singapore Artillery 100th Anniversary: 1888–1988. Singapore: HQ Singapore Artillery and Public Affairs Department, Ministry of Defence, 1988.

Supporting Our NSmen: An Employers' Guide. Singapore: MINDEF Public Affairs, n.d.

The Scimitar: Magazine of the Singapore Armed Forces Training Institute, Mar. 1968.

To Be One. Singapore: 40th Battalion, Singapore Armoured Regiment, 2002.

Two Thousand Two Hundred and Sixty-Three Days 2007–2013: Operation Blue Ridge – The SAF's Six-Year Mission in Afghanistan. Singapore: Ministry of Defence, 2013.

Theses and Research Projects by MINDEF and SAF Personnel

Chan, Kim-Yin. "Toward a Theory of Individual Differences and Leadership: Understanding the Motivation to Lead", PhD dissertation, University of Illinois at Urbana-Champaign, 1999.

Chiang, Hock Woon. "Young Singaporeans' Perspectives of Compulsory Military Conscription: How They Manage the National Service Experience in Relation to Their Education, Development and Careers", PhD dissertation, University of Leicester, 2011.

Goh, Kee Nguan. "The Singapore Army Moving Decisively beyond the Conventional", USAWC Strategy Research Project at the US Army War College, 2004.

Lim, Beng Chong. "Do the Leader and Member Make the Team? The Role of Personality and Cognitive Ability", PhD dissertation, University of Maryland, 2003.

Soh, Star. "Organizational Socialization of Newcomers: A Longitudinal Study of Organizational Enculturation Processes and Outcomes", PhD dissertation, Ohio State University, 2000.

Tse, Lian Tian. "Application of Logistic Regression and Survival Analysis to the Study of CEP, Manpower Performance and Attrition", master's thesis, US Naval Postgraduate School, 1993.

Yip, Kin Cheng. "The Professional Soldier: Organisational and Occupational Commitment of Regular Officers in the Singapore Army", honours thesis, National University of Singapore, 2002.

Archived Periodicals

Air Force News (first published in 1985) – incomplete collection available at SAFTI MI library; and Level 11, Lee Kong Chian Reference Library.

Army News (first published in 1995) – complete collection available at SAFTI MI library.

Asian Defence Journal – available at Clementi Public Library.

Bosun's Call (Newsletter of the SAF Yacht Club) – selected issues available at www.safyc. org.sg/bosuns-call.php.

Connections (Newsletter of Temasek Club – SAF Officers' Club) – selected issues available at www.temasekclub.org.sg.

E.Ngage (Newsletter of the Future Systems Directorate) – selected issues (Apr. 2010– Sept. 2011), available online until website was decommissioned.

Local press (*Straits Times, TODAY, Singapore Monitor, New Nation*) – microfilm archive at Level 11, Lee Kong Chian Reference Library.

Officer biographies in *Pointer: Journal of the Singapore Armed Forces* – incomplete collection available at SAFTI library.

MEDLink (Newsletter of the SAF Medical Corps) – complete collection available at SAFTI library.

National Pioneer/Pioneer Magazine – incomplete collection available at SAFTI MI library; Level 11, Lee Kong Chian Reference Library; and Pioneer editorial team at Defence Technology Tower B, Central Manpower Base.

Navy News (first published in 1983) – incomplete collection available at SAFTI MI library; and Level 11, Lee Kong Chian Reference Library (1983–87; 1988–82; 1997– 99; 2001–03).

Pinnacle Club of ASEAN newsletter – selected issues available at www.pinnacle-asean. org.

Public Service Commission Annual Reports – incomplete collection available at Level 11, Lee Kong Chian Reference Library on reels NL9775 (1951–72, 1947–76); NL24084 (1970, 1972–81); NL24085 (1982–94, 1996); NL24229 (1998, 1999); and NL27188 (2000, 2001). The annual reports for 1995 and 1997 were not available on microfilm. Annual Reports from 2002 onward are available at psc.gov.sg.

SAFSA iNews (Newsletter of the Singapore Armed Forces Sporting Association) – complete collection available at SAFTI library.

SAFTI Link (Newsletter of SAFTI Military Institute) – complete collection available at SAFTI library.

Sembawang Country Club (SAF Golf Club) newsletter – selected issues available at www. sembawanggolf.org.sg.

Internet Sources

Armed Forces Journal – www.armedforcesjournal.com.

AsiaOne – www.asiaone.com.

Associated Press – www.ap.org.

Cable News Network (CNN) – www.cnn.com.

Challenge (Magazine of the Singapore Public Service) – www.challenge.gov.sg.

Channel NewsAsia – www.channelnewsasia.com.

Cyberpioneer – www.mindef.gov.sg/content/imindef/resourcelibrary/cyberpioneer/index.html.

Defence Science and Technology Agency – www.dsta.gov.sg.

Economist – www.economist.com.

Guardian – www.guardian.co.uk.

InfopediaTalk (National Library Board Singapore) – infopedia.nl.sg.

Institute of Engineers Singapore – www.ies.org.sg.

Ministry of Defence (MINDEF) – www.mindcf.gov.sg.

Prime Minister's Office – www.pmo.gov.sg.

Public Service Commission Scholarships – www.pscscholarships.gov.sg.

Scholars' Choice (*Straits Times*) – www.cats.com.sg/scholarschoice.

Scholarship Guide – scholarshipguide.wordpress.com.

Singapore Gazette – www.egazcttc.com.sg/Welcome.aspx.

Singapore Government Data Portal – data.gov.sg.

Singapore Government Directory Interactive – www.sgdi.gov.sg.

Singapore Medical Association News – www.sma.org.sg.

Singapore Youth Flying Club – www.syfc.sg.

St. Stephen's School – www.ststephens.moe.edu.sg.

Straits Times – www.straitstimes.com.

Sydney Morning Herald – www.smh.com.au.

TODAY – www.todayonline.com.

Yale Daily News – www.yaledailynews.com.

Books and Monographs

Alfred, Hedwig. *Living the Mission: The SJI Story 1852–2002*. Singapore: Archipelago Press, 2002.

Barr, Michael D. *Lee Kuan Yew: The Beliefs behind the Man*. Richmond: Curzon, 2000.

———. *The Ruling Elite of Singapore: Networks of Power and Influence*. London and New York: I.B. Tauris, 2014.

Bass, Bernard Morris. *Transformational Leadership: Industrial, Military and Educational Impact*. Mahwah: Lawrence Erlbaum Associates, 1998.

Batson, C. Daniel. *The Altruism Question: Toward a Social-Psychological Answer*. Hillsdale: Lawrence Erlbaum Associates, 1991.

Behrman, Greg. *The Most Noble Adventure: The Marshall Plan and the Reconstruction of Post-War Europe*. London: Aurum Press, 2008.

Blackburn, Kevin and Karl Hack. *War Memory and the Making of Modern Malaysia and Singapore*. Singapore: NUS Press, 2012.

Bourdieu, Pierre. *The State Nobility: Elite Schools in the Field of Power*. Stanford: Stanford University Press, 1996.

Chan, Heng Chee. *Singapore: The Politics of Survival 1965–1967*. Singapore: Oxford University Press, 1971.

Chua, Mui Hoong. *Pioneers Once More: The Singapore Public Service 1959–2009*. Singapore: Straits Times Press, 2010.

Cutts, Robert L. *An Empire of Schools: Japan's Universities and the Molding of a National Power Elite*. Armonk: M.E. Sharpe, 1997.

Desker, Barry and Kwa Chong Guan, eds. *Goh Keng Swee: A Public Career Remembered*. Singapore: World Scientific Publishing, 2012.

Djiwandono, J. Soedjati and Yong Mun Cheong, eds. *Soldiers and Stability in Southeast Asia*. Singapore: Institute of Southeast Asian Studies, 1988.

Elman, Benjamin A. *A Cultural History of Civil Examinations in Late Imperial China*. Berkeley and Los Angeles: University of California Press, 2000.

Esipova, Neli, Julie Ray and Rajesh Srinivasan. *The World's Potential Migrants: Who They Are, Where They Want to Go, and Why It Matters*. Washington, DC: Gallup, 2010.

Fernandez, Warren. *Without Fear or Favour: 50 Years of Singapore's Public Service Commission*. Singapore: Times Media for the Public Service Commission, 2001.

Franke, Volker. *Preparing for Peace: Military Identity, Value Orientations, and Professional Military Education*. Westport and London: Praeger, 1999.

Goh, Keng Swee. *The Practice of Economic Growth*. Singapore: Federal Publications, 1977.

Guderian, Heinz. *Achtung – Panzer! The Development of Tank Warfare*, transl. Christopher Duffy, introduction and notes by Paul Harris. London: Cassell, 1999.

Hack, Karl. *Defence and Decolonisation in South-East Asia: Britain, Malaya and Singapore 1941–1968*. Richmond: Curzon, 2001.

Han, Fook Kwang, Zuraidah Ibrahim, Chua Mui Hoong, Lydia Lim, Ignatius Low, Rachel Lin and Robin Chan. *Lee Kuan Yew: Hard Truths to Keep Singapore Going*. Singapore: Straits Times Press, 2011.

Hartmann, Michael. *The Sociology of Elites*. Abingdon and New York: Routledge, 2004.

Ho, Shu Huang and Samuel Chan Ling Wei. *Defence*. Singapore: Straits Times Press and Institute of Policy Studies, 2015.

Hobbes, Thomas. *Leviathan or the Matter, Forme and Power of a Common-Wealth Ecclesiasticall and Civill* (1651), Chapter 17: Of the Causes, Generation, and Definition of a Commonwealth.

Horner, David and Jean Bou, eds. *Duty First: A History of the Royal Australian Regiment*. Crows Nest: Allen & Unwin, 2008.

Huntington, Samuel P. *The Soldier and the State: The Theory and Politics of Civil-Military Relations*. Cambridge: The Belknap Press of Harvard University Press, 1964.

Huxley, Tim. *Defending the Lion City: The Armed Forces of Singapore*. St Leonards: Allen & Unwin, 2000.

Janowitz, Morris. *The Professional Soldier: A Social and Political Portrait*. New York: Free Press, 1971.

Jans, Nicholas with Stephen Mugford, Jamie Cullens and Judy Frazer-Jans. *The Chiefs: A Study of Strategic Leadership*. Canberra: Centre for Defence Leadership and Ethics, Australian Defence College, 2013.

Josey, Alex. *Lee Kuan Yew: The Struggle for Singapore*. Sydney: Angus & Robertson, 1976.

Keegan, John. *World Armies*. London: Macmillan, 1983.

Lam, Chun See. *Good Morning Yesterday: Growing Up in Singapore in the 1950s and 1960s*. Singapore: Hoshin Consulting, 2012.

Lam, Peng Er and Kevin Yew Lee Tan. *Lee's Lieutenants: Singapore's Old Guard*. St Leonards: Allen & Unwin, 1999.

Langer, J.F. *From the Spitfire Cockpit to the Cabinet Office: The Memoirs of Air Commodore J F "Johnny" Langer CBE AFC DL*. Barnsley: Pen & Sword Aviation, 2016.

Lasswell, Harold D. *On Political Sociology*, ed. and intro. Dwaine Marvick. Chicago: University of Chicago Press, 1977.

Lau, Albert. *A Moment of Anguish: Singapore in Malaysia and the Politics of Disengagement*. Singapore: Times Academic Press, 1998.

Lee, Edwin. *Singapore: The Unexpected Nation*. Singapore: Institute of Southeast Asian Studies, 2008.

Lee, Kuan Yew. *The Singapore Story: Memoirs of Lee Kuan Yew*. Singapore: Times Editions and Simon & Schuster, 1998.

———. *From Third World to First—The Singapore Story: 1965–2000*. Singapore: Times Editions, 2000.

Lee, Terence. *Defect or Defend: Military Responses to Popular Protests in Authoritarian Asia*. Singapore: ISEAS Publishing and Johns Hopkins University Press, 2015.

Leong, Choon Cheong. *Youth in the Army*. Singapore: Federal Publications, 1978.

Lim, Peter H.L., ed. *Chronicle of Singapore: Fifty Years of Headline News*. Singapore: Editions Didier Millet in association with the National Library Board, 2009.

Lindsay, Neville. *Loyalty and Service: The Officer Cadet School Portsea*. Kenmore: Historia Productions, 1995.

Loh, Kah Seng and Liew Kai Shiun, eds. *The Makers & Keepers of Singapore History*. Singapore: Ethos Books and Singapore Heritage Society, 2010.

Low, Kar Tiang and Peter K.G. Dunlop, eds. *Who's Who in Singapore*. Singapore: Who's Who Publishing, 2000.

Low, Linda, ed. *Wealth of East Asian Nations: Speeches and Writings by Goh Keng Swee*. Singapore: Federal Publications, 1995.

Low, Linda and Douglas M. Johnston, eds. *Singapore Inc.: Public Policy Options in the Third Millennium*. Singapore: Asia Pacific Press, 2001.

MacMillan English Dictionary for Advanced Learners. International Student Edition. Oxford: Macmillan Education, 2002.

Mahbubani, Kishore. *The New Asian Hemisphere: The Irresistible Shift of Global Power to the East*. New York: PublicAffairs, 2008.

Maslow, Abraham H. *Motivation and Personality*. New York: Addison Wesley Longman, 1970.

McNamee, Stephen J. and Robert K. Miller Jr. *The Meritocracy Myth*. Lanham: Rowman & Littlefield, 2004.

Moffatt, Jonathan and Paul Riches. *In Orient Primus: A History of the Volunteer Forces in Malaya and Singapore*. Trowbridge: Cromwell Press Group, 2010.

Murfett, Malcolm H., John H. Miksic, Brian P. Farrell and Chiang Ming Shun. *Between Two Oceans: A Military History of Singapore from First Settlement to Final British Withdrawal*. Oxford: Oxford University Press, 1999.

Nadarajan, Ben. *Close Watch: A Nation's Resolve to Secure Singapore*. Singapore: Straits Times Press, 2012.

Nathan, S.R. with Timothy Auger. *An Unexpected Journey: Path to the Presidency*. Singapore: Editions Didier Millet, 2011.

Newman, Aubrey S. *What Are Generals Made Of?* Novato: Presidio Press, 1987.

Ooi, Kee Beng. *In Lieu of Ideology: The Intellectual Biography of Goh Keng Swee*. Singapore: Institute of Southeast Asian Studies, 2010.

Park, Eugene Y. *Between Dreams and Reality: The Military Examination in Late Chosŏn Korea, 1600–1894*. Harvard East Asian Monograph No. 281. Cambridge: Harvard University Press, 2007.

Parry, Geraint. *Political Elites*. Colchester: European Consortium for Political Research, 2005.

Pearsall, Judy, ed. *The Concise Oxford Dictionary*, 10th ed. Oxford: Oxford University Press, 1999.

Peled, Alon. *A Question of Loyalty: Military Manpower Policy in Multiethnic States*. Ithaca and London: Cornell University Press, 1998.

Plate, Thomas. *Conversations with Lee Kuan Yew: Citizen Singapore: How to Build a Nation*. Singapore: Marshall Cavendish, 2010.

Quah, Jon Siew Tien. *Public Administration Singapore Style*. Singapore: Talisman Publishing, 2010.

Samuel, Dhoraisingam S. *Working for Dr. Goh Keng Swee: Collection of Anecdotes*. Singapore: Dhoraisingam S. Samuel, Nov. 2011.

Scott, John. *Power*. Cambridge: Polity Press, 2001.

Stevens, Mitchell L. *Creating a Class: College Admissions and the Education of Elites*. Cambridge: Harvard University Press, 2009.

Tamney, Joseph B. *The Struggle over Singapore's Soul: Western Modernization and Asian Culture*. Berlin: de Gruyter, 1996.

Tan, Guan Heng. *100 Inspiring Rafflesians 1823–2003*. Singapore: World Scientific Publishing, 2008.

Tan, Yong Soon. *Living the Singapore Dream*. Singapore: SNP International, 2007.

The Military Balance 2015. London: International Institute for Strategic Studies, 2015.

Tng, Ying Hui. *Not Born in Singapore: Fifty Personalities Who Shaped the Nation*. Singapore: Epigram Books for Institute of Public Policy, Lee Kuan Yew School of Public Policy, 2015.

Tremewan, Christopher. *The Political Economy of Social Control in Singapore*. New York: St. Martin's Press, 1994.

Trocki, Carl A. *Singapore: Wealth, Power and the Culture of Control*. Abingdon and New York: Routledge, 2006.

Vogel, Ezra F. *The Four Little Dragons: The Spread of Industrialization in East Asia*. Cambridge: Harvard University Press, 1991.

Worthington, Ross. *Governance in Singapore*. London and New York: RoutledgeCurzon, 2003.

Year Book of the United Nations 2003. New York: United Nations Publications, 2005.

Book Chapters

Alagappa, Muthiah. "Asian Civil Military Relations: Key Developments, Explanations, and Trajectories", in *Coercion and Governance: The Declining Political Role of the Military in Asia*, ed. Muthiah Alagappa. Stanford: Stanford University Press, 2001, pp. 433–98.

Bachrach, Peter. "Introduction", in *Political Elites in a Democracy*, ed. Peter Bachrach. New York: Atherton Press, 1971, pp. 1–12.

Batson, C. Daniel, Nadia Ahmad and E.L. Stocks. "Four Forms of Prosocial Motivation: Egoism, Altruism, Collectivism, and Principlism", in *Social Motivation*, ed. David Dunning. New York and Hove: Psychology Press, 2011, pp. 103–27.

Bedlington, Stanley S. "Ethnicity and the Armed Forces in Singapore", in *Ethnicity and the Military in Asia*, ed. DeWitt C. Ellinwood and Cynthia H. Enloe. New Brunswick: Transaction Books, 1981, pp. 242–66.

Blackburn, Kevin. "Colonial Forces as Postcolonial Memories: The Commemoration and Memory of the Malay Regiment in Modern Malaysia and Singapore", in *Colonial Armies in Southeast Asia*, ed. Karl Hack and Tobias Retting. Abingdon and New York: Routledge, 2006, pp. 302–26.

Bulmer, Martin. "Concepts in the Analysis of Qualitative Data", in *Sociological Research Methods: An Introduction*, 2nd ed., ed. Martin Bulmer. Piscataway: Transaction Publishers, 1984, pp. 241–62.

Chan, Heng Chee. "Singapore", in *Military-Civilian Relations in South-East Asia*, ed. Zakaria Haji Ahmad and Harold Crouch. Singapore: Oxford University Press, 1985, pp. 136–56.

Chan, Samuel. "Strategic Gains Without the Strategic Corporal: The Singapore Armed Forces in Afghanistan (2007–13)", in *The Strategic Corporal Re-Visited: Challenges for Combatants in Twenty-First Century Warfare*, ed. David W. Lovell and Deane-Peter Baker. Cape Town: UCT Press, 2017, pp. 147–71.

Chin, Kin Wah. "Singapore: Threat Perception and Defence Spending in a City-State", in *Defence Spending in Southeast Asia*, ed. Chin Kin Wah. Singapore: Institute of Southeast Asian Studies, 1987, pp. 194–223.

Chong, Li Choy. "Durable Stability with Prosperity and Legitimacy: Perceptual Leadership in Singapore", in *Durable Stability in Southeast Asia*, ed. Kusama Snitwongse and Sukhumbhand Paribatra. Singapore: Institute of Southeast Asian Studies, 1987, pp. 169–86.

Choo, Winston. "A Soldier in Diplomacy", in *The Little Red Dot: Reflections by Singapore's Diplomats*, ed. Tommy Koh and Chang Li Lin. Singapore: World Scientific Publishing, 2008, pp. 171–8.

Dandeker, Christopher. "Building Flexible Forces for the 21st Century: Key Challenges for the Contemporary Armed Services", in *Handbook of the Sociology of the Military*, ed. Giuseppe Caforio. New York: Kluwer Academic/Plenum Publishers, 2003, pp. 405–16.

Deck, Richard A. "Singapore: Comprehensive Security—Total Defence", in *Strategic Cultures in the Asia-Pacific Region*, ed. Ken Booth and Russell Trood. New York: St. Martin's Press, 1999, pp. 247–69.

Holstein, James A. and Jaber F. Gubrium. "Inside Interviewing: Transcription Quality", *SAGE Research Methods*. Thousand Oaks: Sage, 2003.

Kakabadse, Nada K., Andrew Kakabadse and Alexander Kouzmin. "From Local Elites to a Globally Convergent Class: A Historical Analytical Perspective", in *Global Elites: The Opaque Nature of Transnational Policy Determination*, ed. Andrew Kakabadse and Nada Kakabadse. Basingstoke: Palgrave Macmillan, 2012, pp. 1–37.

Lasswell, Harold D., Daniel Lerner and C. Easton Rothwell. "The Elite Concept", in *Political Elites in a Democracy*, ed. Peter Bachrach. New York: Atherton Press, 1971, pp. 13–26.

Lee, Boon Hiok. "Leadership and Security in Singapore: The Prevailing Paradigm", in *Leadership Perceptions and National Security: The Southeast Asian Experience*, ed. Mohammed Ayoob and Chai-Anan Samudavanija. Singapore: Institute of Southeast Asian Studies, 1989, pp. 160–80.

Liow, Joseph Chinyong. "Confronting the Weight of History: Singapore and Key Neighbours", in *Impressions of the Goh Chok Tong Years in Singapore*, ed. Bridget Welsh, James Chin, Arun Mahizhnan and Tan Tarn How. Singapore: NUS Press, 2009, pp. 144–52.

Margolin, Jean-Louis. "Foreign Models in Singapore's Development and the Idea of a Singaporean Model", in *Singapore Changes Guard: Social, Political and Economic Directions in the 1990s*, ed. Garry Rodan. Melbourne: Longman Cheshire, 1993.

Mayerchak, Patrick M. "The Role of the Military in Singapore", in *The Armed Forces in Contemporary Asian Societies*, ed. Edward A. Olsen and Stephen Jurika Jr. Boulder and London: Westview Press, 1986, pp. 170–85.

Moskos, Charles C. "Institutional and Occupational Trends in Armed Forces", in *The Military: More Than Just a Job?* ed. Charles C. Moskos and Frank R. Wood. New York: Pergamon Press, 1988, pp. 15–26.

Moskos, Charles C. and Frank R. Wood. "Introduction", in *The Military: More Than Just a Job?* ed. Charles C. Moskos and Frank R. Wood. New York: Pergamon Press, 1988, pp. 3–14.

Nair, Elizabeth. "Nation-Building through Conscript Service in Singapore", in *The Military in the Service of Society and Democracy*, ed. Daniella Ashkenazy. Westport: Greenwood Press, 1994, pp. 101–10.

Scott, John. "Modes of Power and the Re-conceptualization of Elites", in *Remembering Elites*, ed. Mike Savage and Karel Williams. Malden: Blackwell, 2008, pp. 27–43.

Seah, Chee Meow. "National Security", in *Management of Success: The Moulding of Modern Singapore,* ed. Kernial Singh Sandhu and Paul Wheatley. Singapore: Institute of Southeast Asian Studies, 1990, pp. 949–62.

Sim, Susan. "Ng Joo Hee, Commissioner of Police, Singapore", in *Trends in Policing: Interviews with Police Leaders across the Globe*, Vol. 5, ed. Bruce F. Baker and Dilip K. Das. Boca Raton: CRC Press, 2017, pp. 213–34.

Tan, Tai Yong. "Singapore: Civil-Military Fusion", in *Coercion and Governance: The Declining Political Role of the Military in Asia*, ed. Muthiah Alagappa. Stanford: Stanford University Press, 2001, pp. 276–93.

————. "The Armed Forces and Politics in Singapore: The Persistence of Civil-Military Fusion", in *The Political Resurgence of the Military in Southeast Asia: Conflict and Leadership*, ed. Marcus Mietzner. Abingdon and New York: Routledge, 2011, pp. 148–66.

Thayer, Carlyle A. "The Five Power Defence Arrangements at Forty (1971–2011)", in *Southeast Asian Affairs 2012*, ed. Daljit Singh and Pushpa Thambipillai. Singapore: Institute of Southeast Asian Studies, 2012, pp. 61–72.

Journal Articles, Working Papers and Reports

Avolioa, Bruce J. and Edwin E. Locke. "Contrasting Different Philosophies of Leader Motivation: Altruism versus Egoism", *Leadership Quarterly* 13, 2 (Apr. 2002): 169–91.

Barak, Oren and Eyal Tsur. "The Military Careers and Second Careers of Israel's Military Elite", *Middle East Journal* 66, 3 (Summer 2012): 473–92.

Barr, Michael D. "Beyond Technocracy: The Culture of Elite Governance in Lee Hsien Loong's Singapore", *Asian Studies Review* 30, 1 (Mar. 2006): 1–18.

———, "The Charade Of Meritocracy", *Far Eastern Economic Review* 169, 8 (Oct. 2006): 18–22.

Beeson, Mark. "Civil-Military Relations in Indonesia and the Philippines: Will the Thai Coup Prove Contagious?" *Armed Forces & Society* 34, 3 (Spring 2008): 474–90.

Ben-Dor, Gabriel Ami Pedahzur, Daphna Canetti-Nisim, Eran Zaidise, Arie Perliger and Shai Bermanis. "I versus We: Collective and Individual Factors of Reserve Service Motivation during War and Peace", *Armed Forces & Society* 34, 4 (July 2008): 565–92.

Bullock, Khalilah. "Reflection on Tan Tock Seng Hospital Clinical Fellowship Experience", *Singapore Medical Association News* (Mar. 2010): 13–7.

Caforio, Giuseppe and Marina Nuciari. "The Officer Profession: Ideal-Type", *Current Sociology* 42, 3 (Winter 1994): 33–56.

Chan, Heng Chee. "Singapore's Foreign Policy, 1965–1968", *Journal of Southeast Asian History* 10, 1 (Mar. 1969): 177–91.

Chan, Kim Yin. "Professionalism in a National Service Army: An Uneasy Combination?" *Pointer* 15, 2 (Apr.–June 1989).

Chang, Felix K. "In Defense of Singapore", *Orbis* 47, 1 (Winter 2003): 107–23.

Cheng, Li and Scott W. Harold. "China's New Military Elite", *China Security* 3, 4 (Autumn 2007): 62–89.

Cheok, C.S.C., Y.G. Ang, W.M. Chew and H.Y. Tan, "Adjusting to Military Life: Servicemen with Problems Coping and Their Outcomes", *Singapore Medical Journal* 41, 5 (May 2000): 218–20.

Chew, Joy Oon Ai. "Civics and Moral Education in Singapore: Lessons for Citizenship Education?" *Journal of Moral Education* 27, 4 (1998): 505–24.

Chia, Aaron Eng Seng. "Are We Military Professionals or Professionals in the Military?" *Pointer* 23, 2 (Apr.–June 1997).

Chong, Alan and Samuel Chan Ling Wei. "Militarizing Civilians in Singapore: Preparing for 'Crisis' within a Calibrated Nationalism", *Pacific Review* 30, 3 (2017): 365–84.

Choy, Yong Kong. "Forcing Strategic Evolution: The SAF as an Adaptive Organization", *Pointer* 38, 1 (2012).

Chua, Beng Huat. "The Cultural Logic of a Capitalist Single-Party State, Singapore", *Postcolonial Studies* 13, 4 (2010): 335–50.

Chung, Tai Ming. "Soldiers and Scholars: Bright Officers Form New National Elite", *Far Eastern Economic Review* 154, 49 (5 Dec. 1991): 15–8.

Clements, Quinton. "A Gracious Society: The Engineering of a New National Goal in Singapore", *History and Anthropology* 11, 2–3 (1999): 257–89.

Cohen, Eliot A. "Twilight of the Citizen-Soldier", *Parameters* (Summer 2001): 23–8.

Da Cunha, Derek. "Sociological Aspects of the Singapore Armed Forces", *Armed Forces & Society* 25, 3 (Spring 1999): 459–75.

Debrah, Yaw A. "Tackling Age Discrimination in Employment in Singapore", *International Journal of Human Resource Management* 7, 4 (1996): 813–31.

Dowd, James J. "Hard Jobs and Good Ambition: U.S. Army Generals and the Rhetoric of Modesty", *Symbolic Interaction* 23, 2 (2000): 183–205.

Etzioni-Halevy, Eva. "Civil-Military Relations and Democracy: The Case of the Military-Political Elites' Connection in Israel", *Armed Forces & Society* 22, 3 (Spring 1996): 401–17.

Feaver, Peter D. "The Civil-Military Problematique: Huntington, Janowitz, and the Question of Civilian Control", *Armed Forces & Society* 23, 2 (Winter 1996): 149–78.

Feaver, Peter D. and Richard H. Kohn. "The Gap: Soldiers, Civilians and Their Mutual Misunderstanding", *National Interest* (Fall 2000): 29–37.

Ferrarie, Kim E. "Processes to Assess Leadership Potential Keep Shell's Talent Pipeline Full", *Journal of Organisational Excellence* 24, 3 (Summer 2005): 17–22.

Frank Knight Research. *The Wealth Report 2012: A Global Perspective on Prime Property and Wealth.* Citigroup, 2012.

Gal, Reuven. "The Motivation for Serving in the IDF: In the Mirror of Time", *Strategic Assessment* 2, 3 (Dec. 1999).

Gan, Wee Hoe, Robin Low Chin Howe and Jarnail Singh. "Aviation Medicine: Global Historical Perspectives and the Development of Aviation Medicine alongside the Growth of Singapore's Aviation Landscape", *Singapore Medical Journal* 52, 5 (May 2011): 324–9.

Gascoigne, John. "Mathematics and Meritocracy: The Emergence of the Cambridge Mathematical Tripos", *Social Studies of Science* 14, 4 (Nov. 1984): 547–84.

Gibson, Jennifer Lee, Brian K. Griepentrog and Sean M. Marsh. "Parental Influence on Youth Propensity to Join the Military", *Journal of Vocational Behavior* 70, 3 (2007): 525–41.

Goldstein, Andrea and Pavida Pananond. "Singapore Inc. Goes Shopping Abroad: Profits and Pitfalls", *Journal of Contemporary Asia* 38, 3 (Aug. 2008): 417–38.

Grebe, Jan and Max M. Mutschler, eds. *Global Militarization Index 2015.* Bonn: Bonn International Center for Conversion, 2015.

Hanna, Willard A. "The New Singapore Armed Forces", *Fieldstaff Reports* 21, 1 (1973).

Horn, Bernd. "The Dark Side to Elites: Elitism as a Catalyst for Disobedience", *Canadian Army Journal* 8, 4 (Winter 2005): 65–79.

———. "Love 'Em or Hate 'Em: Learning to Live with Elites", *Canadian Military Journal* 8, 4 (Winter 2007–08): 32–43.

Huxley, Tim. "The Political Role of the Singapore Armed Forces' Officer Corps: Towards a Military-Administrative State", Strategic and Defence Studies Centre Working Paper, No. 279 (Dec. 1993).

Ibrahim, Yasmin. "SARS and the Rhetoric of War in Singapore", *Crossroads: An Interdisciplinary Journal of Southeast Asian Studies* 18, 2 (2007): 90–119.

Janowitz, Morris. "Military Elites and the Study of War", *Conflict Resolution* 1, 1 (Mar. 1957): 9–18.

Jones, David Seth. "Recent Reforms in Singapore's Administrative Elite: Responding to the Challenges of a Rapidly Changing Economy and Society", *Asian Journal of Political Science* 10, 2 (2002): 70–93.

Keling, Mohamad Faisol, Md. Shukri Shuib and Mohd Na'eim Ajis. "The Impact of Singapore's Military Development on Malaysia's Security", *Journal of Politics and Law* 2, 2 (June 2009): 68–79.

Killian, Lewis K. "Generals, the Talented Tenth, and Affirmative Action", *Society* (Sept./ Oct. 1999): 33–40.

Kim, Insoo and Tyler Crabb. "Collective Identity and Promotion Prospects in the South Korean Army", *Armed Forces & Society* 40, 2 (Apr. 2014): 295–309.

Koh, Gillian and Ooi Giok Ling. "Singapore: A Home, a Nation?" *Southeast Asian Affairs* (2002): 255–81.

Lau, Teik Soon. "Malaysia-Singapore Relations: Crisis of Adjustment, 1965–68", *Journal of Southeast Asian History* 10, 1 (Mar. 1969): 155–76.

Leander, Anna. "Drafting Community: Understanding the Fate of Conscription", *Armed Forces & Society* 30, 4 (Summer 2004): 571–99.

Lee, Terence. "The Politics of Civil Society in Singapore", *Asian Studies Review* 26, 1 (Mar. 2002): 97–117.

Leong, Y.K. "Béla Bollobás: Graphs Extremal and Random", *Imprints* (Institute for Mathematical Sciences, NUS) 11 (Sept. 2007).

Li, Norman P., Amy J.Y. Lim, Tsai Ming-Hong and O. Jiaqing, "Too Materialistic to Get Married and Have Children?" *PLoS ONE* (May 2015): 1–12.

Lim, Irvin Fang Jau. "Viewpoints: Pointers from the Past, Foresight into the Future", *Pointer* 30, 3 (2004).

Lim, Keak Cheng. "Post-Independence Population Planning and Social Development in Singapore", *GeoJournal* 18, 2 (Mar. 1989): 163–74.

Lim, Stanley Wee Tong. "Discourse on Army Recruitment: In the Context of Generation Y", *Pointer* 36, 3–4 (2011).

Lin, Kuo-Wei, Chia-Mu Kuan and Chi-Hao Lu. "Analysis of Intention to Continue Services among Recruited Voluntary Soldiers", *Journal of Social Sciences* 8, 4 (2012): 479–84.

Low, Linda. "Singapore Inc.: A Success Story", *South African Journal of International Affairs* 10, 7 (Summer 2003): 49–63.

Matthews, Ron and Nellie Zhang Yan. "Small Country 'Total Defence': A Case Study of Singapore", *Defence Studies* 7, 3 (Sept. 2007): 376–95.

McDougall, Derek. "The Wilson Government and the British Defence Commitment in Malaysia-Singapore", *Journal of Southeast Asian Studies* 4, 2 (Sept. 1973): 229–40.

Moore, David W. and B. Thomas Trout. "Military Advancement: The Visibility Theory of Promotion", *American Political Science Review* 72, 2 (June 1978): 452–68.

Moskos, Charles C. "The Emergent Military: Civil, Traditional, or Plural?" *Pacific Sociological Review* 16, 2 (Apr. 1973): 255–80.

———. "From Institution to Occupation: Trends in Military Organization", *Armed Forces & Society* 4, 1 (Nov. 1977): 41–50.

———. "Institutional/Occupational Trends in Armed Forces: An Update", *Armed Forces & Society* 12, 3 (Spring 1986): 377–82.

Mulligan, Casey B. and Andrei Shleifer. "Conscription as Regulation", *American Law and Economics Review* 7, 1 (2005): 85–111.

Nair, Elizabeth. "The Singapore Soldier", *Pointer* 12, 2 (Jan.–Mar. 1986).

———. "Conscription and Nation-Building in Singapore: A Psychological Analysis", *Journal of Human Values* 1, 1 (1995): 93–102.

Ng, Pak Shun. "From 'Poisonous Shrimp' to 'Porcupine': An Analysis of Singapore's Defence Posture Change in the Early 1980s", Strategic and Defence Studies Centre Working Paper (Australian National University), No. 397 (2005).

———. "'Why Not a Volunteer Army?' Reexamining the Impact of Military Conscription on Economic Growth for Singapore", *Singapore Economic Review* (National University of Singapore) 50, 1 (2005): 47–67.

Ng, Yih Yng and Lionel Cheng. "In Remembrance: Wong Yue Sie (1960–2010)", *Singapore Medical Association News* (June 2010): 12–3.

Powell, Jonathan M. and Clayton L. Thyne. "Global Instances of Coups from 1950 to 2010: A New Dataset", *Journal of Peace Research* 48, 2 (Mar. 2011): 249–59.

Quah, Jon S.T. "Singapore: Towards a National Identity", *Southeast Asian Affairs* (1977): 207–19.

Rahim, Lily Zubaidah. "Governing Muslims in Singapore's Secular Authoritarian State", *Australian Journal of International Affairs* 66, 2 (Apr. 2012): 169–85.

Raska, Michael. "'Soldier-Scholars' and Pragmatic Professionalism: The Case of Civil-Military Relations in Singapore", South-South Collaborative Programme Occasional Paper Series, No. 12 (2012).

Rayner, Leonard. "A Review of British Defence and Foreign Policies and Their Effects on Singapore and the Rest of the Region", *Southeast Asian Affairs* (1976): 348–53.

Richardson, Michael. "Marching to Self-sufficiency in Arms as Well as Defence", *Far Eastern Economic Review* 119, 2 (13 Jan. 1983): 28–30.

Rodan, Garry. "Singapore: Emerging Tensions in the 'Dictatorship of the Middle Class'", *Pacific Review* 5, 4 (Jan. 1992): 370–81.

Satana, Nil S. "Transformation of the Turkish Military and the Path to Democracy", *Armed Forces & Society* 34, 3 (Spring 2008): 357–88.

Sebastian, Leonard C. "The Logic of the Guardian State: Governance in Singapore's Development Experience", *Southeast Asian Affairs* (1997): 278–98.

Seet, Benjamin, Tien Yin Wong, Donald T.H. Tan, Seang Mei Saw, Vivian Balakrishnan, Lionel K.H. Lee and Arthur S.M. Lim. "Myopia in Singapore: Taking a Public Health Approach", *British Journal of Ophthalmology* 85, 5 (2001): 521–6.

Segal, David R. "Selective Promotion in Officer Cohorts", *Sociological Quarterly* 8, 2 (Mar. 1967): 199–206.

———. "Measuring the Institutional/Occupational Change Thesis", *Armed Forces & Society* 12, 3 (Spring 1986): 351–76.

Segal, David R. and Mady Wechsler Segal. "Change in Military Organization", *Annual Review of Sociology* 9 (1983): 151–70.

Shachar, Ayelet. "Picking Winners: Olympic Citizenship and the Global Race for Talent", *Yale Law Journal* 120, 8 (2011): 2088–139.

Sim, Jasmine B.-Y. "The Burden of Responsibility: Elite Students' Understandings of Civic Participation in Singapore", *Educational Review* 64, 2 (May 2012): 195–210.

Sim, Jasmine B.-Y. and Murray Print. "Citizenship Education in Singapore: Controlling or Empowering Teacher Understanding and Practice?" *Oxford Review of Education* 35, 6 (Dec. 2009): 705–23.

Singh, Kuldip, Yoke Fai Fong and S.S. Ratnam. "A Reversal of Fertility Trends in Singapore", *Journal of Biological Social Science* 23, 1 (Jan. 1991): 73–8.

Smith, Hugh. "What Costs Will Democracies Bear? A Review of Popular Theories of Casualty Aversion", *Armed Forces & Society* 31, 4 (Summer 2005): 487–512.

Smith, Patrick and Philip Bowring. "The Citizen Soldier: Singapore Stresses Security as an Arm of Nation-Building", *Far Eastern Economic Review* 119, 2 (13 Jan. 1983): 26–9.

Tan, Bernard. "Putting People First in Our Army", *Pointer* 30, 3 (2004).

Tan, Cheong Hin and Lim Lay Ching. "Potential Appraisal: The Shell Appraisal System", NTU School of Accountancy and Business Working Paper Series, No. 29 (1993).

Tan, Kenneth Paul. "Meritocracy and Elitism in a Global City: Ideological Shifts in Singapore", *International Political Science Review* 29, 1 (Jan. 2008): 7–27.

Tan, Peng Ann. "Viewpoints: Learning from the Past: An Old Soldier's Advice", *Pointer* 30, 3 (2004).

Tay, Lim Heng. "The Regular Military Career: From Profession to Occupation?" *Pointer* 17, 2 (Apr.–June 1991).

Teo, Peggy. "Population Planning and Change in Singapore", *Population and Environment* 16, 3 (Jan. 1995): 237–51.

Teo, Peggy, Elspeth Graham, Brenda S.A. Yeoh and Susan Levy. "Values, Change and Inter-generational Ties between Two Generations of Women in Singapore", *Ageing & Society* 23, 3 (May 2003): 327–47.

Thomson, George G. "Britain's Plan to Leave Asia", *Round Table: The Commonwealth Journal of International Affairs* 58, 230 (1968): 117–25.

Toh, Weisong. "High Flyers: Implications of Short Officer Careers in the SAF", *Pointer* 38, 3 (2012).

Vallance, Sarah. "Performance Appraisal in Singapore, Thailand, and the Philippines: A Cultural Perspective", *Australian Journal of Public Administration* 58, 3 (Dec. 1999): 78–95.

Van Ham, Peter. "The Rise of the Brand State: The Postmodern Politics of Image and Reputation", *Foreign Affairs* 80, 5 (2001): 2–6.

Walsh, Sean P. "The Roar of the Lion City: Ethnicity, Gender, and Culture in the Singapore Armed Forces", *Armed Forces & Society* 33, 2 (Jan. 2007): 265–85.

Wan, Fook Kee and Margaret Loh. "Singapore", *Studies in Family Planning* 5, 5 (May 1974): 163–5.

Wee, C.J. W.-L. "'Asian Values', Singapore, and the Third Way: Re-Working Individualism and Collectivism", *Sojourn: Journal of Social Issues in Southeast Asia* 14, 2 (Oct. 1999): 332–58.

Wilson, H.E. "Education as an Instrument of Policy in Southeast Asia: The Singapore Example", *Journal of Southeast Asian Studies* 8, 1 (Mar. 1977): 75–84.

Wong, Sher Maine. "The Boy Who Scored with Ds", *Voices: Magazine for the Central Singapore District* 61 (Nov.–Dec. 2011): 8.

Yeung, Henry Wai-Chung and Kris Olds. "Singapore's Global Reach: Situating the City-State in the Global Economy", *International Journal of Urban Sciences* 2, 1 (1998): 24–47.

Index